ROWAN AND MAYNE

A BIOGRAPHY OF THE FIRST LONDON POLICE COMMISSIONERS

TONY MOORE

BLUE LAMP
BOOKS

First Edition published 2021.

Copyright © Tony Moore, 2021

The right of Tony Moore to be identified as the author
of this work has been asserted in accordance with
the Copyright, Designs & Patents Act 1988.

All rights reserved. No part of this book may be reprinted or reproduced or utilised in any form or by any electronic, mechanical or other means, now known or hereafter invented, including photocopying and recording, or in any information storage or retrieval system, without the prior permission in writing of the publishers.

Unless otherwise stated, images are from the author's collection. Whilst every effort has been made to credit all images to the appropriate source/copyright holder, the author apologises for any oversight, which we would be happy to correct in future editions.

ISBN: 978-1-914277-21-4 (hardcover)

Published by Blue Lamp Books

An imprint of

Mango Books Ltd
www.MangoBooks.co.uk
18 Soho Square
London W1D 3QL

ROWAN AND MAYNE

A BIOGRAPHY OF THE FIRST
LONDON POLICE COMMISSIONERS

CONTENTS

Acknowledgements..i
About the Author iv
Introduction..1

1. The Rowans and Maynes of Ireland.........................7
2. The Making of an Officer................................18
3. Rowan as a Staff Officer under Wellington...............33
4. Rowan as a Regimental Officer...........................51
5. The Battle of Waterloo and the Occupation of France.....65
6. Life in London 1800-1870................................80
7. Rowan and Mayne appointed Joint Commissioners...........94
8. External Problems I: The City of London................111
9. External Problems II: The Magistrates and the Police Offices...124
10. Internal Problems I: Recruiting, Discipline and Complaints....141
11. Internal Problems II: Conditions of Service............158
12. The Early Years..171
13. The Battle for Cold Bath Fields, 1833.................184
14. The Remainder of the 1830s.............................203
15. The Rise of Chartism...................................218
16. The Detective Force....................................231
17. The Late 1840s...246
18. Personal Life and Death of Sir Charles Rowan..........263
19. Mayne and Hay as Commissioners.........................280
20. The First Battle for Hyde Park.........................296
21. Mayne in Sole Charge...................................314
22. The Second Battle for Hyde Park........................330
23. The End of an Era......................................344
24. Personal Life and Death of Sir Richard Mayne..........360
25. The Legacy of Rowan and Mayne..........................375

Appendix: Reith's Nine Principles of Policing..................391
Bibliography...397
Index..409

ACKNOWLEDGEMENTS

This book has been some time in the writing. The vast majority of it has been completed at my home in Turkey and I could not have achieved what I have done without the valuable assistance of a number of people, particularly in England, with whom I was able to correspond by email, and visit on the various occasions when I travelled to London to carry out research. If, in my attempts to thank all of these people, I have omitted anyone, then I apologise most profusely.

When undertaking research of this magnitude, the assistance of archivists and libraries is an essential ingredient to success. Most of the records of the Metropolitan Police for the period are in the National Archives at Kew, and I spent quite a few days there. I am grateful to all the staff at Kew, including the catering staff, who on a number of occasions served me lunch in the excellent cafeteria, and the security staff, who on one occasion rescued some research papers that I had inadvertently left on the top of a locker in the locker room. I also spent three days at the Metropolitan Police Heritage Centre, where some additional records are stored, and I am more than grateful to Phillip Barnes-Warden, now retired, but who, at the time, virtually ran the Heritage Centre on his own. His helpful guidance, along with the occasional tea and biscuits, made this a particularly pleasant place to visit. Finally, the Parliamentary Archives very kindly provided me with copies of the many Parliamentary Papers relating to the police for the period 1829 to 1868. Again, the staff were extremely helpful in assisting me find what I required.

Personal correspondence either originated or received by Charles Rowan was spread between the West Sussex Archives at Chichester, the British Library and University College Archives in London, and the National Library of Scotland in Edinburgh. Most of these only entailed a single visit, but the correspondence between Rowan and the Duke of Richmond was such that I spent three days, on two of which I was assisted by my daughter Helen, at the West Sussex Archives going through the various letters. Towards the end of Rowan's life Richard Mayne also exchanged a number of letters with the Duke. My thanks to the staff of all four noted establishments for their generous assistance, but I am particularly grateful to Frances Lansley and her staff at the West Sussex Archives, who provided me with the list of the folio numbers of all the relevant letters which made it that much easier to trace them amongst the huge volume of papers which go to make up the Goodwood Papers. Other personal letters written and received by Richard Mayne were archived in two other places; the Metropolitan Police Heritage Centre in London, which had copies of a number of letters written in his official capacity, and the Wigan Archives in Lancashire, where I found copies of letters Mayne wrote to his wife over a number of years, in the Hall Collection. At Wigan, I am grateful for the assistance given by Alex Miller, both before and during my visit. From the City of London Metropolitan Archives, in Clerkenwell, I was able to establish where both men lived and stayed at various periods during their lives. Again, a huge thank you to the staff there, who were extremely helpful.

I am hugely grateful to all those historians who have already written about Rowan and Mayne and the early years of the Metropolitan Police, or have written about particular incidents that occurred during those first thirty-nine years. They are too numerous to mention individually – their books or articles can be found in the bibliography – but I must single out a former colleague, Lawrence Roach, who wrote a very perceptive thesis for the award of his doctorate at Loughborough University in 2005. Lawrence and I served together in the Metropolitan Police, as chief superintendents on what was then B District, in the early 1980s. Unfortunately, Lawrence died in January 2011 after suffering a brain haemorrhage. Media accounts were no more neutral in the 19th century than they are today in the 21st century. They should be approached with some caution, and consideration of the dominant ideas which existed in the society of the period. Yet they are a rich source of life during the period covered by this book. To all those journalists who provided such a rich source of material go my thanks.

I am particularly grateful to a number of individuals who assisted me, either by answering queries or by providing me with information once they became aware of the task I had undertaken. These include my dear friend and former colleague Roger Young; a former Metropolitan Police officer, Alan Moss, who has a deep interest in police history; and Jennie De Protari, Archivist at the Athenaeum Club in Pall Mall, who was able to confirm that Richard Mayne had been a member of the club from the time it opened until his death. Two other dear friends then had the arduous job of reading everything I had written whilst it was in draft form; Jeff Little,

Acknowledgements

a former Brigadier in the army, very kindly read the chapters dealing with the Rowan's military career, and Keith Weston read all the remaining chapters. Both made a number of helpful suggestions. That said, any errors or omissions in the book are mine. My thanks also go to Adam Wood and David Green of Mango Books. Without Adam's enthusiasm the book might never have been finished, and without David's meticulous attention to detail, it would not have been so accurate as I believe it to be. That said, any errors or omissions in the book are mine

Finally, my thanks go to five members of my family. To my brother Chris and daughter Tabitha, who acted as post-boxes for the many books about the Napoleonic Wars and the Metropolitan Police I purchased and had delivered to their home addresses; to my younger brother Nick, who, then an Associate Professor at Brock University in St Catherine's, Canada, was a huge help in providing me with obscure articles about the early days of the Metropolitan Police; to my daughter Helen, who is the family genealogist, who uncovered for me details of the Rowan and Mayne families, and who accompanied me on those two occasions to the West Sussex Archives; I am especially grateful for the information she was able to provide which enabled me to compile the two family trees. And, finally, to my wife, Hamide, who, once again, showed great patience in giving me the time and space to complete the book, and provide me with copious cups of tea and coffee.

Tony Moore
Izmir, Turkey
January 2020

ABOUT THE AUTHOR

After four years in the British Army, during which time he served in Germany and Aden, Tony Moore joined the Metropolitan Police. In a career spanning twenty-eight years he served successively at Commercial Street, Holborn, Bethnal Green, City Road, New Scotland Yard, Islington, Caledonian Road, Leyton, Kensington and Notting Hill. He served twice on the staff at The Police Staff College.

An experienced public order commander, he was involved in the policing of a number of high profile events, including the Iranian Embassy Siege, Notting Hill Carnival, the wedding of Prince Charles to Lady Diana Spencer, and, over a period of time, football hooliganism and clashes between right and left-wing demonstrators.

On leaving the police, he became Associate Director of the Resilience Centre at that part of Cranfield University based within what was originally known as the Royal Military College of Science but then became the Defence College of Management and Technology, at Shrivenham. There he taught on a number of Masters Courses, primarily on crisis and disaster management, and leadership and decision-making, but also ran short courses overseas on behalf of the UK Foreign and Commonwealth Office and the Ministry of Defence.

He holds a Master of Philosophy degree (M.Phil) from the University of Southampton, is a President Emeritus of the Institute of Civil Protection and Emergency Management, and a member of the Police History Society, the Metropolitan Police History Society and London Historians.

Apart from many articles on policing and emergency management, Tony's publications include *Tolley's Principles and Practice of Disaster Management* (as co-editor) (three editions 2002-2006); *Disaster and Emergency Management Systems* (2008); *Policing Notting Hill: Fifty Years of Turbulence* (2013); and *The Killing of Constable Keith Blakelock: The Broadwater Farm Riot* (2015).

INTRODUCTION

There have been many famous partnerships in history. The Wright brothers gave the world flight, Marie and Pierre Curie made incredible advances in medicine, Larry Page and Sergey Brin started the company that became Google, now an integral part of information technology, Gilbert and Sullivan gave us the light opera, Lennon and McCartney were the dynamic duo that changed popular music for ever, and there are many others. But in all the lists that have been conjured up, one partnership is always missing.

This is the story of that missing partnership: Charles Rowan and Richard Mayne, brought together by a third man, Robert Peel, to found the Metropolitan Police in 1829. It is just possible Peel may have briefly met Rowan when he visited Paris after the Battle of Waterloo, but he had certainly not met Mayne before inviting them to take up the appointments as joint commissioners; he certainly did not interview them. They were appointed entirely on the recommendations of influential people who knew them, or knew of them. But here, Peel had a remarkable 'fluke of good fortune', because they went on to form one of the most influential partnerships in British history. For it is out of their 'inventive competence' that the modern police service grew.[1] Their shaping of the Office of Commissioner and their consolidation of the operational independence of the police – since recently eroded somewhat by the introduction of Police and Crime Commissioners by a Tory/Liberal Coalition Government[2] – were their ultimate achievement, for it was an example to all future commissioners and, indeed, chief officers throughout the United Kingdom and beyond.

In the United Kingdom, the lives of many great people such as James

---

[1] Cowley, Richard (2011). *A History of the British Police from its Earliest Beginnings to the Present Day*. Stroud, Gloucestershire: The History Press, p.23.
[2] Mawby, Rob I, and Kreseda Smith (2017). 'Civilian oversight of the police in England and Wales: The election of Police and Crime Commissioners in 2012 and 2016'. In *International Journal of Police Studies and Management*, Vol. 19, Issue 1, pp.23-30.

Watt, who gave us the steam engine, Rowland Hill, the postage stamp, and Humphry Davy, the first electric light, together with literally hundreds of politicians, philanthropists and military commanders, such as the Duke of Wellington, have been commemorated in biographies. Houses in which they lived have been identified by the famous blue plaque, installed by English Heritage; statues have been erected. But there have been none to commemorate the achievements of Rowan and Mayne.

Fido and Skinner, in their groundbreaking book *The Official Encyclopedia of New Scotland Yard*, claim it is 'scandalous that there is no official standard biography of Rowan, or, better, of the partnership of Rowan and Mayne.'[3] The notable police historian Charles Reith wrote the nearest to a biography of Rowan in 1956 when his *A New Study of Police History* devoted the first seven chapters to his military career before describing the appointment of the two Commissioners and the setting up of the Metropolitan Police. However, there are gaps in Reith's study of Rowan, some of which I have been able to fill. For instance, he suggests that between 1822 and 1829, with one exception, 'there appears to be no trace of Charles Rowan in records of any kind.'[4] Some authors suggest he became a magistrate in Ireland but that is erroneous. From various sources, e.g. newspaper reports and the records of the United Service Club of which Rowan was a member, it will be seen that he was in London for the greater part of this period. He never wrote about his experiences, but much can be gleaned from two officers, General Sir George Napier[5] and Captain John Dobbs,[6] who served with him in the 52nd Regiment, and from one of his former commanding officers, Sir John Colborne.[7]

A number of books, on both the history of the police generally and of the Metropolitan Police in particular, mention Mayne's contribution, but none describe his life. All writers agree that Rowan and Mayne worked well together. But it is now clear that, for the latter part of their partnership, particularly when Rowan's health was deteriorating, Mayne was hoping he would retire and he then would become the sole Commissioner.[8]

Never was a government better served than the British government was

---

3 Fido, Martin, and Skinner, Keith (1999). *The Official Encyclopedia of Scotland Yard*. London: Virgin Books, p.228.
4 Reith, Charles (1956). *A New Study of Police History*. Edinburgh: Oliver and Boyd, p.5.
5 Napier, Sir George Thomas, and William Craig Emilius Napier (1884). *Passages in the Early Military Life of General Sir George T. Napier*. London: John Murray.
6 Dobbs, John, and Knowles, Robert (2008). *Gentlemen in Red: Two accounts of British Infantry Officers during the Peninsular War*. Available online at www.leonaur.com
7 Moore Smith, G.C (1903). *The Life of John Colborne, Field Marshal Lord Seaton*. London: John Murray.
8 See Chapter Seventeen.

by Charles Rowan and Richard Mayne during the first ten years of the life of the Metropolitan Police. With their combined abilities and an industry, seldom equalled, they formed and led a police force that was equalled by none. But they faced many obstacles brought about in part by the inadequacies of the arrangements made by Robert Peel in setting up the police. For instance, there was some uncertainty about the legal position of the Commissioners; and Peel left five systems of policing operating in parallel with the new Metropolitan Police. Nevertheless, if there was some uncertainty about their legal position, there was none about their power. Together they were a powerful combination. Rowan's success in masking all the problems and difficulties during the early period was made possible for him by his experiences during his time in the Peninsular during the Napoleonic Wars.

Unfortunately, within fourteen months of the Metropolitan Police taking to the streets Rowan and Mayne lost their greatest ally, Robert Peel, when the Tory government suddenly fell, primarily over Catholic emancipation. This brought in a Whig government which, with the exception of a brief four months in 1834, remained in power for nearly eleven years. The Whigs had been opposed to the setting up of the Metropolitan Police in the first place, and, whilst they quickly recognised to disband it would have been extremely foolish, the first two Whig Home Secretaries, Melbourne and Duncannon, made it particularly uncomfortable at times for the Commissioners.

The early years were filled with intrigue, often emanating from the Home Office, but particularly from the Chief Magistrates' Office at Bow Street, which was occupied firstly by Sir Robert Bernie, who died in 1832, and then by Sir Frederick Roe from 1831 to 1839. Both, particularly Roe, fought an unedifying campaign with the Commissioners, primarily through the police officers they came into contact with during their day-to-day activities.

These problems placed an unnecessary burden on the Commissioners during the early period. They constantly brought them to the attention of the government, either through official correspondence with the Home Office or in the evidence they gave to various select committees, of which there were a number. Frequently they were met by vexatious opposition. The ministers, it appeared, were incapable of providing solutions, frequently neglecting the most obvious means of rectifying the problem. Moreover, whilst listening to every intriguing advisor, they frequently ignored the advice given by the Commissioners.

Yet, despite the difficulties, they became one of the most iconic partnerships in London's long and often turbulent history. It is impossible to accurately measure the effect it had, not only on London but the remainder of the United Kingdom, what was then the Empire, now the Commonwealth, and a number of other Western democracies. From the actions they took in those early days stems the policing system that still exists in many countries today. And yet the part played by Rowan and Mayne remains largely unrecognised.[9]

Any attempt to capture their lives, or the problems they faced in setting up the Metropolitan Police, within a simple chronological narrative would only produce mush. Instead, while some chapters in this book do focus on a period, others focus on a particular theme. In some places, it is necessary to zoom in from the general to the specific and then back out again.

Part I of the book consists of six chapters; a chapter outlining the ancestral history of the Rowan and Mayne families, four chapters on the Napoleonic Wars, and a chapter on London as it was during the first half of the nineteenth century. It should, perhaps, be pointed out that Chapters Two to Five are not meant to be an authoritative history of the Napoleonic Wars. Although lacking in detail due to an absence of specific information, it is an attempt to show what Rowan went through during his military career and the experiences he gained, firstly as a regimental officer and then as a staff officer before returning to regimental duties. Similarly, neither is the remainder of the book meant to be an authoritative history of the Metropolitan Police. Rather, it is the story of two men from totally different walks of life, with different skills, coming together to form one of the most famous partnerships in the history of London.

Part II, which includes Chapters Seven to Eighteen, describes how, in just twenty years, the two men worked together to produce the most competent police force the world had seen. Following Rowan's retirement at the beginning of 1850, Part III – Chapters Nineteen to Twenty-five – describes how Mayne continued for five years in a very unsatisfactory partnership with Captain William Hay, before taking sole command for the last thirteen years of his life. However, as the force grew in size from 3,000 to 8,000 men, it became increasingly difficult for Mayne to maintain the standards that had been set by Rowan and himself during those first twenty years. Finally, the story would be incomplete if it finished without discussing the controversy that exists over the legacy they left, not only in the United Kingdom but in many parts of the free democratic world.

Since the formation of the Metropolitan Police in 1829, twenty-seven

---

9   Charles Reith is an exception to this comment.

Introduction

people have held the role of Commissioner. The great commissioners were leaders who confronted and overcame difficulties, but none made a greater contribution than Rowan and Mayne. As Reith pointed out in 1943, 'the story of the struggle' of Rowan and Mayne 'and the eventual triumph of their courage, tact, consummate patience and single-mindedness of purpose, which were at first their only defence against the misguided hostility of King, Ministers, and populace, is an overlooked and forgotten, but very significant item in the history of the British nation.'[10]

This, then, is the story of Charles Rowan and Richard Mayne.

---

10   Reith, Charles (1943). *British Police and the Democratic Ideal*. Oxford: Oxford University Press, p.26.

CHAPTER ONE

THE ROWANS AND MAYNES OF IRELAND

Ireland's contribution to the Metropolitan Police, indeed policing in many parts of the former British Empire, cannot be over-estimated. Like several famous people of the time, the most famous of whom was the Duke of Wellington, who led British Forces in the defeat of Napoleon, Charles Rowan and Richard Mayne were children of eighteenth century Ireland, although neither of their families originated from there. Rowan's ancestors were from Scotland, Mayne's from England. Mayne's ancestors beat Rowan's ancestors to Ireland by about twenty-five years, both arriving during the Plantation of Ulster, a period in history that saw many people from England and Scotland settle in the northern part of Ireland.

In 1594 Gaelic Irish Chieftains rose against English rule resulting in the Nine Years War that ended in 1603, when most of the native Gaelic chiefs fled to Europe. This led to the forfeiture of their lands.[11] Much of Ireland, especially Ulster, was therefore left leaderless. The end of the War coincided with the death of Queen Elizabeth I, who had no immediate heirs, so King James VI, who had been on the Scottish throne since 1567, also became James I of England. Despite having the same monarch, the two countries continued as individual sovereign states, with their own parliaments, until the Act of Union in 1707. One of the first acts James took following his accession to the throne of England was to replace the Gaelic chiefs with suitable nominees, referred to as 'Undertakers', from England and Scotland. This became known as 'the Plantation of Ulster', in which arable land was offered to the Undertakers in plots of 1,000, 1,500 or 2,000 acres.[12]

---

11 For an insight into the war, see O'Neill, James (2017). *The Nine Years War, 1593-1603*. Dublin: Four Courts Press.
12 Gillespie, Raymond (2007). 'After the Flight: the plantation of Ulster', in *History Ireland*, Volume 15, issue 4 (Jul-Aug), pp.40-45.

Richard Mayne was a descendant of the Sedborough Mayne family which can be traced back to 1629, when John Mayne, believed to be from Ulster, married Barbara Sedborough, the granddaughter of John Sedborough, who originated from Porlock in Somerset. John Sedborough, had been awarded 1,000 acres in 1614 and therefore became an Undertaker. When he died in 1629, he left all his property to Barbara and her husband, John.[13]

For the next twelve years, John and Barbara lived a relatively peaceful and productive life at Mount Sedborough in County Fermanagh, but the 23 October 1641 saw the first day of a rebellion by Irish Catholics. In one of their first acts approximately 40 people, led by an Irish Catholic nobleman named Connor Maguire, arrived at Mount Sedborough, broke into the house, stole everything worth taking and drove off the couple's livestock. The following day John Mayne attempted to escape from the property with his wife and infant child, also named John, but they had only gone two miles before they were intercepted by the same gang, again led by Maguire, which 'fell upon [Mayne] and greavously [sic] wounded and killed him.'[14] Barbara and the infant child were spared and made their way to Dublin. Connor Maguire was subsequently arrested, tried for high treason and sentenced to be hung, drawn and quartered.[15]

John Mayne Jr. was educated in England but eventually returned to Mount Sedborough, where he married Anne Morton, the daughter of Edward Morton of Calnacough, also in County Fermanagh. They had five children, the youngest being Robert. Robert Mayne married Rebecca Pearce, the daughter of the Reverend Edward Pearce. Rebecca's mother, Margaret, was the daughter of Richard Dawson of Dawson's Grove who owned a considerable amount of land. Quite how he acquired it is uncertain. One unconfirmed source suggested that an ancestor of Richard's had been an officer in Cromwell's army, and had been given it; another, also unconfirmed but the more likely, that he was a speculator in Irish lands, and had bought land allocated to Cromwell's soldiers. Two months before John Mayne Jr. died in 1710 he transferred to Robert 'four townlands,[16] the mountain of Knockalossetbeag, the Corn mill and its Moulter, and the Courts Leet and Courts Baron of Mount Sedborough.'[17] One of the

---

13   Sedborough-Mayne of Ireland. See tr.scribd.com/doc/75988391 [accessed 6 July 2017].
14   Statement made by Barbara Mayne in Dublin in January 1842, the original of which is at Trinity College, Dublin (MS 835, folios 36v.-17).
15   For an insight into this rebellion, see Perceval-Maxwell, M (1994). *Outbreak of the Irish Rebellion of 1641*. Montreal: McGill-Queen's Press.
16   A townland was a small geographical area of land.
17   Sedborough-Mayne of Ireland, op. cit. 13. The purpose of the courts was to preserve the rights of the landowner, on the one hand, and regulate the relationships between the tenants, on the other. The courts leet also dealt with any criminal matters.

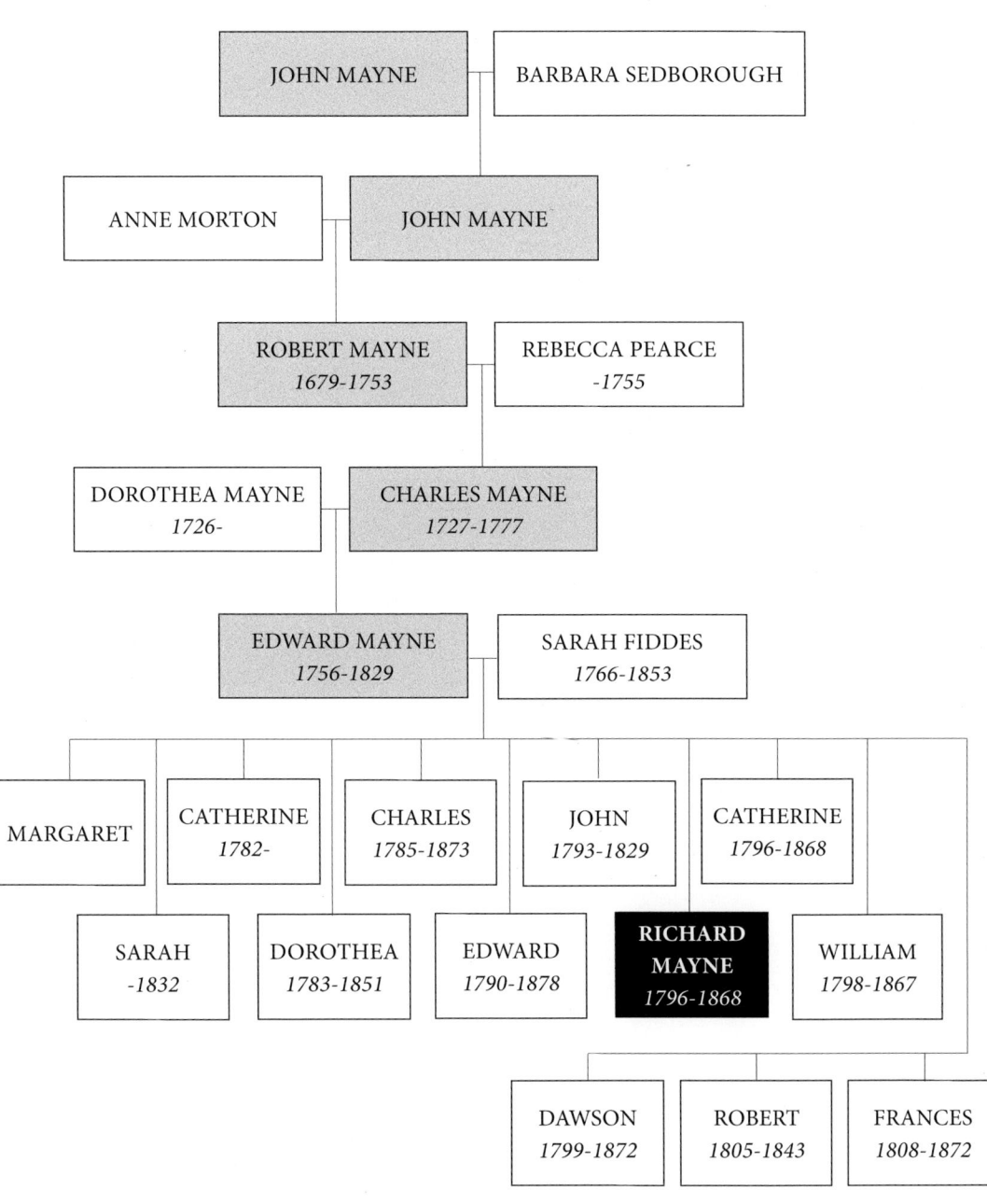

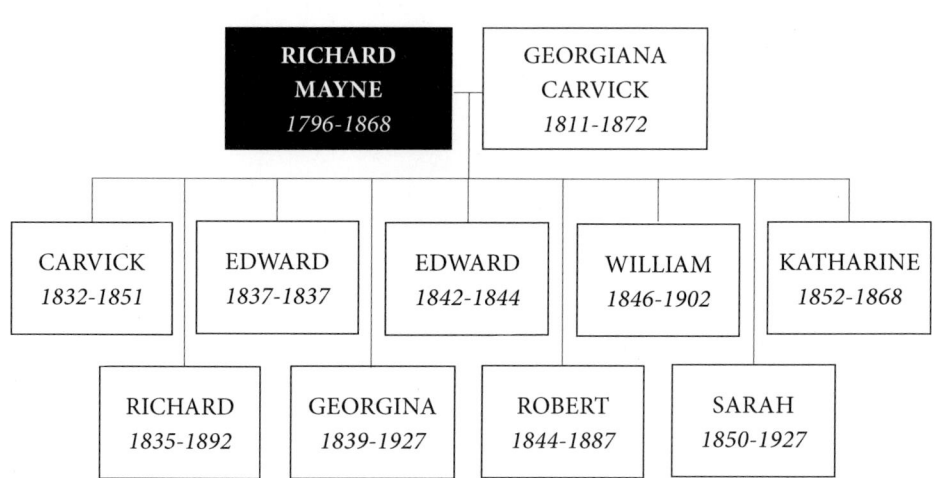

children of the marriage between Robert Mayne and Rebecca was Richard's grandfather, Charles Mayne. Charles built a magnificent house at Freame Mount in 1772. The house overlooked the Dartrey Estate, which was owned by Thomas Dawson, who was also Charles's cousin and benefactor. In fact, Charles named the house after Thomas's wife, Philadelphia Hannah Freame, the granddaughter of William Penn of Pennsylvania. Thomas was the Member of Parliament for Monaghan from 1749 to 1768. In 1770 he was raised to the Peerage of Ireland as Baron Dartrey of Dawson's Grove. In 1785, he became Viscount Cremorne. When Charles married a first cousin, Dorothea Mayne, he effectively became head of the family from his home in Cootehill, County Cavan.[18]

In 1764, a great-uncle of Richard's, Edward Mayne, was tried for murder, although there was little chance of a conviction given the circumstances that led to the trial. Edward served as a lieutenant in the 93rd Regiment of Foot until 1763 when, aged 38 years, he retired from the army and returned to Cootehill. Earlier, a movement known as the Oakboys had been formed to protest local taxation. When Charles Coote, the local magistrate, was faced with having to protect lives and homesteads from the Oakboy Movement[19] in 1763, it was natural he should call on the recently-retired Lieutenant Edward Mayne, acting as a private citizen, to advise him. The Oakboy Movement was well organised, often marching in companies, each with a standard or colours displayed, and could, in total, amount to several thousands. Usually, when opposed by military units the Oakboys would disperse but, on this occasion, they did not. On 17th July Coote, accompanied by Edward Mayne, together with fourteen of Coote's tenants and a troop of light horse, rode to Castleblayney, where the Oakboys had assembled in numbers. Arriving at about 2.00pm, they saw the streets were full of Oakboys. Coote and his party retired to a nearby hostelry to await the arrival of Colonel Roberts, who was in command of local military units. After dining and toasting the King's health, Mayne and Coote went out to meet Colonel Roberts but were set upon by a number of the Oakboys. Armed only with swords, they managed to make their escape but not before one of the Oakboys' leaders, Alexander McDonald, had been fatally injured. The following year, Coote and Edward Mayne stood trial jointly for the murder of McDonald, but given the opposition that existed against the Oakboys a conviction was never likely. In fact, Coote was subsequently knighted for his enthusiasm in putting down the

---

18   Sedborough-Mayne of Ireland, op. cit. 13.
19   For more about the Oakboys, see Donnell, James (1981). 'Hearts of Oak, Hearts of Steel'. In *Studia Hibernica* (21) published by Liverpool University press, pp.7-73.

rebellion.[20]

Charles and Dorothea Mayne had seven children, five sons of whom the first born was Edward, Richard's father, and two daughters. Edward enrolled at Trinity College, Dublin, in 1772 with the intention of pursuing a career in law. He graduated in 1777, the year his father died. As the eldest son the estate at Freame Mount passed to him. Rather than abandon his career in law, he passed over the responsibility for running the estate to his younger brother William and, for a short time, he became a Justice of the Peace and High Sheriff of County Monaghan. However, in 1779 he went to London and entered the Middle Temple, from which he graduated as a barrister two years later. In the meantime, he had married Sarah Fiddes, daughter of John Fiddes, who was an Attorney in Dublin. Returning to Ireland, helped initially by his father-in-law, Edward built up a successful career as a barrister in Dublin and moved his family to 28 St. Stephen's Green North, then one of a terrace of impressive five-storey houses, with basements and attics. It is now part of the Shelbourne Hotel.[21]

*

Charles Rowan's ancestors arrived in Ireland following the rebellion by Irish Catholics. Because of the number of 'Undertakers' in Ulster from Scotland, in the summer of 1842, about nine months after the rebellion had broken out, the Scottish parliament sent some 10,000 soldiers to protect them. Based in Carrickfergus, the Scottish army fought against the rebels until 1650, but whilst they successfully protected the Undertakers they were less successful in quelling the rebellion. During this period, chaplains of the Scottish army moved away from the Church of Scotland and set up the Presbytery of Ulster. In 1656, the congregation of Clough in County Antrim petitioned the Presbytery of Ulster to provide a minister. As a result, the Reverend Andrew Rowan, son of John Rowan, who was known as 'The Laird' of Greenhead in the parish of Govan in Ayrshire, and great-great-great grandfather to Charles Rowan, came to Clough as a minister. But things were not straightforward. King Charles I had been executed on 30th January 1649, and the Commonwealth of England, under Oliver Cromwell, came into being. Partly as a result of this, when the Reverend Andrew Rowan arrived in Ireland there existed what was known as a period of Episcopalian tolerance.[22]

---

20 Sedborough-Mayne of Ireland, op. cit. 13.
21 Ibid.
22 James, Francis Godwin (1979). 'The Church of Ireland in the Early 18th Century' in *Historical Magazine of the Protestant Episcopal Church*. Vol. 48, no. 4, pp.435-445.

Episcopacy involved a system of church government based on the offices of the ministry, bishops, priests and deacons. But, following the restoration of the Monarchy in 1660, after Cromwell's brief reign as Lord Protector, the period of religious tolerance came to an end with the passing of the Act of Conformity in 1662, which stipulated that all church ceremonies must be in accordance with the Book of Common Prayer.

Andrew Rowan was 'one of eight minsters', out of a total of seventy-two, who refused, preferring to continue with Episcopacy. In doing so 'he incurred the disrespect and severe condemnation of Presbyterians' but, for himself and his family, 'it paved the way to prosperity'. Still regarded by the Irish administration as a Presbyterian minister, he was paid a stipend. He also became a friend of the Earl and Countess of Antrim. The Earl, formerly Alexander MacDonnell, had been appointed *custos rotulorum* (the principal justice of the peace of a county) for Antrim in 1680, and became the Earl of Antrim two years later on the death of his brother. Resident in Glenarm Castle on the coast of the County of Antrim, Andrew's friendship with the Earl and Countess resulted in him becoming a man of some wealth, 'a pluralist, a money lender and a large farmer.'[23]

Andrew had, in the meantime, married Eliza MacPhedris, daughter of Captain William MacPhedris, in 1658. The couple's second son became the Reverend John Rowan, who married Margaret Stewart, of County Down, in 1692. They had a number of children including Robert Rowan who, in 1753, married Letitia, daughter of Captain Stewart of Lisbon, County Antrim. Their son, also named John after his grandfather, married another Stewart, Rose Stewart. Their eldest son and heir, Robert, was Charles Rowan's father.

In 1777 Robert married Eliza, daughter of Hill Wilson of Purdysburn, County Down. Although Robert had inherited property, it was 'heavily encumbered with debts' because of 'negligence by trustees, and his natural improvidence ensured that he was impecunious all his life.' As a result, he had to leave the family home at Belleisle, and he took 'a small house near Carrickfergus,' in County Antrim.[24]

Ireland in the late Eighteenth century and early Nineteenth century when the two future Commissioners of the Metropolitan Police were being brought into this world bore little resemblance to what it does today. The population had grown from 2 million in 1700 to just over 5 million in 1800. By 1770, nearly 100% of the land was owned by non-Irish landowners

---

23 Glens of Antrim Historical Society (2013). 'A Church at Clough', see antrimhistory.net/a-church-at-clough, [accessed on 15 September 2017].
24 Reith, Charles (1956). *A New Study of Police History*. London: Oliver and Boyd, p.5.

and the native Irishmen had mainly become tenant farmers. The rural population tended to live in small, windowless, mud cabins. Furniture consisted of a bed and some chairs. It was normal for farm animals, pigs and chickens, to sleep in the cabin with the human occupants. However, after 1770, greedy landowners increased their rental incomes by dividing and sub-dividing their land again and again, until many families were forced to exist on less than an acre. As potatoes were such an efficient crop, by the late 18th century it was practically the only crop being grown by tenant farmers. Many during their lifetime did not taste meat or even bread. Their staple diet was potato and perhaps buttermilk.[25]

At the time Dublin, where Richard's father had settled, was a growing city; by 1800, the population had grown to 180,000, The movement of the seat of government from Dublin to Westminster in accordance with the Act of Union, which came into force on 1 January 1801, caused a steep political and economic decline in the city, bringing with it poverty and disease.[26] A police force had been established in 1786,[27] but it is doubtful that Richard had any contact with it, although his father may have as a practising attorney.

This then was the country to which first Charles and then Richard were born. Charles was born in County Antrim in 1782, the fifth of the ten children born of the union between Robert and Eliza Rowan. Indeed, their first eight children were all boys, born between 1778 and 1789. The two girls were born in 1791 and 1793. All were educated at the local school in Carrickfergus, run by the Reverend Snowden Cupples, who had been appointed Curate there in 1781. Cupples provided the children with an 'excellent education', and it is suggested their father's improvidence 'was amply compensated by the happy home life and strict training in high principles which he and their mother provided for them'. Indeed, their mother, Eliza, was reportedly 'famed for her vivacity and wit.'[28] Unsurprisingly, given the lack of opportunity for the children of impoverished families, there is a similarity in the careers pursued by Charles Rowan and his brothers in that the boys gravitated towards the military.

Charles was destined for the army from an early age for, at the age of

---

25   Smith, Cynthia E (1993). 'The Land-Tenure System in Ireland: A Fatal Regime', in 76, *Maraquette Law Review* 469, available at scholarship.law.maraquette.edu/mulr/vol76/iss2/6 [accessed 20 July 2018].
26   'The Irish Famine' at historycooperative.org/the-irsh-famine [accessed 20 July 2018].
27   Henry, Brian (1993). 'The First Modern Police in the British Isles: Dublin, 1786-1795', in *Police Studies*, volume 16, no. 4, p.167-178.
28   Reith, op. cit. 24, p.5.

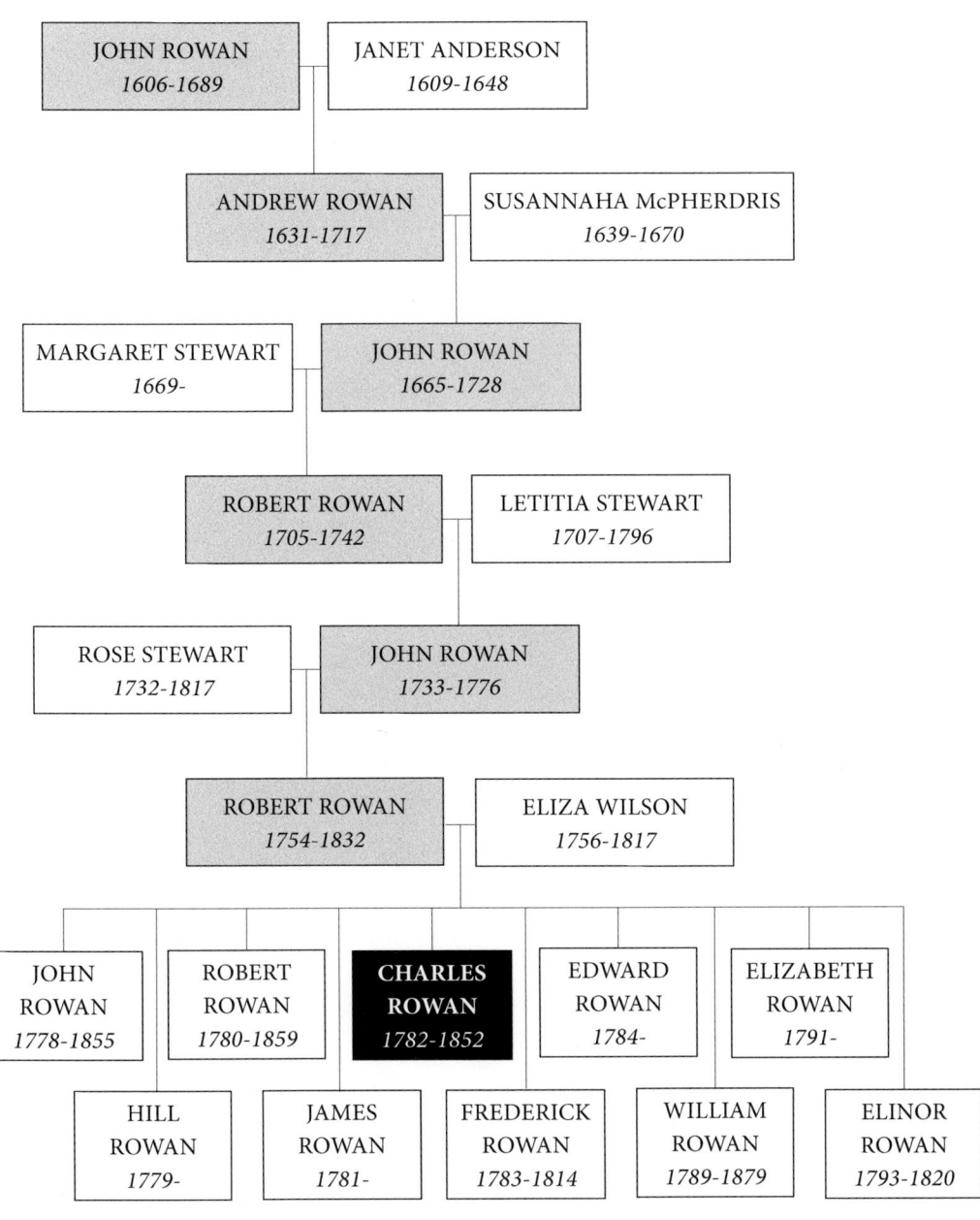

fourteen, he joined the 52nd Regiment as an ensign. In those days if a person wanted to join the army as an officer it was necessary to purchase a commission, but quite how or who paid for it in the case of Charles is unknown. At first his choice of the 52nd Regiment, subsequently named the Oxfordshire Light Infantry, may seem strange, but it is not surprising, perhaps, given that he already had an uncle of the same name, Charles, serving as a captain in the regiment.[29] The future Commissioner's eldest brother, Major John Rowan, was already an officer in the Antrim Militia, an Irish Regiment of the British Army that took a leading part in quelling yet another Irish Rebellion which lasted from May to September 1798. In a letter from the Marquess Cornwallis, then Lord Lieutenant and Commander-in-Chief of British Forces in Ireland, John Rowan, then a lieutenant, was singled out for praise following an attack by 'many thousands' of rebels on the military post at Hacketstown in June which was successfully repulsed.[30] He was promoted to the rank of Major on 16 April 1808.[31] In 1814, having left the army, he was appointed High Sheriff of County Antrim. He also became chair of Ireland's Justice of the Peace Association, and in 1839 the first chair of the Board of Guardians, responsible for overseeing the running of Poor Houses in Belfast.[32] Born three years after Charles, another brother, James, initially joined the Antrim Militia, but on 7 February 1800 became an Ensign in the 64th Regiment, rising to the rank of Major before leaving and being appointed Chief Police Magistrate for the Town and Territory of Gibraltar in 1830,[33] shortly after Charles was appointed Commissioner of the newly-founded Metropolitan Police in London.

Robert Rowan, who was two years older than Charles, followed his younger brother into the 52nd Regiment in 1799. Rising to the rank of Captain, he decided to leave in 1807, after seeing action at Ferrol and in Sicily.[34] Quite what he did after he left is unknown. Suffice to say he had three wives who produced twelve children in total.

Charles's youngest brother, William, seven years his junior, served with

---

29 See Chapter Two.
30 Letter from Cornwallis to the Duke of Portland, dated 25 June 1898, which appeared in the *London Gazette* on 3 July 1798.
31 War Office (1809). *A List of the Officers of the Militia of the United Kingdom; with an index.* London: C. Roworth, p.95.
32 *London Gazette*, 8 April 1800, Issue 15246, p.346.
33 HM Government of Gibraltar (2015). Press Release No. 247/2015 dated 22 April. 'Freedom of the City of Gibraltar to be bestowed upon the Royal Gibraltar Police'.
34 Moorsom, W.S (Ed)(1860). *Historical Record of the Fifty-Second Regiment (Oxfordshire Light Infantry) from the Year 1755 to the year 1858.* Uckfield, Sussex: The Naval and Military Press, p.444; see also Chapter Two.

him in the 52nd Regiment, although not always in the same battalion. William went on to be the most successful military officer in the Rowan family. Attaining the rank of Lieutenant-Colonel in 1830, he was appointed Military and Civil Secretary to the Lieutenant Governor of Upper Canada, Sir John Colborne, who had been one of Charles Rowan's commanding officer's during the Napoleonic Wars. When Colborne was appointed Acting Governor General of British North America during a rebellion by French-Quebecers against the British colonial power, sometimes known as the Patriot War, in 1837,[35] William Rowan was promoted to Colonel. He returned to England in June 1839 but ten years later, having in the meantime been promoted Major-General, he returned to Canada as Commander-in-Chief, North America. Promoted Lieutenant-General in 1854, he went back to England the following year when he retired from active service. He was promoted full General in 1862, knighted in 1865 and promoted Field Marshall in 1877, two years before his death.[36]

Born the year after Charles, a fourth brother, Frederick Rowan joined the 64th Regiment as an Ensign in April 1800,[37] on exactly the same day as his brother James transferred from the Militia, also as an Ensign, but subsequently Frederick transferred to 4th West Indies Regiment. He was slightly wounded leading the forlorn hope[38] on a successful assault on the Fortress of Morne Fortuné against the French on the island of St Lucia in 1803.[39] Frederick married Sarah Prom from Bergen in Norway. The couple had two daughters, the second Frederica born just six months before Frederick's tragic death, from disease, in October 1814.[40] In between these two events he had been promoted to Brevet Major.[41] Returning from the West Indies, Sarah took her two daughters to live successively in Copenhagen, Weimer and Paris before settling in London. As a result, Frederica was fluent in four languages and became a notable author and translator.[42] By then, firmly established as Commissioner of Police, Charles Rowan effectively became their benefactor, as will be seen later.[43]

---

35 Greer, Alan (1995). '1837-1838 Rebellion Reconsidered' in *Canadian Historical Review* 76.1, pp.1-18.
36 Preston, Richard (2003), 'Rowan, Sir William' in *Dictionary of Canadian Biography*, vol. 10, University of Toronto. See www.biographi.ca/en/bio/rowan_william_10E.html, [accessed 26 August 2017].
37 *London Gazette*, 8 April 1800, Issue 15246, p.346.
38 A forlorn hope is fully described in Chapter Three.
39 *London Gazette*, 26 July 1803, Issue 15605, p.918.
40 *The United Services Journal and Navy and Military Magazine 1836; Table-talk of an Old Campaigner II*. London: Henry Cockburn, p.214.
41 *London Gazette*, 7 June 1814, Issue 169, p.1185.
42 *Dictionary of National Biography*, Volume 49. London: Macmillan, p.336.
43 See Chapter Eighteen.

Charles's two sisters were Elizabeth Rowan, born in 1791, of whom little is known, and Elinor Rowan, born in 1793. It is not clear why, but it appears that his mother and father, Robert and Eliza, moved to the Isle of Man with at least one daughter, Elinor. Eliza, Charles's mother, unfortunately died at Castletown in November 1817.[44] Elinor went on to marry a lawyer, John Heywood, a member of a long-established Manx family who was the proprietor of Bemahague, on 5 May 1819 at Malew, Isle of Man. Bemahague was bought by the Isle of Man Government in 1904 and is now Government House. Unfortunately the marriage did not last long, because Elinor died giving birth to a daughter the following year. In 1821, Heywood was appointed as one of Her Majesty's Deemsters[45] for the island, a position he held until his death in 1855. Despite the loss of his wife and daughter Robert stayed on the Isle of Man, surviving to see his son Charles, appointed as Commissioner of the Metropolitan Police. He died at Douglas on 13 September 1832.[46]

Meanwhile, Edward and Sarah Mayne had thirteen children. Twelve reached adulthood, with only the first, Catherine, born in 1782, dying as a child. The second child, also a girl Dorothea, was born the following year. In 1813 Dorothea married a first cousin, Captain John Mayne, who served briefly in the 9th Light Dragoons from 1795 to 1803. The 9th Light Dragoons played an active part in putting down the Irish Rebellion of 1798, during which several members of the regiment were either killed or wounded. The third child, Charles Mayne, the first son, was born in 1785. He initially followed his father into the legal profession, being called to the Irish Bar in 1808 after attending both the King's Inn in Dublin and Middle Temple, London. However, he later became a clergyman, becoming successively Rector of Kilmastulla and Vicar General of the Diocese of Cashel in County Clare. The fourth child, another son, Edward, born in 1791, also became a lawyer, but little is known about him. The fifth child, another girl, Sarah, about who, again, very little is known, other than it is believed she married a clergyman, the Reverend R. French, in 1830, but she died two years later, possibly during child-birth. The sixth child, John, was born in 1793. After attending Trinity College, Dublin, he became a solicitor before he subsequently attended Lincoln's Inn in London and became a barrister, but he died in 1829, at the age of 36. At the time of his death, John was Clerk of the Peace for County Cavan. The seventh child, another daughter, named Catherine after the first daughter who had died,

---

44 *Saunders's News-Letter*, 17 September 1817, p.2.
45 A Deemster was a High Court judge in the Isle of Man.
46 *Belfast Newsletter*, 21 September 1832, p.2.

was born in 1795. She married Major Basil Heron, of the Royal Artillery, who had been wounded at Vitoria during the Peninsula War; he died in Gibraltar in 1841.[47]

Richard Mayne, the future Commissioner of the Metropolitan Police, was the eighth child to be born, on 27 November 1796. However, in 1805, when Richard was just nine years old, his father, Edward, was appointed a Judge of the Court of Common Pleas of Ireland. In 1816 he became a Judge of the Court of King's Bench (Ireland), but was forced to resign two years later due to ill-health.[48] This was three years before Richard embarked on a career as a barrister. In poor health, Edward lived out his life at the home of his eldest son, Charles, at Cashel. He died in May 1829,[49] a mere two months before Richard was appointed as one of the two commissioners of the Metropolitan Police.

Richard was educated at a private school near Dublin before entering Trinity College, Dublin in 1815. The university already had a long history, having been founded by royal charter in the reign of Queen Elizabeth I in 1592. Richard was awarded a degree in 1819 and in the same year he applied for admission to Lincoln's Inn, whose history goes back even further to 1422. Whilst there, he entered Trinity College, Cambridge, yet another seat of learning with an ancient history. It was created by Henry VIII as a result of the merging of two older places of learning, King's Hall and Michaelhouse, which dated from 1317 and 1324 respectively. His original intention appears to have been to study for a Bachelor of Arts degree but, in the end, he was awarded a Master of Arts degree. He was called to the Bar in 1822. He went on the Northern Circuit and appeared mainly at West Riding Sessions.[50]

The ninth child was William about who, again, very little is known. It is suggested he may have served in the army and reached the rank of Lieutenant-Colonel, but that cannot be verified. The tenth child, another son, Dawson, was born in 1799. He enjoyed a distinguished career in the Royal Navy. On his retirement, he became the first chief officer of the newly-formed Shropshire Constabulary in February 1840. He retired in 1859 but continued to live with his wife, Mary Elizabeth, in Shrewsbury. However, towards the end of his life, it seems they separated and he returned to Killaloe in County Clare, where he lived out his last few years with his unmarried younger sister, Frances Rebecca. He died there

---

47 Sedborough-Mayne of Ireland, op. cit. 13.
48 Ibid.
49 *Dublin Morning Register*, 12 May 1829, p.2.
50 Sedborough-Mayne of Ireland, op. cit. 13.

on 25 September 1872.[51] His wife, Mary Elizabeth, died three years later at Sidmouth in Devon on 21 September.[52] Nothing is known about the eleventh child, Margaret, other than it is believed she married a medical practitioner named Dr Beatty, possibly in 1827.[53] The twelfth child, Robert, born in 1805, joined the 86th Regiment of Foot, which later became the Royal Irish Fusiliers, as an Ensign in 1825. He spent 12 years in the army, which included a tour in the West Indies from 1826 to 1831, rising to the rank of Captain.[54] Retiring in 1837 he joined two of his cousins, Captain Edward Mayne and William Mayne, in Queensland, Australia, where he died six years later at the age of 43 years.[55] The last, a daughter, Frances Rebecca, known as Fanny, never married. She lived for some time with her brother Richard in London, when he was Commissioner of the Metropolitan Police, but on his death she returned to Killaloe in County Clare, where, as just mentioned, she lived out the last few years of her life with her brother Dawson. She died, aged 64 years, on 29 October 1872.[56]

So the two young men who would be the first Commissioners of the Metropolitan Police, although both came from large families, which was common at the time, had very different experiences of Ireland in their formative years. The son of a highly-regarded Dublin Attorney, Richard was educated at a private school and then went to university before becoming a barrister like his father. Charles, in the meantime, was born into an impoverished family, went to the local village school and joined the army at fourteen years of age.

---

51 *Morning Post*, 2 October 1872, p.8.
52 *London Evening Standard*, 25 September 1875, p.7.
53 Sedborough- Mayne of Ireland, op. cit. 13.
54 *London Gazette*, 11 October 1859, p.2082.
55 Sedborough-Mayne of Ireland, op. cit. 13.
56 *Morning Post*, 30 October 1872, p.7.

CHAPTER TWO

THE MAKING OF AN OFFICER

Charles Rowan joined the 52nd Regiment in July 1798[57] and served continuously either at Regimental Duty with the 1st Battalion or at Formation Headquarters in staff appointments until his retirement in April 1822. The War of the First Coalition (1792-1797) had just come to an end. It had been the first attempt by the European monarchies to defeat Revolutionary France, but had effectively ended in victory for the French. During this period a young French officer, Napoleon Bonaparte, had become increasingly influential, not only in military matters but in French politics. The 52nd Regiment had just returned from a lengthy tour of duty in India and Rowan joined the battalion at Chatham. A number of sources incorrectly claim he was appointed paymaster on 8 November 1798,[58] but it was an uncle, also named Charles Rowan,[59] then a captain, who was appointed to this role on the Regiment's return from India.[60] In December, the Regiment moved to Colchester and then, in early 1799, to Barking where Rowan attained the rank of lieutenant by purchase.[61] Given the impecunious state of his parents it is not known how he paid for it. For reasons that are not immediately apparent, other than it seems to have been normal practice to keep them on the move, the regiment moved to Ashford in July, and then to Chelmsford in December.[62]

On 25 June 1800, Rowan sailed with the 1/52nd Regiment from Southampton as 'part of a force which was being collected for a secret service'. Landing on the tiny Isle de Houat in Quiberon Bay, just off the

---

57 *London Gazette*, 17 July 1898, Issue 15042, p.670.
58 Fido, Martin, and Martin Skinner (1999). *The Official Encyclopedia of Scotland Yard*. London: Virgin Books, p.226.
59 Uncle Charles Rowan was the younger brother of the future Commissioner's father.
60 *London Gazette*, 10 November 1798, Issue 15079, p.1073.
61 *London Gazette*, 16 March 1799, Issue 15116, p.251.
62 Moorsom, W.S (Ed)(1860). *Historical Record of the Fifty-Second Regiment (Oxfordshire Light Infantry) from the Year 1755 to the year 1858*. Uckfied, Sussex: The Naval and Military Press, pp.57-58.

north coast of France, they came under the command of Brigadier-General the Honourable Thomas Maitland. Maitland had been given instructions to go to the aid of an anticipated royalist uprising in France, but it never materialised. Consequently, after staying with two other regiments on a very crowded island only 3 miles long and a mile wide for just under three weeks, the 1/52nd re-embarked and joined an expedition under Lieutenant-General Sir James Pulteney, destined for Spain.[63] The 2nd battalion of the 52nd Regiment was already part of the expedition. On 25 August, in an obscure and largely forgotten attempt to capture Ferrol, a small port on the northern coast of Spain, both battalions of the 52nd Regiment were put ashore. Rowan saw his first military action the following morning when they attacked 'and gained possession of the heights above the town'. Rowan's battalion 'had the principal share in this action',[64] losing one officer and eight rank-and-file killed and a further 40 wounded. However, after seeing the strength of the fortifications around the town and harbour, Pulteney decided his forces were insufficient to mount an effective assault and re-embarked the troops.[65]

From there, both battalions went to Cadiz in southern Spain, but a plan to take the town was abandoned. Rough seas meant the fleet could not venture close to the landing points. Thus there was a danger that the troops could not be evacuated if it became necessary once they were ashore. An added complication in Cadiz was the plague, which was causing up to 300 deaths a day. Eventually both battalions landed at Lisbon where they stayed for two months before returning to Ramsgate. Disembarking on 26 January 1801, 1/52nd marched to Canterbury, with the 2nd Battalion going to Ashford. On 8 May Major-General John Moore, Colonel-Commandant of the 2/52nd Regiment, was appointed Colonel of the whole Regiment by King George III. In November, the 1st Battalion marched to Deal and the 2nd Battalion moved to Dover. A year later both battalions moved to Chatham, where they remained until 1803.[66]

Britain had largely stayed out of the War of the Second Coalition, in which France was opposed primarily by Russia and Austria. It came to an end in March 1802, with Britain and France signing the Treaty of Amiens. This brought peace to Europe, but it lasted only for fourteen months. By May 1803, Britain and France were again at war and it was feared that Napoleon was planning an invasion of Britain. But units of the British

---

63 Ibid, p.58.
64 Official despatch of Lt. Gen. Sir James Pulteney, dated 27 August 1800 quoted in Moorsom, op. cit. 62, p.59.
65 Moorsom, op. cit. 62, p.58-59.
66 Ibid, p.61.

army, strung out as they were along the south coast, were 'creaking with inefficiency' and in no position to mount a serious defence of the island. This was recognised by the Commander-in-Chief of the British army, His Royal Highness The Duke of York, second son of King George III. He appointed General Sir David Dundas to command Southern District, with his headquarters initially at Chatham before it moved to Canterbury. Southern District was then divided into two, with Sussex being under Lieutenant-General Pulteney, later to be replaced by Lieutenant-General Charles Lennox, who became the 4th Duke of Richmond on the death of his uncle in 1806, and Kent being under Major-General Moore.[67]

Whilst the 1/52nd Regiment was at Chatham it was joined by a young officer, George Napier, who eventually rose to become a Lieutenant-General. Napier, like Rowan from Ireland, served briefly in the Dragoons and the 46th Regiment, but claimed 'he had learned nothing of use to him in his military career' until he joined the 52nd Regiment. Like many young officers at the time who did not come from well-off families, Napier, along with two other young officers, was in debt to the regimental paymaster. The other two were Lieutenant Charles Rowan and his brother Robert. When the 1/52nd Regiment moved to Canterbury in May 1802, although Napier suggested it was 'disagreeable', the three decided to move out of the officers' mess and live on 'plain bread and milk' in lodgings until the debts were paid off.[68]

In January 1803 the second battalion was renumbered the 96th Regiment,[69] but suitable officers could opt to transfer to the first battalion. Amongst those who did was an older brother of Charles Rowan, Robert, who had joined in 1799 and was now a lieutenant.[70] At the same time, the 1/52nd was designated as Light Infantry,[71] not that it meant much at the time. Despite his debt, it was clear Moore regarded the young Lieutenant Charles Rowan as an officer of some talent. The next three years were to prove invaluable to him for the remainder of his military career and in his later appointment as Commissioner of the Metropolitan Police.

On 12 June 1803 Moore wrote to Messrs Cox, Greenwood and Cox, the foremost military agents of the time, because he thought it 'but a shabby proceeding in Government to oblige the first lieutenants of regiments to

---

67 Summerfield, Stephen, and Susan Law (2016). *Sir John Moore and the Universal Soldier. Volume I: The Man, the Commander and the Shorncliffe System of Training.* Huntingdon: Ken Trotman, p.134.
68 Napier, General Sir George T (1884). *Passages in the Early Military Life of General Sir George T. Napier.* London: John Murray, pp.15-16.
69 Moorsom, op. cit. 62, p.61.
70 Ibid, p.64.
71 Ibid, p.61.

raise men for rank, as they are in general a class of officer without money, and have already had the mortification to see several of their juniors purchase over them.' He then went on to explain that

> 'Lieutenant Charles Rowan, the eldest lieutenant of the 52nd Regiment, is exactly in this predicament, but as he is a good young man, and an attentive officer, the want of a few hundred pounds shall not make him lose his rank upon this occasion. I shall advance whatever is necessary to enable him to raise the thirty men required. I beg, therefore, that you will have the goodness to place to his credit three hundred pounds. I shall write by this post to Messrs Drummonds to sell some money I have in Stocks and to lodge an equal share with you, but in the meantime I shall thank you much to give credit, to the amount stated, to Lieutenant Rowan, that he may commence recruiting without delay. If this sum is not found sufficient, I shall order more to be lodged with you. Lieutenant Rowan goes to town, and is advised to fix himself in London for the purpose of raising his men; but all the recruiting parties of the regiment are also instructed to enlist for him; therefore Lieutenant-Colonel M'Kenzie [sic], who commands the 52nd, and to whom the parties will report their success, must, as well as Lieutenant Rowan, have the power of giving credit upon his £300; but upon this part of the subject I am not conversant, and shall take it as a favour if you will see Lieutenant Rowan when he calls, and direct him in what manner it should be arranged. I take the liberty to enclose a letter for him, which I beg may be delivered when he calls at the office.'[72]

What was in the letter Moore had enclosed is unknown, but a month later Rowan was promoted to Captain,[73] the promotion being purchased by Moore himself. His promotion coincided with the 1/52nd moving to Shorncliffe, where it was subsequently joined by two other regiments, the 43rd Regiment and the 95th Rifles. In a list of the officers of the 52nd Regiment at this time, three members of the Rowan family were shown: Charles as a captain, his Uncle Charles, also a captain, was still paymaster, and his brother, Robert, was shown as a lieutenant.[74]

Most regiments in the British Army fought in tight formations which allowed for the easy administration of orders in which troops fired in volleys on a given command. Trained to fight 'over open ground', they kept to stereotype formations, maintaining correct distances and only firing

---

72 Maurice, J.F (1904). *Diary of Sir John Moore, Volume II*. London: Edward Arnold, pp.80-81.
73 *London Gazette*, 9 July 1803, Issue 15600, p.834.
74 Moorsom, op. cit. 62, p.64.

when ordered to do so. Some regiments had what was known as light companies within them which could operate in small detachments often as skirmishers ahead of the main force, but they were few. Neither was efficient for the type of warfare that was evolving, in which troops were forced to fight in close country such as mountainous or wooded areas or open ground strewn with boulders and rocks.[75]

The lower ranks of the British Army consisted primarily of working-class young men, many of them prone to drunkenness if the opportunity arose, as indeed, as will be seen later, when the first constables were recruited into the New Police as it was first known when formed in 1829; many recruits into the army also had criminal tendencies. A further issue was that many of the older lags who had been in the unit for many years and were well set in their ways, simply did not relate to the younger recruits who would join fresh from their basic training. Consequently, the army functioned on a system of repression in which officers imposed summary discipline through fear. Flogging was the standard punishment and for more serious offences, soldiers could be hung or shot.[76]

Moore 'did not believe this "mechanical discipline," which made a mere automaton of the soldier',[77] and it would be extremely difficult to get small detachments to operate efficiently if this means of discipline was retained – such skirmishers needed to employ innovation and creativity in their tactics which rigid drill manoeuvres simply did not allow. He therefore introduced a new system of training, based on his own experience and that of his officers,[78] which he divided into two: moral and military.

The moral training came first because, as the 'pre-requisite to all other reforms and improvements', it was necessary 'to eradicate the brutality, drunkenness and criminal activities that pervaded the ranks of officers and men alike' before the military training could commence. In reading what follows, it is important to consider how the New Police was organised and operated because there is a remarkable similarity with what took place at Shorncliffe. Moore's plan for moral training was to instil in officers the necessity to do everything they could *to prevent crime* within the ranks and he sought to emphasise that *the infrequency of crime*, not punishments awarded, was the yardstick by which he would judge the

---

75	Henderson, Colonel G.F.R (1912). *The Science of War: A Collection of Essays and Lectures*. London: Longmans, Green, and Company, p.344.
76	See for example, Summerfield, op. cit. 67, pp.157-160.
77	Mockler-Ferryman, A.F (1913). *The Life of a Regimental Officer During the Great War 1793-1815*. London: William Blackwood and Sons, p.113.
78	Fuller, Colonel J.F.G (1924). *Sir John Moore's System of Training*. London: Hutchinson & Co, p.102.

state of discipline within the three regiments now under his command.[79] He was not against discipline, other than extreme forms, but recognised that achieving an effective system of discipline required 'two modes of action… encouragement and punishment'. Although the first was always preferable, the latter was necessary 'to bring bad men into a state of good order.'[80]

Insofar as the military training was concerned, Moore believed some regiments should be trained to work in small groups operating either in front or behind the main body of troops, taking careful aim at specific targets and firing at will. To be effective, Moore felt he had to do away with officers who were docile subordinates capable of obeying orders to the letter, but incapable of acting on their own initiative, and replace them with officers with the skill, resolution and judgement who, when left alone, would assume responsibility in leading their sections or companies, and almost invariably do the right thing. The aim was to institute in the officers a system of discipline, instruction and command which would enable even the junior officers to anticipate what he required, without waiting for orders.[81] The principle survives to this day as 'thinking 2 up and 2 down.'

In the summer of 1803 Moore commenced work with the three regiments, the 43rd, 52nd and 95th Rifles, which formed his brigade at Shorncliffe Camp. He was permitted to select his own officers and, realising that his day-to-day duties as the commander responsible for the defence of the south-coast from Dover to Dungeness would often take him away from Shorncliffe, one of his first appointments was to make Lieutenant-colonel Kenneth Mackenzie commanding officer of the 52nd whilst the training was undertaken. A highly-experienced officer, Mackenzie had served with Moore in Egypt and was, according to Napier, 'generally considered to be the best commanding officer in the army.'[82] Although it was under Moore's supervision and direction, much of the training was devised and undertaken by Mackenzie, who was responsible for many of the drills and exercises which became known as the "Shorncliffe System".[83]

A man of high standards, Moore ensured that all officers of his brigade, which included Charles Rowan, worked hard. He believed a battalion would 'be good if it had a good commanding officer and bad if it had a bad one.' Under his scheme 'every individual captain' was 'responsible for the efficiency of his company, both officers and men.' Similarly, 'the

---

79 Napier, op. cit. 68, p.14.
80 Ibid, p.155.
81 Henderson, op. cit. 75, p.348.
82 Napier, op. cit. 68, p.12.
83 Summerfield, op. cit. 67, p.145; see also Fuller, op. cit. 78, pp.43-45.

commanding officer' was 'responsible for the captains and for the whole [regiment].' Such a scheme 'increased the interest of every officer in his work.'[84] His methods were severe. Officers who failed to measure up to his requirements were replaced

> 'with good and reliable officers, establishing a chain of responsibility from highest to lowest, with a thorough organisation of battalions on the company system, with non-commissioned officers and men no longer ruled with a rod of iron, but respecting and relying on their officers...'[85]

He did not confine his operations to the junior officers, as is evident in this extract from a letter he wrote to the Adjutant-General of the Army in 1803:

> 'Some commanding officers, the state of whose regiments justify it, must be told to retire from the service, the duties of which they are unequal to. The command must not be allowed to devolve upon their majors, who may be equally incapable, but be given to officers of approved talents. One or two measures of this sort generally known would excite an exertion which at present is much wanted.'[86]

Colonel Mackenzie began the training with the officers,

> 'telling them that the only way of having a regiment in good order was by every individual thoroughly knowing and performing his duty; and that if the officers did not fully understand their duty it would be quite impossible to expect that the men either could or would perform theirs as they ought; therefore the best and surest method was to commence by drilling the whole of the officers, and when they became perfectly acquainted with the system they could teach the men, and by their zeal, knowledge, and, above all, good temper and kind treatment of the soldier, make the regiment the best in the Service.'[87]

In early November, Charles and Robert were joined by their younger brother William in the 1/52nd Regiment.[88] Still only 14 years of age, he had joined as an Ensign.[89] The regiment then went into its winter encampment in Hythe. By mid-June the following summer, the three regiments were

---

84   Ibid, p.163.
85   Mockler-Ferryman, op. cit. 77, pp.113-114.
86   Summerfield, op. cit. 67, p.162.
87   Napier, op. cit. 68, p.17.
88   It is not known whether the uncle, Captain Charles Rowan, was still serving with the battalion at this time.
89   *London Gazette*, 8 November 1803, Issue 15642, pp.1545-46.

back at Shorncliffe. William was promoted Lieutenant on 15 June, three days before his 15th birthday.[90] The influence the training had on the three regiments became apparent when, on 23 August, the Commander-in-Chief, the Duke of York, reviewed the Brigade. The next day, 'the 52nd Regiment manoeuvred singly' in his presence after which 'he expressed his entire satisfaction of its very high state of discipline.' This was followed by a letter from Lieutenant-Colonel James W. Gordon, Military Secretary to the Duke of York, in which it was stated that he had been commanded by His Royal Highness to tell Major-General Moore that, as a result of his finding the 1/52nd Regiment 'in a superior state' during his visit, he had recommended to the King that the promotion should be more extensive in that corps and hoped that his Majesty's approbation would 'be a strong inducement to the officers to persevere in the same course of industry, zeal and intelligence.'[91]

As a result, Moore issued a regimental order:

'The promotion given to the Regiment on this occasion exceeds perhaps whatever at any one period has been accorded to a regiment. The officers owe it to their own good conduct, and to the attention they have paid to their duty, but above all to the zeal with which they have followed the instructions of Lieut.-Colonel Mackenzie, to whose talents and to whose example the Regiment is indebted for its discipline and the character so justly acquired.'[92]

The pattern was repeated in the winter of 1804/05. The 43rd Regiment and 95th Rifles went to Hythe but, on this occasion, the 1/52nd Regiment moved from their summer tented accommodation in November into the barracks at Shorncliffe. In the meantime, the 52nd Regiment had been authorised to recruit a second battalion to which Charles Rowan's brother Robert was posted as it was being formed. In early 1805 Moore was knighted.[93] The three regiments came together again in June 1805 to continue their training, before once again returning to winter encampments. As Mackenzie predicted, the Light Brigade, as the three regiments were known, was to become 'the finest and best-behaved corps... that was ever seen.'[94]

The following summer there was a serious outbreak of ophthalmia in

---

90 Heathcote, T.A. (2012). *Dictionary of Field Marshals of the British Army*. Barnsley, South Yorkshire: Pen and Sword, p.256.
91 Moorsom, op. cit. 62, p.67.
92 Regimental Order, 31 August 1804, quoted in Moorsom, op. cit. 62, p.68.
93 *London Gazette*, 13 November 1804, Issue 15754, p.1392.
94 Napier, op, cit. 68, p.17.

the regiment. Consequently, when the 1/52nd Regiment received orders in mid-July to be ready for embarkation as part of an expeditionary force, all those who were sick were ordered to the 2/52nd Regiment and those who were fit to the 1/52nd Regiment. The fit included Captain Robert Rowan, who rejoined his brothers. With both Charles and Robert commanding companies, 1/52nd Regiment set sail from England on 25 September 1806 and landed at Messina in Sicily, to join the reserve army of the British Forces in the Mediterranean. Following what turned out to be an uneventful tour of duty, the 1/52nd Regiment returned to England on 8 January 1808, and was initially based at Canterbury. Immediately on the regiment's return, Robert Rowan resigned from the army. Having served in the same regiment, although not always in the same battalion, since he joined in 1799, just under ten years previously,[95] no doubt Charles would have been sad to see his brother leave. However, he still had younger brother William with him and over the next ten years they would experience much together.

The 1/52nd Regiment did not stay long in England. On 30 April, in what turned out to be a waste of time, it embarked for Sweden as part of a force under the now Lieutenant-General Sir John Moore, sent by the British Government to assist King Gustavus IV, who was threatened by France, Russia and Denmark. Reaching Gothenburg between 17 and 20 May, the King demanded Moore carry out a plan of action which the latter felt was foolhardy in the extreme because he did not have sufficient resources to fulfil it, so the whole force returned to England two months later.[96]

Arriving at Portsmouth on 21 July 1808, the Regiment spent only ten days there before being ordered to Portugal. The ships transporting them duly anchored in Mondego Bay on 21 August, but due to a 'high surf' the troops could not come ashore until five days later.[97] One of Rowan's fellow company commanders described how they

> 'attempted to land in the flat-bottomed boats, but, one or two of the first that attempted it were swamped by the surf, and the men drowned. It was therefore found necessary to use the men-at-war boats, and we changed into them, in which operation I had a narrow escape of losing my leg between the two boats; I however escaped with a severe bruise.'

They eventually gained the shore with 'only the clothes [they] wore, one blanket and a few days' provisions in [their] haversacks', and, that night, bivouacked in huts previously built by the French from 'branches

---

95   Moorsom, op. cit. 62, pp.74 and 444.
96   Summerville, Christopher (2003). *March of Death: Sir John Moore's Retreat to Corunna, 1808-1809*. London: Greenhill Books, p.22; see also Moorsom, op. cit. 62, pp.81-82.
97   Moorsom, op. cit. 62, p.83.

of trees' with 'small branches serving for thatch.' The following day it was a short march to Lisbon, 'but the weight each man had to carry was tremendous in addition to heavy knapsacks; there were their muskets and accoutrements, seventy rounds of ammunition, a blanket, a mess kettle, and wooden canteen.' The men and the officers 'had three days' provisions.' Having no change of clothes, 'they took advantage of some running stream to wash [their] shirts as well as they could, sitting by till they dried.'[98] The 2/52nd Regiment had landed in Portugal a week earlier and was already part of Sir Arthur Wellesley's (the future Duke of Wellington) army that defeated the French in the Battle of Vimeiro on 21 August.[99] But shortly afterwards Wellesley was recalled to England along with two other senior officers, General Sir Hew Dalrymple, the officer in overall command, and Lieutenant-General Sir Harry Burrard, his deputy, to face an inquiry into the Convention of Cintra. Under this Convention the French army had agreed to quit Portugal 'in return for a safe passage home in British ships, together with their weapons, colours and accumulated Portuguese plunder.' The departure of these three officers left the British army in the Peninsula under the command of Lieutenant-General Moore,[100] who had travelled there direct from his Swedish escapade. On its arrival, the 1/52nd Regiment became part of 1 Brigade under the command of Brigadier-General Robert Anstruthers whilst the 2/52nd Regiment was part of 2 Brigade, within the 1st Infantry Division commanded by Major-General William Carr Beresford.[101]

On 5 October, 1/52nd Regiment arrived at Estremoz, where they occupied two convents. Fourteen days later Charles' younger brother William, still only 19 years of age, was promoted captain and transferred to 2/52nd Regiment to take charge of a company. On 1 November, 1/52nd Regiment left Estremoz as part of Moore's army, with Charles still in charge of a company, and marched each day until it reached Ciudad Rodrigo on 16 November. Following a day's rest Moore continued the march, arriving at Salamanca on 21 November, where he waited for the arrival of additional troops under Lieutenant-General Sir John Hope, who had gone by a different route, and Lieutenant-General Sir David Baird, who had been sent from England. Hope arrived on 6 December and a week later, without waiting for Baird, and marching eleven hours a day, Moore took his army eastwards. By 20 December he was at Mayorga, where he was finally joined

98   Dobbs, John, and Knowles, Robert (2008). *Gentlemen in Red: Two accounts of British Infantry Officers during the Peninsular War*. Driffield, Yorkshire: Leonaur.
99   Moorsom, op. cit. 62, pp.84-87.
100 Summerville, op. cit. 96, p.20
101 Moorsom, op. cit. 62, pp.89-90.

by Baird. Moore pressed on to Sahagún, where they found an advance post of French cavalry. Quickly driving them out, Moore established his headquarters there.[102]

Moore had reorganised his army on 1 December, although the 1/52nd Regiment was not affected, remaining under Brigadier-General Anstruthers as part of 2 Brigade. However, the 2/52nd Regiment became part of the 1st Flank Brigade under Colonel Robert Craufurd.[103] Just before dusk on 23 December, with snow lying several inches deep on the ground, Moore's army, including both battalions of the 52nd Regiment, started out on a night march to attack French forces under the command of Marshal Soult. They had not gone far when Moore received information that Napoleon was advancing against him with 40,000 troops and was a mere three day's march from his position. Knowing he was 'outnumbered' and facing possible 'encirclement and annihilation',[104] Moore ordered the troops to counter-march and they returned to Sahagún. Moore's initial plan was to conduct a tactical withdrawal to Corunna along the route Baird had taken on his arrival from England. Because Baird knew the route, Moore sent him west to Valencia. The vanguard was formed by the troops of Hope and Major-General Alexander Fraser, with the Reserve Division under Major-General Edward Paget forming the rear guard. The withdrawal commenced at daylight on 24 December.[105]

The next twenty days involved exhausting marches in appalling conditions through some of the most inhospitable terrain in northern Spain, with the French constantly snapping at their heels. The 'situation was exacerbated' by a sudden outbreak of 'typhus, a highly contagious louse-borne disease, which thrives in the wake of squalor and wretchedness'; symptoms vary, ranging from headaches, fever and delirium, to abscesses, gangrene, dysentery and even death.[106]

When the withdrawal commenced Charles Rowan was still with the 1/52nd Regiment, which was now part of the 5th (Reserve) Division which had left with Moore. However, the 2/52nd Regiment, in which his brother William was commanding a company, was part of the 1st Flank Brigade, initially part of the rear guard, and it remained at Sahagún for twenty-four hours to overwatch the departure of the other troops. Meanwhile, two light cavalry brigades under the command of Major-General Sir

---

102   Summerville, op. cit. 96, p.37.
103   Moorsom, op. cit. 62, p.91.
104   Summerville, op. cit. 96, p.40.
105   What follows is only a brief summary of the retreat and is taken largely from Summerville, op. cit. 96, pp. 49-177.
106   Summerville, op, cit. 96, p.46.

The Making of an Officer

Edward Paget screened all French movements, keeping Soult in the dark about the withdrawal for as long as possible by aggressively pushing patrols towards Carrion.[107] Craufurd's 1st Flank Brigade were 'the last foot soldiers to file out' of Sahagún at nightfall on the 25th December. Several hours later they were followed by Paget's cavalry. At Astorga, which was reached on 31 December, Moore decided to send Colonel Craufurd in command of 4,500 men, including the 2/52nd Regiment, to Vigo, which was further south on the Portuguese coast, to board ships to return to England, whilst he continued with the remainder of the army, including 1/52nd Regiment, to Corunna. Thus the brothers William and Charles Rowan became separated. Although the troops under Craufurd, like those under Moore, suffered 'from hunger, fatigue and appalling weather',[108] they were not constantly being harried by the pursuing French forces. By 2 January, Napoleon realised that he had missed the opportunity to encircle Moore's army and he returned to France, leaving the pursuit in the hands of Marshal Soult.[109]

With the Flank Brigades gone to Vigo, the 1/52nd Regiment, along with 1/95th Rifles and the cavalry, became the rear guard under Paget's command. During the whole retreat, Moore was invariably with the rear guard which was frequently involved in skirmishes with the French pursuers. When the army left Villafranca on 4 January two companies of the 52nd Regiment commanded by Captains Charles Rowan and John Hunt formed the rear guard – a delaying force.[110] Indeed, if it were not for the rear guard, which consisted primarily of regiments trained personally by Moore at Shorncliffe, all of whom 'behaved throughout with conspicuous gallantry', Moore's now 'disorganised army' could well have been overwhelmed by 'Soult's pursuing force'.[111] Moore did stop briefly at Lugo on 6 January in the hope that he could engage Soult in battle, but the French army in pursuit was too strung out. Many of Moore's men were by this time 'so worn with hunger, cold and exhaustion, they were almost dead on their feet and literally sleepwalking.'[112]

Harry Smith, a lieutenant with the 95th Rifles which was part of the rear guard, along with the 1/52nd Regiment, and who later became a life-long friend of Rowan's, described how they 'lost their baggage at Calcavellos' and, for three weeks,

---

107 Ibid, p.43.
108 Ibid, p.88.
109 Ibid, pp.91-92.
110 Moorsom, op. cit. 62, p.98.
111 Mockler Ferryman, op. cit. 77, p.135.
112 Summerville, op, cit, 96, p.45.

'had no clothes but those on our backs; we were literally covered and almost eaten up with vermin, most of us suffering from ague and dysentery, every man a living [but] still active skeleton.'[113]

Several times discipline in many regiments broke down completely and, much to the fear and disappointment of the local population, British troops pillaged and looted, particularly at Benavente on 28 December and Bembibre on 2 January. Smith claimed the main body of the army was 'totally disorganised' throughout the withdrawal, and only the rear guard kept their discipline.[114] Moore's army finally reached Corunna on 11 January, only to find the transport ships to evacuate them had not arrived. By 13 January the French had caught up and Moore deployed his whole army on a mile front about two miles in front of the town. The following afternoon, the left of the British line came under artillery fire. The transport ships arrived that evening and Moore immediately began embarking the artillery, cavalry, the sick and the baggage. By the morning of 16 January this was almost complete, and the Rear Guard had been warned to be ready to embark at 4.00pm. However, the French had other ideas. Advancing at around 2.00pm they threatened to outflank the right of the British line. Not only was the attack repulsed, but 1/52nd Regiment, together with five companies of the 95th Rifles, 'established themselves firmly on a part of the enemy's position.' Unfortunately, during the battle, no doubt much to Rowan's sadness, his benefactor Lieutenant-General Sir John Moore was fatally injured and, wrapped in a military cloak, his body was interred by the officers of his staff in the citadel of Corunna.[115]

With the army now under the command of Sir David Baird, Rowan sailed from Corunna with 1/52nd Regiment on 17 January 1809, arriving at Portsmouth eight days later. The 1/52nd Regiment was forced to remain on the ship for ten days 'waiting for a fair wind', and the troops did not finally disembark at Ramsgate until 14 February, from whence they marched to Deal the following day. Two officers had been seriously wounded, along with a sergeant and 30 rank and file. Despite being regularly in contact with the enemy, only five rank and file were known to have been killed, although 90 were missing. Whilst they had lost few in battle, the effects on their health was such that by 1 March only 26 sergeants and 277 rank and file were fit for duty; 22 sergeants and 448 rank and file were in hospital.[116]

---

113 Moore Smith, G.C (1903). *The Autobiography of Lieutenant-General Sir Harry Smith. Baronet of Aliwal on the Sutlej, G.C.B., in Two Volumes, Volume I*. London: John Murray, p.17.
114 Ibid.
115 Moorsom, op. cit. 62, pp.106-107.
116 Ibid, p.110.

Moore's training had been revolutionary. Glover described him as 'the finest trainer of troops the British army has ever known',[117] setting 'in train a revolution in the relationship between officers and men.'[118] Before his death, Moore himself noted 'with satisfaction that in the 52nd Regiment it was 'evident that not only the officers, but that each individual soldier [knew] perfectly what he [had] to do; the discipline [was] carried out without severity, the officers [were] attached to the men and the men to the officers.'[119] Moorsom claimed that 'under [Moore's] personal instruction... the 52nd acquired that admirable discipline and that system of light-infantry drill which contributed so largely to the honour of the British army throughout the war of the Peninsula and the campaign of Waterloo.'[120] As Colonel Mackenzie predicted, the 52nd Regiment, of which Charles Rowan was a part throughout its transition to light infantry, became a model for the British Army and became the nucleus of the soon to be formed Light Infantry Brigade.[121] Over the next 30 years an astounding number of officers, who had learned their trade in the Light Brigade, obtained high command in the expanding Empire.[122]

Rowan's thoughts on the training he underwent at Shorncliffe are not recorded but they are likely to have been similar to George Napier's, who expressed his thoughts in his autobiography:

> 'I am not an advocate for treating soldiers as if they were mere brutes, without either sense, feeling, or character. On the contrary, I have rarely met with a private soldier who has not feelings, and keen ones too; though often indeed they had been blunted by bad example and harsh treatment. Still, by perseverance and kindness and letting them see that you look upon them as rational beings and as fellow-men, you will seldom fail to bring them back to their original dispositions. The officer who considers himself a better man than the private, except from his superior education and intelligence, is a presumptuous fool! For what would he be or what could he do without the private? Nothing! The fact being that upon the physical strength and moral courage of the British soldier mainly depends the success of our greatest generals... So it is the interest as well as the moral duty of all officers to treat the men committed to their charge with every kindness, justice, and respect, for

---

117 Glover, Michael (2001). *The Peninsular War 1807-1814: A Concise Military History.* Harmondsworth: Penguin Classic, p.73.
118 Ibid, p.59.
119 Maurice, op. cit. 72, p.272.
120 Moorsom, op. cit. 62, p.107.
121 Napier, op. cit. 68, p.13.
122 Summerfield, op. cit. 67, p.164.

that is no improper word.'[123]

Many years later, as will be seen in Chapter Seven, Rowan adapted what he had learned at Shorncliffe when he set up the New Police in London, with Richard Mayne. It was set up along the lines of a battalion of light infantry with superintendents in command of companies. Indeed, Rowan initially referred to superintendents being in charge of companies. And, what Moore expected of company commanders and their subordinate officers, Rowan expected of his superintendents and subordinate officers as he made clear in the instructions to them. Similarly, referring to Napier's thoughts, it can be argued little would have been achieved by Rowan and Mayne had it not been for the physical strength and moral courage, and, on occasions, gallantry of the constables and sergeants who patrolled the streets of London during those early years.

---

[123] Napier, op. cit. 68, pp.125-126.

CHAPTER THREE

ROWAN AS A STAFF OFFICER UNDER WELLINGTON

Having recovered from the painful retreat to Corunna and evacuation from Portugal, within three months the three light infantry regiments – 1/43rd, 1/52nd and 1/95th – were formed into the Light Brigade under the command of the recently-promoted Brigadier-General Robert Craufurd. Known as 'Black Bob'[124] because however well he shaved he still had a swarthy chin, he believed in strict discipline which included having men 'lashed' for what today would be regarded as minor breaches. However, he possessed 'accomplished tactical skills on the battlefield'.[125] As a result, although he was at times unpredictable, he did have 'moments of inspired brilliance'.[126] He was also a 'stickler for logistics'. So much so that when someone in the commissary department[127] once complained to Wellington that Craufurd had threatened to hang him 'if supplies were not produced by a certain time,' Wellington is alleged to have replied, 'Then I advise you to produce them, for he is quite certain to do it.'[128]

Charles Rowan's capabilities were recognised by Craufurd almost immediately, because in April 1809, whilst still a captain, he was appointed Brigade Major of the Light Brigade, and promoted brevet major the following month. Thus he became Craufurd's chief of staff, responsible for co-ordinating brigade headquarters. Amongst his many duties, he was expected to expand on any outline plans Craufurd made, and to make sure they were carried out. It was a highly sought-after appointment. In addition to the responsibilities it carried, it brought Rowan into contact

---

124   Snow, Peter (2011). *To War with Wellington: From the Peninsular to Waterloo*. London: John Murray, pp.40-41.
125   Ibid, p.72.
126   Ibid, p.103.
127   The Commissariat was part of Her Majesty's Treasury, although its members wore a uniform and were subject to military discipline.
128   Snow, op. cit. 124, p.72.

with officers of similar appointments both in other brigades and with the army commander, Lieutenant-General Arthur Wellesley. As he was without independent means, the additional pay that went with the appointment will also have pleased Rowan. Given he held staff appointments for the next four years, he learned much.

Wellesley had returned to the Peninsula in April 1809, with instructions to defend Portugal but 'not mount operations in Spain without the government's authority',[129] but the Light Brigade was not with him. It did not arrive in Portugal until late June. With Napoleon heavily involved in France's war with Austria, which had broken out the previous month, and the subsequent reduction in the numbers of French troops in Portugal, Wellesley quickly liberated Portugal for a second time.[130] Leaving the defence of Portugal to the embryonic Portuguese army, stiffened by a few newly-landed British battalions, he was keen to move into Spain; but it was not until 11 June that he received permission from London to do so.[131] Consequently, he did not cross the frontier at Zarza la Mayor until 2 July. A major battle with the French at Talavera on 26 and 27 July resulted in a British victory but at substantial cost. Wellesley's army was reduced by over 5,000 men, which included 800 killed, leaving him with barely 15,000 fit men.[132]

Meanwhile the Light Brigade, composed of some 3,000 infantry and a troop of Horse Artillery, under Craufurd's command, had been seriously delayed off the Isle of Wight for two weeks by appalling weather in the English Channel.[133] Arriving in Lisbon on 29 June, Captain Jonathan Leach of the 95th Rifles wrote of their arrival:

> '...I may observe that unprejudiced persons, and those neither directly nor indirectly connected with it, have pronounced it the finest and most splendid Brigade that ever took the field. I will venture to go so far as to assert that, if it has been equalled, it has never been surpassed in any army, whether the materials of which it was composed, its fine appointments and arms, its spirit du corps, its style of marching and manoeuvring, and in short every requisite for a Light Brigade, be considered.'[134]

---

129 Holmes, Richard (2003). *Wellington: The Iron Duke*. London: Harper Perennial, p.129.
130 Snow, op, cit. 124, p.69.
131 Glover, Michael (2001). *The Peninsular War 1807-1814: A Concise Military History*. Harmondsworth: Penguin Classic, p.103.
132 Ibid, pp.106-112.
133 Snow, op. cit. 124, p.55.
134 Leach, C.B., Lieut.-Colonel J (1831). *Rough Sketches of the Life of an Old Soldier*. London: Longman, Rees, Orme, Brown, and Green, p.71-72.

This then was Craufurd's Brigade of which Charles Rowan was the Brigade Major. For the first few days, they were engaged in purchasing horses for the officers, and mules, packsaddles and other necessities for the months ahead.[135] The Brigade then set off on a series of gruelling marches 'in excessively hot weather'[136] to join Wellesley's army. Captain Leach again:

> 'Each soldier carried from sixty to eighty rounds of ammunition, a musket or a rifle, a great coat, and (if I recollect rightly) a blanket, a knapsack complete with shoes, shirts, etc., a canteen and haversack, bayonet, belts, etc. Such a load, carried so great a distance, would be considered a hard day's work for a horse…'[137]

Much to Wellesley's 'great relief' the Light Brigade eventually arrived at Talavera on the morning of 29 July, having marched the last 52 miles in 26 hours,[138] a remarkable achievement in those days. Harry Smith, then a Lieutenant with the 95th Regiment, described the battlefield as being 'literally covered with dead and dying', adding 'the stench was horrible.'[139] Some of the Brigade were deployed to a string of outposts, but others spent the day 'collecting the dead bodies and putting them in large heaps mixed with faggots and burning them.'[140]

When news of the victory reached London, Wellesley was ennobled as Viscount Wellington. But the celebrations were short-lived. With French forces converging on the area, Wellington, without supplies from England and with food and forage hard to find locally, decided to return to Portugal where he could be better supplied.[141] So, for a second time within six months, Rowan, and many others found themselves part of an army in withdrawal. By the evening of 4 August almost the whole British Army had crossed the River Tagus at Arzobispo, but Wellington was concerned that if the French crossed to the south bank of the Tagus in strength he would be forced to retreat to Cadiz. Therefore he sent the Light Brigade 'on a desperate scramble over the hills, racing to reach the Almaraz bridge' before the French advance guard. Marching for fifteen hours on 6 August on a diet of 'boiled wheat and dried peas, without salt, bread or meat'

---

135 Craufurd, Alexander H. (undated). *General Craufurd and his Light Division*. London: Griffith Farran Okeden & Welsh, p.65.
136 Moorsom, W.S (Ed)(1860). *Historical Record of the Fifty-Second Regiment (Oxfordshire Light Infantry) from the Year 1755 to the year 1858*. Uckfield, Sussex: The Naval and Military Press, p.115.
137 Leach, op cit. 134, p.83.
138 Moorsom, op, cit. 136, p.115; Snow, op. cit. 124, p.72, quoting Napier says 62 miles.
139 Moore Smith, G.C (1903). *The Autobiography of Lieutenant-General Sir Harry Smith. Baronet of Aliwal on the Sutlej, G.C.B, in Two Volumes, Volume I*. London: John Murray, p.19.
140 Glover, op. cit. 131, p.112 quoting Simmons, p.22.
141 Ibid, pp.113-114; Holmes, op. cit. 129, p.141.

they arrived just in time.[142] His withdrawal into Portugal now secure, Wellington's army went into cantonments for the winter whilst he planned an advance into Spain for the third time.

In the spring of 1810 Wellington attached two Battalions of Portuguese Chasseurs, plus some German cavalry, to the Light Brigade, at the same time renaming it the Light Division.[143] Still a Brigadier-General, Craufurd remained in command with increased responsibilities; Charles Rowan remained his chief of staff. By mid-March it was known that the French, under Marshal Masséna, intended to try and take Lisbon. Masséna decided to take the northern route, which meant he had to take the fortress of Ciudad Rodrigo, which was about 16 miles from the Portuguese border, and held by Spanish troops. Wellington sent the newly-formed Light Division forward, 'as a corps of observation', onto the east bank of the River Coa, whilst he assembled the remainder of his force on the west bank around Almeida. To reach Almeida, Masséna, who had now been joined by Marshal Ney, increasing French troops to around 70,000, had to cross the River Coa. Craufurd's instructions were 'to delay the French without engaging them in a pitched battle' but Craufurd, having arrived just too late to take part in the Battle of Talavera, was keen to prove that the Light Division 'could perform outstanding feats of arms'.[144] The result was a major battle by the Light Division, in which Major Charles Rowan 'distinguished himself'.[145]

The Battle of the River Coa, sometimes referred to as the Battle of Almeida, took place on 24 July 1810. The countryside in which the Light Division was deployed was amongst the roughest in Portugal for the Coa ran 'through a deep gorge with steep, rocky sides cluttered with boulders', which 'severely restricted movement'. Because of an early morning storm, the river itself was in full flood and could only be crossed by one narrow bridge.[146]

When Ney advanced with 24,000 men,[147] Craufurd's outposts were forced to withdraw. The French attack intensified and the Light Division was in danger of being cut off from its only avenue of retreat, the narrow bridge across the Coa. Belatedly, Craufurd ordered the guns and baggage to withdraw over the bridge. Several companies of the 52nd Regiment were

---

142   Leach, op. cit. 134, p.93.
143   Snow, op. cit. 124, p.83.
144   Ibid, p.84.
145   Moorsom, op. cit. 136, p.444.
146   Snow, op. cit. 124, p.84.
147   Glover, op. cit. 131, p.133.

'instructed …to prevent the enemy approaching the bridge'.[148] Charles Napier, then a Major on Craufurd's staff, described how 'the fire was hot'[149] as the troops of the Light Division 'retreated through the tortuous rock formations and vineyards, [and] over field walls', fighting off the French every inch of the way. Protected by several companies of the 52nd and 95th, who had taken up positions on 'the rocky hillocks' overlooking the bridge, the Light Division continued its withdrawal over the bridge. But the French, by sheer weight of numbers, drove the companies of the 95th Rifles off the hillocks, isolating five companies of the 52nd Regiment, who were in danger of being cut off and either killed or captured. It was then that Major Charles Rowan gathered together a detachment of the 43rd Foot, together with some companies of the 95th Rifles and 3rd Cacadores, and led a bayonet charge on the hillocks. Major Charles MacLeod of the 43rd Regiment was also aware of the importance of the hillocks if the five companies were to be saved, and took the remaining units of the 95th Rifles and a contingent of the 43rd Regiment forward. Despite intense fire from the French troops, the efforts of Rowan and MacLeod resulted in the recapturing and holding of the hillocks sufficiently long enough for the five companies to make their escape over the bridge. Once everyone was across some units were posted along the western bank, whilst others 'lodged themselves among the rocks of Cabeco Negro which formed an amphitheatre above the bridge'.[150] Ney made three determined attempts to cross the bridge but all failed, leaving him with at least 400 dead and many wounded 'to no purpose' whatsoever.[151]

The officers and men of the Light Division had carried out a tactical withdrawal whilst faced with overwhelming force. No guns or baggage were lost, and very few prisoners were taken by the French. Snow described the Battle of the Coa as 'one of the most heroic though controversial clashes of the Peninsula War'.[152] But Craufurd was accused of 'fighting a very dangerous battle… with a hardihood bordering on rashness',[153] and remaining 'much too long before a vast superiority of the enemy' resulting

---

148 Horwood, Donald D (1980). '"The Dreadful Day": Wellington and Massena on the Coa, 1810.' *Military Affairs*, Vol. 44, No. 4 (December), p.165.
149 Napier, Lieut.-General Sir William (1857). *The Life and Opinions of General Sir Charles James Napier (edited by William Napier). In Four Volumes, Volume I*. London: John Murray, p.138.
150 Horwood, op. cit. 148, pp.165-167.
151 Weller, Jac (2012). *Wellington in the Peninsula 1808-1814*. London: Greenhill Books, pp.120-121.
152 Snow, op. cit. 124, p.84
153 Grattan, William (1902). *Adventures with the Connaught Rangers 1809-1814* (edited by Charles Oman). London: Edward Arnold, p.98.

in the loss of 30 officers and 400 men.[154] It was seen by Wellington as a rare lapse in judgement that almost saw him remove Craufurd from his command. Instead, he censured him for his conduct but, at the same time, his despatch to London reported: 'I am informed that throughout this trying day, the commanding officers of the 43rd, 52nd and 95th regiments, Lieut.-Colonels Beckwith, Barclay and Hall, and all the officers and soldiers of these excellent regiments distinguished themselves.'[155] What he failed to mention was the losses would have been far greater had it not been for the actions of Rowan and McLeod.

In the face of a much superior French force Wellington's army fell back, in stages, to 'a prominent mountain ridge' called Bussaco. He strung his army along the ridge, facing east, with the Light Brigade under Craufurd left of centre as it faced the enemy. Two attempts by the French to break through, one in the centre and one towards the northern end of the ridge, had already been thwarted when, on 27 September 1810, Marshal Ney attacked what he thought was a battery of British guns immediately in front of the Light Division's position. But as the French neared them the guns were quickly withdrawn, and all the French could see was the solitary figure of Robert Craufurd, 'sitting on a fine horse.' Behind him, lying in a sunken road, were 2,000 men of the 43rd and 1/52nd Regiments. When the French came close he quickly turned to the 1/52nd Regiment and called out, 'Now! Fifty Second, avenge Moore!'[156] In a subsequent letter, an artillery officer standing nearby described how the French column

> 'had reached to within nine or ten yards of the summit of the hill: I had watched it advance and was attentively observing it, when the shout of our troops astonished me. I never experienced a sensation like that produced by that 'huzza!' and instant charge. I cannot describe the exhilaration of the feeling. The enemy scarcely stood a moment, but the massive column, so formidable in appearance, flew like lightening down the descent. The French locked up in columns could not act; it was a carnage, not a conflict.'[157]

Having won this defensive battle, Wellington resumed his withdrawal south into the previously fortified Lines of Torres Vedras, 'a network of redoubts and ramparts in the hills west of Lisbon.'[158] Pursued by the

---

154 Lieutenant-Colonel Alexander Gordon, who was at the time Wellington's ADC, quoted in Snow, op. cit. 124, p.84.
155 Moorsom, op. cit. 136, p.122.
156 Weller, op. cit. 151, p.118.
157 Whinyates, Edward, then a Lieutenant in the Royal Artillery, quoted in Glover, op. cit. 131, p.138.
158 Snow, op. cit. 124, p.96.

French, he reached these by 10 October. Finding the lines too strong to attack, the French withdrew during the night of 14 November, pursued by the Light Division which harried the French rear-guard.[159]

The French withdrew to the town of Santarém, where Wellington was content to leave them for the remainder of the winter.[160] Craufurd, meanwhile, returned to England at the beginning of February 1811, leaving the Light Division under the temporary command of Colonel George Drummond of the 24th Regiment, pending the arrival of Major-General Sir William Erskine. The Light Division, having followed the retreat to Santarém, went into cantonments at Valle, with 'its pickets occupying the mined bridge over the Rio Mayor' whilst French sentries were posted at the other end of the long causeway. Thus, except for Almeida close to the border, Wellington had relieved Portugal from French occupation again.

Masséna continued his retreat, pursued by the Light Division, now commanded by Erskine.[161] Catching up with the French rearguard on 11 March, for the next five days, despite Erskine's 'fumbling direction,'[162] the Light Division were involved in repeated clashes. A major clash arose on 12 March, when the 52nd Regiment and one of the Cacadore regiments dislodged a contingent of the French army from some woods two miles south of Redinha, which caused Wellington to remark, in a despatch to London 'I have never seen the French infantry driven out from a wood in more gallant style.'[163]

On 15 March Ney made a fatal error when 'he left three brigades on the allied side of the River Ceira and did not ensure that they posted adequate guards.' But when the Light Division came in sight, Erskine refused to attack. Wellington arrived and ordered an immediate advance. With rifle companies infiltrating behind French lines, the Light Division attacked from the front, supported by the 3rd Division on the French left. Appalled to find riflemen behind them, the French centre panicked and the fleeing soldiers jammed the single bridge; others 'were drowned trying to ford the Ceira.'[164] By the following day the remainder of the army had caught up, and the Light Division then embarked on a series of daily marches until, finally, on 24 March it arrived at Navazienis. Remaining there on the following day, it was reinforced by the arrival of the 2/52nd Regiment

---

159   Moorsom, op. cit. 136, pp.127-128.
160   Snow, op. cit. 124, p.99.
161   Moorsom, op. cit. 136, suggests on p.130, that Drummond was in command when the pursuit commenced on 6 March, but by 11 March Erskine had taken over, pp.133-134.
162   Glover, op. cit. 131, p.144.
163   Moorsom, op. cit. 136, p.136.
164   Glover, op. cit. 131, p.145.

which was put into 2 Brigade with 1/52nd Regiment, the 1 Portuguese Cacadores and the four companies of the 95th Rifles.[165]

The French continued to retreat but Masséna decided to do battle with Wellington one more time before he left Portugal, this time at Sabugal where the River Coa provided him with 'a line of defence against the advancing British.'[166] Wellington's plan was for the Light Division and two brigades of cavalry to circle behind the French open left flank whilst his remaining four divisions attacked the front. On the day of the battle, 3 April 1811, 'a thick fog blanketed the entire valley of the Coa' and there was intermittent rain.[167] With the exception of Erskine, the divisional commanders decided to wait until visibility improved. But Erskine sent 1 Brigade, consisting of the 43rd Regiment and four companies of the 95th Rifles under the command of Lieutenant-Colonel Thomas Beckwith, forward. In the fog, Beckwith crossed at the wrong location and, advancing up the slope on the eastern side of the river, came up against the French left flank, consisting of 12,000 troops, complete with supporting cavalry and guns. When Erskine realised what had happened, he became cautious and issued explicit instructions to Colonel Drummond, in command of 2 Brigade, not to support Beckwith. At this point, Erskine rode off to join the cavalry, leaving the Light Division leaderless for the rest of the battle.

Despite repulsing one French counterattack, during which Beckwith was wounded, the sheer weight of numbers forced his Brigade back towards the River Coa. On the far bank Drummond heard the sounds of battle approaching, and deduced that Beckwith's men were retreating. Disobeying Erskine's order Drummond led 2 Brigade across the River Coa, joined Beckwith and the two Brigades 'surged up the hill.' The fog lifted and the remaining four divisions of Wellington's army swept across the River Coa, causing the French to beat a hasty retreat into Spain.[168] Subsequently, in a despatch to Lord Liverpool, the Secretary of State for War and the Colonies, Wellington wrote that he considered 'the action that was fought by the Light Division, by Colonel Beckwith's brigade principally, with the whole of 2 corps, to be one of the most glorious that British troops were ever engaged in.'[169]

At around this time, Rowan ceased to be the Brigade Major of the Light Division but remained on its staff, taking up an appointment as

---

165   Moorsom, op. cit. 136, p.137.
166   Snow, op. cit. 124, p.106.
167   Weller, op. cit. 156, p.153.
168   Glover, op. cit. 131, pp.146-147.
169   Moorsom, op. cit. 136, p.141.

Assistant Adjutant-General, a position he held until May 1813.[170] Rowan's new appointment made him responsible for unit returns, discipline, correspondence and the transmission of orders and communications within the Light Division. As such he again met many of the senior commanders, including Wellington, over the next two years. Quite why the change was made is not known but it is doubtful that, at that moment, Rowan was sorry. Erskine was the most incompetent commander he served under during the whole of the Peninsular War. Snow described him as being a 'near disaster',[171] whilst Holmes called him 'notoriously incompetent'.[172]

Much to Wellington's delight, Craufurd returned from leave just in time to resume command of the Light Division before the battle for the village of Fuentes de Onoro, which took place from 3 to 5 May 1811. It was 'one of the fiercest battles of the Peninsular War', in which the Light Division 'played a decisive role'. Marshal Massena, with 48,000 troops, had crossed back into Portugal, where Wellington with 37,000 troops was waiting for him.[173] On 3 May Masséna launched a frontal assault against British and Portuguese troops holding the village. Fighting, much of it hand-to-hand, lasted all day, but by evening the French had withdrawn and the village of Fuentes de Oñoro remained in Allied hands. There was a lull the following day, but on 5 May Masséna launched another attack, this time against Wellington's right flank held by the 7th Division. Realising the 7th Division was in danger of being over-run by the far superior French forces, Wellington sent the Light Division, with Rowan in his new role of Assistant Adjutant-General, to extricate it. Craufurd first drew some of the French infantry and cavalry away from the 7th Division, allowing it to withdraw 'steadily in close columns' protected by British cavalry.[174] Once this was done the Light Division, 'consisting of fewer than 4,000 men supported by a battery of Royal Horse Artillery and 1,500 cavalry', faced 'three or four times their number'. But they now 'demonstrated a mastery of fire and movement', as Snow described:

> 'Supported by the small force of cavalry, who charged again and again at the advancing French, they formed mobile squares to protect themselves from the massed French cavalry attacks. All the time they

170 *General Orders, Spain and Portugal: January 1st to December 31st 1811, Volume III*. London: T. Egerton, Whitehall Military Library, p.292, item 15.
171 Snow, op. cit. 124, p.103.
172 Holmes, op. cit. 129, p.150.
173 Snow, op. cit. 124, p.107.
174 Glover, op. cit. 131, p.153.

edged backwards towards Wellington's new line, somehow keeping at bay the continual onslaughts from French infantry and cavalry.'[175]

It was claimed that 'never perhaps in modern war was a more beautiful movement made, nor at a more critical moment, than by the Light Division on this occasion'. The French cavalry,

> 'numbering 5,000 sabres, and flushed with their advantage, pressed round the battalion squares without daring to storm them; the French artillery plunged into the close ranks wherever a clear range could be got; and for nearly three miles, these veterans held in their conduct the fate of the British army.'

This series of rapid moves, combined with the disciplined forming of squares off the line of march, was a spectacle that few could have believed to have been possible. The eminent military historian Richard Holmes claimed Craufurd's extrication 'of his own troops' was 'a remarkable display of disciplined minor tactics.'[176] At the same time as this was taking place, Masséna had some success when he made a second assault on the village of Fuentes de Onoro, although he was eventually driven out by 2 Brigade of the Light Division and the French were pushed back to the banks of the River Dos Casas.[177] There was another fierce battle in mid-May, this time at Albuera, but the Light Division was not involved.

On 18 July 1811 Lieutenant-Colonel John Colborne became the commanding officer of 1/52nd. Colborne was the third of the senior military officers who influenced Charles Rowan. He had already enjoyed a distinguished career and had, at one time, been military secretary to Sir John Moore; he had been with him when killed at Corunna. He had been in the Peninsula since the late summer of 1809 and had, even though still a lieutenant-colonel, temporarily commanded a brigade.[178]

For the remainder of 1811 there were no further major engagements between the two armies. Craufurd took the opportunity to re-equip the Light Division, and the Duke of Wellington ordered them to march from Agueda to Larade, not far from Guinaldo 'for his inspection.' Harry Smith, who was then Brigade Major of 2 Brigade, described how he was riding a horse which he had purchased from 'Charlie Rowan' because it had thrown him.[179]

175 Snow, op. cit. 124, p.113.
176 Holmes, op. cit. 129, p.148.
177 Moorsom, op. cit. 136, p.61.
178 Moore Smith, G.C (1903). *The Life of John Colborne, Field Marshal Lord Seaton*. London: John Murray, p.163.
179 Moore Smith, G.C (1903). *The Autobiography of Lieutenant-General Sir Harry Smith.Baronet of Aliwal on the Sutlej, G.C.B., in Two Volumes, Volume I*. London: John Murray, p.51.

Rowan featured in another story told by Smith of that autumn. Whilst dining with Wellington, Rowan had apparently told the story of an occasion when 'a very facetious Portuguese gentleman' had produced an estimate of British forces 'that was so incorrect that General Drummond had laughed at it.' Because he spoke Portuguese, Smith was sent 150 miles to bring the Portuguese gentleman before the Duke. Smith described it as being a most unpleasant ride, and commented, 'many was the blessing I bestowed on Charlie Rowan's tongue.'[180]

The walls of Ciudad Rodrigo looked extremely formidable; they were 'built largely of rubble', but five hundred yards to the north the fortress was dominated by a 600-foot hill, Greater Teson, on which the French had built a redoubt.[181] Wellington gave Craufurd the job of capturing the redoubt; Craufurd, in turn, gave it to Colborne, who did it brilliantly on 8 January 1812. The assault force comprised ten companies, commanded by senior captains from each regiment: two from the 43rd Regiment, four from the 52nd Regiment, two from the 95th Regiment, and one each from the two Portuguese Cacadore battalions. Four companies were the advance guard to occupy the crest of the glacis and give covering fire, whilst the remainder advanced behind with ladders. It was on this basis that the operation was undertaken.

> 'When about fifty yards from the redoubt, Colonel Colborne gave the word double quick. This movement, and the rattling of the canteens alarmed the garrison, but the defenders had only time to fire one round from their guns before each company had taken its post on the crest of the glacis, and opened fire. All this was effected without the least confusion, and not a man was seen on the redoubt after the fire had commenced.'

The redoubt was entered simultaneously through a gate which had been forced at the rear, and by means of the ladders at the front. By the morning 'the redoubt had been converted into an efficient lodgement under cover, with a communication to the rear, and the first parallel was thrown up for a length of 600 yards.' The achievement was fully recognised by Wellington in his despatch to London:

> 'Major-general Craufurd directed a detachment of the Light Division, under Lieut.-colonel Colborne of the 52nd Regiment, to attack the work shortly after dark; the attack was very ably conducted by Lieut.-

---

180　Ibid, p.54.
181　A redoubt was a smaller fort, usually built of stone or brick, but sometimes of earthworks, to provide a first line of defence to a larger more established fort.

colonel Colborne, and the work was taken by storm in a short time; 2 captains and 47 men were made prisoners, and the remainder put to the sword. We took three pieces of cannon. I cannot sufficiently applaud the conduct of Lieut.-colonel Colborne, and the detachment under his command.'[182]

Within a week, despite 'constant fire from French guns in the fort' and the ground being like concrete due to heavy overnight frost, all the necessary trenches had been dug 'to within 150 yards of the [fortress] wall.' By 14 January the massive, unwieldy guns had been 'dragged into their firing positions, readied and fired, over the next five days,'[183] by which time two breaches had been created.[184]

The assault commenced at 7.00pm on the evening of 19 January with the Light Division focusing on the smaller breach at the centre of the north wall. Each assault was led by a band of soldiers, about 25 in number – known as a forlorn hope[185] - followed by a storming party which generally consisted of 100 soldiers. All were volunteers. Whilst the majority would be killed or wounded, those who survived could expect to be rewarded either with promotion or cash gifts. The intention was for some members of the forlorn hope to survive long enough to gain a foothold in a breach to enable the storming party following up to press home the attack. The forlorn hope party of the Light Division was led by Lieutenant Gurwood of the 1st/52nd Regiment. The storming party, which consisted of men from each of the three British regiments – the 43rd, 52nd and 95th – was led by Rowan's friend, Major George Napier. Before they set off, Craufurd 'gave a stirring speech', in which he said:

> 'Soldiers! The eyes of our country are upon you. Be steady, be cool, be firm in the assault. The town must be yours this night. Once masters of the wall, let your first duty be to clear the ramparts, and in doing this keep together.'[186]

Contrary to the original arrangements, Craufurd himself led the assault. The breach was quickly taken, but Craufurd was seriously wounded and was dragged back to safety by his aide-de-camp, James Shaw.[187] The assault

---

182 Moorsom, op. cit. 136, pp.152-156.
183 Snow, op. cit. 124, pp.127-129.
184 Glover, op. cit. 131, p.180.
185 Snow, op. cit. 124, pp.130-134. The term 'forlorn hope' comes from the Dutch ver loren hoop, which literally means lost troop.
186 Craufurd, op. cit. 135, p.193.
187 This was the same James Shaw whom Robert Peel first approached to be the military commissioner of the New Police in 1829. See Chapter Seven.

on the larger breach was equally successful, and 'Wellington had captured the northern gateway to Spain.'[188]

But it was at a cost. In addition to Craufurd, both Lieutenant-Colonel Colborne and Major Napier were wounded; so too, was Lieutenant Gurwood. Lieutenant John Kincaid, who was serving with the 95th Rifles in the Light Division, and who was another of Rowan's friends in later life, described how

> 'a town taken by storm presents a frightful scene of outrage. The soldiers no sooner obtain possession of it, than they think themselves at liberty to do what they please… without considering that the poor inhabitants may nevertheless be friends and allies… and nothing but the most extraordinary exertions on the part of the officers can bring them back to a sense of duty.'[189]

Rowan would meet with Kincaid and other former military colleagues in London many years later.[190]

Writing home two days after the successful assault, an officer of the 52nd Regiment expressed the views of many of his colleagues:

> 'We have, as a division, sustained a very heavy loss in General Craufurd, who is not expected to recover from his wounds; but, as a regiment, a much more severe one, though we heartily trust it is only temporary, in Colonel Colborne, who, though he has only commanded us a few months, has gained the hearts of every officer and soldier in the regiment.'[191]

Craufurd died from his wounds on 24 January and 'was buried at the foot of the breach which his troops had so gallantly carried five days before.'[192] Rowan's impressions of Craufurd are unrecorded. Given that he had been on his staff for nearly three years, it is likely that he admired Craufurd's military abilities but, as a disciple of Sir John Moore, did not always agree with his approach to discipline. Others, however, did record their sentiments about his death. Despite the need to censure him over his actions at the River Coa, Wellington called Craufurd's death 'the bitterest blow of the war.'[193] Colborne said he 'was a fine fellow, though

---

188 Glover, op. cit. 131, p.181.
189 Kincaid, John (1847). *Adventures in the Rifle Brigade in the Peninsula, France the Netherlands, from 1809 to 1815*. London: T and W. Boone, p.118.
190 See Chapter Eighteen.
191 Moore Smith, op. cit. 178, p.96.
192 Moorsom, op. cit. 136, p.161.
193 Edwards, Peter (2008). *Albuera: Wellington's Fourth Peninsula Campaign, 1811*. Marlborough: The Crowood Press, p.227.

very stern and tyrannical, but after all, that was the way he got his division into such fine order.'[194] Kincaid claimed he had been very unpopular at the beginning, 'and it was not until a short time before he was lost to us for ever that we were capable of appreciating his merits'.[195] Craufurd had been rigid in insisting that regiments in the Light Division

> 'should never deviate from the line of march, and on the way back from [his] funeral the leading files found a marshy pool in their way. They marched straight through the icy, thigh-deep water, and every officer and man followed them in silence.'[196]

Colborne was sent back to England to receive treatment for his injuries. Napier had his right arm amputated; Gurwood survived and was promoted captain.[197]

Wellington now turned his attention to the 'far more forbidding stronghold at Badajoz, 150 miles to the south', which commanded the road to Madrid.[198] Glover described the task ahead:

> 'Along the northern frontier of the town ran the River Guadiana, nowhere less than 300 yards wide. The town was surrounded by a curtain wall 23-26 feet high in which eight bastions, each 30 feet high, which had been rebuilt sixty years earlier.'

In the north-eastern corner of the walls stood a castle, which was 'on a hill rising sharply a hundred feet from the river level.' The slope was 'precipitous, only to be climbed with hands as well as feet.'[199] To the south on either side of the road to Seville were two smaller forts, Fort Pardeleras and Fort Picurina. To the north, on a hill which was over 700 feet high, was Fort San Cristobal.

The siege, which began on 17 March, was one of the bloodiest of the Napoleonic Wars. Wellington decided to attack from the south-east and he began the preparations by ordering the digging of trenches, parallels and earthworks to protect the heavy siege artillery. Prolonged rain meant that the troops were frequently digging in ankle-deep mud. By 25 March the guns were firing at the outworks.[200] By 6 April, three large gaps had been made in the wall. Diversionary attacks were made to the north and east by

---

194   Moore Smith, op. cit. 178, p.171.
195   Kincaid, op. cit. 189, p.118.
196   Holmes, op. cit. 129, p.156.
197   Moorsom, op. cit. 136, pp.158-159.
198   Snow, op. cit. 124, p.138.
199   Glover, op. cit. 131, p.184.
200   Snow, op. cit. 124, p.144.

Portuguese and British soldiers of the 5th Division. At 10.00pm two of the breaches, again led by forlorn hope, were assaulted by the 4th Division. The third breach was attacked by the Light Division, now under the temporary command of Colonel Andrew Barnard, of the 95th Regiment, following the death of Craufurd and the absence of Colborne.[201]

The French had prepared their defences with precision, as Harry Smith described at the Light Divisions point of entry:

> 'The breach was covered by a breastwork from behind and ably defended at the top by *chevaux de fries* of sword blades, sharp as razors, chained to the ground, while the ascent to the top of the breach was covered with planks with sharp nails in them.'[202]

What followed 'was a scene of unimaginable slaughter' as 'again and again waves of British soldiers threw themselves into the breaches only to be gunned down or skewered on the hideous obstructions studded with spikes and sword blades.'[203] As they raced forward the soldiers were illuminated by fire bombs propelled into the ditches below the walls, and were cut down by 'a fusillade from French muskets, mortars and guns firing grapeshot.'[204] The fortress was eventually taken by a combination of the efforts of the 3rd and 5th Divisions.[205] Once taken, the survivors of the 4th and Light Divisions were able to advance into the town. But the cost had been enormous. In the main breach

> 'there lay a frightful heap of thirteen or fourteen hundred British soldiers, many dead but still warm, mixed with the desperately wounded, to whom no assistance could yet be given. There lay the burned and blackened corpses of those who had perished by the explosions, mixed with those that were torn to pieces by round shot or grape, and killed by musketry, stiffening in the gore, body piled on body, involved and intertwined into one mass of carnage …The smell of burning flesh was shockingly strong and disgusting.'[206]

Although numbers differ slightly depending on the source, the assault and earlier skirmishes had left the Allies with approximately 5,000 casualties. Rowan's division, the Light Division, suffered particularly badly, losing approximately 40% of its fighting strength. The 1/52nd Regiment alone lost

---

201 Moorsom, op. cit. 136, p.166.
202 Moore Smith, op. cit. 139, pp.64-65.
203 Snow, op. cit. 124, p.147.
204 Ibid, p.144.
205 Ibid, p.150.
206 Henry, Walter (1843). *Events of a Military Life*. London: William Pickering, pp.64-65.

five officers, killed along with 64 other ranks; the wounded amounted to 17 officers, including the commanding officer, Brevet Lieutenant-Colonel Edward Gibbs, and 329 other ranks.[207]

Because Wellington's soldiers 'had lost countless comrades, the sacking of Badajoz that followed was one of the worst orgies of military indiscipline in British military history.' It lasted for three days as drunken soldiers plundered houses and raped the local women.[208] But there was one human story that emerged from it all, when two young Spanish ladies approached two British officers to ask for their protection after they had been attacked by British troops. Both 'had blood trickling down their necks where their ear rings had been torn off them.' One of the officers was Rowan's friend, Major Harry Smith, who married the younger of the two ladies, Juana, three days later and they remained happily married for the remainder of their lives.[209]

Meanwhile, Marshal Marmont had re-entered Portugal and was threatening Almeida. On 11 April Wellington therefore moved the bulk of his army, including the Light Division, northwards, eventually arriving at Salamanca on 16 June. In the meantime, Charles Rowan was promoted to Brevet Lieutenant Colonel.[210]

The Battle of Salamanca took place on 22 July 1812. Now under the command of Major-General Charles Alten, the Light Division was held in reserve and did not take a major part in the fight although, on 29 July, it did pursue the rear of the French army to the banks of the River Douro.[211] A victory at Salamanca and the abandonment of Madrid by King Joseph Bonaparte in favour of Valencia enabled Wellington to take over the Spanish capital, which he did on 12 August. However, the build-up of French forces in the north threatened his grasp on the city and, to forestall a French attack, he attempted to capture Burgos, an important French supply base some 140 miles away. Leaving the three divisions that had borne the brunt of activity at Ciudad Rodrigo and Badajoz, of which the Light Division was one, under the overall command of Lieutenant-General Sir Rowland Hill, Wellington set off for Burgos.[212] But he underestimated the enemy's strength and, fearing that he would be encircled by French

---

207 Moorsom, op. cit. 136, p.170.
208 Snow, op. cit. 124, pp.151-153.
209 See Moore Smith, op. cit. 139.
210 *London Gazette*, 25 April 1812, Issue 10597, p.781.
211 Moorsom, op. cit. 136, p.173.
212 Heyer, Georgette (2005). *The Spanish Bride*. London: Arrow Books. In her historical novel, Heyer tells the story of Harry Smith's wife, Juana. As was the case with a number of wives during the Peninsular War, following her marriage to Smith, Juana followed her husband throughout.

forces advancing from the north-east and south-east, on 21 October abandoned the siege of Burgos and his 'deeply demoralised army' withdrew to Salamanca.[213] At the same time, he ordered Hill to abandon Madrid and head north to meet him at Salamanca.

Hill left Madrid a little after dark on 31 October and, with the Light Division forming the rear-guard, arrived at Salamanca on 10 November, two days after Wellington had arrived from Burgos. Five days later, again with the Light Division forming the rear-guard, the whole army withdrew towards Portugal again. On 16 November the rear-guard was constantly harassed by French forces, including their light cavalry, but 'without gaining any advantage.' However, 17 November 'was the worst day of the retreat.' Colonel Gordon, the Quartermaster-General, described as 'arrogant and incompetent',[214] for some reason 'sent the rear-guard of cavalry away to a flank' without telling the Light Division 'that there was nothing between them and the French'. Consequently, the Light Division were attacked before they had even broken camp and 'only its suburb training and discipline saved it.' Later that day, as it was crossing the River Huebra at San Munoz, the Light Division came under attack again on a number of occasions, but each time the attack was repulsed.[215]

Although still on the Quartermaster-General's staff, Rowan was with the 52nd Regiment during this period.[216] It was the last fighting of the year and, on 19 November, with Wellington's army in Ciudad Rodrigo, they were back where 'they started twelve months previously.' The troops 'had marched hundreds of miles and routed the French army in Portugal, but they seemed to have achieved nothing.'[217]

By the end of November, Wellington's army was once again in winter quarters. The headquarters of 2 Brigade of the Light Division were in Fuentes de Onoro, where the Allied forces had defeated the French eighteen months previously. Harry Smith found lodgings in a widower's house at one end of the village. His wife Juana had learned to cook a 'mouth-watering' stew and Harry's officer friends were frequent visitors. One of them was Major Charles Rowan, who regularly updated them on the condition of Colonel Colborne.[218]

There was virtually no contact between the two armies in the Iberian Peninsula for six months during which 'the character of the war in Europe changed.' Napoleon arrived in Paris on 18 December having been forced

---

213   Snow, op. cit. 124, p.177.
214   Glover, op. cit. 131, p.219.
215   Glover, op. cit. 131, p.220; Moorsom, op. cit. 136, pp.180-182.
216   Heyer, op. cit. 212, p.138.
217   Glover, op. cit. 131, p.221.
218   Heyer, op. cit. 212, p.159.

into the great retreat from Moscow. Meanwhile, Wellington began to prepare for a major campaign in the spring of 1813. The greatest threat to the troops, apart from the usual diseases that came from poor sanitation, was the penetrating winter cold. Up to 500 people in the army died each week according to his deputy judge advocate, Francis Larpent.[219]

---

219 Glover, op. cit. 131, p.225.

CHAPTER FOUR
ROWAN AS A REGIMENTAL OFFICER

In April 1813, Rowan was rejoined in the Light Division by his brother William, who arrived at Guinaldo, in command of four subalterns, a surgeon, five sergeants and 97 rank and file.[220] A month later Rowan left his appointment as Assistant Adjutant-General with the Light Division and returned to the 1/52nd Regiment. With the exception of the month of April in 1814 when it appears that he briefly returned to perform the duties of Assistant Adjutant-General, he remained with the Regiment until the end of his service in 1822.

On 20 May 1813 the Light Division, under the command of Major-General Charles Alten, quit its winter quarters near Capio and, as part of the right-wing of Wellington's army, marched towards Salamanca, crossing the frontier into Spain on 22 May. Just under two weeks later it crossed the River Douro using ladders and planks erected across the bridge partly destroyed by the retreating French army. On 12 June it spent the whole day supporting light cavalry and artillery harassing the French rear-guard. After crossing the River Ebro at Puente Arenas, on 18 June it came upon two separate brigades of French infantry. 1 Brigade, led by Major-General James Kempt, inflicted heavy losses on the first of these French brigades. Meanwhile, on coming across the second of the French brigades, the 95th Rifles, a part of 2 Brigade, under Major-General Sir John Vandeleur, immediately extended 'in the brushwood' and 'commenced fire on the rear' of the French troops. At the same time,

> 'the 1/52nd Regiment, pushed on at double-quick time along the flank of the French column. As soon as they were in position, they charged

---

[220] Moorsom, W.S (Ed) (1860). *Historical Record of the Fifty-Second Regiment (Oxfordshire Light Infantry) from the Year 1755 to the year 1858*. Uckfield, Sussex: The Naval and Military Press, p.183.

the French column, and took three hundred prisoners and a great quantity of baggage, the remainder of the enemy dispersing among the mountains.'[221]

Wellington quickly took Salamanca and forced the French to flee the fortress at Burgos, which blew up as they left.[222] But it was clear the French would make a stand at Vitoria. Wellington deployed his army between the Rivers Bayas and Zadorra, hidden from the French by a high range of hills. The battle actually took place in the valley of the River Zadorra on 21 June 1813. Wellington attacked the French army, commanded by Napoleon's brother and erstwhile King of Spain, Joseph Bonaparte, and Marshal Jourdan, in four columns. Two advanced on the French positions from the west and two 'struck through the hills to the north, feeling for the French flanks.'[223] The Light Division, still under Alten's command, were part of the Right Centre Column under the overall command of Lieutenant-General Lowry Cole. The 1/52nd Regiment was now part of 2 Brigade under the command of Vandeleur, whilst Kempt remained in command of 1 Brigade. Both Brigades of the Light Division were fully engaged. Kempt's brigade, followed by the 3rd Division, moved rapidly against the village of Arinez, whilst Vandeleur's brigade, headed by the 1/52nd Regiment, 'charged and carried the Margarita height and village, from whence the fire of a powerful battery had been directed on them and on the 7th division.'[224]

Now on the southern side of the river, Vandeleur's brigade, moving eastwards towards the bridges, came under fire from six French guns on a hill a short distance away. The 1/52nd Regiment formed up in a 'line on some rising ground directly opposite, and those who witnessed it, long afterwards spoke with admiration of the steadiness and accuracy with which the alignment was completed.' Advancing rapidly up the hill in front of them,[225] French morale collapsed and its army fled from the field, many on the trace horses, leaving behind their guns. Soon the road was jammed with a mass of wagons and carriages. About 5,000 French soldiers were killed or wounded and 3,000 taken prisoner. Wellington's forces suffered about 5,000 killed or wounded, but captured 152 cannons. King Joseph

---

221 Ibid, pp.183-185.
222 Glover, Michael (2001). *The Peninsular War 1807-1814: A Concise Military History*. Harmondsworth: Penguin Classic, p.233; Snow, Peter (2011). *To War with Wellington: From the Peninsula to Waterloo*. London: John Murray, p.188.
223 Snow, Peter (2011). *To War with Wellington: From the Peninsula to Waterloo*. London: John Murray.
224 Moorsom, op. cit. 220, pp.188-189.
225 Ibid, p.190.

Bonaparte narrowly escaped capture, but the battle effectively led to the collapse of Napoleonic rule in Spain.[226]

Subsequently, in his despatch following the battle, Wellington wrote:

> 'General Vandeleur's brigade (52nd, 95th, 1st Caçadores) of the Light Division was, during the advance upon Vitoria, detached to the support of the 7th division, and the Earl of Dalhousie has reported most favourably of its conduct.'[227]

Having defeated the French forces, 'what should have been a glorious day for Wellington's men, ended in disgrace.' Snow describes how

> 'the British Army abandoned its pursuit of the French and turned to highway robbery. In their desperation to flee, Joseph Bonaparte, his retinue and his army's senior commanders left behind a great trail of gun carriages, coaches and wagons stuffed with their belongings. Joseph himself narrowly escaped being seized by two hussar officers who threw open the door of his coach just as he leapt out and on to the back of a horse the other side. Within minutes a chaotic convoy of abandoned vehicles littered the first few miles of road to Pamplona. They contained all the wealth the French high command had amassed and the treasures they had plundered from the palaces of Spain in six years of occupation. Throughout the evening of 21 June whole units of the British army threw order to the winds and indulged in an orgy of looting that dwarfed what had happened at Badajoz.'[228]

Holmes referred to it as 'larceny on a gigantic scale in which officers participated enthusiastically.'[229] However, the highly-disciplined Light Division took no part in the plundering and set off in pursuit of the fleeing French forces.

But it wasn't over yet. To evict the last French forces from Spain, Wellington needed to take San Sebastian and Pamplona. The two were 40 miles apart. Pamplona commanded two of three roads into France. San Sebastian stood on a peninsula, which ran from north to south, and extended into the Bay of Biscay. It was close to the third road but, more importantly perhaps, had a good port which was needed to bring supplies from Britain. Lacking the resources to attack both simultaneously, he ordered Major-General The Earl of Dalhousie to blockade Pamplona whilst Lieutenant-General

---

226 Glover, op. cit. 222, pp.242-246.
227 Moorsom, op. cit. 220, p.194.
228 Ibid, p.197.
229 Holmes, Richard (2003). *Wellington: The Iron Duke*. London: Harper Perennial, pp.186-187.

Above: Peninsular War battles 1808-1813
Below: The Battle of Waterloo, 18 June 1815 at 11 a.m.

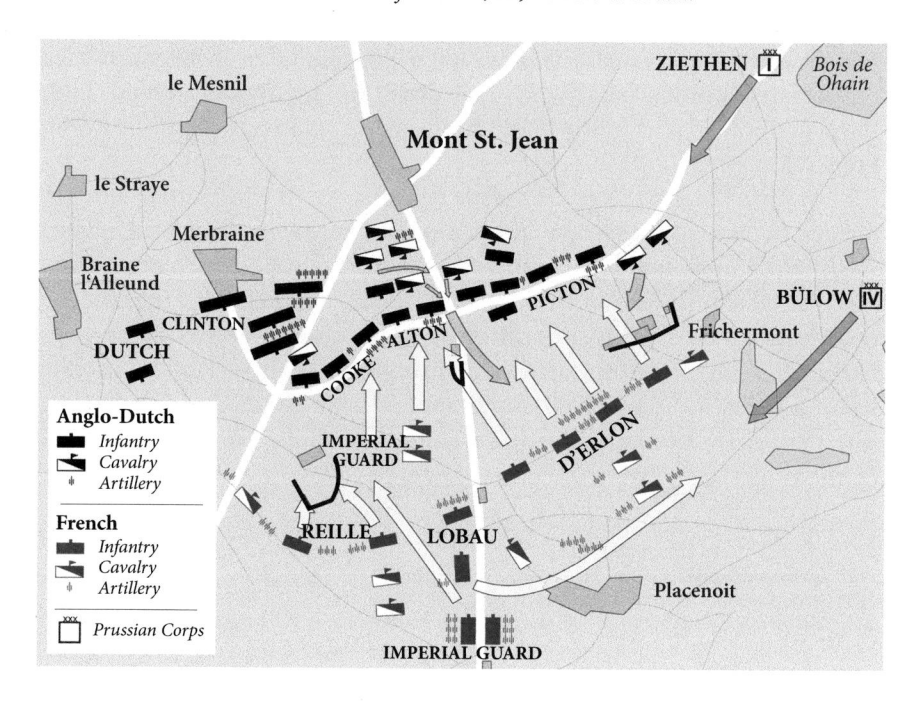

Thomas Graham began a siege of San Sebastian.[230] Attempts to breach the walls of San Sebastian with artillery fire began on 20 July and, five days later, Graham believed that sufficient progress had been made to storm the city. But as the storming parties advanced just before dawn, 'across atrociously rough ground' they were met by a 'terrific fire of musketry and shells from the ramparts' and 'a heavy discharge of grape' from a battery 'which flanked the approach to the beach'. The few who made it to the breach 'were mown down by concentrated musket fire'. This unsuccessful attempt resulted in 'more than 500 British dead or wounded'.[231]

The same day the Light Division, which did not take part in the first siege of San Sebastian, fell back to Lesaca. There, much to everyone's delight, the 1/52nd Regiment were rejoined by Lieutenant-Colonel Colborne who had recovered sufficiently from the wound he had received at Ciudad Rodrigo to play an active part in the remainder of the Peninsula campaign.

The French forces were now under the command of Marshal Soult, whom Napoleon had sent to Spain as soon as he heard of the defeat at Vitoria. Soult decided that he would march first on Pamplona with 60,000 men. But first he had to get past Lieutenant-General Charles Stewart, who was guarding the Maya pass with two brigades from the Second Division, and Roncesvalles, where Major-General Cole had 11,000 men. Faced by vastly superior numbers, both British generals retreated and by 27 July had reached Sorauren.[232]

The Light Division played no part in the battle that took place at Sorauren on 28 July. It was 'a fierce one' that ended with Soult withdrawing his forces.[233] Nevertheless, the allies lost 2,652 men killed, wounded or taken prisoner.[234] By 2 August Soult's army had returned to France. Altogether, in the Battle of Sorauren and the subsequent retreat, the French suffered 7,500 casualties.[235]

Having forced Soult to withdraw, Wellington would have liked to have moved towards France but he was conscious of the fact that San Sebastian and Pamplona were still in French hands. He therefore renewed his efforts to take San Sebastian on 26 August. Fifteen heavy cannon launched an assault on the town's fortifications from the south; a further 48 cannons fired from the east. Meanwhile, 200 men rowed out into the bay to the west of San Sebastian and after a brief fight captured a small island, Santa Clara,

---

230   Snow, op. cit. 223, p.205.
231   Ibid, pp.206-209.
232   Glover, op. cit. 222, pp.250-254.
233   Snow, op. cit. 223, pp.212-215.
234   Glover, op, cit. 222, p.256.
235   Ibid, p.258.

on which they located a six-gun battery. Five days later 'the guns had made two breaches in the walls of San Sebastian.' This time, the forlorn hope was 'backed up' by a storming party 'from the crack Light Division',[236] led by Brevet Lieutenant-colonel John Hunt of 1/52nd Regiment.[237] The attack began at 11.00am, the first major daylight assault on a fortress during the Peninsular War. The forlorn hope, which came from Graham's 5th Division, followed by the Light Division's storming party, scrambled from the trenches and dashed the 180 yards to the breach with very few losses. But then they were hit by ferocious fire from the French inside. As a result, a number of British soldiers were killed. Unbeknown to the British, the French had built an inner wall which stopped the troops from gaining access. Despite the danger to the survivors of the forlorn hope and storming party, Graham decided to open fire on the inner wall and created a breach through which the British spilled out into the city. The French retreated to a fortress on the hill of Urgull, leaving the British in occupation of the town. By 8 September the French commander had had enough and formally surrendered the fortress.[238]

Out of the three officers, three sergeants and 35 rank and file from the 1/52nd Regiment in the storming party, one officer and two rank and file were killed, and two officers, including Hunt, two sergeants and fourteen rank and file were wounded.[239] Unfortunately, the success was 'marred by the depressingly familiar pillage that followed',[240] which included the sacking and setting on fire of buildings, by soldiers 'maddened by drink' and 'desperate for revenge for their fallen comrades', of which there were 3,000.[241]

Meanwhile, on 31 August Soult forded the River Bidasoa in a desperate attempt 'to claw back territory in Spain.' But on this occasion he was driven back by Spanish forces. Soult's retreat was made the more difficult by rising river levels, as a result of which the fords were impassable so they made for the bridge at Vera. Brigadier-General John Skerrett, who had replaced Vandeleur as commander of 2 Brigade of the Light Division, sent a 70-man company of the 95th Regiment, under the command of Captain Daniel Cadoux, to hold it.

Time and again the French troops attempted to cross but, in the pouring rain, their muskets would not fire but the British riflemen were secure with

---

236 Snow, op. cit. 223, p.214.
237 Moorsom, op. cit. 220, pp.207-209.
238 Glover, op. cit. 222, pp.259-262.
239 Moorsom, op. cit. 220, pp.207-209.
240 Holmes, op. cit. 229, p.188.
241 Snow, op, cit. 223, p.216.

dry gunpowder in loopholed buildings. The French attacked with bayonets but were mown down by the British. Cadoux sent for assistance from the Skerrett. He refused; instead he twice ordered Cadoux to withdraw. By the time he did, at dawn, the rain had ceased, the French now had dry gunpowder and Cadoux, along with 16 of his men, was killed. Rowan's friend Harry Smith claimed that Wellington was 'awfully annoyed' when he heard what had happened. A short while later, Skerrett was taken ill and went back to England. Much to the delight of everyone in the brigade, Wellington appointed Colborne the new brigade commander.[242]

Now in possession of the whole of Spain, Wellington kept his forces around the River Bidasoa for the whole of September. Then, on 7 October, he commenced to battle his way into France by crossing the River Bidasoa and mounting a twin assault on Hendaya and Vera, in the foothills of the Pyrenees. Hendaya was quickly taken.[243] Vera was more difficult, and had been given to the Light Brigade. As 1 Brigade under Major-General Kempt advanced on the town from the right, 2 Brigade under Colonel Colborne advanced from the left. Communication between the two brigades was prevented by 'a deep rugged ravine which ran down between the ridges of the main range of mountains', so each was fighting independently of the other.[244] 1 Brigade had 'more trouble with the country than from the French',[245] as Captain Cooke of the 43rd Regiment explained:

> 'The obstacles on each side of the way rendered the mountain fearfully difficult of ascent; and it was so intersected with rocks, trees, brushwood and briar that our hands and limbs were pierced with thorns and the trousers were literally torn from our legs.'[246]

2 Brigade 'had a more difficult task.' The ridge it attacked had 'a stone-built redoubt known as La Bayonette' at the top. Colborne initially sent out riflemen, but the French attacked them downhill and drove them back. The French success was short-lived. Almost immediately the 1/52nd Regiment, under the command of Brevet Major William Mein, emerged from the trees at the bottom of the spur 'and Colborne led them uphill on a charge before the French had time to reform.' As a result La Bayonette was taken.[247] The taking of four other redoubts quickly followed, with 2

242 Ibid, p.218.
243 Glover, op, cit. 222, p.284.
244 Moorsom, op. cit. 220, p.210.
245 Glover, op. cit. 222, p.284.
246 Cooke, John (1831). *The Personal Narrative of Captain Cooke of the 43rd Regiment Light Infantry. In Memoirs of the Late War, Volume II*. London: Henry Cockburn and Richard Bentley. p.28.
247 Glover, op, cit. 222, pp.285-286.

Brigade taking possession of three pieces of artillery in the last. In the pursuit of the French forces, the Brigade also took 22 officers and nearly four hundred rank and file prisoner. Unfortunately, 1/52nd Regiment lost 12 rank and file killed, and six officers and 66 rank and file wounded. Amongst the officers was Mein, who was seriously wounded.[248]

Rowan would have learned from the example set by Colborne prior to the assault on 7 October, as Moorsom describes:

> 'The affair of Vera may serve to show how much mutually depends upon good leaders and good troops. Colonel Colborne during the short time that the camp of his brigade was in this neighbourhood was constantly on horseback from morning till night, reconnoitring the country over which his brigade might have to act. Thus when he led the troops into action he knew the ground, and was enabled to take advantage of every inequality for cover from the enemy's fire, and of any other accidental irregularity that favoured his movement at the moment. He thus inspired the highest confidence in the mind of every officer and soldier whom he led, that whatever they might have to do would be done in the best manner and with the least exposure to loss.'[249]

For the next month, occasionally visited by Wellington, Colborne 'watched the French fortifying the line of the next river beyond the Bidasoa, the Nivelle, which runs down from the Pyrenees to its mouth at Saint-Jean-de-Luz on the coast.'[250] The key to the French defences were two peaks, known as the Rhune and the Lesser Rhune, separated by a ravine. The Lesser Rhune was about 700 yards in front of the Rhune, and would need to be taken first. But it 'was crowned by three stone-built redoubts.'[251] The Light Division were given the very difficult task[252] of taking the Lesser Rhune and, during the night of 9 November, it 'silently approached within 300 yards of the advanced point of the enemy's fortified heights', waiting for the remainder of the night, in a ravine.[253]

The Battle of Nivelle, started just before dawn the following morning. By 8.00am, all the fortifications and trenches on the Lesser Rhune were in Allied hands. This allowed Wellington to advance 'nine Allied divisions on

---

248 Moorsom, op. cit. 220, pp.211-213.
249 Ibid; see also Snow, op. cit. 223, pp.220-221. Compare this with Rowan's actions at Cold Bath Fields in 1833.
250 Snow, op. cit. 223, p.223.
251 Glover, op. cit. 222, p.288.
252 Weller, Jac (2012). *Wellington in the Peninsula 1808-1814*. London: Greenhill Books, p.321.
253 Moorsom, op. cit. 220, p.214.

a front of about five miles.' Once the redoubts of St. Barbe and Grenade and the village of Sare had been occupied, Alten sent the Light Division forward 'through the St Ignace Valley and up the far side, capturing two redoubts' and more entrenchments. This left the well-fortified Signals Redoubt. After 'two bloody assaults', by the 1/52nd Regiment, during which Charles Rowan's brother, Captain William Rowan, played a leading role, Colborne approached the fort under a flag of truce, pointed out to the French commander that he was totally cut off from the remainder of the French army, and 'threatened to turn any survivors over to the Spaniards, if further fighting was necessary to take the fortifications.'

Short of food and water, the French commander surrendered. Once the fortifications had been taken, the main assault commenced with nine divisions fanning out over a five-mile front. When the 3rd Division took the Bridge at Amotz, all French resistance broke. By 2.00pm they were streaming east across the River Nivelle, having lost 4,351 men to Wellington's 2,450.

The 1/52nd Regiment had paid a particularly high price. Two sergeants and 30 rank and file had been killed; six officers, seven sergeants, three buglers and 192 rank and file were wounded. Following the battle, 2 Brigade stayed in the village of Arbonne for five days before moving to the chateau of Casteleur, near Arcangues on 24 November. On 10 December, the Light Division's post at Arcangues was attacked by the French but it appears Colborne was prepared and after two days, the enemy retired.[254]

During January and the first half of February 1814, the weather made any progress impossible and the two armies remained in winter quarters. But, by the middle of February the weather had improved sufficiently enough 'for Wellington to order his men forward again'. Not wanting 'to leave such a formidable fortress in his wake without at least neutralising it', Bayonne was besieged. Wellington's main force, meanwhile, pressed east from the Nive leaving Bayonne surrounded but untaken behind them. Only when they had crossed four more rivers was there serious opposition from Soult at the town of Orthez.[255]

Soult had taken up a formidable position on a great ridge.[256] In front of the French position was a deep marsh. The only way to dislodge him was for Wellington's men to fight their way up three steep spurs. By this time, 2 Brigade had come under the command of Colonel Barnard, and Colborne returned to command 1/52nd Regiment. On 27 February, 4th and 7th

---

254   Moorsom, op. cit. 220, pp.217-223.
255   Snow, op. cit. 223, pp.227-228.
256   Ibid, p.228.

Divisions, under Marshal William Beresford,[257] attacked the western end of the ridge with the intention of taking the village of St Boes; the 3rd and 6th Divisions, under Lieutenant-General Thomas Picton, was supposed to pin down the French centre on the ridge; and Lieutenant-General Rowland Hill led the 2nd Division and a Portuguese Division across the River Gave de Pau above Orthez, with the intention of turning the French left. The Light Division was held 'in reserve on a spur on the main ridge of St Boes'.[258]

Beresford initially succeeded in taking the capturing the church in St Boes, but was unable to force his way into the village itself. Then, in a counterattack, the French drove Beresford's forces from the church.

Seeing this reversal, Wellington changed his plan. His holding attack with the 3rd and 6th Divisions would be converted into a head-on assault, and the Light Division would be committed between the efforts of Beresford's 4th and 7th Divisions against the French right and the all-out assault on the French centre by Picton's 3rd and 6th Divisions.

Led by the 1/52nd Regiment, the Light Division advanced up the narrow spur from the Roman Camp, driving a wedge between the French right-wing and its centre divisions.[259] Colborne describes how 1/52nd Regiment advanced 'diagonally up the ridge to cut off the defenders of St Boes from the rest of the French line.' Adding that 'they did it beautifully', Colborne went on to describe how, despite heavy fire from the French, he 'rode to the top of the hill and waved [his] cap, and though the men were over their knees in mud in the marsh, they trotted up in the finest order.' As soon as they reached the top, he 'ordered them to halt and open fire' which immediately resulted in the French beginning their retreat.[260]

George Napier, who was at the time a major with the 1/52nd described the same incident slightly differently. Within

> 'a few minutes we were in full march, up to our knees every step in the bog, the enemy pouring fire upon us from the height above, which we could not return. I never saw our fellows behave more steadily or more gallantly; but owing to the ground our line was not very correct …

---

257 Beresford was a Brigadier-General in the British Army when he was sent to Portugal originally to overhaul the Portuguese army and bring it in line with the British, which he did with vigour. Given the rank of Marshal, he then commanded the Portuguese forces that fought with Wellington.
258 Moorsom, op. cit. 220, p.233.
259 Glover, op. cit. 222, pp. 320-322.
260 Moore Smith, G.C (1903). *The Life of John Colborne, Field Marshal Lord Seaton*. London: John Murray, p.202.

At last we made the enemy retire and gained the brow of the hill, and then dressed our line and commenced a heavy rolling fire in our turn, advancing at the same time.'

Neither the left nor the right of the British army made much progress, but when Marshal Soult found the 52nd Regiment had succeeded in penetrating the centre and was still advancing, he gave orders for the French to retire to Toulouse. Unfortunately one of Rowan's closest friends in later life, Lord March, then a captain in the 1/52nd Regiment, who would become the 5th Duke of Richmond on the death of his father in 1819, was shot in the chest. At first it was thought to be serious but he recovered sufficiently to enable him to rejoin the regiment at Toulouse.[261]

On 31 March 1814, the eastern allied armies entered Paris. Six days later Napoleon abdicated. The following day, emissaries left the French capital to convey the news to Wellington but they did not reach him until 12 April.[262] In the meantime, Soult had taken his now 'defeated and demoralised army'[263] and was holed up in the fortified city of Toulouse, which stands on the east bank of the River Garonne. The battle that followed was 'one of the bloodiest' as well as being 'the most pointless' of the whole war.[264] Wellington, having surrounded the city on three sides, began his attack on 10 April. Hoping to divert some of Soult's forces from their defensive positions, Lieutenant-General Hill with the 2nd Division and a Portuguese Division, who were on the west bank of the river, attacked the suburb of St-Cyprien. The remainder of the army was still on the east bank. Lieutenant-General Sir Thomas Picton, commanding the 3rd Division, 'cleared some outworks with ease' but when 'he tried to storm the redoubt north of the river' he failed, suffering 400 casualties in the process. Meanwhile Marshal Beresford's troops, required to deploy across ploughed fields which left the troops 'ankle-deep in mud', eventually 'gained the summit of the ridge', capturing two redoubts which were quickly lost in a counter-attack. However, the Great Redoubt at the northern end remained in Allied hands and when Soult realised Wellington's artillery would soon be in a position to open fire he withdrew his army into a fortified part of the city. In the east, Marshal Beresford faced the north-west canal line with the Light Division to the east.

By nightfall, Soult had withdrawn all his troops into the inner defences

---

261   Napier, Sir George Thomas, and William Craig Emilius Napier (1884). *Passages in the Early Military Life of General Sir George T. Napier*. London: John Murray, p.243-246.
262   Glover, op. cit. 222, p.326.
263   Ibid, p.323.
264   Snow, op. cit. 223, p.231.

of the city. The allied army suffered 4,500 dead or wounded, compared with Soult's figure of 3,236.[265] On the evening of 10 April, Marshal Soult received an official communique from Paris informing him that Napoleon had surrendered to the Coalition forces in northern France. Unsure of what to do, Soult's generals advised him to surrender the city, as reinforcements were unlikely to arrive. When further news reached Toulouse that French armies across the whole country had surrendered, Soult took the advice of his generals and surrendered.

Thus ended the Peninsular War, and the 1/52nd Regiment went into cantonments at Castel Sarrasin.[266]

Wellington did conduct 'a special review of his Peninsular army before it split up for the last time.' In a General Order, he also conveyed 'his admiration and thanks for all the soldiers had done to push France out of Spain and Portugal.' The General Order concluded with the sentence:

> 'The commander of forces… assures them that he shall never cease to feel the warmest interest in their welfare and honour, and that he will be at all times happy to be of any service to those whose conduct, discipline and gallantry their country is so much indebted.'

Regrettably,

> 'it was a pledge that many felt he failed to honour. Army pensions remained at a basic minimum for a long time and the government was unable or unwilling to approve a peninsula medal until 1847 when many of the veterans were dead.'

Consequently, many of Wellington's soldiers felt let down and angry at what they saw as a failure to recognise their sacrifice.[267]

The 1/52nd Regiment left Castel Sarrasin, which is some 130 miles west of Toulouse, on 3 June and marched to Bordeaux. Whilst on the march, the 1st and 3rd Portuguese Cacadores, which had been part of the Light Division since its formation four years previously, left Wellington's Army at Bargas to return to Portugal. The 1/52nd Regiment arrived at Bordeaux on 14 June.[268]

Quite how Rowan got back to England is unclear, for he had set off on a jaunt with George Napier. Describing Rowan as 'one of the best and cleverest, gallant, honourable men in existence, as well as a staunch and true friend', the two men left Bordeaux and travelled down a river to board

---

265 Glover, op, cit. 222, p.323.
266 Moosom, op. cit. 220, p.239.
267 Snow, op. cit. 223, p.238.
268 Moorsom, op. cit. 220, pp.239-240.

transport for the return to England. At one point, Napier described how they

> 'went ashore to look at a curious village cut in the rock. Each house was perfectly separate, but cut in the rock; bed-rooms, kitchen, etc, etc, with regular communications, exactly like the inside of a house; not the least difference, except that all the rooms were in line and looking towards the river otherwise there would have been a want of light; but there were chambers one above the other, with steps cut in the rock to enable one to get up to each storey.'

Napier was in uniform and, because of this they were immediately recognised as British officers. Unfortunately, most of the male inhabitants 'were sailors just released by the peace from prisons and hulks – where, to the eternal disgrace and shame of the British government, they had been most infamously and inhumanly treated', and Napier described how 'they were determined to insult us.' They began by 'throwing stones and abusing us most desperately', and such was their rage the two British officers thought it best to retreat to their boat as fast as they could. However, Napier was 'very angry' and drew one of his pistols, but said

> 'Rowan, being a wiser and cooler-headed fellow, very properly prevented my doing so, and luckily for us, as, in a few moments, the whole village turned out, and we had but just time to regain the boat and shove out, and, a breeze springing up, we made all sail into the middle of the river, which was very broad, and escaped their fury, for they certainly would have murdered us without mercy.'

But that was not the end of their adventure. Having got on board the small sailing boat, Napier was so seasick that he could not remain on the boat and 'Rowan very good humouredly' got out with him. Napier goes on to describe how they 'waded up to [their] middle through a long mile of mud, as the tide was out; and at last, having gained the bank', saw a light some way off that turned out to be a house. They knocked on the door, were given food and wine and a bed for the night and the occupier, who spoke 'broken English', even loaned them some clothes whilst theirs, which were by now very muddy, were cleaned and dried. The following morning, they continued on their way and boarded the ships that would take them to England.[269] With or without Rowan and Napier, the 1/52nd Regiment embarked at Panillac on HMS *Dublin* and landed at Plymouth on 28 June. They then went to Tavistock and from there to Hythe, where

---

269   Napier, op. cit. 261, pp.276-280.

they received a draft of 357 men from the 2nd Battalion. The Battalion then moved to Chatham.[270]

The Light Division had been the strongest Division in the British army during the Peninsular War. It proved its tough nature in the numerous actions it had been involved in from the infamous retreat to Corunna right up to the invasion of France and the conclusion of the war at the Battle of Toulouse. Sometime later, Napier summed up what those who had been with the Light Brigade and then the Light Division for the duration of the war, which included Rowan, had achieved. They

> 'had won nineteen pitched battles and innumerable combats; had made or sustained ten sieges, and taken four great fortresses; had twice expelled the French from Portugal, and once from Spain; had penetrated France, and killed, wounded or captured two hundred thousand enemies, leaving their own number forty thousand whose bones whiten the plains and mountains of the Peninsula.'[271]

Rowan was present throughout either in a staff role, firstly with the Light Brigade and then with the Light Division, or as regimental officer with the 1/52nd Regiment. He served under some of the best military commanders of that era. He learned much that would stand him in good stead after Peel invited him to undertake the formation of the Metropolitan Police, along with Richard Mayne.

---

270 Moorsom, op. cit. 220, pp.240-241.
271 Napier, Lieut.-General Sir William Napier, KCB (1879). *English Battles and Sieges in the Peninsula*. London: John Murray. p.469.

CHAPTER FIVE

THE BATTLE OF WATERLOO AND THE OCCUPATION OF FRANCE

Rowan left Hythe with the 1/52 Regiment on 31 August 1814 and arrived in Chatham two days later, where the battalion was issued with new arms and accoutrements. Immediately after Christmas it marched to Portsmouth, where the troops embarked on ships. On 4 January 1815 the ships sailed for Ireland with the intention that the regiment should travel to America to join British troops in the War of 1812, which was still ongoing. Arriving at Cork on 20 January, gales twice prevented the ships from sailing any further. By the time conditions had improved, news had reached England of Napoleon's escape from Elba and his arrival in France to an enthusiastic welcome.[272] Quickly 're-establishing political and military authority over most of the country', he marched northwards with is army towards the Belgian border.[273]

The 1/52nd Regiment was recalled to Plymouth before being sent, under Charles Rowan's temporary command, to Belgium,[274] where two armies were being formed: the Anglo-Allies, which included British, Dutch and German contingents, initially under the Duke of Orange, and the Prussians, under General Gebhard von Blücher. Rowan arrived with his 'battle-hardened' battalion[275] in Ostend on 31 March, marched to Brussels, arriving on 4 April, and then onto Grammont, arriving on 7 April, where

---

272 Snow, Peter (2011). *To War with Wellington: From the Peninsula to Waterloo*. London: John Murray, pp.246 and.251-252.
273 Freemont-Barnes, Gregory (2014). *Waterloo 1815: The British Army's Day of Destiny*. Stroud: The History Press, p.34.
274 Colborne did not arrive in Belgium until 16 May, see Leeke, William (1866). *The History of Lord Seaton's Regiment (The 52nd Light Infantry) at the Battle of Waterloo*. London: Hatchard, p.6.
275 Glover, Gareth (2015). *Waterloo: The Defeat of Napoleon's Imperial Guard*. Barnsley, South Yorkshire: Frontline Books, p.27.

he joined up with a seriously-depleted 2/52 Regiment, which was already in Holland.[276] Here, nine sergeants and 224 rank and file deemed to be fit for active service in the 2nd Battalion were transferred to Rowan's battalion, at the same time, 26 sergeants, eight buglers and 284 rank and file, deemed unfit for service, were transferred from the 1/52nd Regiment to the 2nd battalion.[277] A week later Wellington arrived to take command of the Anglo-Allied army.[278]

Along with 1/71st, 2/95th and part of 3/95th, 1/52nd Regiment was assigned to 2 Brigade, under the command of Major-General Frederick Adam. 2 Brigade was part of Lieutenant-General Sir Henry Clinton's 2nd Division, which in turn was a part of Lieutenant-General Sir Rowland Hill's II Corps. As a response to Napoleon's advance, on 15 June, II Corps were posted west and southwest of Brussels, with a cavalry screen. However, 1/52nd Regiment was dispersed, with two companies in Ligne, four between Moulbaix and Bliquy and four 'in hovels' St. Amand and Villers.[279] On 12 April 1/52nd Regiment, still with Rowan temporarily in command, was inspected by Clinton. Clinton had been with Wellington in a number of the major battles during the Peninsular War, and was known for 'his rigid insistence on total obedience to orders', highlighting 'even the most minor failures… in minute detail.'[280] In the only criticism to be found of Rowan as a soldier, Clinton wrote in his report that he did not think he was 'quite equal to the command of [such a] strong battalion', suggesting that the 1/52nd Regiment was 'past its best and far too arrogant to accept advice on how to improve.' Rowan excused 'the awkward manner… [his] regiment moved' in drills carried out before Clinton by pointing out 'they had been for five months on board ship.'[281] Although it had been 'in almost continuous combat since 1806', over half had joined since the last battle,[282] and, with the companies now separated, they could not drill or train together as a regiment. Colborne was already in Belgium, acting as Military Secretary to the Prince of Orange, so was recalled to take command of the regiment. When he arrived, he supported Rowan's complaint about the companies being scattered and pointed out that it would prevent him using

---

276 Ibid, p.36.
277 Moorsom, W.S (Ed)(1860). *Historical Record of the Fifty-Second Regiment (Oxfordshire 227 Light Infantry) from the Year 1755 to the year 1858*. Uckfield, Sussex: The Naval and Military Press, pp.241-242.
278 Holmes, Richard (2003). *Wellington: The Iron Duke*. London: Harper Perennial, p.208.
279 Glover, op. cit. 275, pp.49-51.
280 Ibid, pp.4-5.
281 Henry Clinton's Inspection Report, dated 14 April 1815 quoted in Glover, ibid, p.49.
282 Cornwall, Bernard (2014). *Waterloo: The History of Four Days, Three Armies and Three Battles*. London: William Collins, p.32.

the three weeks he had before Napoleon was likely to reach the Belgian border, to get the regiment into battle order. Clinton was not immediately responsive to his request, suggesting that 'if the company officers were up to the standard that they were in Spain' it should not be necessary to 'bring the regiment together.' But he did eventually agree to Colborne's request and the battalion was brought together at Lessines on 27 April.[283]

William Leeke, who joined the 1/52nd Regiment as a volunteer prior to being gazetted as an ensign and eventually wrote a history of Colborne's regiment at Waterloo, mentions being greeted by Rowan on his arrival and the change-over of command to Colborne. He recalls 'there was a full sixty officers with the regiment', who dined 'at the same hotel, in two separate rooms' before going on to describe how, after dinner 'each day, between thirty and forty horses' were paraded, which enabled 'some excellent steeple-chasing or rather brook-leaping' to take place 'in the meadows adjoining the town.'[284]

Wellington, meanwhile, was unsure of where Napoleon would cross the border into Belgium,[285] so his army was strung out in an attempt to cover all eventualities. Leading components of Napoleon's army reached the Belgian frontier at 3.30pm on 15 June, crossing into it about eight miles south of Charleroi, which was the hinge between Wellington's and von Blücher's armies. Napoleon's intention was to 'destroy the Prussians, who were concentrated around Ligny, 25 miles south-east of Brussels', before turning on the Anglo-Allies.[286]

Charles Lennox, the 4th Duke of Richmond, was in command of a reserve force in Brussels, to protect the city. On the evening of the 15 June 1815 his wife, the Duchess of Richmond, gave what has been described as 'the most famous ball in history'[287] in the large workshop of a coachbuilder on the Rue de la Blanchisserie. Despite Napoleon's presence in Belgium, although it was unknown to the Allies and the Prussians at the time, Wellington allowed the ball to go ahead because 'it was important to preserve calm in the city, and a sudden cancellation' or the absence 'of many of the leading guests, would give precisely the wrong impression.'[288] With the exception of three generals, including Hill and Clinton, all the senior officers in Wellington's army were 'there to be seen'. Amongst them was Lieutenant

---

283 Glover, op. cit. 275, p.50-51.
284 Leeke, op. cit, 274, pp.6-8.
285 Holmes, op. cit. 278, pp.223-225.
286 Snow, op. cit. 272, p.258.
287 Longford, Elizabeth (1971). *Wellington: The Years of the Sword*. London: HarperCollins.
288 Holmes, op. cit. 278, p.227.

Colonel Charles Rowan of the 1/52nd Regiment.[289]

Believing that his army was at a high state of readiness[290] the Duke of Wellington arrived at the ball with his personal staff at some time between 11.00pm and midnight.[291] Supper was taken at around 1.00am,[292] It was during supper that Wellington was told that Bonaparte had crossed the Belgian frontier and was close to Quatre Bras. He continued with his supper for another twenty minutes before retiring with the Duke of Richmond to study a map of the area.[293] Wellington told him that he intended to concentrate his forces immediately at Quatre Bras but the battle would take place at Waterloo, which was halfway between Brussels and Quatre Bras.[294]

Two battles took place on 16 June. The Prussians were 'roundly defeated' at Ligny in a 'bloody' battle and retreated some eighteen miles to Wavre. A section of Wellington's Anglo-Allied army fought out a draw at Quatre Bras.[295] Following the ball, Rowan had returned to his regiment in the early hours of the morning, where preparations were being made for it to go to a nearby meadow for drill. Suddenly, orders were received for Clinton's division to form up about a mile away on the road to Ath at 10.00am. Once formed up, the division skirted the town of Ath and took the road towards Enghien but were diverted to Soignies. Whilst on the road, although some 22 miles away, sounds emanating from 'fierce' fighting at Quatre Bras were heard. Towards midnight it reached Braine-le-Comte, where it halted for a short while in pouring rain. By 2.00am on 17 June, it was on the march again and reached Nivelles at around 7.00am, where it remained for four hours. Accompanied by British artillery and cavalry, and troops from the Netherlands, the division then moved towards the village of Waterloo.[296] At 7.30pm, it was ordered to move to the highlands immediately east of Merbe Braine after which it settled down to a 'wet and disagreeable night'. Due to the incessant heavy rain it was 'impossible to light fires to cook by

---

289   Swinton, Georgiana (1893). *A Sketch of the Life of Georgiana, Lady de Ros: With Some Reminiscences of her friends including the Duke of Wellington*. London: John Murray, pp.124-132.
290   Holmes, op. cit. 278, p.226.
291   Clayton, Tim (2014). *Four Days that Changed Europe's Destiny*. Little, Brown Book Group, p. 76, says around 11.00pm; Miller, David (2005). *The Duchess of Richmond's Ball*, Spellmount, p. 67, says midnight.
292   Hastings, Max (1986). "Anecdote 194" *The Oxford Book of Military Anecdotes*, Oxford University Press, pp.233-34.
293   Dowager Lady Roos, Georgina (July 1889) "Personal Recollections of the Duke of Great Wellington" *Murrays Magazine* (January or February).
294   Snow, op. cit. 272, p.259.
295   Ibid, pp.260-275; see also Glover, op. cit. 275, pp.88-93.
296   Moorsom, op. cit. 277, pp.244-245.

or even warm the men a little.' Shelter was almost non-existent, so 'most of the men simply had to lie in the mud, covered by their blanket, and attempt to gain a few fitful moments of rest, whilst trying to ignore their hunger pangs, the cold and the unpleasantness of lying in a sea of mud, whilst a veritable river ran beneath and around them.'[297]

The field at Waterloo was approximately six miles south-south-east of Brussels. It was just over two miles wide, with two parallel ridges running west to east, creating a shallow valley one mile across. On the morning of 18 June, Wellington deployed his forces along a two-and-a-half-mile front just below the crest of the northern-most of the two ridges. In front of the ridge were three positions that could be fortified. On the extreme right flank of Wellington's line was a building known as Hougoumont, in the centre was a farmhouse known as La Haye Sante. And on the left flank was the hamlet of Papelotte. Wellington used all three as outposts.

Initially, the 2nd Division, including the 52nd Regiment, were held in reserve away from the front-line, 'hidden from sight on the gentle sloping ground behind the [northern] ridge.'[298] Once units had been deployed, Wellington rode from unit to unit on the basis that the more visibly he was seen to be

> 'exercising command and control even down to the level of the battalion, the more he reckoned he would give his men the will and confidence to win. His way of inspiring his men was to radiate cool self-confidence and to reassure them that he would make the right decisions and be in the right place at the right time, often at great personal risk.'[299]

Meanwhile, on the slopes of the southern ridge, Napoleon deployed his army. Fearing that his artillery and cavalry might get bogged down in the soft ground, Napoleon delayed the start of the battle. His plan was to mount a series of 'major frontal attacks' with massive artillery support. The battle commenced at 11.30am. During the first phase the French artillery opened up on the Anglo-Allied lines. At the same time, three divisions of French infantry attacked Wellington's outpost at Hougoumont. Wellington ordered three brigades of his artillery into a position from which it could provide some covering fire to support those defending the Hougoumont, and Clinton's 2nd Division 'was ordered forward to protect artillery positions'. The guns then 'became a target for the French batteries' and the

---

297   Glover, op. cit. 275, p.94.
298   Ibid, p.105.
299   Snow, op. cit. 272, p.280.

2nd Division, including 1/52nd Regiment, 'began to suffer casualties'.[300]

When it appeared likely that the French might capture the Hougoumont at around 4.00pm, 2nd Division was ordered to move 'in advance of the existing front line'.[301] Adam's Brigade, of which 1/52nd Regiment was a part, marched 'over the [northern] ridge line and down the forward slope of the ridge' at which time the troops were 'very vulnerable and suffered accordingly'.[302] Having arrived in position, it formed into squares before being attacked by French cavalry. Rowan addressed the regiment, telling officers and men that he did not think 'those fellows would come near', but if they did they would get 'a warm reception'.[303] At one stage, in the square in which Rowan happened to be talking to Colonel William Nicolay of the Royal Staff Corps,[304] a shell fell in their midst, injuring seven men. Rowan immediately yelled, 'Steady men!' Nicolay later commented, 'I never saw men steadier in my life'.[305]

In lulls between the cavalry attacks they came under the fire of French skirmishers hidden in a nearby orchard.[306] Blunted by coming continuously up against the disciplined squares of Adam's Brigade, the French cavalry attacks ceased, and Wellington ordered the brigade to move to a more protected position. It therefore 'retired in a four-deep line behind the ridge and formed up to the right of Maitland's Guards Brigade'.[307]

By now some of Wellington's units were down to half strength and 'the whole of the Anglo-allied line was under severe pressure'.[308] At around 7.00pm a deserting French cuirassier colonel told Colborne that Napoleon had decided to commit his so-far undefeated Imperial Guard. They were his elite troops, paid twice as much as other French soldiers. Napoleon brought up eight battalions, five of the Middle Guard and three of the Old Guard[309] – around 5,000 men – to the bottom of the slope which led up to the British line and handed them over to Marshal Ney for the assault. Ney launched them against Wellington's right centre. The 1/52 Regiment 'was towards the west end of the British line'. The mounted officers, including Colborne and Charles Rowan were at the front.[310]

300 Glover, op. cit. 275, pp.114-115.
301 Ibid, p.120.
302 Ibid, p.128.
303 Leeke, op. cit. 274, p.29.
304 The Royal Staff Corps was responsible for military engineering.
305 Leeke, op. cit. 274, p.34.
306 Glover, op. cit. 275, pp.120-132.
307 Ibid, p.139.
308 Snow, op. cit. 272, p.301.
309 The Old Guard was Napoleon's personal unit, consisting of experienced veterans. The Middle Guard were less experienced.
310 Leeke, op. cit. 274, p.46.

Recognizing that the approaching Imperial Guard 'represented a major threat to the Allied lines', Colborne discussed with Rowan the need to menace 'the flank of the French Columns'. Then, acting on his own initiative, and assisted by Rowan, he took the 1/52nd Regiment out of the line formed by Adams Brigade, moved into the empty ground ahead and wheeled the Regiment to its left so the troops faced the flank of the advancing Guards.[311] But, as the regiment wheeled to the left, Charles Rowan was knocked off his horse, according to his brother William 'by the fire from the flank men of the French column'.[312] At the same time William's horse was killed, as was Colborne's. Fortunately the officers were both uninjured, and with many loose, saddled horses roaming the battlefield, they were quickly remounted.[313]

However, historian Nigel Sale suggests that Charles Rowan may have been the victim of friendly fire. He explains:

> 'It is much more likely that the animals and Charles Rowan, and possibly many of Colborne's men, especially the two companies that were acting as skirmishes and markers[314] – were hit by canisters shot from [an] over-keen gunner of Major Rogers' battery of 9-pounders, which was on the ridge.'[315]

Remounted, Colborne then ordered the regiment to 'make that column feel our fire'.[316] The advancing troops of the Imperial Guard were caught in a murderous crossfire, with the men of the 1/52nd Regiment firing at their flank and the main British line shooting straight at their front. Colborne's battalion was unusually strong, a thousand men in lines, nearly all of them, unlike the French, able to fire their weapons at the enemy. Assuming each musket fired a round every thirty seconds, the 1/52nd Regiment discharged around 2,000 balls a minute at the French guardsmen. It was too much even for Napoleon's Imperial Guard.[317]

Seeing the 1/52nd Regiment advancing, Wellington ordered, 'Go on,

---

311 Siborne, H.T. (ed). Waterloo Letters, memorandum with Letter No. 123 from Colonel Sir John Colborne, p.284, quoted in Sale, Nigel (2014). *The Lie at the Heart of Waterloo: The Battle's Hidden Last Hour*. Stroud, Gloucestershire: Spellmount, an imprint of The History Press, p. 109.
312 Letter No. 118 from Captain William Rowan in Glover, Gareth (ed)(2004) *Letters from the Battle of Waterloo*. London: Greenhill Books.
313 Sale, op. cit. 311, p.121.
314 Colborne had already ordered No. 10 Company under Lieutenant Anderson forward as skirmishers and wheeled No. 9 Company, under Captain Cross to act as left marker as the 1/52nd Regiment changed its position. See Sale, op. cit. 311, p.111.
315 Ibid, pp,121-122.
316 Siborne, op. cit. 311.
317 Snow, op. cit. 272, p.303.

Colborne! Go on! They won't stand! Don't give them time to rally.'[318] Colborne's men did not wait to reload, but 'gave one lusty cheer and advanced immediately towards the shattered column in a determined bayonet charge.' Adam ordered the remainder of his brigade to follow. The Imperial Guard broke, forced into retreat; thus the western most end of the French advance had been destroyed literally in minutes. Pursuing the French down the escarpment of Mont St Jean, the 1/52nd Regiment crossed the valley floor, that had separated the armies at the start of the battle and, on the other side, attacked a square of Old Guard, part of Napoleon's personal bodyguard, that had formed up to the British right, forcing it to retreat.[319]

On the night after the battle, the 1/52nd Regiment 'bivouacked …close to the farm of Ronssomme on the rising ground to the left of the Charleroi road'.[320] There, Major William Rowan asked Colborne if he could 'go and look after his brother'. Whilst on his way to do so, he met with Major-General Sir John Byng, commanding the Guards Division, who, when told of Rowan's regiment, said, 'Ah, we saw the 52nd advancing gloriously, as they always do.' William 'found his brother and all the 52nd wounded officers' in a house close to Waterloo.[321] Fortunately, Charles Rowan's injury was not serious and, after treatment, he returned to active duty.

The battle, in terms of human life, was expensive. The Anglo-Allied army lost 15,000 dead and wounded; Blücher lost 7,000, and Napoleon more than 25,000. Casualties among officers, was particularly high because 'they had been out in front taking the lead in every action.'[322] Compared with some divisions, Clinton's got off relatively lightly. The total number killed was 211, which included six officers and four ensigns. However, 1,118 were wounded; this included a colonel, four lieutenant-colonels, six majors, fourteen captains, 41 lieutenants and seven ensigns. Charles Rowan was the most senior officer in the 52nd Regiment to be wounded, along with two captains and five lieutenants; eight sergeants and 183 rank and file were also wounded. One ensign was killed, along with sixteen rank and file.[323]

Having received 'favourable reports' from the Brigade Commanders, Clinton submitted a list of names to Lord Hill, the Commander of II Corps, with the request that they be laid 'before the commander of the forces in

---

318   Ibid, p.249
319   Moorsom, op. cit. 277, pp.265-266.
320   Ibid, p.268.
321   Leeke, op. cit. 274, pp.71-72.
322   Snow, op. cit. 272, p.306.
323   Glover, op. cit. 275, p.176.

the hope that His Grace will recommend them for promotion'. Amongst the names was Brevet Lieutenant-Colonel Charles Rowan.[324] Following the battle, Wellington also submitted the names of all the officers who were to be awarded honours as a result of their involvement in the Napoleonic Wars. The list included Lieutenant Colonel Charles Rowan, who was made a Companion of the Bath (CB).[325] Rowan also received the Waterloo Medal, sometimes referred to as the Waterloo Gold Medal, two clasps – one for action at Ciudad Rodrigo, the other for Badajoz and Salamanca.[326] It was the practice at that time only to award medals to officers. The Duke of Richmond fought this injustice for many years and in 1847, 22 years after the defeat of Napoleon, the Government finally relented by introducing the Military General Service Medal to be awarded to all ranks and which was backdated for various campaigns to 1793. As a result, five years before his death, Rowan received the Military General Service Medal, sometimes referred to as the Silver Medal, with three clasps on it; for Coruna, Bussaco and Fuentes de Oñoro.[327]

Shaw Kennedy, then a member of the Quartermaster-general's staff serving with the 3rd Division, which occupied the centre part of Wellington's line, had a good view of the whole battlefield.[328] Commenting on the final phase of the battle, he said:

> 'The discipline of the 52nd Regiment was at all times admirable; and Colborne caused the movements on this occasion to be made with a precision which ensured coolness, gave security against all attack, and rendered both the firing and the advance in line of the battalion of the most formidable character.'[329]

Despite this, the initial, credit for the defeat of the French Imperial Guard was given to the Brigade of Guards. This was due to Wellington's Waterloo Despatch following the battle, in which he praised the division of Guards as having 'set an example which was followed by all', in effect, giving them 'credit for the victory'. But he made no mention of Adam's Brigade or the 1/52nd Regiment.[330] It was an injustice that rankled with many of the officers in the 1/52nd Regiment but not, it seems, with their commanding officer, Colonel Colborne.

---

324   Ibid, p.172.
325   *London Gazette*, 16 September 1815, issue 17061, p.1881.
326   *London Gazette*, 5 October 1813, issue 16785, p.1980.
327   Hart, Major H.G (1851). *The New Annual Army List for 1851*. London: John Murray, p.84.
328   Shaw Kennedy, James (undated). *An Autobiographical Memoir and Notes of the Battle of Waterloo*. London: Forgotten Books (Classic Reprint Series), p.52.
329   Ibid, p.144.
330   Sale, op. cit. 311, p.222.

Many years later, at a dinner party in London, Charles Rowan recounted the story to Colborne's eldest daughter, Lady Jane Montgomery-Moore, of the occasion that the subject was being discussed in the 1/52nd Regiment's Officers Mess in Paris when the blame for the injustice was laid firmly at the Wellington's door. Overhearing them, Colborne 'said quietly and emphatically, "For shame, gentlemen! One would think you forgot that the 52nd had ever been in battle before!" The matter was never mentioned again, and 'it became a point of honour to take it as the Colonel did.'[331]

Perhaps the last word should be left to Shaw Kennedy. He was of the view that it was 'perhaps impossible to point out in history any other instance in which so small a force as that with which Colborne acted had so powerful an influence on the result of a great battle, in which the numbers engaged on each side were so large.'[332]

Such is Charles Rowan's military legacy.

The morning after the battle the 1/52nd Regiment, together with the remainder of the Brigade, set off towards Paris. On 20 June, the Brigade was near Binck, on 21 June close to Bavay, and on 22 June it reached the neighbourhood of Le Cateau-Cambrésis, where it remained for the next two days. For the six days commencing 25 June Adam's Brigade was constantly on the move, passing through, Joucour, Beauvoir and Lanchy, Roye, Petit Crevecoeur and Clermont before reaching La Chapelle.[333]

On 1 July, from a piece of rising ground called Jardin de Paris, Rowan looked down on the Dome of the Invalides, the plain of St Denis, and Montmartre. It was his first view of Paris, which was still occupied by remnants of the French army. The following day the regiment was alone at Argenteuil, and Captain McNair's company crossed the River Seine in boats to take possession of a country house overlooking the river whilst a pontoon bridge was constructed. That afternoon, the 1/52nd Regiment crossed the Seine and marched to the bridge of Neuilly, which Colborne had been instructed to cross. However, a contingent of the French army refused to retire so two companies of the 1/52nd Regiment were ordered forward with fixed bayonets. Colborne gave the French commander five minutes to give up the bridge or have it stormed. After two or three minutes the French commander retreated, the village of Neuilly was occupied,[334] and the 1/52nd Regiment spent the night camped in a walled graveyard with French dragoons still in very close proximity. Rowan apparently told

---

331 Moore Smith, G.C. (1903). *The Life of John Colborne, Field-Marshal Lord Seaton: Compiled from his letters, records of his conversations and other sources.* London: John Murray, p.235.
332 Shaw Kennedy, op. cit. 328, p.147.
333 Moorsom, op. cit. 277, pp.268-269.
334 Ibid, pp.269-270.

Colborne the next morning that he had 'never spent such a night' and claimed he had not thought 'of closing his eyes the whole time.'[335]

The following day, the remnants of the French army quit Paris and the 1/52nd Regiment went to Bois de Boulogne, remaining there until the 7 July. That morning 'General Adam's Brigade, the 52nd, 71st and 95th, had the honour of entering Paris by the Barriere de l'Etoile'. Led by its commanding officer, Colonel Colborne, and its second in command, Charles Rowan, the 1/52nd Regiment proudly marched down the centre of the road leading through the Champs Elysees, the Place Louis Quinze and the Tuileries.

Adam's Brigade was the only British troops to occupy the French capital; the rest of the army remained in the Bois de Boulogne. The Brigade was encamped in the Champs Elysees, the 52nd to the left, the 71st and 95th to the right of the road towards the Seine. Two companies and the quarter-guard were close to the garden wall of the Duke of Wellington's house, the Chateau de St. Martin, with the remainder of the regiment about a hundred yards off in the direction of the barrier.[336]

At the time of the Battle of Waterloo, Robert Peel, who was instrumental in the formation of the Metropolitan Police fourteen years later in which Rowan would play such a significant role, was the Chief Secretary for Ireland, and had been since 1812. Immediately following the battle he obtained permission from the Lord Lieutenant of Ireland, Lord Whitworth, to go to the continent, together with two of his closest friends, William Fitzgerald, Chancellor of the Irish Exchequer and first lord of the Irish treasury, and John Wilson Croker, Secretary of the Admiralty. The three men travelled from Dover to Boulogne and reached Paris on 11 July, by which time British troops were patrolling the streets. Wellington introduced them to the King of France, the Emperors of Austria and Russia and a 'bevy' of French marshals. On 19 July, he arranged a dinner for them, at which 'Peel had the honour of sitting next to the Duke and hearing all the details of the battle.' On leaving Paris, the three men spent a couple of days with the Duke and Duchess of Richmond in Brussels before returning to England.[337] Given that Rowan was second-in-command of the regiment responsible for guarding the Duke's French residence in Paris, it is quite possible that he was present at the dinner.

The 52nd Regiment remained in Paris for four months before moving to

---

335 Moore Smith, op. cit. 331, p.240.
336 Moorsom, op. cit. 277, p.271.
337 Gash, Norman (2011). *Mr Secretary Peel: The Life of Sir Robert Peel to 1830*. London: Faber and Faber, pp.136-137.

Versailles on 2 November, where it stayed for a further five weeks, moving, on 10 December, to Saint-Germain, where the men occupied the palace and the officers were quartered in the town. In mid-December, Colborne obtained a lengthy leave of absence, leaving Rowan in command.[338]

Rowan remained in France as commanding officer of 1/52nd Regiment until Colborne's return in late May or early June 1817, when he reverted to second-in-command. Following an inspection by Major-General Sir Denis Pack, immediately following Colborne's return, a General Order was issued:

> 'Major-General Sir Denis Pack feels much pleasure in recording his opinion that the appearance of the 52nd Regiment on his late inspection, justified all he heard in praise of the system established in that corps. He thinks particular praise is due to the officers for the good example they set by their strict uniformity of dress and officer-like appearance in every respect.'[339]

It is worth noting that Rowan had been in command in the six months leading up to this inspection.

For the remainder of the year the regiment made its way slowly towards Calais from whence, as the last of the British army to leave, it embarked on a ship that took them back to Plymouth.[340]

Meanwhile, the 1/52nd Regiment had landed at Ramsgate on 26 November 1818, from whence they went first to Uxbridge before settling for the next six months in Chester and Liverpool. In the summer of 1819, due to 'the military authorities being greatly exercised about the disturbed state of the manufacturing districts,' it was moved to the Midlands where contingents were stationed at Weedon, Northampton and Daventry. Over the next eighteen months either the whole regiment or companies of the regiment were successively stationed at Lichfield, Newcastle-under-Lyme, Derby, Hull and Scarborough.[341] It was during this period that Rowan gained some experience of 'policing', and recognized the importance of getting the people on your side, arranging for the officers of the regiment to host 'a magnificent ball and supper' in Chester in March 1919,[342] and allowing the regimental band to take part in a concert in Lichfield in December.[343]

---

338 Moore Smith, op. cit. 331, pp.246-248.
339 Moorsom, op. cit.277, p.274.
340 Ibid, p.275.
341 Ibid, pp.276-277.
342 *Morning Post*, 26 March 1819, p.3.
343 *Staffordshire Advertiser*, 20 November 1819, p.1.

In March 1821 Colborne received a letter from Major General Sir Henry Torrens, the Adjutant General of the Forces, which must have pleased Rowan greatly:

> 'I have the honour to acquaint you, by direction of the Commander-in-Chief, that his Majesty has been pleased to approve of the 52nd regiment being permitted to bear on its colours and appointments, in addition to any other badges or devices which may have hitherto been granted to the regiment, the words –
>
> | | | |
> |---|---|---|
> | Hindoostan. | Nive. | Ciudad Rodrigo. |
> | Corunna. | Toulouse. | Salamanca. |
> | Fuentes de Oñoro. | Vimeira. | Nivelle. |
> | Badajoz. | Bussaco. | Orthez. |
> | | Vitoria.'[344] | |

Thus, the regiment was awarded thirteen battle honours, all of which, with the exception of Hindoostan[345] and Vitoria, Rowan had been present.

Having received orders to move to Ireland, Colborne received a District Order from Major-General Sir John Byng, the General Officer commanding Northern District, on 3 June 1821, in which he said he could not permit the 1/52nd Regiment 'to leave the district without an acknowledgement of their service, and very excellent conduct in every quarter they have been under his command, which has been even creditable to their previous distinguished character.' The District Order ended with Byng assuring 'the regiment of his sincere good wishes for their future happiness and prosperity.'[346]

The high standards first set by Major-General Sir John Moore from 1803 to 1805, and carried on by Craufurd and Colborne, still existed. But they could not have been implemented and maintained without officers who were committed to maintain those high standards. Charles Rowan had been with, or close to, the regiment without a break from the start.

Shortly after, Colborne was appointed Lieutenant-Governor of the island of Guernsey.[347] George Napier, who like Rowan, had served in Wellington's army throughout the Peninsular Campaign either with the 52nd Regiment or in a staff appointment, claimed that, with the exception

---

344   Moorsom, op. cit. 277, pp.277-278.
345   The 1/52nd Regiment were authorized to bear this honour on its colours and appointments in commemoration of the distinguished services it performed in several actions in which it was engaged in India from September 1790 to September 1793. Ibid, p.56.
346   Ibid, pp.278-279.
347   *London Gazette*, 14 August 1821, issue 17737, p.1682.

of the Duke of Wellington, he knew of no other officer in the army that was Colonel Colborne's equal. He went on: 'His expansive mind is capable of grasping anything, however difficult or abstruse: his genius in war so powerful that it overcomes all obstacles; and his splendid talents and long experience have gained him the admiration and confidence of the whole army.' Pointing out that from the time he had first been promoted to the rank of lieutenant-colonel, the Duke of Wellington had

> 'always placed the most entire confidence in him, and …employed him constantly in every enterprise of difficulty and danger, and never did he fail once. He has, with the most intrepid bravery, a coolness of head in the very heat of action which never fails him, and thus he penetrates with eagle eye into the enemy's intentions, and is sure to baffle his designs when least expected. Nothing can take him by surprise or flurry him; and I am confident, if Colborne was suddenly awoke out of his sleep and told he was surrounded by an army treble his numbers, it would only have the effect of making him, if possible, still more calm and collected, and that if it was possible for mortal man to get out of the scrape, he would.'[348]

Colborne's departure meant Rowan was once again in command of the regiment he had joined as a young ensign, 23 years earlier, as it moved to Ireland. Arriving in Dublin on 20 June 1821, he led the regiment into Richmond Barracks. Two months later 1/52nd Regiment was amongst British army units reviewed by His Majesty George IV. On 25 August 1821, in common with many other regiments in the British army, the establishment of the 1/52nd Regiment was reduced to eight companies, each of 72 rank and file.[349]

After nine months in command of the regiment in Ireland, on 26 April 1822 Rowan retired by selling his commission, as was the practice in those days, although he kept the title of Colonel.[350] Quite why he did so at this precise moment remains something of a mystery. But, by this time, he had served in the army for just under 24 years and the following year, the regiment, with his brother, Brevet Lieutenant-Colonel William Rowan in command, went to North America where it remained for the next nine years.[351] By the time it returned in 1831 its former commanding officer,

---

348 Napier, Sir George Thomas, and William Craig Emilius Napier (1884). *Passages in the Early Military Life of General Sir George T. Napier*. London: John Murray, p.60.
349 Moorsom, op. cit. 277, pp.275-279.
350 Reith, Charles (1956). *A New Study of Police History*. Edinburgh: Oliver and Boyd, p.116.
351 Moosom, op. cit. 277, pp.280-297.

Lieutenant-Colonel Charles Rowan, had been Commissioner of the newly-formed Metropolitan Police for two years.

CHAPTER SIX
LIFE IN LONDON 1800-1870

The London that first Mayne and then Rowan came to in the early 1820s was very different to the city it is today. There was no telegraph, no gas, and no electric-light; there were no railways, no cabs and no buses. Coal-fires, as the only means of heating homes and offices, meant the city was frequently enveloped in thick fog. A foul smell prevailed over the city from the raw sewage that flowed into and through many streets. More dangerously, for health, it also flowed into the River Thames, from whence many people obtained water for washing and drinking. In 1852, Punch magazine described the River Thames as 'one vast gutter' in which the leavings of the city were dumped, which included a host of materials from the lime of Vauxhall to the bone deposits of Lambeth and the slaughter-houses of Whitechapel. It was rancid.[352]

The only way to travel other than on foot was by a horse-drawn vehicle or by a boat on the River Thames. Many of the iconic places and buildings, such as Trafalgar Square and the National Gallery, Big Ben and the Houses of Parliament, and the Royal Albert Hall did not exist; and the reigning monarch still lived at St James's Palace.

But it was an important industrial centre. There were flourmills, sugar refineries and breweries; clothes were made, along with accessories, such as hats and boots; so, too, was jewellery, including clocks and watches. Furniture was manufactured, as were machines and tools. Chemicals were developed; horse-drawn carriages were built to meet the increasing demand of people to move about using transport. As was to be expected with such a flourishing city with access to the sea, it had become an important port by the beginning of the 19th century. But, the River Thames could not cater for the number of ships wanting to tie up on its banks to off-load and take on new cargoes. So, new docks were built: West India Docks (1802),

---

352   Ackroyd, Peter (2009). *Thames: The Biography*. London: Anchor, p.273.

London dock (1805), and East India dock (1806). Another, St Katherine's dock (1828), opened shortly before Rowan and Mayne were appointed to set up the New Police, and before Mayne's death in 1868, another two, Victoria dock (1855) and Millwall dock (1868) had opened.[353]

To cater for this increased activity, London needed a larger workforce and it became a city of huge contrast. Many people grew wealthy as it became a major financial and trading centre. The West End, particularly Belgravia and Mayfair, was home to the very rich, with Regent Street attracting 'posh shoppers',[354] but it was also a city of poverty. Much of London consisted of decaying streets, with 'taverns, and pawnshops and brothels and low lodgings for sailors' abutting the streets. Thousands lived in overcrowded and unsanitary conditions. They lacked basic facilities like fresh water, efficient sewage and, more importantly, adequate food. At night, the streets 'were clothed with an inky blackness broken only by distant and diminished lights.'[355]

Giving evidence to the Select Committee on Metropolis Improvements in 1840, James Pennethorne described how in the East End of London there was still no drainage, so 'the privies and cesspools' which were 'scarcely ever emptied flowed over into the streets'. The Medical Officer to the Whitechapel Poor Law Authorities, Samuel Byles, described 'a dozen places …as hot beds of fever.' Claiming Rose Lane as being better than its neighbours, he said that even so he had 'seen the place completely flooded with blood from the slaughter-house.' The people inhabiting this area were 'intolerably filthy.'[356]

In the slum district of Belle Isle, near King's Cross, kilns produced bricks and tiles to contribute towards the building of the metropolis, but the drainage was poor; open sewers ran between the shacks and houses, sewage oozed through the cellar walls of the houses; many of the residents kept pigs and the houses themselves were filthy. Running right through the middle from 1852 onwards was a 'sooty, smoky railway line'. There was a knackers-yard, in which pieces of dead horses were suspended in full view of the slowing trains. Animal carcasses were cooked in vast copper vats to be sold as cat food; as a result, many shacks and cottages were set amidst a nauseating stench.[357]

353 Stone, Peter (2017). *The History of the Port of London*, Chapter 4: New Docks of the Early Nineteenth Century. Barnsley: Pen and Sword.
354 Keller, Lisa (2010). *Triumph of Order: Democracy and Public Space*. Columbia: Columbia University Press, p.ix.
355 Ackroyd, op. cit. 352, p.181.
356 White, Jerry (2008). *London in the 19th Century*, London: Vintage, p.33.
357 Bullman, Joseph, Neil Hegarty and Brian Hill (2013). *The Secret History of Our Streets: A Story of London*. London: BBC Books, pp.199-200.

As industrialisation intensified so the population, which stood at 1.1 million in 1800,[358] steadily grew, to 2.6 million in 1850 and then to 3.2 million by 1860. With it

> 'the filth and pollution of east London grew apace; glue factories and soap factories and match factories lent the very air a malodorous aspect, the water became filthy, tributaries of the Thames such as the Lea and Barking Creek ran with dirt… The area was infamous for its crime and its dangers and ambience of subhumanity; these features seemed soaked into the old bricks and rotting timbers of the buildings, as the smoke from the factories clung and hung in the air.'[359]

The cramped and unsanitary conditions under which people lived led to the outbreak of infectious diseases such as diphtheria, dysentery, scarlet fever, smallpox and typhoid fever. Typhus was referred to as the poor man's disease because it was linked to overcrowding and a lack of hygiene, poor housing and poverty. There were four outbreaks of cholera in London, in 1832-33, 1848-49, 1854 and 1866[360] before Mayne's death at the end of 1868.

Much of this would change during Rowan's lifetime; even more during Mayne's. A working system of the electric telegraph was introduced in London from 1837 onwards;[361] gas light had been installed in Pall Mall in 1807, but it wasn't until 1840 that it was being used to light many of London's streets,[362] whilst the electric-light bulb was not patented[363] until eleven years after Mayne's death.

When constables of the New Police walked out onto the streets for the first time, the area where Trafalgar Square and the National Gallery now sit was still the Great Mews, the stabling for the old Whitehall Palace, which had been destroyed by fire in 1698. Work started on building the National Gallery in 1832. Three years later the Great Mews was demolished, and worked commenced on the construction of Trafalgar Square. The National Gallery opened in 1838; Trafalgar Square, which included Nelson's column

---

358 Keller, op. cit. 354, p.36.
359 Bullman, op. cit. 357, p.144.
360 *The Gazette*: Official Public Records: Sources at www.thegazette.co.uk/all-notices/content/100519 [accessed on 24 April 2019].
361 Liffen, John (2010). 'The Introduction of the Electric Telegraph in Britain, a Reappraisal of the Work of Cooke and Wheatstone'. In the *International Journal for the History of Engineering and Technology*, Volume 80, Issue 2, pp.268-299.
362 White, op. cit. 356, pp.21-22.
363 Matthews, John R (2005). *The Light Bulb: Inventions That Shaped the World*. New York: Franklin Watts.

and a statue of George IV, was eventually opened to the public in 1844.[364] Two more statues were added in the 1850s, one of which, had he still been alive, would have given Rowan considerable pleasure. It was of General Sir Charles Napier, a fellow British Army officer who served in the Peninsular and 1812 campaigns.[365]

The Houses of Parliament, sometimes called the Palace of Westminster because it was the home of the reigning monarch until the 16th century, burned down five years after the formation of the New Police.[366] The current building took 30 years to complete, with Big Ben first chiming in 1859. When Rowan and Mayne were first appointed commissioners, what is now Buckingham Palace was known as The Queen's House. Built by the Duke of Buckingham in 1703, it had been acquired by King George III in 1761 as a private residence for Queen Charlotte. It did not become the residence of the reigning monarch until 1837, having undergone major structural alterations and extensive renovations. Foreign officials to the United Kingdom are still accredited to the 'Court of St James'.[367]

The introduction of horse-drawn omnibuses in 1829 coincided with Rowan and Mayne's appointment as Commissioners of the New Police. The initial fare of sixpence was far too expensive for the average working person, but a price war reduced the cost of a journey to one penny and it became more affordable. Routes connecting London suburbs to the centre quickly followed. The coaches, pulled by four horses, carried four to six people inside and twelve on the outside. The journeys were slow, with many stops en route. Different individuals set up their own horse-drawn omnibus companies and the streets quickly became overcrowded as different companies competed for business. In addition, approximately four hundred coaches left London to all parts of the country, most of them daily. It took an inordinate amount of time to reach some distant places. For instance, around 1830 a coach starting from Eden in Cumberland took three days and two nights to reach London. Approaching London, these coaches were often 'swamped' by passengers.[368]

The large number of horses being used meant a huge amount of dung was deposited daily on the streets. Following the introduction of a new method of surfacing roads by the Scottish engineer John McAdam, some had been

---

364   Mace, Rodney (2005). *Trafalgar Square: Emblem of Empire*. London: Lawrence and Wishart, pp.86-110.
365   Ibid, pp.113-117.
366   See Chapter Fourteen.
367   The official website of the British Monarchy: www.royal.gov.uk/TheRoyalResidences/StJamessPalace/History.aspx [accessed 14 February 2018].
368   White, op. cit. 356, p.18.

'macadamised' by the time the New Police walked the streets, but many were not paved until midway through the century. In good weather, great clouds of dust were blown up from the streets; in wet weather, many of the roads turned into thick mud. Some of the smarter streets were frequented by crossing sweepers who, for a penny, would sweep the street in front of people to enable them to cross the street without stepping into horse dung. Only in the 1830s was wooden paving introduced in some of the main streets of the metropolis, including Oxford Street and the Strand.[369]

Steam boats were introduced on the River Thames in 1818, and Londoners increasingly took day trips to attractions outside the capital such as downriver to Gravesend and Margate, or upriver to Richmond, Henley, Hampton Court and Windsor. By 1850 it was estimated approximately a million people were making such trips each year. Other than by ferry, there were only a limited number of ways to cross the River Thames when Rowan and Mayne first settled in London. Putney Bridge, sometimes known as Fulham Bridge during its early life, had opened as a toll-bridge in 1729.[370] Westminster Bridge opened in 1750; the original bridge was replaced in 1862. Blackfriars Bridge opened in 1769 and Waterloo Bridge opened in 1817, also originally as a toll bridge. Southwark Bridge, originally known as Queen Street Bridge, opened in 1819. Although there had been a series of bridges since the Roman occupation across the River Thames where London Bridge now stands, most were destroyed during wars or by fire. A new bridge was built in 1831.[371] A tunnel under the River Thames from Wapping to Rotherhithe was started in 1823, but building was halted on a number of occasions because the river burst in and flooded the workings. Designed for foot passengers, it eventually opened in 1843, and in the first four months nearly one million people passed through.[372]

One of the most extraordinary transformations during Rowan's and, particularly, Mayne's time, in terms of travel, was the development of the railways. The first railway to be opened was a short line between Bermondsey and Deptford in 1836. This was followed by the opening of rail termini linking London to most parts of Britain. Euston, connecting the capital with Birmingham, opened in 1837. In 1838, a temporary station was opened by the Great Western Railway at Bishop's Bridge Road (now known as Paddington), connecting London with Maidenhead, eventually

---

369 Renier, Hannah (2012). 'Streets of London' *London Historians* at www.londonhistorians.org/index.php?s=file_download&ic=64 [accessed 18 May 2018].
370 In 1845 it became the starting point of the famous Oxford v Cambridge Boat Race.
371 Matthews, Peter (2008). *London's Bridges*. Oxford: Shire Publications.
372 In 1870 it was converted into an underground railway by the East London Railway Company; Ackroyd, op. cit. 352, p.147.

reaching Bristol in 1841 and Plymouth in 1848; a new station was opened on the site of the temporary station in 1854. Fenchurch Street was opened in the City of London in 1841, eventually connecting London with Southend in 1858. The London and the South Western Railway opened a station at Nine Elms in 1840, connecting London with Southampton and eventually with most parts of the south coast; eight years later, the company opened a new terminus at Waterloo. In 1850 a temporary station, to act as the terminus for the Great Northern Railway's east coast mainline to North-East England and Scotland, was opened in Maiden Lane (now York Way). Queen Victoria left here the following year to journey to Scotland; a station on the current site of King's Cross was opened in 1852.

Thus, in fifteen years, London had been connected to virtually all parts of Britain by rail. Another station, St Pancras, was opened as its London terminus by the Midland Railway Company two months before Mayne's death. Five years before his death, the world's first underground railway, between Bishop's Bridge Road and Farringdon, now part of the Metropolitan and Circle Lines, was opened. Another section opened in the year of his death, this time from South Kensington to Westminster, now part of the District and Circle Lines.[373] The huge expansion in transport, using road, the River Thames and rail meant Greater London, as it was to eventually become known, 'spread out like an ink stain' with many new middle-class settling in newly-created suburbs.[374]

Although there were a number of markets in London; three of the largest – Leadenhall, Newgate and Smithfield- were not in the metropolis, but in the City. The last of these was the most controversial. Begun in 1615 in open fields, by the beginning of the 19th century Smithfield was 'in the centre of the metropolis', but, by 1852, had become a serious public nuisance. Every Sunday night thousands of cattle and sheep would be driven through the streets of the metropolis to Smithfield, and on Monday those that had not been slaughtered would be driven back again. Frequently, the route to market was London's main shopping streets, including Oxford Street. Bringing 'chaos to …traffic and danger to life and limb,' shoppers and shopkeepers alike were terrified when bullocks suddenly veered off the road into shops and coffee houses. Some animals would become so distressed on the drive to market that they were slaughtered in the street.[375] In an attempt to alleviate this problem, the City of London Corporation built the Metropolitan Market in Islington, which had space for 7,000 cattle, 42,000

---

373 White, op. cit. 356, pp.43-45 and 55.
374 Keller, op. cit. 354, p.36.
375 White, op, cit. 356, pp.187-189.

sheep and eight abattoirs, on the west side of Caledonian Road in 1855 as a market for live animals, leaving Smithfield to concentrate on dead meat.

Some nine years later, whilst patrolling the market at night, Inspector John Terry tripped over a sleeping dog and suffered a compound fracture of his left leg. The fracture failed to heal and he died nearly three weeks later as surgeons operated to amputate the leg.[376]

Within the City of London, fish and seafood were initially sold from stalls and sheds around Billingsgate Dock, but it moved to a purpose-built building in 1850. Meanwhile, within the Metropolitan Police District, the Covent Garden Market established itself between 1835 and 1845. On three days a week farmers would attend to sell their produce. Spitalfields Market in London's East End, like Covent Garden, catered for farm produce.[377]

Despite many of the so-called improvements, Keller succinctly summed up the appalling conditions in London at around the time of Rowan's death in 1852:

'Only 10 per cent of London was connected to sewers; cattle were still slaughtered downtown; black clouds of pollution hung over dimly lit streets; the erratic water supply contributed to frequent outbreaks of cholera, infant diarrhoea and typhus; and housing was substandard beyond imagination. Traffic was abysmal, made worse by pedlars and markets, and to cross the street one needed to pay a street urchin to clear the manure and night soil in order to pass.'[378]

By the early 1830s, churches in Central London had run out of space in which to bury the dead and companies were authorised to open large cemeteries in and around London's suburbs. The first was at Kensal Green, established by the General Cemetery Company in 1833. Others followed at West Norwood (1836), Highgate (1839), Nunhead (1840), Abney Park, Stoke Newington (1840), Brompton (1840) and Stepney (1841).[379] The bodies of both Rowan and Mayne were buried at Kensal Green, in 1852 and 1869 respectively.

Throughout much of the 19th century, leisure time was at a premium for the working classes. Most people worked for six full days, with only Sundays being recognised as a day off.[380] There were no paid holidays,

---

376 *Morning Post*, 7 October 1864, p.5.
377 White, op. cit. 356, p.188.
378 Keller, op. cit. 354, p.37.
379 Turpin, John, and Derrick Knight (2011). *Magnificent Seven: London's First Landscaped Cemeteries*. Stroud: Amberley Publishing.
380 Not until the 1870s were some skilled workers granted Saturday afternoons off.

although some clerks and skilled workers were granted one week's holiday a year.

The passing of the Theatres Act of 1843[381] led to a rapid growth in the number of theatres. At the commencement of the century the only art collection accessible to a limited section of the public was at The Foundling Hospital. To increase the leisure facilities a new building, the National Gallery, was erected on the northern side of what would eventually become Trafalgar Square. The British Museum, located in Old Montague House in Bloomsbury, desperately needed more space for its growing collection. Therefore, commencing in 1823 its facilities were gradually increased. Two zoos were established, the first in Regent's Park in 1828, the second, known as the Zoological Gardens, originally opened at Kennington in 1831 but subsequently transferred to Kew in 1877. Construction of the Royal Albert Hall began in the year before Mayne's death, in 1867, but he did not live to see it opened.[382]

Despite the efforts of people such as the Fielding brothers and Patrick Colquhoun, policing in London was still organised on an ad-hoc basis when Rowan and Mayne came to London. There were about 450 full-time policemen, all nominally under the direction of the Home Secretary, but for all practical purposes they were under the control of individual magistrates. The nine police offices set up by the 1792 Middlesex Justices Act originally had six policemen, increased to twelve in 1811, attached to each court, a figure, it was suggested 'was too small and centralised to have any perceptible effect on the state of the metropolis.'[383]

The Marine Police, set up by Colquhoun in 1800 after he had warned 'there were no fewer than 10,000 thieves, footpads, prostitutes, and pilferers at work on the jetties and quays that lined the riverside', numbered 'sixty salaried officers' and originally came under his control.[384]

In 1805 the chief magistrate at Bow Street, John Ford, stationed 60 mounted policemen on the various roads leading into and out of London. Described as 'a closely-knit caste of speculators in the detection of crime, self-seeking and unscrupulous', they were 'daring and efficient when daring and efficiency coincided with their private interest.'[385] There were also two foot patrols of 100 policemen each, one designed to start four or five miles from London and walk inwards, the other starting from inner London and

---

381   6 & 7, Victoria, c.68.
382   Ibid, p.263 and 86.
383   Gash, Norman (2011). *Mr Secretary Peel: The Life of Sir Robert Peel to 1830*. London: Faber and Faber, p.311.
384   Critchley, T.A. (1979). *A History of Police in England and Wales*. London: Constable, p.42.
385   Ibid, p.43, quoting Radzinowicz, L (1956). *A History of English Criminal Law*, vol. 2, p.263.

walking outwards, the intention being that the two should meet.[386]

Rowan's arrival in London in 1822 coincided with the appointment of Robert Peel as Home Secretary. Peel immediately set about rationalizing the criminal justice system.[387] One of the things he did was to recruit 27 men to provide a 'preventative force' against daylight robberies.[388] But, as Critchley succinctly pointed out, 'the main burden of maintaining law and order still rested on the elderly, ailing or indifferent shoulders of isolated pockets of parish constables and watchmen.'[389]

Meanwhile, it could be argued, law and order in London was deteriorating. In 1815, 'around a quarter of a million men were demobilised on to a contracting labour market' at the end of the Napoleonic Wars.[390] Crime was rife, from pickpocketing and house-breaking to violent assaults and murder. There were at least three notorious areas known as rookeries, a term used to describe areas of high population living in slum conditions. The most famous was St Giles, at the southern tip of the current London Borough of Camden. This was closely followed by two others; Jacob's Island, a slum in Bermondsey on the south bank of the River Thames, and Saffron Hill, an area around the existing Saffron Hill which runs adjacent to Farringdon Street between Clerkenwell and Holborn.

St Giles has been described as consisting of 'an almost endless intricacy of courts and yards, crossing each other' to the extent that the place was 'like a rabbit warren'. Buckridge Street 'was full of 'thieves, prostitutes and cadgers' (beggars);[391] Jones Court was 'inhabited by coiners (forgers of bank notes and coins), utterers of base coin (people who passed forged currency as real), and thieves';[392] Ivy Lane, better known as Rat's Castle, 'was a large dirty building occupied by thieves and prostitutes, and boys who live by plunder', those who forcibly stole goods.[393]

Dickens used the rookeries for his novel *Oliver Twist*, published in 1838. The Saffron rookery was inhabited by Bill Sikes and Nancy, and Fagin's 'den of thieves' was on the edge of it. Having murdered Nancy, Sikes fled

---

386 Ibid, p.44.
387 Emsley, Clive (1987). *Crime and Society in England 1750-1900*. London: Longman, p.22.
388 Critchley, op. cit. 384, p.44.
389 Ibid, p.38.
390 Emsley, op. cit. 381, p.32.
391 An excellent description of the St Giles Rookery as it was around 1860 is given by John Binney in *Mayhew, Henry and Others* (2005). *The London Underworld in the Victorian Period: Authentic First-Person Accounts by Beggars, Thieves and Prostitutes*. New York: Dover Publications, pp.144-156; the original version first published in London by Griffin, Bohn and Company in 1861.
392 Ibid, p.153.
393 Ibid, p.154.

to the Jacob's Island rookery in his attempt to escape justice.[394] All the rookeries had well-developed self-defences against incursions from the law and intricate escape routes, built into the houses and garrets, were designed to allow fugitives to get away if pursued. The yards and multi-occupied buildings were threaded with escape routes, together with traps and places in which to hide. In the basements, there were holes in cellar walls so a fugitive could quickly pass from one part of the rookery to another without being seen. Similarly, he could go over the rooftops by routes specially constructed for that purpose.[395]

Nothing was done by the authorities to eradicate these slums until shortly before Mayne's death. They were difficult and dangerous areas to police when Rowan and Mayne arrived in London, as, indeed, they were for much of the time they were the Commissioners.

Two of the two most common problems in London were drunkenness, as Rowan and Mayne would quickly find out when they were recruiting for the New Police, and prostitution. Concerns about drunkenness in men and women, the latter caused frequently by the consumption of gin, had been growing for forty years. Prostitution was a substantial industry. Theatreland was a parade ground for prostitutes, with the smartest soliciting at Covent Garden and Drury Lane outside the Italian Opera and Haymarket Theatres. Many of the women handed out printed business cards to likely clients.[396] In some parts of London prostitution was the main industry. For instance Granby Street, a new suburban development of 92 terraced houses built shortly after the New Police was formed, became 'one of the most notorious patches of vice'[397] and would remain so until 1866 or 1867, when the South Western Railway Company bought up all the houses to extend Waterloo Station. Visiting the area in 1839, Flora Tristan found it full of prostitutes 'looking out of windows or seated at their doorsteps' and was much struck by their 'fancy men', 'very good-looking, young, tall and strong'.[398] Norton Street near Portland Place, Wych Street off the Strand, and the area round Friar Street in Southwark, all had women importuning regularly from doorways and windows.

*

On his arrival in London to train as a barrister in 1821, Mayne lived in

---

394 Dickens, Charles (1998). *Oliver Twist*. London: Macmillan.
395 Binney, op. cit. 391, 152-153.
396 White, op. cit. 356, p.297.
397 Ibid, p.296.
398 Tristan, Flora (1840). *Flora Tristan's London Journal, 1840*, pp.74-75.

lodgings at Mitre Court in Temple.[399] Once qualified, he was appointed to the Northern Circuit and spent a considerable amount of time in the north of England, probably based in Yorkshire. Nothing is known of Rowan between the time he left the army in 1822 until July 1825, when he attended 'a select circle' in Grosvenor Street in London to celebrate the baptism the previous day of the Duke and Duchess of Richmond's son, Alexander. Amongst the guests was Lady Julia Peel, wife of Sir Robert.[400] The Duke, then the Earl of March, had served with Rowan in the Peninsula and would become a life-long friend.

Later that year Rowan was appointed a Foreign Office Commissioner to look into the flourishing slave trade between Africa and America, which, although outlawed by Britain in 1807, still existed.[401] Ships would leave Europe for West Africa loaded with beads, ceramics, guns, rum, textiles and tobacco, where they were traded for gold, ivory, pepper and slaves before heading to America and the Caribbean. There, the slaves were sold to work on the plantations in exchange for sugar, cotton and tobacco.

Although the involvement of British merchant ships had, by this time, been suppressed by a Royal Navy task force known as the West African Squadron, which intercepted and seized ships suspected of carrying slaves, their place had been quickly taken by French, Portuguese and Spanish slave-traders. So, during the 1820s, the exportation of slaves from Africa was still rife.

Two areas under British control from whence the slaves were being shipped were the West African protectorate of Sierra Leone and a part of the British colony, Gold Coast (now Ghana) known as Cape Coast. Along the coasts of both were forts which had dungeons, in which slaves would frequently be kept for up to twelve weeks while waiting for the next ship to transport them across the Atlantic.

Writing home, one officer on the Royal Navy warship *Maidstone*, one of the seven ships which made up the task force, described how they had chased and boarded a French ship which had a cargo of 700 slaves, chained by the neck or by the legs to the deck. Rowan's appointment meant, with others, he was required to visit the West Coast of Africa to examine the slave forts and in November 1825 he made the lengthy and perilous journey on the sailing vessel Despatch.[402]

---

399   Royal and Sun Alliance Insurance Group Collection at the London Metropolitan Archives, reference CLC/B/192/F/001/MS11936/545/1199269.
400   *Morning Post*, 21 July 1825, p.3.
401   For more about the navy's role in stopping the slave trade, see Lloyd, Christopher (1968). *Navy and the Slave Trade*. London: F. Cass.
402   *Public Ledger and Daily Advertiser*, 26 November 1825, p.2.

It is not known what he found or when he returned to England, but he was certainly back by March of the following year because he was appointed to a committee set up to oversee the building of new premises for the United Service Club.

Just over ten years previously, on 31 May 1815, Lord Lynedoch, who had only just been raised to the peerage and was better known at the time as Lieutenant-General Sir Thomas Graham, met with 80 senior army officers at the Thatched House Tavern in St James's Street with the intention of forming such a club.[403] A month later the existing Navy Club 'expressed a desire to unite with the soldiers' and the name became the 'United Service Club.'[404] The Duke of Wellington accepted an invitation to become a member in a letter to Lord Lynedoch, written five days before the Battle of Waterloo. A branch committee was established for the officers who were still on the continent and this met at Lord Hill's quarters in Paris on 23 July.[405] It is likely that Rowan became a member either at this meeting or shortly afterwards.

Originally renting property at 23 Albemarle Street, the Club opened its doors on 13 January 1816. By the time Rowan came to London, possibly in 1822, the United Service Club had moved to premises in Charles Street[406] but four years later 'there was much discontent over the inadequacy of the accommodation and, at an Extraordinary General Meeting on the 28 February, it was resolved to build a new house.' This coincided with a decision by the Government to demolish Carlton House in Pall Mall, which had been the home of the Prince Regent until he ascended to the thrown in 1820 as George IV.

At the meeting it was announced that the United Service Club had been granted a lease to build a new club. A building committee was appointed under the Chairmanship of Lord Grantham with Rowan as one of its members. Plans were submitted on 13 October and the management committee authorised the building committee to enter into a building contract.[407] Prior to the application by the United Service Club another club, the Athenaeum, had also been granted a lease to build premises. The Athenaeum had been formed in 1824 and was using temporary premises at 12, Waterloo Place. Amongst the list of founder members was a young,

---

403 Jackson, Major-General Sir Louis C (1937). *History of the United Service Club*. Aldershot: Gale & Polden, p.1.
404 Ibid, p.9.
405 Ibid, p.5.
406 Ibid, p.14.
407 Ibid, pp.18-19.

up-and-coming barrister, Richard Mayne.[408]

The owners of the land, the Commissioner of Woods, Forest and Land Revenues, insisted the external facade of the two buildings should be similar. A memorandum of agreement between the two clubs, dated 7 December 1826, was signed on behalf of the United Service Club by Major-General Samuel Brown, Colonel Alexander Caldwell and Colonel Charles Rowan.

The United Service Club opened the door of its newly-built premises to members on 28 November 1828, with the Athenaeum opening its doors some fifteen months later, on 8 February 1830.[409]

Thus, throughout their service as Joint Commissioners, Charles Rowan and Richard Mayne were members of adjoining clubs. Indeed, both remained members of their respective clubs until their deaths. The Athenaeum Club exists to this day but, unfortunately, the United Service Club closed its doors for the last time in 1977. The building is now occupied by the Institute of Directors.[410]

In August 1827 Rowan spent some time at the New Steyne Hotel in Brighton,[411] described seven years later as 'a superior hotel of the most respectable description, principally resorted to by families of distinction'.[412]

In 1828 Major-General Sir William Napier, who briefly served with Rowan in the 52nd Regiment before transferring to the 43rd, published the first of what was to be six volumes of the *History of the War of the Peninsula*. Rowan wrote to him on 5 June 1828, just a year before he was invited to become one of the commissioners of the newly-formed Metropolitan Police.

> My dear Napier,
>
> It was only yesterday that I learned your address from Cork whom I met accidently, otherwise I should long ago have permitted myself the pleasure of heartedly congratulating you on the well-merited success of your book. I have read it with a degree of interest and of satisfaction greater than I can tell you – I had permitted myself, I suppose from

---

408 Mayne became a member of the Athenaeum in 1824, the date being confirmed in an exchange of emails with the Club Archivist, Jennie De Protani, on 3 May 2016.

409 *Pall Mall, South Side, Existing Buildings: The United Services Club, The Athenaeum' in Survey of London: Volumes 29 and 30, St James Westminster, Part 1*, ed. F.H.W.Sheppard (London, 1960), pp.386-399. www.british-history.ac.uk/survey-london/vols29-30/pt1/pp386-389 [accessed 26 November 2015].

410 History of 116 Pall Mall at www.116pallmall.com/116-history [accessed 26 November 2015].

411 *Sussex Advertiser*, 27 August 1827, p.3.

412 *Wallis's Royal Edition: Brighton as it is, 1834: Exhibiting all the latest improvements in that fashionable watering place*. Dover: W. Batcheller, p.76.

mere weakness, at various times, to be biased by the opinion of others as to the merits of Sir John's retreat, and it always made me unhappy and uncomfortable when I did so.

By telling you now the honest truth on reading your book, you will, perhaps, be inclined to undervalue my manhood, but you will, I Hope, be charitable for the sake of the immediate cause. The simple fact is that at the distance of twenty years I literally cried like a child with pleasure at the complete and triumphant vindication of that dear man's measures. Tis avowal would no doubt raise a smile of pity if not contempt from many, for such weakness, but I hope it will not in you.

I sincerely trust that the forthcoming volumes may equal the sample you have given us of your work, in which case my very humble opinion is it will be a classical and scientific study for all future generations.

I shall not occupy your time by giving you my accounts of any criticisms I have heard upon it, and which, of course, every work must be subject to, nor in which of them I might be inclined to some degree to concern myself. These however can only relate to mere trifling points. It is on such alone that most men can presume to give any opinion on the first perusal of such a work, for to comprehend the scientific part, or, I should rather say, to be able to pronounce judgement on that, requires no trifling study. Having added that I think the narrative the most clear and perspicuous that I have ever read, and having asked to be forgiven for presuming to offer you my opinion at all, (which I merely do for the pleasure it gives me as an old fellow soldier, as John Brown calls it), again, having neither place nor pension to give me that I know of, I subscribe myself, My dear Napier, Ever Sincerely yours,

    C. Rowan[413]

There are traces of only two cases in which Mayne might have been involved whilst on the Northern Circuit. In the first, on 26 July 1828, a Mr Mayne prosecuted James Walsworth at the Yorkshire Assizes for setting fire to a lock-up house at Keighley. In the second at the beginning of 1829, a Richard Mayne prosecuted a Thomas Brown at the West Riding Sessions for stealing the body of Hannah Heesom from the churchyard at Whitkirk on the night of 31 December 1828.[414]

---

413   Reith, Charles (1956). *A New Study of Police History*. Edinburgh: Oliver and Boyd, p.117.
414   *Leeds Mercury*, 26 July 1828, p.3; *Leeds Intelligencer*, 22 January 1829, p.3.

CHAPTER SEVEN

ROWAN AND MAYNE APPOINTED JOINT COMMISSIONERS

Appointed Chief Secretary for Ireland in 1812, Robert Peel had been instrumental in the setting up of the Royal Irish Constabulary two years later. It was unsurprising, therefore, that on his appointment as Home Secretary in 1822 he immediately tried to introduce a police force in London, but hostility to such a move both in Parliament and throughout the country resulted in failure. By 1828 the mood, certainly in Parliament, had changed. A report by a House of Commons Select Committee recommended

> 'That there should be constituted an Office of Police acting under the immediate directions of the Secretary of State for the Home Department, upon which should be devolved the general control over the whole of the Establishments of Police of every denomination...'[415]

In April the following year, Peel laid a 'Bill for Improving the Police in and Near the Metropolis' before the House of Commons, calling for the appointment of 'two fit Persons as justices of the Peace' to run the operational side of the force, and a third person to control its finances. At the same time, Wellington placed it before the House of Lords. It passed both Houses without serious disagreement and received Royal Assent on 19 June 1829 as the Metropolitan Police Act 1829.[416]

Peel's approach to the reform of policing in the metropolis was not 'the revolutionary approach subsequently widely attributed to him.' There was very little change to the 'system of crime prevention' and the prosecution of offenders, and the detection of crime was broadly left in the hands of the London magistrates and their own constables. Indeed, at the same time as

---

415 PP 1828 [533]. Report from the Select Committee on the Police of the Metropolis, p.30.
416 Act of 10 Geo 4 Cap 64 for improving the Police in, and near the Metropolis.

the Metropolitan Police Bill was going through Parliament, Peel pushed through the Justice of the Peace Act 1829 which confirmed all the powers the London magistrates had been given by the original 1792 Middlesex Justices Act. All the Metropolitan Police Act did was to replace one failed part of the criminal justice system – 'the parochial watch and ward' – with the New Police. All other parts of the system remained intact.[417]

It was assumed Peel would look for people who had military experience to fill the posts of the two Justices of the Peace. Within days of the publication of the Bill, Charles Rowan wrote to Lieutenant-General Sir George Murray, who was Secretary of State for War and the Colonies at the time, expressing his interest. Murray had served as Wellington's Quartermaster-General from 1808 to 1811 during the Peninsula War, at a time when Rowan held a staff appointment under General Craufurd. Murray then served in Ireland and Canada but following Napoleon's escape from Elba returned to Europe where he remained in Paris until 1819 as Chief of Staff of the Army of Occupation. Rowan received a same-day reply from Sir George's Military Secretary, Lieutenant-Colonel Alexander Wedderburn, another veteran of the Peninsular War and the Army of Occupation:

Downing Street, 2nd May, 1829.

Lieut.-Col. Rowan

Sir,

I am directed by Sir George Murray to acquaint you, in reply to your letter of this day, that if the appointments under the new Police Bill are, as you suppose, to be allotted to military men, he will have great pleasure in mentioning your name to Mr Peel.[418]

Two days later, Wedderburn wrote again:

Downing Street, 4th May, 1829.

Lieut.-Col Rowan

Sir,

With reference to my note of the 2nd, Sir George Murray desires me to acquaint you that he lost no time in speaking to Mr Peel, but was told by him that he had not yet made up his mind in regard to the

---

417   Roach, Lawrence (2004). 'The Origins and Impact of the Function of the Crime Investigation and Detection in the British Police Service: A thesis submitted in partial fulfilment of the requirements for the degree of Doctor of Philosophy of Loughborough University'. Loughborough: Loughborough University's Institutional Repository, p.43.
418   Sir George Murray Archives 1772-1846 in the National Library of Scotland, Vol. 174, p.128.

description of persons who would be employed under the new Police Bill.[419]

Less than a month later Peel had decided on the kind of people he wanted, for he wrote to William Gregory, who had been his Under-Secretary for most of the time he had held the post of Chief Secretary for Ireland and was still in post under the current Chief Secretary, Lord Francis Leveson-Gower. After telling Gregory he had 'completed a work, which had given [him] great trouble' as a result of which he now had the power 'to reorganise on a very intensive scale a new system of Police', Peel asked him whether there might be 'a military man conversant in the details of the police system in Ireland' who might be 'usefully employed' in London. After pointing out to Gregory that the man chosen 'must be a very superior man to what [he] recollected of Police Magistrates in Ireland', he elaborated on what he required:

'I require a man of great energy, great activity both of body and mind, accustomed to strict discipline and with the power of enforcing it, and taking interest in the duty to be assigned to him then he must be a gentleman and entirely trustworthy…

There will be a force of between two and three thousand men ultimately under his command. With the soldier I would unite a sensible lawyer as the other magistrate.'[420]

Gregory was equally dubious of there being anyone in Ireland that would fit Peel's requirements. However, some use was made of Irish police knowledge, and in July Captain Hunter, a Chief Constable recommended by Gregory, was given leave of absence to travel to England for a short period to assist in the early stages of the Metropolitan Police,[421] although it is unclear exactly what his contribution was, if any.

The Metropolitan Police Act became law on 19 June. Although Rowan's name had already been mentioned to Peel, he initially ignored it. Instead, he offered the post to Colonel James Shaw. Shaw had joined the army in 1805, some six years after Rowan, but their careers had taken similar paths. He had been commissioned into the 43rd Regiment, joining at a time when both the 43rd and 52nd Regiments were under Sir John Moore at Shorncliffe. He was involved in the retreat from Corunna, when the

---

419 Sir George Murray Archives 1772-1846 in the National Library of Scotland, Vol. 174, p.130.
420 Charles Reith, *A New Study of Police History*. London: Oliver and Boyd, p.126.
421 Peel Papers at the British Museum (C.S. Parker's Sir Robert Peel (v. infra) 40334, folios 292, 294, 302, 320; Peel's Memoirs, Volume II, 114)

43rd Regiment fought a rear-guard action with the 52nd. On his return to England he suffered from a severe fever which was to cause him serious ill-health later in life. However, in 1809, he returned to the Peninsula with the 43rd Regiment and, along with the 52nd Regiment, took part in the 250-mile march from Lisbon to Talavera. He was also Robert Craufurd's aide-de-camp during 1809 and 1810, at the time Rowan was Craufurd's brigade major. Unlike Rowan, who had quit the army in 1822, Shaw had remained and, in 1826, had been appointed to the Northern District, where his skill in dealing with disorder during industrial disputes brought him to the notice of the Home Department.[422]

In offering him the job Peel wrote:

'My dear Sir,

An Act has lately been passed for the Improvement of the Police of the Metropolis.

By that Act the Secretary of State is empowered to appoint two Magistrates, whose particular duties are defined in the Act, of which I enclose a copy.

For one of these appointments I mean to select a Military man, and my intention is to take that Officer whom I believe to be the best qualified to discharge the confidential and very important duties which will devolve upon him. I will not make the offer to anyone without first ascertaining whether you are willing to accept. If you are, I shall have the greatest pleasure in nominating you, and you still possess my entire confidence.

The salary, as you will see by the Act, is £800 a year. If you should accept the appointment I would name you the first of the two Magistrates, and I trust, as it will be manifest for the Public Interest that the Chief Magistrate should be constantly on the spot, I could make arrangement by which, in addition to the salary, apartments could be allotted to you in the house destined for the office.

Your military rank would proceed, and I am confident the Commander of the Forces would entirely approve of an Officer of distinction acting in this capacity. I fear the half-pay would, by some recent regulations, be suspended during the continuance of the appointment.

Pray turn these matters in your mind, and let me hear from you as

---

[422] Shaw Kennedy, General Sir James (2015). *Autobiographical Memoir of General Sir James Shaw Kennedy. K.C.B. in Notes of the Battle of Waterloo.* London: Forgotten Books, p.36.

soon as you conveniently can. As the experiment is a novel one, and the undertaking arduous, there will I think be a great opportunity for distinction, and the Office will become more important every day.

As legal advice on many points might be very desirable, my inclination is to select a Barrister for the other Magisterial Office. As you will perceive by the Act, the law makes no distinction between the functions of the two Magistrates.

It will at once appear to you that at the outset when the New Police force is organized, the exertion requisite will be unremitting and severe. If you are not disinclined to the undertaking on other grounds, I earnestly hope that the state of your health is not such as to deter you from it.

I have written in great haste, but I trust I have said enough to give you a tolerably accurate view of the nature of the Appointment. I think if a Military Man is at the head of the Office, he would be consulted by the Horse Guards on all points relating to the public peace in the Metropolis which can be connected with the employment of a Military force.'[423]

Four days later, Peel received his reply. It was terse and to the point.

> Manchester, 29th June, 1829.
>
> Sir,
>
> I have the honour to acknowledge the receipt of your letter of the 25th instant.
>
> The situation of Magistrate under the new Police Act for which you so kindly offer to nominate me, I beg to decline.
>
> Permit me to assure you, with the greatest possibly sincerity, that I feel most highly gratified and flattered by the kindness of your letter.
>
> I have the Honour to be, Sir,
>
> Your most faithful servant,
>
> J. Shaw[424]

Shaw gave no reason for his response, but some years later he explained that he 'was reluctant to leave his own profession'. However, he was not altogether averse to becoming a police officer because, seven years later, he agreed to become Inspector-General of the Royal Irish Constabulary

---

[423] Peel Papers, op. cit. 421, Ibid, 40399, folio 262.
[424] Ibid, folio 269.

Rowan and Mayne Appointed Joint Commissioners

(RIC).

He explained:

> 'The feeling which caused my refusing the first of these situations, and accepting the second was, that the constabulary force was of a more extensive command, and was more of a military character than the other.'

But he was only in post for just under two years before resigning. He was subsequently appointed Commissioner of the Manchester Police in October 1839 by the Home Secretary, a post he held for three years.[425]

Following Shaw's refusal, Peel quickly turned to Charles Rowan. It is not clear precisely when and how Peel approached him, but almost certainly it was on the recommendation of Murray, although a number of authors suggest it was at Lord Wellington's recommendation.[426]

Whatever the circumstances of Peel's approach to Rowan, by 7 July the Home Secretary had made his decision as to who the two Magistrates were to be. It was set out in a letter to Lord Rosslyn, the Lord Privy Seal, who had put forward the name of his eldest son, Lieutenant-Colonel James Alexander St Clair, a relatively inexperienced army officer, for one of the posts:

7th July 1829.

Dear Lord Rosslyn,

> I have not proceeded further with my New Police arrangements than to appoint the two Magistrates.
>
> I have on the Recommendation of the highest Military Authorities taken for the Military Magistrate Colonel Rowan of the 52nd Regt., who I am told brought that Regt., to the highest state of discipline. The two Magistrates after considering the matter are to submit to me a detailed plan for organizing the Police.
>
> I shall be glad if there is an opportunity of employing Lieut. Col. St. Clair, but I should rather fear that the subordinate situations in the Police would not suit an Officer of such rank, and that the duties attached to them would not be very agreeable.

---

425 Shaw Kennedy, op. cit. 422, p.38.
426 For example, see Glover, Michael (1968). *Wellington as Military Commander*, London: B.T. Batsford Ltd, p.251; Howard, George (1953). *Guardians of the Queen's Peace: The Development and Work of Britain's Police*. London: Odham's Press, p.127; Gash, Norman (1961). *Mr Secretary Peel: The Life of Sir Robert Peel to 1830*. London: Faber & Faber, p.499.

However I will keep myself free from all engagements until I have the plan before me.

I am, etc.,

Robert Peel.[427]

The other was Richard Mayne. His main sponsor was William Gregson who had been a barrister on the northern circuit before becoming Peel's legal adviser following the latter's appointment as Home Secretary.[428] In a speech to the House of Commons when introducing a new bill on 9 March 1826, Peel had referred to Gregson as a 'barrister of high eminence on the northern circuit, justly respected by all who know him.'[429] Gregson had been involved in drafting the Bill which Peel had placed before the House of Commons in April 1829.

There is written evidence of Gregson's support in an undated letter which was sent to Mayne prior to his appointment:

My dear Mayne,

Since I wrote my note to Mr Peel I have had some conversation with him; he seems strongly impressed with the nature of your qualifications for the office, and said that, of all the names mentioned to him, yours was decidedly the best. He has not however as yet decided upon any of the appointments, as he has many schemes floating in his mind, and will probably require some little time to mature his Plans. You may depend upon my keeping your interests in mind, and in the meantime I shall not mention the subject to anyone.

I am expecting Dundas and some other Circuiteers to dine with me on Saturday next at ½ before seven, and it will give me great pleasure if you join the party.

Ever yours truly,

W. Gregson
Mitre Court,
        Wednesday, ½ past 4.[430]

---

427 Peel Papers, op. cit. 421, 40399, folio 280.
428 Some authors, e.g. Ascoli, claim that Gregson was one of Peel's Under-Secretaries, but that is incorrect. He did not become an Under-Secretary of State until January 1835 (*Spectator: A Weekly Journal of News and Politics, Literature and Science. Volume III*, week-ending January 10, 1835, p.32).
429 Peel. Sir Robert (1826). *Substance of the Speech of the Right Honourable Robert Peel, in the House of Commons on Thursday, March 9th, 1826, on moving for leave to bring in a Bill for the Amendment of The Criminal Law, and a Bill for Consolidating the Laws relating to Larceny*. London: J. Hatchard and Son, p.48.
430 Letters sent to Sir Richard Mayne 1829-1868, p.1. These are contained in a file at the Metropolitan Police Heritage Centre presented by J.H.R. Heathcote in 1955.

Robert Dundas, the son of the 1st Viscount Melville, had graduated from Lincoln's Inn in 1788 and had practised law for a short time before becoming his father's private secretary. He was briefly Chief Secretary of Ireland in 1809, and was First Lord of the Admiralty from 1812 to 1827 and again from 1828 to 1830. In 1822 he succeeded his father's title to become the 2nd Viscount Melville. Peel and his wife Julia had been known to stay at Melville Castle, the family home near Edinburgh.[431] In 1821 and 1822 Peel, keen to take his wife and children away from the smoke and fogs in London, had rented Lulworth Castle in Dorset and, on one occasion, Melville was amongst a number of people who joined Peel for a shooting party.[432]

Mayne had two other sponsors for his candidature, in addition to Gregson. They were Henry Brougham and Sir James Alan Park.[433] Brougham had been admitted to the Faculty of Advocacy in Scotland in 1800, entered Lincoln's Inn in 1803 and was subsequently called to the Bar in 1808. Four years later he became the chief legal adviser to Caroline of Brunswick, the estranged wife of George IV, who was then the Prince of Wales, defending her when she was brought before the House of Lords accused of adultery. A large proportion of the British public supported Caroline, and, as a result Brougham's practice on the Northern Circuit had increased five-fold. In 1816, Brougham was elected Member of Parliament for Winchelsea and was reportedly one of the most forceful speakers in the House of Commons when Peel sought his advice about Mayne.[434] Park, better known as Justice Park, had also been a former student at Lincoln's Inn before becoming leader of the Northern Circuit, although this was prior to Mayne joining the circuit. By the time Mayne did qualify, Justice Park was a member of the Bench of Common Pleas, which involved hearing cases between subject and subject which did not involve the Crown.[435]

Amongst the many letters currently in the Metropolitan Police Heritage collection is a note, written by Mayne to himself, almost as though it was a diary entry:

> 'On Sunday, July 5th, I received a note from Mr Peel, desiring me to come to him next morning. I saw him on Monday at his house, when he said, that he was going to appoint two persons to organise and direct

---

431 Gash, op. cit. 426, pp.301-302.
432 Ibid, p.269.
433 Ibid, p.499.
434 Chisholm, Hugh (ed)(1911). 'Brougham and Vaux, Henry Peter Brougham, 1st Baron'. *Encyclopaedia Britannica 4* (11th edition). Cambridge: University Press.
435 The Court of Common Pleas was created in the late 12th or early 13th century and existed until December 1880 to hear actions between subject and subject.

the new Police, under 10 G. 4 c. 44, that he had sent for me to offer one of these places to me, that if the places suited my views he was happy in offering it. I accepted the appointment with acknowledgements for the handsome manner in which it was given, and same day, was introduced to Lt. Col. Rowan, my coadjutor, by Mr. Peel at the Home Office, Whitehall.

We commenced operations immediately. Thus terminates my course at the Bar.'[436]

The two Commissioners were appointed 'by Special Warrant under the King's Sign Manual to execute at the Metropolitan Police Office generally the duties of a Justice of the Peace in all parts of those several Counties and Liberties' mentioned in the act, 'for improving the Police in and near the Metropolis'.

Their salary was £800 per annum. At the same time John Wray, like Mayne a barrister and, at the time, Chairman of the University Insurance Society,[437] was appointed by Special Warrant 'to receive all sums of money applicable to the purposes of the above recited Act and to be called the Receiver of the Metropolitan Police District.' His salary was £700 per annum.[438]

Peel's Act was a mere skeleton of what was required. Working from a room at the Home Office because no accommodation had been identified or allocated, organising the 'new police' was a gigantic task.'[439] Fortunately, the two men 'took an instinctive liking to each other' and over the following twenty years there appears to have been little disagreement between them. Indeed, 'the political abuse and political chicanery with which they had to contend during the early years of their partnership' almost certainly 'cemented their feelings of mutual respect and affection.'[440]

Rowan and Mayne's first priority was to submit an initial plan to Peel outlining how they thought the New Police should operate and how many officers they needed. It outlined the setting up of six divisions, lettered from A to F, each with a superintendent in charge, and recommended the number of officers required in each rank. In response, Peel set out the

---

436 Letters to Sir Richard Mayne, op. cit. 430, p.1.
437 Moylan, J.F (1929). *Scotland Yard and The Metropolitan Police*. London: G.P. Putnam's Sons, p.254.
438 TNA HO 65/11, folios 1 and 2.
439 Cowley, Richard (2011). *A History of the British Police*. Stroud, Gloucestershire: The History Press, p.23. The term 'new police' was given to it at the time to differentiate it from the old system of parish constables and watchmen.
440 Ascoli, David (1979). *The Queen's Peace: The origins and development of the Metropolitan Police 1829-1995*. London: Hamish Hamilton, p.80.

initial establishment of the Metropolitan Police, including the salaries to be paid to each rank, in a letter to the Commissioners on 29 July 1829:[441]

OFFICE ESTABLISHMENT

Commissioners Clerks	**Receivers Clerks**
One Chief Clerk	One Chief Clerk
One Second Clerk	One Second Clerk
One Third Clerk	

Police Force
8 Superintendents 20 Inspectors 88 Serjeants 895 Constables

Once the outline plan had been agreed, with the assistance of Wray, Rowan and Mayne had four priorities; firstly, to recruit the required number of officers, secondly to develop a code of operations under which they would operate, thirdly, to design a uniform, which did not make the police officers resemble soldiers, and finally to find accommodation from which to operate.

The two Chief Clerks were quickly appointed. For the Commissioners' Office it was Maurice Dowling, and for the Receivers' office it was Thomas Golden.[442] When the two Commissioners appeared before the Select Committee on Policing in 1834, Rowan described how the superintendents were selected 'after mature deliberation, from a particular class of persons'. By May 1830, 17 had been appointed, and Rowan told the Committee:

> 'Thirteen had been sergeant-majors in the army, who were highly recommended; a sergeant-major is raised from the ranks entirely on his own merit; when the regiments are strong, he must have attained that rank by raising himself above a thousand, or probably a much greater number; he is a man usually of great intelligence, integrity and activity; he is not disinclined to do what men of superior acquirements in point of education and higher station in life would think beneath them; it is therefore considered best to select highly recommended persons of that class as superintendents.'[443]

The immediate priority was to recruit six to command the divisions being set up initially. The first two, Joseph Thomas and Thomas Baker, were appointed on 20 July. They were followed by William Bull on 29 July, John

---

441 TNA HO 65/11, folios 3 and 4.
442 TNA HO 65/11, folios 3 and 4.
443 PP 1834 [600]. Report from the Select Committee on the Police of the Metropolis; with minutes of evidence, appendix and index, minutes of evidence, p.2, q/a 33.

May, who effectively became a staff officer to the two Commissioners, on 30 July, Alexander Skene on 4 August, and Edward Lowry on 10 August.[444]

With regard to the appointment of constables and sergeants, Rowan told the Committee:

> 'The Commissioners receive recommendations and testimonials of character; registers are kept of those, and the parties are summoned by letter for examination, as occasion requires; they are then examined by the surgeon as to their physical qualifications and general intelligence, also by an officer of the department, Mr May; they are afterwards approved and sworn by the Commissioners, and appointed by the Secretary of State; they are then posted as vacancies occur. There is strict enquiry, according to a printed form sent out, after the examination of the candidate, by a confidential officer, who sees the parties recommending them, and enquiries carefully into their conduct and character, and it is upon that final report that they are recommended to the Secretary of State.'[445]

Rowan also told the Committee that by mid-1831 appointments to the sergeant rank were being made from constables.[446] When asked what class of men the Commissioners found did the duty best, Rowan replied, 'Non-commissioned officers of the army and marines; some are admitted a little above the regulated age, which is 35.'[447]

Much has been written already about the development of a code of operations, often referred to as Peel's Principles of Policing.[448] To refer to them as such is a total misrepresentation of how they were developed and fails to take account of the part played in their development by the two Commissioners, about which more will be said in the final chapter. Whilst the Secretary of State approved the regulations, it is clear from Rowan's answer to a question on this matter from the Select Committee on Policing that 'everything that has been done since the commencement has originated with the Commissioners.'[449]

The initial code was divided into two parts: the general instructions under which the force would be organised and would operate, and the legal powers the police possessed as a result of the common law and statutes. Comparison with the instructions Rowan received at Shorncliffe suggest

---

444   TNA HO 65/11, folio 12.
445   PP 1834 [600], op. cit. 443, p.2, q/a 33.
446   Ibid, p.23, q/a 379.
447   Ibid, p.5, q/a 54.
448   In *A History of Police in England*. London: Methuen, p.242, Captain Melville Lee suggests it was Mayne 'who drew up the regulations.'
449   PP 1834 [600], op. cit. 443, p.27, q/a 432.

that the general instructions were almost certainly the work of Rowan. Indeed, when he was researching into Rowan's background in 1952 the eminent police historian Charles Reith discovered a proof copy of the original handbook issued to all police officers in the library at Scotland Yard, which had some marginal notes in Rowan's handwriting.[450]

Pointing out that his 'General Instructions for… the Police Force' were 'not to be understood as containing rules of conduct applicable to every variety of circumstances that may occur in the performance of their duty,' Rowan said 'according to the degree in which they show themselves possessed of these qualities and to their zeal, activity, and judgement, on all occasions, will be their claims to future promotion and reward.'

He continued:

'It should be understood, at the outset, that the principal[451] object to be attained is the Prevention of Crime.

To this great end every effort of the Police is to be directed. The security of person and property, the preservation of the public tranquillity, and all the other objects of a Police Establishment, will thus be better effected, than by the detection and punishment of the offender, after he has succeeded in committing the crime. This should constantly be kept in mind by every member of the Police Force, as the guide for his own conduct. Officers and Police Constables should endeavour to distinguish themselves by such vigilance and activity, as may render it extremely difficult for anyone to commit a crime within that portion of the town under their charge.

When in any Division offences are frequently committed there must be reason to suspect, that the Police is not in that Division properly conducted. The absence of crime will be considered the best possible proof of the complete efficiency of the Police. In Divisions, where this security and good order have been effected, the Officers and Men belonging to it may feel assured that such conduct will be noticed by rewards and promotion.'[452]

The comments about the detection of crime were deliberate. Rowan and Mayne were aware that the detection of crime had been left untouched

---

450 Reith, Charles (1952). 'Charles Rowan: 1792-1852' in *Police Review*, 9 May, p.326. The library at New Scotland Yard was closed some time ago and the location of this proof copy of the handbook is unknown.
451 The word 'principle' was not in the first draft but seems to have been added by Peel. See Footnote on p.85 in Browne, Douglas G (1956). *The Rise of Scotland Yard: A History of the Metropolitan Police*. London: George G. Harrop.
452 Reith, op. cit. 420, pp.135-136. Notes by Mayne in preparing the Primary Objects are contained in TNA MEPO 2/5800.

by Peel in practice, because, as already indicated, he had been careful not to trespass on the responsibilities of the magistrates and the officers they employed.[453]

Rowan then set out the arrangements into how the new police force would be organised, using the headings Local Divisions and Police Force.

Local Divisions

He divided the area up into what was effectively six Divisions, each being given a local name and one of the first six letters of the alphabet, A to F. Each Division was sub-divided into eight sections, with each section having eight beats. Each Division would have a station or watch-house, and, insofar as was practical, the men would lodge together near their place of duty, so they could be called out quickly in case of emergency.

Police Force

Each Division would be policed by a Company under the command of a superintendent. It would consist of four inspectors who would each be in charge of four parties, each consisting of nine constables under a sergeant. Each man would 'be conspicuously marked' with the divisional letter and an individual number on their uniform, with the first sixteen numbers being reserved for the sergeants. One Company would be attached to the Office of the Commissioners, for the duty in the immediate neighbourhood, and to act as a general reserve.[454]

Rowan had based the organisation of the new Police Force on a regiment with himself and Mayne in command, divided into six companies in total, each under the command of a superintendent. The system of beats was an adaptation of Moore's 'outpost' plan for Light Infantry, in which a company formed a line of outlying sentries, based on pickets under sergeants, linked with company headquarters.

Of particular interest were his instructions to superintendents:

- He will be responsible for the general conduct and good order of the Officers and Men under his charge. He should make himself well acquainted, by frequent personal intercourse, with the Inspectors and Serjeants, and through them with the character and conduct of every Man in the Company under his orders; he will be firm and just, at the same time kind and conciliatory towards them, in his behaviour on all occasions.
- He will take care that the Standing Orders and Regulations, and all

---

453 Roach, op. cit. 417, p.41.
454 Reith, op. cit. 420, pp.136-137.

others given out from time to time, are promptly and strictly obeyed. Much must be done by himself, and under his own immediate inspection. And as he will be held responsible for the general performance of the duties of the police, within his own Division, he must give clear and precise instructions to the Officer under him...

- It will be expected that he should at all times be able to furnish the Commissioners with particular information respecting the state of every part of his Division.[455]

Once again, the influence of the Shorncliffe experiment is shown in this instruction, emphasising the importance of the relationship between commissioned officers and men, most notably in the use of such words as 'firm and just, at the same time kind and conciliatory.'[456]

The influence of the same experiment was to be seen again in the instructions written for Constables. They were told to:

- 'be civil and attentive to all persons, of every rank and class' and warned that 'insolence and incivility' would not be tolerated.
- 'be particularly cautious not to interfere idly and unnecessarily' but 'when required to act' they should 'do so with decision and boldness'.
- 'remember that there [was] no qualification more indispensable to a Police Officer than a perfect command of temper' and they should not allow themselves 'to be moved in the slightest degree, by any language or threats that may be used'; it was also pointed out that if they performed their duty 'in a quiet and determined manner,' it was more likely to 'induce well-disposed bystanders to assist them should they require it.[457]

The general instructions, which were issued to each constable, were intended to be confidential for police use only partly because experience would dictate which paragraphs would need to be altered. Despite its confidentiality, chief clerk Maurice Dowling released some of the passages to the media and they were published in many of the leading newspapers on 29 September. Quite why Dowling did this is uncertain,[458] but it annoyed Peel who wrote to him in the following terms:

---

455 Reith, op. cit. 420, p.138.
456 See Chapter Two.
457 Reith, op. cit. 420, p.140.
458 A journalist working for several publications at the time, Vincent George Dowling, may have been the person to whom the information was originally passed. The suggestion is that he was a distant cousin of Maurice Dowling. See Fairfax, Norman (March 2012). 'The Rise and Fall of Maurice Dowling' retrieved from liverpoolcitypolice.co.uk/#/dowling/4562128598 [accessed 7 January 2016].

'After the breach of trust which you have committed and considering the injurious effect which it is calculated to have on the new police establishment, I do not consider myself justified in retaining you in office of so confidential a nature as that of Chief Clerk in the Metropolitan Police Office.'[459]

Dowling resigned, but clearly neither Rowan nor Mayne took the same view as Peel, for less than six months later he was appointed as the superintendent of the newly-formed L Division (Lambeth).[460] Dowling was replaced by Charles Yardley,[461] who had served in the Commissariat during the Napoleonic Wars. Initially coming on one month's trial in October 1829, he remained in post until retiring in 1864.[462]

Precisely how the force operated was briefly outlined by Rowan again when the two Commissioners appeared before the Select Committee in 1834. He explained that 'two-thirds of the Force' were 'on duty during the night' which was from 9.00pm to 6.00am, and 'one-third during the day'. Officers would undertake 'two months' night duty and one month's day duty'. He described how 'supervision of the constables started with the sergeants and inspectors who report to the superintendent.' Superintendent May, who was in command of Whitehall Division, was 'sent out mounted by the Commissioners to visit the police stations, to observe generally how the duty [was] done, and the Commissioners themselves [took] frequent opportunities of seeing how the men [were] doing their duty on the streets.'[463]

Rowan felt that 'the uniform should be "quiet", and the design adopted resembled a civilian livery.' Except for the buttons and the letter on the collar 'the new policeman was scarcely distinguishable from any other citizen.'[464] The uniform consisted of a blue tailcoat and two pairs of trousers, blue for winter and white for summer, a greatcoat for bad weather, boots and a leather top hat, the crown of which contained supports so the patrolman could use it as a stool for peering over walls. For protection, they carried a baton and they were also provided with sword belts although, as it turned out, only a few carried swords on duty. To summon assistance, they were

459 Ibid.
460 Later, he became the Chief Officer of the Liverpool Dock Police and then, in 1845, Liverpool Police. Ibid.
461 TNA HO 65/11, folio 17.
462 Fido, Martin, and Skinner, Keith (1999). *The Official Encyclopedia of Scotland Yard*. London: Virgin, p.295.
463 PP 1834 [600], op. cit. 449, p.4, q/a 47-50.
464 Browne, op. cit. 451, p.82.

provided with a rattle.[465]

Four clothing contractors were invited to attend the Commissioners' Room in the Home Office, where they were acquainted with the 'Patterns of the Dress to be worn by the Metropolitan Police Force' and requested to state in writing the Terms under which they could supply all or some of the items 'for 500 or 1,000 men, specifying the differences in price if paid in ready money or at six months' credit.'[466] Three of the four were old-established army contractors. The exception was Charles Hibbert of 8 Pall Mall East, who was informed on 3 August that his quotations for coats, trousers, greatcoats and boots had been accepted.[467] Edward Moore of Piccadilly secured the order for top hats, Mr Henry Tatham of 36 Charing Cross the order for 'Sword Belts',[468] and Mr Parker of Holborn the order for 1,000 rattles and a similar number of batons.[469]

Not only had no accommodation been allocated to the Commissioners, but no buildings had been identified from which the new police would work. Fortunately, under the Metropolitan Police Act 1829, all existing watch houses were transferred to the Receiver.[470]

No. 4 Whitehall Place was one of a terrace of six three-storey houses with basements that had been built by John Garden between 1814 and 1816, just to the south of but parallel to a street known as Great Scotland Yard; in fact, No. 4 backed onto Great Scotland Yard. It had recently been vacated by Sir Richard Vyvyan who was, at the time, the Member of Parliament for Cornwall. On one side, No. 3 was occupied by the Earl of Kingston; on the other, No. 5 was one of two buildings occupied by the Office for Auditing the Public Accounts.[471] The top floor of No. 4 was made into bachelor quarters for Colonel Rowan whilst the remainder became office accommodation for the two commissioners, the receiver and their respective staffs. The servants' quarters at the back of the house were converted into a police station for A Division and a recruiting office. The total cost of the alterations, fittings and furniture was £1,255 5s 0d.[472]

Also living on the premises were an office keeper and a housekeeper.

---

465   TNA MEPO 1/1.
466   Ibid, folio 2.
467   Ibid, folio 4.
468   PP 1834 [600], op. cit. 449, p.51, q/a 754.
469   TNA MEPO 1/1, folio 31.
470   PP 1834 [600], op. cit. 449, p.51, q/a 754.
471   Cater, GH and EP Wheeler (eds)(1935). *Survey of London: Volume 16, St Martin-in-the-Fields I: Charing Cross*. London: London County Council, pp.197-202. Retrieved from www.british-history.ac.uk/survey-london/vol16/pt1/pp197-202 [accessed 7 January 2016]. Hibbert, Christopher, Ben Weinrob, Julia Keay, John Keay (2010). *The London Encyclopaedia* (3rd Edition). London: Macmillan.
472   TNA HO 65/11, folio 7. Approved by the Home Secretary on 5 September 1829.

The office keeper also acted as doorman. The housekeeper was responsible for taking care of the offices, but she also acted as a servant to Rowan. Originally, the Secretary of State stated that the housekeeper should be paid from the police fund, but shortly afterwards it appears it became Rowan's personal responsibility.[473]

---

473 PP 1834 [600], op. cit. 449, p.58, q/a 855-857.

CHAPTER EIGHT

EXTERNAL PROBLEMS I: THE CITY OF LONDON

Rowan and Mayne quickly became aware of external factors that would cause them difficulties over the first ten years and, in one case, beyond. They all arose from Peel's failure to make the commissioners responsible for all aspects of policing within the Metropolis.

Thus, although the foot patrols emanating from Bow Street had been disbanded – indeed, some officers had been incorporated into the Metropolitan Police – the Bow Street Horse Patrol had been left under the control of the chief magistrate. Similarly, whilst the two commissioners were responsible for policing the land on either side of that part of the River Thames that flowed through the Metropolis, the relatively narrow stretch of water itself was the responsibility of a separate force, the River Police. The policing of the inside of the Royal palaces came under the jurisdiction of the Chief Magistrate at Bow Street Court, with two Bow Street officers and, when necessary, specially employed 'marshal men' being used.[474] The policing of the Palace of Westminster, i.e. the Houses of Parliament, was the responsibility of the High Bailiff, who employed a High Constable, who was in charge of a number of constables.[475] And finally, the magistrates at the nine Police Offices had their own constables to investigate crime coming to their notice and execute warrants granted by them. Peel had made no provisions as to how these various parallel systems would work.

Most will be dealt with in the next chapter, but it was the exclusion of the City of London that caused Rowan and Mayne early problems. Indeed,

---

474 PP 1837-38 [578]. Report from Select Committee on Metropolitan Police Offices; with the Minutes of Evidence, Appendix and Index. Evidence of Sir F.B. Watson, Master of Her Majesty's Household, pp.109-110, q/a.1133-1141.
475 Ibid, p.10.

Mayne was still grappling with this shortly before his death. When the Metropolitan Police were formed in 1829, policing in the City of London was still under the control of a relatively ad-hoc system which involved a day police and a night watch system who never communicated with each other.[476] However, the authorities in the City held considerable power and, fearing he would not get his police bill through Parliament, Peel had deliberately excluded the City, claiming that it was something with which he 'should be afraid to meddle'.[477] Consequently, when the committee appointed to inquire into the policing of the Metropolis reported in July 1828, it said, 'there was no intention of interfering with the existing powers of the City authorities'.[478] But this omission quickly caused problems as 'the riff-raff of the town gathered each evening at the gates of the City – particularly at Temple Bar – to watch crooks and rowdies flying to sanctuary' with constables of the Metropolitan Police, often referred to as the New Police in the year following its formation, 'standing outside the City boundaries unable to follow them' because they had no jurisdiction.[479]

Nevertheless, in February 1830, only four months after the Metropolitan Police had been formed, at the request of the Sub-Nightly Watch Committee of the City of London, Rowan appeared before it and gave a general view of how the newly-formed Metropolitan Police operated. This included how it was structured and financed, the rates of pay for each rank, the provision of equipment, discipline, gratuities and promotion.[480] Nothing changed!

When the Commissioners appeared before the Select Committee on the Metropolitan Police in 1833, they were asked whether they had 'found any inconvenience' because their authority did not extend into the City of London. Answering on behalf of both himself and Mayne, Rowan said 'Yes, especially in cases of public disturbances.' As examples, he briefly mentioned two occasions, one in 1830, the other in 1832, when crowds driven from the metropolis had reassembled in the City.[481] Asked whether he thought it would be desirable to have an arrangement by which the City of London and the Metropolitan Police should be under one head, Rowan

---

476   TNA MEPO 2/5796
477   Gash, Norman (2011). *Mr Secretary Peel: The Life of Sir Robert Peel to 1830*. London: Faber and Faber, p.492.
478   Ibid, p.495
479   Howard, George (1953). *Guardians of the Queen's Peace: The Development and Work of Britain's Police*. London: Odham's Press, p.135.
480   TNA MEPO 2/5796.
481   PP 1834 [600]. Report from the Select Committee on the Police of the Metropolis; with minutes of evidence, appendix and index, p.15, q/a.250-257. These incidents are elaborated on in Chapter Twelve.

said he thought 'it would be very advantageous.'[482]

Meanwhile, before the 1833 Select Committee had reported, on 10 February 1834 the Commissioners directed Charles Yardley to write to Henry Woodthorpe, Town Clerk of the City of London, explaining 'they were desirous of establishing a reciprocal communication' between the Metropolitan Police and the City Police, 'with reference to criminal offenders and the recovery of stolen property', and would be happy to discuss it with any person deputed by the City. As a result Mayne met with the City Police Committee of Alderman, and, as a consequence of that meeting, Woodthorpe responded on 11 March:

> '...the court of aldermen have given directions to the marshal or superintendent to transmit to the office of the commissioners at Scotland-yard, an account of all cases of burglary, robbery or stolen property which shall come to the knowledge of any of the police officers of this city, together with a description of stolen property, and every circumstance which may be useful for the tracing and recovery of the same.'[483]

Soon afterwards the Secretary of State authorised the publication of city cases in the Bow Street Police Report, and the Mansion House office and the justices sitting at the Guildhall were instructed to send reports to it for publication. But Mayne told the Second Sitting of the Select Committee on Police Offices in 1838 that very few city cases had ever been inserted.[484]

When the two Commissioners were recalled by the reconvened Committee in 1834 they were asked, again, whether any suggestions could be offered by which the system of policing in London could be improved. They returned to the 'union of the police in the city of London with the Metropolitan Police', with Mayne telling the Committee that 'on several occasions great public evil' had arisen as a result of this division of responsibility, because the Metropolitan Police had 'no authority to act within the City' and vice versa.[485]

As will be seen in later chapters, the Metropolitan Police successfully prevented serious disorder on many occasions by breaking up groups as they assembled. But difficulties arose when officers drove crowds of protesters eastwards along the Strand and they reached the City boundary at Temple Bar. Metropolitan officers were under strict instructions not to

---

482 Ibid, p.16, q/a 260.
483 PP 1837-1838 [578], op. cit. 474, minutes of evidence, pp.107-108, q/a 1124.
484 Ibid.
485 PP 1834 [600], op. cit. 481. p.319, q/a.4271-4275.

enter the City and the crowd, therefore, was able to reassemble, throwing stones and occasionally rushing out to attack the police, who drove them back again.

Mayne elaborated slightly on the two occasions Rowan had mentioned at the previous hearing. The first was in November 1830, when it was anticipated there would be mass disturbances if the King was to visit the City to attend the Lord Mayor's dinner. As will be seen later, he did not go but there were outbreaks of violence.[486] The Metropolitan Police broke up the crowds in the metropolis, and by nightfall had driven a large crowd up the Strand to Temple Bar. Not being allowed to enter the City, the crowd congregated 'for a length of time, throwing stones, and occasionally rushing out' to attack the police before they were driven back.

The second occasion occurred in March 1832 during the fast-day riots.[487] A meeting in Finsbury Square, which bordered on the City, at which Mayne himself was present, degenerated into violence with the mob pulling up iron-railings and throwing stones at both lookers-on and the police. Driving the crowd before them the police cleared the square, but the crowd reassembled 'just across the street, within the City, and the police were kept for some hours unable to act.' Stones continued to be thrown and several officers were wounded.[488]

Asked whether he thought things would be improved by authorizing the police constables of the City to act within the Metropolis, and the constables of the Metropolitan Police to act within the limits of the City, Mayne replied, 'I think that would a great improvement, but certainly the police would not be so efficient as if they were all under one head throughout the town.'[489] Indeed, Mayne told the Committee that if the Metropolitan Police had been able to follow the mob into the City 'the affair would not have lasted but a very short time.'[490]

When it finally reported in 1834, the Committee found it to be 'most desirable' if the responsibilities of the Commissioners for policing the Metropolis 'could be extended throughout the City of London', and quoted from a comment by the Finance Committee in 1798, when reporting on the expenses and effects of certain branches of Police:

'…it would be most unfortunate indeed if any local jealousies, founded upon no just grounds, though entertained by very honourable minds,

---

486 See Chapter Twelve for the reasons behind the cancellation.
487 See Chapter Twelve for the causes of these riots.
488 PP 1834 [600], op. cit. 481, p.319, q/a.4274.
489 Ibid, p.320, q/a. 4277.
490 Ibid, p.319, q/a.4272.

should continue to deprive ...the inhabitants of the City ...of that security, which a more permanent attendance ...could not fail to produce.'[491]

Despite this, the Whig administration failed to act on any of the recommendations made by the Select Committee, as the Committee set up three years later to inquire into Metropolitan Police Offices was quick to point out when it reported. Following this Committee's report, Home Secretary Lord John Russell, assisted by his Under-Secretary, Fox Maule, did bring a Bill 'for further improving the Police in and near the Metropolis' before the House of Commons the following year. The Bill envisaged the City of London and responsibility for policing the River Thames being brought under the control of the Metropolitan Police Commissioners.[492] However, the City Authorities moved quickly to avert what they saw as a takeover by the Metropolitan Police, when its Members in the House of Commons gained sufficient support to pass the City of London Police Act 1839. This set up a separate police force with its own Commissioner, appointed not by the Home Secretary, as was the case in the Metropolis, but by the Court of Common Council.[493]

Some fifteen years later, a Royal Commission was appointed to inquire into the state of the Corporation of the City of London and recommend measures for its future government.[494] The resultant report was sent to the Home Office on 28 April 1854. In it, the Commission carefully considered why such 'a small portion of the metropolis' should continue to remain separate in terms of policing, and came to the conclusion that incorporating 'the City with the larger district by which it is environed' was a measure to be recommended on the grounds of 'efficiency and economy.'[495]

Despite three Committees and a Royal Commission making recommendations that the two should be amalgamated, the two distinctly separate police forces co-existed without major problems until 1863. But two incidents in the City in March of that year led to another move to bring the policing of the City under the control of the Metropolitan Police Commissioner, Sir Richard Mayne. Both occurred due to unsatisfactory

---

491 PP 1834 [600], op. cit. 481, Report, p.17.
492 HC Deb, 21 April 1863, vol. 170, cc 481-525. Speech in the House of Commons by Sir George Grey.
493 Made up of Aldermen and Common Councilmen elected from the City's wards, the Court of Common Council is the main decision-making body of the City of London Corporation, presided over by the Lord Mayor.
494 PP 1854 [1772]. Royal Commission appointed to inquire into the existing state of the Corporation of the City of London.
495 HC Deb 21 April 1863, vol. 170, cc 481-525, op. cit. 492.

arrangements in the City in the lead up to and following the marriage of Albert Edward, the Prince of Wales, to Princess Alexandra of Denmark. The Princess was due to arrive in England on 7 March, and there would be 'illuminations' throughout the country following the wedding on 10 March.

Unfortunately for the City, Commissioner of Police Daniel Whittle Harvey, who had been in post since the formation of the Force in 1839, died just over a week before the proposed celebrations and his deputy, Captain Charles Hodgson, took command.

The royal couple would arrive by train at the Bricklayer's Arms Terminus on 7 March and then travel by carriage in a procession to Paddington Station. From the Bricklayer's Arms Terminus to London Bridge and from Temple Bar to Paddington Station the route would be policed by the Metropolitan Police, but from London Bridge, through the City via Mansion House, where the Lord Mayor would make a presentation to the royal couple, to Temple Bar, the route would be the responsibility of the City of London Police.

On 28 February a deputation of five officials from the City, which, possibly because it was the day following Commissioner Harvey's death, did not include a representative from the City of London Police, attended a meeting at Sir Richard Mayne's office in Whitehall, at which he offered to send his officers to assist in keeping the route clear through the City. The offer was declined, Sir Richard being assured by the officials that 'they were so much accustomed to great pageants in the City' and 'there would be no difficulty in managing that of the 7th March.' Mayne did meet with Acting Commissioner Hodgson three days later, when he was told that the City Police did not intend to line the route 'because they never did, except on the occasion of the Emperor of France's visit to the Guildhall when the Metropolitan Police had kept a line from Temple Bar to St Paul's.'[496] When Hodgson met with Colonel Sir David Wood of the Royal Artillery about the deployment of the military, the latter made a number of suggestions regarding the placing of temporary barricades, but it was alleged that Hodgson replied, 'I know how to manage a mob.'[497]

---

496 PP 1862 [233]. Letter, dated 24 April 1863, from Sir Richard Mayne to the Secretary of State for Home Department, as to the Police Arrangements and Employment of Troops in the City and in the Borough of Southwark, on the occasion of the Procession on the 7th of March last.
497 PP 1863 [276]. Return of the troops employed on the 7th March last in connexion with the procession of the Princess Alexandra on, or in the vicinity of, the line of route, from the Bricklayers' Arms Station, through the city of London, to the railway station at Paddington; &c. Copies of reports made by officers in command of troops in the city to the Horse Guards or other authorities. Colonel Sir David Wood, in a Memorandum to the Deputy Adjutant-General of the Royal Artillery, dated 23 March 1863.

The Operational Order for the Metropolitan Police, covering the arrival and procession of the couple on 7 March and the wedding at Windsor Castle, together with the illuminations on 10 March, was extremely detailed, amounting to twelve pages of close-typed script. The Metropolitan Police deployed nearly 4,200 men within its area; the City of London Police just under 500 men. In the Metropolitan area the men lined the route, with between seven and ten yards between each man.[498] By and large these arrangements were successful on both days. However, within the City of London it was a different matter.

On 7 March, Princess Alexandra was met by the Prince of Wales on her arrival at Gravesend, and the couple travelled by train into London, arriving at the Bricklayer's Arms Terminus at the southern end of the Old Kent Road from whence the Royal Procession left at 2.00pm. Reaching the Surrey side of London Bridge at 2.30pm, the procession only got to the centre of the bridge before it 'came to a dead stop, evidently from some obstruction far away in the distance, which lasted nearly half an hour.' Eventually, 'the procession continued its progress', but more delays occurred

> 'on the way to Mansion House, which was not reached until near 3 o'clock, a whole hour having elapsed from the start from the other side of the bridge. Some terrible squeezing and crushing took place at intervals, which once or twice seemed to slightly alarm the Princess.'

The Royal Carriage had great difficulty in turning 'the corner at the Mansion House', but no sooner had it done so than pressure from the rear of the crowd pushed people forward hemming the Royal Carriage in. Indeed, the intensity of the pressure was such 'as to threaten danger to the occupants of the carriage themselves', but 'fortunately, the carriage was extricated.'[499]

Colonel Price, the officer in command of troops from the Royal Horse Artillery in the City on the day, claimed that on his arrival at shortly after 11 o'clock he found the processional route 'blocked up with carriages of all sorts, public and private', and 'a dense mass of people' which extended from London Bridge to St Paul's Churchyard. He saw only a few policemen other than at Mansion House, where the Lady Mayoress was due to make her presentation.[500]

---

498 PP 1863 [196]. Procession and illumination accidents, &c. (metropolis).
499 *The Examiner*, 14 March 1863, p.9.
500 PP 1863 [276], op. cit. 497. Memorandum by Colonel C. Price to Colonel Sir D.E. Wood, dated 21 March 1863.

A stinging indictment of Hodgson's arrangements was subsequently delivered by Colonel Wood, in overall command of the three contingents of Royal Horse Artillery troops deployed that day, in the concluding paragraph of his report:

> 'I venture to assert that no difficulty would have occurred, nor would the military or police have been overpowered by the dense mass of people which assembled, if more efficient barricades, and a greater number, had been erected at the Mansion House and across the streets, converging there, and those leading into the route of the procession; and I would also remark, that the City should have been cleared of carriages and vehicles at 10 o'clock, instead of 1 o'clock, and police should have been placed at the side streets (leading into the main line), and by preventing an overflow of people entering them, an egress would have been allowed to the mob from the main route. As it was, there was no egress to the side streets or from them, and the whole route of the procession was consequently crammed to an overwhelming and dangerous degree.'[501]

Tragically two people died, although neither death was directly attributable to the inadequacy of the policing. It later transpired that only 372 City police officers had been available 'to keep the whole line of the procession' between London Bridge and Temple Bar, which, according to Lord Alfred Paget, a Liberal politician and former soldier, was 'manifestly inadequate'.[502]

The wedding ceremony took place at St George's Chapel in Windsor Castle on 10 March. For the wedding itself, Mayne deployed ten inspectors, 27 sergeants and 284 constables, plus 24 constables in plain clothes, under the command of a superintendent, to preserve order and keep the line of procession in and around Windsor. In the evening he deployed one inspector, one sergeant and ten constables to the Terrace of Windsor Castle to maintain order during the firework display. The day was made a national holiday, and festivities, including illuminations, were held throughout the country. Assistant Commissioner Captain Labalmondière was in command of arrangements throughout metropolis for the illuminations, deploying 15 superintendents, 46 inspectors, 159 sergeants and 1,630 constables with another 96 in plain clothes.[503] The

---

501 PP 1863 [276], op. cit. 25. Colonel David Wood, in a Memorandum to the Deputy Adjutant-General of the Royal Artillery, dated 23 March 1863.
502 Quoting from the blue-book published by the Corporation, containing an account of the arrangements on 7th March at HC Deb 13 March 1863, vol. 169 cc 1396-409.
503 PP 1863 [196], op. cit. 498.

illuminations attracted particularly large crowds in the City of London. Unfortunately, poor management of the crowd by the police resulted in at least seven people being killed and over a hundred injured. Many of the injured suffered broken limbs, fractured ribs and the like.[504]

The delays that had occurred in the City on 7 March led to a debate in the House of Commons. Opening the debate, Sir George Grey said:

> 'There can be no doubt that on Saturday last there was a serious obstruction to the passage of the Royal carriages through the City, and I have felt it my duty to write to the Lord Mayor on the subject, calling his attention to the reports I have received, and reminding him that the route was fixed, and obtained the sanction of Her Majesty, on the distinct understanding that every effectual means would be taken to prevent confusion and delay. It is well known that from the Bricklayer's Arms to London Bridge, and from Temple Bar to Paddington, although the whole route was crowded by vast multitudes, there was not the slightest obstruction or delay; but no sooner had the procession entered the City then its progress was obstructed by dense masses of people, a stoppage of nearly twenty minutes taking place on London Bridge. At the Mansion House also a considerable delay occurred; I have been informed by gentlemen who were in attendance on the Prince and Princess that there appeared to be an absence of any authority, and a want of those efficient arrangements which should have been made on such an occasion.'[505]

This led to questions being asked about the advisability of amalgamating the City Police and the Metropolitan Police. The Earl of Dalhousie, with whom Rowan had often stayed during his holidays in Scotland,[506] pointed out that everything went smoothly within the Metropolitan area but as soon as the procession arrived at London Bridge it became 'a scene of confusion and certainly delay, which would not have taken place if proper precautions had been observed.' There was then a further delay opposite the Mansion House, and such confusion that people were able to 'lay hands on the carriages in which [the Royal Party] were seated'. He went on to suggest that it had been a great mistake for the City Police to decline the assistance of the Metropolitan Police, 'on the ground that they were able to perform this duty by means of their own force.' Pointing out that the City Police Commissioner had just died and a new one was yet to be

---

504 *London Daily News*, 12 March 1863, p.5; *The Standard*, 16 March 1863, p.6.
505 HC Deb 13 March 1863, vol.169 cc 1396-409.
506 See Chapter Eighteen.

appointed, he suggested it was an ideal opportunity for an amalgamation to take place.[507]

Approximately six weeks later, Sir George Grey introduced a Bill for the Amalgamation of the City of London Police with the Metropolitan Police in the House of Commons. The debate which accompanied the introduction of the Bill was lively. Mr. Alderman Sidney from the City suggested that whilst the regulations issued by Sir Richard Mayne on 7 March were effective in that the processional route through the Metropolitan Police District was kept clear, all the streets surrounding the route were jammed. The Lord Mayor, Alderman Rose, made a more personal attack on the Metropolitan Police, telling the House that 'the City Police had a better physique, they possessed more intelligence, and in everything that made a policeman valuable, they were far superior to the Metropolitan Police'. He went on to say that 'the City Police was not only more efficient, but less expensive, than the Metropolitan Police'.[508]

The comments in the House of Commons by those representing the City of London were anathema to Mayne, who, it seems, was the only person who was not 'afraid to meddle with the city'.[509] On 29 April he wrote to Henry Bruce, then Under-Secretary at the Home Office, claiming he would 'not have entered into any discussion of the comparative merits of the two Forces, had not assertions been made of the superior efficiency of the City Force.' He started by pointing out that the cost of a Metropolitan Police officer was £65 9s 3d per annum, whereas a City of London officer cost £13 15s 4d more at £79 4s 7d. He continued:

> 'I do not desire to disparage [the City of London Police]; it has been organised exactly upon the model of the Metropolitan, and the general regulations for their government and instructional for the guidance of the men in the performance of their duties seem to be taken from those of the Metropolitan Police...
>
> The City Police are under great disadvantage from the confined area in which they act, and their waste of knowledge of the suspected and criminal characters in the great surrounding district who may go into the City to commit crime.
>
> Except for the execution of warrants by 2 & 3 Vic, cap 94,[510] sec. 23 they have no legal authority as constables beyond the precincts of the City.

---

507   HL Deb 09 March 1863, vol 169 cc 1220-4.
508   HC Deb 21 April 1863, vol 170 cc 481-525.
509   See Browne, Douglas G (1956). *The Rise of Scotland Yard: A History of the Metropolitan Police*. London: Harrap, footnote on p.76.
510   City of London Police Act, 1839.

It cannot be expected that either Force will take much interest in the prevention of crime out of their own district. A system is constantly in operation throughout the Metropolitan District by which constables obtain a knowledge of the criminal and suspected characters in all parts of the District, and communications are made to defeat peculiar modes of committing crime as they are discovered in each division. Such intercommunication can never be effected between separate bodies of police, under different authorities.

I deem it my duty to submit these statements, as it appears to me of great importance, more especially with reference to the consideration of the Bill now before the House of Commons for the amalgamation of the Metropolitan and City Police, that the facts should be known.'[511]

Meanwhile, residents of the City of London conducted a leaflet campaign. The leaflets outlined criticisms of the Metropolitan Police that had recently appeared in the newspapers, and posed two questions:

- Do the Citizens of London desire to be under the rule of the Metropolitan Police?
- Are they a fit body to be brought into the City of London to protect the property and the persons of the Merchants, Bankers and Tradesmen of the City?[512]

Three thousand 'influential citizens' of the City of London met at the Guildhall at the beginning of May. Among the three resolutions passed, all unanimously, was one proposed by Kirkman Hodgson, the Governor of the Bank of England:

That the Police Force of this City is as able and efficient as, if not superior to, any force in these realms for the protection of life and property, for the detection of crime, and for the regulation of the immense traffic which throngs the streets of the City, and that it is unwise and inexpedient to interfere with its management and control so long as its duties continue to be efficiently performed.'[513]

In its battle to save its police force, the City of London was joined by other cities throughout the United Kingdom, who saw their forces being swallowed up by the surrounding counties.[514]

511 TNA MEPO 3/39. Letter, dated 29 April 1863, to Mr Bruce MP.
512 TNA MEPO 3/39
513 *Shoreditch Observer*, 9 May 1863, p.1.
514 HC Deb, 21 April 1863, op. cit. 18. See the speeches by Mr Norris, Sir George Bowyer and Mr Hibbert in the debate in the House of Commons.

Nevertheless, Mayne remained determined to bring the City of London under his control for policing purposes. On 1 June he sent a lengthy letter to the Home Office. After setting out the financial benefits of such an amalgamation, in a clear reference to what had recently occurred in the City, he outlined the advantages in 'times of public commotion and on great public occasions':

> 'The numbers and organisation of the metropolitan police give the means of bringing together whatever amount of the civil power may be required to preserve the peace and maintain good order without the intervention of military or other extraordinary force. The small numbers of the City police do not admit of such arrangements; and the City authorities, therefore, if left to their own resources are unable to provide for the public safety, and lamentable consequences have ensured. This was foreseen and in some degree provided for by the City Police Act,[515] by which the Secretary of State for the Home Department, on the application of the Lord Mayor in any case of special emergency, may grant the assistance of the metropolitan police to act within the City; but the Lord Mayor can hardly judge of the actual necessity or know the amount of assistance that ought to be applied for. Moreover, the principle of such dependence is unfair to the inhabitants of the metropolitan districts, who are thus, at times (most frequently times of great excitement) deprived of their proper protection, and for which they can receive no equivalent from the City force.
>
> I beg leave, in conclusion to state that the existence of a detached police force in the heart of the metropolis is at variance with the principle on which the police is established in every other town in the kingdom. The continuance of such an extraordinary exception in the metropolis has, after lengthened inquiry and careful consideration, been condemned by two select committees of the House of Commons and by two Royal Commissions appointed to inquire into the state of the corporation of the City of London. On the last occasion, in the year 1854, the commissioners, the Right Hon. H. Labouchere (now Lord Taunton), the late Sir George C. Lewis, and Mr. Justice Patteson, in their report to the Queen, thus expressed their deliberate opinion with regard to the police:
>
> *"We believe that the incorporation of the City with the larger districts by which it is surrounded is a measure recommended alike by consideration*

---

515   2nd and 3rd Vict. Cap. 94, sec.24.

of efficiency and economy.'"[516]

Some two-and-a-half months after it had been written it was released to the newspapers;[517] by whom it is not known. Was it Mayne or was it the Home Office, once again engaged in causing mischief? In any event, in an editorial the following day the *Morning Post* pointed out that the Corporation of the City of London had 'considered it beneath their dignity to accept proffered aid of the Metropolitan Police and in consequence the safety of the Heir Apparent to the Throne and his affianced bride were really jeopardised, and several lives were, on the night of the illuminations, actually lost.' Thus, the editorial suggested, it had been 'abundantly demonstrated' that the City Police were 'unequal to the preservation of order within their proper precincts whenever large multitudes' congregated. Supporting the proposed amalgamation, the editorial claimed, 'the public have a right to demand that such measures will be taken as may prevent a repetition in the City of London of the scenes of the 7th and 10th March 1863.'[518]

The City Press took a different view. Claiming that Sir Richard Mayne was 'the jackal to the lion of the Home Office', it suggested that he 'avowedly hungered to be the Caesar of the Blue Brigade' and looked 'on the independence of the City with envious jealousy'. Pointing out that no-one could question Sir Richard's experience on police matters, his statements on the relative ineffectiveness of the City of London Police under certain circumstances should not be accepted for 'the simple reason' he was 'partisan', and 'too much bent on seeking undivided power to be capable of impartiality.'[519]

The idea was temporarily dropped, at least for the remainder of Sir Richard Mayne's life, and, indeed, the City of London Police remain responsible for policing just over one square mile in the centre of the much larger Metropolitan Police District to this day.

---

516   TNA MEPO 3/39.
517   See the *Morning Post* 14 August 1863, p.4.
518   *Morning Post*, 15 August 1863, p.4.
519   *The City Press*, 22 August 1863, p.4.

CHAPTER NINE

EXTERNAL PROBLEMS II: THE MAGISTRATES AND THE POLICE OFFICES

If Peel's exclusion of the City of London from his policing bill gave them operational problems, the exclusion of the various bodies of police then in existence gave the Commissioners both administrative and operational difficulties. Under the Middlesex Justices Act 1792, seven Police Offices,[520] each run by three justices of the peace, had been set up along the lines of Bow Street, which had been in existence since 1714. Six men, later increased to twelve, were appointed to act as constables at each office, and given the power to arrest those persons who had committed crime. The justices also issued arrest warrants and search warrants as necessary for their constables to act upon. The constables brought those arrested before the justices of their respective Police Offices, which acted as courts of summary jurisdiction. The justices also held pre-trial hearings if the crime was one which could only be dealt with by a higher court, such as the Old Bailey or the Middlesex Assizes.

Peel had deliberately allowed what would effectively be a dual system of policing to continue by carefully not trespassing 'on the responsibilities of the magistrates and the officers they deployed'. In fact, on the same day as his Metropolitan Police Act became law in June 1829, another Act emanating from the Home Office, Justices of the Peace, Metropolis Act,[521] was passed which extended the Police Offices Act, the successor to the Middlesex Justices Act 1792, and preserved the 'rights, status and privileges of the magistrates and Police Offices of the Metropolis' for a

---

520   Six north of the Thames – Queen's Square, Westminster, Great Marlborough Street, Hatton Garden, Shoreditch, Whitechapel and Shadwell – and one south of the river at Southwark.
521   10 Geo 4, cap 45.

further three years.[522]

The failure of Peel to anticipate how this dual system would operate caused Rowan and Mayne considerable discomfort for the first ten years. Seeing that the Metropolitan Police was not under their control, some magistrates were antagonistic towards officers appearing before them; and, in their desire to retain their own constables to investigate crimes brought to their notice, they confined the execution of search warrants to their own constables. Additionally, led by the Chief Magistrate Sir Richard Birnie at Bow Street, some magistrates sought to belittle the activities of Rowan and Mayne's Metropolitan Police.

The problem was first addressed in February 1831, when the Commissioners wrote to Samuel Phillipps, the Under Secretary of State at the Home Office, expressing their disquiet at Mr Rawlinson whilst sitting at Marylebone Court because he had expressed, in the strongest possible terms, his disapproval of the instructions given to the Metropolitan Police for their guidance in cases of assault.[523] The instructions were that a constable could not arrest an assailant unless he had witnessed the assault or there was physical evidence, e.g. blood could be seen emanating from the victim's injury. It is unclear to what precisely Rawlinson referred, but, on this occasion, the Home Secretary did send a circular to the magistrates at the Police Offices reminding them that:

> 'A constable is not authorized to arrest or assist in arresting, or take into custody, a person charged with an assault when the assault was not committed in the presence, or within the view of the Constable, but, if a person has been cut or wounded, and gives into custody, the party charged with having given the cut or wound, the Constable is authorized to take the party into his custody and keep him in safe custody until he can be brought before a Magistrate.'[524]

The circular had little effect. Six years later Rawlinson again made his feelings public, commenting, in open court, during a case where two constables had declined to arrest an alleged assailant, that it was 'an absurd regulation', claiming that 'a person could be half-murdered, and unless the police witnessed the outrage, the perpetrator had every facility to escape.'[525]

---

522 Roach, Lawrence (2004). 'The Origins and Impact of the Function of the Crime Investigation and Detection in the British Police Service: A thesis submitted in partial fulfilment of the requirements for the degree of Doctor of Philosophy of Loughborough University'. Loughborough: Loughborough University's Institutional Repository, p.41.
523 TNA MEPO 1/41, Letter 18227, dated 2 February 1831.
524 TNA MEPO 1/41, Folio 18449.
525 *Bell's Life in London and Sporting Chronicle*. 30 July 1837, p.1.

Mayne explained to the 1834 Committee why this regulation existed. When police officers first went on to the streets in 1829, they would arrest for assault on the allegations of another party. However, as a result, 'two actions were brought and some indictments preferred against police officers for doing so'. The Commissioners had therefore sought the opinion of the law officers of the Crown and, on their advice, had 'given orders to the police not to interfere in such cases, or take the parties into custody.'[526]

In May 1831 Mayne had cause to write again to Phillipps, this time on a different matter. Pointing out that when, on 23 April, several constables had been assaulted by a 'large body of sailors and others in Stepney', two people had been arrested at the time. However, when the officers from the Metropolitan Police applied for a warrant the next morning at Thames Police Office for the arrest of several others who had been involved, it was granted not to the officers who made the application but to one of the constables of the Thames Police Office. Mayne continued:

> 'The Commissioners have since learned that three of the leaders of the mob... are now on board His Majesty's Ship Donegal, lying at Chatham, but the Magistrates' Warrant against them remains unexecuted.
>
> The Commissioners have to express their opinion that under the circumstances of this case, it is desirable for the sake of public example, that the parties should be brought to justice.'[527]

Whether they were finally brought to justice is unknown.

On the death of Sir Richard Birnie in 1832, Rowan took the opportunity to write to Phillipps, pointing out that the Commissioners had been led to believe that the proper timing for suggesting any alterations in the arrangement between the Metropolitan Police and Police Offices would be when the situation of Chief Magistrate became vacant. In his letter, Rowan accused some of the magistrates of being less than cordial in their co-operation because of the failure of the Home Office to 'define the duties to be performed by the Police Magistrate and by the Commissioners respectively'.

He then pointed out some of the difficulties that had occurred:

- Metropolitan Police officers and officers of the magistrates had sometimes been working on the same case, without being aware of it. The resultant 'clashing of authority and jealousy' was 'prejudicial to the public service'.

---

526 PP 1834 [600]. Report from the Select Committee on the Police of the Metropolis; with minutes of evidence, appendix and index. Minutes of evidence,, p.29, q/a 451-453.
527 TNA MEPO 1/5, folio 6116. Letter from Richard Mayne to Phillipps, dated 6 May 1831.

- Magistrates would only grant search warrants to their own officers, not to Metropolitan Police officers. Thus, Metropolitan Police officers were tempted to act without the protection of a warrant because they knew if they applied to a magistrate, the case would be taken out of their hands.
- Officers dismissed from the Metropolitan Police were being employed by the Magistrates to act as constables in the police offices.

Rowan made a number of recommendations which included:

- The duties of the magistrates and their officers should be purely judicial whilst the Metropolitan Police should be purely executive.
- Metropolitan Police officers should be employed in the Police Offices of the magistrates.

He also took the opportunity to suggest that if some changes were not made to the law, it would 'not be possible for the Police to act with the same effect' as they had done to date. Amongst a long list, he identified assaults not committed in the presence of a constable; persons collecting in the streets at night; women of the town; drunken persons; regulations for carts, carriages and wagons when blocking or obstructing the streets and highways; public houses, beer shops, coffee-shops, oyster-shops and eating houses; and persons assembling in the vicinity of the Palace or the Houses of Parliament.[528]

Melbourne ignored Rowan's letter and instead, 'possibly being deliberately provocative',[529] replaced Sir Richard Birnie with Frederick Roe, who was promptly given a knighthood.[530]

The Commissioners had already crossed swords with Roe, and experienced Melbourne's duplicity the previous year. Under the leadership of Francis Place, Moderate Radicals, who believed reform could be achieved by peaceful means, had formed the National Political Union (NPU). In an effort to seize control of the NPU, the Ultras, who, in contrast, believed reform could only be achieved by revolutionary action, arranged to hold a mass meeting on 7 November 1831 at White Conduit House. The ultimate purpose of the meeting was to have a pitched battle with the police and it was alleged 'bludgeons and other weapons were …distributed'. But Rowan received such detailed information regarding the meeting, possibly from

---

528 TNA MEPO 1/44, folios 41-48. Letter from Rowan to S.M. Phillipps, dated 20 June 1832; see also PP 1834 (600): Report from the Select Committee on the Police of the Metropolis; with minutes of evidence, appendix and index, Appendix 12.
529 Cowley, Richard (2011). *A History of the British Police from its Earliest Beginnings to the Present Day*. Stroud, Gloucestershire: The History Press, p.30.
530 *London Gazette*, 7 September 1832, Issue 18974, p.2032.

the NPU, 'that he was able to take precautions by a disposal of his forces which prevented people assembling in strength or anywhere near the arranged meeting place.'[531]

Melbourne also knew about the meeting and, without informing either Rowan or Mayne, directed Roe and another magistrate from Great Marlborough Street Police Office to attend. Roe felt the two magistrates should be in charge of the police on such an occasion, claiming should there be a riot, they were answerable for all that might take place. Sending for the superintendent he asked for details of the police deployment, which the former politely refused to give. Roe claimed that the superintendent clearly did not understand that he should look to the magistrates for directions.[532]

The following day Rowan accidentally met Roe at the Home Office. In a letter to George Lamb, Under Secretary of State at the Home Office, Rowan described what had taken place. Roe, apparently,

> 'took occasion to cast reflections on the official conduct of the Commissioners by saying that it was the opinion of himself and a colleague, Mr. Laing, that the Commissioners had intentionally slighted them on the previous day when they were on duty at White Conduit House and that the whole of the official conduct of the Commissioners of Police was most extraordinary and unaccountable.'

Rowan felt this was an unjust censure and told Lamb so.[533] Two weeks later a letter from Phillipps told the Commissioners that 'Lord Melbourne has no doubt, but that on any future occasion, he will be able to make such arrangement that will prevent the recurrence of any similar inconvenience or misunderstanding.'[534]

At about the same time, Phillipps told Roe in a letter:

> 'Lord Melbourne has not, nor ever had any intention to place the Metropolitan Police Force in any respect, under the control or direction of the Magistrates of the Police Offices, Lord Melbourne being fully aware that by the constitution of the Metropolitan Police, all regulations for the general government, as well as for the particular services of the officers of the Police, are to be made by the Commissioners, subject to

---

531 Reith, Charles (1956). *A New Study of Police History*. Edinburgh: Oliver and Boyd, p.159.
532 Roe in evidence to the Select Committee. Select Committee on the Police of the Metropolis; with minutes of evidence, appendix and index, p.93, Q/A 1459-1461; see also TNA MEPO 2/5798 folio 1A.
533 TNA HO 2/5798, folio 2A. Rowan in a letter, 16 November 1831, to George Lamb.
534 Ibid, folio 6A. Phillipps, in a letter, 25 November 1831, to the Commissioners.

the approbation of the Secretary of State.'[535]

And there the matter ended – on this occasion. But, having been appointed chief magistrate, and with a Whig government in power for the next decade (except the five months from 14 November 1834 to 18 April 1835), 'Roe embarked on a long series of petty interferences with the work of the [Metropolitan Police] which the Commissioners… were obliged to suffer with patience.'[536] Any complaints the Commissioners made to the Home Office about Roe and his fellow magistrates, and the constables attached to the various Police Offices, were passed immediately to Roe without comment from the Home Secretary. It was, perhaps, unfortunate that Mayne, whose personality was more rigid and potentially abrasive than that of Rowan, rapidly crossed swords with Phillipps at the beginning of this period. He apparently 'disliked Phillipps on sight', and 'Phillipps returned the feeling'. This 'personality clash …left an undercurrent of friction' between Mayne, in particular, and the Home Office civil servants.[537] However Rowan, in his usual impeccable way, relied on 'civility and moderation.' The two men 'refused to be distracted by overt acts of hostility and worked patiently towards their goal of building a police force, which by its conduct, would eventually achieve the ultimate accolade of public regard and acceptance.'[538] This would be ultimately tested to the full over an incident in 1834 which resulted in a superintendent and an inspector being dismissed from the force on the instructions of the Home Secretary.

In January 1833 Rowan wrote to Phillipps, suggesting it should be put to Lord Melbourne that when the King conducted his official duties at any place where the attendance of the Metropolitan Police was required, one of the Commissioners should be in attendance on his Majesty. Rowan concluded,

> 'It would be very satisfactory to the Commissioners if they are to look upon this as an established regulation – that they should have an official position which would be recognised by the Royal Household.'

Phillipps' reply reflected Melbourne's antagonism towards the Commissioners in favour of Roe. He pointed out that Sir Frederick Roe was 'in attendance when the King leaves the Palace and when he alights

---

535   Ibid, folio 9B. Phillipps in a letter, 30 November 1831, to Roe.
536   Reith, op. cit. 531, p.172.
537   Fido, Martin, and Keith Skinner (1999). *The Official Encyclopedia of Scotland Yard*. London: Virgin Books, p.11.
538   Ascoli, David (1979). *The Queen's Peace: The origins and development of the Metropolitan Police 1829-1995*. London: Hamish Hamilton, p.95.

from his carriage', stating 'Lord Melbourne does not desire, or intend either of the Commissioners to be in attendance on the King or out on the streets' and that a superintendent should be in charge of any Metropolitan Police officers in attendance.

Perhaps the worst example of Roe's antagonism towards the commissioners came ten days after Duncannon – possibly, with the exception of Walpole, the least effective Home Secretary of the 19th century – took over from Melbourne in 1834 on the latter's elevation to Prime Minister. Out of the blue, the Commissioners received a letter from Phillipps:

> 'Viscount Duncannon, having received information that a charge was lately made against Inspector Wovenden by the Superintendent of the 'D' Division for his conduct towards a female at night in one of the Station Houses, directs me to request the Commissioners to transmit for his Lordship's information a report of the charge, and all that has taken place thereupon.'[539]

The reason for the letter was an allegation by Ruth Morris, a notorious prostitute, that she had been raped by Inspector Wovenden in a cell whilst detained at Marylebone Station House. She had been arrested on 19 June for being drunk and disorderly, indecent behaviour, and refusing to pay a cab fare. Too drunk to answer questions, she had been placed in a cell for the night and brought up before the officer-in-charge of D Division, Superintendent Lazenby, in the morning. After being charged, she alleged to Lazenby that she had been raped in the cell by an inspector and identified the early turn Inspector William Wiggins as the perpetrator. When Wiggins pointed out that he had only just come on duty, she then accused Inspector Squire Wovenden. However, it was clear to Lazenby that her allegation as to what had happened was physically impossible and, after Morris had been taken to court, he went personally to Whitehall Place to report the allegation to the Commissioners. They instructed Lazenby to charge Wovenden and take him before the magistrate.

The committal proceedings before Roe at Bow Street Magistrates' Court took place on 24 August, at the end of which Inspector Wovenden was committed to Newgate Prison to await trial. However, in concluding the proceedings, Roe launched a scathing attack on the Metropolitan Police. He accused Lazenby of not immediately bringing Wovenden before the magistrates, but instead of merely reporting the matter to the Commissioners.

An investigation having been ordered by Lord Duncannon, Roe said:

---

539   Letter from Samuel Phillipps, dated 30 July 1834, quoted in Reith, op. cit. 531, p.172.

'I found the greatest difficulties thrown in my way by those who should be the first to afford me every assistance. Instead of the police constables evincing an anxiety to expose the truth, I met nothing from them but prevarication upon prevarication, contradiction upon contradiction, and falsehood upon falsehood, in short, the whole tenor of their evidence from first to last was a tissue of prevarication and the most degrading, disgraceful contradictions …I can only say that having been a magistrate for nearly thirteen years I never in the course of my experience during that time found in any set of witnesses conduct so likely to impede and subvert the ends of justice as that which I experienced in my attempt to investigate this case, and I feel I should be wrong if I did not say so.'[540]

Wovenden appeared before a Grand Jury at Middlesex Sessions three days later where the charge of aggravated assault by Morris was thrown out.[541] In September it was announced that Wovenden had been discharged at the Old Bailey by order of the Middlesex Magistrates.[542] Following Wovenden's discharge the Commissioners held an internal inquiry, which found that Lazenby and Wovenden were innocent of any wrongdoing, and forwarded to the Home Office a bundle of documents which supported this assertion. Without commenting on the documents, Duncannon's reply was short and succinct. Both Lazenby and Wovenden were to be dismissed from the service.[543]

Duncannon was no doubt hoping that the Commissioners would resign and 'their successors, whoever they might be, would be appointed with infinitely less than even the vague and undefined degree of authority which had been conferred on them by Peel, and that police administration would become largely the joint function of magistrates and the Home Office.' The effects of such a course on later history are difficult to imagine.

Duncannon's intransigence left the Commissioners in a dilemma. Loyalty to Lazenby and Wovenden, neither of whom had done anything wrong, and the need to support them may seem to have required their resignation. But they also had a loyalty to all the other officers whom they had recruited and trained, and on whom the withdrawal of their leadership 'would have inflicted even worse disaster than had befallen the two victims of Duncannon's despotism.'[544]

540 *The Times*, 25 August 1834.
541 *Morning Post*, 28 August 1834, p.4.
542 *Morning Advertiser*, 11 September 1834.
543 Reith, op. cit. 531, p.177.
544 Ibid, p.178.

The Commissioners' response to Duncannon's letter, which Rowan signed but which, no doubt, was composed together, was a masterful example of tact and diplomacy. It commenced by saying the two officers had been dismissed in accordance with his instructions. After pointing out, in a 'clear vindication of Lazenby, that, at the time, there was no order which required him to immediately take an officer accused of a crime before the magistrates', the letter concluded:

> 'The Commissioners are compelled to feel, which they do with the deepest regret, by the mode in which the late proceedings in Mr Wovenden's case were originated, and have been carried on, that they have failed to obtain the confidence of the Secretary of State in their management of the Police Force. They are fully sensible how greatly the anxieties of their positions are thereby increased; and they cannot but feel that, after the experience they have had, it would be a dereliction of their duty were they to abstain from declaring to Viscount Duncannon, most respectfully, but most earnestly, their opinion that, if their authority over the numerous body of the police entrusted to their immediate charge should in any degree be impaired, or the respect for the Commissioners, so necessary for maintaining the organization of the police be at all shaken, it will become extremely difficult, if not impossible, for them to carry on the service with credit to themselves or advantage to the public.'[545]

Duncannon's response, in a letter to the Commissioners signed by Phillipps, said:

> 'On that part of your letter in which you have made a reflection or insinuation – which Viscount Duncannon thinks it became you not to make – upon the mode in which the proceedings in the case of Inspector Wovenden were originated and carried on, his Lordship directs me to observe to you that these proceedings were according to the ordinary and regular course, and that this was the only course which could be properly adopted in such a case.
>
> Viscount Duncannon cannot think there is the least reason for assuming that the decision or proceedings in this case can in any degree impair the authority of the Commissioners. On the contrary, Viscount Duncannon believes that they will have a good effect upon the discipline of the police, and tend to the public good.'[546]

---

545 Letter to Phillipps, dated 6 November 1834, quoted in Reith, op. cit. 531, p.179.
546 Letter from Phillipps, quoted in Reith, op. cit. 531, p.179.

Roe's apparent popularity with the Whig administration was further evidenced when, in February 1836, he was made a Baronet of the United Kingdom, following which he was referred to as Sir Frederick Arthur Roe of Brundish in the county of Suffolk.[547]

Meanwhile the Commissioners, in their evidence to the Select Committee set up in 1833 'to inquire into the state of the Police of the Metropolis within the Metropolitan District', had told the Committee about the conflict that existed between officers of the Metropolitan Police and officers of the Police Offices.[548] During the concluding meeting of the Committee, in answer to a question as to whether there should be any alterations, Mayne replied:

> 'The officers belonging to the magistrates' offices [should] be discontinued, and the duties there done by some of the Metropolitan Police, to be attached to the offices for that purpose.'[549]

This followed the recommendations made by Rowan in his letter to the Secretary of State, dated 21 June 1832.[550]

Roe pre-empted his evidence to the Committee by making what was clearly an implied criticism of Peel and the previous Tory government, by complaining that 'no communication' had been made to him, nor, as far as he was aware, any other magistrate about 'the regulations and organisation of the Metropolitan Police Force', so, in giving his reasons, he was offering an opinion. Roe disagreed with a suggestion that officers from the Metropolitan Police should be attached to Police Offices.[551] Referring to them as a corps, when asked for his reasons, he said that the 'system of subordination' was based on 'military discipline' in that

> 'the private is subject to the control of the sergeant, the sergeant to that of the inspector, and the inspector to that of the superintendent, so completely that they form together a body regulated and governed in the strictest way, one of the results of which is that everything that occurs to any individual of that force, in his character of constable, is reported to the chiefs, that they look to them, and to them exclusively, for orders and directions; that it has been a principle laid down, that they should consider the magistrate simply as a person having judicial authority, but to whom they are not to look in any other way

---

547   *London Gazette*, 23 February 1836, Issue 19359, p.358.
548   PP 1834 [600]: Report from the Select Committee on the Police of the Metropolis; with minutes of evidence, appendix and index, Minutes of Evidence, p.14/15, q/a 239-249.
549   Ibid, p.385, q/a 6183.
550   TNA MEPO 1/44, folios 41-48. Letter from Rowan, 20 June 1832, to Phillipps.
551   PP 1834 [600], op. cit. 526, pp.88-89, q/a 1425-1426.

whatever; that, excepting as far as deference and civility go, which I must say I have experienced in the fullest degree, the corps at large consider themselves as being in no way subject to the authority of the magistrates.'[552]

He claimed that the Metropolitan Police had been jealous of the officers employed by the courts from the beginning, accusing Superintendents in the Metropolitan Police of having 'great powers' and accused them of not informing the Commissioners of the true number that were discharged by them from Station Houses without being charged.[553] He claimed the skill of officers attached to the Police Offices was 'superior to all the skill of the Metropolitan Police officers.' He went further, suggesting that they would never acquire the same skills as his officers because the 'probability of success' was unlikely due to the 'rigid discipline' insisted on by the Commissioners.[554]

When asked whether 'the authority of the superintendent' might 'clash with that of the magistrate' if constables from the Metropolitan Police were attached to Police Offices', Roe replied:

'the serjeant, inspector and superintendent, all exercise the most extraordinary powers …the men would more fear the superintendent and inspector than he would even the magistrate …who must write to the Commissioners if he is dissatisfied, and desire another to be put in his place. It seems to me utterly contrary to the original and constitutional intercourse between magistrate and constable, to suppose that a man to execute my orders should be under the control of, and subordinate to, so many different persons, and least of all to the magistrate.'[555]

Roe was gracious enough on this occasion to tell the Committee that due to 'the general conduct and efficiency of the [Metropolitan] Police', the streets were 'in very good order, that they conduct themselves very well, that they are a useful body of men, and I find them personally particularly anxious to please the magistrates.'[556] But that was before the Lazenby/Wovenden case had come before him.

Despite strenuous objections by Roe and other magistrates, the Committee recommended that the constables 'allotted to the several Police

---

552   Ibid, p.91, q/a. 1439.
553   Ibid, pp.90-93, q/a 1443 and 1454-1458.
554   Ibid, pp.102-104, q/a 1538-1539.
555   Ibid, p.91, q/a 1439.
556   Ibid, p.105, q/a 1555.

External Problems II: The Magistrates and the Police Office

Offices' should be incorporated with as little delay as possible within the Metropolitan Police, so that although under the direct and immediate control of the Police Magistrates for all the business of their respective offices, and immediately responsible to them for its due performance, they may, as to pay, clothing and general discipline, be subject to the regulations and ultimate control by which the general body is governed.'[557] The Whig government failed to act on the recommendation.

William IV died on 20 June 1837. By this time, Lord John Russell was the Home Secretary. Arrangements were made for the public to pay homage to the deceased monarch on 7 July. On 4 July, Rowan was alone at Whitehall Place when, at 7.00pm, he received two letters. The first was from Samuel Phillipps, and read:

> 'Application having been made by the Board of Green Cloth[558] for the assistance of the Police during the Ceremonial of the Lying in State and Funeral of His Late Majesty, I am directed by Lord John Russell to desire that you will give the necessary orders for the attendance of one hundred of the Metropolitan Police at Windsor Castle on Friday and Saturday next.
>
> Lord John Russell thinks it will be desirable that the whole of the men should be at Windsor on Thursday night and requests you will direct the superior officers whom you select for the duty to communicate with the Chief Magistrate who will be at Windsor on Thursday night, and to receive his instructions, in conjunction with those of the Lord Steward of the Household, as to the precise nature of the duties they will be required to perform.'[559]

The second was from Roe himself, and was addressed to Rowan by name:

> 'I find Lord John Russell has received the usual application for Police at Windsor Castle, and that Mr. Phillipps has written to request you to send 100 men. This is about the number which Capes, the resident [Bow Street] officer at the Castle thought would be required when I was at Windsor on Saturday to meet Sir F. Watson.[560] I afterwards went over the ground and am satisfied that we shall do very well.

---

557   Ibid, Report, p.17.
558   A board of officials belonging to the Royal Household, chaired by the Lord Steward, on this occasion the Duke of Argyll; it took its name from the green baize that covered the table around which they met.
559   Reith, op. cit. 531, p.191.
560   Sir Frederick Watson was the Master of Her Majesty's Household and a member of the Board of Green Cloth.

Would you have the goodness to let the superior officer get down by 4 o'clock Thursday, as he will naturally act with my directions. I could go over all the ground with him on that afternoon. The difficulty will I am afraid be in getting lodgings for your men …perhaps you will allow me to suggest sending somebody tonight to see what arrangement can be made for their accommodation.'[561]

Clearly annoyed by these two letters, Rowan immediately despatched a letter to Mayne, who was at home:

My dear Mayne,

It is after 7 o'clock. I have only time to say that I have this instant received a letter from Phillipps, official, desiring one hundred men to go to Windsor, and take instructions from Sir F.R. the Chief Magistrate.

I have an unofficial letter from Sir F. at the same time to the same effect.

This has made me quite sick at heart seeing what it must lead to.

I shall be afraid to write without your concurrence and I therefore fear you must come up early in the morning.

Yours in great haste,

C.R.[562]

The following day the two Commissioners composed a lengthy letter, addressed to Phillipps. After saying that 'the necessary orders' would be given 'for the attendance of one hundred Metropolitan Police at Windsor' they pointed out, for the benefit of Lord John Russell, that this would be 'the first occasion since the establishment of the Metropolitan Police', that the Commissioners had been directed 'to place a party' of their officers 'under the orders of the Chief Magistrate, or any of the Police Magistrates.'

The letter then pointed out that such an arrangement 'would break down the immediate link of direct communication between the Commissioners and all ranks of the Police' which was 'necessary…when engaged in any particular service'. They proposed that one of them should go to Windsor to act as a magistrate 'as may be necessary for the direction of the Police there, and thus secure the efficient performance of their duties, under the direction of their own known and responsible heads.' A reply was received the same day to the effect that the Metropolitan Police would 'act under the orders of their own officers, who will receive the necessary instructions

---

561   Reith, op. cit. 531, p.192.
562   Ibid.

External Problems II: The Magistrates and the Police Office

from the Lord Steward[563] instead of the Chief Magistrate.'

Mayne immediately went to Windsor but 'found endless difficulties', because although the Home Office had informed Roe it had informed no-one else of the change of instructions.[564] Meanwhile, Rowan wrote to Roe to inform him that he had sent an inspector to acquire quarters for the men before writing:

> 'In what I am now going to say I feel assured you will allow me to deal frankly with you, and that you will not for a moment imagine there can be anything intended personal to yourself, but we feel called upon, with respect to our own position, to make representation to the Secretary of State as to former decisions, that our men were to be solely under our orders and directions, subject to the approbation of the Secretary of State, and to ask permission officially for one of ourselves to attend on the occasion to obviate the difficulty. Personally, I believe that none of us much covet the job, but you know too much of the world not to be aware that we all like to maintain our privileges.'[565]

He received the following reply from Roe, addressed to 'My Dear Rowan':

> 'I assure you I am quite satisfied that in the course you adopt there is nothing personal to myself and, tho' I hope I should be as considerate in the directions I gave to your men as the magistrates under whom they are placed either at Epsom or Egham,[566] or when they are sent into distant counties, I can in no way find fault with you for taking the course you do.'[567]

The final success 'in dealing with an unscrupulous and inveterate enemy' rested with Rowan, and it was the last occasion that he and Roe actually did battle.

But it was not quite over. In 1837 another Select Committee was appointed, this time 'to inquire into Metropolitan Police Offices with a view to the further Improvement of the same'. The first witness was Phillipps, the Under Secretary of State at the Home Office, who spent two days before the Committee. He was first asked whether the recommendations made by the 1834 Committee had been implemented. He responded by

---

563 The Lord Steward was generally a member of the aristocracy belonging to the governing party; see op. cit. 40.
564 Reith, op. cit. 531, pp.192-194.
565 Ibid, p.194.
566 Reference to Epsom or Egham was Roe's way of reminding the Commissioners that when Metropolitan Police officers were sent to do duty outside the metropolis, they cease to come under the Commissioners' control but took their orders from local magistrates.
567 Reith, op. cit. 531, p.194.

saying that 'the Bow Street mounted horse patrol' had 'been transferred to the Commissioners', but none of the other recommended mergers had occurred.[568] He attempted to undermine the Commissioners, by arguing against the river police being brought under their control on the grounds that the business of the Thames Office water police' was 'of a peculiar and difficult nature'. He added that he thought 'the Thames Police magistrates would be able to decide much better than the Commissioners in Whitehall' as to 'the duties of the river police officers, and how they ought to act on particular occasions.'[569] When he was reminded that one of the Commissioners was a barrister, Phillipps claimed that he would be unable to interpret the particular Acts of Parliament relative to the river, as well as the magistrate at the Thames Office.[570] He then claimed that 'no inconvenience whatsoever' was 'experienced from the river police being separated from the land police, and that if both these services of the river and land were in the Commissioners hands, the public would not derive benefit or convenience from the alteration.'[571]

Insofar as the current arrangement whereby magistrates in Police Offices employed their own constables, Phillipps told the Committee he did not believe the posting of Metropolitan Police Officers to the Police Offices would remedy the inconvenience complained of in Rowan's letter.[572] When asked whether there was any practical objection to implementing the recommendation by the 1834 Committee, Phillipps responded, 'I think it will fail.'[573] However, no doubt to the delight of Rowan and Mayne, when William Ballantine, the senior magistrate at the Thames Police Office was asked whether there would be any practical difficulties or principle standing in the way of the Commissioners taking over the river police, he replied, 'There is no objection be it on the score of principle, and I think it is quite practicable.'[574]

Once again, in his evidence, Roe attempted to belittle the Metropolitan Police. He made it clear that he did not have a very high opinion of the ability of superintendents and inspectors in presenting cases at court. When asked whether they might receive advice from Mayne, being a barrister, he replied, 'I do not think that unless the head of executive police was in the

---

568   PP 1837 [451] Report from the Select Committee on Police Offices, with minutes of evidence, appendix and index, Minutes of Evidence, p.1, q/a. 4-5.
569   Ibid, p.2, q/a 11.
570   Ibid, p.2, q/a 14.
571   Ibid, p.3, q/a 19.
572   Ibid, p.5, q/a 44.
573   Ibid, p.8, q/a 57.
574   Ibid, p.94, q/a 906.

habit of acting as a magistrate, that he would ever be competent.'[575]

But time was running out for Roe. Supported by three other magistrates – Hardwick, Murray and Broughton – he continued to object to any 'union of the Office Constables with the Metropolitan Police', but two other magistrates – Traill and Codd – broke ranks to side with the Commissioners.[576] The thrust of the evidence provided by Rowan and Mayne was again that there were good reasons, including one of financial savings, for the consolidation of the various police forces in the metropolis, including the City and the river.[577] With particular reference to the Police Offices, the Commissioners again told a Select Committee they saw no practical difficulties if all the police constables came under their jurisdiction rather than the magistrates and discussed the role of police inspectors being the prosecutors, although they suggested there would be an advantage in having public prosecutors.[578]

On 11 July 1838 the long-awaited report was published. It made thirteen recommendations, the majority of which related to the qualification and duties of magistrates or changes in the law. But two were particularly relevant to the Metropolitan Police. Firstly, the Committee recommended the consolidation of 'the several Constabulary Forces of the Metropolis, including those of the City of London and the River Thames, under one authority, responsible to the Secretary of State.'[579] Secondly, the Committee reported that it could 'not see any reason to doubt, that out of the body of 3,000 and upwards of constables of the Metropolitan Police, a sufficient number [could] be found who are fully equal to the performance of all the duties which can be required of them by the Magistrates'. As a consequence, the Committee recommended that Police Magistrates should only be concerned with duties of a judicial nature, whilst the Metropolitan Police Force should take responsibility for duties of an executive nature.[580]

Three pieces of legislation that followed the 1837 Select Committee's report must have given Rowan and Mayne great satisfaction. The two, the Metropolitan Police Courts Acts of 1839 and 1840, renamed Police Offices, Police Courts, and stipulated that magistrates could no longer recruit their own constables; thus, for administrative purposes all constables

---

575 PP 1837 [451] Report from the Select Committee on Police Offices, with minutes of evidence, appendix and index, Minutes of Evidence, pp.112-113, q/a 1158-1164 and 1167.
576 For Trail, Ibid, pp.31-33, q/a 336-349; for Codd, PP 1837-1838 [578]. Report from the Select Committee on Police Offices, with minutes of evidence, appendix and index, Minutes of Evidence, pp.9-11, q/a 78-97.
577 PP 1837-1838 [578], op. cit. 576, Minutes of Evidence, pp.80-82, q/a 842-857.
578 Ibid, pp.82-84, q/a 858-873.
579 Ibid, Report, Recommendation 1 on p.12.
580 Ibid, Recommendation 2 on p.14.

employed at the new Police Courts would come under the jurisdiction of the Commissioners.[581] Also, the Metropolitan Police Act 1839 did make the Commissioners responsible for policing that part of the River Thames which flowed through the Metropolitan Police District,[582] and the River Police became Thames Division of the Metropolitan Police. The Act also gave the Commissioners power to administer an oath to constables of the Metropolitan Police to execute the office of constable within the Royal Palaces of Her Majesty,[583] effectively making the Commissioners responsible for policing the royal residences as well.

The Metropolitan Police Act also effectively brought an end to a source of criticism of some of the magistrates in that constables could take into custody, without warrant, any person charged by another person with committing any aggravated assault providing the constable had good reason to believe the assault had taken place. Under section 65, he no longer had to be present. The Commissioners, Rowan in particular, must have been even more pleased when, finally accepting defeat, Sir Frederick Roe of Brandish in the County of Suffolk resigned as Chief Magistrate at Bow Street.[584]

So, by constantly bringing to the attention of the government, through letters to the Home Office and evidence given to a number of Committees, the anomalies that existed following the setting up of the Metropolitan Police had been rectified. All policing in the metropolis was now under the control of the Commissioners.

---

581 2 & 3, Vict, c.72 and 3 & 4, Vict, c.84.
582 2 & 3, Vict, c.47, section 5.
583 Ibid, section 7.
584 *Morning Post*, 4 September 1839, p.4.

CHAPTER TEN

INTERNAL PROBLEMS I: RECRUITING, DISCIPLINE AND HANDLING COMPLAINTS

The two Commissioners had no problems in recruiting men to fill the initial establishment, despite Peel's insistence that 'all nominations for employment in the Police ...should depend exclusively upon the Character, Qualifications and Services of the Person selected.'[585] But patronage was rife and right from the start they were inundated with letters, many from nobility, even royalty, some from future Home Secretaries, recommending people for employment in the Metropolitan Police – frequently referred in the newspapers during the first year or so, as the New Police – and sometimes for promotion. There is room here for but a small example from the many recommendations received.

As early as December 1829, a letter was received from future Home Secretary Lord Melbourne recommending that Constable John Kinhan be promoted to sergeant. In their customary, polite way, the Commissioners acknowledged receipt of the letter and, after presenting 'their compliments to Lord Melbourne' informed him they would 'be glad to attend to his Lordship's wishes' if it appeared 'that the man is deserving of promotion.'[586] On another occasion, in May 1831, future Home Secretary Lord Duncannon recommended to Melbourne, by then Home Secretary, that John Walsh be employed as a constable to which the Commissioners must have had some delight in responding to the effect that Walsh 'had previously been in the Police Force and had been dismissed for misconduct.' The Commissioners concluded the letter by suggesting that Walsh had 'endeavoured to smuggle himself back into the Police Force without revealing these facts.'[587]

---

585   TNA MEPO 2/38.
586   TNA MEPO 1/1, folio 321
587   Ibid, folio 428.

Many of the recommendations came to Rowan personally from his friend, the Duke of Richmond. But this curried no favour, even shortly before he retired. On the Duke's recommendation, a Robert Wilson joined the Metropolitan Police on 27 August 1849. However, he did not last long. Shortly before he retired, Rowan wrote to the Duke on 8 December to say that Wilson had been found absent from his beat for 25 minutes and found in a beer shop on 10 October, for which he was cautioned and fined 2s 6d. Sixteen days later he was found to be drunk on duty, as a result of which he was dismissed the service and fined 5s.[588]

In December 1829, when contemplating the additional divisions to the original six, thereby anticipating the increase in the size of the Metropolitan Police from approximately 1,000 men to 3,000 men, Peel reinforced his views upon the selection being dependent on the individual's 'Character, Qualification, and Services' in a letter to the Commissioners informing them that he was satisfied they were following his wishes.

He added:

'When the whole Establishment shall be completed, and in full operation, it will be deserving of serious consideration whether it may not be fit to establish as a fixed and invariable rule, that all appointments to situations above that of the common constable shall take place from the Ranks of the Police.'[589]

Therefore, when in April 1831 Rowan received a request from the Duke of Richmond asking whether an Inspector Hartley could be considered for promotion to superintendent, Rowan responded 'I fear he does not stand [as] one of the foremost on the list and I feel quite certain you would not desire me to recommend him if we have men we think would do the thing better.'[590]

In April 1835 the Duke of Richmond forwarded the names of two candidates for the Metropolitan Police which had been given to him by a fellow-member of the House of Lords. Rowan refused to accept either of them, writing to the Duke, 'I find they have both been dismissed from their situations in the Post Office for being intoxicated when on duty.'[591]

---

588 The Goodwood Estate Archives. Family Papers. Charles Lennox (afterwards Gordon Lennox) 5th Duke of Richmond, Lennox, and Aubigny. Contains letters written by Charles Rowan and Richard Mayne to the Duke. Held at the West Sussex Record Office, vol. 1727, folios 1585-1586.
589 TNA MEPO 2.38. Letter from Peel to the Commissioners, dated 10 December 1829.
590 Goodwood Family Papers, op. cit. 588, vol. 1448, folio N158. Letter from Rowan to the Duke of Richmond, dated 16 April 1831.
591 Goodwood Family Papers, op. cit. 588, vol. 1572, folio 330. Letter from Rowan to the Duke of Richmond, dated 17 April 1835.

Internal Problems I: Recruiting, Discipline and Handling Complaints

By 1838 the Home Secretary was pointing out the rules under which the Commissioners recommended people for promotion. In February 1838 Lord John Russell received a recommendation from Count de Ludolf, the representative of the Kingdom of the Two Sicilies in London, recommending that Police Sergeant Henry Thompson should be promoted. The request was forwarded to Rowan by Phillipps, together with the reply that had been sent to Count de Ludolf:

> 'Lord J. Russell begs to inform Count de Ludolf that He would have had great pleasure in entertaining his application. But having laid down an invariable rule to make promotions in the Met. Pol. only on the recommendation by the Commrs of those men they consider most meritorious Lord John Russell has transmitted Count de Ludolf's letter for their consideration.'[592]

So, whilst recruitment was not a problem, retaining those who had already been recruited was. Regular drinking, particularly of beer, punctuated the working day in eighteenth and nineteenth-century Britain. Indeed, excessive drinking in early Victorian London was a serious social problem. Whilst many of the early recruits followed what was regarded as common practice, some sought Dutch courage by drinking to face the rigours of the beat,[593] and, 'within two years of being established', over half 'had been sacked for drink-related offences and absenteeism'.[594] For instance, between 29 September 1829 and 31 December 1830, 1,586 constables were dismissed and 736 had resigned. In 1831, 814 were dismissed and 574 had resigned.

However, by 1832 the tide had begun to turn. There were only 403 dismissals compared with 516 resignations.[595] Not surprising, perhaps, given that Rowan had experienced huge problems with drunkenness whilst in the army, the Commissioners adopted a 'zero-tolerance' approach to drink-related offences, such as drinking on duty or coming on duty drunk. This zero-tolerance approach to drink continued right until Mayne's death in 1868. Cavanagh described how he had issued an order one December in the 1860s to the effect that any officer 'reported for drunkenness at Christmas-time would be dismissed.' Apparently, about 60 men appeared

---

592 TNA HO 65/12, folio 402. 5 February 1838.
593 Howard, George (1953). *Guardians of the Queen's Peace: The Development and Work of Britain's Police*. London: Odham's Press, pp.135-136.
594 Mason, Gary (2004). *The Official History of the Metropolitan Police*. London: Carlton Books, p.13.
595 PP 1834 [600]. Report from the Select Committee on the Police of the Metropolis; with minutes of evidence, appendix and index. Minutes of evidence, p 7, q/a 106.

before him on Boxing Day charged with the offence of drunkenness and he dismissed them all from the force, despite some having served for over twenty years.[596]

The reasons for officers resigning were varied. The Commissioners did their upmost 'to ensure that their men behaved on their beats as instructed'. They 'set strict regulations for the manner in which constables were required to perform their duties', and these were rigidly enforced. They 'were required to patrol their beats at a measured steady pace, set initially at three miles an hour' but 'later reduced to two-and-a-half'. They 'were forbidden to talk to each other or gossip with members of the public.' They 'were not allowed to drink, or even enter a pub, while on duty.'[597] Officers were not allowed to receive gratuities without the sanction of the Commissioners.[598]

The Commissioners could dismiss those who failed to conform to the operational procedures laid down by them from the very beginning rarely showed leniency if police officers broke the regulations, 'as they sought to crack down on behaviour that might damage the good image and reputation of the police.'[599] For minor breaches of discipline the transgressor could choose between a fine[600] and dismissal.

But the consequence of this was that many people outside the force looked upon the discipline used to enforce the regulations as being too militaristic. Many of the early recruits 'had difficulty adjusting to something that was so alien to the practices of most early-nineteenth century civilian labour,'[601] and realised the work was not for them. They could not come to terms with the discipline and resigned; others loathed the work and the violence associated with it. Police officers were frequently attacked and 'many of the less-courageous men', appalled by the violence associated with the job, also left.[602]

In dealing with complaints and discipline, the two Commissioners worked as a team. In the main, Rowan dealt with 'the "gentlemen's

---

596 Cavanagh, Timothy (1893). *Scotland Yard, Past and Present: Experiences of thirty-seven years.* London: Chatto & Windus kindle edition from www.amazon.com, loc. 686.
597 Emsley, Clive (2009). *The Great British Bobby: A History of British Policing from the 18th Century to the Present.* London: Quercus, p.42-43.
598 PP 1834 [600]. Report from the Select Committee on the Police of the Metropolis; with minutes of evidence, appendix and index, minutes of evidence, pp.6-8, q/a 72-107.
599 Emsley, op, cit. 597, p.44.
600 Fines for misconduct were put into a fund from which the Commissioners distributed small sums amongst the men for general good conduct. PP 1834 [600]. Report from the Select Committee on the Police of the Metropolis; with minutes of evidence, appendix and index, minutes of evidence, pp.6-8, q/a 72-107.
601 Emsley, op. cit. 597, pp.42-43.
602 Howard, op. cit. 593, p.135.

complaints," those off-the-record awkward situations best dealt with by tact and courtesy', and those occasions when complaints were made against inspectors, certainly in the early days.[603]

Typical of the complaints dealt with by Rowan was one made by the Liberal Member of Parliament for Coventry, Henry Bulwer, in June 1834. He complained to the Home Secretary that when he approached parliament in the company of Colonel George Williams, the Liberal member for Ashton-under-Lyne, his horse was checked violently by two constables, despite the fact they knew him to be a member of parliament. Subsequently, when on foot, the same two officers had been 'very abrupt and rude' in their behaviour. Efforts by the commissioners to trace the two officers failed, but Rowan was quick to point out in a letter to Lord Viscount Howick, the eldest son of the then-Prime Minister Lord Grey, and briefly Under-Secretary of State for the Home Office, that

> 'if strict attention had not been paid on that day by the Police to stop all carriages going towards Westminster Abbey, to ascertain that they were not going to remain there, the approaches to the Parliament House and the thoroughfare through Westminster would have been altogether blocked up.'

He then went on to explain that

> 'the Police had at all times, but on that day particularly, received the strongest injunctions to keep the way clear for, and give every facility to the passage of Members of Parliament; that on many occasions some hundreds of the Police had been employed for that purpose, and that an increased number were always on duty to keep the way clear during the sitting of Parliament; and on the day in questions, besides those on duty in the streets, a Police Sergeant and five Constables were appointed expressly to keep the door of the House of Commons clear from obstruction.'[604]

Nevertheless, Rowan said, if it was likely that Bulwer could recognise them, he would arrange for all the officers on duty at the time to attend their office at any hour convenient to Bulwer. But there is no record of Bulwer taking up Rowan's offer.

---

603 Keller, Lisa (2010). *Triumph of Order: Democracy and Public Space*. Columbia: Columbia University Press, p.71; see also TNA MEPO 1/45: 1836.
604 PP 1834 [434]. Metropolitan Police. Correspondence relative to the conduct of the Metropolitan Police on Tuesday, 24 June 1834. Letter from Rowan to Lord Viscount Howick, dated 30 June 1834.

Sometimes, letters of complaint came direct to the Commissioners. For instance, three years earlier, in June 1831, a Mr Davies Baker made a complaint about the conduct of Inspector Hornsby. Apparently, Hornsby had refused to release an employee of Baker, despite him offering to stand surety, as a result of which the latter had 'sustained a serious loss', and in doing so had been rude.

In his reply, Rowan wrote:

> 'The conduct of Mr. Hornsby appears to the Commissioners to have been highly improper and directly contrary to the orders of the Commissioners have separately given for the conduct of Inspectors and others at the watch houses. Mr Hornsby has been severely censured by the Commissioners who are desirous of knowing from you in what further manner they can cause him to make some amends to you for the loss you have sustained.'[605]

Mayne, meanwhile, 'developed an efficient system for the more common and widespread complaints, in which the accused constable [was] immediately sent before the Police Magistrate,' or, if the complainant refused to appear before the magistrate, 'the Commissioners [dealt] with the constable …according to the best of their judgement.'[606]

Rowan and Mayne worked hard to raise the public's image of the New Police, scouring the newspapers for stories about the force and demanding an explanation from 'the appropriate divisional superintendent when a critical report was printed'. Even in cases which were not widely publicised but somehow still came to the attention of the Commissioners, further details were sought.[607] Many of the complaints were about the actions or behaviour of their officers. Some were legitimate, but many originated from 'members of the public who hoped to ruin a constable's career by making wild charges of brutal assault.' Even if the complaint was anonymous it was investigated. No matter what the provocation, no constable 'was permitted to exceed his duty, and those who broke the regulations were dismissed.'[608]

The Commissioners frequently held court against officers who had been complained about. For instance, on an evening in October 1830 a John Lever had received permission from the landlord of The Windmill public house in Lambeth to sell boots and shoes from a table outside the premises, but he was told to remove the goods by Constable Henry Castle, attached

---

605 TNA MEPO 1/6, folio 6891.
606 Keller, op. cit. 603, p.71.
607 Emsley, op. cit. 597, p.45.
608 Howard, op. cit. 593, p.135.

to L Division. When Lever refused to do so, it was alleged that Castle began throwing the boots and shoes about the street. He was then alleged to have struck Lever and two other people who remonstrated with him, and all three were arrested for obstructing the constable in the execution of his duty. At the Station House the inspector refused to accept the charge, and all three people were released. Two days later the three appeared before Colonel Rowan to make a formal complaint.[609] As a result, a hearing was arranged for the Tuesday morning at which the three people gave evidence in the presence of Castle. At the conclusion of the hearing Colonel Rowan said 'nothing could pollute such a gross outrage on the public,' and said Castle 'had exceeded the rules and regulations laid down for the guidance of the constables.' He was immediately dismissed.[610]

However, where it was felt that media criticism was unjust, Rowan, in particular, during the early years frequently wrote to the editors seeking justification for the report and requesting further information which might 'lead to the discovery of any misconduct on the part of the [Metropolitan] Police which justified the opinion expressed.' Sometimes he would enclose reports from inspectors and superintendents about the incidents.[611] He was not adverse to admonishing the newspaper, as he did with *The Times* in a letter dated 24 August 1830, in which he told the Editor that the Commissioners 'consider it unworthy of the general correctness and freedom from prejudice of *The Times* newspaper.'[612]

Members of the public wrote regularly to the Home Secretary, complaining about the activities of the police. Again, there is space to mention only a few. For instance, a Mr Shoobart wrote to Viscount Melbourne complaining he had been stopped by a constable one evening. When Melbourne passed it to the Commissioners, it elicited an abrupt response from Mayne, who forwarded a copy of the instructions given to officers:

'At Night

If after sunset, and before sun rising, the Constable shall see any one carrying a bundle or goods which he suspects were stolen, he should stop and examine the person and may detain him, but here also he should judge from the circumstances (such as the appearance and

---

609 Normally, this type of complaint would have been dealt with by Mayne.
610 *The Globe*, 9 October 1830, p.4.
611 These letters are contained in TNA MEPO 1/44 as follows: to *The Times*, 22 April 1830, ff.1/2; 23 July 1830, f.12; 24 August 1830, f.13; and 16 October 1830, f.16; to the *John Bull* newspaper, 19 September 1832, f.49; to the *Morning Chronicle*, 20 September 1832, f.50; f.51; to the *Morning Herald*, 18 October 1832, ff.71-72.
612 TNA MEPO 1/44, folio 13.

manner of the party, his account of himself, and the like) whether he has really got stolen goods, before he actually takes him into custody.'

He then added, 'the complainant, Mr Shoobart, had the opportunity… of relieving himself immediately of any inconvenience by stating his name, and satisfying the Constable of his respectability.'[613]

The Commissioners also had cause to complain about the actions of the public occasionally. One such letter from Rowan who, during the early period of his commissionership, attended the same church in Regent Street as the wife of Sir Robert Peel, wrote to a Mr Richards on 5 May 1831:

'Col Rowan presents his compliments to Mr Richards and begs to acquaint him that on Sunday morning last at St Philip's Chapel when handing Lady Peel to her carriage he witnessed what appeared to him to be a very improper and under the circumstances of time and place, indecent breach of propriety on the part of Mr Richards coachman in attempting violently to take a place out of his turn in front of Lady Peel's carriage in consequence of which her Ladyship's carriage was damaged, and an injury was inflicted on one of her horses – they were very spirited and forced upon the flagway amongst the departing Congregation thereby causing them great fear and annoyance. Col Rowan thinks it justice to Mr Richards as an eye witness to make him acquainted with the conduct of his servant on this occasion.'[614]

But the discipline imposed by Rowan, and particularly Mayne, sometimes had unfortunate consequences. In September 1837 two men, referred to only as Day and Sheen, dressed in the rags of the Spanish Foreign Legion were brought before the magistrate at Marlborough Street Police Office charged with begging. One of them had been a police sergeant on N Division who had been caught 'sitting down and asleep when on duty.' When he had appeared before Mayne, he was told he had 'better resign' as he 'was getting on in years.' He resigned and, not being able to get work elsewhere, had joined the Spanish Foreign Legion. At the end of his engagement he returned to Portsmouth with two certificates entitling him to £20, which he was told would be paid to him by the Spanish Ambassador in London. But it was not, and both Day and Sheen had been forced to beg. The magistrate let them go on the condition they would 'sort themselves out'.[615]

On another occasion, in 1845, when a complaint was made against Police Sergeant Thomas Peters, then stationed at Sutton, he appeared before the

613 TNA MEPO 1/5. Letter from Mayne to Phillipps, dated 22 March 1831.
614 TNA MEPO 1/5, un-numbered but immediately after folio 6177.
615 *Morning Advertiser*, 23 September 1837. p.3.

police commissioners, was reduced in rank to constable and posted to Park Place, Lock's Fields. Because it was not convenient to take his family with him, he had to take lodgings. He complained frequently that he had been treated harshly and felt he had suffered an injustice. One morning in November he committed suicide by cutting his throat.[616]

Later, between 1856 and 1866, the number of dismissals from the Metropolitan Police fell quite dramatically, averaging between 182 and 299 each year, but the number of resignations remained high, averaging between 571 and 800. During the same period 535 officers were charged with offences which went before a magistrates' court, 100 of them on the personal directions of Mayne. The majority of the one hundred taken before the courts on Mayne's directions tended to be charged with such offences as neglect of duty, unlawfully withdrawing themselves from their duties, drunk when on duty, and assaulting a superior officer or other constables. The majority resulted in convictions. But in many of the remaining 435 cases, officers went before a magistrates' court as a result of a complaint from a member of the public.

What it showed was just how precarious the life of a police officer could be in those days, because he was required to defend himself. In 373 cases, the officers were found not guilty, with the magistrates frequently commenting that there were 'no grounds for the charge'. For instance, in 1856, when two officers were charged with 'excess of duty in improperly taking a person into custody', the magistrate felt bound to comment that they had 'acted most properly, and in due execution of duty' before dismissing the case against them. Another officer charged in 1858 with 'violation of duty' was told by the magistrate that it was 'a monstrous charge' and the officer had 'acted most judiciously'. In a case in which an officer was charged with 'perjury', the magistrate said there were 'not the slightest grounds for the charge'. Similarly, in 1859, a constable charged with 'violation of duty' was told by the magistrate that he had 'acted very properly'; an officer, charged with assault was told by the magistrate that there was 'not the slightest grounds for [the] charge'; and a third officer charged with 'neglect of duty' was told that he had been quite justified in not interfering in the matter to which he had been called. In 1866, in discharging an officer charged with 'simple larceny', the magistrate said there was 'not the slightest evidence to justify even suspicion'.

Sometimes the complainant was ordered to pay costs. A magistrate found that a constable charged with 'violation of duty' had been charged most unfairly and ordered the complainant to pay 40s costs. In 1863, in

---

616 *Morning Post*, 17 November 1845, p.8.

dismissing a charge of 'assault' against a constable, the magistrate ordered the complainant to pay 14s costs towards the constable's expenses or be imprisoned. In 1865, following the discharge of three officers charged with 'violation of duty', the magistrate ordered the complainant to pay 42s costs.[617]

The circumstances surrounding the dismissal of Superintendent Lazenby and Inspector Wovenden have already been discussed in the previous chapter. Despite the failure of Rowan and Mayne to get Duncannon to change his mind about those two officers, they continued to support officers who they felt had been unfairly dealt with by magistrates. Two such cases happened in September 1838, when the commissioners sought the approval of the Home Secretary for the officers to stay. In one case, Police Constable Turvey had been fined for misconduct, although the exact nature of the misconduct is undisclosed. In the other case, two sergeants, Henry Grifs and James Selway, had been convicted of 'taking improper liberties with a female', but again the improper liberties were not disclosed. In both cases, Phillipps wrote back to say that Lord John Russell had agreed to them remaining in the Force, although in the case of the two sergeants they were to be admonished by the Commissioners.[618]

There were occasions when magistrates, although finding officers guilty, felt bound to recommend that they should be allowed to remain in the police. Two such officers went on to be superintendents. The first, George Martin, who was frequently sent to different parts of the country to deal with outbreaks of disorder had, as a sergeant, been severely injured under such circumstances in Huddersfield,[619] and the Commissioners had already brought his 'meritorious' conduct to the notice of the Home Secretary as this letter from Phillipps indicated:

> 'I have laid before Lord John Russell your letter of the 21st instant, recommending to his favourable consideration the case of Sergeant George Martin, a meritorious officer, who received several severe injuries in the execution of his police duty while suppressing a riot

---

617 PP 1867 [161] Metropolitan Police. Returns of the total number of the Metropolitan Police Force employed in each division, in each year from 1855, specifying the average number on day and on night duty; of the number of men resigned and dismissed from each division in each year since 1855; and, of the number of men of the force charged at the police courts with offences since 1855 to the close of 1866; &c.

618 PP 1867 [161] Metropolitan Police. Returns of the total number of the Metropolitan Police Force employed in each division, in each year from 1855, specifying the average number on day and on night duty; of the number of men resigned and dismissed from each division in each year since 1855; and, of the number of men of the force charged at the police courts with offences since 1855 to the close of 1866; &c.

619 TNA HO 65/12, folios 458 and 456.

under circumstances of great difficulty, and I am to inform you that Lord John Russell has been pleased to direct that a gratuity of 30 [shillings] shall be paid to Sergeant Martin.'[620]

Following this incident Martin had been promoted to inspector but, in March 1838, he appeared before a court, charged with common assault on a female. He was not on duty at the time and in plain clothes. He was found guilty and fined 40s. However, the convicting magistrate, Sir Frederick Roe, in a total turnabout to the way he handled the Lazenby and Wovenden case, wrote to the Commissioners:

March 20, 1838.

Dear Sirs,

I trust you will permit me to draw your attention to the case of Inspector Martin of the A Division, who was lately brought before me on a charge of assault on a female, and being convicted of that offence is, I understand, in danger of being dismissed from the police force. I should at the time have made an entry on the sheet that it was the magistrates' opinion that the fine inflicted was ample punishment for the offence, had I not considered the impropriety he was guilty of was entirely in his individual character, in no way connected with his public situation (he being in plain clothes and not on duty), that it would be almost unfair to draw the Commissioners' attention to his case, and I beg now to represent to you that it was my brother magistrate's feeling [at that time two magistrates heard the case] as well as my own that the penalty was quite sufficient punishment, and that we hope that it may be consistent with your regulations to take no further notice of his misconduct.[621]

Replying to the Commissioners' letter, Phillipps wrote:

'I have laid before Lord John Russell your letter of the 22nd instant with reference to the case of Inspector Martin, reported in your former letter, and I am to inform you that Lord John Russell, having considered the statements made in the letter from Sir Frederick Roe, which you enclosed, approves of Inspector Martin's being retained in the service.'[622]

---

620 PP 1856 [2016]. Report of Her Majesty's commissioners appointed to inquire into the alleged disturbance of the public peace in Hyde Park on Sunday, July 1st, 1855; and the conduct of the Metropolitan Police in connexion with the same. Together with the minutes of evidence, appendix, and index, minutes of evidence, p.259, q/a 6676.
621 Ibid, p.259, q/a 6675.
622 Ibid.

The second such case related to Superintendent Samuel Hughes, who subsequently commanded the police on the ground in Hyde Park in 1855.[623] He had joined the Metropolitan Police as a constable in October 1830 and been posted to H Division. Five days later he resigned as a result of an injury received whilst on duty. He then rejoined less than a month later and was posted to A Division. A year later, he was promoted sergeant and in June 1836 to inspector, remaining on A Division. On the instructions of the Commissioners, Hughes had been charged with entering the house of a Mr. Stoddart without a warrant and 'applying epithets to him of an offensive description' in May 1842. After hearing the evidence, the magistrate remarked upon Hughes' improper conduct in entering Stoddart's house 'without being armed with authority from a magistrate, in the strongest possible terms, and fined him 40s, which was immediately paid.' Before sentence, Stoddart had apparently told the magistrate that 'he had no wish [that] a severe punishment should be inflicted'. In a letter to the Commissioners, Mr. Cottingham, the magistrate, said 'he considered the punishment of 40s was sufficiently severe for a mere error of judgment', whereupon representation was made to the Secretary of State, who authorized his being retained in the service.[624]

In May 1846, on the directions of the Commissioners, Superintendent Pearce appeared before the magistrate, Mr Henry, at Bow Street Court to answer a complaint that on 24 April he had exceeded his duty during a visit to the house of William Clarke, the landlord of The Artichoke public house in Covent Garden, where it was alleged he had used language to the landlord's wife and daughter calculated to provoke a breach of the peace. In cross-examination after he had given evidence of the alleged offence, Clarke admitted that before becoming a publican he had been in the Metropolitan Police, from which he had been allowed to resign after being found talking to a woman who, it was alleged, was a receiver of stolen goods. On hearing this, after consulting with his client Clarke's counsel withdrew the charge. Mr Henry discharged Superintendent Pearce, saying that, in his opinion, nothing had been shown which suggested the superintendent had exceeded his duty.[625]

The Commissioners were not immune from appearing before the courts themselves. Indeed, Rowan was a defendant twice within a month. In March 1831 Catherine Green had been charged with stealing a £5 bank note, now in the possession of the police, from a John Williams and

---

623 See Chapter Twenty.
624 PP 1856 [2016], op. cit. 620, pp.235-236, q/a 6285-6288.
625 *The Globe*, 7 May 1846, p.4.

committed for trial at the Old Bailey, but Williams failed to appear and she was discharged. During the hearing Green claimed that Williams had given it to her for safe custody, but when defending counsel applied for the money to be returned to her the judge, Lord Tenterden, declined to make such an order, saying she had no claim to it.[626] Nevertheless, Green pursued her claim to the money, and some four years later, in May 1835, sued Rowan and Mayne in the Court of the Exchequer for the £5 note to be returned to her. However, Mr. Baron Gurney ruled that there was no evidence to render the defendants liable and refused to make such an order.[627]

The following month Rowan was again the defendant, this time in a case brought by Frederick Taylor, heard before Lord Abinger, Lord Chief Baron of the Exchequer, and a jury. Taylor had purchased his discharge from the 8th Hussars in 1832, and had been given a certificate by his commanding officer on which it stated his length of service and that 'he had always borne a good character.' On leaving the army he had successfully applied to join the Metropolitan Police, and had been required to submit his certificate of discharge and other documents but had subsequently been dismissed. He applied for the return of the army discharge certificate, but when it was returned to him there was written in large red letters 'Dismissed from the Police Office', which Taylor alleged was in Rowan's handwriting. On leaving the police he had been provisionally accepted as a turnkey at a House of Correction, but on submitting the now-defaced army discharge certificate the offer was withdrawn. Taylor brought an action against Rowan in an attempt 'to recover compensation in damages for injury', which the former claimed he had sustained through a 'wrongful act' by the latter. He claimed Rowan had no right to deface the certificate, thus rendering it 'useless' with the obvious 'intention to injure him and prevent him from obtaining other employment.' At the conclusion of Taylor's case, Lord Abinger suggested to his counsel that the case, which had been brought as an action for trespass, had not been made out. The plaintiff had not proved 'the red marking was in [Rowan's] handwriting', and recommended that Taylor withdraw his complaint. However, Taylor preferred the matter be left to the jury. After retiring to consider its verdict, the jury found in Rowan's favour.[628]

In October 1856 former police constable John Casey, whom Mayne had dismissed, appeared at Greenwich Police Court charged with sending a

---

626   Old Bailey Proceedings Online (www.old.baileyonline.org, version 7.2, 17 February 2018), April 1831, trial of CATHERİNE GREEN, alias COCKBURN (t18310407-268).
627   *London Courier*, 5 May 1835, p.4.
628   *Morning Advertiser*, 25 June 1835, p.4.

letter to the Divisional Commander, Superintendent Francis Mallalieu, in which he threatened to murder Sir Richard. The chief clerk read an extract from the letter to the court:

> 'I will make [Sir Richard Mayne] a living momento of my vengeance, no matter what the suffering afterwards. It will be a terrible lesson for other commissioners, and teach them how to act in a fair manner to all under them.'

Another extract read:

> 'I have no hesitation in saying that his tyrannical conduct in my case has made me as deadly and inveterate an enemy against him as can be. I have endeavoured by all means in my power to obtain a living, no matter how degrading. I will not exist without having a terrible revenge on him. My mind is made up, and should I be drove to it I will make him suffer much, if not more, then he has made me experience for the last three years.'

At the initial hearing Casey was remanded for further inquiries to be made. When he re-appeared, Mallalieu was asked whether Mayne wished the case to go to trial, to which he replied he believed not. However, he told the court that Sir Richard 'wished that notice should be taken of the letter for the sake of example to others.' The magistrate then addressed 'some severe remarks' about Casey's conduct, but also referred to 'the high-minded character of the Chief Commissioner' before requiring Casey to find two sureties, each in the sum of £50, and himself in the sum of £100, to be of good behaviour towards Sir Richard and all Her Majesty's subjects for the next twelve months.'[629]

Mayne was a defendant shortly before his death in a case of libel brought against him by an inspector he had dismissed from the service. It was probably the start of one of the most unsavoury episodes in his career when he suspended three inspectors working in the Public Carriage Office. The repercussions no doubt caused him considerable anguish right up to his death. The head of the Public Carriage Office was Lieutenant-Colonel G.F. Paschal, who had originally been recruited by Mayne to superintend Foreign and Provincial Police and Interpreters at the Great Exhibition in 1851.[630]

During this period the Commissioners were increasingly made responsible for implementing a number of laws which were not strictly

---

[629] *Morning Chronicle*, 22 October 1856, p.3 and 29 October 1856, p.8.
[630] See Chapter Nineteen.

a police function. The first of these was the Common Lodging Houses Act of 1851,[631] introduced in an attempt to improve the conditions in lodging houses. The new Act required the owners of all lodging houses to register with the Commissioners, who were responsible for seeing certain standards were met. Therefore, following the Great Exhibition Paschal's services were retained to bring the Act into operation on behalf of the Commissioners. This contract was terminated in February 1852. However, in June 1853 he was rehired to implement another piece of legislation, the London Hackney Carriage Act 1853,[632] which required the owners of all hackney carriages to register with the Commissioners, who were required to ensure all such carriages were fit for public use. Appointed as the Chief Inspector of the Public Carriage Office, Paschal held this position until his retirement on 30 May 1969, approximately five months after Mayne's death.

But to return to the case; when the expenses submitted by Inspectors Robert Jackson, William Clatworthy and Thomas Brook, who were all employed in the Public Carriage Office, came before him for approval in 1866, Mayne doubted 'their correctness', and refused to authorise payment. Instead, he appointed a panel consisting of Paschal, Edmund May, who had replaced Yardley as Chief Clerk,[633] together with Chief Superintendent Walker, to examine the accuracy of the expenses incurred. Claiming that, as their immediate supervisor, the inquiry would be more independent if he was not part of the panel, Paschal was excused. During the investigation it was alleged that Jackson had admitted to May and Walker that he had claimed for omnibus fares when he had made journeys on foot. This Jackson denied. The subsequent report by Walker and May found that each of the three inspectors had made claims which were contrary to regulations and, in some cases, had claimed travelling expenses when omnibuses were not running. All three inspectors were dismissed by Mayne,[634] and a printed circular was sent to all police stations setting out the reason for the dismissal:

> 'For having made out accounts for the payment claimed to be due to them founded upon misrepresentation by each of them of the duties alleged to have been performed, expenses charged not incurred, and in many cases expenses being charged which, if incurred, were not authorised by any regulation.'

631   14 & 15 Vict, chap. 28.
632   16 & 17 Vict, chap. 33; HC Deb 21 April 1853, cc. 231-234.
633   Charles Yardley retired in 1864; Edmund May was the son of Superintendent John May.
634   TNA MEPO 1/47. Letter from Mayne, 21 January 1867, to The Rt Hon. H. Waddington.

It was signed by Richard Mayne. This statement was read to police officers at all stations[635] and, as a result, Inspector Jackson sued the Commissioner for libel.

In the meantime, Mayne had suggested to Paschal that it would be better if he stayed away from the Public Carriage Office until the inquiry was complete. Paschal took the view he had been suspended, and appealed to the Home Office. Mayne was asked by the then Home Secretary, Spencer Walpole for his version of the events following which Walpole declared there were insufficient grounds for the suspension which was declared 'irregular'. Walpole left office in May 1867 to be replaced by Gathorne Hardy who, in June 1867 caused a letter, signed by his Under-Secretary of State, Lord Belmore, to be sent to Mayne:

> 'Under the circumstances it became your duty at once to acquiesce in the decision of the Secretary of State, and to allow Colonel Paschal to resume the regular performance of his duties. It was most painful to Mr. Hardy, therefore, to receive a letter in which you state that "you must decline to employ" this officer upon grounds into which he will not repeat as they have been before his predecessor, and his opinion has been given authoritatively upon them. It is impossible to allow that opinion to be absolutely disregarded and if you have any complaint to make, the restoration must be preliminary to it being taken into consideration.
>
> Mr Hardy's knowledge and full appreciation of your zeal and intelligence in your office make it extremely disagreeable to him to insist upon what is distasteful to you, but it is impossible to allow such resistance to the directions which were given by Mr. Walpole after long and impartial consideration of the facts or to assent to the exclusion of an officer from the discharge of functions which he has been appointed to fulfil, in defiance of the authority by which he was appointed, and which has been appealed by yourself.'[636]

Mayne reinstated Paschal on 7 June and informed the Home Office.

The case came before Mr Justice Keating and a jury at the Court of Common Pleas in Westminster Hall on 5 and 7 December 1868, just three weeks before Mayne's death. In justifying the dismissal of the three officers, Mayne gave evidence of the part he had played, whilst Chief Superintendent Walker gave evidence of the investigation. At the conclusion of the case

---

635 *Morning Post*, 7 December 1868, p.7.
636 TNA MEPO 2/18, Letter, dated 3 June 1867.

for Jackson, the Attorney General submitted that the alleged libel was a privileged communication, but Mr Justice Keating rejected this. On behalf of Sir Richard, defending counsel alleged Jackson had claimed expenses which he ought not to have done, and that the statements in the alleged libel were true. In his summing up to the jury, Mr Justice Keating expressed the view that a libel had been committed, although, in law, he was required to leave the decision of whether that was so to the jury. The jury was also to decide whether damages should be paid. Retiring to consider their verdict, the jury could not agree, and Mr Justice Keating dismissed them.[637] There the matter ended, due almost certainly to Mayne's death less than three weeks later.

---

[637] *Morning Post*, 8 December 1868; *Lloyds Weekly Newspaper*, Sunday, 13 December 1868.

CHAPTER ELEVEN

INTERNAL PROBLEMS II: CONDITIONS OF SERVICE

An attempt by Peel to impose further restrictions on appointees to the New Police was received by the Commissioners in November 1829. Phillipps forwarded to them a letter Peel had received from the Chief Secretary of Ireland which outlined the 'inconvenience which had been experienced in the Constabulary Police of Ireland', and suggested 'the same inconvenience could happen in London.' As a result, Peel suggested the rules laid down in the military relating to the marriage of privates and non-commissioned officers subsequent to their enrolment could be applied to the Metropolitan Police. The restrictions on the military were quite extensive and Mayne, responding on behalf of the Commissioners, no doubt influenced by Rowan's extensive experience in the military, sent back a lengthy letter concluding as follows:

> 'The Commissioners finally take leave to suggest that the powers they at present possess to dismiss any Constable of the Force who may be considered unfit to belong to the Police Force, may be found applicable to cases when the Constables marry under circumstances which shall make them in any respect less qualified for the duties they are to perform, and that at present it is not necessary to establish any more precise rule upon the subject of marriage by the Constable of the Police Force.
>
> With respect to persons to be selected to fill vacancies in the Force attention will always be paid to such circumstances as upon each occasion may make it most desirable that the individual should be married or single.'[638]

638 TNA MEPO 1/1, folios 201-206.

Internal Problems II: Conditions of Service

From the start, the Commissioners paid attention to the conditions of service under which the men would operate. Learning from his military experience, one of the first tasks Rowan identified was the need to acquire a regular medical service for the police officers, but the initial suggestion to the Home Office to appoint a 'medical man' was turned down by Peel. He considered the 'salary and allowances would be too expensive', and asked the Commissioners to 'work out the best and most economical mode of procuring medical attendance.'[639] The Commissioners responded and, as a consequence, Phillipps wrote to the six leading London hospitals[640] on behalf of Peel, asking them what facilities they were prepared to offer officers of the Metropolitan Police who attended or were received in their respective hospitals.[641] Most responded by saying that police officers would be treated like any other patient, but the Westminster Hospital offered a detached and separate ward for police patients.[642]

Towards the end of January 1830 Mayne wrote to John W. Fisher, who had been surgeon for the Bow Street Dismounted Patrol which had been absorbed into the Metropolitan Police, to inform him that Peel had agreed to the appointment of a Superintending Surgeon at £350 per annum. Mayne was also able to tell him that the Westminster Hospital would keep a separate ward for the use of police patients.[643] Initially Fisher was required to examine recruits and attend sick constables throughout the Metropolitan Police District, but later this task was reduced when Divisional Surgeons were appointed to act under his supervision. By 1834, there were 23 divisional surgeons.[644]

Mayne explained the duties of the surgeons to the 1834 Select Committee, commencing with the superintending surgeon, which was

> 'to consult with the Commissioners, and advise upon all questions that relate to the health of the men, and the medical department of the Force, and to carry the result into effect; to carefully examine every candidate as to his fitness, before he is admitted, and report the same; to visit and examine every man who has been long on the sick list; the Commissioners frequently desire the principal surgeon to examine men, to ascertain whether they are likely to recover; to consult

---

639 TNA HO 65/11, Phillipps, 26 October 1829, to the Commissioners.
640 Guys, London, St Bartholomews, St George's, St Thomas's and Westminster.
641 Phillipps to London Hospitals, 17-18 November 1829 in TNA HO 65/11, folios 27-28.
642 TNA HO 65/11 folios 39-42.
643 Mayne to Fisher, 27 January 1829, in TNA MEPO 1/2, p.51; see also TNA HO 65/11, folio 58.
644 PP 1834 [600]. Report from the Select Committee on the Police of the Metropolis; with minutes of evidence, appendix and index. Minutes of evidence, p.66, q/a 997.

with the divisional surgeons, and given his assistance in all cases of accident and danger to the constables in every part of the district; to perform operations when required, and to see that every case that cannot be properly attended to in the section houses, is removed to the most convenient hospital; to visit the various station-houses, and examine as to their salubrity and cleanliness, as also the cells of the watch-houses; to attend to all matters of general reference from the Commissioners, the superintendents of divisions and the divisional surgeons, and pay the latter their respective stipends, and report on the merits of candidates for a vacancy; to visit the police patients in the various hospitals about town, and to observe that the whole of medical arrangements are followed.[645]

An expenditure that Peel had not considered in agreeing to the setting up of the New Police was accommodation for the police officers. Presumably he had anticipated that they would either have lodgings or, if coming from distance, would find accommodation in the same way as any other employee. Rowan, however, felt that it was 'absolutely necessary' for them to be kept together. Indeed, in his evidence to the 1834 Committee he went so far as to say that if it had not been authorised by the Secretary of State, 'we should not have been able to establish the police at all.'[646]

By 1833 the total number of station and section houses was 47. Single men were charged one shilling a week rent, whilst married men were charged between two shillings and sixpence and three shillings depending on the number of rooms they occupied.[647] In addition, each man was provided with an allowance of coal, the amount varying depending on whether he was married or single. Rooms were provided with grates, coal baskets and fire irons. In addition, each man was furnished with a bedstead and bedding, including blanket and sheets. Finally, each section house was provided with tables and chairs, the quantity depending on the number of people occupying the premises.[648]

Rowan and Mayne were conscious of the dangers officers faced on the streets. Almost from the beginning they fought to get the government to introduce a superannuation fund from which officers who had been killed, injured or were unfit to continue, or their families, could be compensated. Officers could be granted a police pensions on a discretionary basis under the 1829 Act, but they had no right to a pension; there was no scale and

---

645 Ibid, p.65, q/a 986.
646 Ibid, p.52, q/a 765.
647 Ibid, p.51, q/a 758.
648 Ibid, pp.56-57, q/a 823-834.

there was no fund from which it could be paid.[649] On the rare occasions, they were granted it was at the whim of the Home Secretary.

Within a year of the formation of the Metropolitan Police, two officers had been killed under violent circumstances. Constable Joseph Grantham was kicked to death while trying to intervene in a fight between two drunken men in Somers Town, near King's Cross, on 29 June 1830. He died the day after his wife gave birth to twins. The coroner's jury concluded that Grantham had brought about his own death by 'over exertion in the discharge of his duty.'[650] There is no evidence of Grantham's widow being offered any compensation.

Less than two months later, Police Constable John Long was stabbed to death in Gray's Inn Road when he stopped three suspected burglars at night.[651] Long left a wife and five children, a fact that did not go unnoticed by Sir Robert Peel's wife. Writing to Mayne from her home at Drayton Manor on 1 September, Lady Julia Peel said:

'Dear Sir,

I trust to your excusing the trouble I am giving you – when I request the favour of you to give the enclosed – in my name – to the poor widow of the unfortunate man John Long for whose family I feel great interest – as belonging to so very brave and meritorious a Policeman.'[652]

On an application being made by the Commissioners, Constable Long's widow was granted a pension of 10s per week by the Home Secretary under the discretionary powers given to him under the Metropolitan Police Act 1829.[653] Nevertheless, Rowan considered such an arrangement was insufficient. As a young officer in the 52nd Regiment he had seen how, in March 1806, Lieutenant-Colonel John Stewart had 'established a fund for the relief of the sick and distressed soldiers' wives and children.' To finance the fund, officers and men donated a small percentage of their salary.[654]

There were two further prominent cases that occurred prior to the Commissioners and the Receiver John Wray giving evidence to the Select

---

649 Critchley, TA (1979). *A History of Police in England and Wales*. London: Constable, p. 168.
650 Mason, Gary (2004). *The Official History of the Metropolitan Police*. London: Carlton Books, p.15.
651 *Globe*, 17 August 1830, p.3.
652 File of letters sent to Sir Richard Mayne 1829-1868; Presented by JHR Heathcoate, 1955, Letter 1. Now held in the Metropolitan Police Heritage Centre.
653 10 Geo IV. C.44 – see PP 1834 [600], op. cit. 644, p.3, q/a 119-122; p.58, q/a 852.
654 Moorsom, W.S (Ed) (1860). *Historical Record of the Fifty-Second Regiment (Oxfordshire Light Infantry) from the Year 1755 to the year 1858*. Uckfield, Sussex: The Naval and Military Press, pp.72-73.

Committee on Policing in 1833 and 1834. The first involved another murdered officer, Police Constable Robert Culley, who left behind a wife pregnant with their first child.[655] Much to the surprise of the Commissioners, small sums of money were donated by many members of the public, and there was a demand by some notable personages for the Home Office to take action. This 'induced Melbourne to grant Mrs Culley the unprecedented sum of two hundred pounds.'[656]

The second involved Police Constable John Terry who had joined the Force on 21 September 1829. Within four years he had been seriously injured on six occasions, as this report from Superintendent W. Grimwood explained:

> 'The first injury he sustained was in 1829 at the time the house of Mr. Rawlinson was on fire in Wells Street, when in saving Miss Rawlinson from the flames he was burnt in the side and the right eye in consequence of which he was under the care of Mr. Fisher, Surgeon of the Police Force, for one month.
>
> The second he received was in May 1830, quelling a disturbance at a public-house in Newman Street kept by Samuel Cross. He had then four ribs broken by being thrown down stairs. He was taken to Middlesex Hospital where he remained for some time.
>
> The third accident occurred on the night of the riot of 9th November 1830, at Temple Bar, upon which occasion his leg was severely hurt, and he was under the care of Mr. Clark, the Divisional Surgeon, for three months.
>
> The fourth accident occurred on the 17th of August 1831, when his head was cut open in preventing a man named Fairbourne from murdering his wife.
>
> The fifth injury was on the 12th November 1831, when his head was cut open again, both back and front. He was on this occasion rendering assistance to Henry Plume, late a P.C. in this Division, who was being ill-used by three men. He was conveyed to the hospital where he remained for some time.
>
> The sixth injury he received was being severely kicked and beaten by a Gentleman named Jonas Binns on the 9th of last month, when his ankle was put out, and the small bone of his leg so much injured that

---

655 Thurston, Gavin (1967). *The Clerkenwell Riot: The Killing of Constable Culley*. London: George Allen & Unwin, p.105.
656 Reith, Charles (1956). *A New Study of Police History*. London: Oliver and Boyd, p.166.

Internal Problems II: Conditions of Service

he will be a cripple for the remainder of his life.'

So, at the age of 39 years, married with five children – the eldest 12 years and the youngest 5½ years – Terry was crippled for the rest of his life. The report from Superintendent Grimwood was forwarded by Rowan to Phillipps at the Home Office on 19 July 1833. Four days later Phillipps wrote back to the Commissioners to say Viscount Melbourne had agreed a payment of £30 to Constable Terry,[657] hardly a generous amount given the circumstances.

When they appeared before the 1834 Committee, the Commissioners took the opportunity to mention the lack of a superannuation fund from which officers who had been injured on duty and forced to retire could receive recompense. Only Police Constable Long's widow was in receipt of a pension, which was 10s per week. This had been authorised by the Secretary of State. The Receiver, John Wray, was asked whether 'any fund had been formed from the pay of the men by order of the Government, or of their own accord, to provide retiring allowances in case of disease or old age', to which he replied, 'there is not any.'[658] The Committee heard from the Commissioners that the retention of those trained as police officers was a problem. In the first four months of 1834, 311 constables had voluntarily resigned, 'of whom about one-half, it is stated, are good men who the Commissioners would have wished to retain.' As a result, the Committee recommended that 'some provision for superannuation allowances and rewards for long and faithful service' should be established 'with as little delay as possible.'[659]

In 1833, fines imposed by the courts on people who had assaulted police officers were paid to the Receiver of the Metropolitan Police. Emphasising that 'a great many men [had] left the force from ill-health, and from hurts which they [had] received in the service, and for which they had received no compensation,' the Commissioners, through Wray, impressed on members of the Select Committee that the £600-£700 received each year from fines imposed on people who had assaulted police officers would be 'a proper source for a superannuation fund.'[660] Later Mayne expanded on the subject, pointing out the Secretary of State was 'authorised to give rewards in cases of men disabled by wounds received actually in service,' under the Act of Parliament. However, he did not have authority to

---

657 TNA MEPO 7/2 folio 303.
658 PP 1834 [600], op. cit. 644, p.58, q/a 852.
659 Ibid, Report, p.18.
660 Ibid, Minutes of Evidence, p.366, q/a 5010-5017.

'reward' those officers who had come into the service with strong health' who had 'become ill from cold, or something of that kind,' in the execution of their duties, and, as a result, had fallen 'into consumption, or some lingering disease' causing the Commissioners 'to discharge him, without any provision whatever.'[661]

As with many of the recommendations contained in the 1834 Report, the Home Office took no action on the Committee's recommendation for a superannuation fund to be set up, and in 1837 Rowan wrote to Phillipps suggesting that fines collected in the Police Offices might be applied to such a fund.

Phillips's response was not encouraging:

'I find that if this were done, there would be such a deduction from the Funds of the Police Offices, it would be necessary for the Treasury to advance a sum of such an amount as would exceed the sum allowed by the Act, and the Treasury would certainly refuse to allow such an increase of Expenditure on the Police Offices. I am afraid the objection cannot be got over.'[662]

A Superannuation Fund was finally set up in 1839 under the Metropolitan Police Act. It bore some similarity to the one set up by Rowan's commanding officer in 1806, in that the fund was to be financed by subscriptions from officers. But it went further, in that monies accrued from stoppages of pay during sickness, fines imposed on constables for misconduct, and from the sale of worn police clothing, was also a source of revenue for the fund. Directions could also be made for a portion of fines to be imposed by magistrates upon drunken persons, or assaults on police officers to be allocated to the fund. Under Section 22, money would be added to the fund by investing in Government Stock and the like. Under Section 23, a constable had to be 60 years of age to receive a pension unless he suffered from ill-health. The rates for those suffering from ill-health were:

- For an officer with 15 years' service but less than 20 years, an annual sum not more than half his pay;
- For an officer with 20 years' service or upwards, an annual sum not more than two-thirds of his pay; but if he was under sixty, it could only be granted if the commissioners provided a certificate to say he was physically or mentally incapable of discharging the duties of his office;

---

661   Ibid, p.395. q/a 6278-6279.
662   TNA HO 65/12 folios 357-358. Phillipps to the Commissioners, 13 March 1839.

- If a constable was disabled from injuries received on duty, he could be granted an allowance not more than the whole of his pay.[663]

Already generous in terms of the scale of the pension, 'a man could retire, for example, on a two-thirds pension after only twenty-four years' service'.[664] A year later, Conservative Home Secretary James Graham made it worse by issuing an order that all gratuities for illness or injury had to be provided out of the Superannuation Fund.[665]

The combination of these two factors was later described by a Permanent Under-Secretary of State at the Home Office as a 'ruinous mistake', and the scheme became unworkable.[666] Within ten years there was no capital, and the contributions, rather than being invested as the legislation demanded, was looked upon as 'current revenue'.[667]

Generous for some, there were also inadequacies in the pension system which were highlighted in 1848 when the then-chief of the detective force, Inspector Shackell, was forced to retire because his veins had become 'ulcerated and diseased' after being kicked in the legs several years earlier. But Shackell had, by this time, only served for just over 13 years, and therefore under the regulations was not entitled to a pension. The Home Office was not anxious to set precedents, but eventually the Commissioners convinced it he should have one.[668]

By 1856, the whole of the fund's capital had been absorbed and, the following year, Parliament authorised the deficit to be made up from the Metropolitan Police Fund.[669] In 1862, the Home Secretary appointed Dr William Farr, who had assisted in the development of a Civil Service Pension Scheme, and he estimated that 'of the Metropolitan policemen pensioned between 1840 and 1860 over a quarter had respiratory or rheumatic complaints,' but only 'a tenth suffered from injuries received while on duty.'[670] In consequence, the awarding of pensions became much less generous. The maximum pension became three-fifths of pay, instead

---

663 Monro, James (1890). 'The Story of Police Pensions'. In *New Review*, No. 16, September, p.198. A copy of the article is contained in TNA MEPO 2/5809.
664 Critchley, op. cit. 649, pp. 168-169.
665 Reith, Charles (1943). *British Police and the Democratic Ideal*. Oxford: Oxford University Press, p.229.
666 Critchley, op. cit. 649, p.168.
667 Munro, op. cit. 663, p.196.
668 Lock, Joan (2014). *Dreadful Deeds and Awful Murders: Scotland Yard's First Detectives 1829-1878*. Jolo Press, p.137.
669 Critchley, op, cit. 649, p.168.
670 The papers of Sir Edwin Chadwick held in the University College London Archives. UCL. Chadwick MSS 16, Folder: POLICE Memoranda etc (1855-69), Printed report to the Secretary of State by William Farr MD, FRS, April 1862.

of two-thirds, and was obtainable only after thirty-two years' service.[671]

These changes led to great dissatisfaction in the Force during the last four years of Mayne's commissionership, which worsened after his death, culminating in some officers refusing to go on duty in 1872. Not until 1890 did the Metropolitan Police have a satisfactory pension scheme, with the passing of the Police Pension Act.[672]

In September 1862 Mayne issued a memorandum reminding officers that 'a Pension or retiring allowance' was granted on the condition that it could be withdrawn by the Secretary of State if the pensioner was convicted of any indictable offence; was knowingly associating with thieves or suspected persons; if he refused to give information or assistance to police in the apprehension of criminals, or in suppressing any disturbance of the public peace. The memorandum also stated that it could be withdrawn if the retired officer 'entered into or carried on any business, occupation or employment' which was, in the opinion of the Secretary of State, deemed to be disgraceful in itself or injurious to the public, or if he made use of his former employment in the Police in a manner which was considered 'to be discreditable and improper.' Mayne concluded that 'the law (2 & 3 Vic, C.47, s.23) does not entitle any Constable absolutely to any superannuation allowance, neither does it prevent him from being dismissed without superannuation allowance.'[673]

The cause of this memorandum was Mayne's dislike of the employment taken up by Detective Inspector Charles Field after he left the Force. Some eight years earlier, Field had resigned his position as head of the Metropolitan Police Detective Force and was granted a pension.[674] He immediately opened a Private Inquiry Office at Eldon Chambers, Devereux Court, Temple, and notices regularly appeared in newspapers claiming that the Office was 'under the direction of Charles Frederick Field, late Chief Inspector of the Detective Police of the Metropolis'. In early 1854 Field was hired by a wealthy individual, a Mr. Evans, who suspected that his wife was having an affair with a Mr. Robinson.

When the case first came before Mr Justice Crowder, it transpired that Field had persuaded the landlady of the property in which Mrs Evans was staying, to take on a Mrs Grocott as a cook. Mrs Grocott was in fact acting under the instructions of Field, and he was paying her a fee. On the instructions of Field Mrs Grocott drilled a hole in the living room wall

---

671 Moylan, J.F (1929). *Scotland Yard and The Metropolitan Police*. London: G.P. Putnam's Sons, pp.263-266.
672 Reith, op. cit. 665, p.219.
673 TNA HO 45/7375. Memorandum, dated 23 September 1862.
674 See Chapter Sixteen.

with a gimlet provided by him, so she could spy on the couple when Mr Robinson visited Mrs Evans.[675] The *London Daily News* still believed Field to be a member of the Detective Force, for the following day, in a leading article, it was reported that the trial had thrown 'rather a startling light on the kind of employment at which our detective police-officers are in the habit of lending themselves'. It went on to suggest that 'if the employment of our "Detectives," after the fashion in which Field appears, from the Liverpool trial, to have been employed, is tolerated, our modern English police will become as intolerable as the old French police in the balmy days of *lettres de cachet*.'[676]

Field attempted to undo the damage by writing to the newspaper:

EVANS v ROBINSON – THE DETECTIVE FORCE

In your journal of this day my attention has been called to a leading article on the subject of the above trial, wherein you inveigh strongly against the use of the Detective Police in private matters. In reply thereto, I have to inform you that after 24 years' honourable service in the Metropolitan Police, I retired from it in November, 1852, since which time, and after the recovery of my health, I have devoted myself, as many others have done before me, to "private inquiries." The celebrated Smyth forgery was, as you are doubtless aware, confided to me; and I have had the satisfaction to receive a flattering testimonial for the services rendered in this case.

It is a duty I owe to the authorities in Scotland-yard publicly to declare that during the whole term of my long period of service, the commissioners never permitted or gave their services to any of the Detective Police being employed on any matter not within the regular routine of police business.

You will therefore perceive that, as a private individual, and "in a free country," I am at liberty to give my services to those who may honour me with employment.

I therefore respectfully beg the immediate insertion of this letter in your next publication.

I am, sir, your obedient servant,

    CHAS FIELD, late Chief Inspector
    of the Detective Police of the Metropolis.

---

675 *London Daily News*, 23 August 1854, pp.6-7.
676 Ibid, 24 August 1854, p.4.

Published the next day, the *Daily News* – whilst accepting that he was no longer a member of the Detective Force – nevertheless claimed to have received letters giving instances of where the detective police had been 'employed outside the range of "regular routine police business"', and called on an 'independent member of parliament [to] interrogate the Home Secretary on the subject as soon as parliament meets again.'[677]

The fallout from this case worsened the following year. Similar evidence of the part played by Field was heard in a retrial before Mr. Justice Cresswell in April 1855. In his summing up before a jury, Mr. Justice Cresswell claimed it was the first time in his life that he had heard a man declare that his profession was that of a private spy, and asked the jury to consider what they thought of a man who might write on his door "Spy; to be hired at so much a day?"

Pointing out that the court had heard how a person had been introduced into a house as a cook, he asked:

> 'Might not a person be introduced as a footman? Might not the servant that dressed your wife by a spy? To what base and villainous purposes might not the services of such people be converted, when once they were introduced into houses.'

Mr Justice Cresswell concluded by claiming 'there was something so revolting, so shocking, in a man standing before the public and proclaiming himself a hired spy by profession.'[678]

The following year, in February, the *Illustrated Times* published a lengthy piece under the title 'A Memoir of Inspector Field' highlighting his police career, at the same time as he was giving evidence at the committal proceedings of William Palmer, known as the Rugeley Poisoner. Although his role in the investigation was relatively minor, acting on behalf of the Prince of Wales Insurance Company in relation to possible insurance fraud, in the newspaper reports Field was given the police rank of inspector.[679]

This, coupled with the fact he continued to advertise himself in offering a private inquiry service as 'Charles Edward Field, late Chief Inspector of the Detective Police of the Metropolis',[680] would have acted as an anathema to Mayne, who brought it to the immediate notice of the Home Secretary, Sir George Grey. Because the media constantly referred to him as Inspector Field, Mayne suggested he was falsely encouraging people to believe that

---

677   Ibid, 25 August 1854, p.4.
678   *Preston Chronicle*, 7 April 1855, p.3.
679   *Illustrated Times*, 2 February 1856, p.6; *Reynolds's Weekly Newspaper*, 25 May 1856, pp.2-4.
680   For instance, see *Leeds Intelligencer*, 25 October 1856, p.2; *West Middlesex Herald*, 9 May 1857, p.1; *West London Observer*, 2 April 1859, p.1.

he was still a member of the Metropolitan Police. This resulted in Grey stopping Field's pension.[681] Field protested the withdrawal of his pension and sought legal advice, in which he was told on 11th December 1861:

> 'We are of the opinion that the Secretary of State has not the power claimed by him in this case, and that Mr Field is still entitled to the Superannuation allowances ordered by Mr Walpole, in the year 1852, and that there is nothing in the form of the Order to interfere with the rights which he has through that Order.
>
> The proper course to recover the arrears of the pension, is to apply to the Queen's Bench for a Mandamus for the Receiver General to pay those arrears to Mr. Field. But before making that application it would be advisable to write to the Secretary of State a final letter such as was suggested in a Consultation.'

Field forwarded this to the Home Office who, on receipt, sought Mayne's view. The report, outlining the facts as the Commissioner saw them, was accompanied by a letter in which he wrote:

> 'I regret that the person mentioned in the enclosed Report [Mr Field] is in receipt of a Pension as a Superannuated Inspector of the Detective Force of the Metropolitan Police. He has appeared very discreditably in Courts of Justice and his conduct has been severely censured by Judges. I think it would have a very useful effect on others if his pension could be withdrawn.'[682]

However, the Treasury Solicitors broadly agreed with legal advice Field had received, stating that 'under the existing circumstances the Secretary of State cannot legally interfere to prevent the continued payment of Mr. Field's Superannuation Allowance.'[683]

Less than two weeks later Field's pension was restored, after he gave assurances to the Secretary of State that he would give no further cause for 'disapprobation', and would take immediate steps to remove 'any impression that may exist that he acts in any connection with the Government.'[684] Despite this, for the next three years Field continued to advertise himself as 'late chief of the Metropolitan Police Detective Force', causing Mayne to again bring it to the notice of the Home Secretary,[685] who, on this occasion,

---

681 TNA MEPO 7/22. Police Order 17 August 1861.
682 TNA TS 25/1165. Letter, dated 20 December 1861, to the Home Secretary.
683 Ibid. Signed by William Atherton and Roundell Palmer, 31 December 1861.
684 TNA MEPO 7/23. Police Order, 7 January 1862.
685 As far as has been identified, the last advertisement offering his services as such appeared in the *London Evening Standard* on 6 July 1865, p.2.

took no action.

Another source of concern to the Commissioners was the reluctance of the Home Office to grant legal aid to officers who prosecuted cases at the criminal courts. These officers, with very little legal training, were often faced with a financially well-off prisoner who, sometimes, had influential friends, and was able to hire trained, and skilful, counsel. The trial would sometimes take place before a hostile magistrate, or judge and jury, and, if they failed to secure a conviction or costs were awarded against the police, they could be personally responsible for paying those costs. If the officer was unable to pay – and it was extremely unlikely a police sergeant or constable could pay – he could be sent to prison. An added burden was the danger of being convicted of assault or wrongful arrest, in which case he could also be sent to prison. As a result, some monstrous injustices occurred.[686]

For the first sixteen years of the Met's existence this was the case, with the Home Office only very rarely providing legal assistance. After 1842, the Home Office did ask the Treasury Solicitors to prosecute in a few cases involving murder, manslaughter and vicious assault. This was put on a more formal footing by the County and Borough Police Act 1856.[687] Despite a suggestion from the Criminal Law Commission in 1845[688] that there ought to be 'a plan of public, as opposed to private prosecutions', not until 1879, with the passing of the Prosecution of Offences Act,[689] would there be a Director of Public Prosecutions to advise the police and personally act in cases of importance.[690] But the prosecution of minor cases remained in the hands of the police until the creation of the Crown Prosecution Service (CPS) in 1986,[691] although the Metropolitan Police did set up its own Solicitors Department in 1935.[692]

---

686 Browne, Douglas G (1956). *The Rise of Scotland Yard; A History of the Metropolitan Police*. London: George G. Harrop, pp.92-93.
687 19 & 20 Vict c.69.
688 PP 1845 [656]. 8th Report of the Criminal Law Commission.
689 Sir John Maule became the first Director in 1880. See Bentley, David (1998). *English Criminal Justice in the 19th Century*. London: Hambledon Press, p.86.
690 Howard, Pendleton (1930). 'Criminal Prosecutions in England II: Public Prosecutions' in *Columbia Law Review*, Vol. 30, No. 1, pp.12-59.
691 Prosecutions of Offences Act, 1986.
692 TNA MEPO 2/10814.

CHAPTER TWELVE

THE EARLY YEARS

The aims of Rowan and Mayne during the first few years were 'unimpeachable,'[693] but the Force suffered at street level. The strict criteria of recruiting working-class men resulted in working-class men enrolled as constables to enforce the laws and regulations they possessed on working-class men, who, by and large, had, until then, been allowed to live as they pleased unless, in the unlikely event, they were caught committing crime by the Bow Street Runners or constables attached to the other Police-offices of the magistrates. The opposition to the New Police was considerable, amounting to a press campaign in selected newspapers, the circulation of posters and broadsheets calling for the abolition of 'Peel's bloody gang' and the 'Blue Lobsters',[694] and verbal and physical assaults on the constables from all sections of society.[695]

The press campaign was particularly virulent during the early years. One newspaper claimed the New Police had been formed not 'for the protection of the lives and property of the community' but as 'a bone for a party', alleging that it would not be 'judged according to the ordinary principles of conservation, but by the bias of political prejudice.'[696] Another accused the New Police of merely 'driving thieves and disorderly persons into the City'.[697] But it was the *London Evening Standard* that voiced the most detailed and prolonged campaign, each day highlighting cases where constables had allegedly interfered with the behaviour of people, which, until the introduction of the New Police, had been acceptable. Thus, on 5

---

693 Emsley, Clive (2009). *The Great British Bobby: A History of British Policing from the 18th Century to the Present*. London: Quercus, p.42.
694 Browne, Douglas G (1956). *The Rise of Scotland Yard: A History of the Metropolitan Police*. London: Harrop, p.93.
695 Cowley, Richard (2011). *A History of the British Police*. Stroud, Gloucestershire: The History Press, p.28.
696 *Atlas*, 4 October 1829, p.10.
697 *Morning Chronicle*, 13 October 1829, p.3.

October *The Standard* described how one constable had compelled a man sitting at his own door smoking a cigarette to go inside the house and shut the door. It quoted an occasion when a constable told a street musician to stop playing in the street and move on, and described how a group of people looking in a shop window had been moved away by a constable who kept jabbing them with his truncheon. The newspaper pointed out that, as far as it was aware, none of these were crimes punishable by law, and complained the existing rules under which the police performed their duties were such that they were open to interpretation by individual constables. It called upon the Commissioners to issue instructions which were 'more distinct and conspicuous.'[698]

Four days later, in a letter to the Editor, a man described how he had walked from the Haymarket Theatre to Temple Bar and did not see a single policeman. He concluded his letter by suggesting the inhabitants of this area may well consider themselves 'in danger', and it would be better to return to the 'watch' system instantly.[699]

Some newspaper reports, although critical, were more constructive. For instance, the *Morning Herald*'s criticism of the police concentrated on the inadequacy of salary and suggested it could lead to corruption:

> 'We have often said that neither the watchman nor the old police were adequately paid. The insufficiency of their means placed them too much within the influence of bribery; their poverty exposed them to all the allurements of venality. The thieves made up to them, or, at least, to most of them, the deficiency in their wages.'

The article went on to say:

> 'We are not better pleased in this respect with the plan of the new police. We say they are not adequately paid. A guinea per week, out of which they have to provide their clothes, is not sufficient for the purpose of ensuring the enlistment in the service of decent and proper men – or if such should find their way into it, from the pressure of immediate want, they are likely to be beset by temptations which virtue, stung by poverty, cannot always resist.'[700]

Pointing out that some instances of misconduct had 'already occurred among the New Police', another leading article in the *Morning Post* suggested this was only to be expected when 'so large a body of men' had

---

698 *London Evening Standard*, 5 October 1829, p.3.
699 Ibid, 9 October 1829, p.3.
700 *Morning Herald*, quoted in the *London Evening Standard*, 2 October 1829, p.3.

'been called to the discharge of duties for which many of them were not perhaps fitted by their previous habits'. However, the article went on to claim it had been 'impossible to pass through the streets' on the previous two nights 'without observing that there appearance was very different from that which they usually presented under the watch system.'[701]

The criticism of the New Police in the newspapers continued for some time. One such complaint published in *The Times* in June 1830 resulted in an exchange of correspondence between the Commissioners and the Editor, as a result of which the Editor agreed to forward any complaints he received against the police to the Commissioners for comment before publication.[702]

But, whilst there was much criticism of the New Police, there was also praise. On one particular occasion in and around the Seven Dials, it was reported in the *Evening Mail* that, in dealing with 'the disgraceful scenes… of drunkenness, riot, and debauchery of every kind', the New Police had 'afforded a practical example of the spirit and determination with which the new civil force [appeared] resolved to act in the performance of this disagreeable but necessary duty.' Initially, the police officers had generally born the taunts and aggressive pushing 'with admirable patience', but eventually they were 'compelled to take two or three into custody.' This resulted in 'a general attack upon the police', but Superintendent Thomas was quickly on the scene with reinforcements of between forty and fifty men and 'nearly 30 of the ringleaders' of this outrageous behaviour 'were secured and carried off to the watchhouses.' Meanwhile, in Covent Garden and James Street, where there were several coffee-shops frequented by 'men and women of the worst character', often going from one gin-shop to another during the night, another body of police cleared the area, thus enabling respectable people 'going to their devotions' to do so without 'witnessing some disgusting exhibitions, or having their ears offended with blasphemous and filthy expressions'.[703]

Mention has already been made in the previous chapter of three of the most extreme attacks on police officers during those early years, but each day police constables faced the danger of violent assault. Again, there is room to mention but one. On 23 September 1832, Constable Robert Davis was severely injured in a brutal attack by three men in the early hours of the morning, with one of the men, James Sutton, kicking him in the face and beating him about the head with an iron bar whilst PC Davis

---

701   *Morning Post*, 6 October 1829, p.4.
702   TNA MEPO 2/9652.
703   *Evening Mail*, 14 October 1829, p.1.

was being held by the other two men. The three men – Sutton, Henry Kempt and Thomas Jones, together with a woman, Elizabeth Lawson – were tried for the attempted murder of the constable. Whilst Lawson was found not guilty and discharged, the three men were each found guilty and sentenced to death. But the judge, Mr Justice Park, recommended Kempt and Jones for mercy, leaving only Sutton to hang.[704] However, a month later it was announced that his life had been 'spared by His Majesty, through the interposition of Colonel Rowan and Mr. Mayne, who together with Constable Davis, petitioned the Throne to extend mercy towards the unhappy man'. Rowan subsequently received a letter from Sutton thanking him for his 'kindness'.[705]

The Commissioners must have been delighted when favourable reports appeared in the newspapers about the action police officers had taken at the scene of a fire in Wells Street less than two months after the formation of the New Police. Describing how 'the aid rendered by the police was most beneficial, in protecting the premises from plunder,' and removing the property to an adjoining house, the report also mentioned that they had assisted in working some of the fire appliances. When it was discovered that one of the family, a Miss Rawlinson, was still in the house after the fire had broken out, it reported how Constable John Terry had 'immediately risked his own life' by going into the burning house and rescuing the young lady by taking her onto the roof and along a parapet into the next house. In doing so, he had been 'badly scorched about the eyes, so that he was obliged to be sent to hospital.'[706]

Whilst disorder on the streets of London took many forms during those early years, as it indeed does today, it was in response to political agitation that the New Police was found to be particularly useful, avoiding the necessity for the Government to deploy troops. Only nine months after its formation, Rowan and Mayne faced a testing period. In May 1830, Richard Carlile, a radical who had been present at the Peterloo Massacre in 1819[707] and had, from that year to 1826, edited the weekly *Republican* newspaper, took over the Rotunda at Blackfriars. Built in 1787, it was originally a

---

704 Old Bailey Proceedings Online (www.oldbaileyonline.org, version 7.2, 02 January 2019), October 1832, trial of JAMES SUTTON, HENRY KEMPT, THOMAS JONES, ELIZABETH LAWSON (t18321018-8).
705 *Bell's Weekly Messenger*, 24 December 1832, p.2.
706 *Morning Post*, 20 November 1829, p.2; the rescued person's name is taken from Superintendent Grimwood's report in the previous chapter; the newspaper report refers to her as Miss Robbins.
707 The Peterloo Massacre occurred at St Peter's Field, Manchester, when a cavalry charge on a crowd of approximately 60,000 people gathered to demand parliamentary reform, resulted in the death of 18 people with hundreds more injured. For more detail, see Reid, Robert (1989). *The Peterloo Massacre*. London: William Heinemann.

museum before becoming a wine and concert room. Several times a week, Carlile and invited speakers would speak to assembled crowds, and it quickly became an important centre for working-class dissent and political reform. Together with five other prominent campaigners,[708] Carlile formed the National Union of the Working Classes (NUWC).

At the time, there was considerable agitation around the country from the economic discontent in the northern industrial areas to agricultural areas in the south where labourers were protesting about winter unemployment.[709] In the south, a revolt by peasants spread 'with startling speed from its focal point in Kent, reaching to Dorset and Gloucestershire in the west, Oxford and Northamptonshire in the north, and penetrating far into Norfolk and Suffolk in the east'. Following the tactics of the Luddites, who had protested against machines replacing people in the Midlands and north some eighteen years previously, protestors going under the name of 'Captain Swing',[710] destroyed 'the new threshing machines that were threatening their livelihood, and fired the ricks and barns of any farmer who refused their demand for higher wages.'[711]

Little of this directly affected the New Police, but it coincided with a seriously weakened Tory government under Wellington which had suffered defections from the party over Catholic emancipation. At the same time, the Tory government was threatened by the increasing power of the Whig Party, under Earl Grey, and its support for parliamentary reform. In London, the nightly meetings of the ultra-radicals[712] at the Rotunda, at which 'excited crowds listened to the outpourings' of William Cobbett,[713] Carlile and other radicals, was followed by demonstrations on the streets afterwards. The Home Office received warnings of a conspiracy against the government, whilst the New Police were subject to 'violent propaganda and physical attacks', which put great strain on their somewhat meagre resources, particularly in November 1830.[714] At the opening of parliament on 2 November, huge crowds lined the route to be taken by the Royal

---

708   William Lovett, Henry Hetherington, James Watson, John Cleave and William Benbow.
709   Gash, Norman (2011). *Mr Secretary Peel: The Life of Sir Robert Peel to 1830*. London: Faber & Faber, p.648.
710   They used the name Captain Swing to spread fear among landowners and avoid the real leaders from being identified – see www.nationalarchives.gov.uk/education/politics/g5 [accessed 1 January 2019].
711   Critchley, T.A (1970). *Conquest of Violence, Order and Liberty in Britain*. London: Constable, p.120.
712   See Chapter Thirteen.
713   William Cobbett was a journalist and publisher of pamphlets in favour of parliamentary reform.
714   Gash, op. cit. 709, p.648.

Procession[715] but, during the day, 'a desperate attack was made on the police without any provocation' as they attempted to arrest pickpockets operating within the crowds lining the processional route. A total of sixty-six police officers were assaulted,[716] and there were calls for the deployment of the military. But Rowan stood firm, successfully pleading for officers of the fledgling force to be allowed to 'do their work alone.'[717]

Traditionally, on the first Lord Mayor's Day[718] after the crowning of a new monarch, the King[719] and his ministers dined at the Guildhall in the city, but there were 'warnings of riot' when it was due to be held on 9 November 1830. Thousands of handbills were circulated, calling Londoners to arms, suggesting they should not lose the opportunity to revenge the wrongs they have suffered, and should 'come armed'. Others claimed '6,000 cutlasses [had] been removed from the Tower [of London] for the immediate use of Peel's Bloody Gang.'[720] Threats were made to assassinate both Peel and Wellington, and it was alleged that Wellington's house at Hyde Park Gate would be attacked. Joseph Hume, the Member of Parliament for Middlesex seen by many as the leader of the movement for electoral reform in the House of Commons, received an invitation 'to head an attack on St James's Palace during the King's absence in the City', in which it was suggested that Manchester radicals would provide pikes and Kent radicals would send eight to ten thousand people. Rather than keep quiet, Hume took the information to Peel at the Home Office. Similarly, Wellington received information from John Key, the Lord-Mayor elect, that 'disaffected elements in the City intended to attack him'. Three days before the event, Peel was told by two Alderman from the City of London that police within the City, such as it was, 'would not be adequate to preserve order... and asked for military aid.'[721]

At a meeting of the cabinet on the afternoon of 7 November, Wellington and Peel decided to cancel the King's visit, and the monarch was duly informed. That evening Colonel Rowan, some magistrates and military commanders met with the cabinet to confirm arrangements for 9 November. Meanwhile, on the evening of 8 November the police dealt with the daily mob outside the Rotunda very 'brusquely' when it came running into Westminster from Blackfriars. Next day, 'the crowds were out

---

715 *Morning Post*, 3 November 1830, p.1.
716 Sir Robert Peel, in an address to the House of Commons, HC Deb 08 November 1830, vol. 1, cc 267-274.
717 Gash, op. cit. 709, p.648.
718 The day a new Lord Mayor took office in the City of London.
719 William IV had become King on 26 June 1830 following the death of George IV.
720 Sir Robert Peel, op. cit. 716.
721 Gash, op. cit. 709, p.649.

in force; disorderly bands of up to a hundred roamed the town, and there was much scattered rioting', but the New Police stood fast.

At Temple Bar, which, being just inside the City of London, 'had long been a favourite no-man's-land for criminals and rioters,' the mob overpowered the City Police and proceeded on their way. However, Rowan's men were made of stiffer material and gave the rioters what the Earl of Ellenborough, then Lord Privy Seal and President of the Board of Control of India, described 'as "a terrible licking" near Southampton Street and again in Piccadilly'.[722]

Although there were substantial military reinforcements on standby, they were not required. Rowan's men had been

> 'completely effective in clearing the streets. There was no bloodshed and, though some of the constables were severely hurt by stones, the authorities remained in control of the situation throughout the 9 November.'[723]

However, unrest in the country was sufficiently serious to persuade Wellington to resign, and he did so on 16 November. The Tories were replaced by a Whig Government, led by Earl Grey. Replacing Peel as the Home Secretary was the truculent Lord Melbourne.

In opposition, the Whig Party had not been supporters of the New Police and had promised to disband it. However, Melbourne could see that this action 'was probably not the wisest of things he could do'.[724] Nevertheless, the Commissioners found that 'the days of close relationship with the Home Office was ended.'[725] Although Peel continued to support them in opposition, during the 1830s the Whig Government and its first two Home Secretaries, Melbourne and Viscount Duncannon, side-tracked the demand for the abolition of the police and, instead, subjected Rowan and Mayne 'to a long course of shameful and not always petty efforts to bully, frustrate and humiliate them.'

The situation was not helped by Mayne's relationship with Samuel Phillipps, the Under-Secretary of State at the Home Office, and it was due mainly to 'the rock-like impregnability of Rowan's dignity', which was built on 'modesty and patience', with the support he received from Mayne, that many of the difficulties were overcome.[726] Not until Lord John Russell became Home Secretary in 1835 did the situation begin to improve.

---

722   Ibid, p.650; see also *Morning Advertiser*, 10 November 1830, p.3.
723   Ibid, p.651.
724   Cowley, op. cit. 695, p.29.
725   Browne, op. cit. 694, p.104.
726   Reith, Charles (1956). *A New Study of Police History*. Edinburgh: Oliver and Boyd, p.158.

The Whigs had only been in power for six months when Grey called a snap General Election after the second reading of the Reform Bill had only been accepted by the House of Commons by one vote. In London, the close vote led to the announcement that an evening of illuminations, in which everyone in favour of the Bill was to light up their windows, would be held. This was arranged for 27 April 1831. That night a mob rampaged along the Strand, breaking the windows of houses that were not illuminated. It went on to break the windows of Northumberland House, London residence of the Duke of Northumberland. The windows of several clubs in the area of Waterloo Place including the United Service Club, of which Rowan was a member, and clubs in the vicinity of St James's Street, which included Crockford's and The Guard's were smashed. The windows in houses in which resided many notable people, including the Duke of Wellington, the Bishop of London, the Duke of Gloucester and Sir Robert Peel were also broken.[727] Despite Rowan arranging for just over 1,100 men – around one-third of the total strength – to be available, it was described as an 'unhappy night' for the police. They did have some success when they were in 'strong parties', but officers who became separated 'were savagely attacked and brutally maimed'. A total of one hundred and sixty-eight people were arrested.[728]

The mood of the country for parliamentary reform led to the new House of Commons being packed with pro-Reformers, and a second reading of the Reform Bill was passed by a substantial majority. It then went to Committee before the amended version returned to the Commons and was passed in September. However, when it went to the House of Lords early the following month, it was refused a second reading by 41 votes.

The response in some parts of the country was to be anticipated. There were serious outbreaks of disorder in Bristol and Nottingham, and violence on a more reduced scale in Birmingham, Derby, Exeter, Leicester, Sherborne and Yeovil. Meanwhile, in London protests started out peacefully but deteriorated into violence on 11 and 12 October. On 11 October, it was confined mainly to attacks on individual or groups of policemen, but on 12 October it was more serious. The unrest followed a peaceful Procession of Parishes to Buckingham Palace to present petitions to the King. As they returned to their respective parishes, a large number of 'windows and policemen's heads and bodies' were damaged.[729]

In a report to the Home Secretary, Rowan described what he had tried

---

727 *Annual Register, 1831*, Chronicle, p.68.
728 Reith, op. cit. 726, pp.90-95.
729 Ibid, pp.96-97.

to do:

> 'During the period that the congregated numbers remained in the neighbourhood of the palace, the Commissioners thought it necessary to keep the police Force together in strong bodies; and part of the mischief which occurred was owing to a misapprehension of the instructions of the Commissioners by the Superintendent of one Division in not having distributed his men to the points to be particularly guarded early after the procession began to leave the Palace. In consequence of this, the rabble which accompanied one of the processions on its return had an opportunity of breaking the windows of Apsley House.[730] A strong body of the police were immediately ordered to the spot but arrived too late to prevent the mischief...
>
> The Commissioners beg to assure you that according to your Lordship's desire, they had taken the greatest pains to dispose of the Force under the directions in a manner they thought best calculated to prevent serious results; and how ever they may regret the damage that has been done, they must bear witness to the zeal and energy shown on every occasion during the day by the police under their orders.'

It was Superintendent Baker who misunderstood his orders and, as a result, failed to post a body of police officers at Apsley House.[731] Nevertheless, it seems that Melbourne was sufficiently pleased with the way the Force had performed. No doubt delighted that London had got off so lightly compared with other parts of the country, he wrote to the Commissioners expressing his 'approbation of their conduct upon the occasion of the late disturbances in parts of the town', following which the Commissioners published a Police Order which was circulated to all Divisions:

> '...the Commissioners have highlighted gratification in finding that no unnecessary use was made by the Police of their Truncheons when called out, and that it has not appeased that in a single instance was an unnecessary degree of violence used. The Commissioners trust that by such firm and temperate behaviour the Police have conciliated the populace and obtained the good will of all respectable persons.
>
> Viscount Melbourne has approved of one shilling extra Pay being given to such of the Police Constables as were called out on Wednesday

---

730 Home of the Duke of Wellington.
731 Reith, op. cit. 726, p.96.

last…'[732]

London, particularly the East End, was hit with a serious outbreak of cholera in 1832. As a result, in February Parliament called for a 'National Day of Fasting and Prayer',[733] to be held on 21 March. The *Poor Man's Guardian* complained that 'to tell the poor to fast would indeed be superfluous', pointing out they were lucky to eat meat once a week, let alone be able to forego it.[734] It became known as a 'farce' day, and the National Union of Working Classes, who wanted to have a 'feast day' instead, called for a public meeting in Finsbury Square on 21 March.

In response, the Home Secretary issued a notice on 19 March prohibiting all processions on 21 March but, despite this, there were a number of clashes in the Metropolis. Both Rowan and Mayne were out on the ground that day in charge of detachments of police, despite being in plain clothes.[735] When one large group of demonstrators, with arms linked, came out of the City with the intention of going to Palace Yard, they were met at Temple Bar by 'a strong body of the F Division under Colonel Rowan… who turned them'. Meanwhile, between 20,000 and 25,000 people had assembled in Finsbury Square, where the police were under the command of Mayne, who was accompanied by a magistrate, a Mr Walker. Sections of the crowd had resorted to various acts of violence by 'hooting and pelting the police with stones and other missiles,' injuring some of them. As a result Mayne, in consultation with Walker, decided to clear the Square. A journalist described how, in order to do this,

> 'the police were divided into six sections or battalions, half of which (formed into front, centre, and rear ranks) were to proceed round one-half of the square, and the other in like manner round the other half. The word of command being given, the men marched in the performance of that very arduous and dangerous duty: the groans and hootings of the populace was deafening: vast numbers of stones were thrown, many of which severely injured the police; we saw about twenty whose heads were badly cut, but the poor fellows bandaged them up, and proceeded in the execution of their duty. Two or three, however, were so severely injured that they were sent off the ground by the orders of the police surgeon, who attended in the square.'

---

732 TNA MEPO 7.2, folios 80/81, Police Order 15 October 1831.
733 The cause of cholera was unknown at the time. It was believed by many that it was proof of the judgement of God and that people needed to atone for their sins.
734 *The Poor Man's Guardian*, 11 February 1832.
735 The Commissioners were not granted a uniform until 1839

It took about half-an-hour to clear the square, but many of the people took refuge in the City, from where they continued to hoot and pelt the police with missiles. On Mayne's instruction, policemen formed cordons across all the streets leading from the City into the Metropolis. According to the same journalist, 'nothing could exceed the excellent temper displayed by the New Police whilst proceeding in the execution of one of the most difficult duties they have had to perform since the establishment of that force.'[736] Mayne subsequently told the 1834 Committee that 'these serious conflicts… could have been wholly prevented had the police been able to follow through the City.'[737]

In another incident on the same day, when a mob marched along Tottenham Street, Superintendent Thomas,[738] in charge of a large body of police, deployed his men in a cordon 'eight deep across the road'. A few stones were thrown and the mob was ordered to disperse. Instead, the stone-throwing intensified and 'the police charged in such excellent order that the mob retreated in all directions towards the New Road, where they again made a stand' and began pelting the police with stones. A second charge by the police 'was made with such effect that the whole took flight.' Seven of the leaders were arrested and taken to Albany Street Station.[739]

This was probably the first occasion the police learned the effectiveness of the baton charge. Its origination is rumoured to have come from a conversation that Francis Place, an English social reformer, had with Superintendent Thomas some time earlier. Place was keen for the New Police to be a success, believing that the use of restrained force was the surest way of avoiding a 'relapse into the vicious circle epitomised by Peterloo – misunderstanding, violence, counter-violence and repression.'[740]

Despite the various problems, the popularity of the police increased steadily during those early years. Grand Juries started to express 'favourable opinion of the merits of the [New Police] generally and their efficiency for the protection and security of the public.'[741] There were a number of examples of this. Twelve months after its formation, the Grand Jury for the County of Middlesex assembled at the quarter sessions at Clerkenwell announced unanimously the policemen

---

736 *Morning Advertiser*, 22 March 1832, p.3.
737 PP 1834 [600]. Report from the Select Committee on the Police of the Metropolis; with minutes of evidence, appendix and index, p.319, q/a 4274.
738 Thomas was one of the few successes that came from the old system of policing. He had been a constable in the St Paul's parish which covered Covent Garden and had been appointed superintendent of G Division, which covered part of his old parish.
739 *The Globe*, 22 March 1832, p.3.
740 Critchley, op. cit. 711, p.125.
741 PP 1834 [600], op, cit. 737, p.28, q/a 444-447.

'called before them have given evidence with great clearness, and very different to evidence given formerly by parochial watchmen. The grand jury are also unanimous in their opinion that the introduction of the new police has already been of great use, and that their continued vigilance will tend to prevent the commission of crimes, and to preserve the peace of the county.'[742]

In 1831, the Commissioners announced in a Police Order circulated throughout the Force that the Grand Jury of Surrey sitting at Kingston had been highly complimentary of 'the New Police, of whom at least fifty were in attendance in different cases of Felony.' Commenting that 'the Grand Jury not only eulogised their vigilance and general intelligence, but the clear and conclusive manner in which they gave their evidence…,' the Commissioners added 'by a continuation of such conduct the Police Force will gain the favourable opinion of the Public and be enabled upon all occasions to perform their duties more agreeably and effectively.'[743]

The Commissioners also sought to reach out to the public in January 1832, circulating to London newspapers a list of police stations where the assistance of officers could 'be obtained when their services [were] required', together with the name of the superintendent in charge of each of the seventeen divisions. In publishing it, the *Morning Advertiser* said 'this document ought to be an advertisement; but being useful to the community we publish it gratis.'[744]

The following month, Rowan and Mayne were embroiled in an extraordinary case of fraud, which, no doubt, particularly to Rowan's disappointment, received some adverse publicity.

Edward Fordham, described as 'a gentleman of fortune', had been arrested, accused of defrauding Esther Tompkins of a sovereign, and detained at Gardner's Lane Station House. At the time he had been accompanied by a friend, Edward Tatham, a partner in a highly-respected firm of sword cutlers. On hearing of the charge Tatham's father went to the United Service Club, where he informed Rowan of the circumstances, and sought his advice as to how he should act and whether bail could be obtained. Rowan apparently listened to him patiently, before saying 'it was a point of law' and 'he would give him a letter to his colleague, Mr Mayne, who was a barrister.' After hearing details of the case, Mayne apparently wrote a letter to the Inspector of A Division, requesting that he grant Fordham bail. Inspector Goodyer, who happened to be on duty at the time, therefore

---

742 *London Evening Standard*, 24 September 1830, p.4.
743 TNA MEPO 7/1, folios 381/382, Police Order 7 April 1831.
744 *Morning Advertiser*, 23 January 1832, p.3.

released Fordham in his own recognizance to appear at court.

When Fordham appeared the next day the magistrate, Mr Marriott, 'expressed his astonishment that such an order should be given, and that a man under such a serious charge should be set at liberty, without proper bail [being] taken.' Presumably, by that he meant one or more persons should have been required to stand as surety for Fordham's appearance.

The charge was eventually dropped, although the magistrate condemned the conduct of the poor inspector, who had merely been following a request given to him, in writing, by Mayne, for letting Fordham go 'without taking bail.'[745]

As will be seen in Chapters Fourteen and Sixteen, the deployment of police officers in plain clothes was a thorny issue for the Commissioners for a number of years because of allegations that the police would be used as spies. Nevertheless, Rowan and Mayne recognised that it was essential if those committing certain crimes were to be caught, and, in taking this decision, they were supported by some magistrates. Less than a month after the formation of the New Police, Sergeant Tyrell arrested three people he had caught pickpocketing in the Strand. When they appeared before Mr Hall sitting at Bow Street Police Office, the magistrate stated it was worthy of notice that 'the Sergeant of Police was not in his uniform when he apprehended the prisoners,' adding, 'I do not think he could have detected them, if he had been in uniform.'[746]

In another case, this time from 1832, three men known to be cracksmen or housebreakers were seen lurking in Church Street, Bethnal Green. It was believed they were about to commit a crime, and two police officers, Sergeant Beale and Constable Savage 'doffed their uniforms, and put on plain clothes' to observe the three men undetected. After watching them for some time, the men were seen attempting to enter a house using false keys and were arrested. Found to be in possession of several skeleton keys and other housebreaking paraphernalia, they were charged with intent to commit a felony. The magistrate, Mr. Broughton, discharged one of the three but sentenced the other two to three months' in a House of Correction.[747] Although Mr. Broughton made no specific comment about the officers 'doffing their uniforms and putting on plain clothes', it is extremely unlikely that Beale and Savage would have been able to observe the men unobtrusively had they not done so.

---

745 *Morning Chronicle*, 2 February 1832, p.4, and 4 February 1832, p.4.
746 *London Courier and Evening Gazette*, 12 October 1829, p.4.
747 *Morning Advertiser*, 4 April 1832, p.4.

CHAPTER THIRTEEN

THE BATTLE FOR COLD BATH FIELDS, 1833

One outbreak of disorder during those early years was significant for two reasons. Firstly, it was during the disorder that the first of three police officers was killed in a riot on the British mainland.[748] Secondly, it was the first occasion since the formation of the New Police that an outbreak of disorder led to a Parliamentary Inquiry.[749]

At a meeting of the National Union of the Working Classes (NUWC), held at the Rotunda in April 1833, members were called upon to meet at Cold Bath Fields in the Clerkenwell district of London on 13 May. A small committee consisting of seven men was set up, including James Mee and Richard Lee, both of whom were to figure prominently on the day.[750] The NUWC was organised throughout London on a district basis. Each district was known as a Class and was allocated a number; thus, for instance, Camberwell was known as the 73rd Class. The number of members in each Class varied from between 80 to 130, and the total membership throughout London was estimated to be about 3,000.[751] Some were more militant than others, and were known to attend meetings armed with pistols, swords and other weapons.[752]

Anticipating opposition from both the Government and the police, it was suggested that the only way to resist the police would be by using arms. During the following few days, notices about the meeting were

---

748 See Moore, Tony (2015). *The Killing of Constable Keith Blakelock*. Hook, Hampshire: Waterside Press, pp.19-28.
749 PP 1833 [718] XIII. Report from the Select Committee on the Cold Bath Fields Meeting with the Minutes of Evidence.
750 Rowe, D.J (1970) (Ed). 'The Radical Club and other papers in London Radicalism 1830-1843: A selection of the Papers of Francis Place'. *British History Online*. Retrieved from www.british-history.ac.uk/london-record-Soc/vol5/pp.119-134 [accessed 9 May 2019].
751 PP 1833 [718] XIII, op. cit. 2, Minutes of Evidence, p.22, q/a.218 and 221.
752 Ibid, p.22, q/a.219.

circulated amongst members of the Union, and large posters signed by the secretary, John Russell, appeared on walls all over London on the evening of 10 May and throughout the 11 May, advertising:

A PUBLIC
MEETING
Will be held on the Calthorpe Estate
COLD BATH FIELDS,
On MONDAY next, May 13th, at Two O'Clock,
To adopt preparatory Measures for holding a
NATIONAL
CONVENTION
The only means of obtaining and securing the
RIGHTS OF THE PEOPLE.
By order of the Committee of the National
Union of the Working Classes

John Russell, Sec.[753]

The two Commissioners, Rowan and Mayne, were summoned to the Home Office two days before the meeting to see the Home Secretary, Lord Melbourne. Also present was Samuel Phillipps, then Permanent Under-Secretary of State. Whilst Section 5 of the 1829 Act required the Commissioners to seek the Home Secretary's approval with regard to changing the way the force was managed, the Secretary of State had no apparent legal authority to give directions about operational matters. This meant the Commissioners had great autonomy, but there were certain types of events which would engage 'the individual attention not only of the Home Secretary, but that of the Prime Minister too.'[754] Mostly, during the commissionership of Rowan and Mayne, they concerned events in which disorder was anticipated, although shortly before the latter's death Fenian terrorism was added to the list. The law on protest and assemblies was extremely vague at the time, and there seems to have been some doubt in the minds of the two Commissioners as to whether the meeting was illegal and, if it was, then when did it become so. Not until after the event did the Courts decree that a meeting called 'to adopt preparatory measures

---

753   Ibid, p.6, q/a 16.
754   Morris, R.M (2004). 'The Metropolitan Police and Government 1860-1920'. Thesis submitted for the degree of Doctor of Philosophy to the Faculty of Arts, Open University. Retrieved from www.oro.open.ac.uk/59576/1/403833.pdf [accessed 12 August 2019], pp.217-218,

for holding a national convention' was an illegal meeting.[755]

The meeting was described as 'unsatisfactory'.[756] During it, the following exchange between Melbourne and Rowan took place:

> Melbourne: Would not the gallant Commissioner, who has reconnoitred – I believe that is the right word? – the battlefield so minutely, deem it advisable to forestall the meeting altogether?
>
> Rowan: I apprehend, my Lord, that there is no legal ground on which we can do this. We are aware of the reports that violence may be contemplated by the unions but, on the face of things, there is insufficient evidence to allow us to place a body of men in advance on Cold Bath Fields.
>
> Melbourne: But, my dear Colonel, many of those present are to be armed – cannot the meeting be anticipated?
>
> Rowan: With respect, my Lord, were we to do this the National Union would merely move elsewhere and collect additional ruffians from the streets as they proceed, leading to the dispersal of our force and making our task the more hazardous.
>
> Melbourne: But this is an illegal meeting, cannot you prevent it?
>
> Rowan: Again, with respect, my Lord, we cannot declare this meeting illegal on the strength of the poster. We are well aware that it may speedily become so and then we can take action for which, depend on it, we are well prepared.
>
> Melbourne: Well then, when the persons get up and talk about a National Convention, you will know that it is the illegal meeting announced by the placard?
>
> Rowan: That is so, my Lord, but most of the ringleaders are already known to us by sight.
>
> Melbourne: Very well, my dear Colonel, you will then arrest the person attempting to hold the meeting and the crowd will undoubtedly disperse as there will be nothing further to command their attention.
>
> Rowan: I would prefer, my Lord, to be permitted a certain discretion according to the circumstances we find in the field.
>
> Melbourne: Naturally, the gallant Commissioner will have my complete

---

755 Rex v Fursey, 1833. In 'Serjeant, The Honourable Thomas (Ed) (1835)'. In the *English Courts of Common Law with Tables of the Cases and Principle Matters, Vol. XXV*. Philadelphia: P.H. Nicklin & T. Johnson, p.293.

756 Emsley (2009). *The Great British Bobby: A history of British policing from the 18th century to the present*. London: Quercus, p.47.

trust and I am sure that he will do whatever is expedient to preserve the public order.[757]

Nothing was put in writing to the Commissioners and, when the events were subsequently reviewed by a Select Committee, there was a dispute as to precisely what had been said.

Later that day, a poster was delivered to Scotland Yard by a messenger from the Home Office. The poster, headed by the Royal Coat of Arms and issued by the order of the Secretary of State, declared the meeting illegal:

> WHEREAS printed papers have been posted up and distributed in various parts of the Metropolis, advertising that a Public Meeting will be held in COLD BATH FIELDS, on Monday next, May 13th, to adopt preparatory measures for holding a NATIONAL CONVENTION, as the only means of obtaining and securing the Rights of the People:
>
> And whereas a Public Meeting holden for such a purpose is dangerous to the Public peace and illegal:
>
> All Classes of his Majesty's subjects are hereby warned not to attend such Meeting, nor to take any part in the proceedings thereof.
>
> And Notice is hereby given, that the Civil Authorities have strict orders to maintain and secure the Public Peace, and to apprehend any persons offending herein, that they may be dealt with according to Law.
>
>   BY ORDER OF THE SECRETARY OF STATE.[758]

The poster must have been at the printers when the Commissioners were at the meeting at the Home Office, but neither Melbourne nor Phillipps saw fit to mention it. However, Mayne saw certain advantages in having the notices posted. Although no mention was made regarding the dispersal of the crowd, it did, in some ways, take the place of a written order that Melbourne had failed to provide.

Meanwhile, at a meeting of the Lambeth Class of the NUWC on the Sunday, some forty men were told:

> 'Tomorrow will be your day of glory. Let every man resist the oppressors to the death. Everyone must go armed. Rally to the flag – Liberty or death – you and your families have endured starvation and poverty, long enough. Arm, arm against the foe. Tomorrow we meet near the

---

757 Thurston, Gavin (1967). *The Clerkenwell Riot; The Killing of Constable Culley.* London: George Allen & Unwin, pp.45-46.
758 PP 1833 [718] XIII, op. cit. 749, p.16, q/a.122.

new Bedlam[759] and march over Blackfriars Bridge to triumph.'[760]

As with many of the meetings at that time, a plainclothes policeman was amongst the audience. Reports of similar meetings at Bethnal Green, Camberwell, Hammersmith and Islington reached the Commissioners. Additionally, at a meeting of the NUWC in Commercial Road it was agreed that 'the Committee should be supported in their aim to secure a national Convention to secure the rights of the people,' and the Home Secretary's warning should be ignored. Again, the report that arrived at Whitehall Place suggested that those attending the meeting would be armed. Subsequently, it was clear that 'many of the marchers certainly did come ready to fight, carrying knives, cudgels, sticks and Maceroni pikes, also called "Maceroni lances".'[761]

As indicated in the exchange between Melbourne and Rowan, the latter had already carried out a reconnaissance of the ground. The area of which Cold Bath Fields was part was known as the Calthorpe Estate. The Fields itself was a piece of ground sloping downwards towards Bagnigge Wells Road,[762] which was its eastern boundary. Surrounded by three-feet high railings, the Fields were sometimes used by local people for the grazing of livestock. To the south lay Cold Bath Prison and Collingbridge's, a coach-builders; to the west was Gray's Inn Lane.[763] Calthorpe Street, running from west to east, was one means of access and egress to and from Cold Bath Fields. Rowan decided that he would be present, in overall command. The ground commander was to be Superintendent John May, the officer in charge of A Division. He would be assisted by a number of superintendents, who would each be in charge of their own contingent of police officers.[764] Thus, Rowan's arrangements for command of the incident was very similar to that which police in Great Britain use today, a three-tier system with Rowan as effectively the Strategic, or Gold, Commander; May as the Tactical, or Silver, Commander; and the remaining superintendents as Operational, or Bronze, Commanders.[765]

---

759   A hospital for the mentally ill. The name comes from the original such hospital, known as Bethlam, set up in 1675-76 at Moorfields which was removed to St George's Fields, Southwark in 1814-15.
760   Thurston, op. cit. 10, p.50.
761   Bloom, Clive (2003). *Violent London; 2,000 Years of Riots, Rebels and Revolts*. London: Pan, p.202. Maceroni lances, named after Francis Maceroni, who was a soldier, diplomat and revolutionary, were about 6 feet long and hinged in the middle for easy carriage.
762   Now King's Cross Road.
763   Now Gray's Inn Road.
764   PP 1833 [718] XIII, op. cit. 749, p.6, q/a.14.
765   See 'Command and Control Structures', retrieved from www.app.college.police.uk/app-content/operations/command-and-control/command-structures [accessed 9 May 2019].

Rowan had something in excess of 900 police officers available to him. Nearest the scene was A Division, consisting of 80 men, together with D and H Divisions (each with 110 men) in Busbridge's Livery Stables. Approximately 100 yards away, in Dawson's Stables, were contingents from C, E, F and S Divisions, each consisting of 110 men. On standby at King's Cross Watch-house, about half-a-mile away, were another 110 men from M Division, under the command of Superintendent James Johnson, and in Rosoman Street, about a quarter-of-a-mile away, 110 men from G Division, under Superintendent James Dixon, were billeted in the watch-house.[766]

The plan drawn up by Rowan in consultation with May was relatively simple. Four or five men in plain clothes would be deployed into the Fields when people started congregating. Their role was to get as near to the spot where the Chairman or anyone else began to address the meeting, take note of what was said, and as soon as uniformed officers appeared, to seize the leaders of the NUWC.[767] A Division, under May, would be deployed to the place where the meeting was being held to 'take into custody the Chairman and any person that might address the meeting and all those who identified themselves with the meeting, by being close to them or on the hustings, or having colours or in any way identifying themselves with the meeting… and to disperse the remainder.' As the officer in overall command, Rowan followed the example of Wellington and decided he would oversee the events from a room in a house which adjoined Busbridge's Livery Stables in the north-east corner, overlooking the whole of Cold Bath Fields.[768] The superintendents, meanwhile, were expected to lead their men from the front.

Meanwhile, Phillipps had called at Whitehall Place. On being told that Rowan was already at Cold Bath Fields, Phillipps wrote him a note, which was timed at 2.30pm:

'My dear Colonel Rowan,
I came over to mention from Lord Melbourne, the necessity of having a magistrate present, in case the military should be called out. As you are on the spot, (as I understand from Mayne, which is very good), you are the best magistrate in the world for the purpose. You have nothing to do (in case there should be a riot and the military are called out), but to read the clause in the Riot Act, which you have, the object and use of which clause is to make rioters guilty of felony if they continue

---

766   PP 1833 [718] XIII, op, cit, 749, p.6, q/a.11 and pp.7-8, q/a.19-21.
767   Ibid, p.7, q/a.31.
768   Ibid, p.6, q/a.14.

together an hour after the reading; the clause of course need not be read before persons taking part in such a meeting are apprehended. If there is a riot, too strong for the police, the magistrate may call upon the military to assist the civil power and disperse the rioters, or in any case in which the civil power is overborne.'[769]

Whilst Melbourne and Phillipps may have been hoping that it would be necessary to call out the military, what they didn't realise was that Rowan had no intention of doing so. He was happy he had the resources to control the crowd, whatever its intention. It is unclear whether the note reached Rowan before he committed his resources to deal with the crowd. But it is, nevertheless, an indication that Melbourne was determined to show that he was in charge.

Rowan frequently 'rode about London in the sober plain clothes favoured by Wellington's officers', and today was no exception.[770] He arrived at Busbridge's Livery Stables between 1.30pm and 1.45pm, with the Riot Act in his pocket. By then there were between 400 and 500 people assembled around Cold Bath Fields, but the meeting was not due to commence until 2.00pm.[771] The time of the meeting came and went. It seemed there was a dispute about procedure and the choice of chairman, and the Union committee was holding an emergency meeting in the Union Tavern in Bagnigge Wells Road, which was directly opposite the east side of Cold Bath Fields. At about 2.45pm, a wagon was driven across Cold Bath Fields from the direction of Bagnigge Wells Road. It stopped at the junction of Gough Street. This was to be the platform from which speeches were to be delivered, but there was then a dispute with the driver and the wagon was quickly driven away. Almost immediately, Richard Lee proposed that James Mee should be the chairman, and the latter duly stood on the railings which surrounded Cold Bath Fields, holding onto a lamppost opposite the Coach Builders Yard owned by Collingbridge. He faced Calthorpe Street and the crowd gathered round.[772]

At about this time between 300 and 400 members of the Union, some carrying flags and banners, or 'colours' as they were known, were marching northwards along Gray's Inn Lane from the direction of the City.[773]

769   Ibid, pp.15-16, q/a.117.
770   Thurston, op. cit. 757, p.44.
771   PP 1833 [718] XIII, op. cit. 749, p.129, q/a.2989.
772   Report of the Commissioners of Police to Viscount Melbourne, dated 20 May 1833. The report is to be found in PP 1833 [718] XIII, op. cit. 749, pp.8-10. This incident is to be found on p.9; The reference to Inspector Carter being hit and John Gurney arrested can be found in Superintendent May's evidence to the Committee, op. cit. 749, p.129, q/a.2990-2991.
773   PP 1833 [718] XIII, op. cit. 749, p.10, q/a.38.

The colours displayed such messages as 'Holy Alliance of the Working Classes', 'Equal Rights and Equal Justice', and 'Liberty or Death'. The last was contained on a black flag with a red border emblazoned with skull-and-crossbones. The American flag, the tricolour and the Phrygian cap of liberty of the French Revolution were also in evidence.

As the procession passed Dawson's Livery Stables there were loud hisses, boos and shouts as they caught sight of the police inside.[774] A stone was thrown from the crowd, hitting Inspector Carter, and a man called John Gurney was arrested.[775] The procession continued northwards along Gray's Inn Lane, turned into Calthorpe Street and joined the meeting, swelling the crowd to between 700 and 800.[776] It was now 2.55pm.

The crowd was grouped in front of Mee, who remained on the railings with his back to Cold Bath Fields. By this time Rowan had received reports that the meeting was the one advertised on the posters, and he left his vantage point overlooking Cold Bath Fields and went to the yard at the rear of Busbridge's Livery Stables, where he warned the A Division contingent, which was formed up ready to be deployed, 'to be temperate, to keep their temper, and not to use more force than was necessary; to take into custody those who were addressing the mob, and those who carried banners, and disperse the remainder.'[777]

Led by Superintendent May, the A Division contingent, with truncheons drawn but held by their side, left by the front entrance to the stables and moved into Gray's Inn Lane. May later told the Select Committee that it was 'a usual thing for them to draw their truncheons when they [went] out in large bodies.'[778] The A Division contingent moved north along Gray's Inn Lane and turned right into Calthorpe Street, where Superintendent May stopped them. Calthorpe Street was full of men, women and children. To enable those who wanted to leave peacefully to do so, May stretched his officers across the street, shoulder-to-shoulder, from gutter to gutter. Thus, people could and some did leave Calthorpe Street along both pavements.[779]

In the meantime, Rowan ordered out the H Division contingent, under Superintendent Thomas Hunter, which had only arrived at Busbridge's Livery Stables about five minutes previously. They left the Stables by a back gate and moved into Gough Street forming up, in four ranks, near the north of the stable exit almost at the junction with Calthorpe Street. They

---

774   Ibid, p.127, q/a.2917 and p.7, q/a.26.
775   Report of the Commissioners, op. cit. 772, p.9.
776   PP 1833 [718] XIII, op. cit. 749, p.10, q/a.38.
777   Ibid, p.127, q/a.2917.
778   Ibid, p.127, q/a.2929.
779   Ibid, p.128, q/a.2937.

stretched across Gough Street, leaving a gap approximately 5 feet wide on the stables side for people to leave peacefully if they wished; no gap was left on the Collingbridge Factory side of the street. Hunter's contingent were to assist A Division in seizing the flags and speakers if necessary.[780]

Superintendent May ordered A Division forward. As the contingent neared the end of Calthorpe Street, a large crowd of men formed up across the street at the junction of Gough Street. Seven or eight banners were displayed. As soon as they came into contact with the crowd May was hit on the ear by a stone; other A Division officers were hit with bludgeons, at least one of which was loaded with lead. A number of people were arrested.[781]

The *Caledonian Mercury* records the events slightly differently. On seeing the police, Mee told the meeting to 'stand firm', but then jumped down off the railings and made good his escape. However,

> 'the police came on, and used their staffs pretty freely, their object evidently being to catch the Chairman and those connected with him in the meeting. The meeting was dispersed in two or three minutes, running in all directions. Many heads were broken…'[782]

Meantime, the C Division contingent, under Superintendent Thomas Baker, had been instructed by Rowan to move from Dawson's Stables northwards along Gray's Inn Lane to assist A Division as necessary, and had reached Calthorpe Street.[783] Turning right to follow A Division, they then stopped after moving about ten yards into Calthorpe Street. They came under immediate attack from people in Calthorpe Street throwing stones and bricks, and several police officers were struck.[784] Like the A Division contingent had, the C Division contingent had drawn their truncheons before leaving Dawson's Stables. Similarly to the A Division contingent, they stretched only across the road, leaving people free to leave the area along the pavements. However, as they advanced along Calthorpe Street they were attacked by individuals from the pavement wielding knives and bludgeons. Some officers were injured; three received stab wounds. Sergeant John Brooks, who had joined the Metropolitan Police straight from the Grenadier Guards in which he had served for 25 years, was stabbed in the side by George Fursey, using 'a brass-handled dagger', as he

---

780   Ibid, p.182, q/a.4533-4537.
781   Ibid, p.128, q/a.2949, 2953, 2970 and 2974.
782   *Caledonian Mercury*, 16 May 1833.
783   PP 1833 [718] XIII, op. cit. 749, p.117, q/a.2633; Colonel de Roos was Brigade major of the Cavalry and was ordered to be present in case military assistance was required.
784   Ibid, pp.136-137, q/a.3210-3214 and p.156, q/a.3831-3837.

ST ANDREW'S BURIAL GROUND

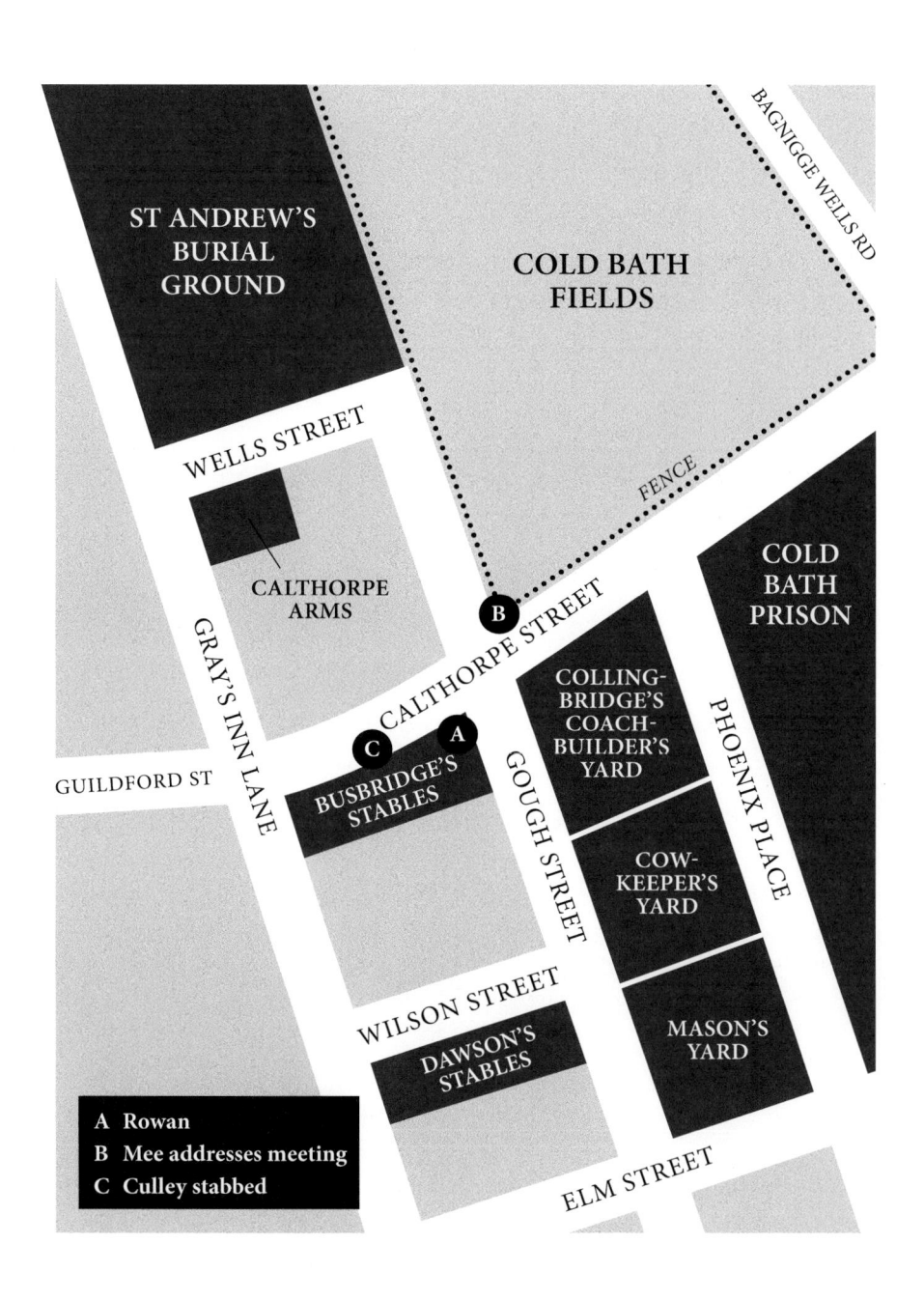

COLD BATH FIELDS

BAGNIGGE WELLS RD

WELLS STREET

FENCE

COLD BATH PRISON

CALTHORPE ARMS

GRAY'S INN LANE

CALTHORPE STREET

B

COLLINGBRIDGE'S COACHBUILDER'S YARD

PHOENIX PLACE

GUILDFORD ST

C A
BUSBRIDGE'S STABLES

GOUGH STREET

COWKEEPER'S YARD

WILSON STREET

DAWSON'S STABLES

MASON'S YARD

ELM STREET

A Rowan
B Mee addresses meeting
C Culley stabbed

went to arrest a man who was carrying what appeared to be an American flag on a pole.[785] Constable Henry Redwood 'heard his sergeant cry out', grabbed at the flagstaff, and at the same time 'tried to wrench it away'. Seeing Fursey with the dagger, Redwood raised his arm to defend himself and was stabbed

> 'through the forearm. Redwood responded by bringing his baton down on the assailant's head and then passed the bloodied and dazed Fursey into the custody of two other constables.'[786]

In the meantime, Constable Robert Culley, together with three other officers, became 'engulfed in a tangle of cursing, sweating men'. Culley claimed to his colleagues that he had been stabbed before he vanished from their sight as the C Division contingent 'battled forward' towards Gough Street. With his uniform becoming bloodsoaked, Culley

> 'staggered back down the street into the Calthorpe Arms pub. In the pub he begged for assistance; a barmaid endeavoured to comfort him, and he died with his head in her lap.'[787]

By the time Superintendent Baker reached Gough Street the meeting had completely broken up, and A Division officers were dispersing the crowd eastwards across Cold Bath Fields towards Bagnigge Wells Road.

The disorder lasted less than five minutes,[788] but Colonel Rowan was determined that members of the Union would not be allowed to re-assemble. He ordered the M Division contingent at King's Cross, under the command of Superintendent Johnson, to move to Wells Street.[789] At the same time he ordered G Division, under the command of Superintendent Dixon, to move from Rosoman Street to Bagnigge Wells Road.[790] Both contingents were instructed to move people away from the area.

In is unclear precisely how many people were arrested. A list that appeared in the report of the subsequent Committee suggested it was thirty, which included Gurney who had thrown the stone that hit Inspector Carter. James Coltman was arrested on suspicion of being concerned in the murder of Police Constable Culley, but was never charged with that offence. Richard Lee was arrested for 'being the person who proposed the Chairman… and making use of seditious language', but Mee escaped.

785 Emsley, op. cit. 756, p.49.
786 Ibid.
787 Ibid.
788 PP 1833 [718] XIII, op, cit. 749, p.8, q/a.36.
789 Ibid, pp.185-186, q/a.4634.
790 Ibid, p.186, q/a.4661-4662.

George Fursey was subsequently charged with stabbing Sergeant Brooks and Constable Redwood; the remainder were arrested and charged with a variety of offences, including throwing stones and bricks, assault, assault with intent to cause grievous bodily harm, exciting a mob to commit violence, attempting to rescue a prisoner, carrying a banner, and threatening language.[791]

At the inquest into Police Constable Culley's death, held in the upstairs room of the Calthorpe Arms, there were heated exchanges between the coroner, Thomas Stirling, who was then 88 years of age, and the jury.[792] At its conclusion, the jury brought in a verdict of justifiable homicide on the grounds that:

> 'no riot act was read, nor any proclamation advising the people to disperse; that the Government did not take proper precautions to prevent the meeting from assembling; and that the conduct of the police was ferocious, brutal and unprovoked by the people; and we moreover, express our anxious hope that the Government will, in future, take better precautions to prevent the recurrence of such disgraceful transactions in the Metropolis.'[793]

The jury was 'feted on its 'glorious verdict'.[794] A few days later, the jury foreman received a package from an anonymous donor. It contained a number of medallions, on one side of each was inscribed the individual name of one of the jurors and on the other was written:

> 'In honour of the men who nobly withstood the diction of the coroner; independent, and conscientious, discharge of their duty; promoted a continued reliance upon the laws under the protection of a British jury.'

A note inside the package asked him to give each of his fellow jurors one of the medallions.

The Milton Street Committee, a group of City men with radical persuasions, arranged a day on the River Thames for the jurors and their families in which they sailed from the City to Twickenham and back. On their arrival at Twickenham they received a cannon salute.

On the first anniversary of the jury's findings the Radical Member of Parliament for Marylebone, Sir Samuel Whalley, hosted a dinner for the jurors at which the Milton Street Committee presented the jurors with

---

791 Mayne presented the Committee with a list of those who had been arrested and the punishments inflicted by the courts, op. cit. 749, pp.206-208, q/a.5153-5157.
792 Thurston, op. cit. 757, pp.68-135.
793 Ibid, p.129.
794 Bloom, op. cit. 761, p.202.

seventeen silver cups. The one presented to the foreman was inscribed:

'This cup was presented on the 20th May 1834 by the Milton Street Committee, City of London to Mr Samuel Stockton, foreman of the memorable Calthorpe-street inquest as a perpetual memorial of their glorious verdict of Justifiable Homicide on the body of Robert Culley a policeman who was slain, while brutally attacking the people when peaceably assembled in Calthorpe-street on 13th May 1833.'

The wording on the other sixteen cups was slightly different, in that it showed the individual name of a juror and indicated that he was 'one of seventeen jurymen who formed the memorable Calthorpe Street inquest.'[795]

The Court of the King's Bench subsequently overturned the verdict of the coroner's court, but did not order a new inquest. Despite this, another Radical, William Cobbett, recently elected as the Member of Parliament for Oldham, stood by the original verdict by the jury, claiming what had been seen at Cold Bath Fields were 'peace officers in uniform embodied in companies and battalions marching in rank and file, commanded by Sergeants and Colonels – under the mock name of Superintendents.' Cobbett suggested that if such practices were to continue, 'the people must arm themselves.'[796]

Meanwhile, Culley's funeral service was held on 17 May, only four days after he had been killed, at St Anne's Church in Soho. About 200 police officers attending the funeral were met by 'a howling mob of about 300 persons, who jeered and booed'. As was pointed out, 'even in the presence of death there was no respect; nothing but hatred'.[797]

A subscription for Culley's pregnant wife raised £188, and the government paid her £200; not inconsiderable sums when one takes into account the fact that a constable's pay was £50 a year.[798] However, she did not receive a pension.

Concerned as to the effect that Culley's death and the subsequent verdict of the coroner's court would have on morale in the Force, the Commissioners drafted an Order which they wanted to circulate and sent it to Phillipps on 27 May with a covering letter signed by Mayne:

---

795 Thurston, op. cit. 757, pp.168-170.
796 Bloom, op. cit. 761, p.202.
797 Thurston, op. cit. 757, p.105.
798 Emsley, op. cit. 756, p.50.

Sir,

                                          4, Whitehall-place, 27 May 1833

The Commissioners of Police having transmitted on the 21st instant, for the information of Lord Melbourne, a full Report of the proceedings in Cold Bath Fields, on Monday the 13th instant, conceived it to be their duty to wait for some information of his Lordship's opinion before any notice was taken by them, in orders to the men, of their conduct on that day; but the Report having been now for some days before his Lordship, and the Commissioners knowing the great anxiety felt by all ranks of the police that their conduct on the late occasion should meet with the approbation of the Secretary of State, and of their own immediate superiors; the Commissioners beg leave respectfully to call his Lordship's immediate attention to the subject, and request that they may be allowed to give an Order to the following effect.

I have the honour to be, Sir,

    Your most obedient Servant

        Richd Mayne

POLICE ORDER

The Commissioners have abstained, up to the present moment, from expressing an opinion of the conduct of the Police, in Cold Bath Fields, on the 13th instant, whilst they have endeavoured by every means in their power to ascertain whether the general charges of misconduct by the Police on that occasion were well founded. Time, also, has been allowed for cases against individuals for violent or improper conduct being brought before the Magistrate, the Commissioners, or any other competent tribunal; and but one such charge has been made, which is in a train for investigation by the Magistrates.

The Commissioners, therefore, now feel that the Police are entitled to an acknowledgement for their services on the 13th instant; and they have very great pleasure in thanking the Police employed, for the effective and steady performance of their duty upon that trying occasion.

The Commissioners desire, at the same time, that it be distinctly understood, should it appear hereafter that any have exceeded their duty, or committed themselves by a wanton or violent exercise of their power, they will be visited by severe punishment by the Commissioners, besides the general consequences to which they are liable by law.

The Commissioners, in conclusion, (in the same spirit as they have at all times endeavoured to instruct and train the Police,) take this opportunity of impressing strongly on the mind of every individual, that his first duty as a constable is to learn self-command; that he must not allow himself to be provoked by offensive or insulting language; and he may rest assured that he shall be at all times duly supported in the discreet and temperate performance of his duty.

The Commissioners have recommended to the most favourable consideration of the Secretary of State the case of the widow of the late police constable, Robert Culley, who unfortunately lost his life; and also the cases of police-serjeant John Brooke and police-constable Henry Chance Redwood, who received wounds by stabbing on the 13th.[799]

A response from Phillipps came two days later:

'I am directed by Viscount Melbourne to acknowledge the receipt of your Letter of the 27th instant, enclosing a General Order relative to the conduct of the Police on the 13th instant, which you propose, to distribute to the Metropolitan Police Force, and request his Lordship's sanction thereto.

And I am to inform you, that as on the trials which are about to take place, the fullest inquiry into all the circumstances which occurred on the occasion referred to will probably be made in a Court of Justice, Lord Melbourne thinks it advisable to withhold, for the present, his sanction to the proposed Order.'[800]

No-one ever stood trial for Police Constable Culley's death. However, on 4 July 1833, about a month after the jury had brought in its verdict of 'justifiable homicide', George Fursey stood trial before Mr Justice Gabelee and a jury at the Old Bailey for stabbing both Sergeant Brooks and Constable Redwood but, for some unapparent reason, the prosecution, which was led by the Solicitor-General, only proceeded with the stabbing of Sergeant Brooks even though Constable Redwood appeared as a witness. Not surprisingly, perhaps, given the verdict brought in by the jury at the coroner's court, Fursey was found Not Guilty.[801]

Although Fursey continued to protest his innocence,[802] some nine years

---

799 PP 1833 [718] XIII, op. cit. 749, pp.14-15, q/a.105.
800 Ibid.
801 Thurston, op. cit. 757, pp.154-163; see also The Proceedings of the Old Bailey at www.oldbaileyonline.org, reference number t18330704-5 [accessed 15 July 2018].
802 Rowe, op. cit. 750. Francis Place interviewed Fursey after the trial and he denied ever having a knife or stabbing any policeman.

later, in a Memorandum to the Home Secretary 'laying out the suggestions for the formation of a Detective Force', Commissioner Mayne, in referring to Culley's death, wrote 'there is no reason whatever to doubt that the party who was tried – but acquitted – did commit the act.'[803] One can only assume that he was referring to Fursey as the person who killed Culley, as well as stabbing Brooks and Redwood.

Of the remainder arrested at Cold Bath Fields, with the exception of three people who were found guilty at the first hearing and were successively fined 40s or awarded one month's imprisonment, fined 20s or one month's imprisonment and fined 40s or two months' imprisonment, there is no evidence that anyone else was convicted.[804]

A Select Committee was appointed by Parliament to inquire into the conduct of the Metropolitan Police in dispersing the meeting. The first main discussion point hinged around what had taken place at the Home Office on the Saturday morning, and more precisely what instructions Lord Melbourne had given the Commissioners. He was therefore summoned to give evidence before the Committee, where he was 'grilled', and did not come out of it with grace.[805] The Committee questioned him 'embarrassingly on the subject of the Home Office habit of refusing to give orders and instructions to the Commissioners in writing,' about which the Commissioners had frequently commented. At a hearing of the earlier 1833 Committee, the Commissioners were asked whether the orders they received from the Secretary of State were in writing or were given verbally. Mayne replied, 'I do not remember that we have ever had orders as to our conduct, or the general management of the Police in writing' other than those involving expenses 'not in the ordinary line of Police duty.'[806]

At the Cold Bath hearing, Melbourne claimed he had 'never found any public inconvenience to have risen from verbal instructions.' But, as Reith pointed out, 'the convenience of being able to deny having given orders to the police was a safety valve in the circumstances of the times that the Home Office was determined not to lose.'[807] Reith goes further, suggesting that Melbourne's behaviour during the whole course of this particular incident illustrated 'the cynical cunning and pettiness in his personality

---

803 TNA HO 45/292. Mayne, Richard (1842). In a Memorandum to the Home Secretary, dated 14 June 1842, laying out the suggestions for the formation of a Detective Police.
804 PP 1833 [718] XIII, op. cit. 749, pp.206-208, q/a.5157.
805 Cowley, Richard (2011). *A History of the British Police*: From its earliest beginnings to the present day. Stroud, Gloucestershire: The History Press, p.33.
806 PP 1834 [600]. Report from the Select Committee on the Police of the Metropolis; with minutes of evidence, appendix and index; minutes of evidence, p.384, q/a 6177-78.
807 Reith, Charles (1956). *A New Study of Police History*. Edinburgh: Oliver and Boyd, pp.164-165.

which so often hampered the exercise of his unquestioned abilities.'[808]

A dispute also arose around what Lord Melbourne actually said to Colonel Rowan at their meeting on 11 May. The Home Secretary definitely ordered Rowan and Mayne to arrest the leaders of the Union as soon as they got up to speak. Despite a view to the contrary, expressed by Phillipps, Colonel Rowan was adamant that Lord Melbourne had told him that, in addition to the arrest of the speakers, the crowd was to be dispersed.[809]

In a report to the Home Secretary following the events, the Commissioners had described in writing their reasons for not occupying the ground early:

- It would be impossible to identify those who had come for the purpose of attending the meeting and those who were there casually, as mere onlookers;
- Any attempt to prevent those who were there casually could lead to confrontations with them questioning the right of the police to remove them; and that a crowd would be collected by such a confrontation;
- It was considered undesirable, in such a public place, to inconvenience members of the public who were not there for the purpose of attending the meeting.
- The police would not be justified in preventing everyone from coming there;
- The police would not be so well organised if the meeting was moved to another place.[810]

When he gave evidence to the Committee, Rowan also reiterated the view he had expressed to Melbourne at the meeting; that if it moved elsewhere, it would have been more difficult to identify it as the meeting declared illegal by the Home Secretary.[811]

The main criticism of the police related to the amount of force used, one claim suggesting they were 'ferocious, brutal and unprovoked by the people.'[812] But there was conflicting evidence both in media reports and in the evidence given by individuals before the Select Committee as to how the disorder had started, and whether the police first attacked the crowd or whether any violence inflicted by the police took place only after people had attacked them with weapons, and stones were thrown at them. Some witnesses claimed that no stones were thrown at all, and accused the police

---

808   Ibid, p.162.
809   PP 1833 [718] XIII, op. cit. 749, p.13, q/a.89-116.
810   Ibid. Cited in p.8 of the Report..
811   Ibid, p.13, q/a.74.
812   Bloom, op. cit. 761, p.202.

of using unreasonable force in dispersing the crowd and leaving no escape routes;[813] some said they had been struck by officers wielding truncheons. Two surgeons, James Brown and John B. Gibson, told the inquiry that some of those examined by them after the riot had sustained superficial cuts, possibly caused by a blunt instrument.[814]

However, the Honourable Colonel William De Roos, a Brigade Major in the Cavalry who was present in plain clothes in case the military was required to act in support of the civil authority, claimed he saw a 'good many' people armed with sticks, and those around the speaker had Maceroni lances and banners. As the police contingent reached the crowd around the banners, he claimed that they were met with 'very determined resistance', and 'there appeared to be a good deal of striking on both sides.' Despite this, he told the Inquiry the police had 'conducted themselves with the utmost steadiness.'

Some witnesses at the Inquiry claimed the police took up the whole street as they advanced, but Colonel De Roos said they only took up the roadway, leaving the pavements free for people to use. Colonel De Roos also saw stones thrown. When specifically asked by a member of the Committee whether he saw any unnecessary act of violence on the part of the police, the Colonel replied, 'No!'[815] Colonel De Roos was accompanied throughout the afternoon by a junior officer, Lieutenant Thomas Bulkeley, who confirmed the evidence given by his senior officer. When asked specifically whether he thought the police had used any unnecessary force, Bulkeley replied, 'decidedly not.'[816]

Other witnesses, such as Samuel Beasley, an architect who had been present as an observer, tended to support the evidence given by the two soldiers. When he was asked whether he considered the police had used greater violence than was necessary, he replied, 'at the time that I saw the collision, they did not use greater violence than was necessary to disperse

---

813 PP 1833 [718] XIII, op. cit. 749. Smallwood, Nathan, op. cit. 2, pp.23-38, q/a.238–621; Brown, James, pp.29-42, q/a. 622-711; Hudson, John, pp.42-47, q/a.712-848; Murray, John, pp.47-50, q/a. 849-942; Burns, Richard, pp.50-55, q/a.943-1054; Nelson, Samuel, pp.55-62, q/a.1055-1221; Sneed, John, pp.62-65, q/a.1222-1308; Walsh, Charles, pp.65–66, q/a.1309 -1339; Read, John, pp.66-69, q/a.1340-1417; Carpenter, William, pp.69-81, q/a.1417-1658; Bowyer, Thomas, pp.81-87, q/a.1659-1806; Wheeler, Charles, pp.87–90, q/a.1807-1867; Clark, Samuel, pp.90-92, q/a.1868-1940; Christopher Best, pp.92-94, q/a.1940-1995; Austin Allen, pp.94-99, q/a.1996-2140; William Robertson, pp.99-104, q/a.2141-2296; William Calf, pp.104-106, q/a.2297-2370; John Browning, pp.106-108, q/a.2371-2418; Thomas Benjamin King, pp.111-115, q/a.2494-2587.
814 Ibid. Browne, James, pp.108-109, q/a.2419-2447; Gibson, John B, pp.109-111, q/a.2448-2493.
815 Ibid, pp.114-124, q/a.2588-2815.
816 Ibid, pp.124-127, q/a.2816-2910.

the people.'[817]

In their report to Melbourne, dated 20 May, the Commissioners had stated that they were:

> 'not prepared to affirm that every blow given by the truncheons of policemen was duly proportionate to the degree of provocation or resistance made by the party struck; and if unnecessary violence can be proved to have been used on the occasion, none would regret it more than the Commissioners.'

However, they requested that 'in judging the conduct of the police on this occasion… due allowance, if such should be necessary, will be made for men in performing, under very peculiar circumstances, so difficult, so responsible and dangerous a duty,' before reminding Melbourne that a police officer had lost his life and two others had been wounded.[818]

The Committee finally reported that it found that the meeting was illegal and that some of the people attending carried 'offensive weapons of a dangerous nature'. No blame was attached to the Commissioners, who were merely carrying out the instructions received from the Secretary of State, and that by not occupying the ground to the north and east of the meeting the police left ample opportunity for people to escape. They concluded that in dispersing the meeting the police used no more force than was necessary to affect their purpose, although, in clearing the wider area, some officers 'in a moment of excitement and irritation, and after much provocation' did individually use unnecessary force.

The report also suggested that, in clearing the area surrounding the meeting place, some police officers followed

> 'persons to a greater distance than was necessary, and that under these circumstances they were not subjected to that efficient control which, in a moment of excitement and irritation, and after much provocation, could alone prevent individual instances of undue exercise or power.'[819]

Having said that, the Committee was quick to point out that no 'dangerous wound or permanent injury' was 'inflicted by them on any individual, while on the other hand one of their own number had been killed with a dagger and two others stabbed while in the discharge of their duty.'

Nevertheless, the Committee felt bound to issue a warning to the effect

---

817   Ibid, p.200, q/a.4975.
818   Ibid. Report, p.10.
819   Ibid, p.3.

that, whilst there was 'no just ground' for complaint about the conduct of the police as a body, superintendents and other officers must be vigilant to check any 'unnecessary violence among their Men on all occasions, but more especially when large bodies of them are employed in the prevention or suppression of disturbance, and the maintenance of the Public Peace.'[820]

Short though it was, the Cold Bath Fields riot caused widespread recognition of the value of police as a means of controlling mobs without inflicting serious casualties or requiring action by troops.[821]

---

820   Ibid, p.4.
821   Reith, op. cit. 807, p.166.

Top: The first Joint Commissioners. Richard Mayne, left, and Charles Rowan, right. Bottom: Sir Robert Peel, Home Secretary, left, and John Wray, the first Receiver, right.

Peel's Police,
RAW LOBSTERS,
Blue Devils,

Or by whatever other appropriate Name they may be known.

Notice is hereby given,

That a Subscription has been entered into, to supply the **PEOPLE** with **STAVES** of a superior Effect, either for Defence or Punishment, which will be in readiness to be gratuitously distributed whenever a similar unprovoked, and therefore unmanly and blood-thirsty Attack, be again made upon Englishmen, by a Force unknown to the British Constitution, and called into existence by a Parliament illegally constituted, legislating for their individual interests, consequently in opposition to the Public good.

—ooo—

" Put not your trust in Princes."—DAVID.
" Help yourself, and Heaven will help you."—FRENCH MOTTO.

Eliz. Soulby, Printer, 91, Gracechurch Street.

Reaction to the formation of the Metropolitan Police.
Above: 'Raw Lobsters' (Courtesy John Murray Archive)
Opposite, top: 'The New Police' (© National Archives). Bottom: Wellington and Peel, in the roles of the body-snatchers Burke and Hare, suffocating John Bull; representing the extinguishing by Wellington and Peel of the constitution of 1688 by Catholic Emancipation (Courtesy Wellcome Collection).

The New Police.

PARISHIONERS.—Ask yourselves the following *Questions*:

Why is an Englishman, if he complains of an outrage or an insult, referred for redress to a Commissioner of Police?

Why is a Commissioner of Police delegated to administer Justice?

Why are the proceedings of this new POLICE COURT *unpublished* and *unknown*? and by what Law of the Land is it recognized?

Why is the British Magistrate stripped of his power? and why is Justice transferred from the Justice Bench?

Why is the Sword of Justice placed in the hands of a MILITARY Man?

Consider these constitutional questions: consider the additional burthen saddled on you—consider all these points, then UNITE in removing such a powerful force from the hands of Government, and let us institute a Police System in the hands of the PEOPLE under *parochial* appointments—

UNITY IS STRENGTH;

THEREFORE,

I.—Let each Parish convene a Meeting.

II.—Let a Committee be chosen, instructed to communicate with other Parishes.

III.—Let Delegates be elected from each Committe to form a

CENTRAL COMMITTEE,

To join your Brother Londoners in one heart, one hand, for the

Abolition of the New Police!

ELLIOT, Printer, 14, Holywell Street, Strand.

Burkeing the Constitution of E—g—d !!!!!

The rear entrance to Great Scotland Yard, home of the New Police.

Chester Square, where Mayne lived with his family at No. 80 from 1856 until his death.

Poster proclaiming a protest at Cold Bath Fields on 13th May 1833, and the result.

Wanted poster for the murderer Daniel Good.
The search for the fugitive led directly to the formation of the Detective Branch.
(© National Archives / Adam Wood)

Captain William Hay, junior Joint Commissioner following Rowan's death

Lieutenant-Colonel Douglas Labalmondière, Assistant Commissioner following Hay's death

Eaton Place, where Hay died at his home, No. 12, in August 1855.

Sir Richard Mayne in the 1860s (Alamy).

Top: The Hyde Park riot of 1866. Bottom: The 1867 Clerkenwell epxlosion. Both events led to Mayne's resignation, albeit refused.

Sir Richard Mayne.
Top: The unveiling of his tomb at
Kensal Green Cemetery, and
Left: the scene today (©Jose Oranto)

CHAPTER FOURTEEN

THE REMAINDER OF THE 1830s

Already required to spend six days before the 1833 Select Committee, earlier in the year, during which Rowan was very much the dominant of the two, immediately following the events at Cold Bath Fields the Commissioners were kept busy appearing before two further Select Committees. A petition, presented to Parliament by members of the National Union of the Working Classes (NUWC), resulted in a Select Committee being set up on 1 July 'to inquire into the matter of a Petition of several Persons complaining that Policemen are employed as spies, and praying that the People may not be taxed to maintain those Spies'.

The allegation was that a sergeant in the Metropolitan Police, William Popay, had infiltrated Union meetings at Camberwell and become an agent provocateur in that he was extremely vocal in his criticisms of government minsters, and induced the members to use stronger language than they would have, encouraged them to practice shooting and the use of the broad-sword and, on one occasion, even paid members' expenses out of his own pocket.

Rowan and Mayne faced some searching questions when they appeared before the Committee,[822] as to how much they knew of Popay's activities, particularly as all the 51 reports by him had been forwarded to them by Superintendent McLean of M Division, Popay's immediate supervisor.[823]

When it reported on 6 August, the Committee declared that Popay's conduct had been 'highly reprehensible', in that he had taken an active part in the proceedings of the Camberwell branch of the National Union of Working Classes when 'his duty only required him to observe'. But, in

---

822 PP 1833 [627]. Report from the Select Committee on the Petition of Frederick Young and Others (police), Minutes of Evidence, pp.78-80, q/a. 1804-1846 and pp.170-178, q/a 3885-4040.
823 Ibid, Minutes of Evidence, p.170, q/a 3885.

a criticism of the Commissioners, they found that had those reports been properly checked, they would have had cause to caution Popay 'as to the manner in which he was obtaining information.'

However, the Committee did declare it 'had no complaint' about the employment of policemen in plain clothes, providing it was 'strictly confined to detect breaches of the law and prevent breaches' if there was no other way of obtaining such information. But, it warned that it regarded 'any approach to the Employment of Spies as a practice most abhorrent to the feelings of the People, and most alien to the spirit of the Constitution.'[824]

The Select Committee on the Metropolitan Police, having made considerable progress during April and May 1833, suspended its proceedings without issuing a detailed report[825] because of the pressure put on Members of Parliament by the necessity to inquire into the events surrounding both the Cold Bath Fields riot[826] and the activities of Sergeant Popay. It reconvened on 6 May 1834.

In addition to those matters already covered in Chapters Eight to Eleven, the Commissioners were questioned about those occasions Metropolitan Police officers were required for duty outside the Metropolitan Police District. The Committee was told that, in 1832, parties of police had been sent to Reigate, Hastings, Hetton Colliery near Durham, Midhurst, Morpeth, Wareham, Spalding, Knowston, Chippenham, Great Yeldham and Godalming; officers had also been sent to establish and take charge of the police permanently in several places.[827] Asked on what grounds such requests were made, Mayne had replied that it was quite often because there were criminals operating in the area and local resources could not cope with them. As an example, he mentioned the occasion three constables had been sent to three parishes in Essex and, upon their return, the Commissioners received letters from the inhabitants, indicating they had been very successful.[828]

The Committee also heard about three day-to-day problems on the streets. The first arose from having to deal with public nuisances and vagrants. The total number of vagrants arrested in the first five months of 1833 was 9,325. Rowan told the Committee that they were taken before the Magistrates, but about half would be discharged immediately whilst

---

824   Ibid, Report, p.2.
825   PP 1833 [675], op, cit. 822, Report from the Select Committee on Metropolitan Police.
826   See Chapter Thirteen.
827   PP 1834 [600]. Report from the Select Committee on the Police of the Metropolis; with minutes of evidence, appendix and index, Minutes of Evidence, p.2, q/a. 23.
828   Ibid, Minutes of Evidence, p.30, q/a 464.

the other half were sentenced to a short-term of imprisonment, returning to vagrancy on being released. Colonel Rowan described how boys, many of them the children of destitute Irish families, would carry a broom to 'sweep crossings', or assemble close to the clubs 'to hold gentlemen's horses.'[829]

The second arose from the supervision of public houses, a number of which kept very irregular hours. When police considered a public house to be disorderly or thought it was the resort of thieves, the Commissioners were informed and permission was given for an officer to appear before magistrates, state the facts and apply for a summons. As a result, a few licenses had been withdrawn and others suspended.[830] However, Rowan pointed out that magistrates had very different views on the subject. Some held that there was nothing wrong with such houses being open all night, despite the fact that 'prostitutes and bad characters' frequented them and they kept irregular hours.

The third arose with oyster shops and coffee shops, some of which sold liquor that was not excisable, such as ginger beer and soda water. The Commissioners believed that such places required regulation.[831]

In its summing-up of the first five years of the Metropolitan Police's existence, the Committee suggested 'it was a matter of surprise that so great a change should have been accomplished, without greater opposition than has been experienced.' Although not mentioning him by name, the report went on to suggest that much of the credit was due to Peel because of the 'judgment and discrimination which was exercised in the selection of the individuals, Colonel Rowan and Mr Mayne' as Commissioners. More importantly, it then went on to say that on 'many critical occasions, and in very difficult circumstances, the sound discretion' exercised by the two Commissioners, coupled with 'the straightforward, open and honourable course' they had 'pursued whenever their conduct' had 'been questioned by the Public', called 'for the strongest expression of approbation on the part of [the] Committee.'[832]

A significant event in 1834 was the fire which seriously damaged the Houses of Parliament. It broke out on the evening of 16 October and quickly took hold. The incident was arguably the first occasion on which there was police/military cooperation, at what would now be termed a major incident, when 'fifty Grenadier Guards marched to the spot and with the

---

829   Ibid, pp.30-33, q/a 479-499.
830   Ibid, p.33, q/a 500-502. TNA MEPO 1/18. Letter, dated 14 May 1835, folio 30028.
831   Ibid, p.34, q/a 505-508.
832   Ibid, Report, p.6.

assistance of a strong body of police, opened up a square space before both Houses, in order that the firemen were not obstructed in their efforts.'[833] Thereafter the police and military cooperated 'to control the crowd, man the pumps, and clear the way for rescuers for many hours.'[834] At one stage, 'the whole structure, from the entrance of the House of Commons to the entrance of the House of Lords, presented a bright sheet of flame,'[835] and sparks were falling 'thick as flakes of snow' on the south side of the River Thames. Given the spectacle that it must have been, it was inevitable that huge crowds would descend on the area. Westminster Bridge was almost impassable, and other bridges – Vauxhall, Waterloo and Blackfriars – up and down the river began to fill up. Despite the sparks, the southern shore of the Thames was thronging with people. Every street and lane leading to the Houses of Parliament was 'thronged by an almost countless multitude of all descriptions of persons.'[836] A number of prominent people attended the scene; as well as Rowan and Mayne, these included Prime Minister Lord Melbourne, Home Secretary Viscount Duncannon, Chancellor of the Exchequer Viscount Althorp, and Lord Hill, commander-in-chief of the army.[837]

Some people arriving at the scene were appalled at the lack of organisation in the fire-fighting, claiming there was no coordination. Amongst them was Captain William Hook of the Royal Navy, who saw that 'each engine crew was accountable only to itself,' with 'no-one coordinating the rescue efforts'. He appealed to the police, but was told 'they were only there to keep order and had no authority over the fire-engine men.'[838] The following morning, firemen continued to pour water 'on the smouldering embers', but there were at least three further outbreaks of fire that day.[839] Captain George Manby, a well-known inventor of various lifesaving equipment,[840] had been at the scene of the fire, following which he had visited Rowan at Whitehall Place to see whether arrangements could be made for him to look over the site. Rowan apparently said there had been 'a want of union among persons in the direction of Fire engines,' and provided him with a police escort to view the ruins of the palace.[841]

---

833   Shenton, Caroline (2012). *The Day Parliament Burned Down*. Oxford: Oxford University Press, p.81.
834   *Bristol Mercury*, 17 October 1834, p.2.
835   *Scotland Yard, Past and Present: Experiences of thirty-seven years.* , 17 October 1834.
836   *Bristol Mercury*, 17 October 1834, p.3.
837   *Morning Chronicle*, 17 October 1834, p.3.
838   Shenton, op. cit. 833 p.82.
839   Ibid, p.230.
840   Ibid, p.99.
841   Ibid, p.244.

The newspapers strongly supported the establishment of a single fire superintendent, and even the institution of a Fire Police, to take charge of public safety on such occasions, with 'one ostensible and responsible head.' The police themselves had been found to be 'firm, temperate and judicious; no number of parish constables could have performed their duty, and ten times the number of soldiers would have been less effective.'[842] The previous year, ten independent insurance companies had united to form the London Fire Engine Establishment (LFEE) and James Braidwood had been appointed as the chief officer. As a result, he now headed an Establishment that had fourteen horse-drawn fire appliances spread across London. In his report to the LFEE board following the fire, Braidwood said:

> 'Although I regret the extent of the fire and the loss which has been sustained by the country, I have the satisfaction of feeling that no exertions were spared, either by myself or the men under me, to arrest the progress of the flames. I also gratefully acknowledge the very efficient assistance of the military in working the engines and of the military and police, in keeping the ground clear.'[843]

In early December, the Committee of the LFEE wrote to the Duke of Wellington, who had briefly returned as Prime Minister, to point out that the private insurance companies making up the Establishment were still duty-bound to their private employers and, if during the fire at Westminster any insured property had been in danger elsewhere, then the Superintendent would have been obliged to redeploy fire engines, leaving 'Westminster Hall and the Public property adjoining' to share 'the fate of the Houses of Parliament.' They recommended that the problem 'would be corrected merely be placing the parochial engines under the inspection of the Commissioners of Police... and by placing the public and parochial engines at fires under the order of one directing officer.'[844]

This was just the first of a number of exchanges between the fire authorities and the Commissioners. In 1835 they received a letter from the Alliance Assurance Company criticising the actions of police at the scene of a fire:

> 'Had [they] not interfered no loss, or next to none, would have been sustained by this Company. Instead of which, from the rough and

---

842 *The Examiner*, 19 October 1834.
843 Guildhall Library, London MS 15728/2, p/83, quoted in Shenton, op. cit. 833, p.245.
844 TNA HO 44/27, folios 318-319. Letter from the London Fire Engine Establishment to the Duke of Wellington.

absurd manner in which goods were thrown out which ought not to have been removed at all, and windows smashed to pieces which would otherwise remained entire, a severe loss will be sustained by that Company.

The police indeed state that they acted under the instructions of the proprietor, Mr. Shackel. This, however, he denies, and even if they had, it would not have justified or accounted for the destruction of property by the panic-stricken style of their operations.'[845]

The Commissioners did not agree, as Mayne's response indicates:

'The Commissioners beg leave to add that in communications they had had with managers of the United Fire Engine Establishments and the respective Insurance Offices, they have endeavoured to meet the views of the Assurance Companies, and all the police regulations on the subject have been framed with a due regard to the interests of the Companies, and the more general services by which it was found the police could render most benefit to the public.

The duties thus devolving upon the police at such times are most arduous and responsible, and from which, with but very few exceptions, they can derive no advantage, and while the Commissioners are at all times ready to check every act of misconduct or indiscretion by any of the police, they are unwilling to allow any undeserved censure to rest upon them, which must have the effect of abating their future exertions.'[846]

Two months later, following further criticism, Mayne wrote to the Committee for Managing the London Fire Engine Establishment:

'The Commissioners lament to find from the statements and spirit of the reports of Mr. Braidwood on these occasions that they cannot hope for that mutual good-will and cordial co-operation between the firemen and the police which it is so much to the interest of the public should exist, and which they are conscious it has at all times been the desire of the Committee and the Commissioners to promote.'[847]

The next thing that taxed the Commissioners' patience was slightly more personal. When the Metropolitan Police was originally set up, Peel

---

845 TNA MEPO 1/18, folio 30028. Letter, dated 14 May 1835, from the Alliance Assurance Company to the Commissioners.
846 Ibid, folio 30030. Letter, dated 16 May 1835, from Mayne to the Alliance Assurance Company.
847 Ibid, folio 30186. Letter dated 20 July 1835, from Mayne to the London Fire Engine Establishment.

obviously thought the management of the force would be conducted in the same way as the Chief Magistrate managed the Bow Street Runners and the Bow Street Horse Patrol – from an office. Therefore, whilst it was a uniform body, there was no need for the Commissioners to have a uniform. However, as will have been noted, the Commissioners were often 'out on the ground'. So, in September 1836, Mayne outlined the problem, requesting that Lord John Russell petition His Majesty to grant them official dress for public occasions:

> 'On such occasions when the police are assembled in great numbers from the several Divisions and it becomes necessary for the efficient control and management of so numerous a body for one of the Commissioners to take the immediate direction of the whole Force, the Commissioners find themselves unknown to many even of the police as well as the soldiers and others on duty. They are impeded in moving about as may be necessary, sometimes unable to make their way through the crowd, and when allowed to pass the lines kept by the police and soldiers, others are encouraged to attempt to pass the lines also…
>
> The Commissioners have abstained from making an earlier representation to your Lordship on the subject from an unwillingness to move in a matter apparently of personal consideration, and are now induced to do so in consequence of having, on a recent public occasion, most forcibly experienced the difficulties to which they have alluded, from which very serious evils might have arisen.'[848]

However, Russell turned down the request[849] and the Commissioners had to wait almost another two years before the matter was resolved, after Queen Victoria's coronation. On this occasion Major-General Sir James Willoughby Gordon, Quartermaster of the Army from 1811 until 1851, no doubt with the encouragement of Rowan, wrote to Lord John Russell suggesting the Commissioners should have a uniform,[850] as a result of which Phillipps wrote to the Commissioners:

> 'Lord John Russell, having observed on the celebration of the late Coronation that it would be for the convenience of the public, and proper also from regard to the Police Force, that the Commissioners

---

848 TNA MEPO 1/4A. Letter, dated 3 September 1836.
849 Letter signed by Maude, dated 8 September 1836.
850 Letter, dated 10 July 1838, from Sir Willoughby Gordon to Lord John Russell. Quoted in Reith, Charles (1943). *British Police and the Democratic Ideal*. Oxford: Oxford University Press, p. 214.

of Police should be dressed in uniform on public occasions (whenever they consider it necessary)… and accordingly one should be adopted.'[851]

Towards the end of the year, Mayne sent details of a uniform he and Rowan thought would be suitable for them to wear for Lord John Russell's approval.[852] Regrettably, it would appear that no details of the uniform have survived.

Whilst they were dealing with the subject of uniforms, the subject of an increase in the Commissioners' salaries also came up and Mayne wrote a personal note, which is on file in the National Archives, in which he outlined why such an increase would be justified:

- The importance of the establishment, not only to the metropolis but to the whole Kingdom, together with difficulties that had been overcome;
- The nature, extent and variety of the responsibilities and duties of the office;
- The favourable comments of the two men contained in various parliamentary reports;
- The number of applications from different foreign nations for information about the system;
- As many as 2,000 uniform Metropolitan police officers have been sent to all parts of the kingdom;
- In what state would the Police of the Metropolis and throughout the Kingdom be now had the experiment failed in the metropolis.[853]

Towards the end of the decade Rowan and Mayne, either together or individually, were involved with three other inquiries. On 21 February 1837 Mayne gave evidence before the Criminal Law Commission, who at that time were enquiring into 'whether it would be advisable to make any distinction in the Mode of Trial between Adult and Juvenile Offenders; and, if not, whether any class of Offenders can be made subject to a more summary proceeding than trial by Jury'.[854]

Mayne's contention was that whilst the current punishments inflicted on juveniles did have some deterrent effect, 'in that no thief [liked] to be caught and imprisoned,' it had 'no effect [in] preventing them from

---

851 Letter, dated 4 July 1838, from Phillipps to the Commissioners. Quoted in Reith, op. cit. 29, p.214.
852 Letter, dated 7 November 1838, from Mayne to Phillipps, quoted in Reith, op. cit. 29, p.214.
853 TNA MEPO 2/5813. Personal memorandum, dated 15 April 1837, written by Mayne.
854 PP 1837[79] Third Report from the Commissioners on Criminal Law. Juvenile Offenders, Report, p.5.

again committing crime.'[855] Therefore, they continued with the same type of criminal activities on their release. Mayne pointed out that, at a time when 'the public [were] continually crying out for prevention,' many of the 'younger thieves' were able to 'assemble uncontrolled at all hours of the night, as well as by day, in public houses and beer-shops,' but under the existing law the police were only authorized to take action when they could 'prove that the party being a reputed thief or suspected person was in such public-house, &c, with intent to devise or plan the commission of felony, or some other offence'. But because 'proof of such intent' could 'very seldom be safely given on oath' the law, as it stood, was, in effect, 'inoperative'.[856]

Mayne also took the opportunity to point out to the Commission that much police time was wasted because police officers were required to attend Sessions at the beginning whilst the 'clerk of indictments' drew up the bills of indictment. As an example, he told them that 'in November 1836, 205 officers of the Metropolitan Police were involved with cases at the Central Criminal Court, and each man spent, on average, two-and-a-half days 'merely in getting the bill prepared to go before the grand jury'. He claimed that, as a result, great difficulty had been experienced 'in carrying on the ordinary police duty of the town.' Mayne suggested that the bill of indictment ought to be prepared at the magistrates' court at the time of committal.[857] A copy of the evidence he had given was subsequently forwarded to Mayne. He showed it to Rowan, who agreed with 'the statements and opinions' Mayne had expressed.[858]

The main body of the report related to the reasons why the inquiry was set up in the first place. But, in its conclusions, the Committee said:

> 'We are persuaded that it is desirable that increased powers should be given to the police to withdraw young persons from public-houses, beer shops, penny theatres, and other notorious places of meeting for the idle and dissolute. Much advantage also might be derived from giving to the police a more distinct authority than they now possess, to disperse or apprehend as vagrants, boys wandering in companies in the streets, or loitering around theatres and other places of public amusement, without any ostensible employment. The evidence given before us by Mr. Mayne, one of the Commissioners of the Metropolitan Police… appears to us to be of the utmost importance upon the subject

---

855   Ibid, Report, p.19.
856   Ibid, Appendix No. 1, p.20.
857   Ibid, p.23.
858   Ibid, dated 9 March 1837, p.23.

of preventing crimes among young persons of the lower classes.'[859]

Next, Rowan was appointed as one of three members of a Royal Commission in October 1837 to inquire

> 'as to the best Means of Establishing an Efficient Constabulary Force in the Counties of England and Wales, especially with a view to the Prevention of Offences, and also with regard to any Proceedings before Trial by which the Detection and Apprehension of Criminals may be rendered more certain; and also for Inquiring as to any public Services which may be obtained from such a Force, either in the Preservation of the Peace and the due Protection of Property, or by enforcing a more regular Observance of the Laws of the Realm; and also for Inquiring as to the Manner in which such a Force should be appointed and paid.'[860]

Rowan's two colleagues on the Committee were already involved in a number of government initiatives. Edwin Chadwick was well known. Called to the bar in 1830, he had been one of the nine commissioners of the Royal Commission into the Operations of the Poor Laws in 1832. When the Poor Law Commission was set up in 1834 to administer poor relief, Chadwick had hoped that he would be one of the three commissioners but instead, much to his disappointment, he had been appointed secretary. As secretary, Chadwick tended to air 'his opinions and disagreements as freely as if he were indeed a fourth commissioner' and 'the initial work of the Commission was entirely his.'[861] The other member, Charles Shaw Lefevre, was a Whig politician whose career had been helped by being the son-in-law of Lady Elizabeth Grey, sister of former Prime Minister Earl Grey.

The idea of such a Commission was Edwin Chadwick's, for, in an undated letter to Lord John Russell in August 1836, he had suggested a 'rural police was needed, not only to deal with beggars, vagrants and casuals, but for the suppression of tumults connected with the administration of relief.' Russell was dubious, particularly if such a police force was to be uniformed. But Chadwick suggested to Russell he should 'let public opinion be moulded by a Royal Commission.' In persuading Russell, Chadwick suggested it need not 'be a real Royal Commission'; all that needed to be done was to 'obtain the sanction of other names,' and Chadwick himself would perform

---

859 Ibid, Report, p.11.
860 PP 1839 [169]. First report of the commissioners appointed to inquire as to the best means of establishing an efficient constabulary force in the counties of England and Wales, pp.iii-iv.
861 Finer, S.E (2017). *The Life and Times of Sir Edwin Chadwick*. Abingdon, Oxon: Routledge, p.117.

all its work in his spare time!'[862]

Other than sign the final report, Shaw Lefevre had little to do with its preparation and neither did he take part in the investigation. True to his word, the final report was written by Chadwick although, given its content, Rowan had some influence, particularly on the final recommendations:

I. A paid constabulary force should be trained, appointed, and organised on the principles of management recognised by the Legislature in the appointment of the new Metropolitan Police Force.

II. That an application in writing, supported by the majority of the justices assembled at any Quarters Sessions of the Peace for the county should be submitted to the Home Office requesting the assistance of the Commissioners of the Metropolitan Police in setting up a constabulary force.

III. The force should be paid one-fourth, from the Consolidated Fund and three-fourths from the county rates, as a part of the general expenses of the whole county.

IV. That the constables so appointed shall report their proceedings to the magistrates of the Quarter and Petty Sessions where they are stationed.

V. The Commissioners would frame the rules and regulations for the general management of each force and those rules and regulations, once approved by the Secretary of State, would be binding.[863]

Chadwick sent the final draft to the Home Secretary without showing it to Rowan, who was not altogether satisfied with it. Two letters suggest this. Firstly, a communication sent subsequently from Rowan to Chadwick stated 'I am now fully satisfied with the Report.'[864] Secondly, Lord John Russell was informed in a letter signed both by Rowan and Chadwick that some minor changes had been made to the proposals contained in the first draft of the Report which had been sent to him earlier.[865]

Chadwick and Rowan felt the time was not right to recommend a

---

862 Letter from Chadwick to Lord John Russell, N.D., August 1836, quoted in Finer, op, cit. 861, p.126.
863 PP 1839 [169], op. cit. 860, pp.184-185.
864 Rowan to Chadwick, March 1839, quoted in Finer, op. cit. 861, p.167.
865 Chadwick Papers. Correspondence, memoranda, pamphlets and newspaper cuttings c.1820-1890, of Sir Edwin Chadwick (1800-1890). 191 boxes. Contains letters written by Charles Rowan to Chadwick and others, whilst serving on the Royal Commission appointed to inquire as to the best means of establishing an efficient constabulary force in the counties of England and Wales PP 1839 (169). Letter, dated 5 March 1839, from Rowan and Chadwick to Lord John Russell, folio 93.

completely centralized and para-military body of trained policemen, primarily because they were 'worried about public reaction' to such a proposal. Rowan's comments upon the completed draft were favourable but anxious, commenting on the one hand that he thought it was 'exceedingly good' and it would 'produce a good effect,'[866] but in his letter to Chadwick, approving the draft a month later, he added as a final comment, 'But what will come of it?'[867]

Rowan and Chadwick made every effort to 'rally friends and possible foes.' Rowan 'prevailed upon the Tory leaders to read it and wrote that "The Duke" and Sir Robert Peel had thanked him for the Report and have said they will read it.'[868] In a private letter to the Duke of Richmond, he expressed his concern that the time had 'not yet arrived' for 'the recommendations to be generally well received'. But, Rowan said that if the report was 'not thought a satisfactory foundation to legislate' then, at least it contained 'much valuable information.'[869]

Rowan's concerns proved to be realistic. Russell took the view that it was politically unacceptable to act on the Royal Commission's main recommendation and rejected it, although his successor as Home Secretary, Lord Normanby, confessed to a friend later that year that he thought it was 'a serious and almost fatal error' not to have brought the new Rural Police 'more closely under the Government.'[870] However, when introducing the County Police Bill in Parliament, although Russell claimed 'the time had come to establish an efficient constabulary force in the counties', the legislation that followed was weak. It allowed magistrates in quarter sessions to establish a police force, but they were not required to do so. Consequently, as Rowan had anticipated, the Act was not a huge success; sixteen years later, only twenty-five of the fifty-five counties had established police forces.[871]

In July 1838 the long-awaited Select Committee Report on the Metropolis Police Offices was published.[872] Evidence was given to the Committee by Rowan and Mayne on three separate occasions, and once again they

---

866 Sir Charles Rowan to Edwin Chadwick, dated 11 February 1839, quoted in Finer, op. cit. 861, p. 167.
867 Rowan to Chadwick, dated 12 March 1839, quoted in Finer, op. cit. 861, p. 168.
868 Sir Charles Rowan to Edwin Chadwick, dated 5 April 1839 quoted in Finer, op. cit. 861, p.173.
869 The Goodwood Estate Archives. Family Papers. Charles Lennox (afterwards Gordon Lennox) 5th Duke of Richmond, Lennox, and Aybigny. Contains letters written by Charles Rowan and Richard Mayne to the Duke. Held at the West Sussex Record Office. Letter from Rowan to the Duke of Richmond, dated 2 April 1839. Folio 1692.
870 Parl. Deb, 3rd ser., Vol. XLIX, July 24th, 1839, cols. 727-30.
871 Grieve, John; Clive Harfield and Allyson MacVean (2007). *Policing!* London: Sage, p.206.
872 PP 1837-1838 [578]. Report from Select Committee on Metropolitan Police Offices; with minutes of evidence, appendix and index.

took the opportunity to raise a number of problems that were peripheral to the main purpose of the inquiry. The main thrust of the inquiry has already been discussed in Chapter Eight, but the Commissioners took the opportunity to again highlight shortcomings in the law relating to minor assaults and the power of the police to liberate people on bail. As they had been arguing since 1829, a constable could not arrest an assailant unless the assault had been committed in his presence; and, as the law stood, the police had no power to liberate on bail any person arrested after the magistrates had adjourned for the day, or on a Sunday, which meant a person 'must remain in custody'.[873]

The Committee were also keen to know the Commissioners' views on receivers of stolen goods, and expressed the view that it would be useful if the police had the right to visit the premises of a convicted Receiver for twelve months.[874] They were also asked about Sunday trading, to which Rowan claimed there was 'a strong and increasing favour' of its suppression 'amongst the respectable part of the community', who looked upon it from 'a religious point of view.' Asked whether, if it was forbidden to expose goods for sale or keep shops open on Sundays, the police would be able to enforce such a law, Mayne responded by saying shopkeepers would close the doors of their shops after admitting customers inside 'and unless a policeman followed the parties into the house, which, of course, the tradesman would not allow him to do, he could have no means of enforcing the law.'[875]

The Committee were also keen to hear the views of the commissioners on the offence of begging. Responding, Rowan submitted a return which revealed that of 4,287 people arrested for begging during 1837, 2,508 had been discharged by magistrates and only 1,779 had been convicted. As a result, the police were discouraged from bringing cases of vagrancy before certain magistrates. Mayne suggested that the remedy was to introduce an improved system in which there

> 'should be some mode, either by consultation amongst the magistrates themselves, through the Secretary of State, or, if it be deemed advisable, by a court of appeal, to bring decisions, where they vary, under review; and that the court, or the Secretary of State, upon legal advice, should lay down a rule for the guidance of all magistrates.'[876]

---

873 Ibid, Minutes of Evidence, pp.84-85, q/a 877-879 and 882-883.
874 Ibid, pp.85-86, q/a 887-894.
875 Ibid, pp.86-87, q/a 895-900.
876 Ibid, pp.100-101, q/a 1074-1080.

Asked whether they thought there had been any alteration in people's conduct when assembled at various public events such as fairs, of which there were a number each year, visiting places such as the Zoological Gardens in St James's Park, the British Museum, which had 120,000 people pass through it during the Easter holidays in 1838, and at elections, the commissioners' views were summed up by Mayne in this brief exchange:

> Q. Can you state whether the attention on the part of the people to the police on these public occasions has been greater than when originally established?
>
> A. Yes, very much so. Even in cases where the police have, strictly speaking, no power, no authority by law, the public now submit from general respect, and feeling that, whatever the regulations are, they are for the general convenience of the public.
>
> Q. You mean to say the moral influence of the police, in their official character, has its effect upon those public occasions in aid of maintaining the peace?
>
> A. Very great indeed; to a very great extent.[877]

The Commissioners again took the opportunity to highlight the number of Metropolitan Police officers being sent to different parts of the country. In response to a question, Rowan told the Committee they had 'sent into the country since the first establishment of the police between 2,000 and 3,000 men at different times.'[878]

Metropolitan Police officers were frequently detached to the provinces during elections and on other occasions. In 1837 the number of officers despatched to the provinces had been 444; the following year it rose again, this time to 764, but as Mather explained, 'many went to perform the more humdrum operation of keeping order at race meetings' rather than in response to riots.[879] In 1839 Metropolitan Police officers were deployed to Bedlington, Bury, Cockermouth, Loughborough, Mansfield and Monmouth.[880]

The movement of Metropolitan Police officers was made easier by the growing railway network that was spreading over the country.[881] Nevertheless, Rowan and Mayne resented 'the depletion of their force

---

877   Ibid, pp.183-185, q/a 2091-2105.
878   PP 1837-1838 [578], op. cit. 51, p.184, q/a 2101.
879   Mather, F.C (1984). *Public Order in the Age of the Chartists*. Westport, Connecticut: Greenwood Press, p.89.
880   Ibid, pp.105-106.
881   See Chapter Six.

which was small enough for the duties it was required to perform in London.' This, coupled with the refusal of the Government to allow them to increase numbers, drove the Commissioners to resist applications from the provinces for the loan of Metropolitan constables in 1837, and again the following year.[882]

The Committee asked the Commissioners whether their officers had the same moral influence when sent outside the Metropolis, to which Rowan replied 'from their reports, and the reports which they invariably bring back with them from those persons by whom they have been employed, magistrates and others, we have every reason to believe that their moral influence at such places has been as great, or perhaps greater, than within their own district'. Mayne added 'and we believe, from the personal good conduct of the men, a general respect in consequence is felt for them.'[883]

In its final report, the Select Committee made thirteen recommendations, most of which related to the qualifications and duties of magistrates or changes in the law. But two were particularly relevant to the Metropolitan Police in the context of this chapter:

- Police Constables should be authorised to take into custody, without warrant, offenders by an aggrieved party and Police Magistrates should have the power to remand such persons in custody for further examination.[884]
- To prevent people being unnecessarily detained, more powers of taking bail or personal recognizance should be provided.[885]

The result was the Metropolitan Police Act of 1839 which, amongst other things, extended the Metropolitan Police area to 15 miles from Charing Cross. It also gave the Commissioners power 'to make regulations for the route to be observed by all carts, carriages, horses and persons' to prevent obstruction of thoroughfares through the Metropolitan Police District.[886]

As has already been mentioned, the Act also abolished the Bow Street Runners and the constables attached to each of the magistrates' offices, and brought the Marine Police into the Metropolitan Police as Thames Division. The strength of the Metropolitan Police now stood at 3,444.[887]

---

882 Reith, Charles (1943). *British Police and the Democratic Ideal.* Oxford: Oxford University Press, p.210 et seq.
883 PP 1837-1838 [578], op. cit. 872, Minutes of Evidence, p.184, q/a 2101.
884 Ibid, Report, Recommendation 10, p.32.
885 Ibid, Recommendation 11, p.34.
886 2 & 3 Vict, c.47, section 2 and section 52 respectively.
887 Goodway, David (2002). *London Chartism 1838-1848.* Cambridge: Cambridge University Press, p.99.

CHAPTER FIFTEEN

THE RISE OF CHARTISM

Throughout the 1840s Rowan and Mayne were kept busy by the Chartists, although the strength of the movement in London was not as strong as it was in other areas of England, Scotland and Wales.[888] Chartism grew from the disillusionment of working people with the government's approach to economic crises in the 1830s. Higher interest rates imposed by the Bank of England, because of a serious decline in the monetary reserves, meant a lack of investment which, in turn, caused increasing unemployment. Whole families were forced into workhouses; efforts to form trade unions largely failed; taxes placed a higher burden on the poor than it did on the rich; food prices were high, not helped by a series of poor harvests.

Arising from this, the London Working Men's Association was set up in 1836. Appealing to respectable skilled craftsmen, its secretary was cabinet-maker William Lovett. Together with master tailor Francis Place, Lovett drew up the People's Charter, which had six key aims – annual general elections, universal suffrage for all men, secret ballots at elections, the abolition of the property qualifications for MPs, the payment of MPs to allow working men to stand, and equally-sized constituencies in terms of the electorate.

Support for the People's Charter grew quickly, particularly from educated and politically-mature working men. Containing 1.2 million signatures, a national petition was presented to Parliament on 14 June 1839 by one of its own members, Thomas Attwood, the Member for Birmingham. Nothing happened, so on 12 July, joined by another Member, John Fielden, who represented Oldham, Attwood proposed that the Commons consider the petition. The newly-elected Benjamin Disraeli, the Member for Maidstone and future leader of the Conservatives, unlike most Tories had a personal

---

[888] For what was happening elsewhere, see Chase, Malcolm (2007). *Chartism: A New History*. Manchester: Manchester University Press.

sympathy for the Chartists and he backed their appeal, but still the motion was defeated by 235 votes to 46. The result was pandemonium.[889]

Rowan and Mayne's attitude towards Chartist agitation was, on the whole, tolerant.[890] This was possibly influenced by instructions from the Whig government in 1839 not to apprehend for political offences 'without previous communication to the Secretary of State,'[891] but there is evidence to suggest that they had no wish to pursue a repressive policy even if they had been free to do so. Indeed, during that year complaint was made to the Home Secretary that the Commissioners were failing in their duty to put down the frequent meetings of the working class which were held on Clerkenwell Green 'to the alarm and annoyance of the property-owning residents of the district.' The Commissioners defended themselves, stating that no breach of the peace had occurred, and interference was therefore unnecessary.[892]

Chartism did not present many problems in the metropolis during its early stages, but as it grew stronger in other parts of the country, much to the dismay of the two Commissioners, the government saw the deployment of Metropolitan Police officers as 'an alternative to sending troops to deal with provincial disorder.'[893] However, Metropolitan Police officers were sometimes less successful in controlling disorderly crowds in the provinces than they were in London for three reasons. Firstly, 'their numbers were often totally inadequate to enable them to cope with the situations which confronted them'. Secondly, 'their knowledge of the territory in which they had to operate' was, in many cases limited and they often 'found themselves subjected to the same kind of hostility they faced during the early years of the Metropolitan Police in London.' Thirdly, 'they had to act under the direction of magistrates whose judgement was often inferior to their own' and who were quick to cast blame on them 'if things went wrong.' There was also a fourth problem in that 'discipline tended to deteriorate when the Metropolitan constables were removed from the immediate oversight of the Commissioners.' One notable occasion occurred in Carmarthenshire, when the Metropolitan police contingent stationed in Llanelly 'refused to obey the orders of a sergeant of the rural

---

889   Hernon, Ian (2006). *Riot! Civil Insurrection from Peterloo to the Present Day*. London: Pluto Press, pp.80-82.
890   Mather, F.C (1984). *Public Order in the Age of the Chartists*. Westport, Connecticut: Greenwood Press, p.104.
891   TNA HO 65/13. Home Office to Rowan, 18 May 1839.
892   Reith, Charles (1943). *British Police and the Democratic Ideal*. Oxford: Oxford University Press, p.239.
893   Emsley, Clive (2009). *The Great British Bobby: A History of British Policing from the 18th Century to the Present*. London: Quercus, pp.51-52.

police'. The newly appointed chief constable wrote to the Home Office to complain but the Home Secretary refused to intervene.[894]

The first major test for the Metropolitan Police came not in London, but in Birmingham when, at the beginning of July 1839, the Chartists were holding evening meetings in the Bull Ring. Although illegal, the meetings were peaceful, 'in spite of the occasional blast of violent rhetoric'. The local magistrates had troops on standby but 'were reluctant to deploy them'.[895] A request was sent to the Home Office for a contingent of Metropolitan Police officers to be sent. A meeting was actually in progress when the police arrived late on the afternoon of 4 July, and the contingent of 61 police officers under the command of Inspector Martin[896] 'was ordered by the magistrates to arrest the speaker.'[897] As a result, they

> 'marched, allegedly with batons drawn, into the Bull Ring and proceeded to disperse the meeting, arrest speakers and pull-down banners. At first the crowd was stunned and gave way, but the more spirited Chartists rapidly recognised their numerical superiority and began a violent resistance. Within minutes the police were on the defensive; they were driven out of the Bull Ring and several were so badly beaten that, in the initial reports, it was suggested that some of them had fatal injuries. The magistrates now felt compelled to call on the army and a detachment of the Rifle Brigade and troopers from the 4th Royal Irish Dragoons rescued the police and secured the Bull Ring.'[898]

One of the magistrates subsequently admitted that the police had been given an impossible task because 'the crowd was so closely intermingled that it was not possible to take the man.'[899] As a result, Rowan sent a further 39 men, under the command of the experienced Superintendent John May.[900] Three days later, now increased to 100 men, the officers 'restored their pride' by dispersing 'a Chartist crowd in the Bull Ring without the aid of troops.'[901]

The Birmingham affair had some repercussions at 4 Whitehall Place. In a letter to his wife, dated 11 July 1839, Mayne expressed his disappointment at not being able to join her at Maisonette, their summer residence in Essex,

---

894 Mather, op. cit. 890, pp.107-109.
895 Ibid, p.107.
896 TNA HO 2/61. Report by Superintendent John May, 4 October 1839.
897 Mather, op. cit. 890, p.107.
898 Emsley, op. cit. 893, p.53.
899 Mather, op. cit. 890, p.
900 May, op. cit. 896.
901 Emsley, op. cit. 893, p.53.

as planned because, 'the Birmingham affair is to be discussed tomorrow evening, and in the morning I have to prepare a Report of our accounts from thence, and probably Maule[902] will wish me to be in the House.' However, in the same letter, he was also able to tell his wife, clearly with some satisfaction, that the House had agreed the previous evening 'after a Division 87 to 7, to award the Commissioners a rise of £400 per annum.' Pointing out that Peel and Lord John Hume[903] had 'expressed approbation' in the 'strongest possible terms' he felt that 'such golden opinions were substantial repayment for many a day of labour [sic] and anxiety.' He added that both Hume and Peel had spoken 'of our never having even hinted to them about any increases of Salary' and Mayne commented that, in dealing 'with gentlemen, gentlemanly feelings have been appreciated.'[904] In the debate, whilst there was some opposition to the proposed increase, some Members of Parliament spoke highly of the two Commissioners. Daniel O'Connell, the Member for the City of Dublin, suggested that 'it could not be denied by any one, that the commissioners had done their duty admirably, and in a manner which exhibited not only good temper but sound and wise discretion'; Sir Robert Inglis, the Member for Oxford University, said that although he had been against the setting up of such a force initially, he was, now 'entirely satisfied with it'; whilst Colonel Charles Sibthorp, the Member for Lincoln, went further, saying that not only were the commissioners entitled to the increase, but he would like to see superintendents and inspectors given an increase of £50 per annum, with the salary of constables being increase by one shilling a week.[905]

Meanwhile, in London, the Metropolitan Police, no doubt encouraged by Rowan, 'were evolving a new technique of controlling disorderly crowds, one which minimized the use of sheer brute force against mobs by combining it with an element of science.' Whether it was a science or an art is debatable, but, according to Mather, in order 'to make possible this economy in physical force a science of crowd control, involving knowledge of the behaviour of human beings in the mass, was being formulated and

---

902 Fox Maule was the Under Secretary of State at the Home Office; there is no trace in Hansard of such a debate taking place.
903 Although a Mr Hume was a Member of Parliament, almost certainly, Mayne meant to write Lord John Russell here; Hume only contributed two sentences to the debate and they were insignificant, HC Deb, 10 July 1839, Vol. 49, cc 113-117).
904 Henry Hall Collection. Collection of diaries, journals, letters, books and miscellaneous papers, donated by Edward Hall (b.1898), a dealer and collector of Manuscripts and books. Includes letters written by Sir Richard Mayne to his wife between 1831 and 1866 in files EHC210/M1251;EHC210A/1252 and EHC 211/M1253. Held in the Wigan Archives. Mayne, in a letter to his wife, dated 11 July 1839, letter 12, pp.23-24.
905 HC Deb, 10 July 1839, Vol. 49, cc 113-117.

put into practice for the first time in British history.'[906]

The Metropolitan Police were increasingly trying to deploy resources 'to prevent violence from breaking out, rather than to suppress it after it had done so.'[907] An early example of this occurred when, to rekindle their flagging cause, Chartist leaders planned to sack and loot the City of London, under cover of darkness, on 16 January 1840. This was to be the signal for other groups of Chartists to rise-up in towns and cities throughout the country. However, Superintendent Pearce of H Division received information that the meeting in London which would be the start of disorder was to be held at Trade Hall in Abbey Street, Bethnal Green. He immediately informed the Commissioners who, 'acting on the principle of preventing disorder by preventing the instigation and formation of riotous mobs,'[908] instructed Pearce to stop the meeting. Gathering a body of police officers together, Pearce raided the Trade Hall. About 500 people were present. Twelve people were arrested and charged, five with attending an illegal meeting with arms in their possession and the other seven with being present at an illegal meeting for an unlawful purpose.[909]

Later, during in the summer, Mayne's wife left town for her annual trip to the country and it would appear that Rowan too, took advantage of the lull in Chartist activity in the capital to absent himself. On 31 July, Mayne wrote to his wife:

'You will say all my economy is vanishing now that I am away from your influence, but that is not so; I fear however I must buy a horse. Rowan has sold his, and having been so long without one, it is hardly right that both Commissioners should be dismounted.'[910]

Writing again on 11 August, Mayne informed her that "The Queen leaves town tomorrow, and I take it there will be nothing to prevent me, Hay being free.' He told her that the bells were ringing as Queen Victoria travelled to Parliament for the closing ceremony before the summer recess. But he had sent 'Hay out' and remained in Whitehall Place.[911] Later the same day, however, the situation had changed because, in a further letter to his wife, he wrote:

'I fear before Parliament is up I cannot move, and that they now say,

---

906 Mather, op. cit. 890, p.98.
907 Critchley, T.A (1970). *The Conquest of Violence: Order and Liberty in Britain*. London: Constable, p.132.
908 Reith, Charles (1956). *A New Study of Police History*. Edinburgh: Oliver and Boyd, p.158.
909 *The Charter*, 19 January 1840, p.3; *Globe*, 22 January, 1840, p.4.
910 Henry Hall Collection, op. cit. 904, Mayne, in a letter to his wife, 31 July 1840, letter 22, p.49.
911 Ibid, 11 August 1840, letter 24, p.55.

will not be until the 22nd. There is to be a meeting of Chartists, ...here tomorrow, but I don't apprehend any disturbance.'[912]

If such a meeting occurred, it did not create any publicity. In fact Chartist activity in August was predominantly confined to Birmingham and some northern cities. However, with the formation of the National Charter Association (NCA) in July, the autumn and winter did 'see the real establishment of Chartism in London' with old bodies being replaced by branches of the new association.[913]

London was quiet, relative to Chartist activity in 1841, but for 2 May 1842, Rowan and Mayne made copious arrangements for the delivery of the Chartist's National Petition, containing nearly three-and-a-half million signatures, to be delivered to the House of Commons. All seventeen Divisional Superintendents were involved, each Division supplying between 50 and 100 men, a total in excess of 1,200 men. The various Chartist associations of the metropolis assembled locally before making their way to Lincoln's Inn Fields. By the time the processions moved off at one o'clock to the House of Commons, Lincoln's Inn Fields was 'densely crowded'. Walking by way of Great Queen Street, Drury Lane, Holborn and Oxford Street, the processions arrived at the House of Commons at quarter-past three where the petition, contained in a number of large boxes, was lodged on the table in front of the Speaker's Chair. That evening, a dinner was arranged at White Conduit House for the principal members of the Chartist Movement who had taken part.[914]

A little later that year, unrest in the provinces 'touched off a sequence of demonstrations' designed to keep London 'in a state of continuous alarm.' Rowan being on holiday in Scotland, Mayne was on his own for most of August which was a particularly busy time. Following the policy, the two Commissioners had adopted since the beginning of Chartist agitation, Mayne continued to be reluctant to interfere with meetings unless there was good reason.[915] Consequently, a meeting on Stepney Green, on 16 August, attended by between 2,000 and 4,000 people, passed off peacefully.[916] However, two days later, at the conclusion of a meeting of between 3,000 and 4,000 people, on Islington Green, although giving the local senior officer every indication they were dispersing, the crowd moved,

[912] Ibid, 11 August 1840, letter 25, p.56.
[913] Goodway, David (2002). London Chartism 1838-1848. Cambridge: Cambridge University Press, pp.38-39.
[914] *Morning Chronicle*, 3 May 1842; the policing arrangements are contained in Police Orders, 2 May 1842.
[915] Goodway, op. cit. 913, p.107.
[916] *London Evening Standard*, 17 August 1842, p.1.

unsupervised by police, towards Clerkenwell Green, despite Mayne having given strict instructions that on no account was it to be allowed to move towards the centre of London. Following a short meeting at Clerkenwell Green, at which the crowd listened to more speeches, it moved off towards Lincoln's Inn Fields. But, within 400 metres of leaving Clerkenwell Green they were into the City Police area and remained so until they reached a point 400 yards from Lincoln's Inn where another meeting was held between 10.00 and 11.00pm. Mayne knew nothing of this but news of this 'multitude' did reach the ears of Prime Minister Robert Peel and Home Secretary Sir James Graham, despite the lateness of the hour, went to the Home Office and demanded of Mayne to know why this had been allowed to occur.[917] In a letter to his wife, Mayne suggested that it had occurred because police action and not been 'altogether satisfactorily done in the early part of the evening'. As a result, he told his wife, he had to ride to Bethnal Green at about 1.00am and did not get to bed until 3.00am.[918] In fact the remnants of the meeting had been ordered to disperse by Mayne. Subsequently, Mayne wrote to the Home Office to point out that 'for a Considerable portion of the whole way they were not under the control nor observation of the Metropolitan Police.'[919]

The incident on 18 August was the trigger for the Home Secretary to direct that such processions and meetings should be banned.[920] As a result, it was decided that another meeting at Clerkenwell Green on 19 August should not be allowed and Mayne went 'to prevent' it. In a letter to his wife, he wrote: 'We had some little skirmishing, and covered ourselves with glory, on one occasion putting the rabble to the rout, letting the wild Beasts (i.e. Police) out, and captured two flags, which we retained as trophies.'[921] However, one slightly unsavoury court case arose from this occasion. An allegation was made to Mayne that a fifteen-year-old boy had allegedly been struck by a mounted officer as a result of which he was rendered unconscious for a short period. As was the practice, Mayne heard from witnesses, but as the officer could not be identified, he took the unusual step of arraigning the only three mounted officers who were in the vicinity of the alleged assault that night before a magistrate. So, on 5 September, Sergeants George Goodman, Arthur Webb and John Lund,

---

917 *Morning Advertiser*, 19 August 1842, p.3.
918 Henry Hall Collection, op. cit. 904, Mayne, in a letter to his wife, 20 August 1842, letter 36, p.42.
919 Goodway, op. cit. 913, p.108.
920 Ibid.
921 Henry Hall Collection, op. cit. 904, Mayne, in a letter to his wife commenced on 21 August 1842 and completed on 22 August, letter 37, pp.80-82.

appeared before Mr Combe, at Clerkenwell Police Court. Immediately there was an exchange between Mr. Combe and Superintendent Maissey of G Division, representing the Commissioner:

> Combe: 'How comes it that three policemen are arraigned here, whereas only one is alleged to have committed the assault?'
>
> Maissey: 'As the complainant was unable to distinguish the policeman who he said committed the assault upon him, the commissioners directed that the only three policemen who were on horseback in Clerkenwell-green on the night in question should be arraigned here.'
>
> Combe (expressing his surprise at the decision made by the commissioners): 'If all the policemen in London were mounted in Clerkenwell-green on the night in question, were they all to be arraigned?'

All three sergeants denied any knowledge of the alleged incident. After hearing all the evidence, Combe announced that there was nothing to show that any of the three had taken part in this incident and dismissed the case.[922] Whilst Maissey, as was the practice, referred to 'the commissioners' in speaking with the magistrate, it was Mayne who made the decision to arraign all three. Rowan was on holiday in Scotland when the incident occurred, and it would be interesting to speculate, given his background, as to whether, he would have come to the same decision as Mayne.

In addition to policing Chartist meetings, the Metropolitan Police were still required to deploy large numbers of officers for other events. For instance, when Queen Victoria went to the House of Lords to close parliament for the summer recess on 12 August, 14 superintendents, 26 inspectors, 116 sergeants and 1180 constables, plus 90 officers in plain clothes, were required. Again, the order stipulated that one half of the officers would be taken from day duty; the other half would come from the night duty who would be relieved at 4 a.m.'[923]

Despite 'their frequent training and drilling' the tactics of the Chartists were generally predictable and not very formidable; for instance there appears to be only one occasion "during the entire period when an English mob erected a barricade."[924] The only recorded barricade was at Stone in Staffordshire in May 1839.[925] Nevertheless, the police did experience some difficulties. In a letter to his wife, written at 12 noon, on 22 August, Mayne

---

922 *Morning Chronicle*, 6 September 1842, p.4.
923 Police Orders, 11 August 1842.
924 Mather, op. cit. 890, pp.20-21.
925 See Napier, Lieut.-General Sir William (1857). *The Life and Opinions of General Sir Charles James Napier (edited by William Napier), Volume I*. London: John Murray, p.27.

told of some of the arrangements that had been made to cover a meeting on Kennington Common that day:

> 'Our preparations are made to meet far worse than I think at all likely to occur, but in these times no risks are to be allowed. In addition to Police assembled in large numbers, and the ordering of troops of the Town kept in Barracks, Sir James has moved a Squadron of the 8th Hussars up from Hounslow and 4 guns from Woolwich. All this sounds very formidable…'[926]

Mayne used one of the new powers given to the commissioners by the Metropolitan Police Act 1839 by issuing instructions to prevent the obstruction of the thoroughfares leading to Kennington Common to take effect from the evening before. The large numbers of police Mayne refers to in his letter amounted to approximately eighteen hundred, many of them out of the view of the public in a church, livery stable and an unoccupied carriage repository at Kennington Cross. Approximately fifty officers were stationed on each bridge. Superintendent McLean of P Division was in command of those in and around Kennington Common; Superintendent Murray had overall command of those stationed on the bridges. Groups of twenty to thirty people started assembling in various parts of the Common at around one o'clock, 'the chief subject of discussion being how the police might be resisted in the event of the meeting being disturbed.' From five o'clock onwards, the crowd rapidly increased and the meeting got under way. After about 20 minutes, a group of mounted police, supported by about five hundred officers on foot, led by Superintendent McLean, approached the meeting from the direction of Kennington Gate. As they neared the crowd, which now numbered between 3,000 and 6,000,[927] their pace quickened and 'little difficulty was experienced in driving them off'. Seven people were arrested. The whole operation was seen by Mr. Traill, a magistrate at Union Hall Police Court, who, together with several influential men residing in the vicinity, 'complimented very highly the tact displayed by the superintendents, in dispersing, without injury, so large an assemblage.' Meanwhile, at another meeting at Paddington, attended by between 2,000 and 3,000, police blocked off the bridge leading to the meeting place and made seventeen arrests as they dispersed the crowd.[928]

In a letter to his wife, which he commenced on 21 August, Mayne mentioned that he had had a letter from Rowan, which suggested he

---

926   Henry Hall Collection, op. cit. 904.
927   The *Morning Chronicle* estimated 6,000; other sources less.
928   *Morning Chronicle*, 23 August, p.3.

would be back either on 23 or 24 August. He then complained how his police duties had interfered with what he saw as his religious duties:

> 'Yesterday was not passed as a Sunday usually should be, but I hope I may be excused for attending to necessary duty. The whole day I was preparing orders, or with Sir James; he deals frankly and confidentially, and those are great points to me. His situation is one of terrible anxiety at such times, any allowance ought to be made for manner, and excess even of precaution.'

The following day he continued with his letter:

> 'I had to work till 12 o'clock tonight. The police were obliged to disperse both meetings, which they did effectively. Sir James well pleased at all that has been done; and as far as I hear at present, all respectable people well satisfied.'[929]

Rowan did return as anticipated, for on 31 August 1842, he and Mayne went 'to look over the new Houses of Parliament' before Mayne called on his sister, Catherine. In the evening, the two Commissioners dined together.[930]

There was a lull in Chartist activity between 1843 and 1848 which is probably just as well, given increasing concern over Rowan's health.[931] Two occurrences stood out in this period. Firstly, for the first time, the arrangements for a state funeral fell predominantly on the commissioners, and secondly, Mayne gave evidence to yet another House of Commons Committee.

The state funeral was that of Prince Augustus, the Duke of Sussex, sixth son of George III and Queen Charlotte, who died at his home at Kensington Palace on 21 April 1843. The Lying-in-State took place at Kensington Palace on 3 May, commencing at 10.00am. The Palace should have closed at 4.00pm, but the crowds were such that it remained open for a further two hours. The instructions for this event had been issued under Rowan's signature which suggested that he took the lead in making the arrangements for both the Lying-in-State and the funeral:

REGULATIONS FOR CARRIAGES TO VIEW THE LYING IN STATE

> Those carriages arriving from London will keep the centre of the road, leaving the south or Brompton side free for the general use of the

---

929 Henry Hall Collection, op. cit. 904.
930 Ibid, dated 31 August 1842, letter 40, p.83.
931 See Chapter Eighteen.

public – and passing on, beyond the Palace gate in Kensington, are to turn round and set down their company at this gate with the horses' heads towards the Kensington turnpike, and, after setting down, will proceed through the turnpike, keeping on the north or park side of the road, and enter the park-gate at Kensington, and wait there under the directions of the police.

The company will be taken up at the garden-gate close by the Old Cavalry Barracks, for the Light Dragoons.

Carriages arriving from the west through Kensington will set down their company in the same order, keeping the north side of the road, and proceed to the park, as before described, to wait and take up.

(Signed) C. Rowan, Commissioner of Police.[932]

The directors of the company that owned the new cemetery at Kensal Green had issued 6,000 tickets of admission for the burial service on 4 May. People with tickets were allowed to enter the grounds from 6.00am, where between 400 and 500 policemen were stationed in various parts of the grounds to keep order.

On the day of the funeral, the cortege, nearly a mile long, left the Palace at eight o'clock and travelled by way of Kensington High Street, Church Street, Church Lane, into Uxbridge Road, along Queen's Road, into Harrow Road, to Kensal Rise. The cortege was accompanied by Rowan and Mayne, both mounted. It was estimated between 25,000 and 30,000 people were assembled along the route. Temporary stands had been erected at suitable locations; other parts of the route were lined with strong barriers behind which members of the public stood. Policemen lined the route, approximately three or four yards apart. All shops in Kensington were closed and 'from many of the houses mourning flags and banners were displayed.' Windows, balconies and roof tops were filled with spectators. No carriages were permitted to remain on any part of the route.[933]

In July 1844, Mayne gave evidence to a Select Committee which had been set up to enquire into Dog Stealing in the Metropolis. He told the Committee that, in 1841 a total of 564 were either lost or stolen; in 1842 it was 615, and in 1843 it was 666, and claimed there was 'an organised system of stealing dogs' for which the thieves were paid money, sometimes very large sums,[934] for their return. Expanding on this, he told how:

---

932 *Morning Post*, 2 May 1843, p.5.
933 *London Evening Standard*, 4 May 1843, p.3.
934 PP 1844 [549]. Report from the Select Committee on Dog Stealing (Metropolis); together with the Minutes of Evidence taken before them, Minutes of Evidence, p.6, q/a 55.

'The party who has the dog keeps it secret and waits for a little time till a reward is offered, and then, through a third or fourth party, according to the circumstances, communicates to the owner that he knows where the dog is, or probably has the means of coming at the dog if he will give either the reward offered, or sometimes more. Then, if the terms are agreed upon, the individual or perhaps some other person, brings back the dog and claims the reward; so that while a corrupt bargain is made, and a benefit is derived by the original stealer, shared with others, it is impossible to bring it home to him; he never appears, and it is impossible to trace back through the different persons to him that he was the original taker of the dog.'[935]

He claimed the police probably knew all the parties engaged in gaining 'their livelihood by buying and selling dogs', many of them stolen dogs, and taking rewards for the return of such dogs.[936] He then told the Committee that in 1841, 51 people were charged with dog stealing, but only 19 were convicted; in 1842, 45 people had been arrested but only 17 convicted and in 1843, 38 people had been charged but only 18 convicted. A member of the committee reminded Mayne it was an offence to be in possession of a dog, knowing it to have been stolen. Mayne responded by pointing out the difficulty of proving that the party had 'guilty knowledge'. Mayne suggested that, to put an end to this corrupt practice, it should be an offence to offer or give a reward and an offence to take a reward.[937]

In its report, the Committee claimed there was an illicit trade occurring with a 'notorious frequency' and found' that 'the present state of the Law gave confidence to those who [made] a profitable trade of the practice'. It went on to suggest 'the success and impunity with which these operations were carried out had combined to reduce the practice into an organized system of theft and extortion'. Although it was an offence to 'steal a dog, beast or bird ordinarily kept in a state of confinement' by virtue of the Larceny Act 1827,[938] the Committee claimed it had little effect on the current practice. Because of the doubts that existed as to whether dogs were property, the Committee said the doubt should be removed, by making the stealing of dogs a misdemeanour. By constituting the offence as a Misdemeanour, 'all parties engaged in this disgraceful transaction, now a daily occurrence,' would be subject to the penalties imposed under the Larceny Act 1827:

935 Ibid, p.3, q/a 29-30.
936 Ibid, p.5, q/a 48
937 Ibid, p.8, q/a 87-90.
938 7 & 8 Geo 4, c.29, sections 31 and 32.

'Every person who shall corruptly take any money or reward, directly or indirectly, under pretence or upon account of helping any person to any chattel, money, valuable security, or other property whatsoever, which shall by any felony or misdemeanour have been stolen, taken, obtained, or converted as aforesaid, shall (unless he causes the offender to be apprehended and brought to trial for the same) be guilty of felony, and, being convicted thereof, shall be liable, at the discretion of the Court, to be transported beyond the seas for life, or for any term not less than seven years, or to be imprisoned for any term not exceeding four years, and, if a male, to be once, twice, or thrice publicly or privately whipped (if the court shall so think fit), in addition to such imprisonment.'[939]

It further added dealers should be required to take out a Licence for their tenements and premises and those premises should be open to inspection by sergeants or inspectors of police at all reasonable hours in the day-time.[940]

---

939 Ibid, section 58.
940 PP 1844 [549], op. cit. 934, Report, pp.iii to vi.

CHAPTER SIXTEEN

THE DETECTIVE FORCE

Rowan and Mayne's reluctance to allow their officers to regularly become involved in the detection of crime was primarily as a result of two things. The first was Peel's failure in 1829 to take any action in relation to the constables of the police offices who, therefore, for the next ten years until they were effectively disbanded in 1839, remained responsible, under their respective magistrates for the investigation of crime. The second arose from Popay's actions in Camberwell in 1833, which 'discouraged the Commissioners from venturing on what was felt to be dangerous ground', the regular employment of officers in plain clothes, although technically, until 1839, the magistrates of the police officers and their constables continued to be 'responsible for the detection and punishment of the offender after he [had] succeeded in committing a crime.'[941] This would change, albeit in a small way.

Between 1836 and 1842, there were a number of sensational cases, particularly murders, in London. In none of these did the constables of the Police Offices play a part in the investigation, but they all aroused considerable public interest as can be identified from newspaper reports.

When James White (see below) appeared before the magistrates at Marylebone Police Office in 1837, 'every avenue leading to the office was crowded with persons anxious to gain a glimpse of the prisoner' long 'before the court commenced business'.[942] When it became known that a person was in custody for the murder of Eliza Davis (see below),

'immense crowds collected in front of the station-house at an early hour ...and at eleven o'clock (the hour at which prisoners [were] removed

---

941 Roach, Lawrence (2004). 'The Origins and Impact of the Function of the Crime Investigation and Detection in the British Police Service: A thesis submitted in partial fulfilment of the requirements for the degree of Doctor of Philosophy of Loughborough University'. Loughborough: Loughborough University's Institutional Repository, p.57.
942 *Morning Post*, 16 May 1837.

to the police office) every street, alley and passage in the vicinity of the watch-house was crowded with people.'

Police constables deployed in 'two contrary directions, divided the crowd, and prisoners were taken down a narrow lane leading into Wapping High Street, in charge of several policemen, who were 'sorely pressed by the curious mob.'[943] Likewise, when it became known that a person had been arrested for the murder of Eliza Grimwood (see below), 'a crowd of persons stationed themselves opposite the front entrance' to Union Hall Police Office 'in order to obtain a view of the suspected offender'. When the arrested person arrived in a coach accompanied by two police officers, 'a scene of almost indescribable confusion' occurred and police officers were deployed to prevent 'the mob from forcing their way into the Justice-room, such was the determination … to gratify their curiosity.'[944] Murders also generated a great number of letters, many of them anonymous, in some of which the writer claimed to be the murderer.[945]

The first of this series of sensational murders occurred on 28 December 1836, when the torso of a woman was found close to the Regents Canal just off Edgware Road, which was situated on T Division. An inquest was held on the unidentified torso and the jury returned a verdict of wilful murder against some person or persons unknown. Inspector George Feltham took charge of the investigation, assisted by the constable who had been first on the scene, Samuel Pegler, who was actually from S Division. From then on, one of Mayne's innovations bore fruit. He had introduced a system in which divisional superintendents were required to submit a report of all crimes for which no one had been arrested, together with details of suspected persons. Called 'route papers', these were circulated by mounted messenger to all the other superintendents in charge of divisions. As a result, when a severed head was found some seven miles away in Stepney, which was on K Division, and the legs were eventually discovered in Camberwell, which was on P Division, seven miles from Stepney and seven miles from where the torso was found, in both cases, the superintendent in charge of T Division was informed. The body was finally identified as that of Hannah Brown by her brother, William Gay, who had been searching for her since he had last seen her just before Christmas 1836 when she left her lodgings saying she was to marry a James Greenacre of Camberwell.

Sometime in early March, a church warden in Paddington, who went by

---

943 *Morning Post*, 12 June 1838, p.6.
944 *Morning Post*, 2 June 1837, p.6.
945 See Inspector Field's evidence in the case against George Hill in the *Morning Post*, 27 August 1845, p.7.

the name of Mr. Thornton, believing that he knew the identity of the body and who her killer might be, sought an interview with Colonel Rowan at Whitehall Place. Following the meeting, Rowan 'instantly gave orders to the different divisions of police to use their utmost endeavours to ascertain if the villain was in the neighbourhood'.[946] Greenacre was finally tracked down on 24 March, just as he was about to emigrate to America with his common-law wife Sarah Gale. The couple stood trial on 3 April, Greenacre for murder and Gale as an accessory. Both were convicted. Sentenced to death, Greenacre was hanged on 2 May 1837; Gale was transported for life.[947]

It was around this time that the Commissioners began to allow divisional Superintendents to respond to local demands and allow them to employ officers, generally inspectors and constables, but sometimes sergeants, in plain clothes to investigate specific crimes, such as murder. But, at the end of the case, they invariably returned to their normal duties. But such a system meant that the Force did not have an intimate knowledge of criminals and their habits, and haunts, and it lacked effective coordination and all the benefits that come from it.[948]

A week later, on 9 May 1837, 21-year-old Eliza Davis, a barmaid at the King's Head Public House in Frederick Street just off the Hampstead Road, was found in a parlour behind the bar with her throat cut. Despite a ten-week investigation by Inspector Aggs, assisted again by Constable Pegler, both from S Division on which the murder had taken place, the killer was never found, although at least four people were arrested for it over the following eight years. Six days after the murder, a James White, who had been arrested in Kent, was brought before Mr. Rawlinson at Marylebone Police Office but, as his description did not match that of the alleged killer which had appeared in *Hue and Cry*,[949] he was discharged.[950]

On 31 May Charles Taylor was taken before Sir Frederick Roe, the chief magistrate at Bow Street Police Office, by Superintendent Sandrock of F Division, 'charged on suspicion of being connected or acquainted with the circumstances of Eliza's murder'. Quite what the circumstances were, is not known because Sir Frederick interviewed the suspect and witnesses in his private room before announcing, 'there appeared no ground for supposing

---

946 *Monmouthshire Merlin*, 1 April 1837, p.3.
947 Old Bailey Proceedings Online (www.oldbaileyonline.org, version 7.2, 13 February 2018), April 1837, trial of JAMES GREENACRE, SARAH GALE (t18370403-917).
948 Roach, op. cit. 941, pp.107-108.
949 The *Police Gazette, or Hue and Cry*, started publication in 1772. It dropped the *Hue and Cry* part of its title in 1839 when the Metropolitan Police assumed responsibility for circulating details of crimes and descriptions of criminals and deserters from the army and navy.
950 *Morning Post*, 16 May 1837, p.4.

the defendant to be implicated' although he did remand him to be dealt with later on another matter, a charge of stealing some shirts.[951]

On 1 June William Rhynd, a seaman, was taken before the magistrates at Thames Police Office, having apparently walked up to a Constable John Mitchell at 1.00am, as he was patrolling his beat on K Division and confessed to the murder of Eliza. At court the next day, Sergeant James Shepherd was asked by the magistrate whether he resembled the description given of the killer at the time and when his reply was negative, the magistrate discharged Rhynd, there being no other evidence against him other than the confession to Constable Mitchell.[952]

Eight years after the murder, on 26 April 1845, Walter Chambers walked into the King's Head Public House and told the barmaid he was the one who had cut Eliza Davis's throat. He was arrested and brought before the magistrate at Marylebone Police Office but, during the examination, it was decided that Chambers had not been involved in the murder and had been drunk when he made the confession. The magistrate bound him over in his own recognisance of 25 shillings to keep the peace and be of good behaviour for six months.[953] Three years later, it was revealed that the police were in possession of further information which might lead to the identification of Eliza's killer but it led nowhere[954] and Davis's killer was never traced.

On 26 May 1838, the body of 'beautiful 28-year-old prostitute' Eliza Grimwood, who was known as 'the Countess', was found in her bedroom at 12, Wellington Terrace, Lambeth. She had been slashed across the throat and repeatedly stabbed. Inspector Charles Frederick Field took charge of the investigation and eventually, her pimp, William Hubbard, who was her cousin, was charged with her murder but was acquitted at the Police Office for lack of evidence. Her killer was never traced.[955] Nevertheless, it was a case that would not go away. Some seven years later, George Hill, a private in the 67th Regiment confessed to her murder but, as he did not fit the description of the person believed to have done it, the magistrate decided that the confession was merely a ruse to get himself discharged from the army.[956] Then, in 1853, a Dane, Peter Lemeschal, was taken before the

---

951 *Evening Standard*, 1 June 1837, p.4.
952 *Morning Advertiser*, 2 June 1837, p.4.
953 *Morning Post*, 28 April 1845, p.7 and 3 May 1845, p.7.
954 *Morning Post*, 31 January 1848, p.4.
955 See Cobb, Belton (1957). *The First Detectives; and the early career of Richard Mayne, Commissioner of Police*. London: Faber and Faber, pp.124-142; and Lock, Joan (2014). *Dreadful Deeds and Awful Murders: Scotland Yard's First Detectives 1829-1878*. Jolo Press, pp.38-43.
956 *Morning Post*, 27 August 1845, p.7.

magistrate at Southwark Police Court by Inspector Teague of the City of London Police. During the proceedings, Charles Goff, who, as a constable in the Metropolitan Police, had been involved in the original investigation but had since left the Force, gave evidence that Lemeschal looked nothing like the person they had been looking for. However, the magistrate, asked Goff to review the papers lodged at Whitehall Place and try to find the hackney carriage driver, Joseph Spechnell, who had picked up Grimwood and her client in theatreland and taken them back to Waterloo Road. At the remand hearing, Goff reported that in 1846, Spechnell had been found guilty of stealing a gentleman's watch, had been transported and was now employed as a coachman to a judge in Hobart, Tasmania.[957] Grimwood's murderer was never traced.

In 1839, any confusion that existed up until then over jurisdiction was removed by virtue of the Metropolitan Police Act and the Magistrates' Courts Act of that year when the executive functions of the police offices were transferred to the Metropolitan Police. However, both acts had been hastily drafted and failed to take into consideration 'the extent and importance of the magistrates' officers in gathering information about, and cultivating informants among active criminals and their associates.' So, whilst there was a need for detective duties of this type to continue, Rowan and Mayne 'neither recognised nor accepted that they had either the powers to carry them on, or any obligation to discharge them.' Instead, they remained focused 'on prevention and on the primacy of uniform patrol and 'quick and fresh pursuit' rather than on the detection and prosecution of unidentified offenders.' Therefore, although the detective role of the magistrates' officers was discontinued by virtue of Section 5 of the Magistrates Courts Act, it was not replaced.[958]

On 17 March 1840, 70-year-old John Templeton was found murdered at this home in St Mary's, Islington. His wrists had been tied with cord and he had been blindfolded with a stocking. He had severe head injuries. Superintendent Johnson, the officer in charge of N Division, appointed Inspector James Miller to undertake the investigation and late that evening he arrested Richard Gould and charged him with the murder. Gould appeared at the Old Bailey on 14 April 1840 but, after an extremely effective closing address by defending counsel, was found not guilty and was discharged.[959]

---

957 *Morning Post*, 6 and 9 September 1853, p.7.
958 Roach, op. cit. 941, pp.103-104.
959 Old Bailey Proceedings Online, op. cit. 947, April 1840, trial of RICHARD GOULD, alias Arthur Nicholson (t18400406-1281).

Following the trial, Gould made immediate plans to leave the country, but, in the meantime, Mayne, having reviewed the case, instructed Sergeant Otway to apply to the magistrate at Bow Street Police Court[960] for a warrant to arrest Gould on a charge of 'having been an accessory after the fact in the murder and robbery of John Templeton'. Receiving information that Gould was on a ship about to leave for Sydney, Otway went to Gravesend on 7 May, where he found him, listed under the assumed named of Kelly. Gould was arrested and subsequently appeared at the Old Bailey on 15 June, this time on an indictment, charging him with burglariously (sic) breaking and entering the dwelling of John Templeton at 11.30pm. 16 March with intent to steal and stealing money. Found guilty he was sentenced to transportation for life.[961] On this occasion, all the evidence pointed to Gould being the murderer.

On the night of 5/6 May 1840, Lord William Russell, a member of the British aristocracy was murdered – his throat had been cut – at his home at 14 Norfolk Street, Park Lane. He was an uncle of Lord John Russell who had recently stood down as Home Secretary. Both the Government and the family of Lord Russell offered rewards, each amounting to £200, for the apprehension of the killer.

Mayne became actively involved in this case, visiting the scene, along with Superintendent Baker, soon after the body was discovered.[962] On 10 May, he attended the house again along with Mr Wynne, the solicitor for the family, and was engaged there for the greater part of the day.[963] The next day, Superintendent Baker told Mayne some 'valuable objects' were missing from the house. After a relatively short investigation, the officer who Mayne had put in charge of the case, Inspector Pearce, acting on Mayne's advice, decided there was sufficient evidence to arrest Sir William's recently employed butler, Francois Courvoisier.[964] Mayne then sent Mr. Yardley, secretary and chief clerk to the Commissioners, to sit in on the committal proceedings at Bow Street Police Court on 11 May. Later that day, at about 4.00pm, Mayne and a Mr. Hobler, jr, solicitor for the prosecution, arrived at the house. They were followed shortly afterwards by Superintendent Baker and Inspector Pearce. Mayne stayed for nearly three hours; Baker and Pearce stayed longer.[965] Mayne also spent 'some

960 By this time the Police Offices, which were run by the magistrates, had been renamed Police Courts.
961 Old Bailey Proceedings Online, op. cit. 947, June 1840, trial of RICHARD GOULD, alias Arthur Nicholson (t18400615-1696).
962 Lock, op. cit. 955, p.60.
963 *London Evening Standard*, 11 May 1840, p.4.
964 Lock, op. cit. 955, pp.61-64.
965 *Morning Post*, 12 May 1840, p.5.

hours at the house' on 20 May.⁹⁶⁶ Courvoisier was tried at the Central Criminal Court and convicted on 15 June.⁹⁶⁷ He was executed on 6 July.

In August, it was announced the £200 offered by the Government for the killer's capture would be divided up. Inspector Pearce was awarded £50, Inspectors Beresford and Tedman £30 each and six constables were each awarded £10 each. Sarah Mancer, the housemaid, was awarded £15, James Ellis, the late valet to Lord Russell, was awarded £10 and the cook, Mary Hannell £5. The family announced that their £200 reward money would be divided in the same way, so, in total, Pearce received £100 and Beresford and Tedman £60 each, substantial sums of money in those days.⁹⁶⁸

Inspector Pearce, who would eventually become the first head of the Detective Force had shown great tenacity earlier in the year, following the theft of letters containing money from Birmingham Post Office by an employee, Thomas Webb. Webb had apparently come down to London from Birmingham on the night train accompanied by a young lady, Mary Stokes. They spent two days in the capital, changing bank notes at three different banks, buying clothes and twice visiting the Drury Lane Theatre before Webb sent Stokes back to Birmingham. Pearce's initial information suggested that Webb was staying at Hatchett's Hotel in Piccadilly or at the Gloucester Coffeehouse but, by the time he enquired at these two places, Webb had left, apparently for Brighton. Inspector Pearce caught the mail coach to Brighton but, on arrival, discovered Webb had gone to Hastings and from there to Dover and then caught a steamship to Calais, which is where the tenacious inspector caught up with him. Webb was staying in a lodging house under the name of Stanley and, at first denied he was the person Pearce was pursuing. Although he had no jurisdiction in France, Pearce persuaded him to return on a steamship to Ramsgate, from whence they returned to London, where Webb was taken before Bow Street Police Court.⁹⁶⁹ Webb was committed to Warwick Assizes for trial and was subsequently sentenced to transportation for fifteen years.⁹⁷⁰

Another case in February 1840, again unsolved, occurred at 29 Welbeck Street, Cavendish Square. The house was occupied by a Mr and Mrs Turner. Mr Turner was away on a visit to the Duke of Rutland. When Mrs Turner went out to dinner she left three servants in the house. When she returned, she found that a jewel case, containing 'trinkets' to the value of

---

966   Ibid, 21 May 1840, p.7.
967   Old Bailey Proceedings Online, op, cit. 947, 25 December 2017), June 1840, trial of FRANCOIS BENJAMIN COURVOISIER (t18400615-1629).
968   *Morning Post*, 19 August 1840, p.4.
969   *Birmingham Journal,* 22 February 1840, p.7.
970   *Northern Standard*, 11 April 1840, p.1.

between £500 and £700, was missing. Inspectors Tedman and Black from D Division attended but, finding no signs of a forced entry, suspicion fell on one of the servants.[971] Rowan issued an instruction for all divisions 'to employ an active and intelligent man' to trace the missing jewels,[972] but the thief or thieves were never found.

It was now becoming clear that the 'preventative system' had 'inherent limitations' and 'there was a mounting fear that police techniques were lagging behind' those of the successful criminals.[973]

Then, in April 1842, 'a murder of a most appalling nature,'[974] was committed in Surrey.'[975] Daniel Good had murdered his common-law wife Jane Jones, dismembered her body and attempted to burn the remains. However, Good was also a thief and had stolen a pair of trousers from a pawnbroker. When Police Constable Gardner was searching a stable attached to Good's home for the missing trousers, he found what he at first thought was the burned carcass of a pig or a goose, but it turned out to be a partially scorched female torso. Good escaped by locking the policeman in the stable. The Government took the unusual step of offering a One Hundred Pounds Reward 'to be paid …to any person who shall have such information and evidence as will lead to the apprehension' of Good.[976]

Meanwhile, criticism of the police was mounting. The *Morning Advertiser* suggested that:

> 'nothing can possibly be worse than the "helter-skelter" mode in which the police proceed. The case of the late-lamented Lord William Russell cannot be forgotten, or the gross blundering of the police, by which a cold-blooded and mercenary murderer was so near escaping the punishment which so justly awaited him, and whose conviction was entirely owing to a mere matter of chance. In the present case, as in that just stated, there are ten times too many officers employed, and each being anxious to acquire some fame by what he may be able to do, they cross one another, the one undoing that which the other has done, and the case is merely "bit by bit".'[977]

971 *Morning Post*, 10 February 1840, p.7.
972 Police Order, 2 February 1840.
973 Durston, Gregory J (2001) 'Criminal and Constable: The Impact of Policing Reform on Crime in Nineteenth Century London. PhD thesis at the London School of Economics'. Retrieved from www.ethesis.lse.ac.uk/2779/1/U615728.pdf, pp.367-368.
974 This was another occasion, in June 1832, when a partly burned body had been found in Leicester.
975 *Morning Post*, 8 April 1842, p.7.
976 Ibid, 12 April 1842, p.6.
977 *Morning Advertiser*, 11 April 1842, p.3.

On the same day, the *London Evening Standard* claimed:

'the conduct of the metropolitan police in the present case, as in those of the unfortunate Eliza Grimwood, Lord William Russell and others, is marked with a looseness and want of decision which prove that unless a decided change is made in the present system, it is idle to expect that it can be an efficient detective police, and that the most desperate offender may escape with immunity.'[978]

Five days later, in pointing out that the 'perpetrator' of the murder, Daniel Good, had been 'at large' for nine days, the *Morning Advertiser* suggested that 'the public had a right to have expected better things from the metropolitan police, a force so great in numerical strength and maintained at so heavy a cost to the country.' It continued:

'The system is so organised, that a quick and ready communication is, or should be, maintained between the officers and the men under them and the head office; and yet this police, which, from its manifold arrangements, would be thought to be perfect, has not succeeded in delivering into the hands of justice an individual who has upon several occasions crossed their path, and all but stayed to be taken and who, be it further stated, is most probably in the metropolis. If the police suffer this man to escape, they will inflict themselves indelible disgrace; and the public will be led to suspect that there is something wrong in its government.'[979]

He remained at large for ten days until finally arrested in Kent after being recognised by a former police constable from Wandsworth who had read about the murder in the newspaper.[980]

The inquiries to trace Good involved officers on different divisions but Rowan and Mayne were clearly dissatisfied with the way they had been conducted because they subsequently suspended a number of officers, including three inspectors. Although they were subsequently reinstated, they did not receive any pay for the period they were suspended.[981]

Meanwhile, there were three attempts on the life of Queen Victoria between June 1840 and 1842. The first occurred on 9 June 1840, during her first pregnancy when 18-year-old Edward Oxford attempted to assassinate her while she was riding in an open-top carriage along Constitution

---

978 *London Evening Standard*, 11 April 1842, p.3.
979 *Morning Advertiser*, 16 April 1842, p.3.
980 Old Bailey Proceedings Online, op. cit. 947, (27 December 2017), May 1842, trial of DANIEL GOOD (t18420509-1705).
981 *London Evening Standard*, 28 April 1842, p.2; *Morning Post* 18 May 1842, p.7.

Hill, accompanied by Prince Albert, to visit her mother. There were two outriders but no other attendants. Oxford had two pistols under his coat and was able to draw them and fire twice at the Queen before he was overpowered by passers-by and handed over to two police officers, Charles Brown and William Smith who quickly arrived on the scene. He was taken to Gardner's Lane Station House. That evening, Inspector Samuel Hughes visited 6 West Place, and found a quantity of property including three ounces of gunpowder, a bullet-mould, five bullets and some percussion caps. Apparently, Oxford had stolen the pistols from a pawnbroker in Blackfriars Road. The pawnbroker 'underwent a long and very strict examination' by both Rowan and Mayne at Whitehall Place 'as to the identification of [the pistols]' before he was able to satisfy the Commissioners that the pistols used by Oxford had been stolen from his premises.[982] Oxford was tried for high treason and found guilty but was acquitted on the grounds of insanity. He was ordered to be detained during Her Majesty's pleasure and committed to a mental institution.[983]

The second attempt occurred on Sunday, 29 May 1842. Queen Victoria and Prince Albert where returning to Buckingham Palace, in a closed carriage, after attending a service at the Royal Chapel in St James's Palace. When they were about halfway down The Mall, John Francis rushed towards the carriage, thrust a pistol through a window and fired. Fortunately, the gun failed to go off but, on this occasion, Francis made his escape. Rowan returned to his office at 4 Whitehall Place[984] from an afternoon stroll at some time between 5 and 6 o'clock, to find that the Home Secretary, Sir James Graham had called and left a message that he wished to see him at the Home Office. There, Sir James told him of the incident that had occurred. The two men then went to Buckingham Palace where the Queen made it clear that she did not wish to 'shut herself away'. It was decided, therefore, Rowan would arrange for a strong force in plain clothes to be deployed in St James's Park in an attempt to 'draw the assassin out the following day'. Rowan had another meeting with Sir James on the Monday afternoon and was sitting in his office issuing further instructions when he received information that 'the Queen had been fired at.'[985]

At around 4.00pm the Queen and Prince Albert had left Buckingham

---

982   *Hull Packet*, 19 June 1840, p.3.
983   Old Bailey Proceedings Online, op. cit. 947, 27 December 2017), July 1840, trial of EDWARD OXFORD (t18400706-1877); see also Charles, Barrie (2012) *Kill the Queen! The Eight Assassination Attempts on Queen Victoria*. Stroud: Amberley Publishing, p.23.
984   This was also Rowan's residence at the time.
985   From a note, dated 29 May, in Rowan's handwriting on file TNA MEPO 3/18.

Palace in an 'open barouche and four'.[986] They were accompanied by their equerries, Colonel George Arbuthnot and Colonel William Wylde, riding on each side of the carriage. Nothing happened on the outward journey but on their return to the Palace, in Constitution Hill, Francis struck again. This time the gun went off, but he missed his target and was seized by Constable William Trounce who, with the aid of passers-by hustled him away to the porter's lodge at the Palace.

Two hours later he was brought to the Home Office where 'assembled dignitaries', including the Duke of Wellington, Prime Minister Sir Robert Peel, Attorney General Sir Frederick Pollock, Police Commissioner Colonel Charles Rowan, and Bow Street Chief Magistrate Mr. Hall, questioned witnesses for an hour-an-a-half. At his trial, Francis was sentenced to death for high treason, but this was commuted to transportation for life.[987]

Stung by the growing criticism, on 14 June 1842, the Commissioners forwarded to the Home Office a lengthy 'Memorandum relative to the Detective Powers of Police' outlining 'a scheme for such a branch'. The Memorandum described how, as a result of Good remaining at large for a time, there had been an assumption that there was a lack of 'skill in the Metropolitan Police, and a defect of general organisation applicable to detective duties.' Mayne counteracted this suggestion by pointing out that, since the formation of the police, there had been 24 murders. In 14 of these cases, the murderer had been convicted and in seven other cases, the guilty parties were known but had either escaped by leaving the UK or there was insufficient 'legal evidence' to obtain a conviction.

The Memorandum concluded by recommending the Detective Force should consist of two inspectors and eight sergeants. The Home Secretary, now Sir James Graham, queried the cost of such a body and wanted to know what regulations would be introduced 'to ensure the proper employment of the detective officers when not immediately occupied in the pursuit of offenders.'

The Commissioners responded to the effect that, when not employed on specific cases, all members of the Detective Force would be 'employed in gaining information as to the facilities' that might 'be afforded from time to time for the commission of particular species of crimes, and by the habits, haunts and persons or parties known or suspected to live by the commission of crime, so as to prepare themselves for tracing and detecting

---

986 A four-wheeled horse-drawn carriage with a retractable hood over the rear half with two seats inside for two couples facing each other; the driver's seat is outside at the front.

987 See TNA MEPO 3/18; Barrie, op. cit. 983, pp.24-43; Old Bailey Proceedings Online, op. cit. 947, 03 (February 2018) July 1842, trial of JOHN FRANCIS (t18420613-1758).

offenders when any case occurred.'[988] On 20 June Sir James gave his formal approval for the Detective Police to be established, but restricted the strength to two inspectors and six sergeants.[989]

Despite seeing the need to form a Detective Force to ward off some of the criticism being levelled at them and the Force, Rowan and Mayne remained reluctant. Chadwick, who, with Rowan had been a member of the Royal Commission, was quoted as saying in 1840 that he knew 'from Sir C. Rowan and Mr Richard Mayne that they disliked detection on principle and only yielded to its adoption on what they deemed superior authority.'[990]

In typical Home Officer fashion, no provision was made for a head of the Detective Police. Nicholas Pearce, who was already attached to A Division, and John Haynes, from P Division, were the two inspectors. The sergeants were Stephen Thornton (E Division), William Gerrett (A Division), Frederick Shaw (R Division), Braddick (F Division) who were already sergeants; two constables, Charles Goff (L Division) and Jonathan Whicher (E Division) were promoted to sergeant to fill the remaining positions. Despite their number being 'inadequate from the beginning', the strength of the Detective Force remained the same for the next twenty-two years. Not until 1864 was there any increase in its size and when Mayne died at the end of 1868, it still numbered only fifteen in a force which then amounted to nearly eight thousand men.[991] The fact that it took thirteen years to employ some officers as full-time detectives was, it has been said, a 'strategic error of judgement,' by Rowan and Mayne.[992]

On 5 July, a mere two weeks after Sir James had given formal approval for the formation of the Detective Police, yet another attempt was made on Queen Victoria's life. It occurred whilst the Queen and Prince Albert, on this occasion accompanied by the King of Belgium, were in the second of three carriages on their way to the Royal Chapel for the Sunday morning service. John Bean, a 17-year-old youth who suffered from a severe spinal deformity, pulled out a gun as the Queen's carriage passed him in the Mall, pointed it at the carriage and pulled the trigger. However, it failed to fire. He was seized by 16-year-old Charles Dassett, who took the gun from him and, with the help of his brother, marched him in the direction in which the

988 TNA HO 45/292.
989 Ibid.
990 Richardson, Benjamin Ward (1887). *The Health of Nations: A Review of the Works of Edwin Chadwick, Volume II*. London: Longman, Green and Co, pp.394-395.
991 Moylan, J.F (1929). *Scotland Yard and The Metropolitan Police*. London: G.P. Putnam's Sons, p.154.
992 White, Jerry (2008). *London in the 19th Century*, London: Vintage, p.396.

three carriages had gone. He came across Constable Hearn, told him what had happened, and showed him the gun, but the constable took it to be a joke. The same happened when he approached Constable Claxton. Now fed up with the failure of the two officers to take him seriously, he let Bean go, but still had the gun. Attracted by the crowd around Dassett, Constable Partridge took a different view, arrested him for being in possession of the gun and took him to Gardner's Lane Station House where, on being questioned by Inspector Hinkman, the full story came out. Hinkman immediately sent word to Rowan, on whose directions Bean's description was circulated to all station-houses.

Both Whitehall Place and Gardner's Lane Station House were besieged by members of both Houses of Parliament, and the Duke of Cambridge, Prince George,[993] visited the latter. Meanwhile, Rowan went to the Cabinet Office where members of the cabinet were assembling for a meeting. At around 2.30pm Dassett was brought to the Cabinet Office, escorted by Superintendent May and other officers.

Later that afternoon the description circulated on Rowan's instructions bore fruit. Bean lived in Clerkenwell, and local policeman Henry Webb, recognising the description, arrested him. On 25 August he appeared at the Old Bailey, where it was decided that the gun was not loaded, and he was found guilty of harassing and alarming the Queen and her subjects, for which he was sentenced to 18 months in the penitentiary at Millbank.[994]

A week later, Prime Minister Peel introduced a Bill for the Better Protection of the Queen's Person, but it did little more than authorize the ordinary courts to deal with offenders like Francis and Bean without recourse to the Privy Council. However, during the preparation of the Bill, there were almost certainly discussions about police protection of the royal family between the Rowan and Mayne, and Home Secretary Graham, and even with the Prime Minister.'[995]

Initially, the Commissioners gave little publicity to the formation of the Detective Police, with only the briefest mention being made in one leading London newspaper:

'Several cases have lately occurred, in which criminals have not been taken into custody so promptly as the public had a right to expect, the

---

993 Prince George was a cousin of Queen Victoria.
994 Barrie, op. cit. 983, pp.44-54; *London Evening Standard*, 4 July 1842, p.3; Old Bailey Proceedings Online, op. cit, 947, 03 February 2018), August 1842, trial of JOHN WILLIAM BEAN (t18420822-2277).
995 Browne, Douglas G (1956). *The Rise of Scotland Yard: A History of the Metropolitan Police*. London: Harrap, p.120.

commissioners of police have arranged that a new company shall be immediately raised out of the present police, to be called the Detective Force.'

There followed a brief description of the make-up of such a Force, which, as it turned out, was incorrect.[996] However, on Rowan's retirement eight years later, Mayne took a different view regarding publicity. By this time, there had been some changes in the personnel of the Detective Force. Nicholas Pearce had been promoted to Superintendent in 1844 and for the next two years Joseph Shackell led it. In 1846 Charles Field, who had been involved in the investigation into the murder of Eliza Grimwood in 1837, became the unofficial chief of the Detective Force for the next six years, heading it until his retirement in 1852.

It was during this time that Charles Dickens became interested in the Detective Police, inviting them all to a social evening at the offices of his journal, *Household Words*, at 16 Wellington Street, an occasion subsequently described by Dickens in an article entitled 'A Detective Police Party' published in 1850.[997] But perhaps the most controversial article published in *Household Words* relating to the police was one entitled 'On Duty' with Inspector Field, published in 1851.[998] The article described how Dickens had accompanied Inspector Field around various notorious spots in London, which would not have been allowed to take place without Mayne's prior agreement.

Despite a considerable increase in the overall size of the Force, Mayne's 'conservatism' kept the size of the Detective Force at its 1842 size until 1864, when an inspector and a sergeant were added. Three years later an inspector and several more sergeants were added, which brought the total up to 16, including a clerk.[999] This led to the Departmental Inquiry appointed by Home Secretary Gathorne Hardy, to inquire into the policing in the metropolis, which announced:

'The detective police, having regard to their number, appear to the Committee to be very efficient for the detection of ordinary crime, but their numbers are wholly inadequate to the present requirements of the metropolis …[and] …their constitution scarcely adapts them to cope with the conspiracies and secret combinations.'

---

996 *Morning Post*, 12 July 1842, p.7; it also appeared in a few provincial newspapers.
997 *Household Words, a Weekly Journal Conducted by Charles Dickens*, No. 18, dated 27 July 1850. It appears that both inspectors and five of the six sergeants attended.
998 Ibid, No. 64, dated 14 June 1851.
999 Roach, op. cit. 941, p.375.

Accordingly, the Committee recommended 'the detective police should form a separate division under the control of a special superintendent and under the immediate command of the head of the police.' But it did not stop there. In what must have been a total anathema to Mayne, it also recommended that 'the officer in command of the detective force should have the power to recommend men for his division, whether or not they have filled the office of constable.'[1000] This went against one of the only two principles Peel laid down in 1829.[1001]

1000 TNA HO 45/A49463/2. Report of the Departmental Committee on the Metropolitan Police 1868, pp, 212-22.
1001 See Chapter Ten.

CHAPTER SEVENTEEN

THE LATE 1840s

During the mid-1840s, much of Mayne's time was spent in attempting to keep the streets of the metropolis free of obstructions from the increasing number of horse-drawn omnibuses. Another source of obstruction occurred in theatre land when special events were held, as the number of carriages used by patrons to arrive for performances and depart after they had finished, increased.

With regard to the first, Mayne became unpopular with omnibus proprietors in May 1845 when between twenty and thirty of them were instructed to attend Whitehall Place, together with their drivers. Summonses had been issued, charging them with 'stopping longer than was necessary for taking up or setting down passengers or loading or unloading' at the Fox and Ball, Knightsbridge, and various other places on the Fulham and Chelsea line. Announcing that 'the Commissioners had no wish to press the summonses' on this occasion other than to obtain an order for costs, Mayne reminded the proprietors that their drivers should not stop for longer than was necessary to take up or set down passengers, and police constables had been 'directed to enforce the regulation.'[1002]

With regard to the second, for the opening ceremony at the Royal Exchange in 1844, Mayne issued specific instructions about the direction from which coaches bringing people to it should approach, where the coaches should wait during the ceremony and the direction from which they should come to pick up their owners after the ceremony.[1003] In theatreland, Mayne frequently issued instructions for the setting down and picking up of patrons attending Covent Garden Opera House[1004] and

---

1002 *London Evening Standard*, 12 May 1845, p.4.
1003 *Evening Mail*, 28 October 1844, p.1.
1004 *Globe*, 22 December 1845, p.2; *Morning Post*, 2 February 1846, p.1; *Morning Advertiser*, 6 April 1847, p.2.

Drury Lane Theatre.[1005] He also issued instructions for events at Exeter Hall, a large hall in the Strand,[1006] which could hold 3,000 people, and the slightly smaller Willis's Rooms in St James,[1007] both of which hosted musical concerts, lectures and evangelical meetings.

By the beginning of 1848, the political scene in England had worsened. A trade depression coincided with an increase in revolutionary movements on the continent; there were rebellions in Austria, Hungary and Germany, but the one that affected Britain most took place in France, where a republic had been declared following the overthrow of King Louise Philippe. In London, the news that Louise Philippe had been deposed led to 'occupants of the cheapest seats, in the pit and gallery', at Sadler's Wells, stopping the evening's performance and 'calling for the Marseillaise to be played.' The Royal Victoria Theatre in Waterloo Road quickly put on a play depicting the French Revolution at which cast and audience ended each performance with a rousing rendition of the Marseillaise. But it was the election of Feargus O'Connor to Parliament as Member for Nottingham that gave the Chartist Movement renewed vigour. This, coupled with news of what was happening on the continent, 'turned the spring and summer of 1848 into the most momentous few months in Victorian history', with many believing that Britain and Ireland were on the verge of revolution.[1008]

The first test for Mayne and the ailing Rowan[1009] was set for Trafalgar Square on 6 March. Although the extent of this being a Chartist initiative is debatable, newspapers and, indeed, the authorities perceived it to be just that. The meeting had been called by Charles Cochrane, a campaigner for the poor who had founded the Poor Man's Guardian Society in 1846, to protest against the imposition of income tax.[1010]

The meeting itself was illegal. It contravened the Seditious Meetings Act of 1817 in that it was being held within one mile of Parliament which was then in session, and Mayne sent a letter to Cochrane on 3 March requesting that he call upon the Commissioners to discuss it.[1011] Cochrane replied that he would call on them at 11 o'clock the following day, 4 March.

1005 *Morning Post*, 27 November 1847, p.1.
1006 *Morning Post*, 11 June 1847, p.1.
1007 *London Daily News*, 21 May 1847, p.1.
1008 Chase, Malcolm (2007). *Chartism: A New History*. Manchester: Manchester University Press, pp.294-295.
1009 See Chapter Eighteen.
1010 Whilst people had been required to pay income tax previously during wartime, the Income Tax Act 1842 (5 and 6 Vict, c.35) was the first occasion that income tax had been imposed during peacetime.
1011 The exchange of letters between Mayne and Cochrane appeared in the *Morning Advertiser*, 7 March 1848, p.2.

But Mayne was unhappy with this and, at 4 o'clock, that afternoon, replied on behalf of the Commissioners regretting that Cochrane could not call on them as he had suggested. The letter then explained the purpose of the meeting was

> 'to point out that, by the Act of 57 George III, cap. 19, sec. 26, it is made illegal to hold a public meeting during the sitting of Parliament, within the distance of one mile from Westminster-hall.
>
> The Commissioners, believing that that the law referred to has probably escaped your notice, trust, that in calling your attention to it now, you will take the requisite steps to change the place of holding the intended meeting on Monday next, as Trafalgar-square is within the limits mentioned.'

The following morning, Cochrane did not 'call upon the Commissioners' but responded again by letter, expressing surprise that the Commissioners thought the intended meeting was illegal. He continued:

> 'I find great difficulty, after your first courteous communication of the same date, in understanding what can have led to this unjust interpretation of the Act towards the meeting referred to, when a few days ago a densely-crowded assemblage of sailors was permitted on the same spot, under great excitement, and countenanced and encouraged by the most stirring party appeals from several of the daily papers. I presume the Commissioners have thought proper to favour me with their two communications under an entire misapprehension of the object of the meeting. I can assure them that it is exclusively limited to the consideration of a petition to Parliament relative to the odious income-tax; and I think I can with confidence guarantee to the Commissioners that the greatest peace and good order will be maintained by the parties assembling, who, in number, will not, I presume, be a tithe of those sailors who were permitted to congregate; and finally, present a petition to Sir George Grey in reference to a law which they considered involved the fate of their future welfare.
>
> I have thought it more advisable at present thus to convey my opinions, and the expression of my feelings to you, rather than trust to the verbal communications of an interview which I proposed having today, lest any misconceptions might take place as to your wishes and intentions.'

Mayne wrote back the same afternoon, suggesting that Cochrane had 'misapprehended the object of the letter'. He continued:

> 'It was not intended to imply that the object of the meeting was illegal,

or that any disturbance of order was apprehended. The Commissioners only desired to point out that by the Act of Parliament referred to, the meeting appeared to them to be one which ought not to be held within one mile of Westminster-hall (unless within the parish of St. Paul, Covent-garden); they felt it their duty to point this out to you, thinking it probable [that Cochrane] might not be aware of the Act in question.'

At 6 o'clock that evening, Cochrane responded, saying it was his 'earnest wish to respect' the law, but enquiring whether they would allow the meeting 'to take place without interruption' or whether it was their intention 'to adopt measures for its prevention'. If they proposed the latter course, he would like to know as soon as possible in order that he could make 'the necessary announcement' that the meeting was prohibited. Mayne's response, dated 5 March, was brief and to the point. Having pointed out the relevant Act of Parliament, the Commissioners would leave it to Cochrane to decide for himself the action he should take. At nine o'clock on the morning of the proposed meeting, Cochrane wrote again, complaining that Mayne had not answered the points he raised in his letter of 6 o'clock on 4 March, particular if it was intended to prevent the meeting, but he had decided to cancel the meeting. Mayne responded, regretting that Cochrane felt he had cause for complaint over a previous letter, informing him that the sole intention was to bring the relevant Act of Parliament to his notice. Once again, Cochrane was told that only he could be the judge 'as to the course of action he thought it proper to take under [the] circumstances'.

Shortly before 1 o'clock, police under the command of Superintendent Pearce appeared in Trafalgar Square 'in considerable numbers'. At the same time several men appeared carrying a placard on which it said:

> 'The Commissioners of Police having declared that the public meeting to be held this day in Trafalgar-square, against the income tax, is illegal, Mr. Cochrane respectfully, but earnestly, requests the public will not congregate or remain in the square, but return quietly and orderly to their homes. He deeply regrets, in consequence of the decision by the Commissioners, he has put the public to so much unnecessary inconvenience.'[1012]

But the crowd was in no mood to disperse. The placard was seized and broken up. Cochrane did not appear, but several Chartists, using 'inflammatory language', addressed the crowd from the balustrades of the

---

1012 *Morning Chronicle* (Evening Edition), 6 March 1848, p.8.

terrace in Trafalgar Square. It was announced that a meeting would be held at Clerkenwell Green at 5 o'clock to discuss the People's Charter and resolutions were passed calling for 'the abolition of the obnoxious tax'. At about 3.00pm, police attempted to clear the Square but failed. By 4.00pm, a section of the crowd had removed the hoarding around Nelson's column, and finding stones behind it, threw them at the police as they tried to maintain a semblance of order. Some lamps in the Square were broken. A running battle broke out which continued for the next hour. During this time, 'individual policemen broke from their colleagues and made sallies into the crowd' to arrest or knock down ringleaders. As Mather points out, such a tactic appeared to have been very highly rated by the exponents of the new police ideal, for the were lauded by Edwin Chadwick in his County Constabulary Report of 1839,[1013] and by Superintendent Martin, an experienced officer of the Metropolitan Police, giving evidence before a parliamentary committee in 1852.[1014] On this occasion, however, they proved quite ineffectual. At about 5.00pm, the main body of people left the Square and headed for St James's Park, breaking lamps and windows as they did so. At 9.00pm, a crowd of about 5,000 was still marauding about the West End but by 11.00pm this number had dwindled down to about 1,500.[1015] The meeting at Clerkenwell Green attracted about 2,000 people and lasted for two hours. The police 'were assembled in considerable force' and there was no disorder.[1016]

The following morning, hundreds of young men gathered in the Square and surrounding streets from an early hour; some indulged in 'general rowdiness'. Their behaviour 'attracted several thousand spectators' on the terraces surrounding the Square. Most businesses in the surrounding streets were closed. Eventually the hoardings around Nelson's statue, which had been replaced overnight, were torn down again, and, armed with splintered pieces of wood, a section of the crowd met with a large body of police, under the personal command of Mayne, as they advanced on the Square. The central area of the Square was eventually cleared by 11.30am, but not before the police had used 'their staves with some severity'. However, some missiles were still being thrown from the terraces.[1017]

At 2.00pm a notice, prohibiting such gatherings, was posted at various

---

1013 PP 1839 [169]. First report of the commissioners appointed to inquire as to the best means of establishing an efficient constabulary force in the counties of England and Wales.
1014 PP 1852-53 [715]. Second report from the Select Committee on Police; together with the proceedings of the committee, minutes of evidence, and appendix. Minutes of evidence. pp. 90-93, q/a 3727-3793.
1015 *Morning Post*, 7 March 1848, p.6.
1016 *Morning Advertiser*, 7 March 1848, p.2.
1017 *Evening Standard*, 8 March 1848, p.1.

places in the area:

NOTICE

Whereas large bodies of Persons assembled yesterday, in the Forenoon and throughout the Day, and of the Night, in TRAFALGAR SQUARE, and in the Neighbourhood, and committed many acts of Violence and Rioting, and serious Breaches of the Peace.

And whereas large bodies of Persons are at this time and there assembled, whereby the Public Peace is greatly disturbed, and the peaceable inhabitants of Neighbourhood are interrupted in their lawful Business and alarmed.

NOTICE IS HEREBY GIVEN

That all such Meetings and Assemblies are

CONTRARY TO LAW.

And orders have been given to the Police to prevent such unlawful Meetings, and to apprehend and take into their Custody all Offenders, that they may be dealt with according to Law.

All Persons are hereby cautioned and strictly enjoined not to attend, or join, or be present at any such Meeting.

And well disposed Persons are hereby called upon and required to aid the Police in the discharge of their duties, and to assist, as far as they may be able, in protection of the public Peace.

WHITEHALL, March 7th, 1848,

Two o'clock

During the course of the afternoon, detachments of police cordoned off the Square.[1018] However, there was trouble in some of the surrounding streets. On hearing there was a considerable number of disorderly people present at Charing Cross, Superintendent May went there with 2 inspectors and 30 constables. On their arrival they found that the hoarding around the King Charles statue had been removed by the mob and thrown at vehicles to prevent them passing. As they advanced on the mob, stones were thrown. May gave the order to disperse them and the officers drew their truncheons and drove them down Cockspur Street and Whitehall but a number of street lamps were smashed. Six ring-leaders were arrested. Meanwhile larger numbers had assembled on the promenade above the Square and the steps of St Martin's Church. Stones were thrown as

---

1018 Ibid.

additional police resources arrived to disperse them.[1019]

The following day, the Commissioners took steps to prevent a recurrence of the previous evening's disorder by stationing small groups of officers, about thirty strong, 'at various points in the Charing Cross area, from which constables could quickly descend on any place where a mob was becoming troublesome, and disperse it.'[1020] One-hundred and three persons, the majority of whom were around twenty years of age, were arrested during the period 6 to 8 March of which 73 were convicted and the remainder conditionally discharged.[1021]

Another demonstration was planned for Kennington Common on 10 April 1848 as this poster suggests:

CHARTIST
DEMONSTRATION
"PEACE and ORDER" is our MOTTO
TO THE WORKING MEN OF LONDON.

Fellow Men – The Press having misrepresented and vilified us and our intentions, the Demonstration Committee therefore consider it to be their duty to state that the grievances of us (the Working Classes) are deep and our demands just. We and our families are pining in misery, want, and starvation! We demand a fair day's wages for a fair day's work! We are the slaves of capital – we demand protection to our labour. We are political serfs – we demand to be free. We therefore invite all well-disposed to join our peaceful procession on

MONDAY NEXT, April 10.

As it is for the food of all that we seek to remove the evils under which we groan.

The following are the places of Meetings of THE CHARTISTS, THE TRADES, THE IRISH CONFEDERATION & REPEAL BODIES:

East Division on Stepney Green at 8 o'clock; City and Finsbury Division on Clerkenwell Green at 9 o'clock; West Division in Russell Square at 9 o'clock; and the South Division in Peckham Fields at 9 o'clock, and proceed from thence to Kennington Common.

Fearing 'a full-scale uprising',[1022] the Government ensured elaborate

---

1019 Report, dated 7 March 1848, by Superintendent John May in TNA MEPO 2/64.
1020 *Evening Standard*, 8 March 1848, p.1.
1021 TNA MEPO 2/64, quoted in Mace, Rodney (2005). *Trafalgar Square: Emblem of Empire*. London: Lawrence and Wishart, p.138.
1022 Chase, op. cit. 1008, p.317.

arrangements were made by both the police and the military. The Commissioners received letters requesting that buildings such as the House of Commons, the Home Office, the Foreign Office, and the Public Record Office should be adequately protected.[1023] But the main body of police would be deployed to stop demonstrators converging on Parliament or Government offices after the meeting. Consequently, the police planned to occupy Blackfriars Bridge, Waterloo Bridge, Hungerford Bridge, Westminster Bridge and Vauxhall Bridge to prevent people from crossing from the south side of the River Thames after the meeting.[1024]

On 9 April, final plans were made at a conference at the Home Office between the Home Secretary, the Duke of Wellington, still the Commander in Chief of the Army, Rowan and Mayne, and the Lord Mayor.'[1025] The plans, both for the military and the police, were almost certainly the work of Rowan. Some years later, Lord John Russell described how, when they were all assembled, he 'requested Sir C. Rowan to read the programme.' When Rowan had finished, Russell turned to the Duke and asked him whether he approved of the plan to which the Duke replied in the affirmative.[1026] The specific military arrangements were the responsibility of the Duke. He deployed 890 cavalry, eleven pieces of artillery, including three 12 lb howitzers, nine brigades of Infantry (approximately 5,000 men) and 12,000 enrolled pensioners to protect, if necessary, all the Parks, the area from Trafalgar Square to the Houses of Parliament, in which Government offices were located, the Tower of London and the Royal Palaces, although the Royal Family had left London to stay at Osborne House on the Isle of Wight.[1027]

On the day, the various groups met as planned and the processions walked 'in perfect order' along the routes specified by the police, to Kennington. Eventually, towards noon, the estimates of the number of people who had assembled varied considerably from 20,000 to 150,000.[1028] In a report to the Home Secretary, Mayne described his meeting with Feargus O'Connor; one report said it was in a nearby public house,[1029] but the letter to his wife (below) suggests otherwise:

1023 TNA MEPO 2/65.
1024 Mace, op. cit. 1021, p.150.
1025 Critchley, T.A (1970). *The Conquest of Violence: Order and Liberty in Britain*. London: Constable, p.139.
1026 Letter, dated 4 August 1872, from Lord John Russell to the Rev. G.R. Gleig. In G.R. Gleig (1891), *The Life of the Duke of Wellington*, revised edition; appendix, p.498.
1027 TNA WO 30/81, folio 28-1. Memoranda by the Duke of Wellington with statement showing distribution of troops.
1028 Mace, op. cit. 1021, p.150.
1029 *Illustrated London News*, 15 April 1848.

¼ to 12
Kennington

I have seen Mr. O'Connor and communicated to him that the petition would be allowed to pass and every facility given for that, and its reaching the House of Commons, but no procession or assemblage of people would be permitted to pass the bridges.

Mr. O'Connor gave me his word that the procession would not attempt to cross the bridges, but he added that the petition should be sent in cabs. I had sent Mr. Mallalieu to ask Mr. O'Connor and two or three of the rioters to come and see me to accept such a communication.

There was considerable excitement among the people as Mr. O'Connor came to see me. It was evidently supposed he was taken into custody. I never saw a man more frightened than he was, and he would I am sure have promised me anything. He had some difficulty in keeping people about us on the road… and got on top of a cab to tell them he had accepted a friendly communication on which he was resolved to act.[1030]

Immediately afterwards, Mayne found the time to drop his wife another quick letter. Timed at approximately the same time, he wrote:

'I sent for Feargus O'Connor, from the meeting, to come to me on the road where I was on horseback; he came, accompanied by a considerable crowd, much excited, supposing he was arrested.

I gave notice of what was intended, and he promised that the procession should not attempt to go with the petition. How far he can prevail on the people to disperse, we shall see. He was evidently terrified, and would have promised me anything.

The meeting is not perhaps above 10,000 people and a few thousand lookers on.

I shall now go to Blackfriars Bridge in case these worthies should attempt to force a passage.'[1031]

Much later, Sergeant Lowe, who escorted Mayne that day, described the conversation:

1030 TNA HO/OS 2410, quoted in Critchley, op. cit. 1025, p.140.
1031 Henry Hall Collection. Collection of diaries, journals, letters, books and miscellaneous papers, donated by Edward Hall (b.1898), a dealer and collector of Manuscripts and books. Includes letters written by Sir Richard Mayne to his wife between 1831 and 1866 in files EHC210/M1251;EHC210A/1252 and EHC 211/M1253, Letter 184, pp.179-180.

O'Connor: What do you intend to do Sir Richard?

Mayne: What do you intend to do. Do you intend to go in procession for if you do I shall stop you by force if necessary.[1032]

Everything went largely according to plan, although there were small skirmishes with the police as people tried to cross Blackfriars Bridge. By 2.00pm

'not more than 100 persons were to be seen upon the Common. Many of these consisted of its usual occupants – boys playing at trap-ball and other games; and, by a quarter past two, a stranger to the day's proceedings would never have guessed, from the appearance of the neighbourhood, that anything extraordinary had taken place.'[1033]

Hearing there was to be another demonstration, this time on 25 April, Mayne wrote again to Charles Cochrane on 22 April:

'The Commissioners of the Metropolitan Police have observed in the *Morning Advertiser* newspaper an advertisement headed 'No Bastilles – Metropolitan Demonstration on East Monday against the cruel Poor-laws; in which it is stated that a very large crowd (upwards of 90,000) of persons have promised to pass by Whitehall on Monday, when the petition to the Queen against the present poor-law will be left by a deputation with Sir George Grey, at the Home Department, and that five oil paintings, illustrating the conditions of the poor in unions and workhouses, will be taken round Trafalgar-square for public exhibition, previous to these being submitted for Sir George Grey's inspection. It also appears that printed addresses to the working classes, with your signature, have been circulated in various districts of the metropolis and other places, calling upon the people to form a very numerous assemblage in Charing-cross, to join the deputation, and that every man is expected to wear on his hat a printed paper, with the words 'No Bastilles' upon it. The commissioners lose no time to acquiring you that such an assemblage would be illegal. It becomes the duty of the commissioners to adopt the necessary measures not to allow the assemblage of a crowd of persons at Charing-cross on the occasion, and directions will be given to the police for preventing the obstruction of the streets and thoroughfares, and the interruption of business, which each procession would occasion.

1032 *Illustrated London News*, 15 April 1848.
1033 'The Oldest Policeman: Reminiscences of London Scenes.' An interview with London's oldest policeman, in *The Globe*, 21 June 1897, p.3.

The commissioners have to acquaint you that the statement in the advertisement of "Sir George Grey having declared he would not interfere with the demonstration" is erroneous, no such declaration having been made by Sir George Grey.'[1034]

On the following day, a placard signed by Mayne was widely circulated:

'Notice – The police have directions to prevent the assemblage of persons in Trafalgar-square or Charing-cross on Monday, April 25, and no procession or crowd of persons will be permitted to pass along Whitehall, or the neighbourhood of her Majesty's palaces or public offices, on Monday, April 25. Any person who wilfully disregards or does not conform himself to the regulations for preventing obstructions in the streets and thoroughfares on this occasion will be immediately taken into custody.'[1035]

The part played by Mayne is interesting in the light of the operational leads taken by Rowan previously. One likely reason was that Rowan was too infirm to ride a horse. Nevertheless, just sixteen days after Rowan's and Mayne's great victory, it was announced that 'Her Majesty has been graciously pleased' to give orders for the appointment of 'Richard Mayne, Esq., one of the Commissioners of the Police of the Metropolis, to be [an] Ordinary Member of the Civil Division of the Third Class, or, Companions of the aforesaid Most Honourable Order of the Bath.'[1036] The following year, obviously riding the crest of a wave, Mayne attended Her Majesty's Drawing Room at St James's Palace to celebrate Her Majesty's birthday.[1037] Mayne had another cause to celebrate at about this time. His nemesis at the Home Office, Phillipps, finally retired.[1038]

Meanwhile, the unpopularity of the decision by O'Connor to conform to Mayne's demands on 12 April, did nothing to dampen the enthusiasm of the London Chartists. Indeed, by the early summer 'emboldened by the restless state of Ireland' their 'commitment to an uprising' became 'extensive.'[1039] The trigger for what was to happen through to August was

---

1034 *Morning Advertiser*, 24 April 1848, p.3.
1035 *Morning Advertiser*, 24 April 1848, p.3.
1036 *London Gazette*, 28 April 1848, Issue 20850, page 1655.
1037 *Morning Post*, 21 May 1849, p.5.
1038 Roach, Lawrence (2004). 'The Origins and Impact of the Function of the Crime Investigation and Detection in the British Police Service: A thesis submitted in partial fulfilment of the requirements for the degree of Doctor of Philosophy of Loughborough University'. Loughborough: Loughborough University's Institutional Repository, p.131.
1039 Chase, op. cit. 1008, p.309.

the arrest, on 13 May, of John Mitchel, editor of the *United Irishman*,[1040] which 'commanded ready sales among British Chartists.'[1041] Mitchel was found guilty of sedition on 27 May and sentenced to transportation for 14 years.[1042]

Whilst there was still much activity during the second half of April and most of May, none of it called for action by the Metropolitan Police. But the large crowds resurfaced on 29 May. Following a meeting on Clerkenwell Green, the crowd set off first for Finsbury Square where some 7,000 people marched around for forty-five minutes by which time more people had joined. They then set off for Smithfield before marching through Holborn to Leicester Square and then on to the Chartist Assembly Rooms in Dean Street, Soho, where they were addressed by Chartist leaders from the windows.

The crowd's next target was Buckingham Palace, but it was prevented from reaching the building by a strong body of police. They therefore returned to Finsbury Square, from where they eventually dispersed.[1043]

Two days later, despite rain, several hundred had assembled at Clerkenwell Green by 6.00pm expecting to hear a number of speakers. However, the conveners had abandoned the meeting 'in the face of immense police precautions'.[1044] The crowd steadily increased until at 9.00pm, not only was the Green densely packed but the surrounding streets were also thronging with people. Suddenly, a large contingent of police officers converged on the area and commenced to clear the streets. In some of the streets leading to the Green, 'several violent attacks' were made on the officers, 'but owing to the admirable organisation of the force,' the officers did not receive 'much personal injury'.[1045]

The Commissioners received information that several meetings would take place the following day, 1 June, in different parts of the metropolis at the conclusion of which the various assemblies would march to Clerkenwell Green. The Commissioners therefore made arrangements to ensure this did not happen by deploying foot and mounted police at different locations around the Metropolis. Later that evening, Rowan and Mayne met with City of London Police Commissioner Daniel Whittle

---

1040 *The United Irishman* was a weekly newspaper, calling for resistance against British rule, founded by Mitchel in February 1848. It was suppressed under the Treason Act 1848. See Dillon, William (1888). *The Life of John Mitchel*. London: K.Paul, Trench and Company.
1041 Chase, op. cit. 1008, p.317.
1042 *Morning Post*, 29 May 1848, p.4.
1043 *Evening Standard*, 30 May 1848, p.1.
1044 Mather, F.C (1984). *Public Order in the Age of the Chartists*. Westport, Connecticut: Greenwood Press, p.101.
1045 *Morning Post*, 1 June 1848, p.4.

Harvey to draw up plans for the future.[1046]

On 2 June, again at around 6.00pm, people began assembling on the Green. On this occasion, a man harangued them for 'their cowardice in not resisting the police the previous night.' At 8.15pm police converged on the Green and within half-an-hour had driven the crowd from it.[1047]

At a Chartist meeting on 4 June 1848, at Bishop Bonner's Fields, a large contingent of police was concealed in a nearby church in case they should be needed. When a section of the crowd realised it, they started to throw stones at the windows of the church. In order to put an end to the stone throwing, the police emerged but met stubborn resistance in trying to clear the crowd from the meeting ground. Some of the demonstrators carried knives, others continued to throw stones. Truncheons 'were used in full force'[1048] but, not, claimed one commenter, 'unnecessarily' in clearing the Field.[1049] A number of officers were injured and an attempt to stab one officer in the stomach was only prevented when he managed to deflect the knife with his hand.[1050] However, in scenes that were slightly reminiscent of the behaviour of some officers at Cold Bath Fields, individual officers, no doubt, angry and 'exasperated by months of emergencies and alarms,' pursued members of the crowd into the surrounding streets, broke into houses and dragged the occupants into the streets, again freely using their truncheons.[1051]

By now the Commissioners were in possession of information that the Chartists and Irish Confederates intended to hold a series of meetings in early June, culminating in a monster one on 12 June, Whit Sunday. The Irish Confederates were an Irish nationalist independence movement founded in 1847 by people in Ireland to demand a national parliament with full legislative and executive powers. A London branch had opened two months later and by early 1848, a union with the London Chartists had been established.[1052] The purpose of the June meetings was to keep 'up the excitement' and tire out the authorities, most notably, the Metropolitan Police.[1053] But the majority of these meetings were prevented by the deployment of large numbers of officers at the venues before the time of the scheduled meeting.

1046 *Morning Advertiser*, 2 June 1848, p.2.
1047 *Morning Post*, 2 June 1848, p.4.
1048 *Morning Post*, 5 June 1848, p.4.
1049 Mather, op. cit. 1044, p.101.
1050 *Morning Post*, 5 June 1848, p.4.
1051 Mather, op. cit. 1044, p.101.
1052 Goodway, David (2002). *London Chartism 1838-1848*. Cambridge: Cambridge University Press, pp.65-67.
1053 *Morning Post*, 5 June 1848, p.4.

Concerned about the proposed meeting called to take place 'in and around the centre of the Metropolis,' on 12 June, the Home Secretary, Lord Grey, chaired a lengthy meeting on 6 June, at which both Rowan and Mayne were present along with the Attorney General and the Solicitor General. The purpose of the meeting was to decide on the measures to be taken to prevent the 12 June meeting from taking place.[1054] Again, elaborate arrangements were made by the police and the military but five days before the planned meeting, in an operation planned by Rowan and Mayne, four prominent London Chartists were arrested for making seditious speeches at meetings at Clerkenwell Green on different occasions in late-May, and the meeting at Bishop Bonner's Fields on 4 June.[1055]

On the day before the meeting Rowan and Mayne briefed all the Superintendents at 4 Whitehall Place. As they had done in March, a proclamation, this time signed by both Rowan and Mayne was issued:

> 'Whereas large meetings of persons, calling themselves Chartists, have lately been held in the open air, in and near the metropolis, at which seditious and inflammatory speeches have been addressed to the persons there assembled, such meetings have created terror and alarm, and have caused serious disturbance of the public peace, and have led to sets of tumult, disorder, and violent resistance to the law. And whereas certain persons styling themselves members of the Executive Committee of the Chartist Association have declared their intention to call together other large meetings in and near the metropolis, on Monday, June the 12th, whereby apprehension is entertained by the peaceable inhabitants of the metropolis that such meetings will be of the same dangerous character, and will lead to the disturbance of the public peace. Notice is hereby given, that such meetings are illegal, and that all necessary measures will be adapted to prevent any such meetings taking place; and all well-disposed persons are hereby cautioned not to attend, be present at, or take part in, any such meeting.'[1056]

On the day preceding the proposed demonstration, a rumour circulated that 300 police officers 'had given in their resignation in consequence of the severe duties which they had been called upon to perform' but this was

---

1054 *Morning Post*, 7 June 1848. p.4.
1055 *Morning Advertiser*, 8 June 1848, p.2; see also Old Bailey Proceedings Online (www.oldbaileyonline.org, version 7.2, 06 January 2019), July 1848, trial of JOSEPH IREANAUS JOHN FUSSELL (t18480703-1677)(Old Bailey Proceedings Online (www.oldbaileyonline.org, version 7.2, 06 January 2019), July 1848, trial of ALEXANDER SHARPE (t18480703-1712)
1056 *Morning Post*, 12 June 1848, p.4.

denied.[1057]

Throughout the afternoon of 12 June, Rowan and Mayne were present at 4 Whitehall Place, receiving reports from Bonner's Fields, Clerkenwell Green, Notting Hill, Regent's Park, Blackheath and Croydon, all venues the Chartists had announced meetings would be held. They were also in regular communication with City of London Police Commissioner Harvey and the Home Secretary. Large bodies of police were posted to the various meeting-points and troops were on standby, out-of-sight, at strategic points. But, by-and-large, they were not needed. Few people turned up at any of the meeting places and, in any event, those that did quickly dispersed when they caught sight of police. As one newspaper announced, despite all the 'sound and fury', the demonstrations did not take place; 'we were promised a revolution' but 'a good thunder shower was sufficient to quench the courage' of the fiercest 'fire eater in the Chartist camp.'[1058]

On 21 June 1848, Rowan again appeared before a Select Committee of the House of Lords, on this occasion, to give evidence to it about regulating the Sale of Beer and other Liquors on Sundays. Places licensed for the sale of intoxicating liquors were closed from Saturday night until 1.00pm on Sunday by virtue of the Metropolitan Police Act 1838 which had come into force in August 1839, resulting, reported Rowan, in a decrease in the number of arrests for drunkenness. Rowan took the opportunity to suggest to the Committee that coffee shops should be brought under the supervision of the police in the same way as public houses and beer shops, because many of the 'low' coffee shops were frequented by thieves and prostitutes.[1059]

Meanwhile, all efforts by the Chartists to-date having failed, some of the more firebrand members were developing plans for an insurrection to take place on the night of 16 August. As these plans developed, Rowan and Mayne were kept abreast of their intentions by two informers, one who was able to attend meetings throughout the summer and the other, a journalist who had close connections with the Chartists. At shortly before 6.00pm, the London conspiracy[1060] ended in an anti-climax,[1061] when fourteen leading conspirators were arrested by a large body of police, some armed, in a raid on The Angel Tavern, in Rotherhithe. A quantity of

---

1057 Ibid.
1058 *Morning Post*, 13 June 1848, p.5.
1059 PP 1847-48 [501]. Minutes of evidence taken before the Select Committee of the House of Lords; to whom was referred the bill, -- for regulating the sale of beer and other liquors on the Lord's Day; together with an appendix. Session 1847-8, Q.1-13; p.3-4.
1060 The name of the planned insurrection; also known as the Orange Tree conspiracy after the second major raid on the conspirators that night.
1061 Chase, op. cit. 1008, pp.322-326.

weapons, including loaded pistols, pikes, spear-heads, daggers and swords were seized. A similar raid, again by a large body of police, this time on the Orange Tree Public House in Webber Street, off Blackfriars Road, resulted in the arrest of a further eleven people and the discovery of knives and three fire-balls.[1062] Later that evening, Mayne wrote to his wife:

> 'I don't know when I may get home. We have done some good work tonight – about 26 or 7 are in custody, taken in different parts – some with Pikes and other such arms or weapons. These were in houses, and I expect now they will hardly venture, as they threatened, any open attack. All has been well done by Police so far, and Sir George writes from the House of Commons approving it.'[1063]

Subsequently, six of the arrested conspirators were transported for life, whilst another fifteen received prison sentences from six to twenty-four months.[1064]

By the end of the summer 1848 Mayne was anticipating Rowan's departure, for contained in a Metropolitan Police file, is a memorandum, in his handwriting, headed 'Memo on the constitution and administration of the Office of Commissioners of Police of the Metropolis and alterations suggested.' It is not clear whether he submitted it to the Home Office, but the main thrust of his argument was that there should be only one commissioner.[1065]

In December 1848, it was announced from Downing Street that along with two others, the Queen had

> 'been graciously pleased to give orders for the appointment... of Lieutenant Colonel Charles Rowan, C.B. to be [an] Ordinary Member of the Civil Division of the Second Class, or Knights Commanders of the said Most Honourable Order.'[1066]

The investiture was held the following year, on 24 February at Buckingham Palace. A number of knight grand crosses were present, including the senior knight grand cross, the Duke of Wellington. During the course of the investiture, Rowan came before Her Majesty between the Bath King of Arms, Algernon Granville, and the Gentleman Usher, Albert William Wood. Kneeling before Her Majesty he was knighted. Rising to his feet, Sir

---

1062 *London Illustrated News*, 19 August 1848, p.7.
1063 Henry Hall Collection, op. cit. 1008, letter 85, p.181.
1064 Chase, op. cit. 7, pp.325-326.
1065 TNA MEPO 2/5814.
1066 *London Gazette*, 26 December 1848, Issue 20930, p.4666.

Charles had the honour of kissing the Sovereign's hand before retiring.[1067] Four days later, the Queen held her second levee[1068] of the season at St James's Palace. Colonel Sir Charles Rowan was present and was formally presented to the Queen by the Home Secretary, Sir George Grey.[1069]

With the exception of a fourth attempt on the life of Queen Victoria in May, 1849 was an uneventful year in the professional lives of the two Commissioners. The attempt on the Queen's life occurred as a carriage in which she was travelling, together with three of her children, including the Prince of Wales, the future Edward VII, descended Constitution Hill. On this occasion, a 24-year-old unemployed bricklayer William Hamilton, standing in almost the same spot as Edward Oxford, nine years earlier, fired a pistol at the royal carriage which fortunately missed its target. Hamilton was immediately arrested and taken to Gardner's Lane Station House which was quickly visited by both Rowan and Mayne.[1070] Hamilton subsequently appeared at the Old Bailey where he pleaded guilty 'to pointing, aiming and discharging a loaded pistol' at and near the Queen 'with intent to alarm Her Majesty and break the peace'. He was sentenced to be transported for seven years.[1071]

Towards the end of 1849, rumours were circulating that Rowan was about to retire due to 'the delicate state of his health'[1072] and would be replaced by the Commissioner of the City Police, Daniel Whittle Harvey.[1073] However, a further report claimed Rowan had 'no intention' of relinquishing his duties and that his health had been 'quite restored.'[1074] However, the rumours turned out to be partly true for, at the end of December, it was announced that Rowan would retire on 3 January 1850, to be replaced not by Harvey, but by Captain William Hay.[1075]

1067 *London Daily News*, 26 February 1849, p.5; *London Evening Standard*, 26 February 1849, p.1.
1068 The Queen held between 3 and 5 levees each year, at which between 150 and 300 people would be presented to Her Majesty. It was for men only and the people being presented were usually government officials, foreign dignitaries, diplomats and military men returning from abroad, etc. See Ellenberger, Nancy W (1990). 'The Transformation of London "Society" at the End of Victoria's Reign: Evidence from the Court Presentation Records' in *Albion: A Quarterly Journal Concerned with British Studies*, Vol. 22, No. 4 (Winter) p.640.
1069 *London Evening Standard*, 1 March 1849, p.3.
1070 *Morning Post*, 2 May 1849, p.5.
1071 Old Bailey Proceedings Online (www.oldbaileyonline.org, version 7.2, 27 December 2018), June 1849, trial of WILLIAM HAMILTON (t18490611-1260; Charles, Barrie (2012). *Kill the Queen! The Eight Assassination Attempts on Queen Victoria*. Stroud, Gloucestershire: Amberley, pp.55-67).
1072 See Chapter Eighteen.
1073 *Morning Advertiser*, 16 November 1849, p.1.
1074 *Globe*, 3 December 1849, p.3.
1075 *Morning Advertiser*, 31 December 1849, p.2.

CHAPTER EIGHTEEN

PERSONAL LIFE AND DEATH OF CHARLES ROWAN

Charles Rowan never married. His private life revolved around former army colleagues in London, Scotland and Sussex. For almost the whole time he was Commissioner, he resided on the top floor of 4 Whitehall Place. The 1841 Census shows that he had two servants, James Murray – almost certainly a veteran from the Napoleonic Wars – and his wife Maria living with him at the time.[1076] However, no doubt anticipating retirement, by December 1846 he had moved his personal quarters to a rented house at 17 Bolton Street.

Built around 1696, Bolton Street extended northwards from Piccadilly to Curzon Street. At the time, it was one of London's fashionable streets. The terraced houses varied between three and four stories with basements and attics; No. 17 consisted of three stories.[1077] According to the 1851 Census, he had at his residence with him William Meighan, a butler; his wife Elizabeth, a housekeeper, and Elizabeth Carter, aged 20, a housemaid.[1078] Whilst the western side of the street has been almost completely replaced by modern buildings, amongst the listed Georgian buildings[1079] on the eastern side No. 17 remains, the exterior very much as it would have been when Rowan was living there.[1080]

Whilst the Commissioners declined to accept patronage in relation to any appointments to the Force, Rowan was not above seeking a little help from his friends when necessary. One of his closest friends was a former

---

1076 1841 Census.
1077 Hibbert, Christopher, Ben Weinrob, Julia Keay, John Keay (2010). *The London Encyclopaedia* (3rd Edition). London: Macmillan, p.81.
1078 1851 Census.
1079 Under the Planning (Listed Buildings and Conservation Areas) Act, 1990, as amended, every effort should be made to preserve No 17, with others on the same side of Bolton Street, because it is regarded as being of special architecture or historical interest.
1080 www.historicengland.org.uk/listing/the-list/list-entry/1357210 accessed 28 September 2018.

lieutenant in the 52nd Regiment, then the Earl of March, but now the 5th Duke of Richmond, having succeeded to the Dukedom on the death of his father in 1819. Already an influential member of the House of Lords, the Duke was appointed to the Privy Council[1081] the year after Rowan became Commissioner. In 1836, the Duke inherited the estates of his mother's brother, as a result of which he also became the Duke of Gordon. Already the owner of a large country estate known as Goodwood House, near Chichester in West Sussex, he also became the owner of Gordon Castle, a grand baronial mansion, at Fochnabers about 8 miles east of Elgin in Scotland.

Less than two years after being appointed Commissioner, Rowan's younger brother, William, who was still in the army, had been living in London without a posting since July 1830. Consequently, he was on half-pay. It was therefore natural for Rowan to write to the Duke of Richmond, in June 1831, to seek his assistance.[1082] Four days later he received the reply:

'My dear Rowan,

Upon my return to Town I found your Letter – I shall be most happy if I can be of any service to your Brother William. Pray tell him to call upon me tomorrow morning at nine o'clock. I will speak to Fitzroy and also Lord Hill.'[1083]

One of Rowan's former commanding officers, John Colborne,[1084] since knighted and now a Major-General, had been appointed Lieutenant-Governor of Upper Canada. The sequel to Rowan's request was William's appointment as Colborne's Military Secretary in 1832. The following year, when Rowan heard a rumour that Colborne was about to leave Canada, he wrote again to the Duke of Richmond to ask whether there was any truth in a report that Colborne was to replace Sir Peregrine Maitland in Nova Scotia.[1085] On 9 March, came the reply:

My dear Rowan,

There is not the slightest intention of removing Colborne from Upper Canada.[1086]

1081 *London Gazette*, 23 November 1830, No. 18748, p.2449.
1082 The Goodwood Estate Archives. Family Papers. Charles Lennox (afterwards Gordon Lennox) 5th Duke of Richmond, Lennox, and Aubigny. Held at the West Sussex Record Office, Volume 1433, folio 329.
1083 Ibid, Volume 1486, page 49. Lord Hill was at that time Commander-in-chief of the British Army and Lord Fitzroy Somerset was the Adjutant Secretary. Both had taken part in the Napoleonic Wars and it is almost certain they both knew Charles Rowan.
1084 See Chapters Four and Five.
1085 The Goodwood Estate Archives, op. cit. 1082, Volume 1462, folio 488.
1086 Ibid, Volume 1484, folio 285.

Rowan wrote again to Richmond in October 1833, this time about a cousin and took the opportunity to mention a mutual friend, the Marquess of Tweeddale:

> My dear Duke,
>
> I feel myself obliged to forward the enclosed to you the writer being a first Cousin of my own tho' I have never seen but once. All I ask is that you will be good enough to treat it upon its own merits and at your leisure.
>
> I shall be in about the 1st and hope to hear of your being quite well.
>
> I have been upwards of a month at Tweeddales. I suppose you know He has taken a house in Town for five years where he now is with all his family.
>
> Yours ever sincerely,
>
> C.Rowan[1087]

Rowan had an active social life. He had 'a wide circle of friends and acquaintances', amongst whom he was extremely popular.[1088] From 1812, people wishing to kill game and to fish required a licence, known as a General Game Certificate. Each year, whilst he was the Commissioner of Police, Rowan purchased such a licence, which originally cost him £3 13s 6d each year,[1089] but which subsequently went up to £4 0s 10d.[1090] This allowed him to pursue his favourite pastimes of salmon fishing and shooting game.[1091]

A letter to the Duke in October 1833 was the first indication that Rowan, who was, by this time, 55 years of age, would increasingly spend periods of time out of London, either in Sussex visiting the Duke himself or travelling around Scotland staying with his various friends, although he did occasionally visit Brighton.[1092]

Horse racing had been held at a race course within the extensive grounds of Goodwood House since 1802 and, from the time Rowan became Commissioner until well after his death, Metropolitan Police officers were sent down each year to police the large crowds that attended the race meetings. In 1840, Rowan took the opportunity to seek alternative

---

1087 Ibid, Volume 1590, folio1164.
1088 Reith, Charles (1956). *A New Study of Police History*. Edinburgh: Oliver and Boyd, p.232.
1089 For example, see under the List of Persons who obtained Game Certificates in London, Middlesex and Westminster in the *London Courier* and Evening Gazette, 21 September 1836, p.1.
1090 See *Bell's Weekly Messenger*, 16 November 1844, p.1; *Globe*, 17 June 1847, p.1.
1091 Reith, op. cit. 1088, p.231.
1092 *Brighton Gazette*, 16 January 1845, p.4., where he stayed at the prestigious Albion Hotel.

employment for an unnamed servant of his, who was finding it increasingly difficult to climb the stairs at 4 Whitehall Place to Rowan's apartment on the top floor. In a letter to the Duke confirming the attendance of police officers at the Goodwood Races in July, Rowan asked him whether he could employ his servant, an ex-Dragoon, who he was forced to get rid of because

> 'of a rupture which makes it expedient for him not to run up and down such a staircase as this. He is a most Excellent and Trustworthy person and his wife a kind … woman without children.'[1093]

There is no record as to whether his request was successful, but given the relationship he had with the Duke and Duchess, it probably was. Some four years later, in 1844, the widow of his brother Frederick, who had died under tragic circumstances in the West Indies[1094] came to London with her two daughters. By this time, Rowan's influence in London circles was such that he felt able to approach the Prime Minister direct. On 1 December he wrote to Sir Robert Peel, outlining Sally Rowan's difficult financial situation and requested she be given the post of Housekeeper in the Department of Stamps and Taxes, which had recently become vacant.[1095] This Peel appears to have done. Rowan had kept a watchful eye on the family since Frederick's death, and must have been delighted when, a little earlier, a series of advertisements appeared in London newspapers[1096] advertising a 'History of the French Revolution; its causes and consequences' written by Frederica Maclean Rowan, the younger of the two daughters. She also published short histories of England and Scotland shortly before Rowan's death in 1852. Later she became secretary to Sir Francis Goldsmid, a barrister and Queen's Counsel who entered Parliament as the Member for Reading in 1860. Following this appointment Frederica's literary work mainly involved translations, one of which, 'Stunden der Andacht' was a favourite of Prince Albert, the Prince Consort.[1097]

Rowan was interested in the various accounts of the Napoleonic Wars that were emerging and, in February 1833, he received a copy of Gawler's account of the Battle of Waterloo which was subsequently published in the *United States Journal* under the title, 'The Crisis and Close of the Action

---

1093 The Goodwood Estate Archives, op. cit. 1082, Volume 1547, folio 155.
1094 See Chapter One.
1095 Reith, op. cit. 1088, p.243, footnote 2.
1096 *Globe*, 15 June 1844, p.1, and 13 December 1845, p.1; *London Illustrated News*, 19 October 1844, p.15; *London Daily News*, 22 June 1846, p.2.
1097 Marzials, Frank Thomas, and Susanne Stark (2004). Rowan, Frederica Maclean (1814-1882). *Oxford Dictionary of National Biography* (online edition). Oxford University Press. doc:10.1093/ref.odnb24193.

at Waterloo'.[1098] Gawler had been commissioned as an Ensign in the 52nd Regiment in 1810[1099] and was a Lieutenant at the time of Waterloo.[1100] Rowan forwarded it to the Duke of Richmond with an accompanying letter, suggesting it was a 'very well written and clear account of the crisis,' and 'very well worth reading'. He continued:

> 'I went up at Daylight to the Position from which the 52nd charged, and my original impression was proved, if such proof was necessary by our men and the Imperial Guard with the Red and Green Leathers laying on the ground wounded and dead – I remember well speaking to your brother William's old servant Samuel who died before I left the Field on that morning and I think Baring an old ADC of the Light Division in the Peninsula who commanded one of Halkett's Regiments of Lt Infantry KGs.[1101] I could corroborate Gawler's statement of the last advance. But I know not why I should endeavour to prove to you what took place as before your wound you must have been a better judge than myself, a better four deep advance was never made, and I recollect having told Jones when he painted the battle of Waterloo for the King[1102] that he ought to have described the triumphant charge and advances of Adams Brigade.'[1103]

In addition to Gordon Castle, his journeys to Scotland in summer involved stays at Dalhousie Castle, overlooking the River Esk, approximately 8 miles south of Edinburgh, home of the 9th and 10th Earls of Dalhousie; the 9th Earl had commanded 7 Division during the latter stages of the Napoleonic Wars. The Earl of Dalhousie, known as Lord Ramsay until 1838, was a Scottish statesman who held various government posts in London until, in 1848, he was appointed Governor-General of India, remaining there until 1856. He married Lady Susan Hay, the daughter of the Marquess of Tweeddale, who died almost to the year after Rowan, on 6 May 1853.[1104] Another of his summer haunts was Dochfour, about 5 miles south-west

---

1098 *United Service Journal 1833*. Gawler eventually reached the rank of lieutenant-colonel and was Governor of South Australia from 1838 to 1841.
1099 *London Gazette*, 6 October 1810, Issue 16411, p.1583.
1100 *London Gazette*, 16 May 1812, Issue 16604. p.931.
1101 Refers to Major George Baring, who commanded the 2nd Light Battalion of the King's German Legion, which was part of Major General Sir Colin Halkett's 5th Division. See Fremont-Barnes, Gregory (2014). *Waterloo 1815: The British Army's Day of Destiny*. Stroud, Gloucestershire: The History Press, pp.174-177.
1102 Painted by the artist George Jones, the picture is now on display at the Royal Chelsea Hospital in London.
1103 The Goodwood Estate Archives, op. cit. 1082, Volume 1468, folio pages 340-342.
1104 Ballhatchet, Kenneth A (1998). 'James Andrew Broun Ramsay, marquess and 10th earl of Dalhousie'. *Encyclopaedia Britannica*. See www.britannica.com/biography/James-Andrew-Braun--Ramsey-Marquess-of-Dalhousie [accessed 16 June 2019].

of Inverness on the west bank of Loch Dochfour, the ancestral home of the Baillie family; quite how Rowan knew this family, other than through some of his other friends in Scotland is uncertain.[1105] Yet a third was Pitfour, a large estate in the Buchan area of north-east Scotland, home of George Ferguson, who was the Member of Parliament for Banffshire from 1832 to 1837. Ferguson was the fifth laird of Pitfour. He had served in the Royal Navy during the Napoleonic Wars. His second marriage – his first wife died in child-birth – was to Elizabeth Rowley whose mother was a niece of the Duke of Wellington.[1106]

But possibly his two favourite haunts were Yester House and Floors Castle. Yester House was a fine mansion of two storeys, with basements and attics and pavilions around the grounds, near Gifford in East Lothian, the centrepiece of the family estate of the Marquess of Tweeddale. Rowan maintained a strong friendship with the Marquess of Tweeddale for much of his life. George Hay, as he was originally, was commissioned into the 52nd Regiment as an ensign in July 1804 at the time the regiment was at Shorncliffe being trained as Light Infantry, but a month later, on becoming the 8th Marquess of Tweeddale on the death of his father, he was promoted lieutenant. In May 1807 he transferred into the Grenadier Guards and then into the 41st Regiment. Like Rowan he spent time during the Peninsular War as a staff officer. Following the Battle of Waterloo, he had returned to the family estate.[1107]

But, possibly his favourite haunt was Floors Castle on the banks of the River Tweed, overlooking the Cheviot Hills at Roxburghe in south-east Scotland. Despite its name, it was a grand country house, embellished with turrets and battlements, rather than a castle in the traditional sense. Rowan was a frequent visitor there in the 1840s and he referred to the Castle as 'my fishing headquarters.'[1108] Quite how he knew the 6th Duke and the Duchess so intimately as to be a frequent visitor there is not known. The Duke was some thirty-four years younger than Rowan and did not have a military background. The only likely explanation is that he may have known them through the Duchess's father, Colonel James Dalbiac, who had seen service through the Peninsular War, albeit in the Dragoons,[1109] and would almost certainly have been a member of Rowan's

---

1105 'Landed Families of Britain and Ireland'. See www.landedfamilies.blogspot.com/2018/02/321-ballie-of-dochfour-and-redcastle.html [accessed 4 January 2019].
1106 Buchan, Alex R (2008). *Pitfour: "The Blenheim of the North."* Peterhead: The Buchan Field Club, pp.38-47.
1107 Heathcote, Tony (1999). *The British Field Marshals, 1736-1997*. Barnsley: Leo Cooper, p.173.
1108 Reith, op. cit. 1088, p.232.
1109 Stephen, Leslie (1888). *Dictionary of National Biography*, Vol, 13. London: Macmillan & Co, p.282.

club in London, the United Service Club.

In June 1837, along with a substantial number of police officers, Rowan suffered an attack of influenza and was 'laid up' with it for some time.[1110] Some seven weeks later, he was in Scotland amongst friends. In late August, he was at Gordon Castle where he met up with the Duke of Richmond,[1111] who was spending part of the summer at his Scottish home. By mid-September 1837 he had moved on to Dochfour,[1112] to visit the Baillies. He was back in London by 20 October 1837 for he wrote to the Duke thanking him 'for the delightful three weeks' he had spent at the Castle.[1113] From the dates of the letters it was likely that he was away for some two months in Scotland, leaving Mayne to run the force on his own.

Unfortunately, the 9th Earl of Dalhousie died the following year, 1838, but Rowan continued to maintain close relationships with the family, partly because the 10th Earl, as Lord Ramsay, had married Lady Susan Hay, a daughter of the Marquess of Tweeddale, at the home of her father, Yester House, in 1836.[1114]

On Thursday, 18 April 1839, Rowan attended the marriage of Arthur, Marquis of Douro, eldest son of the Duke of Wellington, to Lady Elizabeth Hay, fourth daughter of the Marquess of Tweeddale at St George's, Hanover Square in London. The reception for 150 invited guests was held at the Marquess of Tweeddale's mansion in Belgrave Square.[1115] Rumour has it that 'Rowan was a disappointed suitor' of Lady Elizabeth. However, 'with no property, and no financial resources other than his police salary, and possibly some part of his Army pension, and with the difference of thirty-seven years between him and Elizabeth, it seems unlikely that he could ever posed seriously as a prospective bridegroom.'[1116] Indeed, an extract from a letter Lord Dalhousie wrote to his sister, Susan, who was unable to attend the marriage, throws some light on the relationship Rowan had with the family. Rowan and Dalhousie had gone to the Church together for the morning service. On their arrival, the vestry was apparently full of brothers and sisters, aunts and uncles. Dalhousie continued:

> 'Rowan... said he had no business to be there for he was neither Uncle nor brother nor near relation. Oh, I said, never mind that, you come, you know, as the Grand Papa.'

1110 The Goodwood Estate Archives, op. cit. 1082, Volume 1589 folio 1151.
1111 Ibid, folio 1287.
1112 Ibid, folio 1298.
1113 Ibid, folio 1310.
1114 *Inverness Courier*, 27 January 1836, p.3.
1115 *Morning Post*, 19 April 1839, p.4.
1116 Reith, op. cit. 1088, p.233.

Later in the letter, he described how he 'went home with Rowan who was as melancholy as I, tho' probably for a different reason, and heigh-hoed [sic] loudly every minute till about 1 we went to the dejeuner.'[1117]

The possibility of any Chartist agitation in London from 1839 onwards did not prevent Rowan from taking his holidays in Scotland. For the latter part of July and most of August of that year, he was in the Highlands at Glenmore Lodge, with the Marquesses of Tweeddale and Douro. In a letter to the Duke of Richmond, written whilst he was there, he apologised that he would most probably have to return to London before the Duke came north but was able to report that there had been good weather the previous day, when he and others had killed 330 brace of grouse.[1118] Meanwhile, Mayne frequently did not know when Rowan would return to London for he wrote to his wife on 3 August 1839:

'I have not heard from Rowan since he left, and am therefore unable to say what chance I may have of getting down for the 13th or 15th as you propose.'[1119]

However, a few days later, in another letter to his wife, Mayne told her he had heard from Rowan, who had been fishing and was clearly in 'very good spirit', as he was going to the Moors the following day with a party which included the Marquesses of Tweeddale and Douro. But he apparently told Mayne that if he was required, he had 'no objection' to returning to London 'for a few days at any time.'[1120]

The Marquess of Tweeddale returned to public service in 1842 when he was appointed Governor of Madras and Commander-in-Chief of the Madras Army where he remained, with his wife, until 1847. Whilst abroad, they had no hesitation in making use of Rowan's friendship, depending on him to make purchases on their behalf in London and send them to forwarding-agents for onward transmission to India. These purchases covered horses, carriages, furniture, books and innumerable other items. One letter states the total cost of purchases to date was £2,487 15s 5d; another mentions the sum of £1,284 9s 6d.[1121]

Now aged 61, Rowan was clearly not well during the early months of 1843, for in late March he wrote to the Duke of Richmond, 'I have not been right for some time, old age coming on I suppose.'[1122] However, this did not

---

1117 Ibid, p.234.
1118 The Goodwood Estate Archive, op. cit. 1082, Volume 1605, folio 1742.
1119 Henry Hall Collection, held in the Wigan Archives in EHC210/M1252, p.19, letter 10.
1120 Ibid, letter 25, p.57.
1121 Reith, op. cit. 1088, p.237.
1122 The Goodwood Estate Archives, op. cit. 1082, Volume 1659, folio 1333.

stop him going to Scotland, for just under a month later, in a letter dated 21 April to his son Richard, Mayne wrote:

> 'I cannot say when I shall be able to get down to see you all, as you know that depends on Colonel Rowan's return, which is uncertain. He writes that he has had a very good fishing and caught several fine salmon. The other day he breakfasted at ½ past seven, rode on a pony with his rod slung behind him. Fished all day and did not get home till after 6 o'clock; the largest fish he caught weighed 3 pounds and a half.'[1123]

In a letter to his wife, the following day, Mayne complained that he could not move because had heard nothing from Rowan as to when he would return.[1124]

In December 1843, Rowan received a letter from a John Cross[1125] who was then residing in Brighton:

> 'I had a letter from Madras written by Col. Logan[1126] at the request of Lord Tweeddale to beg that I would send him a copy of the 52nd Shorncliffe Standing Orders and also mentioning that you would be good enough to have them forwarded.
>
> I have therefore arranged and classified many orders that was (sic) issued at that period bearing on the discipline and interior economy of the Regt., which I send herewith in [the hope] that you will be able kindly to forward to Lord Tweeddale.'[1127]

In April 1844, Rowan was again in Scotland, this time at Floors Castle, mentioning in a letter to the Marquess of Dalhousie, that 'the reception is always as kind and friendly as heart can wish', although he did mention 'the season has been desperately bad, we have had but few fishing days and but few salmon yet, altho' plenty of kelts ....'[1128]

Writing to the Duke of Richmond on 19 January 1845, Rowan said:

> 'I know I shall be fully occupied tomorrow and therefore seize the day of rest to thank you for your considerate friendship in sending such a

---

1123 Henry Hall Collection, op. cit. 1119, pp.89-90, letter no. 41.
1124 Ibid, p.90, letter 42.
1125 Lieutenant-Colonel John Cross had served in the Peninsula and was present at Waterloo. He went on to command the 68th Light İnfantry – see Moorsom, W.S (Ed) (1860). *Historical Record of the Fifty-Second Regiment (Oxfordshire Light İnfantry) from the Year 1755 to the year 1858*. Uckfield, Sussex: The Naval and Military Press, p.428.
1126 Colonel Logan served in the Rifle Brigade during the Napoleonic War.
1127 Asian and African Studies, MSS Eur F 96, Folio 344. Rowan, letters to Lord Tweeddale in the British Library.
1128 Ibid.

supply of game to my Brother and to say that he is very grateful – I can imagine how it came about that it should be sent, but how it found him I am at a loss to make out, but find him it did.'[1129]

It is difficult to know what Rowan meant when he mentioned he would be fully occupied the next day. It may have been something of a private nature because nothing of any significance occurred in the metropolis on 20 January.

Much later that year, whilst Rowan was yet again in Scotland, Mayne wrote to his wife:

'I have a letter this morning from Rowan, and I fear he is suffering and out of spirits; this latter may be partly from a Home Office letter I could not help letting him see; but he is evidently not well, and even talks of resigning as soon as his house is ready – I will write and do what I can to cheer him up, for in truth there is nothing in the letter that ought to dispirit him, though an improper and offensive one.'[1130]

It is not known to what this Home Office letter referred. Clearly, whilst the letter would have been addressed to the Commissioners, Mayne found it necessary to forward it on to Rowan.

Meanwhile, Rowan frequently met up with former military colleagues in London. During the late 1830s and 1840s, he was an annual visitor to Apsley House, the Duke of Wellington's home situated at Hyde Park Gate. Originally built between 1771 and 1778, it was purchased by the Duke of Wellington in 1817. Commencing in 1820, Wellington held an annual dinner known as the Waterloo Banquet to celebrate the defeat of Napoleon. However, the dining room could only seat 35 which meant only the most senior officers were invited. So, between 1828 and 1830, he added on the Waterloo Gallery, a magnificent dining facility which could seat 85 people. This allowed him to invite many more of those officers who had helped him to victory. It is not known when Rowan first attended but he was certainly present in 1836 when William Salter painted his famous picture of the Banquet which currently hangs in the Portico Drawing Room at Apsley House. The picture shows the Duke of Wellington proposing the loyal toast. Rowan is seated almost opposite to the Duke.[1131]

In 1846, one of Rowan's long-term friends, Harry Smith, by this time a Major General serving in India, led British and Indian troops of the

---

1129 The Goodwood Estate Archives, op. cit. 1082, Volume 1666, folio 4.
1130 Henry Hall Collection, op. cit. 1119, p.162.
1131 Bryant, Julius (undated). *Apsley House: The Wellington Collection*. London: English Heritage, pp.12.

Bengal Presidency to a decisive victory in the Anglo-Sikh war.[1132] As a result, members of the House of Commons gave a vote of thanks to Smith, Knight Commander of the Bath, and two other named officers 'for the distinguished services rendered by them in the eminently successful operations in the battle of Sobraon.'[1133]

On the day that Smith was congratulated by the House of Commons, Charles Beckwith

> 'invited Barnard, Johnny Kincaid, Rowan, Alix MacDonald and others of your old friends and comrades to dine with me, and we drank a bumper to your health and that of Lady Smith.'[1134]

Beckwith had served with the Light Division, firstly with the 95th Rifles and later in staff appointments. At the Battle of Waterloo he had lost a leg.[1135] General Sir Andrew Barnard had also been appointed to command the 3rd Battalion of the 95th Rifles when it was raised in 1810 and in 1814, was appointed to command the 2nd Brigade of the Light Infantry Division, which included the 52nd Regiment and had command of the British troops occupying Paris following the Battle of Waterloo.[1136] Kincaid had also been with the 95th Rifles, writing two books about his experiences, but had retired from the army in 1831.[1137] Later that year, in September, Beckwith wrote:

> 'The last enemy has done his worst on very many of our Peninsular companions. Sir Andrew and some Riflemen still remain to dine together in Albermarle Street. Charley Rowan is letter A, No. 1 Old Duffy regulates the Club, Johnny Bell cultivates dahlias at Staines. Will Napier misgoverns the Guernsey men, Johnny Kincaid regulates the secrets of a prison-house, Jonathan Leach writes histories...'[1138]

But, by this time, Rowan was not a well man, informing the Duke of Richmond that the doctors were currently in charge of when he could go

---

1132 This was the final battle in the First Anglo-Sikh War which took place in 1845-1846.
1133 HC Deb 02 April 1846. Vol. 85, cc 436-62.
1134 Moore Smith, G.C (1903). *The Autobiography of Lieutenant-General Sir Harry Smith. Baronet of Aliwal on the Sutlej, G.C.B., Volume II*. London: John Murray, pp.210-211.
1135 Dalton, Charles (1904). *The Waterloo roll call, with biographical notes and anecdotes*. London: Eyre & Spottiswoode, p.36.
1136 Stephen op. cit. 1109, pp.235-236.
1137 Kincaid, John (1847). *Adventures in the Rifle Brigade in the Peninsula, France the Netherlands, from 1809 to 1815*. London: T and W. Boone.
1138 Moore Smith, op. cit. 1134, pp.210-211. Lieutenant-General Sir John Bell served in the Peninsula from 1808 to 1814 mainly on the staff of the Quartermaster-General, with the Light, 3rd and 4th Divisions. By this time Kincaid had become a government inspector of prisons in Scotland.

out.[1139] Nevertheless, two days later he accepted an invitation from the Duke to visit Goodwood on the 15 June.[1140] Taking advantage of the train, he travelled down with Lord Fitzroy.[1141] Back in London, Rowan wrote to the Duke on 31 December, to tell him, without naming them, he had 'asked a few old Peninsula [friends] to meet for dinner on the 7th,' and asked him to join them.[1142]

Following the announcement that the Marquess of Tweeddale would relinquish his appointment as Governor of Madras, Rowan, who was in Scotland, wrote to him from Floors Castle on 21 October:

'Delighted at the prospect of seeing you once more… I wonder whether you will take quietly to former pursuits again, or whether you will at least at first require some… employment for the mind, after five years of important mental work – you will see by the papers what a deplorable state the Mercantile world is in here at present, and I much doubt if we have yet seen the worst, the truth is that we are a nation of Mercantile Gamblers and Speculators…'[1143]

Despite his declining health, Rowan continued to lead a busy social life and occasionally gave dinner parties in town for invited guests in 1848. For instance, on Monday, 24 July, he entertained Lord and Lady Tweeddale, Lord Fitzroy and the Duke of Richmond.[1144] Earlier, it did not stop him being amongst 'upwards of two hundred noblemen and gentlemen' who attended a dinner, along with Prince Albert and the Duke of Wellington, at the United Service Club on 7 April 1848, to welcome the return to Britain of Lieutenant-General Viscount Hardinge, who had just completed a four-year appointment as Governor-General of India.[1145] As successively a captain, major and lieutenant-colonel, Hardinge had been involved in many of the battles Rowan had taken part in during the Peninsular War. Following Napoleon's escape from Elba, Hardinge returned to military service as a brigadier-general attached to the Prussian army and was wounded at the Battle of Ligny, resulting in the amputation of a hand two

---

1139 The Goodwood Estate Archives, op. cit. 1082, Volume 1694, folio 2139.
1140 Ibid, folio 2141.
1141 Ibid, folio 2142.
1142 Ibid, folio 2151.
1143 Rowan, letters to Lord Tweeddale, op. cit. 1127.
1144 The Goodwood Estate, Archives, op. cit. 7, Volume 1713, folios 1457 & 1459. Lord Fitzroy refers to Lord Fitzroy Somerset, later Lord Raglan, more famously known as being the commander of British troops in the Crimea from 1853 to 1855. Much earlier, however, he had been Wellington's aide-de-camp or military secretary during the Peninsula campaign. At this time he was military secretary to the Duke of Wellington, who was then Commander-in-chief of the British Army.
1145 *Morning Post*, 8 April 1848, p.6.

days before the Battle of Waterloo.[1146] A few days later, Rowan wrote to the Duke of Richmond to thank him for his invitation to visit Goodwood for 'a day or two', but added 'if I can get away'. He then pointed out that Chartist meetings were making things difficult.[1147] He wrote again the following month, by which time he had moved out of his bachelor quarters in Whitehall Place to the three-story, terraced house at 17 Bolton Street:

> 'I am so anxious for a little peace and fresh air, that I shall gladly avail myself of your kind offer in your note of Friday last the 21st. It is now 12 o'clock and Mr. Cochrane's great demonstration was to take place at… o'clock. All our preparations are made to prevent it but it does not appear that we are to have much trouble… but the anxiety that we should make no mistakes is beginning to sicken me of the situation. I feel that I am getting too old for it and do not think I have had a days' good health all winter. I shall probably go by the 2 o'clock train from here. I presume it does not stop at Drayton, I shall therefore go on to Chichester.'[1148]

In March 1849, Rowan was again in Scotland, for he sent his apologies to the Duke of Richmond for not attending a meeting in London, explaining he had been unwell. In fact, his doctors recommended that he 'leave London for some time' and he added 'the life I lead here ought to do me good.' He also mentioned to the Duke that the doctors in London claimed he had a tumour in the mesenteric gland. However, whilst in Scotland, the Marquis of Tweeddale arranged for him to see a distinguished Professor of Medicine at Edinburgh University, Dr. William Alison, who disagreed; he thought the tumour was in the rectum. At the same time, Rowan told the Duke he had become a member of a new club, the Military and Country Club 'because it is nearest my house and I am getting so old that I shall shortly be unable to walk so far as the United Service.'[1149]

Nevertheless, although clearly still unwell, he was back in London by mid-April, for, in response to a letter to him from Matthew Dowling, the Chief Constable of Liverpool, the Chief Clerk, Charles Yardley, wrote 'Sir Charles Rowan is in Town and feeling but indifferently well…'.

According to the records of the Metropolitan Police, Rowan signed his

---

1146 See Holmes, Richard (2003). *Wellington: The Iron Duke*. London: Harper Perennial, pp.229 and 233.
1147 The Goodwood Estate Archives, op. cit. 1082, Volume 1713, folio 1429.
1148 Ibid, Volume 1713, folio 1437.
1149 Ibid, Volume 1727, folio 1531. The Military and Country Club, for active and retired military officers, including those from the East India Company, militia and yeomanry, was opened in November 1848, taking over the premises of Crockford's at 50, St James's Street, which had closed earlier in the year.

last official letter in his role as Commissioner on 23 May 1849.[1150] Thereafter, until his retirement some seven months later, the administration of the Force was left entirely to Mayne.

Just over two months later, on 6 August, the *Morning Post* reported that Rowan was in 'so precarious a state of health as to cause much anxiety amongst his friends.'[1151] However, three days later it was reported that he had 'quite recovered from his recent indisposition, which at one time assumed a serious aspect' and he would shortly leave London 'on a tour of visits in Scotland'.[1152]

But the following month, it was reported that his delicate state of health would prevent him from resuming 'his arduous duties.' Instead, he would travel on a visit to the Duke of Roxburghe at Floors Castle, and from there he would go to Yester, the seat of the Marquis of Tweeddale, to spend the winter.[1153] He was reported to have spent a night at the Queen's Head in Newcastle,[1154] presumably on his way to Floors Castle. He would make one more visit to Scotland, a place which, over the years, had given him much peace and tranquillity, in addition to enjoying the company of people he mixed with throughout his adult life.

Standing down as Commissioner at the end of 1849, for the next twelve months Rowan continued to enjoy an active social life. In June, 1850, together with many other dignitaries including the Duke of Wellington, he attended an assembly given by Angela Burdett-Coutts at her mansion in Stratton Street.[1155] The grand-daughter of Thomas Coutts, the founder of Coutts Bank, she was the wealthiest woman in Britain, inheriting nearly £2 million[1156] following the death of her stepmother.

In late September and early October Rowan visited Scotland for the last time, staying with the Marquis and Marchioness of Tweeddale at Yester House before moving on to visit James Maitland, the 9th Earl of Lauderdale at Thirlestane Castle.[1157] Returning to London, he attended the wedding Alexander Stuart, eldest son of Lieutenant-General the Honourable Sir Patrick Stuart, and the Honourable Elizabeth Lennox, daughter of Lord and Lady John George Lennox at St. George's, Hanover Square in November 1850.[1158] He would have been invited by the bride's

---

1150 TNA MEPO 1/46.
1151 *Morning Post*, 6 August 1849, p.6.
1152 *London Evening Standard*, 9 August 1849, p.1.
1153 *Morning Post*, 7 September 1849, p.3.
1154 *Newcastle Journal*, 15 September 1849, p.2.
1155 *Morning Post*, 1 July 1850, p.5.
1156 Equivalent to £160 million in 1980.
1157 *Caledonian Mercury*, 30 September 1850, p.3; *Globe*, 11 October 1850, p.3.
1158 *Morning Post*, 13 November 1850.

parents, Lord John Lennox being the younger brother of the current Duke of Richmond. Lord John himself was also a Peninsula veteran, having joined the army in 1811 and been ADC to the Duke of Wellington from 1813 to 1818 which included the Battle of Waterloo.

As his health deteriorated, so did the number of his social engagements. In June 1851 he attended Miss Burdett-Coutts's last 'soirée' of the season; again the Duke of Wellington was present.[1159] In August he spent six days at the Norfolk Hotel in Brighton.[1160] Built in 1824, and originally known as the Norfolk Arms, it was a three-storey building, rising to four floors in the centre, with a balcony and verandah on Ionic columns.[1161]

By November 1851 Rowan's condition had deteriorated, as this excerpt from a letter written by Mayne to the Duke of Richmond indicates:

> 'I went to Dr. Bright today and he gives a good account of Rowan, he says he is certainly better than he has been and he thinks altogether less unfavourably of the case than he did. At the same time there is cause for anxiety considering the length of time he has been suffering and the season of the year. I thought his spirits much improved when I last saw him on Sunday.'[1162]

The following month, two letters from Rowan to the Duke of Richmond were an indication of his worsening condition. In the first he wrote, 'I am quite forbidden to think of going down, in fact it appears to me that nothing but close watching, care and time will bring me round...'[1163] This was followed by another letter ten days later in which he commenced by wishing the Duke, his wife and daughters, many happy returns. At the same time he expressed his regret at not being able to do it in person because Dr. Bright, when he had seen him the previous day, had been 'thoroughly opposed' to him going to Goodwood.[1164] At around the same time, Mayne wrote to the Duke acknowledging receipt of a brace of pheasant, but he then said, 'I am sorry to give you a very indifferent account of Rowan, he is I fear very ill.' After describing a number of symptoms, including a 'total loss of appetite' Mayne continued:

> 'These are bad symptoms and I cannot but fear he is much worse than

---

1159 *Morning Post*, 31 July 1851, p.5.
1160 *Brighton Gazette*, 21 August 1851, p.4, and 25 August 1851, p.4.
1161 www.mybrightonandhove.org.uk.places.placehotel/norfolk-hotel/norfolk-resort-hotel [accessed 7 December 2019].
1162 The Goodwood Estate Archives, op. cit. 1082, Volume 1749, folio 838. Dr Richard Bright was a famed English physician, who is associated with the identification of a kidney disease, known as Bright's disease.
1163 Ibid, Volume 1751, folio 1054.
1164 Ibid, Volume 1751, folio 978.

I have before known him. I have not seen his medical attendants but fear their opinion is inoperable. I grieve to have such an account to give, but I think you would like to know the actual state of the case.'[1165]

Less than six months later, Rowan was dead. He died on 8 May 1852 at 26 Norfolk Street, Park Lane, incorrectly referred to in some newspaper reports as his home address.[1166]

Mystery surrounds why Rowan was at 26 Norfolk Street when he died. Living there at the time was the wealthy widow of a Church of England clergyman, the Reverend Edward Pearce Serocold who had died two-and-half years earlier. Serocold's first wife, Georgiana Elizabeth, had died in childbirth in 1828. He married the occupant of 26 Norfolk Street, his second wife, Charlotte Eleanor, the daughter of Colonel Vansittart of Shottesbrook in Berkshire, at St. George's in Hanover Square, in 1842. At the time of Rowan's death Charlotte was relatively young, at 41 years of age, and living at the address with her two daughters, the eldest also named Charlotte, aged 7, and her younger sister, Teresa Eden, aged 4, along with her stepson Charles, then aged 23 years. She also had three live-in staff, a butler, a housemaid and a governess for the children.[1167]

How Rowan knew Charlotte to the extent that she was prepared to have him stay in her home for his final days is part of the mystery. Although in different colleges, Mayne was at Cambridge with her deceased husband Edward, and may have introduced them. It is unlikely that Rowan met her through her father, for he was only a colonel in the Berkshire Militia and, in any event, had died in 1829. It is possible, but again unlikely, that he met her deceased husband in his capacity as a Justice of the Peace in Cambridgeshire. A more likely scenario is that following Rowan's move from Whitehall Place to Bolton Street, they both attended St. George's in Hanover Square, the parish church of Mayfair.

When writing his book in 1956, Reith claimed he approached the living descendants of Charlotte, but they were unable to throw any light on why Rowan died in her house. He claimed that one view of her was of 'a very forbidding old woman, cross and grumbling, and a terror to children', and 'not the sort of person to take in and nurse a dying man'.[1168] Unfortunately, he does not say where this view came from. Given that she had two very

---

1165 Ibid, Volume 1761, folio 1110.
1166 For example, *Evening Mail*, 10 May 1852 and many other newspapers.
1167 Charlotte's residency at 26 Norfolk Street at this time has been confirmed from the 1851 census, op. cit. 1078, and from the *Post Office London Directory* for 1851. London: W. Kelly & Co.
1168 Reith, op. cit. 1088, p.243, footnote 1.

young daughters, she is hardly likely to have been the 'terror of children', and, at 47 years of age, she could hardly be described as 'old'. And it is unlikely that she did too much nursing, given that Rowan, too, had three live-in staff at 17 Bolton Street. Almost certainly, his man-servant at least would have accompanied him to 26 Norfolk Street.

Norfolk Street no long exists; it was renamed Dunraven Street by the London County Council in 1939. Nos. 25 to 31 of what was Norfolk Street were replaced by Avenfield House between 1959 and 1961 after some of the existing houses had suffered serious damage during World War II.[1169]

There were no military honours; not even any police honours. Instead, Sir Charles Rowan, one of the heroes of the Battle of Waterloo and the senior member of the Rowan and Mayne partnership, who against considerable odds founded the Metropolitan Police, was buried at a 'strictly private' ceremony in a private vault at Kensal Green Cemetery on 14 May.[1170]

Knowing that his condition was deteriorating, Rowan had taken the precaution of making his will five months earlier. He made a number of personal legacies, which included his gold watch to Lieutenant-General Sir George Napier; his guns, fishing rods and tackle to his godson, Lord Charles Innes-Ker, the second son of the Duke and Duchess of Roxburghe; and a hundred guineas to another godson, Richard Charles Mayne, son of his former colleague, Sir Richard. Two items, a diamond snuff box and an oil painting of Sir Charles by William Salter, had already been given to the Duke of Richmond and the Marquess of Tweeddale respectively. In addition, the executor of the will, his brother James, who was living in London, was instructed to have made and to present to the Duke and Duchess of Roxburghe a mourning ring 'as tokens of affectionate regard'. The remainder of his property was to be equally divided between his brothers, John, Hill Wilson, Robert, James and William and the widow of his brother Frederick, Sally Rowan.[1171] Interestingly, but in accordance with what seems to have been tradition in the Victorian period, he left nothing to his surviving sister, Elizabeth.

1169 *Survey of London: Volume 40, the Grosvenor Estate in Mayfair, Part 2 (The Buildings)*. London: London County Council, 1980. See 'Park Lane', in *Survey of London: Volume 40, the Grosvenor Estate in Mayfair, Part 2 (The Buildings)*, ed F.H. Shepherd (London 1980), pp. 264-289. www.british-history.ac.uk/survey-london/vol40/pt2/pp264-289, accessed 7 January 2016.
1170 *London Evening Standard*, 15 May 1852, p.2.
1171 TNA: PROB 11/2153/305. Copy in possession of the author.

CHAPTER NINETEEN

MAYNE AND HAY AS COMMISSIONERS

Prior to Rowan's departure, anticipating the Home Office would continue with two Commissioners, Rowan and Mayne had 'made joint representation' to the Home Secretary on 26 November 1849, for there to be a written distribution of duties. This was formally approved by the Secretary of State and issued as a Regulation on 2 January 1850. It stipulated 'that one Commissioner should be principally responsible, as the First Commissioner, for the general management of the service. The Second Commissioner was appointed on the understanding that such a distinction existed and he would 'feel it his duty to act in concert with the First…' Amongst Mayne's specific responsibilities was listed 'arrangements for the Police on public occasions, or whenever required to act together in times of commotion.'[1172]

Much to Mayne's displeasure, the Home Office did continue with two Commissioners, appointing the Inspecting Superintendent, Captain Hay, to replace Rowan. Possibly as a result of the regulation, some newspapers reported that Mayne had become Chief Commissioner with Hay being appointed Commissioner.[1173] Five years later, in announcing the death of Hay, the *London Evening News* referred to him as the 'Junior Commissioner'.[1174] But this was not technically correct because the Home Office carefully avoided the term Chief Commissioner.

Hay's appointment as the second Commissioner meant that there was a vacancy for an Inspecting Superintendent. For the second time, rather

---

1172 PP 1856 [2016]. Report of Her Majesty's commissioners appointed to inquire into the alleged disturbance of the public peace in Hyde Park on Sunday, July 1st, 1855; and the conduct of the Metropolitan Police in connexion with the same. Together with the minutes of evidence, appendix, and index, pp.508-509, q/a 18,822-18,824, and p.550, Appendix No. 2.
1173 *Illustrated London News*, 5 January 1850, p.7.
1174 *London Evening News*, 30 August 1855, p.2.

than promote someone from inside the force, the Home Office preferred to go outside and appointed an army captain, Douglas Labalmondière, at the time serving in India. Whether Mayne was consulted about this appointment is unknown, but it seems it was a relatively successful one because he tended to turn to Labalmondière for assistance rather than Hay. An indication of Rowan's increasingly poor health in 1849, can be gleaned from the fact that Mayne took over the response to much of the correspondence sent by the Duke of Richmond on official matters such as arranging each year for parties of Metropolitan Police Officers to attend the Goodwood Races.[1175] This continued for a number of years, even after Rowan's death, but his letter to the Duke in June 1853 also revealed that Superintendent May, the officer both Commissioners had relied on, particularly for handling disorder, had been very ill:

> 'I have been obliged very unwillingly to make an alteration as to some of the Police Officers for the duty at Goodwood. I enclose a list of those who go. You will see there are three Inspectors instead of the Superintendents. I believe these will be found well qualified. I do not feel justified in sending any of the Superintendents away from their Divisions as some unpleasant symptoms of discontent have appeared amongst some of the Constables. I believed it is confined to [a] few, but careful observation is required as to what is going on.
>
> P.S. Supt. May has been very ill but is better.'[1176]

The discontent to which Mayne referred to, was a growing belief amongst some constables and sergeants that they were not being financially rewarded sufficiently for the long hours of duty they were required to perform coupled with dissatisfaction over the pension arrangements. Although there had been some small increases to police pay, it had fallen behind industrial wages. Mayne, as the letter indicates, was aware of the grievance and from time to time pressed the Home Office for an increase. But his requests fell on deaf ears until in the year following the Hyde Park riot of 1866, the Home Secretary did sanction 'enhanced rates of pay… which were not over-generous', at least to the lower ranks.[1177] As has already been mentioned in Chapter Eleven, there was also resentment of the 'ill-considered' Superannuation Fund that had

---

1175 The Goodwood Estate Archives. Family Papers. Charles Lennox (afterwards Gordon Lennox) 5th Duke of Richmond, Lennox, and Aubigny. Contains letters written by Charles Rowan and Richard Mayne to the Duke. Held at the West Sussex Record Office.
1176 Ibid, Volume, 1774, folio 918.
1177 Browne, Douglas G (1956). *The Rise of Scotland Yard; A History of the Metropolitan Police.* London: George G. Harrop, pp.133-134.

been set up under the Metropolitan Police Act 1839.[1178] The dissatisfaction with pay and conditions led, eventually four years after Mayne's death, to a few London policemen refusing to go out on duty 'because one of the constables organising a committee to press for better conditions had been dismissed.'[1179]

Barely a year had passed since the previous attempt on the life of Queen Victoria when there was yet another – the fifth. Given that the assailant was arrested only with a cane, it can hardly be described as a serious attempt to kill her, but, nevertheless, it was the only occasion in which she suffered physical injury. It happened on 27 June 1850, just as the Queen was leaving Cambridge House, in Piccadilly about a quarter of a mile east of Hyde Park Corner after visiting her dying uncle. The Queen was travelling in an open barouche, with three of her children, when a retired army officer, Robert Pate, stepped from the crowd of about two hundred people assembled for a view of Her Majesty, and struck her with his cane. He was immediately seized by people in the crowd and given into the custody of Police Sergeant Silver. The following day, Mayne and Hay were present at the Home Office when Pate was brought before a meeting of dignitaries, chaired by the Home Secretary, Sir George Grey. Mayne read out the charge and the enquiry began.[1180] Pate eventually appeared at the Old Bailey charged with unlawfully assaulting the Queen with intent to injure her. His defence pleaded that he was unfit to stand trial but this was rejected. He was found guilty and, like Hamilton a year earlier, was sentenced to transportation for seven years.[1181]

Mayne's first real test in dealing with major public events without the guiding hand of Rowan came in 1851 with the Great Exhibition. Held in Hyde Park from 1 May to 11 October, it was the brain-child of Henry Cole, then a council member of the Royal Society for the Encouragement of Arts, Manufactures and Commerce, and later the first director of the South Kensington Museum.[1182] He had strong support from Queen Victoria's husband, Prince Albert. It was the first in a series of exhibitions of culture and industry that became increasingly popular around the world in the 19th century and was a much-anticipated event. A massive glass house, nicknamed the Crystal Palace, 1851 feet (564 metres) long by 454 (about

---

1178 See Chapter Eleven.
1179 Browne, op. cit. 1177, p.156.
1180 *Morning Chronicle*, 29 June 1850, p.7.
1181 Old Bailey Proceedings Online (www.oldbaileyonline.org, version 7.2, 27 December 2018), July 1850, trial of ROBERT PATE (t18500708-1300; Charles, Barrie (2012). *Kill the Queen! The Eight Assassination Attempts on Queen Victoria*. Stroud, Gloucestershire: Amberley, pp. 68-94.
1182 Now the Victorian and Albert Museum.

138 metres) wide, constructed from cast iron-frame components and glass made almost exclusively in Birmingham and Smethwick, was erected in which the show would take place.

Initially, strong arguments were put forward to employ the military for security and crowd arrangements at the Exhibition because it was claimed that the Police, being 'a comparatively new institution... had little or no experience of the kind required for such an enormous task.'[1183] But eventually Mayne was given the job although it did pose some problems for the Metropolitan Police. Traffic control would be relatively simple, but vast numbers of people had to be supervised. The revolutions abroad three years earlier had filled London with political refugees, and there was an influx of foreign criminals who were unknown to the police. Realising that a large number of officers would be needed to police the Exhibition each day, Mayne asked the Royal Commissioners responsible for the arrangements surrounding the Exhibition, which included paying for any services the police might provide, for an increase in establishment of 500 men. In his letter to Home Secretary Sir George Grey, Mayne wrote:

'it must be expected from the unprecedented character of the Exhibition, and the invitation given to the whole world to take part in it, that a vastly greater number than have ever been brought together on any previous occasion, such an assemblage necessarily increasing in an immense degree the responsibility and labours of the Police. Large and continuing demands on the Police would thus be made for measures of observation and precaution; provision would thus be made for the protection, by day and night, of the Exhibition Building, the safety of the property of such enormous value deposited in it, and the protection of visitors from theft, insult, etc.'[1184]

The Royal Commissioners replied to the effect that

'if the expected two million visitors came to London for the Exhibition, and each visitor stayed two days, there would be an average effective increase in London's population of 1 in 80; an equivalent increase in the strength of the Police – that is to say, 63 men – would be quite sufficient to deal with the general situation. In the second place, the special problem of the security of the building could be adequately dealt with by a corps of pensioned policemen.'[1185]

1183 Williams, T.C. (1951). 'Police at the Great Exhibition of 1851'. In *Police College Magazine*, September. Ryton-upon-Dunsmore: Police College, p.106.
1184 Ibid, p.107.
1185 Ibid, p.108.

Mayne's response was brief but succinct. He ignored the suggestion that 63 men would suffice but pointed out virtually all retired policemen were 'so worn out or disabled as to be quite useless.' Subsequently, the Home Secretary granted an increase of 13 inspectors, 51 sergeants and 1,031 constables with effect from 1 January 1851. Mayne also had a small police station built at the Princess' Gate entrance to the Park.[1186] At the same time, he saw an opportunity for innovation. The commercial use of the newly invented electric telegraph had been growing since 1838 and, in February, Mayne asked the Home Secretary for electric telegraph to be installed between 4 Whitehall Place and the exhibition building, emphasising that it would be used 'especially in cases of disturbance or tumult requiring reinforcements of police' when 'it would be important to have means of instantaneous communication to prevent alarm on account of accidents that may occur on the unfounded rumours of such at the Exhibition.' The request was approved by the Home Office.[1187]

Superintendent Pearce, of F Division, took charge of the Exhibition Building with effect from 11 February, together with three inspectors, five sergeants and fifty constables to ensure the safety of exhibits. In accordance with the Home Secretary's Regulation regarding the specific duties of the Commissioners, Mayne kept a tight control on the policing arrangements for the Exhibition, giving Hay no part in it whatsoever. Instead, he gave the responsibility for traffic arrangements to Captain Labalmondière, the new Inspecting Superintendent.[1188] Mayne also recruited a Major Paschal at one guinea a day, to be responsible for the police officers drafted in from all over Europe who were sent to provide information about and supervise refugees and foreign criminals.[1189]

Exhibits started to arrive in February, although the Exhibition was not due to open until 1 May. Just over 6 million people, equivalent to a third of the entire population of Britain at the time, visited the Great Exhibition. The average daily attendance was 42,831, with a peak attendance on 7 October of 109,915. Notable figures of the time attended, including Charles Darwin, and the writers Charlotte Bronte, Charles Dickens, Lewis Carroll, George Eliot and Alfred Tennyson. Queen Victoria visited the Exhibition on no fewer than thirty-two occasions.[1190]

Once the exhibition closed, the Royal Commissioners wrote to the Home Secretary expressing their pleasure at the 'admirable conduct of

---

1186 Ibid, pp.108-109.
1187 Bunker, John (1988). *From Rattle to Radio*. Warwickshire: Brewin Books, p.19.
1188 TNA MEPO 2/90, File 1.
1189 TNA MEPO 2/90, File 2.
1190 Williams, op. cit. 1183, p.115.

the whole of the Police Force employed in connection with the Exhibition throughout the entire period' which had been praised by all visitors, whether from 'this 'Country or from abroad.' In publishing this letter for the benefit of the whole Force, Mayne wrote:

> 'The Commissioners are assured that every man in the Police Force will feel proud of the testimony thus borne to the value of their services, and it will always remain a valuable record of the great and universally acknowledged merit of the Police Force of the Metropolis on so memorable an occasion.'[1191]

Despite his obvious annoyance at the Home Office decision to appoint a second commissioner, Mayne continued with the practice he and Rowan had adopted from the start, insisting that all written communications emanating from Whitehall Place came from 'the Commissioners'. Mayne's reward for the successful policing arrangements was the announcement in October of his Knighthood. Despite the fact he had played no part in the policing of the exhibition, Hay was appointed to be a Companion of the Most Honourable Order of the Bath, thus allowing him to place CB after his name.[1192]

In August 1852, it was reported that 'various police stations in the metropolis and its outskirts' would shortly 'be connected with one and another and the railways by electric telegraph'.[1193] It did not happen. Correspondence at around that time did confirm there was 'telegraphic communication between Whitehall Place and Sir Richard Mayne's home,'[1194] but whether this was installed at the same time as the exhibition building was connected to Whitehall Place is unclear. However, Mayne was 'unimpressed by the value of the telegraph for everyday policing', for, following a demand for payment from The Electric Telegraph Company, in a letter to the Receiver dated 17 September 1852, written whilst he was holidaying in Brighton, he wrote:

> 'The letter from the Electric Telegraph Company of the 8th Inst. is referred to the Receiver that the claim may be settled according to the agreement entered into by him.
>
> I have no intention of recommending to the Secretary of State the proposal of the Company for a general communication to the Police Stations by the Telegraph and this single line of communication is of

---

1191 Ibid, p.118.
1192 *London Gazette*, 28 October 1851, Issue 21257, page 2813.
1193 *The Times*, 3 August 1852.
1194 Bunker, op. cit. 1187, p.40.

no use. I think therefore it should be closed.'

It cost £500 to remove the line.[1195] It would be another seven years before the subject would be considered again. In 1859, a memorandum was circulated to all Superintendents asking them for a list of stations and other places that would be suitable for the 'installation of the telegraph.' But there is no record of any installations taking place.[1196]

Mayne's next test came in November 1852, when on the first of the month, along with the Lord Mayor elect of the City, the City Police Commissioner, Daniel Whittle Harvey, and the Dean of St Paul's Cathedral, he attended a meeting, chaired by Lord Hardinge, Commander-in-Chief of the British Army,[1197] to discuss the funeral arrangements for the Duke of Wellington.

The Duke had died suddenly on 14 September 1852 at Walmer Castle, his honorary residence as Lord Warden of the Cinque Ports.[1198] The delay on making the arrangements was caused by both Houses of Parliament being in recess and nothing could be done until it reconvened. By the beginning of November, all had been resolved.

The Duke's body was brought by train from Deal to London on the night of 10/11 November where arrangements had been made for it to lie-in-state at Chelsea Hospital from 12 to 16 November.[1199] Mayne made all the police arrangements assisted by Captain Labalmondière. Again, Hay was given no part to play. The first day passed off relatively uneventfully, when 16,800 people filed through the hall in which the body was lying. However, on the second day, a Saturday, more than double that number attended; there was a crush at the entrance, during which two women died and many others suffered 'broken bones, dislocations, severe bruises, wounds from being thrown down and trodden under foot, and permanent injury to health from pressure and extreme fright.'[1200]

Following this unfortunate incident, Mayne insisted on checking the arrangements personally each day, but, unfortunately, whilst doing so on 15 November, he was thrown from his horse. Mayne was immediately assisted by several police officers and taken to his home in Spring Gardens. A surgeon was summoned who decided he had been severely concussed, and suggested he rest 'for several days.'[1201] Two days later, however, he

---

1195 Ibid, p.41.
1196 Ibid, p.43.
1197 *London Evening Standard*, 2 November 1852, p.3.
1198 Holmes, Richard (2007). *Wellington: The Iron Duke*. London: Harper Perennial, p.293.
1199 Evidence of Sir Richard Mayne at the inquest into the death of the two women, see *London Daily News*, 17 November 1852, p.5.
1200 *Evening Mail*, 15 November 1852, p.5.
1201 *Lloyds Weekly Newspaper*, 21 November 1852, p.4.

attended the inquest into the death of the two women and gave evidence. After giving details of the police deployment to the coroner, he admitted he had not been 'prepared for anything like the number of persons who were present on this occasion'.

The inquest verdict was accidental death, but the jury added a rider that it regretted 'that better arrangements were not adopted by the police authorities for the public safety on Saturday morning last.'[1202] Fortunately, although attended by huge crowds, the funeral on 18 November passed off without any trouble. To dissociate himself from what had happened, Captain Hay contacted several newspapers and persuaded them to print the following sentence: 'the police arrangements connected with the lying-in state' were

> 'conducted from the commencement under the personal direction of Sir Richard Mayne himself, assisted by Captain Labalmondière, Inspecting Superintendent, and a statement, which has appeared in some papers, that Captain Hay, Sir Richard's colleague, conducted them is quite unfounded.'[1203]

Mayne saw this as an act of betrayal and was much angered.

In 1853, a Select Committee was appointed 'to consider the Expediency of adopting a more Uniform System of Policing in England and Wales, and Scotland'. Still concerned with the number of occasions the Metropolitan Police were asked to send officers out of London, Mayne saw this as an opportunity to make his feelings known, although he resisted the temptation to once again appear before a Select Committee to give evidence on a subject on which he had previously made his feelings known. Instead, he nominated Superintendents Mallalieu and Martin to do so. But, first to give evidence on 26 May was Captain William Harris, who, two years later would be appointed an Assistant Commissioner in the Metropolitan Police on the death of Captain Hay, but, who then commanded the Hampshire Constabulary. Hampshire had been one of the first counties to form a police force following the County Police Act 1839. It was apparent that Harris had a good knowledge of what was happening in the remainder of England and Wales, for he was able to tell the Committee that the Act had been adopted as a whole in 22 counties, partly adopted in seven others, but in 22 counties the old parochial system continued.[1204]

1202 *London Daily News*, 17 November 1852, p.5.
1203 For instance, see *The Times,* 15 November 1852, p.3. *Globe*, 15 November 1852, p.3; *Evening Mail* 15 November 1852, p.5.
1204 PP 1852-53 (603). First report from the Select Committee on Police; with the minutes of evidence, Minutes of Evidence, pp.1-2, q/a 4-9.

Superintendent Mallalieu had been present at all the major outbreaks of disorder in the metropolis, including the Cold Bath Fields riot and the public gatherings in 1848 on Kennington Common and elsewhere. He had also been briefly in charge of the Bristol Police in 1838 following the death of the incumbent chief officer.[1205] He had also been sent out to the West Indies to organise the Island of Barbados Police.[1206] Pointing out his division contained parts of the metropolis that extended into the rural county of Kent, he told the Committee that the county had a superintending constable system which he described as 'a great failure'.[1207] He then described what happened to men joining the Metropolitan Police:

'A man is retained in the probationary section for two or three weeks, where he receives the rudiments of his police education and drill; he then joins a division, and he is employed usually at head-quarters, on an average perhaps of 12 months, in the more populous parts of the district, in order that he may have an opportunity of frequenting the police courts to see how the police cases are managed; during that period he is also made more efficient in his drill. The men of the Metropolitan force are now well-drilled, and made efficient in the practice of the sword.'[1208]

Asked whether he thought soldiers were the 'class of man' most suitable to policing, he replied, 'I never considered them the most efficient men for the purpose; I have been rather disposed to think that the intelligent part of the agricultural labouring community after training made the best policemen.'[1209] When asked whether he thought discipline had improved from some of the earlier difficulties, he replied 'I think we have made rapid strides within the last few years', and 'I feel proud of the establishment, in comparison with what it was about 15 years ago.'[1210]

Superintendent George Martin told the Committee how, as an inspector, he had been sent to Wales during the Rebecca riots when 'there was very great disorder' with 'regularly organised gangs breaking down the turnpike-gates all over the country' but 'there was no police of any kind whatever, except one policeman at Carmarthen, and two or three at Haverford-west.' Asked whether he received any assistance from the local constables, he

---

1205 PP 1852-53 (715). Second report from the Select Committee on Police; together with the proceedings of the committee, minutes of evidence, and appendix. Minutes of Evidence, p.18, q/a 2831-2836.
1206 Ibid, p.18, q/a 2842.
1207 Ibid, p.19, q/a 2850.
1208 Ibid, p.20, q/a 2869.
1209 Ibid, q/a 2872.
1210 Ibid, p.21, q/a 2874-2875.

replied 'No'. Describing how he went to Carmarthenshire with 22 men, went into Pembrokeshire with a party of 100 and took a detachment of 32 men (two sergeants and thirty constables) to be stationed at Pembroke, he said he was there for ten months.[1211] Also, he went to Huddersfield with twelve men in 1837, as a result of an application to the Secretary of State. He then described how 'there was great excitement in opposition to the poor laws' as a result of which 'a very serious disturbance took place', the military were called out and the Riot Act was read. Several of his men including himself were injured.[1212]

He was asked about the value of special constables, to which he replied that at Huddersfield a great many special constables were sworn in, about 400, adding 'we had a serious fight, and the special constables ran away, with the exception of one only who remained with us.'[1213] He placed little reliance on the special constables in Wales, because they were mixed up with the gate-breakers.[1214] He had also taken thirty men to Dewsbury in 1838, where they had faced a crowd armed with stones and bludgeons. Again the military had been called out and the Riot Act had been read. Some of his men had been injured, fortunately not seriously.[1215]

Martin had also been sent, with sixty men, to Lewes in Sussex two or three years previously, to deal with the threat of crowd disorder on the occasion of bonfire night. Although there was an organised police force in Lewes, it was felt insufficient to deal with the threat. However, Martin pointed out that if the county force and Brighton force had been under one command, Brighton would have had sufficient men to obviate the need for the Metropolitan contingent.[1216] Martin was asked, in the light of his great experience with riots, whether he thought that policemen were 'much more efficient for the suppression of riots and the dispersion of a mob than the military'. He replied, 'Decidedly so; and more especially when they get to know the people; if a constable knows a number of these low characters, he can do more than a dozen strange constables; they do not like to resist for fear of the after consequences.'[1217]

In its final report, the Committee found that:

- The County Police Act 1839 'failed to provide such a general and uniform Constabulary Force as… is essentially required for the

---

1211 Ibid, p.90, q/a 3727-3736.
1212 Ibid, p.91, q/a 3737-3744.
1213 Ibid, q/a 3745.
1214 Ibid.
1215 Ibid, p.92, q/a 3748-3755.
1216 Ibid, p.93, q/a 3785-3793.
1217 Ibid, p.93, q/a 3763-3768.

prevention of crime and security of property'. (Resolution 1)

- Where the Act has been adopted it had 'proved highly advantageous to those districts in the detection and apprehension of offenders, the maintenance of order, vagrancy has decreased and, in some cases, almost entirely suppressed, and property has been greatly protected. (Resolution 2)

- Any system of policing dependent on Parochial Constables has proved largely ineffectual. (Resolution 3)

- That the efficiency of all existing Police Forces is materially impaired by the lack of co-operation between the Rural Police and Borough Police. Therefore smaller boroughs should be consolidated with districts or counties for police purposes and police in the larger boroughs should be under a similar management system to those of the counties. (Resolution 6)

- The Government should consider defraying the cost of an improved system, without interfering with the local management of the Force. (Resolution 7)

- Finally, the Committee recommended that it was 'most desirable that legislative measures should be introduced without delay by Her Majesty's Government, rendering the adoption of an efficient Police Force on a uniform principle imperative throughout Great Britain. (Resolution 8)[1218]

During the summer of 1853 what was known as the Great Camp was held on Chobham Common. It was the first large-scale military manoeuvres in Britain since the Napoleonic Wars. Under the command of Lieutenant-General John Colborne, by then Lord Seaton, Rowan's former commanding officer amongst other things, it consisted of a full-scale exercise, involving 8,000 troops, cavalry and artillery.[1219] Many of those that took part, including the Light Brigade, would be involved later in the Crimea War. When Queen Victoria went there to inspect her Army, Mayne ignored Hay and gave Labalmondière charge of the police contingent sent to ensure her safety.[1220]

By the end of 1853 the relationship between Mayne and Hay had deteriorated still further, to the extent that they were not talking to each other but were only communicating, if at all, through the Chief Clerk,

---

1218 Ibid, Report, pp.iii-iv.
1219 *Sun* (London), 28 June 1853, p.5.
1220 *Morning Post*, 22 June 1853, p.5; see also National Army Museum Online collection at www.nam.ac.uk/online-collection/detail.php?acc=1999-09-39-1 [accessed] 3 May 2016.

Charles Yardley. In Mayne's absence, presumably on holiday, Hay had sought to introduce a new system of policing which would have meant 'shorter periods of relief than at present'. On his return at the beginning of December, Mayne wrote at length, in rather rambling fashion, to Under Secretary of State Horatio Waddington at the Home Office requesting him to bring the letter to the notice of the new Home Secretary, Viscount Palmerston:

> 'Superintendent Pearce mentioned to me yesterday that Captain Hay had spoken to him about a plan for carrying on the duties of the Police which had been submitted to the Secretary of State by Captain Hay, and it was intended by him to try the plan on one Division. Captain Hay desires the experiment to be made in the Division of which Mr. Pearce was Superintendent.
>
> The plan seemed open to so many objections that Mr Pearce consulted upon another Superintendent, Mr Mallalieu, in whose judgement he had great confidence. Mr Mallalieu concurred with Mr Pearce, and said that the plan having sometime before been shewn to him by the Chief Clerk of the Commissioners, he had then expressed a decided opinion against it. Upon making enquiry I learnt that several weeks ago Captain Hay consulted with the Chief Clerk about allowing the mode of performing the Police duties in the Divisions, and the Chief Clerk gave the plan in question which had been drawn up many years ago, to Captain Hay – I may here mention that such matters do not come within the duties of the Chief Clerk. Mr Yardley has no opportunities for forming any sound opinion as to the best mode of carrying on Police duties, and I should not consider his authority of any weight in such a matter.
>
> I do not think this a proper occasion for making observations on the plan, and I therefore abstain from doing so, but I ought to state that having heard four weeks ago that Captain Hay had such a plan in contemplation, I requested him to acquaint me with the details, and was informed through the Chief Clerk by Captain Hay's desire that he declined to do so.
>
> Subsequently Mr Fitzroy[1221] spoke to me upon the subject of an alteration proposed by Captain Hay and seeing the plan, I at once stated what I considered fatal objections to it, not having heard more of it I supposed the plan was given up.

1221 Henry Fitzroy was the Under-Secretary of State at the Home Office from 1852 to 1855.

I was surprised on hearing now that there had recently been consultation between Captain Hay and the Chief Clerk about such a plan that it had been shewn by the Chief Clerk to one Superintendent and his opinion asked, that Captain Hay had proposed to another of the Superintendents to carry the plan into execution in his Division, and that all these steps had been taken without any communication to me.

It is my duty to state for the information of Lord Palmerston that such a course is in direct violation of the Regulations approved by the Secretary of State, Sir George Grey, in January 1850, on the appointment of Captain Hay for the guidance of the Commissioners in the performance of their respective duties and which remain in force.

The course now taken by Captain Hay sends, I submit to disorganise the Office of the Commissioners and brings the Commissioners themselves into open collision, impairing their authority and influence over the Officers of Police which it is essential to maintain and which cannot be weakened without injury to the Public Service.

It becomes impossible to maintain and enforce by two Commissioners that discipline over so large a body of Men as the Police Force which has hitherto preserved the Force in a state of thorough efficiency, if the general principles for carrying on the duties can be altered by one Commissioner without the knowledge and consent of the other.

I may perhaps be permitted to refer to the opinions I have on former occasions submitted to the Secretary of State as to the unsound constitution of the Office of the Commissioners of Police in giving two Commissioners equal powers and a coordinate authority, and a case having now arisen such as I have represented, I am compelled with great regret to bring the circumstances under the consideration of the Secretary of State.

I have the honour to be,
Sir,
    Your most obedient Servant,
        R.Mayne[1222]

Fitzroy wrote to Captain Hay requesting an explanation to which Hay replied:

[1222] TNA HO 45/4726, letter from Mayne to Home Office, dated 2 December 1853.

> 'I have the honour to acknowledge the receipt of your letter of this days' date, stating that "Lord Palmerston has been informed that I have ordered Superintendents Pearce and Mallalieu to carry out a new scheme of Police duty on their respective Districts, and you are directed by His Lordship to enquire whether such orders have been given by me."
> I request you will do me the favour to inform Viscount Palmerston that I have given no orders to Superintendent Pearce or Superintendent Mallalieu, to carry out a new scheme of Police Duty in their respective Districts. I had a conversation with Superintendent Pearce, and directed him to give me his opinion upon the Scheme I submitted to the Home Office, and three months ago I wrote to Superintendent Mallalieu from Brighton requesting his opinion on the same subject.'[1223]

In the meantime, Mayne had asked for a report from Superintendent Pearce:

> 'I beg to report that about the 28th ultimo, I was asked by Captain Hay to look at a plan which Mr. Yardley had for the alteration of the Police Duties, in shorter periods of relief than at present, and to give him my opinion on the same, that he had shown it to the Secretary of State who wishes it to be tried, and that my name was mentioned as the person to give it a trial in my Division. I mentioned to Captain Hay at the time that I considered it would be advisable to try the effect on more than one Division, Captain Hay replied that it was his desire that the change should take place in all Divisions at once, but the Secretary of State thought it best to try one Division first.
> Believing that I should be called upon to carry the new plan into effect and Sir Richard Mayne having on the first instant come down to settle Men's Reports he, (after being out of Town for some weeks) I thought it my duty to mention the circumstances to him.'[1224]

In typical Home Office fashion, the whole situation was left in abeyance without being resolved, other than the fact that Hay's suggestion was not implemented.

Mayne remained concerned about officers employed in plain clothes because he issued the following Memorandum on 23 January 1854:

1223 Ibid, letter from Mayne, to Home Office, dated 12 December 1853.
1224 Ibid, report from Superintendent Pearce.

'I find a considerable number of Sergeants and Constables employed in plain clothes, 15 Sergeants and 55 Constables permanently and 2 Sergeants and 102 Constables temporarily...

The Superintendents are reminded that there is no regulation of the Service authorizing the employment of Police in plain clothes, and by doing so two very important objects are lost sight of, namely the prevention of Crime by the presence so that it shall be known of a Constable, and [the satisfaction] that in some cases parties may be detected by Police in plain clothes that would not be detected by men in uniform, but this does not counterbalance the general objection to the practice Public seeing that a Constable is at the place; also such constables are not under the control of public observation not being known from the duties to belong to the Police, and such practice gives occasion to a charge of Police being employed as Spies and in other improper ways – I am also aware.

Each Superintendent will report the objects of his employing the number of Sergeants and Constables in plain clothes.'[1225]

On 17 April 1855, City Police Commissioner, Daniel Whittle Harvey, wrote to Mayne about the arrangements he was making for the visit to the City of the Emperor Napoleon and the Empress. He commenced the letter by expressing his disappointment 'in the pleasure of seeing you yesterday afternoon, as I had proposed, and being well aware of your manifold and important engagements at the present time, I consider it desirable to give you in writing the amount of assistance we shall need on Thursday next, when the Emperor Napoleon and the Empress will honour the city with their presence at Guildhall.' There followed details of the arrangements he was proposing including the area he had assigned to the Metropolitan Police which was

> 'the entire ground from Temple-bar to the west end of Cheapside, crossing in line directly from the corner of St Paul's Churchyard to the Obelisk, and thence to the opposite side of Cheapside, near Foster-lane, as will be indicated by barriers. The entire distance so to be occupied is 1,289 yards.'

There followed further details of the proposed arrangements including the setting up of a joint command at the Obelisk, Cheapside. He concluded the letter:

1225 TNA MEPO 2/28. Memorandum from Mayne to Superintendents, dated 28 January 1854.

'You doubtless will have received instructions from Sir G. Grey, as one of Her Majesty's Principal Secretaries of State, upon the subject of this communication, the Lord Mayor having authorized the metropolitan police to act within the city upon the present occasion. Though the ordinary sphere of our respective services is distinct, our duties are identical, and I feel satisfied that it will be the ambition of us both to act together in entire and friendly concert, and thereby show to our gallant allies that, upon the appearance of their illustrious Emperor and Empress, the peace and order of this great city were intrusted without reserve to the keeping of the civil authorities, strengthened, as I feel confident we shall be, by the good sense and loyal devotion of the people...'

Clearly Harvey had an appointment with Mayne which the latter did not keep. Neither, it would appear, did he arrange for either Captain Hay or Superintendent Labalmondière, whom he had used as his second-in-command on previous occasions, to meet Harvey to finalise the arrangements. But, stranger still, Harvey sent a copy of the letter he sent to Mayne to *The Times* which published it two days later.[1226] Did this suggest that Harvey did not trust Mayne, possibly after the deaths of the two women at Chelsea Hospital just over two years previously?

As it turned out, the event went off without any problems. On 18 April, Mayne and Captain Labalmondière rode in advance of the procession in which the Emperor Napoleon and the Empress went into the City where they were met by Harvey. A subsequent newspaper report claimed that 'owing to the admirable way that the City and metropolitan police worked together in the City, and being aided by the Horseguards, many accidents were prevented, which otherwise would have been inevitable.'[1227]

1226 *The Times*, 19 April 1855, p.9.
1227 *London Evening Standard*, 19 April 1855, p.2.

CHAPTER TWENTY

THE FIRST BATTLE FOR HYDE PARK

The origins of what was to take place on 1 July 1855 are to be found approximately twelve months previously, on 13 July 1854, when, under pressure from those who wanted Sunday to be retained as a day of prayer, Parliament rushed through the Sale of Beer Act which effectively meant that beer could only be sold between 1.00pm and 2.30pm, and again between 6.00pm and 10.00pm on a Sunday.[1228]

Over the ensuing months, 'popular feeling' against the Act increased.[1229] So, when Lord Grosvenor introduced a Bill in Parliament, with the intention of severely restricting the selling of all types of goods on Sundays in 1855,[1230] there was considerable opposition. Supported by an article in *The Times*,[1231] the working classes saw it as a blatant piece of class legislation that would alter their way of life. Mayne opposed it for different reasons. Repeating the views he and Rowan had expressed when a similar prohibition was being considered in 1832, he said the enforcement of any such legislation 'would cause public hostility and defiance' and, in any event, any such law would be difficult to enforce.[1232] The response to the introduction to the Bill was the appearance of posters announcing a meeting in Hyde Park on Sunday, 24 June 1855:

> 'New Sunday Bill to put down newspapers, shaving, smoking, eating and drinking and all kinds of food or recreation for body or mind at present enjoyed by 'poor people'. An open-air meeting of the artisans, mechanics and 'the lower orders' of the metropolis will take place

---

1228 17 & 18 Vict, ch.79.
1229 Harrison, Brian (1965). 'The Sunday Trading Riots of 1855.' *The Historical Journal*, Vol. 8, No. 2, p.220.
1230 Ibid, pp.220-221.
1231 *The Times*, 15 June 1855.
1232 See Chapter Fourteen.

in Hyde-park on Sunday afternoon next to see how religiously the aristocracy observe the Sabbath and how careful they are not to work their servants and cattle on that day! *Vide* the Lord Robert Grosvenor' speech. The meeting is summoned for three o'clock on the right bank of the Serpentine looking towards Kensington-gardens. Come! and bring your wives and families with you! That they may benefit by the example of their betters!'[1233]

As a result, Mayne arranged for an inspector with two sergeants and thirty constables to be at the Triumphal Arch[1234] at 2 o'clock, and a few constables to be deployed near the Serpentine. He gave instructions that should any person begin to address a meeting, that person was to be told that the park regulations did not allow it, and if he persisted he was to be removed.[1235]

That afternoon, accompanied by his daughter, Georgina, Sir Richard entered the park at some time between 3 and 4 o'clock with the intention of walking across it and exiting via the Victoria Gate, but he heard 'such a hooting and yelling and noise' that he turned towards the Serpentine. Each time a carriage or a horseman went anywhere near the assembled crowd, the hooting increased. According to Mayne, ladies in the carriages and horses were frightened to the extent that he 'saw most serious accidents nearly being caused'. Indeed, on one occasion a carriage and horses, driven at full gallop, passed the crowd and continued towards the magazine and Kensington Gardens with the 'coachman endeavouring to stop them without succeeding.'[1236] Consequently, Sir Richard instructed additional police officers to come to the Park and the crowd was eventually dispersed.[1237]

The following week handbills and placards, calling upon people to assemble in large numbers in Hyde Park on 1 July, were distributed around London. The Home Secretary, Sir George Grey, took the view that the assembly had been arranged 'with the evident intention of creating

---

1233 *Morning Chronicle*, 25 June 1855, p.5.
1234 The Triumphal Arch, known also as the Wellington Arch or Constitutional Arch, originally stood close to the Duke of Wellington's home at Apsley House, Hyde Park Corner. But in 1886, it was moved to its current location, a large traffic island, between Hyde Park and Green Park, facing down Constitution Hill.
1235 PP 1856 [2016]. Her Majesty's Commissioners (1856). Report of Her Majesty's Commissioners appointed to Inquire into the alleged Disturbances of the public peace in Hyde Park on Sunday, 1st July 1855 and the conduct of the metropolitan police in connection with the same, together with the Minutes of Evidence, Appendix and Index. London: Eyre and Spottiswoode. Minutes of evidence, p.226. q/a 6164.
1236 Ibid, q/a 6166.
1237 Ibid, p.227, q/a 6171-6178.

disturbances and disorder' and, at a meeting at the Home Office on 29 June, he instructed Mayne to issue 'a notice, warning persons against assembly for the purposes contemplated.'

This Mayne did. The notice requested 'well-disposed persons to abstain from joining or attending the meeting... in Hyde-park' and warned that all necessary means 'would be taken to prevent [it] and preserve the public peace.'

It was published in the morning papers on 30 June and was posted at all the entrances to the Park in the afternoon,[1238] but it had little effect.

The same day, Mayne issued written instructions relating to the deployment of police. With effect from 9.30am, an inspector, two sergeants and twenty constables, under the command of Superintendent O'Brien of C Division, would be responsible for policing the area around Lord Grosvenor's house which was in nearby Park Street. An additional inspector, five sergeants and fifty constables would be on reserve to give support if necessary. Should disorder occur and the number of officers be insufficient, 'an immediate notice' should be sent to the superintendents of A and D divisions to each provide an inspector, five sergeants and fifty constables.

As for Hyde Park, four superintendents, six inspectors, twenty-four sergeants and 250 constables would parade at 2.00pm as follows:

- B Division: one superintendent (Superintendent Gibbs), one inspector, two sergeants and twenty-five constables and a further one inspector, two sergeants and twenty-five constables (two parties) to be deployed on the grass on the south side of the road between the entrance from Hyde Park Corner and the hill at the head of the Serpentine, near the Knightsbridge Road.

- D Division: one superintendent (Superintendent Hughes), one inspector, five sergeants, fifty constables, together with M Division – one inspector, five sergeants, fifty constables, to be deployed on the grass north of the road between the statue of Achilles and the Humane Society's House.

- G Division: one superintendent (Superintendent Martin), one inspector, five sergeants, fifty constables, to be deployed on the grass on the north side of the road between the Humane Society's house and Kensington Gardens.

- A Division: one superintendent (Superintendent May), one inspector,

---

1238 Thurmond Smith, Phillip (1985). *Policing Victorian London: Political Policing, Public Order, and the London Metropolitan Police.* Westport, Connecticut: Greenwood, p.131.

five sergeants and fifty constables to be on standby at the Magazine Barracks.

In addition, the following reserves would be available from 2.00pm:

- A Division: one inspector, five sergeants and fifty constables at Triumphal Arch.
- B Division: one inspector, five sergeants and fifty constables at Walton Street Police House, near Lowndes Square.
- C Division: one superintendent (Superintendent O'Brien), one inspector, five sergeants and fifty constables at Stanhope Gate (It should be noted that this is, those officers who are also on standby for Lord Grosvenor's House).
- D Division: one inspector, five sergeants and fifty constables at Marble Arch.
- T Division: one inspector, three sergeants and twenty-five constables at Kensington Police House.[1239]

The instructions originally stipulated that Superintendent May, by far the most experienced public order commander, would be in overall command, but on the morning of 1 July he was taken ill; so Superintendent Hughes was designated to replace him at the last minute. Hughes had been in the force for 25 years and had policed large crowds at Epsom and Ascot Race Courses and the Opening of Parliament. But, of course, by and large these were peaceful crowds.[1240] Mayne would be in overall command at Scotland Yard.

There is some dispute as to the type of briefing that occurred. At a meeting attended by a number of superintendents on 30 June, Superintendent O'Brien, who was responsible for safeguarding Lord Grosvenor's house, claimed that Sir Richard merely read out the written instructions.[1241] When asked whether he had been consulted about the original notice issued by Sir Richard, he replied, 'No; it is not usual for the Chief Commissioner to ask his officers their opinions.' Asked whether it was 'not usual for Sir Richard to consult his superintendents', O'Brien answered, 'Not at all.'[1242]

Although Superintendent May had been present on the previous Sunday and was the deputed ground commander for 1 July, and Mayne had seen him each day in the intervening period, May told the Commission that

---
1239 TNA MEPO 7/17. Police Order, 30 June 1855.
1240 PP 1856 [2016], op. cit. 1235, Minutes of Evidence, pp.469-470, q/a 12775-12784.
1241 Ibid, p.448, q/a 12239-12240.
1242 Ibid, p.449, q/a 12270-12271.

he was not consulted as to what they were to do on that day.[1243] However, he added that he would have received instructions from Sir Richard on the Sunday morning had he not been taken ill. Instead, Mayne spoke to Hughes[1244] and told him that if there was any disorder or hooting, the crowd was to be cleared back from the rails which ran along the carriageways.[1245]

On the Saturday evening Mayne wrote to his wife:

> 'I have been somewhat busy today, preparing amongst other things for Hyde-park tomorrow, where they threaten a repetition of last Sunday's proceedings. Lord Grosvenor called yesterday and spoke penitently, and acknowledged I had given good advice against such bills.'[1246]

All officers taking up their posts in Hyde Park the next day were told of the Commissioner's written order and instructed that the directions contained in it were to be firmly enforced. They were further told that any person commencing a meeting or assemblage, or shouting, or making a noise, or acting in any way calculated to cause a disturbance or frighten horses pulling carriages, were to be cautioned and requested to desist and, if they failed to do so, they were to be removed and, if necessary, taken into custody and sent to Vine Street Police House. Finally, directions were given to the men that they were to sit or lie down quietly on the grass, and not to interfere unless it became absolutely necessary.[1247]

Mayne told Superintendent Hughes to send him reports every half-hour from 2.00pm onwards, or more frequently if the situation warranted.[1248] A few people arrived before 2.30pm, and those that did were generally quiet and orderly. During the next half-an-hour, there was a steady increase of people arriving in the Park. By 3.00pm *The Times* reported a 'dense mass'[1249] on the north side of the Serpentine, especially near the Humane Society's Receiving House.[1250] Hughes merely told Mayne there was an increasing number of people in the vicinity of the Receiving House, but there were no speakers and everything was quiet. The crowd consisted of the middle and

---

1243 Ibid, p.476, q/a 12917-12919.
1244 Ibid, p.459, q/a 12525.
1245 Ibid, p.464, q/a 12638.
1246 Henry Hall Collection. Collection of diaries, journals, letters, books and miscellaneous papers, donated by Edward Hall (b.1898), a dealer and collector of Manuscripts and books. Includes letters written by Sir Richard Mayne to his wife between 1831 and 1866 in files EHC210/M1251 and EHC210A/1252. Held in the Wigan Archives, letter 100 from Mayne to his wife, dated 30 June 1855, p.214.
1247 PP 1856 [2016], op. cit. 1235. Report, p.v.
1248 These reports are shown in PP 1856 [2016], op. cit. 1235, p.233, q/a 6249.
1249 *The Times* estimated that by early afternoon, 150,000 members of the 'respectable class' had assembled. *The Times*, 2 July 1855.
1250 First erected in 1794 by the Royal Humane Society, to rescue people from the Serpentine. It was replaced in 1834.

working classes who could broadly be divided into five categories:
- Some were present simply for the ordinary and legitimate purposes of exercise and recreation to which the Park was specially dedicated;
- Some were there out of curiosity as to what would occur;
- Some were present with the specific intention of expressing their disapproval of the Sunday Trading Bill; and
- Also present were a large number of 'lads' and 'young men' who were there to loudly express their disapproval of the upper classes who use the Carriageway for a Sunday afternoon drive.
- Finally, amongst them, were a mixture of thieves, pickpockets, and 'other reckless and disorderly persons, bent on plunder and mischief.'[1251]

Soon after 3.00pm, people lining the rails of the Drive, leading westwards from Hyde Park Corner towards Kensington Palace (now known as Rotten Row) started shouting and yelling at passing carriages; occasionally a missile, usually a clod of earth or a piece of hurdle, was thrown. Police officers at the entrance to the Park advised carriages to turn back, and some did. Others, who, in the main supported the demonstration, insisted on entering the Park.[1252]

By 3.30pm, the danger to carriages from the throng of 'disorderly persons' gathered in front of the rails on the south side of the Drive near the Receiving House, had increased. Superintendent Hughes, after consulting with Superintendent Martin, decided that the time had come 'to use more vigorous measures to clear the carriageway,' following the directions given by Mayne, 'to clear the crowd back to some distance from the railings.'[1253] He therefore gave orders to the police to clear the road using their staves, during which some arrests were made. Coinciding with this, the police near the Serpentine were provoked when 'some of the mob managed to get an enormous eel out of the Serpentine' and started 'throwing it over the heads of the people and, at last, at the police.'

In response to his 4.00pm report, Mayne instructed Hughes to call up a reserve squad from Vine Street Police Station to replace those he had deployed from Marble Arch.[1254]

Responding to Hughes' 4.30pm report, Mayne sent a written note informing him he had ordered reserves from Walton Street and Kensington to report to him in the Park, and told Hughes 'You may now

1251 PP 1856 [2016], op. cit. 1235. Report, pp.vi-vii.
1252 Ibid, p.vii.
1253 Ibid, pp.xxviii to xxx.
1254 Ibid, p.x.

act vigorously in compelling all rioters to move to a distance from the road, and disperse and apprehend rioters.'[1255] To clear those who were in front of the rails, police officers 'advanced with their truncheons drawn along the carriageway road of the Drive, clearing it of people.' Those that refused to move 'were pushed, struck or roughly handled.' Other police officers passed along the Drive, striking the rails with their truncheons or brandishing them over their heads, to get the crowd to fall back from the rails. If anyone failed to move they were struck.

Another contingent of police officers, again with truncheons drawn, went along the footpath between the Drive and the Serpentine near the Receiving House, again driving the people back from the rails, in an easterly direction along the bank of the Serpentine. Because of the narrow space, this particular part of the operation was 'attended with great confusion' and some people, including well-dressed women, were forced ankle-deep into the water; others were struck with truncheons. Yet another contingent of police officers passed behind the rails on the north side of the Drive, and drove the people back thirty or forty yards, and, in some cases, further.[1256]

These various operations by the police produced or increased 'irritation or ill-feeling' amongst the crowd, many of whom shouted abuse or threw stones at officers, to the extent that the subsequent inquiry found that, from 5.00pm to 5.30pm, 'a state of tumult and disturbance prevailed.' Those arrested were taken initially to the yard of Dairy Lodge[1257] near the Receiving House, which was used as a temporary place of custody, before being taken by cab or on foot to Vine Street Police Station.[1258]

The deployment of an increasing number of police led to a reduction in disorder in the vicinity of the Drive by 6.00pm, and for the next hour, groups in various parts of the Park were dispersed; again, some stone-throwers were arrested. Soon after 7.00pm, some young soldiers of the Guards began to mingle with those still in the park and Superintendent Hughes sent to the nearby Magazine Barracks for a military picket to take them into custody. Again, some stones were thrown whilst this was in progress and a crowd followed the soldiers to the barracks, before being dispersed. At 9.00pm Superintendent Hughes instructed about 100 police officers to form an open line, with between two and three yards between each, extending northwards from the Serpentine, and he then led them eastwards towards Hyde Park Corner and Stanhope Gate, sweeping

---

1255 Ibid.
1256 Ibid, p.xi.
1257 Ibid.
1258 Ibid, p.xii.

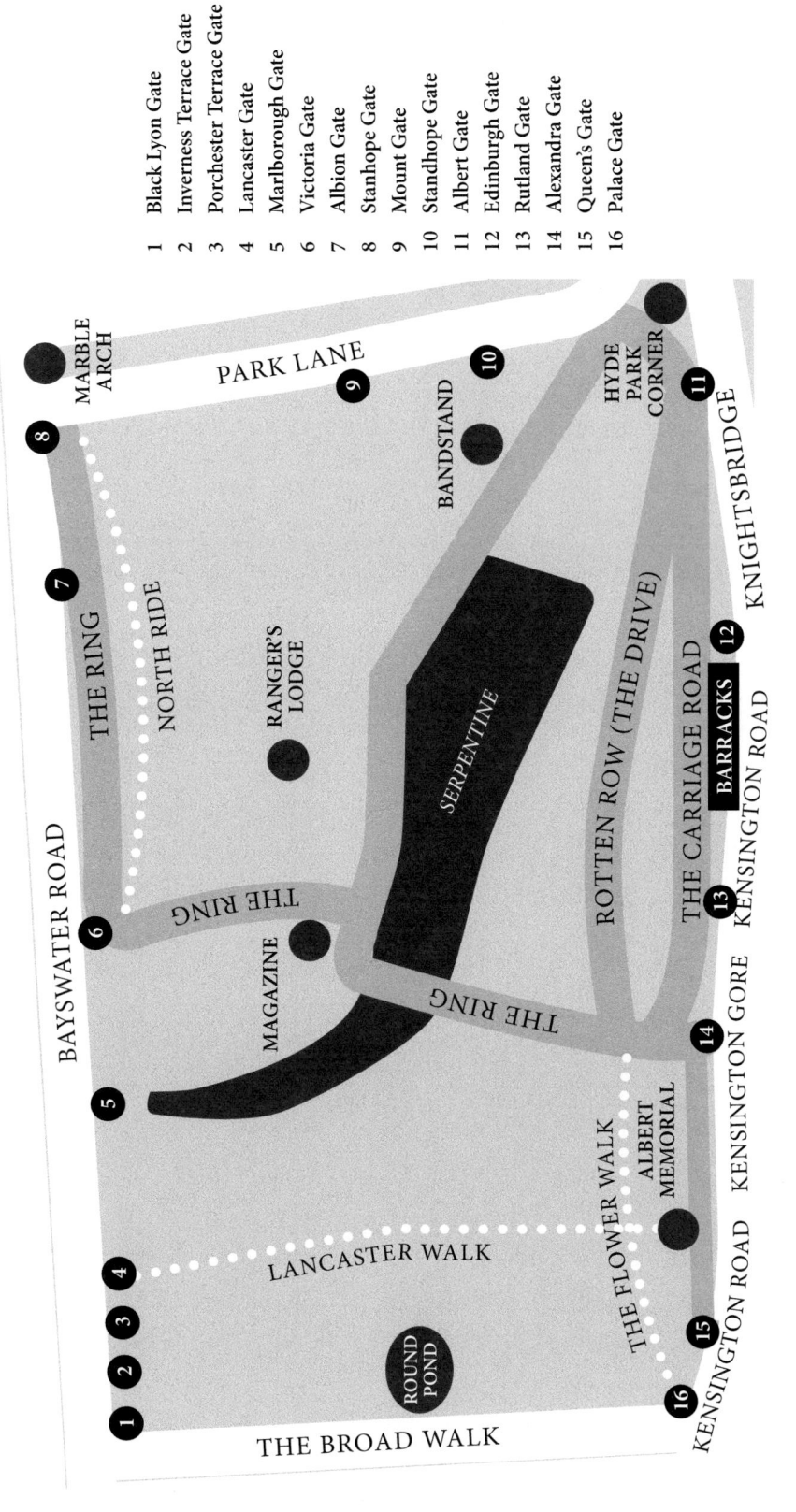

1 Black Lyon Gate
2 Inverness Terrace Gate
3 Porchester Terrace Gate
4 Lancaster Gate
5 Marlborough Gate
6 Victoria Gate
7 Albion Gate
8 Stanhope Gate
9 Mount Gate
10 Standhope Gate
11 Albert Gate
12 Edinburgh Gate
13 Rutland Gate
14 Alexandra Gate
15 Queen's Gate
16 Palace Gate

everyone before them.[1259]

Meanwhile, in Park Street, Superintendent O'Brien had arrived soon after 2.00pm and he immediately sent Inspector Webb, two sergeants and twenty constables to the vicinity of Lord Grosvenor's house. An additional sergeant and ten constables were deployed to 5 Park Street, about 300 yards from Lord Grosvenor's house, and another sergeant and ten constables to 1A Park Street, which was about 200 yards from Lord Grosvenor's house. Of these, two or three constables were posted outside Lord Grosvenor's house.[1260]

At around 6.00pm, a crowd was seen moving from Hyde Park towards Grosvenor Gate. O'Brien was told by passers-by they were headed for Lord Grosvenor's house and some had stones in their pockets. O'Brien immediately sent a constable to confirm that they had in fact gone to Lord Grosvenor's house; the constable rapidly returned to say that there were between 2,000 and 4,000 people present. Initially a small body of police officers mingled with the crowd in an effort to persuade them to disperse peacefully but this failed. Superintendent O'Brien led 50 men from Stanhope Gate, bringing them in at the southern end of Park Street in five columns of ten. Seeing this, some people dispersed, but many turned to confront the advancing police officers. In a loud voice, Superintendent O'Brien ordered them to disperse, but he then tripped and fell and, in doing so, hurt his knee; as a result he was incapacitated for a brief period and unable to command his men.[1261] With truncheons drawn, the police officers, under the command of an inspector, rushed forward. Although the crowd offered no serious resistance, people were struck by the officers, some of whom, it was said, 'acted with violence, inflicting severe injuries on several persons who were not shown to have been guilty of any violence, but who refused to move off when requested so to do, or who, being inoffensively there, ran or stood still when the police came up the street.'[1262]

A total of seventy-two people were arrested; seventy-one in Hyde Park and one in Park Street. Ten were charged with simple theft or theft from the person (pickpocketing); twenty-four with riot or stone-throwing; twenty with riot or assault on police; and eighteen were charged with obstructing police. Forty-nine police officers were injured. Twenty-seven were struck with stones, thirteen were struck with sticks of pieces of hurdle; and seven

1259 Ibid, p.xxxi.
1260 Ibid, p.xi.
1261 Quoted in Thurmond-Smith, op. cit. 1238, p.118.
1262 PP 1856 [2016], op. cit. 1235, Report, p.vii.

were kicked and knocked down. It is not recorded how the remaining two were injured.[1263]

In the aftermath of the disorder, Lord Grosvenor withdrew his Bill. This meant there was no reason to continue to demonstrate. Even so, around 4,000 people gathered in the Park on Sunday, 8 July, although the dress of those who assembled on this occasion 'was less respectable.'[1264] Mayne deployed approximately eight hundred police officers on this occasion and the military were again on standby. Despite this relatively large number, when some youths left the Park and went on the rampage they broke seven hundred and forty-nine panes of glass in the windows of mansions in Upper Belgrave Street, Wilkin Street and Haton Street in a fifteen-minute spree.[1265]

Following the events of 1 July, there was widespread condemnation of the police. One newspaper suggested that 'an indiscriminate attack was made by a body of police on a crowd of men and women, and many were knocked down by police bludgeons';[1266] another that the police 'made unsparing use of their truncheons on every person within reach';[1267] and a third accused the police of using 'their truncheons freely over the heads of young and old' and of acting in a way that went 'far beyond the justification of necessity'.[1268] Even the more moderate *Morning Advertiser* suggested the police had, 'in many instances, exceeded their duty' and had 'resorted to force where no force was necessary.'[1269]

A letter to *The Times* on 3 July protested against 'the outrageous brutality displayed by the police force', accusing them of making 'periodical onslaughts among the crowd, striking indiscriminately with their truncheons all who happened to be in their way' whilst another letter likened the police unto 'a group of armed highwaymen.'[1270] Meanwhile, led by Thomas Duncombe, the Radical Member of Parliament for Finsbury, there were calls in the House of Commons for an inquiry to be set up to examine the conduct of the police.[1271]

Five days after the events, on 6 July, Mayne wrote to his wife:

1263 Ibid, p.xi.
1264 Ibid, p.xxxii.
1265 Ibid, pp.xxxii to xxxiii.
1266 *London Daily News*, 2 July 1855, p.5.
1267 *Illustrated London News*, 7 July 1855, p.11.
1268 *John Bull*, 2 July 1855, p.16.
1269 *Morning Advertiser*, 2 July 1855, p.4.
1270 *The Times*, 3 July 1855.
1271 HC Deb 05 July and 06 July 1855, vol, 139, cc 452-63 and 519-31.

> 'Sir George has acted very well, but I expect will yield to the demands for enquiry by a Commission Committee of the House of Commons; to that enquiry I object, as there is no ground shewn for it, and all such enquiries weaken authority, and the Tribunal is a bad one for enquiry; however I personally fear no enquiry. Waddington[1272] is decided in favour of all that has been done by Police, and says the only reason to make him assent to House of Commons enquiry, would be to show a set of Bobbies how wrong they are.'[1273]

Two days later, Mayne wrote again to his wife, this time at some length. It will be seen that, after a brief comment about the problems the police faced on the previous day, most of the letter was concerned with his relationship with Hay and this, together with comments made in a letter to his wife on 8 July, show just how far the relationship between the two Commissioners had broken down:

> 'Yesterday was a day of riots and Police movements. You will see by Newspapers that there was much damage done in Belgravia and other parts, by breaking windows. I am sorry to say, likewise, that Sir George Seymour was severely cut on the head by stones; Altogether the rioting was most disgraceful and I should be ashamed for Police; but after all the abuse by Press and Parliament (some MPs) during the past week, it will be useful to let the Public feel what a riotous mob is. I was at work until past 12 o'clock night. Sir G. Grey and Waddington approve of Police operations, and I believe so do the Community. The Newspapers behaved infamously; there is in *The Times* of this morning, one of the most untruthful and disgraceful Articles I have ever read. I may mention to you that Sir G had asked on Saturday for Captain Hay – said he wished to see him – that he was a Commissioner of Police and might complain if he were not consulted, etc. I only replied that Captain H was I believe in Blackheath, and had been unwell. Sir G however desired Waddington to write to him – that he had asked to see him – but not, if he were unwell, to give him the trouble of coming up on Sunday. But the Captain however came up, and I met him with all due civility; he talked in the silliest way possible, and having him up to the Park, again talked mischievous nonsense. I said nothing at the time, but resolved on my course; this morning, after a short preface, I told

---

1272 Horatio Waddington was the permanent under-secretary in the Home Office from 1848 to 1867.
1273 Henry Hall Collection, op. cit. 1246, letter 101, from Mayne to his wife, dated 6 July 1855, p.215.

Waddington, referring to what passed yesterday, that I must distinctly let Sir G know I could not continue to carry on Police operations jointly with Captain Hay. W at once said he had never heard such proofs of imbecility, and that he, Captain H, was evidently unfit for the situation; and he thought Sir G would see that from what had passed yesterday, and he would speak to Sir G on the subject. I have since told Sir G the same as I had to W; he said W had spoken to him, and he asked where Captain H was today. I said he had not come up to town. So you see the long agitated question is thus brought to a climax.'[1274]

In a letter to his wife, dated 12 July, Mayne wrote:

'These are, I can assure you, no idle times for me. In addition to ordinary and extraordinary Police work, I have been before a Committee of the House of Commons for a long time this morning. I told them my opinion, which will I dare say make some people consider me a mere Heathen, that I thought the law closing public houses from half past two to 8 o'clock on Sundays, was unreasonable, and ought not to be maintained.'[1275]

Three days later, in another letter to his wife, Mayne wrote:

'I have seen Sir George and Waddington, and we to have a consultation tomorrow as to arrangements for next Sunday. I don't know what the chances are of a row – by the bye, I have heard no more of Captain Hay, and he has not been at the office since Sunday. I am sure his exhibition of talent and discretion on that day, ought to bring his official course to a close, but I dare say he does not think so. I suspect he has had a hint to keep away, from high quarters. I wish sincerely for his own sake as well as on other accounts, that he would resign.'[1276]

The 1855 Commission had the higher status of a Royal Commission.[1277] Therefore, unlike the committee set up twelve years previously to examine the circumstances surrounding Cold Bath Fields, which had been made up of some twenty parliamentarians, this Commission consisted of just three barristers, the Rt Hon James Wortley MP, who had been appointed a Queen's Council in 1841, the year before he was elected as the Member of Parliament for Bute; Robert Baynes Armstrong, former Recorder of Hull,

---

1274 Henry Hall Collection, op. cit. 1246, letter 102, from Mayne to his wife, dated 8 July 1855, pp.216-218.
1275 Ibid, letter 104, from Mayne to his wife, dated 12 July 1855, pp.219-220.
1276 Ibid, letter 105, from Mayne to his wife, dated 15 July 1855, pp.221-222.
1277 Critchley, T.A (1970). *The Conquest of Violence: Order and Liberty in Britain*. London: Constable, p.146.

Leeds, Manchester and Bolton; and Gilbert Henderson, former Recorder of Liverpool. On being told the make-up of the Commission, Mayne wrote to his wife on 10 July:

> 'Waddington tells me the Commission to enquire into the conduct of the Police on Sunday last, are Armstrong (you may remember meeting at Heywoods), Henderson of Liverpool (has a pretty wife), and Wortley. These are good men for the work, and I shall be surprised if we (Police) don't make out a good case.'[1278]

Mayne's confidence in the three Commissioners turned out to be somewhat misplaced given their findings. Not only were the witnesses rigorously questioned by the three Commissioners but some were subjected to more questions from two barristers, a Mr. Mitchell, 'a respectable and intelligent attorney', who represented some of the complainants, and a Mr. Ellis, 'who conducted the case on behalf of the police'.[1279] In many respects, therefore, it was more like a criminal court.

The Commission began its work on 17 July, investigating allegations against the conduct of individual police officers, including Superintendent Hughes and, to a lesser extent, Superintendent O'Brien, and the more general complaints of a failure to grant bail to those arrested for minor offences, together with the overcrowded and unsatisfactory conditions under which they were detained at Vine Street Police Station.

The Commission sat for 15 days between its commencement and 2 August, during which time it heard evidence from around 120 members of the public, including military officers and barristers, most of whom had been present in Hyde Park or in the vicinity of Lord Grosvenor's House on 1 July, and nearly 60 police officers. Most were constables, sergeants and inspectors, but they included Sir Richard Mayne and Superintendents Hughes, Martin and O'Brien. A clearly unwell Superintendent May also gave evidence[1280] but he died a short while later, on 7 December 1855.

Mayne gave evidence before the Commission on the opening day. Clearly under some pressure by this time, Mayne had written to his wife on the previous day:

> 'I have not been at Church for 3 Sundays. So much for the effects on me of Lord R. Grosvenor's Bill for the better observance of the Sabbath. Today, between 12 and 1, I walked quietly round the enclosure, St James's Park, meditating and praying, which I hope I did as effectively

---

1278 Henry Hall Collection, op. cit. 1246, letter 103, from Mayne to his wife, dated 10 July, p.218.
1279 PP 1856 [2016], op. cit. 1235. Report, p.v.
1280 Ibid.

as if I had been in Church.'[1281]

He also mentions that, each morning, he read 'a few verses of The Epistle to the Romans'.

When it reported, the Commission refused to recognize any right to public assembly in Hyde Park. Meetings should be 'interdicted or suppressed' it said, for 'to make Hyde-park an arena for the discussion of popular and exciting topics would be inconsistent with the chief purpose for which it was thrown open to and used by the public.'[1282] The Commission decided that the police had two objectives on 1 July:

- Firstly, to protect persons using the Drive and keep the carriageway clear.

- Secondly, to check shouts and noise and other behaviour which might alarm horses, thus endangering the health of those using the carriageway for recreational purposes.

The most effective way to do this, suggested the Commission, was to remove and keep people some distance from the rails so that the noises and gestures of the crowd would produce less effect.[1283]

In his letter to his wife on 16 July, Mayne wrote 'I have no grounds whatsoever for believing that the Police did use unnecessary force in the Park'[1284] but the inquiry pointed out that the number of witnesses accusing the police of using unnecessary force were 'numerous'. Amongst these were nine of the seventy-two people who had been arrested[1285] and twelve people who had made specific complaints against individual officers who it was claimed they could identify.[1286] But, 'there were also many witnesses who came forward, impelled', they said, 'by a sense of justice, and bore testimony to the good conduct of the police in all that fell under their observation.'[1287]

The Commission found that 'none of the crowd came armed in any manner, and that no violence seems to have been contemplated by the general mass even of those who conducted themselves in a disorderly or riotous manner.' Rather, 'their intention seems to have been, to limit their interference to shouts and petty annoyances to those riding or driving in

---

1281 Henry Hall Collection, op. cit. 1246, letter 106 from Mayne to his wife, dated 16 July 1855, p.226.
1282 Critchley, op. cit. 1277. pp.146-147.
1283 PP 1856 [2016], op. cit. 1235, Report, pp.x-xi.
1284 Henry Hall Collection, op. cit. 1246 and 1281.
1285 PP 1856 [2016], op. cit. 1235. Report, pp.xviii-xxiv.
1286 Ibid, pp.xxviii-xxx.
1287 Ibid, p.x.

the Park.' However, the Commission did point out the crowd contained 'a sprinkling of bad and dangerous persons, who required the control of the police, and who, but for such control, might have led the way and been followed by the thoughtless and inconsiderate to mischief and damage to property, the extent of which would only have been limited by the resistance met with.' Whatever is said about 'the conduct of police, their presence and acts on the 1st of July,' the Commission felt their presence had prevented such mischief and damage to property. [1288]

Nevertheless, the Commission found that excessive and unnecessary force was used on a number of occasions and seemed to place most of the blame initially on Superintendent Hughes, although Mayne did not escape some of the blame. Insofar as Superintendent Hughes was concerned, he was accused of 'undue excitement', of using improper language, of many assaults with his horsewhip, with directing officers to use their truncheons without sufficient grounds and, having done so, of failing to control the police under his command.

Throughout the operation Superintendent Hughes was on horseback, and he was accused 'failing to control many excesses on the part of police under his command.'[1289] In his evidence to the Commission about the use of truncheons, Hughes claimed the situation had reached a critical stage, when, unless they were controlled, 'the dangerous elements in the crowd would become unmanageable' and cause 'serious mischief'. However, the Commission pointed out that after weighing all the evidence, the resort to violence at this stage was not warranted because:

- No attack had been made by the people;
- No combined or serious resistance had been made to the police; the carriages and riders passing were few; and
- Many 'inoffensive individuals' were mixed up with the disorderly portion of the crowd.

Insofar as the accusation of 'undue excitement' was concerned, the Commission felt that allowances ought to be made considering the 'difficulties' he faced. In response to the use of the horsewhip on people, no-one came forward to say they had been struck with the whip and the Commission accepted Superintendent Hughes' assertion that he had merely 'cut the air' to encourage people to move.[1290]

However, the Commission was critical of the use of truncheons, claiming

1288 Ibid.
1289 Ibid, p.xii.
1290 Ibid.

that 'if the order to use staves had been strictly limited to the clearance of the road,' it might have been justified.[1291] But, the Commission report continued, 'there was not the same necessity to drive the crowds from the railings, and still less to clear the space between the rails and the water of the Serpentine, to which object it is clear the order extended, and it was in the course of executing it' that a number of people were struck. Indeed, 'up to a late hour in the evening, when groups were collected even at a distance from the drive, parties of police came rushing forwards, and used staves to disperse them.'[1292]

Whilst, as already stated, the Commission appreciated the difficulties that the police faced on the day, it decided that he 'exercised less control over his men than a due regard for the safety of unoffending individuals required' and suggested that had Hughes adopted 'a more calm and forbearing course... much excitement at the time and complaint afterwards would have been avoided.'[1293]

Mayne had apparently mentioned this in the forenoon verbally to Superintendent Hughes, and confirmed it in writing at 5.00pm. However, the Commission pointed out that it was 'an operation requiring judicious management, not to be attempted with an inadequate force, and every precaution which, tact and temper in dealing with a crowd, could supply.'[1294]

The Home Secretary received a copy of the report prior to publication, and he instructed the Under-Secretary of State, William Massey, to send a copy to Mayne together with a covering letter. The content of the letter would have been of considerable concern to him, because whilst it commenced by saying that although the 'interference of the police was indispensably necessary' in that it 'had the effect of preventing... mischief and damage to property', he nevertheless found 'with great regret' that 'charges of serious misconduct on the part of some members of the force' had been upheld.[1295]

Sir George said that he presumed that 'Superintendent Hughes was not responsible for the amount of the force at first employed, which must have been determined by the Commissioners of Police, and that the strong reinforcements which arrived between half-past 3 and half-past 5 o'clock were sent on his application.'

1291 Ibid, p.xi.
1292 Massey's letter to Mayne, 16 November 1855, contained in PP 1856 [2016], op. cit. 1235. Report, p.xxxi. William Massey, the Member of Parliament for Oldham, was the under-secretary of state in the Home Office from 1855 to 1858.
1293 Ibid.
1294 Ibid.
1295 Massey's letter to Mayne, ibid, p.xxxi.

However, Sir George continued,

'there can be no question but that calmness and forbearance are as essential as firmness and resolution in an officer placed in command of a body of men engaged in preserving the public peace, and that a marked or habitual absence of these qualities would render a man wholly unfit for such a position. Sir George Grey has carefully considered the facts of the case as stated in the Report, and the opinion of the Commissioners, in order to determine whether the conduct of Superintendent Hughes, under the circumstances in which he as placed on the 1st July, was such as to disqualify him from holding the office of a Superintendent of Police' but 'after taking in account all the circumstances as detailed by the Commissioners, and after considering the long service of Superintendent Hughes in the force, and the general approval with which he had during such service discharged duties requiring great judgement and discretion, Sir George Grey is of the opinion that, while it is necessary to mark with censure the conduct which the Commissioners have thought justly liable to blame, his dismissal from his office would be harsh and uncalled for.'

As a result, Mayne was instructed to convey the disapproval of the Secretary of State to Superintendent Hughes and impress upon him, 'in the strongest possible terms, the necessity of maintaining perfect self-control in the performance of his highly responsible duties, and of checking, both by his example and his orders, any necessary violence on the part of those under his command.'[1296]

The next section of Sir George's letter was, to a large extent a criticism of Sir Richard in that the Secretary of State supported the view of the Commissioners that a 'superior officer of the police' should have been on the spot and that on such occasions 'a force fully adequate for the duty it may be called upon to perform' should be present.[1297]

The letter then went on to identify eight officers, seven constables and a sergeant, against whom criminal charges should be brought, two cases of 'unjustifiable apprehension' and six cases of 'unnecessary', 'illegal' or 'reckless' violence against people who were present either in the Park or in the vicinity of Lord Grosvenor's house.[1298]

The letter then detailed the action Mayne was expected to take in respect of the accused officers:

1296 PP 1856 [2016], op. cit. 1235, Report, p.xxxii.
1297 Ibid.
1298 Ibid, pp.xxxii-xxxiii.

- Police Constable 398A William Gearing, to be charged with the apprehension, without sufficient ground of J.J. White, and of inexcusable violence to him while in custody.
- Police Constable 363A George Thorpe, to be charged with the unjustifiable apprehension of Henry Austin.
- Police Constable 20D William Bewley, to be charged with the unnecessary violence towards William Floyd and James Vassie.
- Police Constable 147A Charles Leach, to be charged with unnecessary and reckless violence towards John Thomas King.
- Police Constable 84C Charles Madgett, to be charged with taking part in violence against William Stephens.
- Police Constables 375A James Teasdale and 385A Thomas Wade, to be charged with violence towards persons who were not known or examined.
- Police Sergeant 21C Vincent Gummer, to be charged with unjustifiable violence in dispersing the crowd in Park Street.

Because the violence inflicted by Gearing, Bewley and Madgett were so 'gross and unprovoked, Sir George Grey instructed Mayne to prefer indictments against each of them with a view to sending them for trial. Insofar as the remainder were concerned, with the exception of Leach, who had left the Force in August, he was instructed to 'award in each case such punishment, either by suspension or dismissal,' as he thought fit, following 'the ordinary course adopted by the Commissioners in the case of constables who are proved to have committed illegal or unjustifiable acts in the performance of their duty.'[1299]

Following the findings of the Commission, Sir George Grey was also critical of the inadequate arrangements made for the large numbers of persons taken to and kept in custody at Vine Street Police Station and the failure to grant bail to those charged with minor offences sufficiently quickly. Finally, he asked Mayne 'to consider whether any alteration can be made in the manner of affixing these numbers and letters in order to afford greater facility for prompt and easy identification.'[1300]

Prior to the publication of the Commission's report, Mayne had already informed the Home Office that the police should not attempt to disperse a disorderly crowd unless they were present in sufficient numbers to do so effectively. Any success by the crowd, he said, could encourage other

---

1299 Ibid.
1300 Ibid, p.xxxiv.

people 'to oppose the police with force and the consequences might be serious.'[1301] In doing so he had obviously learnt a lesson from the events in Birmingham in 1839 as well as this latest incident, and might well have been anticipating the Commission's judgement on the latter.

In its final report, the Commission criticised the dispersal operation for not occupying and keeping 'a line along the cleared space, so as to prevent the return of the people; consequently crowds collected along the rails again, and were again driven back repeatedly, with more or less violence and confusion.'[1302]

The Commission went on to suggest that had 'the attempt' to disperse the crowds 'been made by an adequate force... the people might have been moved without resorting to the use of staves; but the attempts made with inadequate force produced much of the violence which cannot be justified.'[1303]

The events in Hyde Park on 1 July 1855 provided the Metropolitan Police with one of its sternest tests to date. Arguably, Mayne had not made sufficient arrangements, particularly in relation to the number of policemen available (it will be recalled that the notice he originally prepared and posted stated that 'all necessary resources would be taken to prevent' the meeting from taking place, and 'to preserve the public peace') to adequately police a crowd that, as he had seen the previous week, had the potential to cause disorder. There being no letters to his wife following the publication of the Commissioners' report – it is assumed she was in London – Mayne's personal views on the Commission's findings and the subsequent action he was ordered to take by the Home Secretary are unknown.

It would be interesting to speculate how Rowan would have policed this event had he been alive and still in the post of Commissioner. It is extremely unlikely that he would have based himself at 4 Whitehall Place for the duration, as Mayne did, relying on half-hourly reports from a superintendent at the scene. At the very least he would have found an observation point overlooking the scene, possibly in Park Lane, from where he would have directed the police response.

1301 Thurmond Smith, op, cit. 1238, p.118.
1302 PP 1856 [2016], op. cit. 1235. Report, p.vii.
1303 Ibid, p.xi.

CHAPTER TWENTY-ONE

MAYNE IN SOLE CHARGE

Captain Hay died at his home address at 12, Eaton Place South, Eaton Square, on 29 August 1855. He was 67 years of age.[1304] Following his death, Mayne assumed sole command. For a brief period, he relied on his Inspecting Superintendent, Labalmondière, for support, sending him off to France for nearly two weeks in August, to accompany Queen Victoria and Prince Albert on a state visit.[1305] The following year the 1856 Metropolitan Police Act[1306] did away with the requirement to have two Commissioners. Instead, it allowed for the appointment of two assistant commissioners, and both were appointed with effect from 3 March. Captain William Charles Harris, formerly of the 68th Regiment and chief constable of the Hampshire County Constabulary from 1843,[1307] was appointed as the first Assistant Commissioner (Executive). He was responsible for the executive business of the force, together with supplies and buildings. Labalmondière became the second Assistant Commissioner and his responsibilities included internal discipline. As such he was required to make quarterly inspections of every station and section house in the Metropolitan Police District.[1308]

Although there were some events that required large-scale planning during the first few years Mayne was in sole charge, there was nothing of huge significance until 1862. In the meantime, the two newly appointed Assistant Commissioners adapted comfortably to their new roles, although Labalmondière had been doing very similar work since his appointment as the Inspecting Superintendent. However, by now Mayne had become

---

1304 *London Evening News*, 30 August 1855, p.2.
1305 Fido, Martin, and Keith Skinner (1999). *The Official Encyclopedia of Scotland Yard*. London: Virgin Books, p. 142. .
1306 19 Vict., c.2.
1307 *London Gazette*, dated 4 March 1856, number 21857, p.918. Captain Harris had been an impressive witness before the 1952-53 Committee on Police (see Chapter Nineteen).
1308 *London Gazette*, dated 4 March 1856, number 21857, p.918.

'somewhat autocratic, reluctant to delegate even minor responsibilities to his two Assistant Commissioners' or 'to receive advice or readily countenance significant change'.[1309]

Only six days after Hay's death, Mayne was required to police the last great Chartist event, the funeral of Feargus O'Connor, who Mayne had persuaded to abandon any attempt to march on Parliament seven years previously. The funeral cortege formed up outside the Prince Albert public house, in Notting Hill, and moved off shortly after two o'clock. Following the cortege were approximately 10,000 people walking four to six abreast. Between 30,000 and 40,000 people lined the streets as the cortege wound its way along Westbourne Grove and into Harrow Road, taking two hours to reach the Kensal Green cemetery. After it entered the cemetery, for some unexplained reason the gates were closed and locked but were 'unceremoniously' broken open. Mayne had instructed police to keep a low profile but plain-clothes officers mingling with the crowds arrested a number of people for pickpocketing.[1310]

In February 1856, Mayne was required to give evidence before a Coroner's Court sitting at the Elephant and Castle to enquire into the death of Elizabeth Saunders, who had been crushed to death when a wall at Messrs Hodgkinson's factory, in Diana Place, collapsed onto houses following an earlier fire. One of the ever-increasing non-police duties placed on the police was a requirement, under the Metropolitan Building Act,[1311] for the Commissioner to have dangerous structures inspected by 'the district surveyor, or some other competent person'. After hearing from Mayne how he had personally complied with the Act, the Coroner said that 'no blame' could be attached 'to the police authorities.'[1312] Mayne must have been particularly pleased when, in September 1858, John Fisher, the chief surgeon virtually since the inception of the force, was knighted.[1313]

Despite the limited time they had off-duty, Metropolitan Police officers increasingly pursued leisure activities that enhanced the reputation of the force. Their involvement in cricket, with teams from within the Metropolitan Police either playing each other or local traders, grew during the late 1850s and early 1860s. The earliest reported match took place towards the end of August 1858 at Plaistow Grove, West Ham, when

---

1309 Roach, Lawrence (2004). 'The Origins and Impact of the Function of the Crime Investigation and Detection in the British Police Service': A thesis submitted in partial fulfilment of the requirements for the Degree of Doctor of Philosophy of Loughborough University: Loughborough University's Institutional Repository, p.374.
1310 *Reynolds's Weekly News*, 5 September & 16 September 1855.
1311 18 & 19 Vict., c.122.
1312 *The Times*, 6 February 1856, p.7.
1313 *Morning Chronicle*, 11 September 1858, p.4.

teams consisting of constables and sergeants from Poplar and West Ham – both then within K Division – met, with the latter winning the match by one run.[1314] The following month two matches between Kingsland and Hackney Sub-divisions were played. Both 'healthy and good-natured contests... excited much interest in the locality', as a result of which the 'police and tradesmen of Kingsland' then met in a match.[1315] The following year, N Division defeated the Kingsland tradesmen by 24 runs.[1316] In June 1860 two teams from N Division, representing Hoxton and Kingsland, met at Victoria Park 'with great spirit and skill' which was 'witnessed with interest by a large number of spectators.' Following the game the players and their friends, including respectable residents of the area, sat down to dinner at the White Lion Tavern, Hackney Wick.[1317] The following year, it was reported the annual cricket match between eleven gentlemen of Islington and N Division of the Metropolitan Police took place at Wood Green, with the police winning by five wickets. After the game, there was a dinner for 70 guests at the Jolly Butchers Tavern, with entertainment provided by the N Division police band.[1318] In April 1862, the first cricket match of the season involving police teams, between Paddington and Marylebone Lane, took place at Kilburn Park, with the former winning by five runs. The match was watched by between two and three hundred people, who were entertained by the D Division police band.[1319] In the summer of 1863 A and T Divisions met twice, firstly on Shepherd's Bush Common and then at a cricket ground in Vincent Square, Westminster; both games were won by T Division.[1320] In the same year, T Division was beaten by a team representing Holland Park Estate at 'Mr Tindall's ground at Holland Park Farm.'[1321]

From 1860 onwards, the number of divisional brass bands grew steadily. In April of that year 'the first instrumental and vocal concert, undertaken solely by the police since the formation of the force, was given by the M or Southwark Division' band. The concert, in front of nearly one thousand people including Sir Richard and Lady Mayne and two of their sons, most likely Robert, then 15, and Charles, 13, was held at the Queen Elizabeth Grammar School in Southwark. The M Division band was assisted by a junior band at the school, and Sir Richard and Lady Mayne were greeted

---

1314 *Chelmsford Chronicle*, 3 September 1858, p.4.
1315 *Globe*, 27 September 1858, p.3.
1316 *Morning Advertiser*, 11 October 1859, p.3.
1317 *Shoreditch Observer*, 30 June 1860, p.3.
1318 *North London News*, 21 September 1861, p.4.
1319 *Morning Advertiser*, 28 April 1862, p.2.
1320 *West London Observer*, 22 August 1863, p.3; *Morning Advertiser*, 8 September 1863, p.3.
1321 *West London Observer*, 22 September 1863, p.3.

'with true military honours' on their arrival by 'a company of young riflemen belonging to the school who were lined up as a guard of honour on both sides of the entrance.' The police band played 'several airs from popular operas' which 'were received with rounds of applause.' The concert ended with the police band, together with the junior band, playing the National Anthem.[1322] Thereafter, regular reports of performances by police bands appeared in newspapers. In May, P Division band gave a performance;[1323] in August, the G (Finsbury) Division band gave a concert at Zion College, London Wall;[1324] and, in December, the H Division band gave a performance of instrumental music at a school in St. Mary Street, Whitechapel, to 'a very large and appreciative audience.'[1325]

Increasingly, police bands were invited to play at events unconnected with the force. In February 1864 the V Division band was reported to have played at several venues in Richmond;[1326] in October, the N Division band played at the North London Industrial Exhibition.[1327] In June 1867 the G Division band played at the Middlesex County Ground, Caledonian Road, Islington,[1328] and in May 1868 the N Division band accompanied the Commodore in a procession of boats to inaugurate the opening of the rowing season on the River Lea.[1329]

Mayne obviously encouraged such off-duty activities. Whilst there is no evidence of him attending a cricket match, he was regularly seen, often with his wife and sometimes his children, at concerts given by police bands. Given Mayne's iron grip on what police officers were permitted and not permitted to do, even when off-duty, it is unlikely that the cricket matches, particularly against outside bodies, took place without his approval.

In May 1860, Mayne opposed a further attempt to restrict Sunday trading when the Selling and Hawking of Goods on Sunday Prevention Bill came before the House of Lords, telling those members of the House who sought his advice[1330] that such restrictions 'could not be carried into effect ... without imposing great and considerable trouble on the force'. He warned that it would 'lead to serious collisions between the people and the

---

1322 *Morning Advertiser*, 16 April 1860, p.3.
1323 *South London Chronicle*, 26 May 1860, p.4.
1324 *London City Press*, 11 August 1860, p.5.
1325 *East London Observer*, 8 December 1860, p.2.
1326 *Surrey Comet*, 27 February 1864, p.4.
1327 *Morning Advertiser*, 24 October 1864, p.1.
1328 *Morning Advertiser*, 10 June 1867; founded on 2 February 1864, Middlesex County Cricket Club played their first match against Sussex County Cricket Club on this ground on 6 & 7 July 1864.
1329 *Sporting Life*, 13 May 1868, p.3.
1330 For instance, see the speech by the Earl of St. Germans in the House of Lords on 3 May 1860. Hansard HL Deb 03 May 1860. Vol.158, cc547-551.

police' which would 'tend to make the police unpopular.'[1331]

A fire in Tooley Street in 1861, described as the greatest fire since the Great Fire of London in 1661 occurred at Cotton's Wharf, where many warehouses, stored with jute, hemp, cotton, spices and coffee, were located. It began on the afternoon of 22 June, and by 6.00pm the London Fire Engine Establishment (LFEE) had fourteen fire engines, including a steam fire engine and a floating engine, at the scene. The fire spread quickly because the iron fire doors, which separated many of the storage rooms in the warehouses, had, contrary to advice, been left open. It took two weeks to finally extinguish. Twenty police officers were present throughout the fire-fighting operation.[1332] Unfortunately the front section of a warehouse collapsed on top of the Superintendent of the LFEE, James Braidwood, killing him instantly.[1333] The total cost of the damage was £2 million and, following this fire, fire insurance companies raised premiums.

Mayne's response was to propose to the Home Office that the Metropolitan Police 'should take responsibility for a metropolitan fire brigade'. But when he submitted his proposal to Home Secretary Sir George Grey, it was too expensive. Instead, the Home Office proposed the government would fund a police-run brigade that would be funded partly by insurance companies. This was immediately challenged by the City of London on the basis that it had its own police force, and the City of London Corporation demanded that its police should run a separate City fire brigade. When this proved unacceptable to the government the Metropolitan Board of Works (MBW) was called upon to raise a fire brigade, thus adding to its growing empire.[1334] The Metropolitan Fire Brigade Act, setting up the Metropolitan Fire Brigade as a public service, eventually came into being at the beginning of 1866.[1335]

R Division had taken over the responsibility of policing Deptford and Woolwich dockyards in April 1841.[1336] Some nineteen years later, in 1860, five dockyard divisions of the Metropolitan Police were formed at Woolwich, Portsmouth, Devonport, Chatham and Sheerness, and Pembroke with a total establishment by 1868 of 710 men.[1337] Having

1331 *Morning Advertiser*, 4 May 1860, p.2.
1332 See www.london-fire.gov.uk/museum/history-and-stories/the-tooley-street-fire accessed 3 February 2019.
1333 *Reynolds's Weekly Newspaper*, 30 June 1861, pp.3-4.
1334 Travers, Tony (2015). *London Boroughs at 50*. London: Biteback Publishing. The pages are unnumbered, but the information is contained in the section entitled 'The growth of London and the need for government.'
1335 Vict. 28-29, ch. 90.
1336 Bunker, John (1988). *From Rattle to Radio*. Studley, Warwickshire: Brewin Books, p.12.
1337 Ibid, p.19.

taken over the policing of the Dockyards, Sir Richard and Lady Mayne, in the company of Superintendent Mallalieu, who had been appointed the Inspecting Superintendent of the Dockyard Police, went on a tour of the various locations in late 1861, visiting Portsmouth in early November, where they also attended a concert given by the Portsmouth Dockyard police band at the drill-hall of the 3rd Hampshire Artillery Corps.[1338] At Chatham in early December, as part of Mayne's tour, he and Lady Mayne attended a lecture given by a Mr Litchfield to the assembled police officers on 'The Past and Present Modes of Conveyance'.[1339] Later, in October 1865, Mayne oversaw the formation of three more Metropolitan Police divisions – W (Clapham), X (Paddington) and Y (Highgate) – and by 1 January 1866 the strength of the force stood at 7,493.[1340]

The year 1862 was the beginning of a six-year period during which Mayne faced an increasing number of problems, some of which, it could be argued, were of his own making; others he had no control over. They included an outbreak of a particularly obnoxious and painful type of crime, a threat on his life, renewed disturbances in Hyde Park, his refusal to allow police officers to administer corporal punishment ordered by juvenile courts, resulting in criticism in the House of Lords, the attempted release of Fenian prisoners from the House of Detention at Clerkenwell, and finally, just before his death, the ignominy of appearing in court as a defendant in a libel case brought by a former inspector he had dismissed from the police.

The cause of the first of these arose because of the substitution of transportation overseas with penal servitude and release on licence, commonly referred to as ticket-of-leave. This was followed by an increase in violent crimes which, according to one author, led to a 'return to something like pre-1829 conditions',[1341] with 'the public, angry and alarmed', and increasingly being 'afraid to go out after dark'. The ticket-of-leave system, a product of the Penal Servitude Act of 1853,[1342] was intended to ensure supervision of convicts released on licence before their sentences expired, but the Home Office had issued instructions that the police were on no account to question or interfere with these men, who

---

1338 *Hampshire Telegraph*, 9 November 1861, p.4.
1339 *Morning Advertiser*, 8 December 1861, p.3.
1340 PP 1867 [392] Police (metropolis). Return of the strength of each division of the Metropolitan Police Force on 1st January 1846, 1865 and 1866, together with the additions made to the force during the above-mentioned periods.
1341 Moylan, J.F (1929). *Scotland Yard and The Metropolitan Police*. London: G.P. Putnam's Sons, p.37.
1342 Browne, Douglas G (1956). *The Rise of Scotland Yard; A History of the Metropolitan Police*. London: George G. Harrop, p.135.

'almost invariably destroyed their licences (which they were not compelled to keep), and, if apprehended for a fresh offence, or on suspicion, stoutly denied that they had previously been convicted: nor was it easy for the authorities to prove the contrary in the absence of any proper system for the registration of convicts.'[1343]

Mayne was disgusted with this 'ill-directed humanitarianism', and washed his hands of the whole affair, telling the House of Commons Select Committee on Transportation in 1856 that 'until a few months before he had never seen a ticket-of-leave and did not know what was endorsed on it.' It was a strange thing for him to say, because 'the non-enforcement of the conditions under which these licences were issued was very much the business of the constable on the beat,' but, even though the criminal was known to him, he could take no action 'unless he caught them actually committing a crime.'[1344]

There had already been a scare in 1856, when there were an increasing number of newspaper reports of the crime of garrotting. However, this quickly subsided following heavy sentences imposed at the Old Bailey in the November.[1345] However, in 1862 the crime received more widespread publicity, leading to questions in the House of Commons, following an attack on Hugh Pilkington, the Member of Parliament for Blackburn. Garrotting occurred when 'one ruffian [came] up behind an unsuspecting wayfarer, put a hand over his shoulder and [compressed] his throat while a confederate rifled his pockets.' Because his throat was compressed the victim could not cry out, and 'he was left writhing on the ground with his tongue protruding' and 'was quite unable to describe his assailants.'[1346] Pilkington was garrotted on 17 July, on his way to his hotel, having just left the House of Commons. When he reached the hotel it was found that he had severe contusions on his head and a cut on his jaw. There were also signs of a garrote, often a piece of wire, having been placed around his throat.[1347] The following day in Parliament Lord Lennox questioned Home Secretary Sir George Grey about the attack, and was told that Sir Richard Mayne had already been asked for a report.[1348] But it was just the beginning

---

1343 Ibid, p.136.
1344 Ibid.
1345 Sindall, R (1987). 'The London garrotting panics of 1856 and 1862'. *Social History*, Vol.12, No.3 (Oct), p.353.
1346 Thomson, Sir Basil (1936). *The Story of Scotland Yard*. New York: The Literary Guild, p.145; the term 'garrotte' came from the Spanish instrument of execution known as 'the garotta'- see Ibid, p.352; in more serious cases, wire would be used to compress the throat.
1347 *Morning Post*, 18 July 1862, p.2.
1348 HC Deb 17 July 1862. Vol. 168, cc. 425-426.

of a series of such attacks. Between June and December there were at least eighty-two cases of garrotting in London alone.[1349] Mayne's response was to order seventeen sergeants and 176 constables to be taken from beat duty and employed in plain clothes between 10.00pm and 2.00am throughout the Force area.[1350] This operation met with some success, and towards the end of the year a number of 'garrotters' appeared at the Central Criminal Court, and were given heavy sentences.[1351]

In giving evidence to the Commission appointed to inquire into the Operation of the Acts relating to Transportation and Penal Servitude in February the following year, Mayne expressed the view that the sentences had had a deterrent effect.[1352] He also told the Commission that a) those released on a ticket-to-leave basis should be required to report to the police station of the area in which they intended to live immediately on arrival and at the commencement of each month thereafter, and b) police officers should be allowed at any time to ask such a person how he obtained his living.[1353]

In October 1862 Mayne was required to attend Bow Street Magistrates' Court during the trial of John Tremlett, who was charged with sending a threatening letter to Sir Richard. When Tremlett claimed he had made no threat against Sir Richard, the magistrate sent for the Commissioner 'to ascertain what interpretation he had put on it.' Mayne said he had received the letter by post and claimed that 'the mention of the murderer Rush,[1354] and also the allusion to the other murderer Williams,[1355] made me think that what was in the writer's mind was, that he contemplated killing me or somebody [else].' Agreeing with Mayne's interpretation, the magistrate freed Tremlett when two sureties entered into recognizances, but 'cautioned him that if he wrote to Sir Richard Mayne, or anyone else, more letters containing similar threats he would be committed for trial.'[1356]

Mainland Britain was remarkably free from serious disorder arising

---

1349 Melville Lee, Captain W.L (1901). *A History of Police in England*. London: Methuen, p.341, footnote 1.
1350 TNA MEPO 7/23. Metropolitan Police Order, 14 August 1862.
1351 For example, see Old Bailey Proceedings Online (www.oldbaileyonline.org, version 8.0, 22 May 2019) November 1862, trial of GEORGE ROBERTS (33), SAMUEL ANDERSON (t18621124-36).
1352 PP 1863 [6457]. Report of the Commission appointed to Inquire into the Operation of the Acts (16 & 17 Vict. c.99 and 20 & 21 Vict. c.3) relating to Transportation and Penal Servitude. Volume II, p.151, q/a 1836.
1353 Ibid, p.131, q/a 1631-1635.
1354 Rush was hanged at Norwich Castle for the murder of a father and son at Stanfield Hall, Norwich.
1355 Williams was the alias of John Murdock, the brother of Tremlett's daughter-in-law, who was hanged at Lewes in 1856 for murder. See *London Evening Standard*, 10 October 1862.
1356 *Morning Post*, 11 October 1862, p.7.

from religious quarrels during the nineteenth century, but the Garibaldi riots, which occurred between 1862 and 1864, went against the trend. So-called after an Italian political figure who was preaching secularism and republicanism in Europe, the riots brought English working men, who professed to support his view, into conflict with Irish workmen, who tended to be papist and monarchist, who were against. The first outbreak of serious disorder took the police by surprise. But given the advance publicity – notices had been widely distributed calling on people to attend a public meeting in favour of Garibaldi in Hyde Park on 28 September 1862 – it ought not to have. When the meeting began there were 12,000 and 15,000 people in attendance. The majority were English admirers of Garibaldi and Irish devotees of the Pope. When the meeting got underway the main speaker, Charles Bradlaugh, an English radical who campaigned for individual liberties, was interrupted when speaking from a mound of earth he was using as a platform by Irish supporters of the Pope. Using clubs, they attacked the Garibaldians on and surrounding the mound and drove them off. Arming themselves with sticks, and supported by a small group of Grenadier Guardsmen,[1357] the Garibaldians struck back and retook the mound, forcing the Irish men and women to flee, but attempts to resume the meeting were drowned out by the noise. The Irish regrouped, and later that afternoon, in even larger in numbers, forced the Garibaldians from the mound for a second time. They were still in occupation when torrential rain drove everyone from the Park. Only a few policemen were in attendance, and a few of the Irish contingent were arrested, although no soldiers or Garibaldians were taken into custody.[1358]

A repeat performance occurred the following Sunday, 5 October. Although no meeting was scheduled, a huge crowd, many of them spectators, assembled. The Garibaldians received even more support from soldiers and there were 'fierce struggles', with both sides armed with clubs and sticks, for control of the mound. Every so often, three or four police officers 'fixed their eyes on some prominent aggressor', and 'would thrust themselves fearlessly into a surging mass of 200 or 300 infuriated men, collar one, cling to him and hold him despite attempts made at escape' before bringing him out and, generally, but not always, 'conveying him away in safe custody.' As the afternoon wore on the number of soldiers involved increased to about 500, all of whom were on the Garibaldian's side.

[1357] *Morning Advertiser*, 29 September 1862, p.3, suggested they were from the Coldstream Guards.
[1358] *London Evening Standard*, 29 September 1862, p.6.

Later that afternoon, Mayne arrived with Assistant Commissioner Captain Harris. Mayne sent for pickets from the Grenadier Guards and the Fusiliers. When about fifty arrived under the command of an officer at around 5.30pm, half took possession of the mound whilst the remainder ordered soldiers back to their barracks. In the meantime, Harris had taken command of approximately four hundred police officers who were on reserve in the vicinity of Marble Arch and led them into the Park. As rain began to fall the crowd thinned out substantially, although, at seven o'clock, one thousand people remained. At least fifteen people were arrested and a further fifteen required treatment at St George's Hospital.[1359]

Following these events, Mayne issued a notice on 9 October which was widely circulated:

> 'Whereas numbers of persons have been in the habit of assembling and holding meetings on Sundays in Hyde Park, and the other parks in the metropolis, for the purpose of hearing and delivering speeches, and for the public discussion of popular and exciting topics; and whereas such meetings are inconsistent with the purpose for which the parks were thrown open to and used by the public; and the excitement occasioned by such discussions at such meetings has frequently led to tumult and disorder, so as to endanger the public peace; and on last Sunday, and the Sunday before large numbers of persons assembled in Hyde Park for the purpose aforesaid, and when so assembled conducted themselves in a riotous and disorderly manner, so as to endanger the public peace, and by the use of sticks, and throwing stones and other missiles, committed many violent assaults upon persons quietly passing along the Park and interrupted the thoroughfare; and whereas it is necessary to prevent such illegal proceedings in future:
>
> Notice is hereby given that no such meeting or assemblage of persons for any of the purposes aforesaid will be allowed hereafter to take place in any of the parks in the metropolis; and all well-disposed persons are hereby cautioned and requested to abstain from joining or attending any such meeting or assemblage.
>
> And notice is further given, that all necessary measures will be adopted to prevent such meetings or assemblages, and effectually to preserve the public peace, and to suppress any attempt at the disturbances thereof.'[1360]

1359 *Morning Post*, 6 October 1862, p.6; *London Evening Standard*, 6 October 1862, p.6.
1360 *London Evening Standard*, 11 October 1862, p.2.

Two days later Mayne issued a Police Order making it clear that on such occasions:

'The police patrolling should not interfere without special directions from the Assistant Commissioner, unless a breach of the peace occurred.

Any person seen committing an assault or other illegal act, such as carrying offensive weapons, is to be taken into custody but only if there are sufficient police present.

Police contingents on reserve at specified places close to Hyde Park will not move into the park until ordered to do so by the Assistant Commissioner.

Should there be any attempt to make a speech, the person is to be cautioned and if he refuses he should be removed from the park but 'it is desirable to avoid taking [such] persons into custody.'

The instruction concluded:

'The police are to be specially cautioned not to notice any offensive or angry language used towards them; if required to interfere, they are to do so with the necessary vigour to effect the object; but to show great forbearance towards all not actually engaged in the commission of illegal acts.'[1361]

For the third Sunday, 12 October, Mayne established a headquarters near the Powder Magazine[1362] in Hyde Park. Whilst Mayne was present – indeed, it is reported that he 'kept patrolling about' issuing instructions that people were not to be interfered with unless ordered to do so by himself or Assistant Commissioner Captain Harris – it was Harris who was effectively in command. At every gate leading into the park, police officers were under strict orders to stop anyone from entering the park carrying anything more formidable than a walking stick or umbrella. Military pickets were stationed at the entrances 'with orders to prevent any solider passing through.' Several hundred police officers, along with military pickets, were also deployed inside the park, the latter under orders to take into custody any soldier found in the park. Large bodies of police were on reserve nearby.

1361 TNA MEPO 7/23. Metropolitan Police Order, 17 October 1862, headed Meetings in Hyde Park or any Park in the Metropolis.
1362 The Powder Magazine had been opened in Hyde Park in 1805 as a Central London store of gunpowder in case of 'foreign invasion'. The building still stands and is now the Serpentine Sackler Gallery.

Despite Mayne's notice, heavy rain and the assumption no meeting would take place, between eight and ten thousand people had assembled in Hyde Park by two o'clock. Some thirty minutes later, 'several bodies of Irish labourers, 100 strong, evidently well-organised, and armed with bludgeons, arrived at the fence around the park.' To gain entry into the Park they broke into small groups and hid their bludgeons under their coats. But there was very little trouble. Anyone attempting to make any kind of speech was told to desist, and the police, acting 'with great forbearance', only stepped in to break-up crowds when the groups got too large. By five o'clock, heavy rain had forced most of the people to leave the park.[1363]

Sporadic outbreaks of disorder between English and Irish working-classes continued throughout 1863 and into the first part of 1864. Prevented from meeting in Hyde Park the confrontations occurred in other areas of London, predominantly – as one would expect – in those areas where there was a substantial Irish population; disorder also occurred in other towns, notably Birkenhead.

In April 1864, Garibaldi was widely acclaimed when he arrived in London, and although he was due to speak in a number of towns throughout England, ill-health forced him to leave before any of these engagements were undertaken. However, before he left he attended a banquet in his honour given by the Duke and Duchess of Sutherland[1364] at Stafford House. Following the banquet, an evening party was held by the Duchess at which many distinguished guests, including Sir Richard and Lady Mayne, and their daughter Georgina, were introduced 'to the distinguished Italian'.[1365]

A week later Mayne was told it was anticipated a large number of people would assemble in Russell Square and march via Bedford Square, Tottenham Court Road, Hampstead Road and Regent's Park Road to Primrose Hill, to take part in the ceremonial planting of an oak tree in commemoration of the 300th birthday of William Shakespeare. Mayne arranged for a total of 223 officers under Superintendent Loxton to police the event, with instructions that the route would not be lined, but officers instead would assemble, in groups, on street corners 'to be ready to act in preserving order and preventing obstruction of the thoroughfares.'[1366] Following the planting of the tree it became clear that it had been a cover for a Garibaldi meeting, when a representative of the Garibaldi Working

---

1363 *Morning Post*, 13 October 1862, p.5.
1364 A friend of Queen Victoria's, the Duchess of Sutherland held a position of high influence in London Society.
1365 *Morning Post*, 14 April 1864, p.5.
1366 TNA MEPO 7/25. Metropolitan Police Orders, 22 October 1864.

Men's Committee started to address the crowd. At this time it was estimated there were 50,000 people in attendance. When Inspector Stokes and Superintendent Loxton spoke to the members of the Committee the meeting was adjourned and people left the area.[1367]

A rare glimpse of Mayne at this time, now 63-years-old, can be seen through the eyes of a police officer serving at the time. Timothy Cavanagh described how he went before him on promotion to sergeant:

> 'I was ushered into his presence, and shall never forget the sensation I felt. It almost amounted to a feeling of awe. He continued writing while I stood to attention for I should say ten minutes, each minute making me feel more uneasy and uncomfortable. At last he put his pen on one side, and, without saying a word, looked me straight in the face – and he knew how to look. His glance seemed to go right through me. At length he said, "Mr Yardley has recommended you for promotion to the accountant's office. It is a very important position. I hope you will give him satisfaction." I bowed and left the room, a weight being lifted as I got outside the door, wondering whether I should ever have the ill-luck to go before him as a "defaulter".'[1368]

Cavanagh described his appearance as being 'about five feet eight inches, spare, but well-built, thin face, a very hard compressed mouth, grey hair and whiskers, an eye like that of a hawk, and a slightly limping gait, due, I believe, to rheumatic affection of the hip-joint.' He went on to describe how

> 'the amount of work done by the Commissioner was enormous. He was frequently at work from ten in the morning till late at night, himself answering most of the letters received, and superintending the most important of the departments of the office.'

Cavanagh acknowledged the role played by Charles Yardley. Pointing out he was about the same age as Mayne, he said "they never tired; and when the staff of 4, Whitehall Place were thoroughly beaten, the two veterans would go home perfectly fresh."[1369] But, shortly afterwards, Mayne suffered a tragic loss when Yardley, who had been the chief clerk virtually from the

---

1367 PP 1864 [252]. Primrose Hill meeting. Copy of the Reports of the Superintendent and Inspector in command of the Police employed at Primrose Hill on Saturday, 23rd April 1864; and of the Instructions to the Police to be on Duty on the occasion of the Meeting held there on that Day.
1368 Cavanagh, Timothy (1893). *Scotland Yard, Past and Present: Experiences of thirty-seven years*. London: Chatto & Windus, under the title Sir Richard Mayne, Loc.661.
1369 Ibid, Loc.674.

beginning, and was probably, to a large extent, Mayne's main confidante since the departure of Rowan, decided to retire. It was said that 'the last four years of Richard Mayne's life were undoubtedly made worse by the lack of the fine Chief Clerk who established the embryo Civil Staff' in the Metropolitan Police.[1370] Had Mayne had the presence of mind to follow Yardley's example, he would have saved himself much aggravation during those final four years.

In January 1865 Mayne issued yet another Police Order relating to the actions of officers on the street, this time concerning the arrest of people for obstructing a police officer. But, on this occasion, the officers concerned appeared in a good light:

> 'Obstructing Police in the Execution of their Duty – The attention of the whole of the Police is specially directed to the Police Orders 3rd June and 21st August 1830; 17 September 1842; and 19th April 1843 and to General Instruction 58 respective Police interfering unnecessarily with persons in the streets, or apprehending persons on charges of obstructing Police in the execution of their duty. As an instance of the support the Police will receive when acting properly and with forbearance and discretion, the case which lately occurred in S Division is referred to. A sergeant was assaulted by three men, who pushed and struck him. The defendants endeavoured to prove that the Sergeant was to blame, but the Magistrate, E. Yardley, Esq., addressing the Prisoners said:
>
> "Your conduct cannot be passed over; it happens that I have knowledge of the officer, who has often been examined before me during the last four years, and I have always observed him to give his evidence in a straightforward manner. You must not imagine that you can do just as you like in the streets. You seem to think it a mere nothing to strike and assault an Officer. You are men of education, and as such ought to conduct yourselves better, and set a good example to others. You must be taught to control yourselves better, and set a good example to others. You must be taught to control your acts, and by way of a caution to deter others from acting as you have done, I must inflict a substantial punishment on you."
>
> The prisoners were then sentenced: one to 14 days, one to 7 days imprisonment and one fined 20s.'[1371]

1370 Fido, Martin, and Keith Skinner (1999). *The Official Encyclopedia of Scotland Yard*. London: Virgin Books, p.295.
1371 TNA MEPO 7/27. Metropolitan Police Order, 6 January 1865.

In January 1865 criticisms of Mayne began to appear with monotonous regularity in the newspapers and during debates in parliament. *Reynolds's Weekly Newspaper* suggested that the people of London were not governed by Queen Victoria, or by the House of Lords or the House of Commons, 'nor any of them combined'. Rather, it was Sir Richard Mayne who controlled the lives of the three million Londoners through 'ordinances and decrees'.[1372]

Two months later Mayne found himself the subject of a debate in the House of Commons after he had been in dispute with magistrates at Barnet. Under the Summary Jurisdiction Act 1848, the magistrates at Barnet had sentenced two boys to be whipped, and had, as they were entitled to do by the legislation, ordered 'the punishment to be inflicted by a constable'. However, when they requested the local Inspector of Police to do so, he told them that it was contrary to his instructions to carry out such a sentence. They protested to Mayne, but he referred them to two cases at Epsom and Richmond which had occurred some twenty or thirty years previously, when the Commissioners had sought the advice of the then Home Secretary, Sir George Grey, whilst he was in post for the first time. On that occasion Grey had said that although the police were not exempt when magistrates ordered the whipping of offenders, he hoped that arrangements might be made 'by which the necessity of throwing it on the police might be obviated'. In a further letter to Mayne the magistrates protested that he was bound to comply with the law. Mayne replied that if the police were to perform this duty, the magistrates were to provide all necessary 'paraphernalia'.

He continued:

> 'I do not think the police ought to be allowed by me to inflict such a punishment unless precautions are taken by the magistrates to guard against any abuse of the power proposed to be given, and that the sentence should not be inflicted if, from the state of health any abuse of the power proposed to be given, and that the sentence should not be inflicted if, from the state of health of the prisoner, or other causes, dangerous consequences might ensue. For these purposes, some persons should attend on the part of the magistrates to see that the punishment is duly inflicted according to the sentence, and a competent medical man, appointed by the magistrates, be present during the punishment.'

Mayne also pointed out that if the sentence was carried out at a police

---

1372 *Reynolds's Weekly Newspaper*, 8 January 1865, p.4.

station, it would be within the hearing of the wives and daughters of the constables who resided there. When the matter was raised in the House of Commons a number of members supported the Barnet magistrates, but Sir George Grey, then serving as Home Secretary for the third time, pointed out that because the cries of the boys being whipped tended to attract a disorderly crowd, 'for some years past the practice of whipping at the police stations had been abandoned, and boys were sentenced to imprisonment, though it might be only for a few days or a few hours.'[1373]

In June 1866, with growing agitation for reform and the likelihood of Fenian troubles, Mayne appeared to have a change of heart about the telegraph. Divisional Superintendents were instructed to report the name and description of any telegraph company having wires near their respective stations.[1374] This was followed by a request to telegraph companies to tender 'for the performance of the telegraph service of the Police of the Metropolis' by 8 October 1866.

Work on the installation of an electric telegraph was finally completed a year later, on 30 September 1867. All Divisions were connected to Scotland Yard, along with the private residences of Richard Mayne at 80 Chester Square, Captain Harris at 17 Porchester Square, and Captain Labalmondière at 13 South Audley Street.

Replying to a question put to him whilst giving evidence to the Committee Appointed to Enquire into the System of Police in 1868, Sir Richard stated, 'each superintendent is first of all responsible for the preservation of peace and the prevention of any disturbances within his own Division as far as his means go, and directions are that he is immediately to communicate by telegraph to me and the Assistant Commissioners and to the superintendents of adjoining Divisions.' Quoting Paddington Police House as an example, it was assessed that within half an hour at night four hundred constables could be assembled.[1375]

1373 HC Deb 03 April 1865, vol 178, cc.719-726.
1374 TNA MEPO 7/27. Metropolitan Police Order, 7 June 1866.
1375 Bunker, op. cit. 1336, pp.48-56.

CHAPTER TWENTY-TWO

THE SECOND BATTLE FOR HYDE PARK

Despite earlier attempts to reform the electoral system, by 1865 only one million of the five million adult males in Britain could vote and there were renewed demands for electoral reform. As a result the Reform League, firmly committed to manhood suffrage and the ballot, as opposed to household suffrage advocated by many Advanced Liberals at the time, was formed on 23 February 1865. Edmond Beales was elected President and George Howell, Secretary. Other senior members included Lieutenant-Colonel Dickson, a British soldier who had served in India and with the British Auxiliary Legion sent to Spain in 1835 to support Queen Isabella II against the Carlists in the First Carlist War.[1376]

In March 1866, William Gladstone, leader of a Liberal government in the House of Commons, together with Earl Russell the Prime Minister introduced a Bill which would have at least increased the number of adult males who were entitled to vote, although it had its critics. Some suggested it went too far; others that it did not go far enough. Three months later, in June, an amendment to the Bill resulted in the resignation of the Russell-Gladstone government,[1377] to be replaced by a minority Tory government with Lord Derby as Prime Minster and Benjamin Disraeli as its leader in the House of Commons. The new government was largely against any reform, and the Bill was dropped.[1378]

Naturally disappointed, the Reform League organised a demonstration

---

1376 Although firmly committed to manhood suffrage, the Reform League had 'no real intention of seeking the enfranchisement of casual labourers.' See Wright, D.W.(1988). *Popular Radicalism: The Working-Class Experience 1780-1880*. London: Longman, p.159; see also Foot, Paul (2012). *The Vote*. London, Penguin, pp.135-138.
1377 HC Deb 26 June 1866, vol. 184, c.654.
1378 Hawkins, Angus (2007). *The Forgotten Prime Minister - The 14th Earl of Derby, Volume II*. New York: Oxford University Press, pp.252-253.

to take place in Trafalgar Square on 27 June 1866. The number of people attending exceeded the expectations of both the Reform League and the Metropolitan Police, but, although a section of the crowd demonstrated outside Gladstone's home, the Reform Club and the Carlton Club following the meeting, there was no disorder.[1379] A second meeting on 2 July 1866 attracted even greater crowds, with one report putting it between 20,000 and 30,000. Again, whilst a section of the crowd carried out minor demonstrations, as it had done on 27 June, there was no disorder.[1380]

Prior to the meetings the then Home Secretary, Sir George Grey, gave directions to Sir Richard Mayne that 'he was not to interfere with the meeting as long as it was legally and peaceable conducted, but that he was to take means to prevent any illegal assemblage of persons afterwards for the purpose of breaking windows and expressing political animosity against individuals.' Grey instructed Sir Richard to send a letter to the President of the Reform League, Mr Edmond Beales, which he did immediately on 2 July:

> 'The Commissioner of Police of the Metropolis has to acquaint the President or Chairman of the public meeting to be held this evening in Trafalgar Square that the police have instructions not to prevent or in any way interfere with the holding of the meeting in a peaceable and quiet manner, but should bodies of persons proceed together about the streets in such a manner as by their numbers, noise, demeanour, or language is calculated to cause a breach of the peace, or excite terror or alarm in the minds of Her Majesty's subjects, it will become the duty of the police to prevent, and, if necessary, put a stop to such proceedings, and apprehend persons encouraging those engaged in them, and others who continue to act with them.'

Following the demonstration, Beales responded to Mayne's letter:

> 'Mr Beales presents his compliments to Sir Richard Mayne, and begs to thank him in all sincerity for his letter relative to the meeting last evening in Trafalgar Square, and the police arrangements made with regard to it. The letter was received with much good feeling, and, in fact, with much applause generally on the part of the very large multitude assembled, and they evinced every desire to adhere to the course of action prescribed in it – a course also strongly urged by the speakers. If there was any procession or clamour in the streets after the proceedings

---

1379 *London Evening Standard*, 28 June 1866, p.3.
1380 *London Daily News*, 3 July 1866, p.2; another newspaper put the figure at 40,000 (see *Morning Advertiser*, 3 July 1866, p.2).

of the meeting were terminated, they could only have been the work of a few boys, as the great bulk of those assembled dispersed quietly to their several homes. It will, as it has been, Mr Beales' constant effort to prevent any constitutional exhibition of popular opinion from being perverted into anything approaching to a breach of the peace or to public disorder.'[1381]

The Reform League then sought to hold a meeting in Hyde Park and announced the date as 23 July 1866. Spencer Walpole, who had replaced Grey as Home Secretary just seventeen days previously, decided to ban the demonstration on the grounds that serious disorder was anticipated, and instructed Sir Richard to issue the appropriate notice which, after outlining why it was being issued, said:

'And Whereas such a Meeting – being inconsistent with the purposes for which the Park is thrown open to and used by the Public – is illegal, and cannot be permitted, and such an assemblage there of large numbers of persons is calculated to lead to riotous and disorderly conduct, and to endanger the public peace:

And Whereas it is necessary to prevent such proceedings, and to preserve the public peace:

NOTICE IS HEREBY GIVEN

That NO SUCH MEETING or ASSEMBLAGE of persons in large numbers will be ALLOWED to take place in HYDE PARK, an all well-disposed persons are hereby cautioned and requested to abstain from joining or attending any such meeting or Assemblage: and Notice is further Given, that all necessary measures will be applied to prevent such Meeting or Assemblage, and effectually to preserve the public peace, and to suppress any attempt at the disturbance thereof.'[1382]

A copy of the notice was sent personally to Edmond Beales, with an accompanying letter in which Mayne said:

'The Commissioner of Police of the Metropolis encloses for the information of Mr. Edmond Beales a copy of the public notice that the meeting announced to be held in Hyde Park on the evening of Monday next, July 23, cannot be permitted. As Mr. Beales name is mentioned in the printed bills calling the meeting, the Commissioner of Police trusts Mr. Beales will exert his influence to prevent any attempt to hold this

---

1381 *Evening Mail*, 25 July 1866, p.
1382 *London Evening Standard*, 19 July 1866, p.7.

meeting.'

Beales responded the next day. In a lengthy letter, he said that he was unable to 'recognise' Mayne's 'power or right to issue such a notice or to take it upon [himself] to declare that the meeting cannot be permitted.' He went on to say that he 'must withhold that recognition' until Mayne could show him 'under what statute or law, or principle of law' he was acting. Referring to Mayne's claim that it was 'inconsistent for which the park is thrown open to and used by the public', Beales said he was unable to accept that it was for the Commissioner of Police to decide what was and what was not illegal.[1383] Meanwhile, the Notices had been distributed all over London and displayed 'in pubs and shops and on park railings', which Thurmond Smith suggested was 'excellent advertising that no doubt increased park attendance.'[1384]

The Reform League responded by sending a copy of a resolution passed at a meeting of the Demonstration Committee to the Home Secretary:

> 'That her Majesty's Secretary of State for the Home Department in prohibiting the proposed reform meeting in Hyde-park, having claimed on behalf of the Crown an unlimited discretionary power with regard to properties vested in it; and that the Crown can of its sole will prevent the people from holding public meetings in the parks, this committee denies that the Crown has any such power, and has determined to test the question by holding a public meeting in favour of reform in Hyde-park on Monday evening, the 23rd instant, at seven o'clock.'

Walpole's reply was succinct.

> 'After the statement which I felt it my duty to make in the House of Commons I had hoped that those who had proposed to convene that meeting would have forborne from calling it together. Should they still persevere in their intentions, which I trust they will not, I gave no other course left open to me but to desire the police to act on the notice issued by Sir Richard Mayne.'[1385]

At 6.00pm on 23 July, people met at nine different locations, including the traditional meeting places of Finsbury Square, Clerkenwell Green and Victoria Park, with the intention of marching in procession to arrive at

---

1383 *Evening Mail*, 20 July 1866, p.5.
1384 Thurmond Smith, Phillip (1985). *Policing Victorian London: Political Policing, Public Order and the London Metropolitan Police*. London: Greenwood Press, p.164.
1385 *Morning Post*, 23 July 1866, p.2.

Marble Arch at 7.00pm. It was also announced that the London Working Men's Association, although not part of the Reform League, would take part, forming up in Lincoln's Inn Fields.[1386] The Demonstration Committee had given instructions that if, on arrival at Hyde Park, a procession was 'prevented from entering', it was to reform 'four deep' and go to Trafalgar Square via Grosvenor Place, Victoria Street and the Houses of Parliament.[1387]

At Clerkenwell Green, by about 5.30pm, two or three hundred people collected round a wagon to hear a speaker denounce the Government for ordering the closure of Hyde Park. At the same time, he appealed for the demonstration to be peaceful. The demonstrators then marched by way of Hatton Garden, to Holborn, Oxford Street to Marble Arch. In the City of London Police area, officers stopped traffic to allow the procession to proceed. In the Metropolitan Police area, the police's primary objective was to allow traffic to proceed.[1388] The progress of the march along Oxford Street towards Marble Arch, led by Mr Beales and Colonel Dickson and other leaders of the Reform movement riding in carriages and cabs, was described as 'triumphal'. Around the route they took,

> 'every spot which could command a view was filled and as they passed along they were greeted with enthusiastic cheering, which hardly ceased. So dense was the crowd that the horses could only proceed at a slow walk, and several times had to stop while a way was made. In the immediate vicinity of Marble Arch the excitement was intense… The roofs and windows of surrounding houses were crowded by people anxious to witness the decision of the question between police and Reformers. As far as the eye could reach in every direction there was a compact mass of people to be seen.'[1389]

Again, Mayne, now seventy years of age, took personal charge of all the arrangements. To ensure the meeting did not take place, he 'assigned 1,613 men, including 105 in plain clothes and 60 on horseback, in locations round the park, with double patrols in the park itself'. As the members of the Reform League were due to assemble at a number of locations throughout London, Mayne also instructed superintendents, on whose divisions such assembly points were designated, to post a reserve of one inspector, two sergeants and twenty constables at the nearest police station.

1386 Ibid.
1387 *Times*, 22 July 1866, p.9.
1388 Ibid, 24 July 1866, p.9.
1389 *Daily Telegraph*, 24 July 1866, p.3.

No doubt haunted by the severe criticism made of police action in 1855, Mayne decided that he would be in uniform on horseback in Hyde Park itself; he also involved his two Assistant Commissioners, posting Captain Harris to Marble Arch and Colonel Labalmondière to Hyde Park Corner. All gates into the Park would be closed to prevent people from entering.[1390]

Two days before the proposed demonstration Mayne had written to Major-General Lord Frederick Paulet, the officer commanding the Brigade of Guards, requesting that a number of military units should be placed on standby on 25 July, prepared to act in support of the civil power. These were:

1 and 2 Life Guards;
2 Bn the Grenadier Guards
2 Bn the Coldstream Guards
1 Bn of the Scots Fusiliers Guards[1391]

The following day Mayne wrote again to Paulet, pointing out that 'the Police on the ground being insufficient for the duties demanding on them in preserving the peace,' requested him in the event of 'the crowd becoming very turbulent', to move the 2nd Regiment of Life Guards and two companies of the Coldstream Guards to his aid.[1392]

In the past the police had frequently kept the initial deployment of police to a minimum, but had reserves nearby. On this occasion, however, there had been a visible build-up of resources during the afternoon. For instance, one journalist reported 'mounted police of K Division were seen riding westwards long the Strand, while bodies of foot constables [converged] by different routes on Hyde Park.'[1393]

At Hyde Park, vast crowds had collected in the neighbourhood by 5.00pm, and the gates into the Park had been closed. But the police left inside the Park large numbers of people who had assembled as spectators; other spectators were assembled on the balconies and at windows of houses overlooking the Park[1394] At each of the main entrances into the Park – at Hyde Park Corner, Stanhope Gate, Grosvenor Gate and Victoria Gate – a sergeant and some constables were drawn up 'in military formation'. The small gates along Park Lane were guarded by a few constables, who allowed people to leave the Park but not to enter. The greatest numbers of police were at the Marble Arch entrance, where a line of foot police was drawn up, with their truncheons in their hands. Behind them was a line of

1390 TNA MEPO 1/27. Police Orders 18 & 21 July 1866.
1391 TNA HO 45/7854, folio 10, letter from Mayne to Paulet, 23 July 1866.
1392 Ibid, folio 11, letter from Mayne to Paulet, 24 July 1866.
1393 *Daily Telegraph*, 24 July 1866, p.3.
1394 *Times*, 24 July 1866, p.9.

mounted police, again with their truncheons in the hands. In reserve were 'several companies'; a mounted troop also patrolled along the Bayswater Road and the drive parallel to Park Lane. Sir Richard Mayne and Captain Harris were stationed here, and personally directed the movement of police.[1395]

The first signs of an incursion by the crowd occurred when, through sheer pressure, it broke the bolts holding one of the gates, as a result of which the gate was forced open. A journalist described what happened next:

> 'Having thus far forced the gate, the foremost persons in the crowd were open to the blows of the truncheons of their opponents, who made unmistakably free and active use of their ugly weapons. Driven back by this attack, and without having actually gained their way into the park, the crowd suddenly paused, and immediately afterwards fell back in confusion.'

A few remained by the marble pillars to which the gates were attached. They were seized by several policemen, who 'without hesitation or provocation commenced in the most savage and unsparing manner to beat them on the head and shoulders with their truncheons.' Another incursion occurred when a number of youths each grasped the top of a rail along a fifty-yard stretch in Bayswater Road, and by swaying backwards and forwards managed to topple it so that it fell inside the Park. As soon as this occurred, hundreds of 'lads and boys' swarmed into the Park before police were rushed to the spot to stem the breach and prevent others from entering.[1396]

Towards seven o'clock, the streets around Marble Arch were completely blocked and foot and mounted police cleared the people away, although there was some 'mild skirmishing' and several people were arrested.[1397] The carriage containing Beales and his entourage approached the main gate, but as they did so 'the crowd immediately closed in, and endeavoured by an "ugly rush" to effect admission.' The police responded, using 'their staves freely to defeat this attempt.' Both Beales and Colonel Dickson 'were struck in the scuffle.'[1398]

Having been refused admission, the leaders announced that they were going to Trafalgar Square and implored those that followed them to refrain

---

1395 *Daily Telegraph*, 24 July 1866, p.3.
1396 Ibid.
1397 *Pall Mall Gazette*, 24 July 1866, p.1.
1398 *Times*, 24 July 1866, p.9.

from any acts of violence. Between ten and fifteen thousand followed to Trafalgar Square, where a meeting was held decrying the closure of the Park. Despite being requested to do so, many of the demonstrators did not follow the leaders; they were looking for an opportunity to create disorder, although it was unlikely they were members of the Reform League.[1399]

Therefore, a huge crowd remained in the vicinity of the Park – one newspaper report put the number at 50,000 people[1400] – and the railings in Park Lane suffered the same fate as those in Bayswater Road, allowing many more to swarm into the Park. As they did so, the police, now clearly insufficient to prevent further incursion into the Park, attacked

> 'using their truncheons indiscriminately. Several of the people were badly beaten, and this so irritated the rest of the crowd that, arming themselves with the broken flagstones and sticks, they closed with the police, and a fair stand-up fight took place, in which, from the overwhelming superiority of numbers, the police came off second best. Several of the constables who had been particularly active in using their truncheons were singled out for special punishment; being surrounded they were pummelled until they appeared to be senseless.'[1401]

The police repeatedly charged the crowd, arresting a number of people 'who were seen in the act of throwing stones'. However, after each charge, the police retreated with their prisoners, allowing the mob to close in, hooting and yelling at the police and hurling another volley of stones. Police were deployed to various parts of the Park bordering onto Park Lane as section after section of the railings were forced in, and hundreds of people swept into the Park adding to those already present before the breach was sealed. Considerable damage was done to the trees as people armed themselves with pieces of wood. On occasions the police got 'very rough treatment from the stones and sticks', and 'in some cases, the stones flew so thick that they rattled off the helmets of the police like hail.' As the heavily outnumbered police fought to control the incursions in to the Park, they continued to use their truncheons, and a number of people were taken to hospital with head injuries. Police officers too were injured, some seriously. At one point, Mayne was surrounded by a section of the crowd and almost thrown from his horse, but he was quickly rescued by both foot and mounted police.[1402]

1399 *Daily Telegraph*, 24 July 1866, p.3.
1400 Ibid, 25 July 1866, p.8.
1401 Ibid, 24 July 1866, p.3.
1402 Ibid.

The increasing numbers and hostility of the crowd towards the police caused Mayne to request the deployment of the military, under the command of Lieutenant-Colonel Lane Fox,[1403] who had command of 50 men from the Grenadier Guards, who were on standby at the Magazine Barracks in the Park, to assist the police for the first time since the formation of the Metropolitan Police some thirty-seven years previously.

In a report to the Adjutant-General the next day, Paulet described how Mayne had already asked Fox to help the police in defending breaches made in the railings on both sides of Marble Arch Gate before his arrival at 7.30pm, but the task was impossible, given Fox had so few men. Paulet therefore summoned reinforcements, which consisted, initially, of two companies of Coldstream Guards from Knightsbridge Barracks. At around 8.00pm they were joined by two Regiments of Life Guards. The Guards detachment, with bayonets fixed, took up a position at Marble Arch whilst the Life Guards patrolled the Bayswater Road, urging the crowds to confine themselves to the footways. At about 8.30pm another company of the Guards arrived, along with half a dozen more squadrons of Life Guards.

This effectively brought the skirmishing between sections of the crowd and the police to an end, and the cordon formed by the detachment of Guards prevented any more 'rushing' movements by the crowds. As the evening progressed people started to drift away, but it was after midnight before Hyde Park had resumed its normal tranquillity and the military and police could be stood down.[1404]

Earlier in the evening, at a meeting hastily convened by a section of the crowd near Marble Arch, a resolution, which reflected the views of many of the people who had been involved, was passed as follows:

> 'That this meeting condemns in the most emphatic and unqualified terms the attempt on the part of the Ministry to rule the country by force and their recklessness in compromising the dignity of the Government by wantonly provoking a collision between the people and the officers appointed to keep the peace, and resolves that a deputation of not more than six persons wait on Her Majesty with a petition, signed by the chairman, in the name of the meeting, requesting the dismissal of Earl Derby and his colleagues, and the appointment of a Ministry who have a better appreciation of the value of the lives of Her Majesty's

---

1403 *Spectator*, 28 July 1866, p.1.
1404 *The Times* 24 July 1866, p.9; see also *Daily Telegraph*, 24 July 1866, p.3 and TNA HO 45/7854, folio 2, report from Paulet to the Adjutant-General, 24 July 1866.

The Second Battle for Hyde Park

subjects, and of what is due to their own high office.'[1405]

The following morning the *Daily Telegraph* reported that 'the gallant Commissioner' rode 'over the field of battle.' Only then was the full extent of the damage to the Park clearly seen. Over two hundred yards of railings from Marble Arch stretching along the Bayswater Road had been 'laid level on the ground'. There was little interruption in the damage to the railings stretching down Park Lane, between Marble Arch and Grosvenor Gate. Many of the trees, shrubs and flowers had been damaged.[1406]

The police had been heavily outnumbered, and 265 officers were injured. Amongst this number was the Commissioner himself, who was 'struck several times' by missiles, one stone hitting him on 'the side of the head causing blood to stream down his face.'[1407] At least 30 people were taken to St George's Hospital.[1408] One person, who attempted to escape over some railings from the police, was seriously injured when one of the spiked railings penetrated his leg. Others were taken to St Mary's Hospital, Paddington. About 100 people were arrested in Marble Arch and the approaches to the Park. They were charged with criminal damage of the railings, throwing stones, assault on police and disorderly conduct.[1409]

But this was not the end of events in the Park. The following day, a crowd, mostly of the ruffian type, rapidly grew but there were few police officers present. The trigger for the disorder on this day occurred at about 2.30pm when a section of the crowd 'hooted and threw mud at the carriages and their occupants as they passed.' The few officers present attempted to protect the carriages, but were forced to retreat when confronted by some 2,000 people. By three o'clock some people had begun to destroy trees and arm themselves with the iron railings toppled the previous night.

Mayne, despite his injuries, was present on horseback near Marble Arch, along with the military commander, this time the Adjutant-General to the Forces, Major-General Lord William Paulet,[1410] and two aides-de-camp. Mayne deployed a strong body of officers who had been waiting nearby, under the command of Chief Superintendent Walker. At about the same time, a regiment of Horse Guards were marched into the Park and more mounted police arrived.

Other than continuous yelling and shouting from the crowd, there were no significant incidents until the arrival of two members of the Reform

---

1405 *The Times*, 24 July 1866, p.9.
1406 *Daily Telegraph*, 25 July 1866, p.8.
1407 Thurmond Smith, op. cit. 1384, p.164.
1408 *Daily Telegraph*, 25 July 1866, p.8; see also *The Times*, 24 July 1866, p.9.
1409 Ibid; see also *The Times*, 25 July 1866, p.5.
1410 *London Gazette*, 11 May 1866, number 23113, p.2899.

League at sometime between six and seven o'clock. Mayne gave them permission to address the crowd and persuade it to disperse, but it had no effect. Lieutenant-Colonel Dickson then urged Mayne to withdraw all police from the Park, threatening him that if they were not withdrawn 'he would not be responsible for the consequences.' Instead, a detachment of Grenadier Guards was deployed to assist in keeping order and dispersing the crowd.[1411]

During the day, a further fifty police officers and at least thirteen members of the public were injured, some seriously. Over forty people were arrested.[1412]

On 30 July, at a meeting of the Reform Movement at the Agriculture Hall, Islington, attended by 25,000 people, the behaviour of the police was denounced and a resolution was passed calling for the appointment of a Committee of Inquiry into the conduct of Sir Richard Mayne and the police under his orders in forcibly preventing the working classes from meeting in Hyde Park on Monday 23 July, and likewise their conduct in ejecting persons from the Park and otherwise maltreating them, on that and the following two days.[1413]

Following the Hyde Park riot of 1866, in answer to a question put to him in the House of Commons, Walpole was asked on whose authority Mayne had issued the notice forbidding the meeting. He replied:

'The order signed by Sir Richard Mayne has been issued under my authority and direction, and I am entirely responsible for it.'

Walpole said the meeting had been prohibited because there was a likelihood that it would 'lead to riotous and disorderly proceedings.'[1414]

Reynolds's Weekly Newspaper again was one of the worst critics of Mayne. Before the riot, it accused him of modelling himself on the continental tyrants such as the Parisian and Muscovite Ministers of Police, suggesting his claim that the meeting was inconsistent with the purposes for which the park was thrown open to, and used by, the public was 'both shallow and a false pretence.'[1415] Later, it accused Sir Richard Mayne and Mr Walpole of being 'the real authors of the riot', claiming had the gates 'not been closed against the people, no riot or disturbance would have taken place.'[1416]

The *London Daily News* accused Mayne of being 'that great promoter

---

1411 *Morning Post*, 25 July 1866, p.6; *London Evening Standard*, 25 July 1866, p.6.
1412 *London Evening Standard*, 25 July 1866, p.5.
1413 *Morning Post*, 31 July 1866, p.3.
1414 HC Deb 19 July 1866, vol. 184, cc 1073-5.
1415 *Reynolds's Weekly Newspaper*, 22 July 1866, p.5.
1416 Ibid, 29 July 1866, p.4.

of disturbances.'[1417] A report in the *Illustrated Times* accused the Commissioner of being 'a very conceited man', who had 'boasted that he had a sufficient force to guard the park.' But as the report pointed out, he deployed between 1,600 and 1,800 men 'to guard an exposed frontier of some three-and-a-half to four miles.'[1418] The *Pall Mall Gazette* also suggested that 'to attempt to guard such a frontier as the whole of Hyde Park was absurd, and to set 1,500 police skirmishing with 50,000 people was worse than absurd.'[1419] The *Pall Mall Gazette* arguably made a more reasoned assessment of the events of 23 July:

> 'The temper of the constables was beyond all praise, and such as, had we not witnessed it ourselves, we could hardly have believed. They were repeatedly struck by heavy stones and also with sticks; attempts, once or twice, successful, were made to pull them from their horses, and even to cut their girths, and they bore it all with admirable patience and good temper.'

But the report then went on to suggest that

> 'the authorities were wrong in their tactics. They should have withdrawn their men as soon as the mob was in the park and the meeting had gone off to Trafalgar Square. Instead of this they sent for soldiers. A more ludicrous sight in its way has seldom been seen, though it is to be regretted that redcoats should ever be seen in this country acting in such a capacity.'[1420]

The *Pall Mall Gazette* thought that in terms of the original cause of the disturbance, 'the Government were right and Mr. Beales and his committee wrong.' It was important 'to establish once and for all the principle that the royal parks [were] not places for public meetings, and when Mr Beales and his friends claimed the legal right of holding the meeting there they made interference inevitable.'[1421]

In fact, two days after the riot, on behalf of Walpole, Waddington wrote to the Attorney-General to enquire whether in the circumstances that existed on 23 July, 'there was any legal authority to disperse such meeting by force.'[1422] The reply came back from two eminent Queen's Counsel, Cavins and Bovill, on 28 July:

1417 *London Daily News*, 25 July 1866, p.4.
1418 *Illustrated Times*, 28 July 1866, p.2-3.
1419 *Pall Mall Gazette*, 24 July 1866, p.1-2.
1420 Ibid.
1421 Ibid.
1422 TNA TS 25/1493. Letter from Waddington to Attorney-General, 25 July 1866.

'...there is not for any practical purpose a legal authority to disperse by force a meeting of the kind supposed consisting of a large number of persons and that whether notice has or has not been given beforehand.'

The suggestion put forward by Counsel was that people used Hyde Park with permission of the owner, Her Majesty the Queen. They should therefore have been treated as trespassers, in which case there was a right to remove each separate individual as such 'using just as much force (and no more) as is necessary for that purpose.'[1423] A week after the riot, the Adjutant-General informed the Under-Secretary of State at the Home Office that the Royal Horse Guards from Aldershot and the HQ and six troops of the 14th Hussars from Hounslow had been moved to Central London 'as a temporary arrangement.'[1424]

Cavanagh suggested that during the 1860s Sir Richard had begun 'to blunder and fall to pieces', claiming that during the riot 'he had lost his nerve' despite 'sticking to his post in the most gallant manner, and giving orders right and left...'[1425] There is no direct evidence that Mayne lost his nerve, other than the fact he called out the military. But, at the time, the police officers on the ground were under huge pressure. There is little doubt that he had underestimated the number of officers required to effectively manage the situation, employing between 1,600 and 1,800 officers out of a total strength of 7,000. Compare this with the occasion in May of the following year, when Mayne deployed over 4,000 police officers when Hyde Park was threatened with a similar meeting.[1426]

Following the events of that evening, the Home Secretary 'received a deputation from the Reform League to who he expressed his personal regrets for the events' that had taken place.[1427] Mayne, who took the view that the principle cause of the riot had been the Home Secretary's decision to ban the meeting from Hyde Park, was disgusted and offered to resign. The offer was refused, and the Home Secretary was criticised by Parliament for banning the meeting in the first place.[1428]

The following year the 1867 Reform Act[1429] doubled the number of

---

1423 TNA TS 25/1493. Letter from Waddington to Attorney-General, 25 July 1866.
1424 TNA HO 45/7854, folio 12. Letter from Adjutant-general to Under Secretary of State at the Home Office, 30 July 1866.
1425 Cavanagh, Timothy (1893). *Scotland Yard, Past and Present: Experiences of thirty-seven years* (Kindle Book). London: Chatto & Windus, under the title Sir Richard Mayne, Loc. 686.
1426 See Chapter Twenty-three.
1427 Ascoli, David (1979). *The Queen's Peace: The origins and development of the Metropolitan Police 1829-1995*. London: Hamish Hamilton, p.133.
1428 Critchley, T.A (1970). *The Conquest of Violence: Order and Liberty in Britain*. London: Constable, p.147.
1429 30 and 31 Vict, c.102. See Himmelfarb, Gertrude (1966). 'The Politics of Democracy: The English Reform Act of 1867' in *Journal of British Studies*, Vol. 6, No. 1 (November), pp.97-138.

adult males who could vote, and by the end of 1868 all adult males who were heads of households could vote. In 1884, the Representation of the People Act (also known as the Third Reform Act), whilst not establishing universal suffrage, did widen the vote considerably, enabling 60% of males – approximately 5.5 million – to vote.[1430]

In August 1866 Sir Richard received a letter from William G. Osborne, the 8th Duke of Leeds, forwarding a cheque for £500, 'the amount of a voluntary subscription collected in the course of a few days from many persons of all classes, who are anxious to show their sense of the courage, temper, and forbearance of the police' on the occasion of the riot in Hyde Park 'and to assist those among them who have been injured or disabled in the performance of an arduous and painful duty.' In his reply, Sir Richard said the 'expression of the approval of the conduct of the police concerned shall be immediately known to the whole force. I know how highly it will be valued by them; it will be an additional encouragement to all to perform their duty in the same exemplary manner on all occasions…'[1431]

Shortly before he died, Mayne was able to tell the whole Force that a total of £836 18s 10d had been subscribed following the 1866 Hyde Park riot, of which £747 had been distributed to those who had been deployed in dealing with the riot, the remaining £89 18s 10d going to the Reward Fund. Individual officers who had been injured or since died had received £25 each. For instance, Constable Stokes of A Division had received £25, and so too had the late Constables Penny, also of A Division, and Hillsden of P Division. He concluded his announcement with these words:

'The Commissioner is highly gratified in making this statement of the final distribution of so large a sum of money voluntarily subscribed by the Public for the Police on the occasion referred to. It proves to the whole Force that important services rendered in support of the law and order are not overlooked, and it must be an additional encouragement to all to perform their duty in the same exemplary manner on all occasions.'[1432]

1430 48 and 49 Vict, c.3. See Glen, William Cunningham, (1885), *The Representation of the People Act 1884.* London: Shaw and Son.
1431 *The Times*, 10 August 1866, p.5.
1432 TNA MEPO 7/27. Police Order, 12 December 1868.

CHAPTER TWENTY-THREE

THE END OF AN ERA

The Hyde Park riot in 1866 was the beginning of the end of an era that commenced in 1829, and the following year, 1867, whilst he had some success, was overall not a good year for Mayne. It started well enough in January when, over a period of three days, bread riots occurred in Deptford and Greenwich. Refused relief by the local relieving officer,[1433] unemployed labourers took to the streets in large numbers on 23 January, entering at least three bakers' shops and a butcher's shop in Deptford High Street and taking all the contents. Order was quickly restored that day by foot and mounted police from the A Division Reserve Force. On the following two days, policemen in pairs patrolled the High Street, whilst mounted police were held in reserve. Nevertheless, at least one baker's shop in one of the side streets was looted, before a section of the mob moved on to Greenwich, where another baker's shop was looted. There were few arrests. On the Saturday night the mobs came out again, but when it rained the streets rapidly emptied.[1434]

In April 1867, it became known that the Reform League would hold another meeting in Hyde Park. On 1 May, acting on Mayne's instructions, Superintendent Durkin interrupted a meeting of the Reform League's General Council, being held in Sussex Hall, Bouverie Street, just off Fleet Street, and served Beales with a notice signed by Walpole:

'Whereas it has been publicly announced that a public meeting will be held in Hyde Park on Monday the 6th of May, for the purpose of political discussion,

And whereas the use of the park for the purpose of holding such a

---

[1433] Under the Poor Law Acts, the relieving officer was responsible for evaluating the cases of all persons applying for medical or poor relief, to authorize emergency relief or entry to the local workhouse.

[1434] *London Evening Standard*, 24 January 1867, p.5; 25 January, p.5; 26 January, p.7 and 28 January, p.5.

meeting is not permitted, and interferes with the object for which her Majesty has opened the park for public use,

Now all persons are hereby warned, and admonished to abstain from attending, aiding, or taking part in any such meeting or from entering the park with the intention of attending such meeting.'

Following Durkin's departure, a 'long and excited discussion' took place before the following resolution was passed unanimously:

'That this meeting, having received the copy of a proclamation, signed by her Majesty's Secretary of State for the Home Department, declaring the use of the park cannot be permitted for holding the public meeting on Monday evening next, denies the existence of any legal or constitutional right in the government to forbid the use of the park for the purpose contemplated, and hereby instructs the council to persevere in holding the meeting under such arrangements as they may think it desirable to make.'[1435]

In the meantime, the Home Secretary's proclamation had been posted in various parts of the Metropolis. Three days later, it was reported that nearly all the proclamations had been either torn down or defaced, or, in some cases, covered by another placard calling 'on the people to disregard [the] proclamation, and to attend in thousands and vindicate their right to hold their meeting in the Park'. On 6 May, at least one newspaper accused the Government of abandoning 'its opposition to the meeting in Hyde Park' and surrendering to 'King Mob'.[1436]

Mayne made copious arrangements, deploying twenty superintendents, seventy-two inspectors, 372 sergeants and 3,708 constables, together with 184 mounted officers. Two-thirds were stationed in and around Hyde Park, whilst the remainder were on standby at police stations. His instructions were brief and to the point:

'Persons are not to be taken into custody in Hyde Park unless by direction of the Commissioner or one of the Assistant Commissioners. The Police are to be specially cautioned not to notice any offensive or angry language used towards them; if required to interfere, they are to do so with necessary vigour to effect the object, but to shew great forbearance towards all not actually engaged in the commission of illegal acts.'[1437]

1435 *London Evening Standard*, 2 May 1867, p.6.
1436 *The Times*, 6 May 1867.
1437 TNA MEPO 7/29. Police Order, Monday 6 May 1867.

As well as the police, the military were on standby in force with three companies of the Grenadier Guards stationed in the gardeners' stores attached to the Magazine Barracks and two or three troops of Life Guards at nearby Knightsbridge Barracks. Mayne and Major-General James Lindsay, the military commander, were present in the Magazine Barracks.[1438]

As the afternoon wore on, branches of the Reform League began arriving. Holborn branch arrived behind a brass band, and Clerkenwell branch, having assembled on the green by the Middlesex Sessions House, marched to Hyde Park 'with drums beating and trumpets blowing.' By seven o'clock in the evening, the time of the proposed meeting, approximately 20,000 people had assembled in the Park.[1439] They were addressed by Beales and Colonel Dickson, amongst others, for about an hour before the meeting began to break up. As the crowd dispersed, policemen, in groups of six under the command of a sergeant, patrolled the park. The park gates were closed at midnight.[1440] There had been no disorder. Mayne's softly, softly approach had paid off. It was one of his few successes during the final two years of his reign.

On 3 June 1867 the City of London Militia, a body of 800 men under the command of Colonel Samuel Wilson, accompanied by 'organised gangs of thieves', allegedly from the metropolis east of the City, marched through the streets from Finsbury to Regent's Park. Whilst the City of London Police Commissioner had been warned and had made appropriate arrangements,[1441] it appeared Mayne was unaware of this event. Thus, Metropolitan Police officers had not been deployed along the route of the march and, more particularly, in Regent's Park. Consequently, the gangs accompanying the march took the opportunity, almost at will, to rob people of their belongings to the extent that the matter was raised in the House of Commons. The Home Secretary, Gathorne Hardy, who had taken over from Walpole following the latter's resignation immediately after the debacle of Hyde Park on 6 May, told the House that he had written to Mayne, asking him for a report. In response, Sir Richard had told him there were 26 robberies on the route of the march and fifteen people had been arrested.[1442] However, it appears that the number of people who had been robbed was considerably greater.[1443] In an attempt to absolve himself

---

1438 *Illustrated London News*, 11 May 1867, p.2.
1439 *The Times* suggested the number was between 40,000 and 50,000, *The Times*, 7 May 1867; the *Daily News*, 7 May 1867. Between 100,000 and 150,000; police estimated the numbers to be between 12,000 and 15,000.
1440 *London Evening Standard*, 7 May 1867.
1441 *Morning Post*, 19 June 1867, p.6.
1442 HC Deb 06 June 1867, Vol. 187, cc.1665-1666.
1443 *Morning Post*, 7 June, p.4 and 19 June 1867, p.6.

of all blame, Colonel Wilson wrote to the newspapers who were, in the main, unsympathetic. Both the *Pall Mall Gazette* and the *Morning Post* pointed out that 'it was legal for any man, whether peace officer or not to prevent breaches of the peace' and queried why Colonel Wilson 'had not detached a sufficient number of pickets to arrest the ruffians who were committing felonies under his very eyes.'[1444]

But, by far the worst incident, insofar as Mayne was concerned – it was the cause of his second offer to resign in less than eighteen months – was the explosion at the Clerkenwell House of Correction on 13 December. Ireland had been under British Rule since 1603, but was frequently in a state of turmoil. In 1856 an Irishman, John O'Mahony, founded the Fenian Brotherhood in the United States. The aim of the Brotherhood was 'to supply arms and officers for revolutionary efforts to sever Ireland from British rule and create a republic.' Two years later, the Irish Revolutionary Brotherhood, later to become known as the Irish Republican Brotherhood, was founded in Ireland by James Stephens with the aim of establishing an independent democratic republic.[1445] The Fenian Movement grew in England, particularly in Birmingham, Liverpool and Manchester.

In August 1866, a number of swords and rifles stolen from the headquarters of the London Irish volunteer companies, were discovered in Liverpool following a tip-off from an informer and four people were arrested. Mayne sent £10 to Liverpool to pay the informant.[1446] The Home Office instructed the Head Constable of Liverpool, Major John Greig, to cooperate with the Metropolitan Police and Mayne despatched two of his detectives, Williamson and Mulvaney, to the city, hoping that their efforts in assisting the local police would crush the Fenians.[1447] At the same time, Mayne stressed that it was 'of great importance that information be now obtained on which the conspiracy should be defeated in Liverpool, where it seems to be widely spread.'[1448]

The problem then moved to Manchester when, on 11 September, two leading members of the Fenian movement, Captain Thomas Kelly and Timothy Deasy, were arrested and held in custody. Exactly one week later, while being transferred from the courthouse to Belle Vue Gaol the police carriage in which they were being transported was attacked by

---

[1444] *Pall Mall Gazette*, 12 June 1867; *Morning Post*, 13 June 1867, p.2.
[1445] Thurmond Smith, Phillip (1985). *Policing Victorian London: Political Policing, Public Order, and the London Metropolitan Police*. Westport, Connecticut: Greenwood Press, p.184.
[1446] Ibid.
[1447] TNA HO 45/7799 folio 120, dated 15 September 1866.
[1448] TNA MEPO 1/47. Mayne to Greig, dated August and 24 September 1866; see also HO 45/7799 folio 118. Dated 12 September 1866.

an armed gang of Fenian supporters, and Kelly and Deasy were freed; tragically Police Sergeant Charles Brett was shot and killed in the attack. Five Fenians suspected of involvement in the escape were tried for Brett's murder and sentenced to death. Opposition to the conviction of the five men grew, and a series of meetings was held in London on Clerkenwell Green. A deputation was sent to the Home Office and a petition was sent to Queen Victoria asking for clemency. These met with some success, for one man was pardoned and another had his sentence commuted. However, the remaining three were hanged at Salford Gaol on the morning of Saturday, 23 November 1867. The following day, there were memorial funeral processions to Hyde Park from various parts of London. About 2,000 people eventually met in the Park, where they heard speeches and prayers for the hanged men. The police made no attempt to prevent this from taking place.[1449]

Meanwhile, in London, Ricard O'Sullivan Burke and Joseph Casey were arrested in Woburn Square by officers, led by Inspector James Thomson. Thomson was in possession of a warrant for Burke's arrest, alleging treason, which had been issued in Dublin.[1450] Burke had tried to organise a revolt against the British Government in Waterford and Tipperary, but it failed. Burke was charged with treason. Casey had resisted arrest and was charged with assaulting a constable. Both men were remanded in custody pending trial, and imprisoned at the Clerkenwell House of Correction. Meanwhile, in Dublin, an informer told police that an attempt would be made to release Burke, and Superintendent Daniel Ryan, of the Royal Irish Constabulary, sent a note to this effect to the Home Office in London, which arrived on the next day, 12 December 1867:

> 'I have to report that I have just received information from a reliable source to the effect that the rescue of Ricard Burke from prison in London is contemplated. The plan is to blow up the Exercise Walls by means of Gunpowder – the hour between 3 and 4 p.m; and the signal for all right, a white ball thrown up outside when he is at exercise.'[1451]

A copy of the message was sent to Great Scotland Yard. Mayne was temporarily absent, and it was received by Captain Labalmondière who took immediate action, writing an instruction for Superintendent Andrew Gernon, the officer in charge of the area in which the Clerkenwell House

---

1449 Thurmond Smith, op. cit. 1445, p.190.
1450 Old Bailey Proceedings Online (www.oldbaileyonline.org) April 1868, Trial of MICHAEL BARRETT t18680406-412.
1451 TNA MEPO 3/1788. Letter, dated 11 December 1867, from Superintendent Ryan, Dublin.

of Correction was located. However, before it had been sent, Mayne returned and made more specific directions on the number of officers to be deployed. The instructions that finally went to Superintendent Gernon read:

> 'Superintendent Gernon – Acquaint the Governor of the House of Detention that information has been received of an intended rescue of the prisoner Burke, to be effected by blowing up the walls of the exercising ground during the hours he is at exercise. Have the external walls carefully examined to ascertain that there has been no attempt to mine, and arrange for strict observation to be kept on them – 12.45 p.m.'

At least five uniformed constables, plus three in plain clothes, were assigned to the immediate vicinity of the House of Correction 'to keep close observation on all persons loitering round the prison walls, and give immediate information to the inspector on duty at King's Cross Station should anything arise.'

Despite this, on 12 December a man was able to wheel a cask of explosives up to the prison wall and light a fuse. A white ball was thrown into the prison yard. When the cask failed to explode, the same man was able to return and take the cask away without any interference from the police officers on duty in the vicinity.

The following day Mayne ordered a double patrol to be posted, with an extra five uniformed and three plain-clothes policemen to watch the area around the walls as had been done the day before.[1452] Despite the police presence, a second attempt was made at 3.45pm, this time using a barrel of gunpowder concealed in a costermonger's barrow. The explosion demolished a 60-foot (18 metres) section of the prison wall, but no-one escaped; the prison authorities had been forewarned and the prisoners were exercised earlier in the day, so they were locked in their cells when the bomb exploded. But the blast seriously damaged several tenement houses in Corporation Lane (now Corporation Row) on the opposite side of the road, killing twelve people and causing many injuries, with estimates ranging from 30 to 120.[1453]

Three people – Jeremiah Allen, Timothy Desmond and Anne Justice – were arrested at the scene. More arrests followed. Charges were laid against eight, but two, Jeremiah Allen and Patrick Mullany, turned

---

1452 HC Deb 9 March 1868, Vol. 190, cc 1215-17; see also TNA HO 65/8, dated 11 March 1868.
1453 Browne, Douglas G (1956). *The Rise of Scotland Yard: A History of the Metropolitan Police*. London: Harrop, p..124; Moylan, p.155; Thurmond Smith, op. cit. 13, p.191.

Queen's evidence, leaving Michael Barrett, brothers William and Timothy Desmond, Nicholas English, John O'Keefe, and Anne Justice to face indictments for the wilful murder of Anne Hodgkinson, who had lived at 3a Corporation Lane.

At the trial, which was held at the Old Bailey from 20-27 April 1868, Barrett protested his innocence, stating that he had been in Glasgow on 13 December, a claim that was supported at the trial by some witnesses, but another witness identified him as being at the scene. Two defendants were acquitted during the trial on the instructions of the presiding judge, Lord Chief Justice Cockburn, leaving the jury to decide upon the fate of the other four. After deliberating for 2½ hours, three of the defendants the Desmond brothers and English were acquitted, but Barrett was convicted of murder and sentenced to death.[1454] At the instigation of the Home Office, further enquiries were made into his claim to have been in Glasgow at the time of the explosion, but they failed to reveal any reason why the sentence should not stand. Barrett was hanged on the morning of Tuesday, 26 May 1868 outside Newgate Gaol. He was the last man to be publicly hanged in England, the practice being ended three days later by the Capital Punishment Amendment Act 1868.[1455]

The trial of Burke and Casey and a third defendant, Henry Shaw, alias Mullidy, began on 28 April, all three being charged with treason. The prosecution claimed that Burke had been involved in finding arms for the Fenians in Birmingham in late 1865 and early 1866, where he was using the name Edward C. Winslow. After a period in the United States, he returned to Liverpool to take part in the preparations for a plan to storm Chester Castle, after which he moved to Ireland. Shaw had been arrested in Ireland, but was alleged to have been a party to the plot which resulted in the rescue of Kelly and Deasy. After court hearings on 28, 29 and 30 April the case against Casey was withdrawn, but Burke and Mullidy were found guilty of treason on 30 April, and sentenced to fifteen years' and seven years' penal servitude respectively. Burke protested that he was not a subject of the Queen, but a soldier of the United States; however, evidence was provided that his mother and sister lived in Ireland, and he was convicted nonetheless.[1456]

There was condemnation of Mayne, in particular, and the Metropolitan Police in general, for their failure to prevent the Clerkenwell explosion.

1454 Trial of Michael Barrett, op. cit. 1450.
1455 Richter, Donald C (1981). Riotous Victorians. London: Ohio University Press, p.32.
1456 Old Bailey Proceedings Online (www.oldbaileyonline.org) April 1868, trial of GEORGE BERRY, alias RICKARD BURKE alias WINSLOW alias WALLACE (35) JOSEPH THEOBALD CASEY (23) HENRY SHAW alias MULLIDY (26) (t18680406-413).

The End of an Era

The Prime Minister, Lord Derby, said:

> 'I find it difficult to come to any other conclusion than that there has been great remissness, or great incapacity, on the part of our Police Authorities. It is not very much to the credit of our detective system that the first intelligence of a conspiracy which must have been known to many persons should have come to us from Ireland. But the information which we thus received was so full and accurate that, if properly acted upon, it should have been impossible to carry out the design.'[1457]

In a letter to Lord Derby, the comments of Benjamin Disraeli, then Chancellor of the Exchequer, were to the point:

> 'It is my opinion that nothing effective can be done in any way in these dangers, if we don't get rid of Mayne. I have spoken to Hardy who says he "wishes to God he would resign", but surely, when even the safety of the State is at stake, there ought to be no false delicacy in such matters… I think you ought to interfere.'[1458]

Derby agreed, and told Disraeli:

> 'It is really lamentable that the peace of the metropolis, and its immunity for wilful devastation, should depend on a body of Police, who, as Detectives, are manifestly incompetent; and under a chief who, whatever may be his other merits, has not the energy, nor, apparently, the skill to find out and employ men fitted for peculiar duties.'[1459]

Lord Mayo, the Chief Secretary for Ireland, was quick to remind Home Secretary Gathorne Hardy that the Metropolitan Police had been 'well warned'. He told Lord Derby:

> 'You will see that we gave ample notice of the Clerkenwell outrage and that it occurred exactly at the hour indicated… Truly the ways of the English Police are wonderful.'[1460]

Hardy wrote in his diary, 'strict enquiry is needed and 'more detection force and skill needed… I must decide whether to ask for more powers.'[1461]

1457 O Broin, Leon (1971). *Fenian fever: an Anglo-American dilemma*. New York: New York University Press, p.216; quoted in Thurmond Smith, op, cit. 1455, p.192.
1458 Queen's College, Oxford (Lord Blake), Derby MSS 146/3, Disraeli to Derby, dated 16 December 1867, quoted in Thurmond Smith, op. cit. 1445, p.192.
1459 O Broin, op. cit. 25, p.216; quoted in Thurmond Smith, op. cit. 1445, p.192.
1460 Cranbrook MSS, T501/270 (19 Dec 1867), Mayo to Hardy. Quoted in O Broin, op, cit. 25, pp. 211-12; Thurmond Smith, op. cit. 1445, p.192.
1461 Cranbrook MSS, 1501/260 (15 December 1867) quoted in Thurmond Smith, op. cit. 1445 p.192.

For a man of Mayne's temperament it is likely that the deaths weighed heavily on his conscience. He was, by this time, 71- years-old, six years beyond the mandatory retirement age for the civil service.[1462] Cavanagh, by now the chief inspector in charge of the Public Carriage Office, suggested he

'was getting in the natural order of things older and less fitted to carry on the onerous and important duties attached to his position. He felt, as many others have done, that he alone could carry on the duties of his office.'

He went on to suggest that it would have been better 'had he resigned some years before.'[1463]

Mayne admitted he had been at fault for the lax security and tendered his resignation. However, it was refused. The Under-Secretary of State at the Home Office at the time, the Honourable Sir Augustus Liddell, is alleged to have said: 'We told Mayne that he had made a damned fool of himself, but we meant to pull him through; we weren't going to throw him over after such long public service.'[1464]

In March 1868, an embarrassed Home Secretary was still trying to explain in Parliament what went wrong. It was revealed then that Mayne interpreted the warning as meaning that the walls were to be blown 'up' from beneath and not blown 'down'. Accordingly, Mayne had instructed Superintendent Gernon to 'have the walls carefully examined to ascertain that there has been no attempt to mine [them].'[1465] Following Gernon's interpretation of this instruction, the police officers in the vicinity paid little attention to the cask that was placed against the wall.

There was a feeling in government that the Metropolitan Police was not competent to deal with such 'secret conspiracies', and the Army's Senior Intelligence Officer in Ireland, Lieutenant-Colonel William Feilding, was attached to the Home Office for a period. His job was to set up 'a temporary secret service organization' in an attempt to determine the extent of the Fenian movement in Britain, and discover whether it had any links with revolutionaries on the Continent. Because of a fear that he might somehow thwart such a move, Mayne was kept largely in the dark about the arrangements, Feilding having been instructed to report direct to

1462 Browne, op. cit. 1453, p.143.
1463 Cavanagh, Timothy (1893). *Scotland Yard, Past and Present: Experiences of thirty-seven years*. London: Chatto & Windus, kindle edition from www.amazon.com, loc. 674
1464 Brown, op. cit.1453, p.143.
1465 HC Deb 09 March 1868, vol. 190, cc 1216.

Liddell at the Home Office.[1466] When the Queen expressed concern about the Fenian Movement, Derby wrote to her, pointing out that the attention of her staff had been directed at her security. However, his opinion of the Metropolitan Police was not particularly high, for he suggested its state was 'far from satisfactory', going on to write:

> 'The men are overworked and dispirited, they have not had a single day's rest throughout the year; and though for the most part [the police] perform their ordinary duties efficiently, they are not equal to the present extraordinary demand. They are especially deficient, however, as a detective force, which is at this time urgently required; and steps have already been taken to supply this deficiency by a separate and secret organisation; and at the same time to diminish pressure upon the regular force by an increase in their numbers.'[1467]

Almost certainly because the military had been called out to assist the police in the Hyde Park riot of July 1866 and had been placed on standby for the Reform League demonstration earlier, the year ended with the Inspector General of the Foot Guards, Major General Lindsay, seeking Mayne's view as to how he saw troops being deployed in an emergency where the civil power was insufficient. In response, Mayne pointed out that he and his two deputies, Harris and Labalmondière, were magistrates and had the power to order troops to move to a specified place. Depending on the nature and location of the disturbance, he would remain at 4 Whitehall Place, whilst one of his deputies would attend as the magistrate at the scene.[1468]

*

The last year of Mayne's life started badly from a personal point of view. Taking up almost two complete columns of its editorial, the *Illustrated Times* launched a scathing attack on the ageing Commissioner:

> 'It is high time that Sir Richard Mayne was relegated to private life – in other words, the Chief Commissioner of the Metropolitan Police must be "allowed to resign." Under his command, the force is rapidly becoming a scandal... The police do not fulfil their proper functions, while they are over-diligent in matters which are better left alone. To protect the persons and property of the lieges – that is, to prevent the

---

1466 Thurmond Smith, op. cit. 1445. p.193.
1467 Buckle, George Earle (Ed) (1926). *The Letters of Queen Victoria: A Selection from Her Majesty's Correspondence and Journal between the years 1862 and 1878*. London: John Murray, p.481.
1468 Letter, dated 30 December 1867.

commission of crime – is, one would fancy, the primary purpose for which the police force is instituted; but the metropolitan police, under the tuition of the Chief Commissioner appear to have long considered prevention but a minor part of their business. They seldom seek to hinder the criminal from carrying out his nefarious designs; they devote their energies mainly to catching him afterwards – if they can. But even in that line they are not over-successful, for cases of detection are about as rare as roses in December – at least, that is so whenever the affair in hand is of special importance.

We are willing to admit that the Metropolitan Police have done good service in the past, though in many respects they might have done much better. Nor will we deny that there are good men in the force, both in superior and subordinate positions. But there is no getting over the facts that they are neither so efficient nor so successful in preventing crime and detecting criminals as they ought to be. And, as an army is what its commander makes of it, we are compelled to attribute the deficiencies of our police army to the shortcomings of its chief. A long course of blundering and failure – faults of commission, as well as omission – seems to establish this point beyond dispute. Whatever may have been Sir Richard Mayne's original recommendations for the post he occupies, it is plain that years of routine and irresponsibility have spoilt a naturally not very brilliant intellect, and induced habits of domineering in small matters and of wrong-headed official conceit that make him unfit to cope with special emergencies. All this is highly detrimental to the public interests; for, constituted as the population of the metropolis now is, and including as it does a large a number of criminals *in posse* or *in esse*, an inefficient police is about the greatest evil with which society can be afflicted.

The editorial went on to suggest that Sir Richard's 'unfitness' had been exhibited too often and should no longer be tolerated, referring, as examples, to the Hyde Park riot of 1866, the marching of the City Militia through the streets of London, and the Clerkenwell explosion of 1867, in which he was accused of taking 'meagre precautions after the warnings.'[1469]

Gathorne Hardy had had enough. The Cabinet had authorised an increase of 1,000 extra officers,[1470] but they came at a price for Mayne; another Committee, but this time an internal one. In announcing it, Hardy

---

1469 *Illustrated Times*, 4 January 1868, p.6.
1470 Morris, R.M (2004). 'The Metropolitan Police and Government 1860-1920. Thesis submitted for the degree of Doctor of Philosophy to the Faculty of Arts'. Open University. See www.oro.open.ac.uk/59576/1/403833.pdf , p.244.

said:

'I think it desirable when the police force is being so largely increased, to inquire into its control, its government and its several divisions. The duties discharged by the Assistant Commissioners, and how far their time is occupied by clerical work, the advisability of appointing persons of higher positions and education as officers between the superintendents and the Assistant Commissioner and the Chief Commissioner. It is difficult to come to conclusions without more knowledge on these points, and I think it will be more rapidly acquired by an inquiry within the office.'[1471]

Mayne had seen the writing on the wall. Earlier he had written to the Home Office to propose that the Inspecting Superintendent post, introduced in 1839 but abolished in 1856, should be revived but with two appointed instead of one. Subsequently, in his oral evidence to the committee, he raised this to four.[1472]

In February Gathorne Hardy appointed a committee of three, all from the Home Office, as an Internal Departmental Committee to inquire into the System of Policing in the Metropolis. The Chairman was Sir James Ferguson, a former soldier who was the Member of Parliament for Ayr and the Under-Secretary of State for the Home Department in 1867/68. The two members were Henry Thring, a civil servant and the lawyer responsible for drafting Home Office bills, and George Everest, a long-serving clerk involved in police business at the Home Office.[1473]

Mayne spent what must have been a gruelling three-and-a-half days before the Committee which, in accordance with Hardy's wishes, took a mere three months to examine witnesses and issue its report.[1474] Ferguson questioned Mayne closely about how the force was organised, pointing out to him that the force had begun 'with the strength of a regiment' but it had 'grown into the strength of a division', and he accused Mayne of 'still working it as a regiment'. As Ferguson was quick to point out, it was only at this late hour that Mayne asked for additional officers.[1475]

The report, when it came at the beginning of May, will not have made pleasant reading for Mayne. It was highly critical of the organisation of the

---

1471 TNA HO 45/A49463/2.
1472 Morris, op, cit. 1470, p.246.
1473 Roach, Lawrence (2004). 'The Origins and Impact of the Function of the Crime Investigation and Detection in the British Police Service: A thesis submitted in partial fulfilment of the requirements for the degree of Doctor of Philosophy of Loughborough University'. Loughborough: Loughborough University's Institutional Repository, p.123.
1474 TNA HO 347/1. Departmental Committee on the Metropolitan Police (1868).
1475 Ibid, Report, p.37.

Force, claiming it was 'extremely centralised' with 'nothing of importance being done except under the direction of the commissioner or assistant commissioners.'[1476] It pointed out that the strength of the Force had increased from its original 3,000 to 8,000 but the number of 'superior officers' had remained virtually the same, thus making it impossible for there to 'be sufficient contact and acquaintance between officers and men to secure confidence and proper supervision'.[1477]

Whilst the Committee made a number of recommendations relating to enlistment, discipline and punishments, drill, lodgings, pay and pensions, the two key recommendations related to organisation. Firstly, the Committee recommended that the Metropolitan District should be divided into four Districts, to be commanded by four assistants to the Commissioner.[1478] The second recommendation, about the Detective Force, has already been described in Chapter Sixteen.

Later that year Mayne made himself extremely unpopular by introducing a series of measures under powers he had been given by the Metropolitan Streets Act of 1867,[1479] an act which had been passed primarily to regulate traffic and give people greater security when passing through the streets of the Metropolis. As a result, he banned the driving of cattle though the streets between 10.00am and 7.00pm, ordered that all dogs on the streets should be muzzled, and instructed police constables to arrest boys throwing snowballs and wheeling large metal hoops through the streets, a popular pursuit at the time.

The *London City Press* accused him of becoming 'reckless' and being 'indifferent to public opinion.'[1480] So, too, did the *London Evening Standard*,[1481] whilst the *Morning Post* accused him of 'ill-judged interference.'[1482] But, as has been pointed out, it was 'ironic that [Sir Richard] had to weather a storm of abuse in the last year of his long career for supposedly becoming obsessed' with these activities 'when he heartedly disliked involving his men in such assignments.'[1483]

During August 1868 Mayne made what would turn out to be his last visit to Ireland, visiting Cork, Killarney, Glengarriff and the Bay of Bawtry. But he and his wife were struck with yet another tragedy when his 16-year-old daughter Katherine died at Nuthurst, on 28 September 1868. The cause of

1476 Ibid, Report, p.12; Roach, op. cit. 1473, p.123.
1477 Ibid, Report, p.17; Roach, ibid, p.124.
1478 Ibid, Report, pp.17-18.
1479 30 and 31, Vict., c.134.
1480 *London City Press*, 5 September 1868, p.4.
1481 *London Evening Standard*, 26 August 1868, p.5.
1482 *Morning Post*, 3 November 1868, p.4.
1483 Winter, James (1993). *London's Teeming Streets, 1830-1914*. London: Psychology Press, p.47.

death was an enlarged spleen, which she had apparently had for at least six months. This letter from Mayne to the editor of *The Times*, John Delane, as well as referring to policing matters, is an indication of just how upset he was:

> 'I have only just returned to Town, and during my absence a sad attendance on a death bed and deep affliction at the death of my daughter prevented my writing to you on the subject to which I now request your attention.'

Continuing the policy he and Rowan had adopted from the beginning of writing to newspapers when they felt the Metropolitan Police had been unfairly criticised, he brought to Delane's attention two letters that had been published in *The Times*, one of which, written by a solicitor, referred to a burglary which had occurred at 4.00pm during the day. As Mayne pointed out, by virtue of an Act of Parliament, a burglary could only be committed at night, defined as between 9.00pm and 6.00am. The other referred to a robbery which Mayne suggested was pure fabrication, because he could find no details of the incident. He concluded his letter:

> 'I am not, I believe, over sensitive about attacks, either personal or on the Police, and readily admit that it is useful to call attention to all cases of neglect or misconduct, which will infallibly occur amongst so humorous [sic] a Body, acting often under very difficult circumstances and exposed to great temptation. All I desire is truth and fair play.'[1484]

In November, in a lengthy editorial, the *Morning Post* suggested 'the glaring inefficiency of our metropolitan police' was 'a disgrace to the country.' Mayne was accused of being 'the autocrat of Scotland Yard', and whilst the newspaper 'had no desire to deal harshly' with him, it pointed out that he was 'no longer young' and it was 'idle to expect the energy of middle age in a man of threescore and ten.' The editorial suggested to retire gracefully 'at the present time' would be 'honourable to himself and advantageous to the community.'[1485]

By the beginning of December, Mayne was clearly not well and reports were circulating about his ill-health. Despite this, he appeared at the Court of Common Pleas on 5 and 7 December.[1486] On 16 December, it was reported that he was 'seriously indisposed.'[1487] Five days later it was

---

1484 TNA MEPO 1/48.
1485 *Morning Post*, 3 November 1868, p.4.
1486 See Chapter Ten.
1487 *Liverpool Daily Post*, 16 December 1868, p.5.

suggested he was 'somewhat better', but still confined to his home'.[1488] Subsequently, in a report following his death, it was suggested he 'had been ailing for about a fortnight', and on 25 December allegedly 'underwent a painful operation'.[1489]

According to the records of the Metropolitan Police held at the National Archives, the final letter written by Mayne in his capacity as Commissioner was an insignificant one on 2 December. Thereafter, the two Assistant Commissioners dealt with all incoming correspondence. However, one signed by Captain Harris and dated 21 December, referred to 'the serious illness of Sir Richard Mayne'.[1490]

A number of reports appeared in the media in those last few days. On 21 December, it was reported that 'on the advice of his family and friends', Mayne would 'shortly tender his resignation, though he had hoped "to die in harness"'. The report suggested he would 'retire on a full pension' and be granted 'a baronetcy'.[1491] Indeed, seven days earlier, a report claimed Sir Richard Mayne was about to have a baronetcy conferred on him.[1492] Whether the baronetcy was mere media 'tittle-tattle' or there was an element of truth in it is unknown.

The last year of his term as Commissioner was summed up perfectly by Browne:

> 'Overworked and disillusioned, and haunted, as a man with his strong sense of responsibility might have been, by the thought of deaths and injuries which foresight might and should have prevented, for the remaining months of his life he was again to be the victim of constant attacks in the newspapers, some of them unmerited and some disgraceful. His energies, however, were still vigorous, and his eye, where petty detail was concerned, all-seeing; and at this very time he was beset by fresh anxieties which he had brewed for himself by his inquisition into the affairs of the Public Carriage Office.[1493]

To this Fido and Skinner added, 'the old autocrat at 72 bore little resemblance to the enthusiastic 39-year-old who had followed Rowan's lead and helped with the tactful and diplomatic face that weathered opposition' in those early days. But 'he had kept the force administration sound, and clear of either corruption or the forms of political tyranny the

---

1488 *Manchester Courier and Lancashire General Advertiser*, 21 December 1868, p.4.
1489 *Belfast Morning News*, 30 December 1868, p.4.
1490 TNA MEPO 1/48.
1491 *London Evening Standard*, 21 December 1868.
1492 *Morning Post*, 14 December 1868, p.4.
1493 Browne, op. cit. 1453, p.144.

The End of an Era

country once dreaded.'[1494]

[1494] Fido, Martin, and Keith Skinner (1999). *The Official Encyclopedia of Scotland Yard*. London: Virgin Books, p.163.

CHAPTER TWENTY-FOUR

PERSONAL LIFE AND DEATH OF SIR RICHARD MAYNE

Mayne was a workaholic. As a consequence his personal life, particularly during the early years, had none of the variety enjoyed by Rowan. Nevertheless, whilst pursuing his career as a barrister on the Northern Circuit he did find time to pursue a young lady, Georgina Marianne Carvick, whom he was determined to marry. Georgina was the eldest daughter of Thomas Carvick of Wyke Manor in Yorkshire, who had acquired the property by virtue of his wife, Marrianne Barbarina,[1495] the only daughter of Thomas Meyer. Meyer had died in July 1826 leaving the Manor to his son, Charles, but the latter himself died within five months of his father's death. Consequently, the property passed to his sister, Marrianne Barbarina.[1496]

Reith suggested that 'Peel persuaded Mayne to sacrifice a promising legal career for the new duty of organising the police'.[1497] In fact, it is doubtful whether he needed much persuasion. Carvick was unimpressed with the prospects of the young barrister, still trying to make his way in the profession. So the opportunity to have a regular salary of £800 per annum on taking up the appointment of Commissioner was too good to miss. Mayne's marriage to Georgina was a success. But there was a problem. As a father, as well as father-in-law, Carvick's behaviour, particularly from a financial point of view, left much to be desired, and it was necessary for Mayne to engage the services of a solicitor, James Tudor Nelthorpe, who

---

1495 The spelling of the name Marrianne given to her daughter, appears slightly different in that it is spelt with only one 'r'.
1496 Burke, John, and John Bernard Burke (1847). *A Genealogical and Heraldic Dictionary of the Landed Gentry of Great Britain & Ireland, Volume 1 A-L*. London, Henry Cockburn, p.194.
1497 Reith, Charles (1943). *British Police and the Democratic Ideal*. Oxford: Oxford University Press, p.34.

became a family friend.[1498] The precise details are unknown.

In addition to owning Wyke Manor, Carvick also owned or rented Mount Moat on Highwood Hill in Middlesex so, quite why the marriage took place at Danbury in Essex is unknown. But, it seems, for a short while, Carvick based himself at Riffham's Lodge in the village of Danbury, about 34 miles from London. In a letter to his sister, in June 1831, Mayne briefly described how he was hoping the family would meet his prospective bride:

'Tomorrow, I go down again to Riffham's and shall remain away for a few days. I hope by the end of next week that all our family in this part of the world will meet there.'[1499]

Six weeks later, on 15 August, Richard and Georgina were married.[1500]

Just prior to his wedding, Mayne attended the Queen's Drawing Room[1501] at the King's Palace, St James, on 24 June 1831, when he was presented to Queen Adelaide and her husband, William IV, by the then Home Secretary, Viscount Melbourne.[1502] Less than a year after their marriage, his wife Georgina was also presented to Queen Adelaide at Her Majesty's Drawing Room by her mother. Dressed in 'a Corinthian gauze dress over a white satin slip, elegantly trimmed with satin and white roses' and wearing a headdress which consisted of 'a handsome plume of ostrich feathers, blonde lappete, with a splendid suit of aquamarine ornaments set in gold', Georgina must have looked stunning.[1503]

Either at the time or shortly after the marriage, Mayne and his wife moved into No. 30 Green Street.[1504] Built largely in the latter half of the 18th Century, the houses on the north side of the street, where Mayne lived, had been substantially refurbished before he took up residence. It is likely to have been a modest Georgian house, probably of three storeys and three windows wide.[1505] In May 1834, not long after moving in, Mayne found some silver plates and cutlery had gone missing and he confronted his butler, Robert Last, who he had recently employed. Last admitted he

---

1498 Heathcote Collection. A collection of letters sent to Richard, later Sir Richard, Mayne between 1829 and 1868. Presented to the Metropolitan Police Heritage Centre by JHR Heathcoate, 1955, p.6.
1499 Ibid, p.8.
1500 These were occasions were people of note were formally presented to the Queen, who was not necessarily the reigning monarch (see later in the chapter).
1501 *Suffolk Chronicle*, 20 August 1831, p.3.
1502 *Morning Post*, 25 June 1831, p.3.
1503 *Morning Chronicle*, 4 May 1832, p.3; *Morning Post*, 4 May 1832, p.3.
1504 Royal and Sun Alliance Insurance Group Collection at the London Metropolitan Archives, reference CLC/B/192/F/001/MS11936/545/1199269.
1505 Sheppard, FHW (ed)(1880). *Survey of London, Volume 40, the Grosvenor Estate in Mayfair, Part5 2 (the buildings)*, pp.185-187.

had taken them.[1506] He was committed for trial and appeared at the Old Bailey at the beginning of July, when he pleaded guilty of stealing seven silver forks and three silver spoons from Richard Mayne, and one silver fork and one silver spoon from his brother, Dawson Mayne, who was staying with him at the time. For his crimes, Last was sentenced to be transported for seven years.[1507]

Over the next twenty-two years the couple had nine children. Within a year of their marriage, a son, who they named Carvick Cox after his maternal grandfather, was born. Three years later, in July 1835, a second son, Richard Charles, was born.[1508] Clearly, the relationship between Rowan and Mayne was particularly strong at this point for Rowan was a godfather to Richard. Mayne was proud of what Richard achieved during the former's lifetime, as will be seen later in this chapter. Richard joined the Royal Navy in 1847 at the age of 12 years. He was promoted Lieutenant in July 1855, Commander in 1861 and Captain in 1864. He eventually retired with the rank of Admiral in 1879.[1509]

During the early years of their married life, each summer Georgina and the children took possession of 'Maisonette', at Ingatestone in Essex. It is apparent from the many nostalgic references to the place in Mayne's letters to his wife that it offered a most desirable rural alternative to noisy, dirty, smelly London. However, it did involve periods of separation, acutely felt, particularly by Mayne, but it was considered a joint parental duty on behalf of the children's health and well-being.[1510] Quite who owned 'Maisonette' is unclear, but Mayne paid the insurance for the property in 1839.[1511] In the run-up to Christmas 1838 it was reported that 'the lady of Richard Mayne' had supplied the poor of Ingatestone and the adjoining parish of Fryerning with a bountiful supply of beef.[1512]

With Rowan in Scotland and his wife and children in Essex, Mayne was frequently left alone, both professionally and privately, in London during the summer months. The principal source of information for this was a series of letters Mayne wrote to his wife between 1837 and 1865. In the first of these, written in January 1837 Mayne announced:

1506 *London Courier and Evening Gazette*, 29 May 1834, p.4.
1507 Old Bailey Proceedings Online (www.oldbaileyonline.org, version 7.2, 18 January 2018) July 1834, trial of ROBERT LAST (t18340703-111).
1508 *Morning Post*, 8 July 1835, p.4.
1509 Lee, Sidney (1894). *Dictionary of National Biography*, Volume 37. London: Elder & Son.
1510 Heathcote Collection, op. cit. 1489, pp.8-9.
1511 Royal and Sun Alliance Insurance Group Collection at the London Metropolitan Archives, reference CLC/B/192/F/001/MS11936/566/1298947.
1512 *Essex Herald*, 1 January 1839, p.3.

'I have seen Rowan for a moment only, but there is no news on Police matters, he says. I don't know whether he will go out of town; but if not this week, I shall be down with you to dine on Saturday...'[1513]

On 11 February 1839 a daughter, Georgina Marianne, was born, this time at 'Maisonette'.[1514] Georgina remained single throughout the remainder of Mayne's life, but just sixteen months after his death, on 23 April 1870, she married Horace Broke, the only son of the late Lieutenant-General Horatio Broke. Interestingly, General Broke had served in the 52nd Regiment with Rowan from 1806 to 1813 before transferring to the 58th Regiment. He had died on 30 August 1860 and was buried at Kensal Green Cemetery,[1515] the same place Sir Richard would be buried just over eight years later. Horace was a lawyer, having been a student at both Inner Temple and Lincoln's Inn. Georgina was his second wife, his first wife having died in 1865, leaving him with three young sons and a daughter.[1516]

As early as 1840 came the first indications that Mayne was looking forward to the day when Rowan retired. For, in a letter to his wife, written whilst Rowan was holidaying in Scotland, he wrote:

'The longer he stays away the better pleased I shall be, while he enjoys it. I really wish he should be idling, and for my part I have several advantages. I like carrying on the business alone, I then feel I am really at work.'

Mayne also mentioned that he had had a letter from Rowan, which suggested the latter would return to London on 23 or 24 August. A deeply religious man, Mayne mentioned how his police duties had interfered with his religious duties:

'Yesterday was not passed as a Sunday usually should be, but I hope I may be excused for attending to necessary duty. The whole day I was preparing orders, or with Sir James [Graham, the Home Secretary]; he deals frankly and confidentially, and those are great points to me. His situation is one of terrible anxiety at such times, any allowance ought

---

1513 Henry Hall Collection of diaries, journals, letters, books and miscellaneous papers, donated by Edward Hall (b.1898), a dealer and collector of Manuscripts and books. Includes letters written by Sir Richard Mayne to his wife between 1831 and 1866 in files EHC210/M1251; EHC210A/1252 and EHC 211/M1253, letter 7 from Mayne to his wife, dated 14 January 1837, pp.11-12.
1514 *Essex Standard*, 1 March 1839, p.3.
1515 *Annual Register 1860*, Appendix, pp.395-396.
1516 Foster, Joseph (1885). *Men-at-the-bar, a biography hand-list of the members of the various Inns of Court, including Her Majesty's Judges, etc.* 2nd edition. London: Hazell, Watson and Viney, p.57.

to be made for manner, and excess even of precaution.'[1517]

At the time of the census of 1841, held at the beginning of June, Mayne, his wife and three children, Carvick Cox, Richard and Georgina, were staying at Nuthurst Lodge, a substantial estate of some 900 acres at Nuthurst, Sussex, as the guest of his solicitor, James Nelthorpe.[1518] Nelthorpe was a widower whose wife, Eliza Sarah, had died in Paris in 1826.[1519]

In April 1844 Rowan was again in Scotland, this time at Floors Castle, Kelso. In a letter to Lord Tweeddale, he explained that he had 'been in some degree turned out of his own house', meaning his bachelor quarters at 4 Whitehall Place, by Richard Mayne and his wife 'who is about to be confined there.' Clearly, he did not mind because he had 'profited by the occasion' coming to fish at Floors Castle, 'where the reception is always as kind and friendly as heart can wish', although he did go on to say 'the season has been desperately bad; we have had but few fishing days and but few salmon yet, altho' plenty of kelts...'[1520] It is difficult to be precise about what Rowan meant here. Mayne's wife duly gave birth to their fourth child, Edward, over six months later, on 30 October, but he was clearly not a well child for he died in August 1846 of brain fever.[1521] It can only be assumed that his wife had a difficult pregnancy from an early stage, and Mayne wanted her close to him whilst he was at work.

The year after Edward's death, Georgina gave birth to another son, Robert Dawson. Robert was educated at Balliol College, Oxford and was following in his father's footsteps at Lincoln's Inn at the time of his father's death. Qualifying in 1869, Robert was appointed a stipendiary justice at Port of Spain in Trinidad, but unfortunately died at the age of 42 years on 9 September 1887.[1522] In April 1846, Georgina gave birth to another son, William John. Little is known of him, other than he is believed to have died around August 1902.[1523]

Although Mayne and his wife had attended the Drawing Rooms of William IV and Queen Adelaide, his attendance at Queen Victoria's

---

1517 Henry Hall Collection, op, cit. 1513, letter 25 from Mayne to his wife, dated 11 August 1840, p.57.
1518 1841 Census.
1519 Dudley, Howard (1830). *The Histories and Antiquities of Horsham and its Vicinity*. London: unknown, p.57.
1520 Rowan, letters to Lord Tweeddale in the British Library – Asian and African Studies, MSS Eur F 96, Folio 344.
1521 Ibid.
1522 Moore, Tony (2017). 'The First Chief Constable of Shropshire, Captain Dawson Mayne'. *Journal of the Police History Society*, No. 31, p.33; see also *Morning Post*, 28 August 1844, p.4.
1523 England, Select Births and Christenings, 1538-1975 via www.ancestry.co.uk/family-tree/person/free/85511544/person/385116117254/facts

Levees and, with his wife, Drawing Rooms became a regular occurrence from 1846 onwards.[1524] Levees, of which the Queen held between three and five each year, each with an attendance initially of between 150 and 300, were only attended by men, consisting of diplomats, newly-appointed government officials, and military men. Drawing Rooms, of which the Queen held approximately three each year, were meant to announce and confirm a woman's position in society. Many of the women attending were debutants, but others included women who had had a change in status through marriage or advancement.[1525] Thus Georgina had been presented to Queen Victoria by her mother, who had already been previously presented, after her marriage to Mayne. Mayne was also amongst 200 people who attended an anniversary lunch of the National Mercantile Life Assurance Company at the London Tavern in Bishopsgate Street.[1526]

In July 1850 Georgina gave birth to a second daughter, Sarah Fanny, whilst living at 13 New Street, Spring Gardens.[1527] Sarah Fanny remained single throughout the remainder of both her father's and mother's lives, eventually getting married at St Thomas's, Portman Square on 8 February 1877 to a Barrister of the Inner Temple and Recorder of Thetford in Norfolk, Charles Edward Malden.[1528] Sarah lived until the age of 77 years, dying in Kensington in April 1927, just four months after her husband had died.[1529] New Street ran between Spring Gardens and St James's Park. The houses generally were of three storeys with basement and attic.[1530] Nine months later, in March 1851, the census shows Mayne still living at 13 New Street with his wife and daughter, Fanny, and a nephew, John. He also had at least five staff, a nurse, a lady's maid, a cook, a nursery maid and a footman. His mother lived with them[1531] until she died in October 1853 at the age of 89 years.[1532] In 1852 his wife gave birth to the last of their eight children, another daughter, Katherine Emily.[1533] But between the birth of their two daughters tragedy struck Richard and Georgina again,

1524 *Sun* (London) 19 February, 1846, p.10; Morning Pose 28 May 1847, p.8; *Globe*, 12 May 1848, p.3.
1525 Ellenberger, Nancy W (1990). 'The transformation of London "Society" at the end of the Victoria's Reign: Evidence from the Court Presentation Records'. *Albion*, Vol. 22, No. 4 (Winter), pp.640-641.
1526 *London Evening Standard*, 31 December 1846, p.4.
1527 *London Evening Standard*, 8 July 1850, p.4.
1528 *John Bull*, 17 February 1877, p.16.
1529 *Yarmouth Independent*, 4 December 1926, p.26.
1530 Gater, G.H., and F.R. Hiorns (1940). 'Spring Gardens', in *Survey of London*; see www.british-history.ac.uk/survey-london.vol20/pt3/pp58-65, [accessed 5 December 2019].
1531 1851 Census; *Freeman's Journal*, 2 November 1853, p.4.
1532 *Morning Post*, 31 October 1853, p.8.
1533 England, Select Births and Christenings, 1538-1975, op. cit. 1523.

when they suffered the loss of a second child. This time it was their first-born Carvick Cox, who died of heart disease at Penhurst in Sussex on 23 September 1851.[1534]

The British elite was dominated by a landowning aristocracy and gentry families who generally regarded their country house as their principal home, but spent several months of the year in London during the social season. During the Victorian era the Social Season coincided with the sitting of Parliament, which was approximately from the beginning of February to the end of June. The Social Season included a number of major occasions, including two big horse-racing events, Epsom, which included the famous Derby, and Ascot, and the annual exhibition at the Royal Academy of Art. Part of the business of the Season was to enable young ladies from the 'right backgrounds' to meet and marry wealthy young men, also from the 'right backgrounds'. Whilst Mayne could never be described as being either from the landowning aristocracy or the gentry, from 1852 onwards he did enter London's High Society, attending a number of 'Fashionable Parties', although his daughters do not seem to have found young men to marry. Perhaps they were put off by Mayne's rather stern approach to life, and his position as Commissioner of Police. The first was in March, when he attended 'a great entertainment' hosted by the Duke and Duchess of Northumberland at Northumberland House.[1535] Two months later, he attended 'an assembly' given by the Countess of Malmesbury, the wife of the then Foreign Secretary at his official residence in Downing Street.[1536] Finally, in November, following 'a grand dinner for the representatives of foreign Sovereigns and armies who attended the funeral of the late Duke of Wellington', the Countess of Derby held a 'reception at which a very brilliant assembly of the aristocracy', Mayne amongst them, 'assembled'.[1537]

For these dinners, Mayne and his son Richard would invariably be dressed in white tie and tails, whilst Georgina would wear a beautiful gown and sparkling jewellery. The dinners, or if it was merely drinks, would be served by butlers, footmen and waiters. There would be solid silver ornaments on the tables, the cutlery would be silver and the food would invariably be served on fine, bone-china plates. Whether Mayne enjoyed such occasions, or attended merely because he felt he ought, is not known.

1534 *London Evening Standard*, 25 September 1851, p.4.
1535 *Morning Post*, 22 March 1852, p.5.
1536 *London Evening Standard*, 27 May 1852, p.1.
1537 *Morning Post*, 29 November 1852, p.5.

At some time during 1856 Mayne moved his family to No. 80 Chester Square,[1538] where he remained until his death. Built around 1835 by Thomas Cubbit, acting on the instructions of Richard Grosvenor, the Second Marquis of Westminster, Chester Square had a rectangular garden in the centre. No. 80 was a four-storey, end of terrace house, with attic and basement; protruding from the first floor was a small terrace. Inadvertently, Mayne's social life seems to have become intertwined with Robert Grosvenor, whose bill had been the cause of the 1855 Hyde Park riot. Richard Grosvenor, who had had some say in the design of the area in which Mayne's house now stood, was the older brother of Robert, and the Duchess of Northumberland was, in fact, Eleanor Grosvenor, the daughter of Richard.

Mayne's neighbours included John Liddell, Director-General of the Medical Department of the Royal Navy from 1855-1864, and senior medical officer of the Royal Hospital at Greenwich, living at No. 72, who died six months before Mayne in June 1868. It was a fashionable area, and has remained so right up to the present day. In more modern times, the top flat of No. 38 was the home of Guy Burgess, one of the Cambridge spies, from 1935 to 1939, Queen Wilhelmina of the Netherlands resided at No. 77 from 1940 to 1945, and Margaret Thatcher lived at No. 73 following her resignation as Prime Minister in 1991 until shortly before her death in 2013. Closer to home, the film actor Steve McQueen and his wife lived at No. 80 during 1961 and 1962 whilst he was filming The War Lover at RAF Bovington in Hertfordshire, RAF Manston in Kent and at Shepperton Studios in Surrey.[1539]

On 10 April, probably just before they moved house, Lady Mayne had the pleasure of presenting her eldest daughter, Georgina (who was, by this time, 17 years of age,) to Queen Victoria, who was accompanied by the Princess Royal, at one of Her Majesty's Drawing Rooms, held at St James's Palace.[1540]

The house move took place shortly before the birth of their ninth and last child, Charles Edward, in August 1856.[1541] Baptised like most of his brothers and sister at St Martin-in-the-Fields,[1542] he was not a particularly strong child, and died as a result of rheumatic fever at the age of 17 years

---

1538 An entry in the *Morning Advertiser*, 8 August 1956, p.8, and a number of other newspapers of the time refers to Lady Mayne residing at 80 Chester Square.
1539 historicengland.org.uk/listing/the-list/list-entry/1001675; *Financial Times* at ft.com/content /6fa4ed8e-ebdd-11e5-a09b-1f8b0d268c39 [both accessed on 27 December 2019].
1540 *London Evening Standard*, 11 April 1856, p.1.
1541 *Morning Advertiser*, 8 August 1856, p.4.
1542 England, Select Births and Christenings, op. cit. 1523.

whilst staying at the home of his tutor, the Reverend William E. Hadow, at South Cerney in Gloucestershire.[1543] He was the fourth of Mayne's nine children to die under the age of 20 years.

From 1855 onwards Mayne frequently travelled outside London on official duties, and he and Lady Mayne increasingly became regular guests at various semi-official and official functions in town. There is insufficient space to give details of them all; suffice to mention a few as an indication that the Commissioner of the Metropolitan Police was now a respected member of London society.

Probably as part of his official duties, Mayne was on the Isle of Wight on 6 August 1857 when Queen Victoria entertained the Emperor Napoleon and the Empress at Osborne House.[1544] Previously that year, he had been in Paris in March when he had been received by the Emperor.[1545] Between these two commitments, he had been amongst the guests when Count and Countess Bernstorff entertained Queen Victoria and other members of the Royal Family at a banquet at Prussia House in London in July.[1546] Bernstorff was the Prussian Ambassador to London from 1853 to 1861.

Sir Richard was again a guest at Prussia House early the following year, when the Count and Countess entertained the Crown Prince and Princess of Prussia whilst they were on a visit to Britain.[1547] In March, Sir Richard and Lady Mayne were guests at an assembly given by the Countess of Derby, wife of three times-Prime Minister the Earl of Derby, at the family mansion in St. James Square. In May, Sir Richard and Lady Mayne were guests of the Duchess of Northumberland, whose husband was a Conservative Member of the House of Lords, at Northumberland House.[1548] No doubt, partly due to son Richard's blossoming career in the Royal Navy, Sir Richard and Lady Mayne attended a number of functions at the First Lord's official residence at The Admiralty,[1549] during which time the post was held firstly by Sir Charles Wood, from 1855 to 1858, and then by Edward Seymour, the 12th Duke of Somerset, from 1859 to 1866.

In January 1861, Sir Richard and Lady Mayne were guests at the wedding of the Countess of Rothes and the Honourable George Waldegrave, whom Mayne is likely to have known as a fellow barrister, at All Souls'

1543 *Stroud News and Gloucestershire Advertiser*, 5 December 1873, p.5.
1544 *Morning Post*, 7 August 1857, p.5.
1545 Ibid, 9 March 1857, p.5.
1546 *Morning Post*, 7 July 1857, p.5.
1547 *Morning Post*, 25 January 1858, p.5.
1548 *Morning Post*, 20 May 1858, p.5.
1549 See, for example, *Saunders's News Letter and Daily Advertiser*, 22 February 1856, p.2; the *Morning Post*, 25 February 1864, p.5.

Church, Langham Place.[1550] In May 1861 Georgina took 'the boys' to Paris. Unfortunately, whilst she was away their daughter Katherine, then aged 9 years, developed rheumatic fever which was initially critical.[1551] Although she recovered on this occasion, she would pass away seven years later. Nevertheless, the same month Mayne received a letter from Captain John Moore, Private Naval Secretary to the First Lord of the Admiralty, then the 12th Duke of Somerset, which must have given him much pleasure:

> 'I am very glad to be desired by the Duke of Somerset to inform you that he has this day promoted your Son. The Duke desires me to add that, whilst he is glad to have the opportunity of expressing his sense of your own services, he is happy to say that your Son's high character has enabled him to promote him, in the belief that he will be a most efficient addition to the list of Commanders.'

In forwarding this letter on to his wife on the continent, Mayne wrote, 'Dearest love, what additional proof of God's protecting, guiding love this is, let us seek to serve Him better and love Him more.'[1552]

In April 1862 Sir Richard and Lady Mayne, eldest daughter Georgina and eldest surviving son Richard, now Captain Mayne RN, were amongst nearly 200 guests at the annual Easter Monday banquet given by the Lord Mayor and Lady Mayoress of the City of London at the Mansion House.[1553] A month later Sir Richard and Lady Mayne, together with Richard, were guests at a function given by the Duchess of Northumberland at Northumberland House at which the principal guests were a number of Ambassadors, members of parliament and senior naval officers.[1554] Mayne also attended a meeting of the Royal Geographical Society where, amongst other things, his son Richard presented a paper on an exploratory journey he had made across Vancouver Island.[1555] At the beginning of March 1867 Sir Richard and Lady Mayne were amongst a select number of guests entertained to dinner by Alexander Beresford-Hope and Lady Mildred Beresford-Hope at Askew House, Connaught Place.[1556]

Towards the end of his life Mayne took regular holidays with his wife. For

---

1550 *The Edinburgh Evening Courant*, 24 January 1861, p.3.
1551 Henry Hall Collection, op. cit. 1513, letter 110 from Mayne to his wife, dated 11 May 1861, pp.232-33.
1552 Ibid, letter 111 from Mayne to his wife, dated 22 May 1861, pp.234-35.
1553 *London Daily News*, 22 April 1862, p.3.
1554 *London Evening Standard*, 22 May 1862, p.3.
1555 *Atlas*, 17 May 1862, p.5.
1556 *Globe*, 4 March 1867, p.3. Alexander was, at the time the Member of Parliament for Stoke-on-Trent and an ardent supporter of the Church of England. His wife, Lady Mildred, was the daughter of the 2nd Marquess of Salisbury and, for many years, was a leading figure in London society.

instance, in September 1863 he was reported to be enjoying 'his autumnal holiday abroad'.[1557] In fact, the previous month, Mayne had embarked alone on a trip to Germany which took in Cologne, Coblenz, Dresden, Frankfurt and Maine. Quite why he made this trip is unclear. Whilst in Dresden he met up with his wife, who was there with son Robert,[1558] now eighteen years old. In October 1864 the couple stayed for a brief period at Sivier's Hotel, which adjoined the Royal Victoria Yacht Club in Ryde on the Isle of Wight,[1559] and they were fairly frequent visitors to Southsea where they stayed in the Portland Hotel.[1560] Both were fashionable resorts of the day. The Sivier's Hotel had been rebuilt during the winter of 1856/57 to provide luxury accommodation.[1561] Their last visit to the Portland at the end of October 1968 was undertaken a mere two months before Sir Richard's death.[1562]

In the summer of 1865 Mayne was a guest of honour of the Royal Navy, during which there was an exchange of courtesies between the British and the French fleet. Quite why he was accorded this honour is not recorded, but it is likely to be for one of two reasons. Either because he was the Commissioner of the Metropolitan Police and was responsible for policing the naval dockyards, or because he was the father of a young rising naval officer. In a letter to his wife he described how he left Portsmouth on 14 August aboard HMS *Osborne*, referring to it as 'a grand spectacle' as it led eleven other Naval ships into Cherbourg harbour. He then told her that the cruise was most enjoyable, and that they would leave on Friday afternoon, stopping on Saturday and Sunday at Guernsey and Jersey respectively, before going on to Brest where they were expected to arrive on Monday morning. On Thursday, they would return to Portsmouth. He also mentioned that he thought at first he had made a mistake in not bringing Gibbs, one of his staff at 80 Chester Square, but had been 'turned over to a trusty Marine, who valets me most effectively.' He concluded:

> 'How extraordinary it seems that I should be here, and on this anniversary writing to you. May God bless you as He has done – may I add, as you deserve. I look with confidence to your restoration to health and strength.'[1563]

1557 *City of London News*, 12 September 1863, p.6.
1558 Henry Hall Collection, op. cit. 1513, letter nos. 112-113 from Mayne to his wife, pp.236-246.
1559 *Isle of Wight Observer*, 1 October 1864, p.1.
1560 *Morning Post* 20 November 1863, p.5, and 9 September 1865, p.5.
1561 *Isle of Wight Observer*, 19 January 1856, p.1.
1562 *Hampshire Telegraph and Sussex Chronicle*, 31 October 1868, p.3.
1563 Henry Hall Collection, op. cit. 1513, letter 114 from Mayne to his wife, dated 15 August 1865, pp.247-260.

A month before the ill-fated Hyde Park demonstration on 23 July 1866, Mayne wrote to his wife:

> 'Your birthday tomorrow reminds me that, no less than 5 and 30 years ago, when I first had a right to an affianced wife; how long a course of married life, happy I believe beyond any other I have known! Gratitude to God, and a prayer for its continuance, are ours in large measure...'[1564]

May 1867 saw the death of his brother William, who was living at 95 Ebury Street, Pimlico.[1565] This was followed by two events in April the following year, one of which will have given Mayne pleasure, the other, no doubt, tinged with sadness. On 1 April his wife attended one of Queen Victoria's Drawing Rooms, along with daughters Sarah and Georgina, where she had the honour of presenting the former to Her Majesty.[1566] Two days later, his sister Catherine died at Dorking in Surrey.[1567] This was followed just over five months later by the death of Katherine.[1568]

After being ill for a few weeks,[1569] Sir Richard Mayne died on 26 December 1868 at his home at 80 Chester Square. His death certificate[1570] shows that he had had a pelvic abscess for three weeks. The following day, Assistant Commissioner Harris distributed the news to the Force:

> 'It is with deep regret that the Assistant Commissioner has to announce to the Force, the lamented death of Sir R. Mayne, KCB, which took place at his residence, 80, Chester Square at 10.30 p.m., 26th inst. During a period of 40 years devoted to the service of his country, Sir R. Mayne has gained the lasting gratitude and esteem of all classes; and to his sound judgment ability, the most unceasing exertions to promote the welfare of the Service, is to be attributed that complete system of organization which has excited the attention even of Foreign Governments.
>
> The Assistant Commissioner thinks that all ranks of the Force will continue by their good conduct and attention to duties to maintain the high reputation acquired under their late distinguished leader.'[1571]

On 28 December the superintendents of the Force submitted to the Assistant Commissioners a request to open a subscription for a memorial:

1564 Ibid, letter no. 118, from Mayne to his wife, dated 16 August 1865, p.261.
1565 Believed to be his sister, Margaret.
1566 *Morning Post*, 2 April 1868, p.5.
1567 London, England, Deaths and Burials, 1813-1980.
1568 See previous chapter.
1569 Ibid.
1570 Copy in possession of the author.
1571 TNA MEPO 7/30, Police Order 27 December 1868.

'We, The Superintendents of the Metropolitan Police, having heard with deep regret of the Death of Sir Richard Mayne, are desirous of testifying our esteem and veneration for his character and uprightness in the discharge of his public duties. We therefore beg the authority of the Assistant Commissioners to open a subscription in each Division for the purpose of raising a Testimonial or Monument to his Memory, with the subscription by each member of the Force not to exceed one day's pay of the rank he holds, or be less than one shilling.

The form of Testimonial or Monument to be decided on hereafter.'

In publishing this suggestion by the superintendents in a Police Order, Assistant Commissioners Harris and Labalmondière added: 'We entirely concur in the proposition to raise a Monument to the Memory of our esteemed and valued chief.' In the same Order, it was announced that Sir Richard Mayne would be interred in Kensal Green Cemetery at 10.00am on Wednesday, 30 December, and that Lieutenant Colonel Douglas Labalmondière had been appointed by the Secretary of State 'to perform the duties of Chief Commissioner of the Metropolitan Police' until a replacement had been decided upon.[1572]

On 30 December 1868, the cortege consisted of a hearse and three mourning coaches which contained two of his sons, William and Robert; two of his brothers, Captain Dawson Mayne, the Chief Constable of Staffordshire, and Mr Edward Mayne, together with his son, also called Edward; Captain William Mayne, and Richard's brother-in-law Thomas Mayor Carvick;[1573] together with the two Assistant Commissioners of Police, Colonel Labalmondière and Captain Harris.

Twenty-one past and present superintendents were present at his funeral in plain clothes. The service was conducted by the Reverend J. Steward, chaplain of the cemetery. Sir Richard was laid beside his brother William Mayne, buried there just over a year previously, and his beloved daughter, Katherine.[1574]

On 11 January 1869 it was announced that the sum of £586 8s 9d had been collected for the Mayne Memorial Fund.[1575] The Monument eventually erected in the Kensal Green Cemetery to the memory of Sir Richard Mayne was unveiled at a special ceremony on 24 January 1871, to

---

[1572] Ibid, Police Order 28 December 1868.
[1573] Interestingly, Thomas Carvick, who originally joined the 78th Regiment, transferred to Rowan's old regiment, the 52nd Regiment, in 1843, whilst Rowan was still Commissioner. See *London Gazette*, 14 April 1843, issue 20213, p.1235.
[1574] *London Illustrated News*, 2 January 1868, p.4.
[1575] TNA MEPO 7/31, Police Order 11 January 1869.

which any police officer was invited to attend if it did not interfere with his duties.[1576] The monument, an obelisk in Pink Peterhead Granite with an Irish granite base, is located on the south side of Centre Avenue. It is the second tallest obelisk in the cemetery, and is Grade II listed.[1577]

On 21 January, the copy of a letter from General Charles Grey, Queen Victoria's private secretary, to the Secretary of State for the Home Department, appeared in Police Orders:

> 'The Queen desires me to say how grieved and concerned she is to hear of Sir R. Mayne's death. Notwithstanding the attacks lately made upon him, Her Majesty believes him to have been a most efficient head of the Police, and to have discharged the duties of his important situation most ably and satisfactorily in very difficult times.'[1578]

Although Mayne died, tired and embittered at his home in Chester Square on Boxing Day 1868, and he had made mistakes, he had achieved astonishing things. The original force of less than 1,000 men had grown to nearly 8,000. The area it policed had increased tenfold, and the system of policing which he and Rowan had implemented had spread to every county and town in the country.

The sole executor of his will was his wife, referred to in the document as 'Dame Georgina Mayne'. After making 'immediate provision' for her, Mayne 'left the residue of his property, real and personal, upon trust as to income, for his wife for life, and as to the capital after her death for his children in such a manner as his wife should by deed or will appoint.'[1579]

Dame Georgiana Mayne was granted a 'Civil List' pension of £150 'in consideration of the personal service of her late husband, Sir Richard Mayne, to the Crown, and of the faithful performance of his duty to the public.'[1580]

Lady Mayne died aged 60 on 12 April 1872 in Boulogne-sur-mer while returning home from a visit to Rome.[1581] Following her death the pension went to Sir Richard's daughter, Sarah Fanny, but at the reduced rate of £90 per annum.[1582] His son, Captain Richard Mayne, was still in occupation of 80 Chester Square in 1872.[1583]

1576 TNA MEPO 7/33, Police Order, 19 January 1871.
1577 The author visited Mayne's grave in November 2018 and was given information on the obelisk at the cemetery office.
1578 TNA MEPO 7/31, Police Order, 11 January 1869.
1579 *Morning Post*, 27 January 1869, p.5.
1580 *Lloyds Weekly Newspaper*, 31 July 1870, p.2.
1581 *Morning Post*, 18 April 1872, p.5.
1582 *London Illustrated News*, 27 July 1862, p.22.
1583 *Post Office London Directory* for 1872. London: W. Kelly & Co., p.233.

Whilst Sir Richard had been subjected to some criticism in his later years, it did not last long. Following the appointment of Sir Edmund Henderson newspapers began to refer back to the time when Sir Richard had been Commissioner. In announcing that Lady Mayne had been awarded her pension, one newspaper felt it necessary to comment further:

> 'When we remember the faithful service of the late Sir Richard Mayne, his lifelong devotions to the interest of the public, and the very inadequate salary he received (£1,500 a year) this pension to his widow is some slight tribute to the memory of a zealous servant of the Crown, whose name will long be remembered in connection with the force he organized and commanded for so many years. That there are faults in the force no one can deny, but these faults have crept in of later years, and in no way detract from the merit of the system of policing originally framed by Sir Richard Mayne. He was a thorough lawyer, and no one knew better than himself the limits beyond which it was unsafe for the police to act. His pride was to preserve the police as a constitutional forcer dependant on Government up to the point at which Government itself is independent but beyond that point the police looked to the acts of Parliament and not to the Home Secretary's directions. Although in the later years of his life, when, overwhelmed by business, his health was declining, he perhaps allowed a little too much drill and suffered the force to assume rather a military aspect, he never forgot that a policeman is a constable and not a soldier, and no private interest or influential entreaties induced him to permit the employment of the police in other than police duties. In his passion for work he undertook duties which, although authorised by Parliament, are not strictly duties of the Metropolitan police, and it would be better for the force, had the duties connected with common-lodging houses, smoke nuisance, dangerous structures, dockyards, military stations, cattle disease, contagious diseases, &c, been entrusted to other hands, and the Metropolitan Police been allowed to confine themselves to their proper mission of keeping order in the streets, and preventing and detecting crime. He died a martyr to overwork and multifarious duties he conscientiously performed. His heart was too much in the work to pay any attention to the insufficiency of the salary allotted for its performance, and in giving this small pension to his widow the country is only somewhat tardily paying some portion of the debt it owed to her husband at the time of his death.'[1584]

1584 *Clerkenwell News*, 29 July 1870, p.3.

CHAPTER TWENTY-FIVE

THE LEGACY OF ROWAN AND MAYNE

So ended almost forty years of police history! Rowan and Mayne had 'raised the [Metropolitan Police] which Peel had founded from a not too popular experiment to an essential institution.'[1585] Although the last few years of Mayne's commissionership were marred by misjudgement and criticism, nearly three years after his death a period of rehabilitation began when the media, in particular, began to look on the influence he had had on the Metropolitan Police, even during those final years, in a more favourable light.

In October 1872, following a meeting of four thousand constables 'to discuss their grievances',[1586] one newspaper suggested the Metropolitan Police had 'steadily gone on from worse to worse';[1587] another that the force was 'in a disjointed and unsettled condition that would surprise and grieve the …late Sir Richard Mayne, who formed it, and for many years drove the team with a success that only failed when ill-health, produced by overwork and anxiety, struck down one of the most valuable public servants that ever served the Crown and the public.'[1588] A month later, the same newspaper pointed out 'the London police, upon which we are dependent for the safety of the capital' was 'not in a satisfactory state, that the men [did] not respect their officers, and that the tone of the whole body [had] been perceptibly lowered since the death of Sir Richard Mayne.' Whilst not knowing what exactly was wrong, the paper said it did know that 'nothing of this spirit' was 'exhibited while Sir Richard Mayne was in command.'[1589]

1585 Browne, Douglas G (1956). *The Rise of Scotland Yard; A History of the Metropolitan Police.* London: George G. Harrop, p.144.
1586 *Pall Mall Gazette,* 19 October 1872, p.4.
1587 *The Examiner,* 23 November 1872, p.4.
1588 *Pall Mall Gazette,* 19 October 1872, p.4.
1589 *Pall Mall Gazette,* 23 November 1872, p.2.

A year later, *Lloyd's* suggested 'the force has been losing in public estimation since the death of Sir Richard Mayne.'[1590]

Ten years after his death, following a number of incidents, letters were published in the *London Evening Standard* which led the newspaper to allege that the police had been 'riotous, violent, and, in addition, seem to have used language of a very gross and objectionable kind.' Suggesting the claims were supported by the magistrate before whom those arrested were taken, in that most were discharged or bound over, a leading article said 'under Sir Richard Mayne, the police considered themselves guardians of the peace', but they now behaved 'as if they believed themselves to be an army in possession, put to keep in order a conquered, disaffected, and rebellious country.' It went on to say:

> 'The late Commissioner was not, it is true, a soldier or master of drill; but he was a sound lawyer and a shrewd man of the world. The one lesson he constantly impressed upon his subordinates was that they were a civil and not a military body, and it [was] for many reasons [a] matter of regret that the traditions which grew up under his rule, and to which Sir Edmund Henderson succeeded, should not have been more carefully preserved.'[1591]

Eighteen months later, it was reported that 'ever since the death of the late Sir Richard Mayne, the Metropolitan Police [had] been steadily deteriorating', and it was no secret that the state of affairs at Scotland Yard had 'been a source of grave anxiety to the Home Office for some time past'. It was then suggested that 'one of most troublesome questions' that the new Home Secretary, Sir William Harcourt, would have to deal with 'was the reorganisation of the administrative department of the Metropolitan Police.'[1592]

Nearly eighteen years after his death, newspapers still referred to Sir Richard Mayne. Thus, when they were calling for the resignation of Colonel Henderson following his mishandling of a riot in Trafalgar Square in 1886,[1593] it was suggested that although pay had increased, hours had been shortened and holidays multiplied, the 'morale of the police force [had] gone down', and there had been no apparent 'increase in efficiency.'

1590 *Lloyd's Weekly Newspaper*, 9 November 1873, p.6.
1591 *London Evening Standard*, 16 November 1878, p.4.
1592 *The Examiner*, 29 May 1880, p.660.
1593 PP 1886 [C.4665]. Report of a committee to inquire and report as to the origin and character of the disturbances which took place in the metropolis on Monday, the 8th of February, and as to the conduct of the police authorities in relation thereto; with minutes of evidence and appendix; with memorandum by the Secretary of State for the Home Department therein.

The *Pall Mall Gazette* pointed out that while they could not 'resuscitate Sir Richard Mayne', what was needed was 'a dash of the Mayne element at Scotland Yard.'[1594]

For the next 77 years, with just two exceptions – James Monro and Sir Edward Henry, who had backgrounds in the Indian Police – the Commissioner of the Metropolitan Police came from a military background. Not until Sir Harold Scott, a career civil servant, was appointed Commissioner in 1945, was the Metropolitan Police again under the command of a commissioner that had neither policing nor military experience, as it had been during Sir Richard Mayne's tenure.[1595]

Rowan and Mayne's legacy should be immense. Indeed, it is immense. Unfortunately, it has largely gone unrecognised because police historians (and, in some cases, police chiefs) have tended, incorrectly, to attribute much of what they achieved during that vital first decade to Sir Robert Peel. He has been referred to as the father of modern policing,[1596] but there are those who take issue with this. Roach, for instance, points out that Peel's contemporary biographers, for example, William Cooke Taylor hardly mention his involvement in the formation of the Metropolitan Police,[1597] and this suggests his fame as the founder 'is a much more recent development.'[1598]

However, without his persistence in driving through legislation that led to the formation of the Metropolitan Police and, perhaps more importantly, his appointment of Rowan and Mayne as the first two commissioners, it might have been very different. Just over a year after the Metropolitan Police had been formed, the Tory government (in which Peel was the Home Secretary) resigned, and for the next eleven years, with the exception of four months approximately halfway through this period, Britain had a Whig government. The Whig party was strongly opposed to

---

1594 *Pall Mall Gazette*, 17 February 1886, p.1.
1595 The background of all Metropolitan Police Commissioners up until 1999 can to be found in Fido, Martin, and Keith Skinner (1999). *The Official Encyclopedia of Scotland Yard*. London: Virgin Books.
1596 Bayley, David, Michael A. Davis, and Ronald L. Davis (2015). 'New Perspectives in Policing: Race and Policing: An Agenda for Action. Laurel MD: Office of Justice Programs', U.S. Department of Justice, p.5; Law Enforcement Action Partnership. law enforcementactionpartnership.org/peel-policing-principles accessed 30 May 2019; Jones, Eric, Chief of the Stockton Police (2017). 'The Evolution of Policing'; a presentation to the Stanford Institute for Economic Policy Research (SIEPR) on 21 April.
1597 Cooke Taylor, W (1851). *The Life and Times of Sir Robert Peel: a biography in 4 Volumes*. London: Peter Jackson, Vol. II, pp.4-10. '
1598 Roach, Lawrence (2004). 'The Origins and Impact of the Function of the Crime Investigation and Detection in the British Police Service: A thesis submitted in partial fulfilment of the requirements for the degree of Doctor of Philosophy of Loughborough University'. Loughborough: Loughborough University's Institutional Repository, p.47.

the formation of such a body. If Peel had not got his legislation through parliament when he did, it is likely it would have been another eleven years before such an opportunity arose again, when Peel, by then the leader of the Tory party, became Prime Minister. But, had that been the case, more tragically, the outstanding partnership of Rowan and Mayne would almost certainly not have existed.

So, whilst it might be said that Peel was the father of modern policing, Rowan and Mayne's contribution to it has been continually undermined by the many references to Peel as the architect of the modern police service.[1599] An architect is a person who plans, designs and reviews the construction of something. It derives from the Greek word for chief builder.[1600] Peel did not plan, design or review the Metropolitan Police. Indeed, having got his Bill through Parliament he left it, primarily to Rowan and Mayne, assisted on occasions by officials at the Home Office, 'to lay the foundation of the modern police service'.[1601] Peel merely provided the Commissioners with a skeleton of what the Metropolitan Police should look like through the legislation he introduced.

There were only two principles – and there is considerable doubt as to whether they can genuinely be termed as principles – that Peel formulated right at the start. Firstly, despite their official title of Justice of the Peace stipulated in the legislation, Rowan and Mayne would be referred to as the Commissioners of Police[1602] to distinguish them from the Justices appointed to the police offices in the Metropolis. The second was that 'jobbery' must be excluded in the selection of people for the Metropolitan Police. Peel insisted people would be appointed on their perceived ability to do the job, not upon the recommendation of some 'highly-placed individual', which was extremely rife in Victorian society at the time. This particularly applied to promotion to the posts of superintendent, inspector and sergeant. Peel was adamant that 'police efficiency' was not to be undermined by 'political influence,' because he wanted the Metropolitan Police to be placed 'on a democratic basis of self-government'. It fell to Rowan and Mayne to uphold this last principle, 'not only against private pressure from highly-placed individuals anxious to find situations for "poor gentlemen" and others, but even against the backsliding on the part

---

1599 Bronitt, Simon, and Philip Sterring (2011). 'Understanding discretion in modern policing', in *Criminal Law Journal* 35(6), pp.319-332, p.323.
1600 www.definitions.net/definition/architect [accessed 22 March 2019].
1601 Roach, op, cit. 1598, p.47.
1602 They did not officially become Commissioners until 1839 by virtue of the Metropolitan Police Act of that year.

of Peel's successors at the Home Office.'[1603] It was Rowan and Mayne who played the crucial role in 'fleshing out the skeleton – providing the force's distinctive features and developing its overall image.'[1604]

Peel, whilst in opposition, was a member of the three committees that sat to inquire into various aspects of the Metropolitan Police in 1833 and 1834,[1605] but he did not chair these committees, and, indeed, there is little evidence that he took an active part. Similarly, he was one of fifteen members of the committee that sat in 1837 and 1838 to enquire into Police Offices. In 1837, whilst he attended the opening session, he attended none of the thirteen sessions in which witnesses were questioned; in 1838, of the eleven sessions, he attended only four.[1606] Again, he chaired neither committee, and other than, perhaps, making some observations when the final report was being discussed, there is again little evidence that he was active.

The issue that denigrates Rowan and Mayne's legacy more than any other is the constant reference by many historians and police chiefs to Peel's Principles of Policing; generally there are nine,[1607] but, occasionally, there are more.[1608] There are many examples, but suffice to highlight a few from around the world at this point. Bryn Caless, an academic and former director of human resources with an English police force, claimed Peel 'formulated nine Principles of Policing.'[1609] David Bayley, et al – Bayley was on the staff of the School of Criminal Justice in New York at the time – stated Peel 'was credited with formulating nine principles of policing'.[1610] Peter Moir, an Australian academic, in questioning some of the basic assumptions of community policing, thought it worthwhile to

---

1603 Moylan, J.F (1929). *Scotland Yard and The Metropolitan Police*. London: G.P. Putnam's Sons, pp.32-33.
1604 Miller, Wilbur R (1999). *Cops and Bobbies: Police Authority in New York and London, 1830-1870* (Second Edition). Columbus: Ohio State University Press, p.2.
1605 PP 1833 [627]. Report from the Select Committee on the Petition of Frederick Young and Others (police); PP 1833 [675]. Report from the Select Committee on Metropolitan Police; PP 1834 [600].Report from the Select Committee on the Police of the Metropolis; with minutes of evidence, appendix and index.
1606 PP 1837 [451]. Report from the Select Committee on Metropolitan Police Offices; with the minutes of evidence, appendix and index; PP 1837-1838 [578]. Report from Select Committee on Metropolitan Police Offices; with minutes of evidence, appendix and index.
1607 Reith, Charles (1956). *A New Study of Police History*. Edinburgh: Oliver and Boyd, pp.287-288.
1608 For instance, twelve are identified by Peake, Kenneth (1993). 'Policing in America: Methods, Issues, Challenges'; Pamela Mayhall in *Community Relations and the Administration of Justice*.
1609 Caless, Bryn (2011). *Policing at the Top: The roles, values and attitudes of chief police officers*. Bristol: Policy Press, footnote on p.215.
1610 Bayley et al (2015), op. cit. 1596, p.5.

use one of Peel's nine Principles of Policing as a starting point.[1611] The website of Law Enforcement Action, an organisation in the United States designed to unite and mobilize the voice of law enforcement in support of criminal justice reforms relating to community safety, states that 'in 1829, Peel established a list of policing principles that remain as crucial and urgent today as they were two centuries ago'.[1612] Merrick Bobb, who reviewed the National Oversight Model for the Eugene Police Department in the United States, claimed that 'Peel formulated a set of principles that made clear that the police were accountable to the wider public of which they were part' and went on to suggest 'Peel's nine principles became the foundation for English policing.'[1613] Timothy Brain, a former chief officer turned historian, refers to 'the principles of preventative policing introduced in London by Sir Robert Peel in 1829.'[1614] Another former chief officer, John Alderson, also credits Peel with these principles.[1615] William J. Bratton, successively Commissioner of Police in Boston, New York and Chief of Police in Los Angeles, claimed on becoming Commissioner of New York Police for the second time in 2014 that Peel's nine Principles were his Bible, and he carried them with him everywhere.[1616] Following a recent spate of fatal shootings involving police officers in the United States, Debo P. Adegbile, in referring to the relationship between law enforcement and the community, referred to 'the Peelian framework of policing, which emphasizes the capacity of community-focused policing to serve our communities through well-calibrated practices and policies', and claimed that 'to make a formal police force acceptable to the public' Peel set 'out nine principles that every officer was to follow.'[1617]

But Peel did not formulate any Principles of Policing other than the two doubtful ones already mentioned, a view clearly articulated by Wilbur Miller, now Professor of History at Stony Brook University in New York, who states categorically that he neither 'originated the concept of preventive police', not 'did he have much impact on the subsequent

---

1611 Moir, Peter (1990). *Community Policing: Questioning some basic assumption.* Canberra City: Australian Institute of Criminology, p.59.
1612 Law Enforcement Action Partnership. lawenforcementactionpartnership.org/peel-policing-principles accessed 30 May 2019.
1613 Bobb, Merrick (2005). *Review of National Police Oversight Models for The Eugene Police Commission.* Los Angeles: Police Assessment Resource Center, p.3.
1614 Brain, Timothy (2010). *A History of Policing in England and Wales from 1974: A Turbulent Journey.* Oxford: Oxford University Press, p.258.
1615 Alderson, John (1979). *Policing Freedom.* Plymouth: Macdonald and Evans, p.198; Alderson, John (1984). *Law and Disorder.* London: Hamish Hamilton, p.134.
1616 Nagle, Michael (2014). 'Sir Robert Peel's Nine Principles of Policing'. *New York Times,* 15 April.
1617 Adegbile, Debo P (2017). 'Policing Through an American Prism' in *Yale Law Journal,* Volume 126. Issue 7/4, pp.2228-2230.

organisation' and, more importantly in the context of Rowan and Mayne's legacy, the 'practice of the force'.[1618] In an examination of Peel's so-called Principles in 2007, Lentz and Chaires conclude that they were 'a later twentieth century invention', although they may have been constructed from 'common themes, values or vent principles' to be 'found in earlier times'. But they go further, claiming that the continued intimation that 'Sir Robert Peel wrote or even held such principles is simply inappropriate'.[1619]

This is not new. The Principles of Policing, so often attributed to Peel, were in fact formulated almost one hundred years after his death by the British police historian Charles Reith. He first articulated the so-called Nine Principles in 1943, suggesting they had been 'evolved, almost unconsciously in ...overcoming the immense difficulties with which [the New Police] was confronted'.[1620] Bayley and Stenning, the latter a Canadian academic who has worked for much of the time in Australia, recently reinforced this by pointing out the so-called Peelian Principles 'were in fact developed by Charles Reith over a hundred years later'.[1621] Another British police historian, Robert Reiner, goes further, referring to them as 'the Reithian Principles', although he then adds, incorrectly, that they were 'derived from those originally formulated by Sir Robert Peel in 1829.'[1622]

Some accept this evidence, but, unfortunately, the so-called Peelian Principles are so embedded in police history it is still felt necessary to refer to them as Peel's Nine Principles of Policing; and, Peel continues to be referred to as the architect of modern policing. For instance, whilst admitting that recent research suggested the Nine Principles were the creation of twentieth century police scholars, in particular Charles Reith, Bronitt, an Australian academic, and Stenning still insist 'the mandate of the modern police is typically traced to the architect of modern British policing, Sir Robert Peel and his Nine Principles of Policing.'[1623] When the UK Government issued a Definition of Policing by Consent in December 2012, it first of all said 'there was no evidence of any link to Sir Robert

---

1618 Miller, op. cit. 1604, p.2.
1619 Lentz, Susan A, and Robert H. Chaires (2006). 'The invention of Peel's principles: A study of policing 'textbook' history' in *Journal of Criminal Justice* 35, p.74.
1620 Reith, Charles (1943). *British Police and the Democratic Ideal*. Oxford: Oxford University Press, p.3.
1621 Bayley, David H, and Philip C. Stenning (2016). *Governing the Police: Experience in Six Democracies*. New Jersey: Transaction, p.44.
1622 Reiner, Robert (2010). *The Politics of the Police*. Fourth Edition. Oxford: Oxford University Press, p.47.
1623 Bronitt, Simon, and Philip Stenning (2011). 'Understanding discretion in modern policing', in *Criminal Law Journal* 35(6), pp.319-332, p.323.

Peel' of the Nine Principles of Policing, claiming 'it was likely devised by the first Commissioners of Police of the Metropolis (Charles Rowan and Richard Mayne).' However it then goes on to suggest that Reith's Nine Principles 'were set out in the "General Instructions" that were issued to every new police officer from 1829.'[1624] Similarly, Reiner claimed, it was the distinctive achievement of the policies pursued by the architects of modern British policing, Sir Robert Peel and his appointees as metropolitan commissioners, Rowan and Mayne, 'that, in setting up the first modern police force, they were able to defuse the anxiety felt by so many that any such force 'would inevitably be a tool of government oppression.'[1625]

The definitive book on the Principles of Policing was written in 1985 by Michael S. Pike, at the time a serving police officer in England, some 43 years after Reith first articulated his Nine Principles of Policing. Pike suggests that although Peel steered the Act through Parliament, 'many details of the new police system' were left to Rowan and Mayne, 'who had considerable discretion in deciding on policy and organisation.'[1626] Pike attributes the drawing up of the instructions for the Metropolitan Police, 'namely the prevention of crime, the protection of life and property and the preservation of public tranquillity' to Mayne,[1627] whilst Rowan 'is generally regarded as having made the greater contribution in organising the force and basing it on military lines.'[1628]

There is evidence from two primary sources that supports the fact that it was Rowan and Mayne who were instrumental in developing the instructions for the Metropolitan Police rather than Peel. The most telling came from Rowan in answering a question from a member of the 1834 Committee, already referred to in Chapter Seven; he said, 'everything that has been done since the commencement has originated with the Commissioners'.[1629] The second comes in a letter Phillipps wrote to Peel on 26 September 1829 following the unfortunate release of the instructions to the press:[1630]

1624 www.gov.uk/government/publications/policing-by-consent/definition-of-policing-by-consent [accessed 9 December 2019]
1625 Reiner, Robert (1992). 'Police Research in the United Kingdom: A Critical Review', in Tonry, Michael and Norral Morris (Eds) (1992). *Modern Policing*. Chicago: University of Chicago Press, pp.435-508, p.436.
1626 Pike, Michael S (1985). *The Principles of Policing*. Basingstoke: MacMillan, p.11.
1627 Ibid, p.36.
1628 Ibid, p.11.
1629 PP 1834 [600]. Report from the Select Committee on the Police of the Metropolis; with minutes of evidence, appendix and index. Minutes of evidence, p.27, q/a 432.
1630 See Chapter Seven.

'The publication of the Regulations was very much to be regretted. For they were in a very new state, and required amendment. That passage which you notice, in pp.50 to 51 is strikingly wrong. I mentioned it yesterday to Mr. Mayne who drew up that part of the Instructions. It is now altered. When you read up [sic] your copy with your remarks, a correct copy shall be immediately printed. There have been no more printed yet.'[1631]

So, whilst Peel approved the 'General Instructions', from which Reith developed the so-called Peelian Principles, it is clear they were written by Rowan and Mayne. It was they, and not Peel, who emphasised, amongst other things, that 'the police would be most effective if they developed close, respectful, and trusting relationships between themselves and the members of the communities they were policing.'[1632]

Melville Lee claims Mayne drew up 'a set of rules and regulations' that embodied the 'principles and maxims upon which our modern police codes rest.'[1633] Charles Reith, who is partly to blame for the controversy that surrounds Peel's so-called Principles of Policing, suggested it was quite clear that 'the conception and invention of many of the theories and ideals' on which policing around much of the democratic world 'is based were the life-work of two men, Charles Rowan and Richard Mayne, whose names and immense services to the nation were forgotten by the public almost as soon as they were dead.' Having provided the skeleton on which the Metropolitan Police was built, and chosen Rowan and Mayne as the first two Commissioners, Peel 'left it to them'. It was they who 'created the Metropolitan Police', providing a 'service' that was, at first, restricted to an area of the Metropolis. But,

'the striking success of the London police force in the face of what had seemed insurmountable difficulties was soon seen and acknowledged in adjoining parishes and country areas. In the course of thirty years, a 'London-model' Police Force was established in every town and county in Great Britain, and in almost every colony and dependency of the empire.'[1634]

The Instructions issued to the Metropolitan Police can be seen in greater detail in Chapter Seven. If a close study is carried out between the

---

1631 British Museum, Peel Papers, 40399, folio 350.
1632 Bailey, David H, and Phillip C. Stenning (2016). *Governing the Police: Experience in Six Democracies*. New Jersey: Transaction, p.44.
1633 Melville Lee, Captain W.L (1901). *A History of Police in England*. London: Methuen, pp.241-242.
1634 Reith, op. cit. 1620, p.26.

Principles developed by Reith in 1943, now frequently referred to as Peel's Principles of Policing, the ideals that emanated from the teachings of Sir John Moore at Shorncliffe between 1804 and 1806,[1635] and the Instructions issued by the Commissioners in 1829 (see Appendix), the similarities will be clearly seen in relation to Principles 1 to 5 and 9. In addition to the initial instructions to the police issued by the Commissioners, they issued a stream of additional instructions each year, either reinforcing the initial ones or introducing new ones as a result of experiences undergone. This is where Reith obtained the information on which he based Principles 6 and 7. Finally, by correspondence with the Home Office and in giving evidence to parliamentary committees, the Commissioners constantly urged the Government to ensure a clear separation between the Judiciary and the Executive, which is the basis for Principle 8.

As a result of Rowan and Mayne's initial Instructions and their continuous attention to detail, in particular, the setting and meeting of standards, an image was constructed 'of ideal policing that had strong resonances around the world.'[1636] The success in forming a model which others could emulate resulted almost immediately in those responsible for setting up forces recruiting 'experienced men from London to guide them during the early years.'[1637] As a result, superintendents, inspectors and sergeants from the Metropolitan Police were extensively employed to establish new police forces elsewhere in Britain, and so the Principles of the Commissioners 'were carried far and wide.'[1638] As a result of the success of the model, 'the early outlook and growing traditions of the Metropolitan Police permeated the whole.'[1639]

*

By 1833, Rowan and Mayne had lost two superintendents. First to go was Joseph Thomas, in command of the Covent Garden Division. Although Manchester did not actually organise its force along the lines of the Metropolitan Police until 1839, Thomas was appointed Deputy Chief Constable of Manchester, at £600 per annum, compared with the £200 per annum he received in London.[1640] In the same year Maurice Dowling, the superintendent in charge of Lambeth Division, left to head up the newly

---

1635 See Chapter Two.
1636 Reiner, op. cit. 1625, p.436.
1637 Reith, op. cit. 1620, pp.252-253.
1638 Moylan, op. cit, 1603. p.34-35; see also Reith, op. cit. 1620, pp.252-253).
1639 Critchley, T.A (1973). 'The Idea of Policing in Britain: Success or Failure?' in Alderson, J.C, and John Stead (1973). *The Police We Deserve*, London: Wolfe, p.30.
1640 Reith, op. cit. 1620, p.136.

founded Liverpool Dockyard Police, transferring, in 1845, to Liverpool City as Chief Officer of Police.[1641]

In 1836 another superintendent, this time Joseph Bishop in charge of Wandsworth Division, took charge of the Bristol force.[1642] Two years later, when Bishop suddenly died, Superintendent Mallalieu was sent as his temporary replacement[1643] until a permanent one was recruited. Frederick Goodyer, an Inspector on A Division, became Chief Constable of Leicester City in 1836; four years later he became Chief Constable of Leicester County.[1644]

Also in 1836, Inspector Stuart carried out a survey of what was required to police the City of York, although he was not appointed to the post of Chief Officer. But in 1841, another Metropolitan officer, Robert Chalk, was appointed and served as the chief officer for the City of York for 20 years.[1645] The same year, Inspector John Enright was appointed Chief Officer of Southampton City Police, and remained in post for 32 years,[1646] and Inspector Andrew McManus became the Chief Officer of the newly-formed Kingston-upon-Hull Police Force. In this particular case, two members of a newly-formed Watch Committee went 'to London to discuss their requirements with Colonel Rowan.' It is said that he must have been impressed by their attitude towards police reform, as he allowed them to study the operating plans of the Metropolitan Police, and recommended to them one of his most senior inspectors, Andrew McManus who at that time was second in line for promotion to Superintendent. McManus insisted in taking Sergeant Edward O'Hara with him, who was given the rank of Acting/Inspector in Kingston-upon-Hull. McManus set up the Kingston-upon-Hull Police remarkably similar to the Metropolitan Police, including the rank structure and the ratio of inspectors to sergeants, and sergeants to constables.[1647] Sergeant Richard Castle was appointed to form the Wolverhampton Borough Police.[1648]

1641 Fairfax, Norman (2012). 'The rise and fall of Maurice Dowling'. See www.liverpoolcitypolice.co.uk/dowling/4562128598 [accessed 28 February 2018].
1642 Morris, R.M (2004). 'The Metropolitan Police and Government 1860-1920'. Thesis submitted for the degree of Doctor of Philosophy to the Faculty of Arts, Open University. See www.oro.open.ac.uk/59576/1/403833.pdf , p.162.
1643 PP 1834 [600], op. cit. 1629, p.18, q/a 1833-1834).
1644 Emsley, Clive (1986). 'Detection and Prevention: The Old English Police and the New 1750-1900'. No. 37, *Crime and Criminal Justice History* (January), p.78.
1645 Morris, op. cit. 1642, p.162.
1646 Cookes, Anne (1972). *The Southampton Police Force, 1836-1856*. City of Southampton, pp. 17-18.
1647 Welsh, David Roy (1997). 'The Reform of Urban Policing in Victorian England: A Study of Kingston-upon-Hull from 1836 to 1866'. Thesis submitted for the Degree of Doctor of Philosophy at the University of Hull, pp.95-97.
1648 Emsley, op. cit. 1644, p.75.

When the Marquess of Tweeddale approached Rowan on behalf of the Commissioners of Supply in Haddingtonshire, also known as East Lothian, for someone to set up and run a local police force, Rowan recommended Alfred List, at the time also an inspector in the Metropolitan Police. He was duly appointed, and spent eight years at Haddingtonshire before being appointed as Chief Constable of Midlothian, where he spent a further 27 years. During that time, he became recognised as 'the most influential writer and thinker on policing in nineteenth century Scotland.'[1649]

In 1840 Sergeants William Cleaver and Stephen Underhill became the superintendents[1650] of Roxburghshire and Berwickshire respectively, and two years later, at the request of the Superintendent of Edinburgh City Police, a W.F.N. Smith was sent from London to assist in re-organising the Force.[1651] A police force had been established in Dumfriesshire in 1838, but following three disastrous appointments the Commissioners of Supply turned to the Metropolitan Police for a replacement in 1843; John Jones, who had spent ten years in the Metropolitan Police, was duly appointed superintendent, serving as chief officer until 1891 – nearly 44 years.[1652] Another former Metropolitan Police officer who made his name in Scotland was Donald Mackay. He left the Metropolitan Police and became an Inspector in Fife but, in 1844, became the Chief Officer of Dundee, where he served for 32 years, seeing the force double in size from 50 to 100 officers.[1653]

Meanwhile, in Wales, Jeremiah Box Stockdale, a five-year veteran of the Metropolitan Police, was appointed by the newly-formed Watch Committee to set up a Police Force in Cardiff at the beginning of 1836. Only 24 years of age, he spent the next 36 years in post, seeing the force grow from four to sixty, and setting up the first fire service in the town.[1654] Twelve years later another Metropolitan Police officer, Stephen English, was appointed chief officer at Newport in Wales, where he remained for four years before moving on to command Norwich in 1853, and then

---

1649 Davidson, N, Jackson, L and Smale, D (2016). 'Police Amalgamation and Reform in Scotland: The long twentieth century.' *Scotland Historical Review*, vol. 95, no.1, pp.88-11, pp.5-7; see also Emsley, Clive (2009). *The Great British Bobby: A History of British Policing from the 18th century to the present*. London: Quercus, p.92-94.

1650 At the time, the chief officers of the emerging police forces in Scotland were known as 'superintendents.

1651 Emsley, op. cit. 1644, p.94.

1652 *Dumfries and Galloway Standard*, 12 September 1894, p.4; see also PP 1852-53 (715). Second report from the Select Committee on Police; together with the proceedings of the committee, minutes of evidence, and appendix, p.119, q/a 4210.

1653 Dumfries and Galloway Standard, 12 September 1894, p.4.

1654 www.roystockdill.wordpress.com/the-iron-copper [accessed 5 December 2019].

Leeds in 1859.[1655]

The influence of Rowan and Mayne did not only extend throughout Britain. As Rowe points out, 'the model developed in London in the nineteenth century has influenced policing in many parts of the world'[1656] Clive Emsley also pointed out that the Metropolitan Police's ability to check crime and disorder did not only provide a model for the rest of Britain, but for the rest of the world.[1657] This view is supported by former Metropolitan Police Commissioner Ian Blair, when he noted that 'what began in London spread across Britain and then, with variations, across the common law, English-speaking world'.[1658]

Superintendent Francis Mallalieu was sent to Barbados in 1834 to organise and run the island's first police force. But disagreements between the British government and local administrators about who controlled the police resulted in Mallalieu resigning and returning to England.[1659] Five years later, at the request of the Colonial Office, Mayne submitted a memorandum relative to policing in the West Indies:

> 'There should be two branches of the police, the Judicial and the Executive or Administrative.
>
> 1st. The Judicial, consisting of the magistrates carrying on the business at their office.
>
> 2nd. The Executive, consisting of the police force, under the Inspector-General and the subordinate officers for the prevention of crime, detection of offenders, bringing cases before the magistrates for adjudication, and enforcing all the laws relative to matters of police for the good order and comfort of society.'[1660]

Indeed, it seems that during the second half of the 1830s Rowan and Mayne were frequently engaged 'in reporting on and re-drafting schemes for police establishments based on the London model' which had been sent to them from various parts of the world.[1661]

In 1840 Sergeant John Colepepper was sent to reorganise the police in Ceylon, taking charge of the district of Kandy, where he remained for five

---

1655 Morris, op. cit. 1642, p.162.
1656 Rowe, Michael (2008). *Introduction to Policing*. London: Sage, p.39.
1657 Emsley, op. cit. 1644, p.75.
1658 Blair, Ian (2009). *Policing Controversy*. London: Profile Books, p. xvi.
1659 Schomburgk, Sir Robert (1847). *The History of Barbados*. London: Longman, Brown, Green and Longmans, pp.463-464;also p.18, para. 2842.
1660 TNA CO 884/1, Section V.
1661 Reith, op. cit. 1620, p.26.

years.[1662] When Victoria, Australia, organised its first police force, as a result of the 1853 Police Regulations Act, the officers 'were clearly identified by their uniforms', which were 'identical to those of the London Metropolitan Police.' Because there were insufficient suitable recruits, 53 police officers were recruited from the Metropolitan Police and they travelled to Australia under the command of Samuel Freeman, who had served in London for fourteen years. Although Freeman was not recruited as the chief of police – a Captain Charles MacMahon was the Chief Commissioner – he was given the rank of superintendent, and policing in Melbourne was based on the civil model of the London Metropolitan Police, the central feature of which was police beats. These were devised by Freeman, and it was intended that the police would be 'a preventative force, discouraging crime and encouraging order through their smart appearance and impeccable manner.' However, it appears Freeman suffered the same problems as the Commissioners did when setting up the Metropolitan Police because not all 'lived up to such ideals', and a number were dismissed for being drunk.[1663] On a wider scale, Keane and Bell state 'the similarities between British and Australian policing structures and law are self-evident. This is to be expected, given the development of Australian policing from the British model.'[1664]

Moving to North America, when cities were first considering setting up police forces, they turned to London for assistance. As early as November 1836, Rowan responded to a request from the Mayor of the City of New York by sending him copies of the General Regulations of the Metropolitan Police, along with 'orders of a general nature' that were issued to constables from time to time, and invited him to send someone from New York 'to shew [sic] them the system in detail'.[1665] The early police departments, including New York, New Orleans, Boston, Baltimore and Newark all took the Metropolitan Police as the model, organizing themselves with quasi-military command structures and identifying their main task as being the prevention of crime and disorder.[1666] In a presentation given to a Conference on Police Accountability and the Quality of Oversight in 2005, Merrick Bobb commenced by referring back to the formation of the

1662 Sinclair, Georgina (2008). 'The 'Irish' policeman and the Empire: influencing the policing of the British Empire – Commonwealth. *Historical Irish Studies*, Vol. 36, No. 142, November, p.183. Emsley, op. cit. 56, p.11.
1663 www.emelbourne.net.au/biogs/EM01154b.htm [accessed 15 November 2019]
1664 Keane, John, and Peter Bell (2013). 'Confidence in the police: balancing public image with community safety: a comparative review of the literature'. *International Journal of Law, Crime and Justice*, 41(3), pp.233-246.
1665 Reith, op. cit. 1620, pp.203-204.
1666 'Early Policing in the United States' at www.britannica.com/topic/police/early-police-in-the-United-States [accessed 17 November 2019].

modern police service in London in 1829, claiming that, from the start, Peel's 'formulation became the foundation' in 1844 when the New York Police Department (NYPD) was formed. But the question right from the outset, he claimed, was who should oversee Peel's so-called principles.[1667] In Canada, Macleod and Schneiderman claimed 'Peel's London model was influential'.[1668]

Painstakingly, beginning with Rowan and Mayne, police leadership in Britain has striven 'to develop an image of the British Bobby as the impartial embodiment of the rule of law and the ethic of public service.'[1669] Ascoli claimed, when writing his book which coincided with the 150th anniversary of the founding of the Metropolitan Police, that 'two men of lesser calibre than Rowan and Mayne would probably have fallen at the first hurdle, but relying on the policy of civility and moderation… they refused to be distracted by overt acts of hostility and worked patiently towards their goal of building a police force, which, by its conduct, would eventually achieve the ultimate accolade of public regard and acceptance.'[1670]

Whilst Peel was instrumental in forming the Metropolitan Police, the credit for the subsequent success of the British police system and the preventative and other principles on which it is founded, is wholly due to the first Commissioners, Charles Rowan and Richard Mayne. They succeeded in overcoming 'the impediments and frustrations which Whig ministers and the public inflicted on them during the first decade of the existence of the New Police in London.'[1671] Miller claimed, 'the organizational history of the mid-nineteenth London price is largely the account of the two commissioners' impact on the institution and their response to the social and political milieu.'[1672] As Rowe pointed out, 'in Britain, perhaps, more than most other countries, the police service forms part of the historical landscape, and the police officer is elevated to the status of national symbol and is a ubiquitous part of the cultural framework.'[1673] Cowley added, 'Charles Rowan and Richard Mayne are to be lauded in their achievement.'[1674]

1667 Bobb, op. cit. 1613, p.3
1668 Macleod, R.C., and David Schneiderman (eds) (1994). *Police Powers in Canada: The Evolution and Practice of Authority*. Toronto: University of Toronto Press, p.xv.
1669 Reiner, Robert (1992). 'Policing a Postmodern Society'. *Modern Law Review*, Vol. 55, No. 6 (November), p.762.
1670 Ascoli, David (1979). *The Queen's Peace: The origins and development of the Metropolitan Police 1829-1995*. London: Hamish Hamilton, p.95.
1671 Reith, op. cit. 1620, p.21.
1672 Miller, op. cit. 1604. p.2.
1673 Rowe, op. cit. 1656, p.3.
1674 Cowley, Richard (2011). *A History of the British Police from its Earliest Beginnings to the Present Day*. Stroud, Gloucestershire: The History Press, p.25.

Whilst there were shortcomings, particularly towards the end of Mayne's tenure as Commissioner, nobody can deny they set the standard and the Metropolitan Police provided the model for subsequent British forces and, indeed, for many police forces around the world.

But the last word is left to the police historian Charles Reith, who, although a great supporter of the achievements of Rowan and Mayne, is arguably the inadvertent cause as to why the two men have not received greater recognition. The British people he claimed should be 'indebted to Rowan and Mayne for the guidance, leadership, vision, and organising ability which gave practical form for the police institutions of Britain and the empire'.[1675]

1675 Reith, op. cit. 1620, p.26.

APPENDIX

REITH'S NINE PRINCIPLES OF POLICING

FIRST PRINCIPLE

Reith
To prevent crime and disorder, as an alternative to their repression by military force and severity of legal punishment.

Rowan and Mayne
It should be understood, at the outset, that the principal object to be attained is the Prevention of Crime. To this great end every effort of the Police is to be directed.

Rowan's military training under Sir John Moore
'The great thing that Sir John Moore and Colonel Mackenzie used to impress upon the minds of the officers was that our duty was to do everything in our power to prevent crime.'[1676]

SECOND PRINCIPLE

Reith
To recognize always that the power of the police to fulfil their functions and duties is dependent on public approval of their existence, actions, and behaviour, and on their ability to secure and maintain public respect.

Rowan and Mayne
'…the Commissioners have highlighted gratification in finding that

---

[1676] Napier, p.13. quoted in Fuller, Colonel J.F.C (1924). *Sir John Moore's System of Training*. London: Hutchinson & Co, p.108.

no unnecessary use was made by the Police of their Truncheons when called out, and that it has not appeased that in a single instance was an unnecessary degree of violence used. The Commissioners trust that by such form and temperate behaviour the Police have conciliated the populace and obtained the good will of all respectable persons.'[1677]

Rowan 'appreciated, perhaps more than the younger man Mayne, that the man on the beat was in the firing line; that the future of the New Police depended entirely on public acceptance; and that the constable – and his conduct – were the yardstick by which the whole police concept would be judged.'[1678]

THIRD PRINCIPLE

Reith
To recognize always that to secure and maintain the respect and approval of the public means also the securing of the willing co-operation of the public in the task of securing observance of laws.

Rowan and Mayne
'Remember there [was] no qualification more indispensible to a Police Officer than a perfect command of temper' and they should not allow themselves 'to be moved in the slightest degree, by an language or threats that may be used'; it was also pointed out that if they performed their duty 'in a quiet and determined manner,' it was more likely to 'induce well-disposed bystanders to assist them should they require it.'[1679]

FOURTH PRINCIPLE

Reith
To recognize always that the extent to which the co-operation of the public can be secured diminishes, proportionately, the necessity of the use of physical force and compulsion for achieving police objectives.

Rowan and Mayne
The Constables are to recollect upon all occasions, that they are required to execute their duty with good temper and discretion; any instance of unnecessary violence by them, in striking a party in their charge, will be

---

1677 TNA MEPO 7/2. Police Order, 15 October 1831.
1678 Ascoli, David (1979). *The Queen's Peace: The origins and development of the Metropolitan Police 1829-1995*. London: Hamish Hamilton, p.86.
1679 Initial instruction.

Appendix

severely punished. A Constable must not use his staff because the party in custody is violent in behaviour or language.[1680]

Rowan and Mayne

In his briefing to officers of A Division immediately before they were deployed to deal with the Cold Bath Fields riot, Rowan personally warned the officers 'to be temperate. To keep their temper, and not to use more force than was necessary; to take into custody those who were addressing the mob, and those who carried banners, and disperse the remainder.'[1681]

FIFTH PRINCIPLE

Reith

To seek and preserve public favour, not be pandering to public opinion, but by constantly demonstrating absolutely impartial service to Law, in complete independence of policy, and without regard to the justice or injustice of the substance of individual laws, by ready offering of individual service and friendship to all members of the public without regard to their wealth or social standing; by ready exercise of courtesy and friendly good-humour; and by ready offering of individual sacrifice in protecting and preserving life.

Rowan and Mayne

To 'be civil and attentive to all persons, of every rank and class' and warned that 'insolence and incivility' would not be tolerated.

SIXTH PRINCIPLE

Reith

To use physical force only when the exercise of persuasion, advice and warning is found to be insufficient to obtain public co-operation to an extent necessary to secure observance of law or to restore order; and to use only the minimum degree of physical force which is necessary on any particular occasion for achieving a police objective.

Rowan and Mayne

'Be particularly cautious not to interfere idly and unnecessarily' but 'when required to act; they should 'do so with decision and boldness'.[1682]

1680 TNA MEPO 7/1. Police Order, 21 August 1830.
1681 PP1833 [718], p.127, q/a 2917.
1682 Initial instructions to the Police.

SEVENTH PRINCIPLE

Reith
To maintain at all times a relationship with the public that gives reality to the historic tradition that the police are the public and that the public are the police; the police being only members of the pubic who are paid to give full-time attention to duties which are incumbent on every citizen, in the interests of community, welfare and existence.

Comment
It is likely that this originates from the Justice of the Peace Act 1361, which established the office of justice of the peace and provided for three or four people from the community to be employed as constables. As far as is known, Peel never uttered such words and neither did Rowan or Mayne.

EIGHTH PRINCIPLE

Reith
To recognize always the need for strict adherence to police-executive functions, and to refrain from even seeming to usurp the powers of the judiciary of avenging individuals or the State, and of authoritatively judging guilt and punishing the guilty.

Rowan and Mayne
The duties of the magistrates and their officers should be purely judicial whilst the Metropolitan Police should be purely executive.[1683]

NINTH PRINCIPLE

Reith
To recognize always that the test of police efficiency is the absence of crime and disorder, and not the visible evidence of police action in dealing with them.

Rowan and Mayne
The security of person and property, the preservation of the public tranquillity, and all other objects of a Police Establishment, will thus be better effected, than by the detection and punishment of the offender, after

---

1683 TNA MEPO 1/44 folios 41-48. Letter, signed by Rowan, to S.M. Phillipps, dated 20 June 1832; see also PP 1834 [600]: Report from the Select Committee on the Police of the Metropolis; with minutes of evidence, appendix and index, Appendix 12.

he has succeeded in committing the crime.[1684]

Rowan's military training under Sir John Moore

'...it is by the unfrequency [sic] of crime in your regiment, and not by the few punishments that may appear in the regiments books, that a general officer will judge of its state of discipline and of your capacity and conduct as a commanding officer.'[1685]

1684 Initial Instructions to Police.
1685 Napier, op. cit. 1676, p. 13.

BIBLIOGRAPHY

PRIMARY SOURCES

The National Archives
HO347/1. Report of the Departmental Committee on the Metropolitan Police, 1868.

PP 1833 [627]. Report from the Select Committee on the Petition of Frederick Young and Others (police)

PP 1833 [675]. Report from the Select Committee on Metropolitan Police.

PP 1834 [434]. Metropolitan Police. Correspondence relative to the conduct of the Metropolitan Police on Tuesday, 24 June 1834.

PP 1834 [600]. Report from the Select Committee on the Police of the Metropolis; with minutes of evidence, appendix and index.

PP 1837 [451]. Report from the Select Committee on Metropolitan Police Offices; with the minutes of evidence, appendix and index.

PP 1837-1838 [578]. Report from Select Committee on Metropolitan Police Offices; with minutes of evidence, appendix and index.

PP 1839 [58]. Metropolitan Police Act. A bill for improving the police in and near the metropolis.

PP 1839 [169]. First report of the commissioners appointed to inquire as to the best means of establishing an efficient constabulary force in the counties of England and Wales.

PP 1844 [549]. Report from the Select Committee on Dog Stealing (Metropolis); together with the Minutes of Evidence taken before them.

PP 1847-48 [501]. Minutes of evidence taken before the Select Committee of the House of Lords; to whom was referred the bill, intitulated, an act for regulating the sale of beer and other liquors on the Lord's Day; together with an appendix.

PP 1852-53 [603]. First report from the Select Committee on Police; with the minutes of evidence.

PP 1852-53 [715]. Second report from the Select Committee on Police; together with the proceedings of the committee, minutes of evidence, and appendix.

PP 1854 (1772). Royal Commission appointed to inquire into the existing state of the Corporation of the City of London.

PP 1856 [2016]. Report of Her Majesty's commissioners appointed to inquire into the alleged disturbance of the public peace in Hyde Park on Sunday, July 1st, 1855; and the conduct of the Metropolitan Police in connexion with the same. Together with the minutes of evidence, appendix, and index.

PP 1863 [6457]. Report of the Commission appointed to Inquire into the Operation of the Acts (16 & 17 Vict. c.99 and 20 & 21 Vict. c.3) relating to Transportation and Penal Servitude.

PP 1864 [252]. Primrose Hill meeting. Copy of the reports of the superintendent and inspector in command of the police employed at Primrose Hill on Saturday, 23rd April 1864; and the instructions to the police ordered to be on duty on the occasion of the meeting held there on the day.

PP 1864 [272]. Public meetings (metropolis). Copy of instructions given to the police with reference to the suppression of meetings for public discussion in the public parks of the metropolis.

PP 1867 [161] Metropolitan Police. Returns of the total number of the Metropolitan Police Force employed in each division, in each year from 1855, specifying the average number on day and on night duty; of the number of men resigned and dismissed from each division in each year since 1855; and, of the number of men of the force charged at the police courts with offences since 1855 to the close of 1866; &c.

PP 1867 [392] Police (metropolis). Return of the strength of each division of the Metropolitan Police Force on 1st January 1846, 1865 and 1866, together with the additions made to the force during the above-mentioned periods.

Special Collections

Asian and African Studies. MSS Eur F96, folio 344. Includes letters between Charles Rowan and Lord Tweeddale. Held at the British Library.

Chadwick Papers.

Correspondence, memoranda, pamphlets and newspaper cuttings c.1820-1890, of Sir Edwin Chadwick (1800-1890). 191 boxes. Contains letters written by Charles Rowan to Chadwick and others, whilst serving on the Royal Commission appointed to inquire as to the best means of establishing an efficient constabulary force in the counties of England and Wales PP 1839 (169). Held at the Archives of University College London.

Heathcote Collection. A collection of letters sent to Richard, later Sir Richard, Mayne between 1829 and 1868. Presented to the Metropolitan Police Heritage Centre, London, by JHR Heathcoate, 1955.

Henry Hall Collection.

Collection of diaries, journals, letters, books and miscellaneous papers, donated by Edward Hall (b.1898), a dealer and collector of Manuscripts and books. Includes letters written by Sir Richard Mayne to his wife between 1831 and 1866 in files EHC210/M1251;EHC210A/1252 and EHC 211/M1253. Held in the Wigan Archives, Lancashire.

Sir George Murray Archives 1772-1846, Volume 174. Includes letters between Charles Rowan and Sir George Murray. Held in the National Archives of Scotland, Edinburgh.

The Goodwood Estate Archives.

Family Papers. Charles Lennox (afterwards Gordon Lennox) 5th Duke of Richmond, Lennox, and Aubigny. Contains letters written by Charles Rowan and Richard Mayne to the Duke. Held at the West Sussex Record Office.

SECONDARY SOURCES

Books

Military career of Colonel Charles Rowan

Cooke, John (1831). *The Personal Narrative of Captain Cooke of the 43rd Regiment Light Infantry. In Memoirs of the Late War, Volume II.* London: Henry Cockburn and Richard Bentley.

Cornwall, Bernard (2014). *Waterloo: The History of Four Days, Three Armies and Three Battles.* London: William Collins.

Craufurd, Alexander H. (undated). *General Craufurd and his Light Division.* London: Griffith Farran Okeden & Welsh.

Dobbs, John, and Knowles, Robert (2008). *Gentlemen in Red: Two accounts of British Infantry Officers during the Peninsular War.* Available online at www.leonaur.com

Edwards, Peter (2008). *Albuera: Wellington's Fourth Peninsular Campaign, 1811.* Marlborough: The Crowood Press.

Freemont-Barnes, Gregory (2014). *Waterloo 1815: The British Army's Day of Destiny*. Stroud: The History Press.

Fuller, Colonel J.F.C (1924). *Sir John Moore's System of Training*. London: Hutchinson & Co.

Glover, Gareth (2015). *Waterloo: The Defeat of Napoleon's Imperial Guard*. Barnsley, South Yorkshire: Frontline Books.

Glover, Michael (1968). *Wellington as Military Commander*. London: B.T. Batsford Ltd.

Glover, Michael (2001). *The Peninsular War 1807-1814: A Concise Military History*. Harmondsworth: Penguin Classic.

Grattan, William (1902). *Adventures with the Connaught Rangers 1809-1814* (edited by Charles Oman). London: Edward Arnold.

Hay, Captain William (1992). *Reminiscences 1808-1815 Under Wellington*. Cambridge: Trotman

Henderson, C.B., Colonel G.F.R. (1912). *The Science of War: A Collection of Essays and Lectures 1891-1903*. London: Longman, Green, and Co.

Heyer, Georgette (2005). *The Spanish Bride*. London: Arrow Books.

Holmes, Richard (2003). *Wellington: The Iron Duke*. London: Harper Perennial.

Kincaid, John (1847). *Adventures in the Rifle Brigade in the Peninsula, France the Netherlands, from 1809 to 1815*. London: T and W. Boone.

Leach, C.B., Lieut.-Colonel J (1831). *Rough Sketches of the Life of an Old Soldier*. London: Longman, Rees, Orme, Brown, and Green.

Leeke, William (1866). *The History of Lord Seaton's Regiment (The 52nd Light Infantry) At the Battle of Waterloo*. London: Hatchard.

Maurice, Major-General Sir J.F (Ed)(1904). *The Diary of Sir John Moore*. London: Edward Arnold.

Mockler-Ferryman, Lieut.-Col. A.F. (1913). *The Life of a Regimental Officer during the Great War 1793-1815*. London: William Blackwood and Sons.

Moore Smith, G.C. (1903). *The Autobiography of Lieutenant-General Sir Harry Smith. Baronet of Aliwal on the Sutlej, G.C.B., in Two Volumes, Volume I*. London: John Murray.

Moore Smith, G.C. (1903). *The Life of John Colborne, Field Marshal Lord Seaton*. London: John Murray.

Moorsom, W.S. (Ed)(1860). *Historical Record of the Fifty-Second Regiment (Oxfordshire Light Infantry) from the Year 1755 to the year 1858*. Uckfield, Sussex: The Naval and Military Press.

Napier, Sir George Thomas, and William Craig Emilius Napier (1884). *Passages in the Early Military Life of General Sir George T. Napier*.

London: John Murray.

Napier, Lieut.-General Sir William (1857). *The Life and Opinions of General Sir Charles James Napier (edited by William Napier). In Four Volumes, Volume I*. London: John Murray.

Napier, Lieut.-General Sir William Napier, KCB (1879). *English Battles and Sieges in the Peninsular*. London: John Murray

Sale, Nigel (2014). *The Lie at the Heart of Waterloo*. Stroud, Gloucestershire: Pellmount.

Shaw Kennedy, James (undated). *An Autobiographical Memoir and Notes of the Battle of Waterloo*. London: Forgotten Books (Classic Reprint Series).

Snow, Peter (2011). *To War with Wellington: From the Peninsula to Waterloo*. London: John Murray.

Summerfield, Stephen, and Susan Law (2016). *Sir John Moore and the Universal Soldier. Volume I: The Man, the Commander and the Shorncliffe System of Training*. Huntingdon: Ken Trotman.

Summerville, Christopher (2003). *March of Death: Sir John Moore's Retreat to Corunna, 1808-1809*. London: Greenhill Books.

Swinton, Georgiana (1893). *A Sketch of the Life of Georgiana, Lady de Ros: With Some Reminiscences of her friends including the Duke of Wellington*. London: John Murray.

Weller, Jac (2012). *Wellington in the Peninsula 1808-1814*. London: Greenhill Books.

As Commissioners of the Metropolitan Police

Ackroyd, Peter (2009). *Thames: The Biography*. London: Anchor.

Alderson, John, and Philip John Stead (1973). *The Police We Deserve*. London: Wolfe.

Alderson, John (1979). *Policing Freedom*. Plymouth: Macdonald and Evans.

Alderson, John (1984). *Law and Disorder*. London: Hamish Hamilton.

Ascoli, David (1979). *The Queen's Peace: The origins and development of the Metropolitan Police 1829-1995*. London: Hamish Hamilton.

Blair, Ian (2009). *Policing Controversy*. London: Profile Books.

Bloom, Clive (2004). *Violent London: 2,000 Years of Riots, Rebels and Revolts*. London: Pan.

Bondeson, Jan (2011). *Queen Victoria's Stalker: The Strange Case of the Boy Jones*. Ohio: The Kate State University Press.

Brain, Timothy (2010). *A History of Policing in England and Wales from 1974: A Turbulent Journey*. Oxford: Oxford University Press.

Browne, Douglas G (1956). *The Rise of Scotland Yard; A History of the Metropolitan Police.* London: George G. Harrop.

Buckle, George Earle (Ed) (1926). *The Letters of Queen Victoria: A Selection from Her Majesty's Correspondence and Journal between the years 1862 and 1878.* London: John Murray.

Bullman, Joseph, Neil Hegarty and Brian Hill (2013). *The Secret History of Our Streets: A Story of London.* London: BBC Books.

Bunker, John (1988). *From Rattle to Radio.* Studley, Warwickshire: Brewin Books.

Cavanagh, Timothy (1893). *Scotland Yard, Past and Present: Experiences of thirty-seven years.* London: Chatto & Windus.

Caless, Bryn (2011). *Policing at the Top: The roles, values and attitudes of chief police officers.* Bristol: Policy Press,

Charles, Barrie (2012). *Kill the Queen! The Eight Assassination Attempts on Queen Victoria.* Stroud, Gloucestershire: Amberley.

Chase, Malcolm (2007). *Chartism: A New History.* Manchester: Manchester University Press.

Clarkson, Charles Tempest and J. Hall Richardson (1889). *Police!* Whitefish, MT: Kessinger Legacy Reprints.

Cobb, Belton (1957). *The First Detectives; and the early career of Richard Mayne, Commissioner of Police.* London: Faber and Faber.

Cowley, Richard (2011). *A History of the British Police from its Earliest Beginnings to the Present Day.* Stroud, Gloucestershire: The History Press.

Critchley, T.A (1970). *The Conquest of Violence: Order and Liberty in Britain.* London: Constable.

Critchley, T.A (1979). *A History of Police in England and Wales.* London: Constable.

Darvall, Frank Ongley (1969). *Popular Disturbances and Public Order in Regency England.* New York: Augustus M. Kelley.

Dillon, William (1888). *The Life of John Mitchel.* London: K.Paul, Trench and Company.

Durston, Gregory J (2001). *Criminal and Constable: The Impact of Policing Reform on Crime in Nineteenth Century London.* PhD thesis at the London School of Economics. See www.ethesis.lse.ac.uk/2779/1/U615728.pdf

Emsley, Clive (1987). *Crime and Society in England 1750-1900.* London: Longman.

Emsley, Clive (1996). *The English Police: A Political and Social History* (Second Edition). London: Longman.

Bibliography

Emsley, Clive (2009). *The Great British Bobby: A History of British Policing from the 18th Century to the Present.* London: Quercus.

Fido, Martin, and Keith Skinner (1999). *The Official Encyclopedia of Scotland Yard.* London: Virgin Books

Finer, S.E (2017). *The Life and Times of Sir Edwin Chadwick.* Abingdon, Oxon: Routledge

Foot, Paul (2012). *The Vote.* London, Penguin.

Gash, Norman (2011). *Mr Secretary Peel: The Life of Sir Robert Peel to 1830.* London: Faber and Faber.

Glen , William Cunningham (1885). *The Representation of the People Act 1884.* London: Shaw and Son.

Goodway, David (2002). *London Chartism 1838-1848.* Cambridge: Cambridge University Press.

Grieve, J.G.D. (2015). 'Historical Perspective: British Policing and the Democratic Ideal' in P. Wankhade, D. Weir (2015). *Police Services.*

Halliday, Stephen (1999). *The Great Stink of London: Sir Joseph Bazalgette and the Cleansing of the Victorian Metropolis.* Stroud, Gloucestershire: Sutton Publishing.

Hawkins, Angus (2007). *The Forgotten Prime Minister – The 14th Earl of Derby, Volume II.* New York: Oxford University Press.

Hernon, Ian (2006). *Riot! Civil Insurrection from Peterloo to the Present Day.* London: Pluto Press.

Howard, George (1953). *Guardians of the Queen's Peace: The Development and Work of Britain's Police.* London: Odham's Press.

Hurd, Douglas (2007). *Robert Peel: A Biography.* London: Weidenfeld & Nicolson.

Jackson, Lee (2015). *Dirty Old London: The Victorian Fight Against Filth.* London: Yale University Press.

Jackson, Major-General Sir Louis C. (1937). *History of the United Service Club.* London: The Committee of the United Service Club.

Johnston, Helen (2015). *Crime in England 1815-1880: Experiencing the criminal justice system.* Abingdon, Oxfordshire: Routlege.

Keller, Lisa (2010). *Triumph of Order: Democracy and Public Space.* Columbia: Columbia University Press.

Lock, Joan (2014). *Dreadful Deeds and Awful Murders: Scotland Yard's First Detectives 1829-1878.* Jolo Press.

Mace, Rodney (2005). *Trafalgar Square: Emblem of Empire.* London: Lawrence and Wishart.

Mason, Gary (2004). *The Official History of the Metropolitan Police*. London: Carlton Books.

Mather, F.C (1984). *Public Order in the Age of the Chartists*. Westport, Connecticut: Greenwood Press.

Mayhew, Henry and Others (2005). *The London Underworld in the Victorian Period: Authentic First-Person Accounts by Beggars, Thieves and Prostitutes*. New York: Dover Publications.

Melville Lee, Captain W.L (1901). *A History of Police in England*. London: Methuen.

Miller, Wilbur R (1999). *Cops and Bobbies: Police Authority in New York and London, 1830-1870* (Second Edition). Columbus: Ohio State University Press.

Moylan, J.F (1929). *Scotland Yard and The Metropolitan Police*. London: G.P. Putnam's Sons.

O Broin, Leon (1971). *Fenian fever: an Anglo-American dilemma*. New York: New York University Press,

Pike, Michael S (1985). *The Principles of Policing*. Basingstoke: MacMillan.

Reith, Charles (1943). *British Police and the Democratic Ideal*. Oxford: Oxford University Press.

Reith, Charles (1956). *A New Study of Police History*. Edinburgh: Oliver and Boyd.

Richardson, Benjamin Ward (1887). *The Health of Nations: A Review of the Works of Edwin Chadwick, Volume II*. London: Longman, Green and Co.

Richter, Donald C (1981). *Riotous Victorians*. London: Ohio University Press.

Saville, John (1990). *1848: The British State and the Chartist Movement*. Cambridge: Cambridge University Press.

Shenton, Caroline (2012). *The Day Parliament Burned Down*. Oxford: Oxford University Press.

Stallion, Martin, and David S. Wall (1999). *The British Police: Police Forces and Chief Officers 1829-2000*. Hook, Hampshire: Police History Society.

Thomson, Sir Basil (1936). *The Story of Scotland Yard*. New York: The Literary Guild.

Thurmond Smith, Phillip (1985). *Policing Victorian London: Political Policing, Public Order, and the London Metropolitan Police*. Westport, Connecticut: Greenwood, p.131.

Thurston, Gavin (1967). *The Clerkenwell Riot: The Killing of Constable Culley*. London: George Allen and Unwin.

Webb, Simon (2015). *Bombers, Rioters and Police Killers; Violent Crime and Disorder in Victorian Britain*. Barnsley, South Yorkshire: Pen and Sword.

White, Jerry (2008). *London in the 19th Century*. London: Vintage.

White, William (1838). *The Police Spy or the Metropolitan Police, its Advantages, Abuses, and Defects*. Whitefish, MT: Kessinger Legacy Reprints.

Williams, David (1967). *Keeping the Peace: The police and public order*. London: Hutchinson.

Williams, Guy R (1972). *The Hidden World of Scotland Yard*. London: Hutchinson.

Winter, James (1993). *London's Teeming Streets, 1830-1914*. London: Psychology Press.

Worrall, John L, and Frank Schmalleger (2011). *Policing!* London: Pearson, p.3.

Wright, D.W. (1988). *Popular Radicalism: The Working-Class Experience 1780-1880*. London: Longman.

Articles

Adegbile, Debo P (2017). 'Policing Through an American Prism'. In *Yale Law Journal*, Volume 126. Issue 7/4, pp.2228-2230.

Bayley, David, Michael A. Davis, and Ronald L. Davis (2015). 'New Perspectives in Policing: Race and Policing: An Agenda for Action'. Laurel MD: Office of Justice Programs, U.S. Department of Justice.

Bronitt, Simon, and Philip Stenning (2011). 'Understanding discretion in modern policing', in *Criminal Law Journal* 35(6), pp.319-332.

Ellenberger, Nancy W (1990). 'The Transformation of London "Society" at the End of Victoria's Reign: Evidence from the Court Presentation Records'. In *Albion: A Quarterly Journal Concerned with British Studies*, Vol. 22, No. 4 (Winter) p.633-653.

Emsley, Clive (1986). 'Detection and Prevention: The Old English Police and the New 1750-1900'. No. 37, *Crime and Criminal Justice History* (January), pp.69-88.

Gilley, Sheridan (1973). 'The Garibaldi Riots of 1862'. *The Historical Journal*, Vol. 16, No. 4, pp.697-732.

Griffin, Rachel (2015). 'Detective Policing and the State in Nineteenth-century England: The Detective Department of the London Metropolitan Police, 1842-1878'. Electronic Thesis and Dissertation Repository, 3427. Ontario: University of Western Ontario, accessed via ir.lib.uwo.ca/etd/3427 on 18 February 2019.

Harrison, Brian (1965). 'The Sunday Trading Riots of 1855.' *The Historical Journal*, Vol. 8, No. 2, pp.219-245.

Himmelfarb, Gertrude (1966). 'The Politics of Democracy: The English Reform Act of 1867'. In *Journal of British Studies*, Vo. 6, No. 1 (November), pp.97-138.

Jones, Eric, Chief of the Stockton Police (2017). 'The Evolution of Policing'; a presentation to the Stanford Institute for Economic Policy Research (SIEPR) on 21 April.

Law Enforcement Action Partnership. law enforcementactionpartnership.org/peel-policing-principles accessed 30 May 2019.

Lentz, Susan A, and Robert H. Chaires (2006). 'The invention of Peel's principles: A study of policing 'textbook' history'. In *Journal of Criminal Justice* 35, pp.69-79.

Mawby, Rob I., and Kreseda Smith (2017). 'Civilian oversight of the police in England and Wales: The election of Police and Crime Commissioners in 2012 and 2016'. In *International Journal of Police Studies and Management*, Vol. 19, Issue 1, pp.23-30.

Moore, Tony (2017). 'The First Chief Constable of Shropshire, Captain Dawson Mayne'. *Journal of the Police History Society*, No. 31.

Reiner, Robert (1992). 'Police Research in the United Kingdom: A Critical Review', in *Modern Policing* (Eds: Michel Tonry and Norral Morris). Chicago: University of Chicago Press, pp.435-508.

Reiner, Robert (1992). 'Policing a Postmodern Society', in *Modern Law Review*, Vol. 55, No. 6 (November), pp.761-781.

Reith, Charles (1952). 'Charles Rowan: 1783-1852.' *Police Review*, 9 May, pp.326-327.

Robinson, Cyril D., and Richard Scaglion (1987). 'The Origin and Evolution of American Policing', in *Law & Society Review*, Vol. 21, No, 1, pp.109-154.

Sinclair, Georgina (2008). 'The 'Irish' policeman and the Empire: influencing the policing of the British Empire – Commonwealth'. *Historical Irish Studies*, Vol. 36, No. 142, November, pp.173-187.

Sindall, R (1987). 'The London garrotting panics of 1856 and 1862.' *Social History*, Vol.12, No.3 (Oct).

Swift, R.E (2007). 'Policing Chartism, 1839-1848: The Role of the 'Specials' Reconsidered'. *English Historical Review*, Vol. CXXII No. 497, pp.669-699.

Taylor, Rosemary (2009), "The City of Dreadful Delight': William Morris in the East End of London.' The *Journal of William Morris Studies*. Volume XVIII, Number 3, Winter, pp.9-28.

Williams, T.C (1951). 'Police at the Great Exhibition of 1851'. *Police College Magazine*, September, pp.106-118.

Doctoral Theses

Morris, R.M (2004). 'The Metropolitan Police and Government 1860-1920: A thesis submitted for the degree of Doctor of Philosophy to the Faculty of Arts', Open University. See www.oro.open.ac.uk/59576/1/403833.pdf.

Roach, Lawrence (2004). 'The Origins and Impact of the Function of the Crime Investigation and Detection in the British Police Service: A thesis submitted in partial fulfilment of the requirements for the Degree of Doctor of Philosophy of Loughborough University': Loughborough University's Institutional Repository.

Welsh, David Roy (1997). *The Reform of Urban Policing in Victorian England: A Study of Kingston-upon-Hull from 1836 to 1866*. Thesis submitted for the Degree of Doctor of Philosophy at the University of Hull. Hull: Hull University's Institutional Repository.

INDEX

Note: Ranks are generally the highest mentioned in the text

9th Light Dragoons, 15
14th Hussars, 342
43rd (Monmouthshire Light Infantry) Regiment: military training at Shorncliffe, 21, 23–5; formed into Light Brigade, 33; at battle of the river Coa, 37; at Bussaco, 38; at Sabugal, 40; assault on Ciudad Rodrigo, 43–5; campaign in Pyrenees, 57
52nd (Oxfordshire) Regiment of Foot: returns from India, 18; in French Revolutionary Wars, 18–19; military training at Shorncliffe, 21, 23–5; new second battalion raised, 25; in Sicily and Sweden, 26; first campaign in Peninsula (1808–9), 26–30; retreat to Corunna and Vigo, 28–30; evacuated to England, 30; as elite army unit, 31; formed into Light Brigade, 33; second campaign in Peninsula (1809–14), 34–62; forced march to Talavera, 35; at battle of the river Coa, 36–8; at Bussaco, 38; at Sabugal, 40; at Fuentes de Oñoro, 41–2; assault on Ciudad Rodrigo, 43–5; at Badajoz, 47–8; advances to Salamanca, 51–2; at battle of Vitoria, 52–3; assault on San Sebastian, 56; campaign in Pyrenees, 56–8; at battle of Orthez, 59–61; at battle of Toulouse, 61–2; returns to England, 62–5, 65; sails to Ireland, 65; in 1815 campaign against Napoleon, 65–74; officer dining and sports, 67; at Waterloo, 69–72, 73, 74; Wellington fails to mention in Waterloo Despatch, 73; enters Paris, 74–5; stationed in France, 75–6; returns to England (1818), 76; policing and domestic peacekeeping in Midlands, 76; colours and honours, 77 & n345; estimation, 77; posted to Dublin, 78; regiment reduced, 78
64th Regiment of Foot, 14
86th Regiment of Foot, 17
95th Regiment of Foot (Rifles): military training at Shorncliffe, 21, 23–5; retreats to Corunna, 29; at Corunna, 30; Andrew Barnard appointed commander, 273; formed into Light Brigade, 33; arrives in Lisbon, 34–5; reaches Talavera, 35; withdraws to Portugal, 35–6; at battle of the river Coa, 37; at Sabugal, 40; assault on Ciudad Rodrigo, 43–5; in 1812 campaign, 49; advances to Salamanca (1813), 51; defends Vera, 56–7; enters Paris after Waterloo, 75

Abinger, Lord, 153
accommodation, for police, 160; *see also* station houses
Act of Conformity (1662), 11
Act of Union (1801), 12
Adam, Major-General Frederick, 66, 72
Adam's Brigade: formed, 66; at Waterloo, 70, 71, 72; Wellington fails to mention in Waterloo Despatch, 73; movements after Waterloo, 74; enters Paris, 75
Adegbile, Debo P., 380
Adelaide, Queen, 361
agents provocateurs, 203
Aggs, Inspector, 233
Albert, Prince Consort: and assassination attempts on Queen

Index

Victoria, 240–1, 242; dines at United Service Club, 274; Great Exhibition, 282; state visit to France, 314; favours *Stunden der Andacht,* 266
Albert Hall, 87
Albuera, battle of (1811), 42
Alderson, John, 380
Alexandra, Princess of Wales (*later* Queen of Edward VII): reception on arrival in London, 116–18; wedding celebrations, 118–19
Alison, Dr William, 275
Allen, Jeremiah, 349–50
Allied Insurance Company, 207–8
Almaraz bridge, Spain, 35
Almeida, Portugal, 36, 39, 48
Alten, Major-General Charles, 48, 51, 59
Althorp, John Charles Spencer, Viscount (*later* 3rd Earl Spencer), 206
Amiens, Treaty of (1802), 19
Angel Tavern, Rotherhithe, 260–1
Anglo-Sikh War, First (1845–6), 272–3
Anstruthers, Brigadier-General Robert, 27, 28
Antrim, County, 10, 11
Antrim Militia, 13
Apsley House, 179, 272
Arbuthnot, Colonel George, 241
Arcangues, France, 59
Armstrong, Robert Baynes, 306–7
arrest powers, assault, 125–6, 140, 215, 217
Arzobispo bridge, Spain, 35
Ascoli, David, *The Queen's Peace: The origins and development of the Metropolitan Police 1829–1995,* 389
assault, and arrest powers, 125–6, 140, 215, 217
assemblies and protest law, 185–6, 247–9, 333, 341–2, 345
Athenaeum (club), Pall Mall, 91–2
Atlantic slave trade, 90
Attwood, Thomas, 218
Australia: early policing, 388

Badajoz, Spain: fortifications, 46; siege and assault on (1812), 46–7; sacking, 48
bail, and detention regulations, 215, 217, 312
Baird, Lieutenant-General Sir David, 27, 28, 30
Baker, Davies, 146

Baker, Superintendent Thomas: appointed superintendent, 103; Apsley House misunderstanding, 179; at Cold Bath Fields riots, 192, 193; and Courvoisier murder case, 236
Ballantine, William, 138
Barbados: first police force, 288, 387
Barbarina, Marrianne *see* Carvick, Marrianne
Baring, Major George, 267 & n1101
Barnard, General Sir Andrew, 47, 59, 273
Barnet magistrates: and corporal punishment of child offenders, 328–9
barouches, 241n986
Barrett, Michael, 350
barricades, 225
batons and baton charges, 108, 181
battalions: raising, 20–1
Bayley, David, 379, 381
Bayonne, siege of, 59
Beale, Sergeant, 183
Beales, Edmond, 330, 331–3, 334, 336–7, 341, 344–5, 346
Bean, John, 242–3
Beasley, Samuel, 200–1
beat system, 106, 144
Beckwith, Charles, 273
Beckwith, Lieutenant-Colonel Thomas, 38, 40
Bedlam, 188n759
beer, 260, 296
begging, 215
Bell, Lieutenant-Colonel Sir John, 273 & n1138
Bell, Peter, 388
Belle Isle (King's Cross), 81
Belmore, Lord, 156
Bemahague, Isle of Man, 15
Benavente, Portugal, 30
Beresford, Inspector, 237
Beresford, Marshal William Carr, 27, 60 & n257, 61
Beresford-Hope, Alexander, 369 & n1556
Beresford-Hope, Lady Mildred, 369 & n1556
Bernstorff, Albrecht, Count von, 368
Bethnal Green: Chartist meetings, 222, 224
Bethnal Green housebreaking gang, 183
Bewley, Constable William, 312
Bidasoa, river, 56–7
Bill for the Better Protection of the

Index

Queen's Person (1842), 243
Billingsgate fish market, 86
bills of indictment, preparing, 211
Birkenhead: Garibaldi riots (1862), 325
Birmingham: Chartist meetings, 223; riots (1839), 220–1, 313
Birmingham Post Office robbery (1840), 237
Birnie, Sir Richard, 125, 126
Bishop, Superintendent Joseph, 385
Bishop Bonner's Fields, 258, 259
Black, Inspector (of D Division), 238
Blair, Ian, *Policing Controversy,* 387
Blücher, General Gebhard von, 65, 72
Board of Green Cloth, 135 & n558
Bobb, Merrick, 380, 388–9
Bolton Street (No. 17), Piccadilly, 263 & n1079, 275
Bonaparte, Joseph, King of Spain, 48, 52–3
Bordeaux, 62
Bow Street Patrols, 87–8, 94, 111, 138, 159, 209
Bow Street Police Office: jurisdiction, 111; as crime reporting centre, 113; Strand pickpocket gang (1829), 183; Wovenden committal hearing (1834), 130–1; Charles Taylor case (1837), 233–4; Thomas Webb case (1840), 237; Richard Gould case (1840), 236; Courvoisier committal hearing (1840), 236; trial of Superintendent Pearce (1846), 152; trial of John Tremlett (1862), 321
Bow Street Runners, 171, 209, 217
Braddick, Sergeant, 242
Bradlaugh, Charles, 322
Braidwood, James, 207, 208; killed on duty, 318
Brain, Timothy, 380
brass bands, police, 316–17, 319
Bratton, William J., 380
bread riots (1867), 344
Brett, Sergeant Charles, 348
Bright, Dr Richard, 277 & n1162
Brighton, 92, 265, 277
Bristol: Reform Bill riots (1831), 178
Bristol Police, 288, 385
Britain, and French invasion threat, 19–20
British army: battle tactics and fighting techniques, 21–2; commissions system, 13; deaths from cold and disease, 50; discipline, 22–3; drunkenness of lower ranks, 22; fever among troops in Spain, 28; ill-discipline among, 30, 48, 53, 56; inadequate recognition for Peninsular veterans, 62; raising, 20–1; training, 22–4
British Museum, 87, 216
Broke, Horace, 363
Broke, Lieutenant-General Horatio, 363
Brook, Inspector Thomas, 155
Brooks, Sergeant John, 192–3, 197
Brougham, Henry, 1st Baron, 101
Broughton, Mr (magistrate), 139, 183
Brown, Constable Charles, 240
Brown, Hannah, 232–3
Brown, James, 200
Brown, Major-General Samuel, 92
Brown, Thomas: body stealing case (1829), 93
Browne, Douglas G, *The Rise of Scotland Yard: A History of the Metropolitan Police,* 358
Bruce, Henry, 120–1
Brussels, 65, 67–8
Buckingham Palace (*formerly* The Queen's House), 83, 178–9, 240
Bulkeley, Lieutenant Thomas, 200
Bull, Superintendent William, 103
Bulwer, Henry (*later* 1st Baron Dalling and Bulwer), 145
Burdett-Coutts, Angela, 276
Burgess, Guy, 367
Burgos, Spain, 48–9, 52
Burke, Ricard O'Sullivan, 348, 349, 350
Burrard, Lieutenant-General Sir Harry, 27
Busbridge's Livery Stables, Cold Bath Fields, 189, 190, 191
Bussaco, battle of (1810), 38
Byles, Samuel, 81
Byng, Major-General Sir John, 72, 77

Cacadores battalions, 37, 39, 40, 43, 62
Cadiz, 19
Cadoux, Captain Daniel, 56–7
Caldwell, Colonel Alexander, 92
Caledonian Mercury, 192
Caless, Bryn, 379
Calthorpe Arms (public house), 193, 194
Calthorpe Estate, 188
Calthorpe Street inquest (1833), 194
Cambridge, Prince George, 2nd Duke

of, 243
Cambridge House, Piccadilly, 282
Canada: early policing, 389
Cape Coast, 90
Capes (Bow Street officer), 135
Capital Punishment Amendment Act (1868), 350
'Captain Swing' movement (1830), 175 & n710
Cardiff Police, 386
Carlile, Richard, 174–5
Carlist War, First (1833–40), 330
Carlton House, Pall Mall, 91
Caroline, Queen of George IV, 101
Carrickfergus, 11, 12
Carter, Inspector, 190n772, 191, 193
Carter, Elizabeth, 263
Carvick, Georgina Marianne *see* Mayne, Georgina Marianne
Carvick, Marrianne (*née* Barbarina; Georgina's mother), 360, 361
Carvick, Thomas (Georgina's father), 360–1
Carvick, Thomas Mayor (RM's brother-in-law), 372
Casey, John, 153–4
Casey, Joseph, 348, 350
Castel Sarrasin, France, 62
Castle, Constable Henry, 146–7
Castle, Sergeant Richard, 385
Catholic Emancipation: Tory attitude to, 175
cattle-driving, 356
Cavanagh, Timothy, 143–4, 326, 342, 352
Cavendish Square murder (1840), 237–8
Ceira, river (Portugal), 39
cemeteries and burial grounds, 86; *see also* Kensal Green Cemetery
Central Criminal Court *see* Old Bailey trials
Ceylon: early policing, 387–8
Chadwick, Edwin, 212–14, 242, 250
Chaires, Robert H., 381
Chalk, Chief Officer Robert, 385
Chambers, Walter, 234
Charing Cross: Chartist meetings, 251, 255–6
Charleroi, Belgium, 67
Charles I, King, 10
Chartist Assembly Rooms, Soho, 257
Chartists: origins and aims, 218; police policy towards, 219, 223; first petition (1839), 218–19; meetings and demonstrations, 219–20, 222–4, 225–7, 250, 252–6, 256–60; planned sacking of City (16 January 1840), 222; second petition (1842), 223; procession through City area (18 August 1842), 224; use of barricades, 225; Feargus O'Connor elected MP (1842), 247; Trafalgar Square riots (6–8 March 1848), 247–52; Kennington Common demonstration (10 April 1848), 252–5; arrest and conviction of John Mitchel, 256–7; union with Irish Confederates, 258; Orange Tree conspiracy, 260–1; funeral of Feargus O'Connor, 315
Chatham, 20, 65
Chatham Dockyard Police, 319
Chelsea Hospital: crush fatalities at (1852), 286, 287, 295
Chester Castle: Fenian plot to storm (1867), 350
Chester Square, London, 329, 367, 371, 373
Chobham Common Great Camp, 290
cholera outbreaks, 82, 180 & n733
Cintra, Convention of (1808), 27
City of London: watch and ward system, 112; excluded from Metropolitan Police Act (1829), 112; resists 'takeover' by Metropolitan Police, 115, 121; Lord Mayor's Day disturbances (8–9 November 1830), 114, 162, 176–7; planned Chartist sacking (16 January 1840), 222; Chartist procession (18 August 1842), 224; and state visit of Emperor Napoleon (1855), 294–5; and fire brigade, 318
City of London Militia: march through London (3 June 1867), 346 & n1439
City of London Police: created (1839), 115; boundary and jurisdiction issues, 112–14, 177, 180, 181; liaison with Metropolitan Police, 113, 257–8, 260, 286, 294–5; proposed amalgamation, 114–15, 119–23, 139; and Royal Procession through London (7 March 1863), 116–18, 119, 123; compared with Met, 120
City of London Police Act (1839), 115, 122
City Press, The, 123
Ciudad Rodrigo, Spain, 27; assault on, 43–5; British troops overwinter in

Index

(1812–13), 49
Clarke, William, 152
Clatworthy, Inspector William, 155
Claxton, Constable, 243
Cleaver, Superintendent William, 386
Clerkenwell Green: demonstrations and meetings, 219, 224, 250, 257–8, 259, 333–4, 348
Clerkenwell News: tribute to Richard Mayne, 374
Clerkenwell Police Court, 225
Clerkenwell Prison bombing and trial (1867–8), 348–51
Clinton, Lieutenant-General Henry, 66–7, 69–70, 72–3
Clough, County Antrim, 10
Coa, river, 40; battle of (1810), 36–8
coaches, 83, 246–7
Cobbett, William, 175, 195
Cochrane, Charles, 247–9, 255–6
Cockburn, Lord Chief Justice, 350
Codd, H.G. (magistrate), 139
coffee shops, regulation of, 205, 260
Colborne, Sir John (*later* 1st Baron Seaton): background, 42; takes command of 1/52nd, 42; attacks redoubt at Ciudad Rodrigo, 43–4, 45; on Craufurd, 45–6; recuperates in England, 46; rejoins 1/52nd, 55; appointed brigade commander, 57; assault on Vera, 57–8; as military commander, 58; at battle of Nivelle, 58–9; defends position at Arcangues, 59; at battle of Orthez, 60; military secretary to Prince of Orange, 66; recalled to take command of 1/52nd, 66–7; at Waterloo, 70–2; on Wellington's failure to recognise distinguished service, 73–4; enters Paris, 74–5; leave of absence, 76; regimental colours and honours, 77; Lieutenant-Governor of Guernsey, 77; later military career, 14, 264; and Chobham Common Great Camp, 290; Napier on, 77–8
Cold Bath Fields riot (1833): planned meeting by NUWC, 184–5; legality of meeting, 185–6, 201; no clear instructions from Melbourne, 187, 198–9; banning order, 187; venue, 188; police operation, 188–90, 191; procession and assembly of demonstrators, 190–1; advance of police, 191–2; fighting and riot, 192–3; Constable Culley killed, 193; arrests, 193–4 & n791; commissioners report to Melbourne, 201; inquest on body of Culley, 194; jury feted, 194–5; reactions, 195–7; convictions, 198; Parliamentary inquiry into police conduct, 184, 198–202
Coldstream Guards, 335, 338
Cole, Henry, 282
Cole, Major-General Lowry, 52, 55
Colepepper, Sergeant John, 387–8
Colquhoun, Patrick, 87
Coltman, James, 193
Combe, Mr (magistrate), 225
Commission of Inquiry into Transportation and Penal Servitude (1863), 321
commissioners: background and qualifications, 96, 377 & n1595; complaints handling, 146, 147–8; constitution and administration, 261, 314; created, 97–8; decision making, 185, 292; distinguished from Justices of the Peace, 378; duties, 154–5, 280, 292, 315; emergency military powers, 353; relations with Home Office, 123, 125, 129–30; relations with London magistrates, 125–8, 129–32, 133–7, 138–9; salary, 97, 102, 210, 221; uniform, 180n735, 209–10; written communications, 285
commissions, army: purchase system, 13
Common Lodging Houses Act (1851), 155
Commons, House of: and police reform proposals, 94, 100, 115, 119–20, 121n514; passes Reform Bill (1831), 178; and Chartist demands, 218–19, 223; vote of thanks to Sir Harry Smith, 273; debates garrotting, 320; debates corporal punishment of juvenile offenders, 329; debates Reform Bill (1866), 330; *see also* Parliament
Commonwealth of England, 10
conditional licences for convicts, 319–20
Conservative Party: view on Catholic Emancipation, 175; fall of Wellington's government (November 1830), 177, 377; and Gladstone's 1866 Reform Bill, 330
constables: attached to Police Offices, 111, 124, 125, 138, 171, 231; general

413

Index

instructions for, 107; mobilisation, 329; parish, 88, 290; recruitment and selection, 104; special, 289; supervision of, 108
Cooke, Captain John, 57
Coote, Charles, 9–10
Cornwallis, Charles, 13
corporal punishment of juvenile offenders, 328–9
Corunna, Spain, battle of (1809), 30
Cottingham, Mr. (magistrate), 152
Cotton's Wharf, Tooley Street, 318
County and Borough Police Act (1856), 170
county constabularies, 212–14, 287–90
County Police Act (1839), 214, 287, 289–90
Court of Common Council, 115n493
Court of Common Pleas, 101 & n435, 156–7
courts leet, 8n17
Courvoisier, Francois, 236–7
Coutts, Thomas, 276
Covent Garden Market, 86
Cowley, Richard, *A History of the British Police*, 389
Cox, Greenwood and Cox (army agents), 20–1
Craufurd, Colonel Robert: commands light infantry in Peninsula, 28, 29, 33, 36; character and strict discipline, 33; at battle of the river Coa, 36–8; at Bussaco, 38; home leave, 39; in battle of Fuentes de Oñoro, 41–2; at Ciudad Rodrigo, 43, 44; mortally wounded, 44, 45; estimation, 45–6
Cresswell, Mr Justice, 168
cricket, police teams, 315–16
crime prevention, emphasis on, 105, 235, 354
crime rate: following Napoleonic Wars, 88; after 1853, 319
criminal intent, proof of, 211
Criminal Law Commission (1837), 210–12
Criminal Law Commission (1845), 170
Critchley, T.A., *A History of Police in England and Wales*, 88
Croker, John Wilson, 75
Cromwell, Oliver, 10–11
Cross, Lieutenant-Colonel John, 271 & n1125
crossing sweepers, 84

crowd and riot control, 113–14, 117–18, 119, 181, 199–200, 219, 221–2, 312–13; *see also* dispersal powers; protest and assemblies law; riots and disturbances
Crowder, Mr Justice, 166
Crown Prosecution Service (CPS), 170
Crystal Palace, 282–3
Culley, Constable Robert: killed on duty, 193; inquest, 194; jury feted for justifiable homicide verdict, 194–5; funeral, 195; bereavement payment for wife, 162, 195; Fursey identified by Mayne as killer, 198
Cupples, Reverend Snowden, 12

Daily Telegraph, 339
Dalbiac, Colonel James, 268–9
Dalhousie, Fox Maule-Ramsay, 11th Earl of *see* Maule, Fox
Dalhousie, George Ramsay, 9th Earl of, 53, 267; death, 269
Dalhousie, James Broun-Ramsay, 10th Earl of, 119–20, 267, 269–70, 271
Dalhousie Castle, near Edinburgh, 267
Dalrymple, Lieutenant-General Sir Hew, 27
Danbury, Essex, 361
dangerous structures, inspection of, 315
Dassett, Charles, 242–3
Davis, Constable Robert, 173–4
Davis, Eliza, 233–4
Dawson, Richard, 8
Dawson, Thomas, 1st Viscount Cremorne, 9
Day and Sheen (beggars), 148
day patrols, 88, 94
De Roos, Colonel William, 192n783, 200
Deasy, Timothy, 347–8, 350
death, injury and ill-health benefits, for police, 160–2, 163–6
'Definition of Policing by Consent' (UK Government information document, 2012), 381–2
Delane, John, 357
Deptford: bread riots (1867), 344
Derby, Countess of, 366, 368
Derby, Edward Geoffrey Stanley, 14th Earl of: forms government (1866), 330; criticises police mishandling of Clerkenwell bombing, 351; on deficiencies of Metropolitan police, 353

Index

Desmond, Timothy, 349–50
Desmond, William, 350
Detective Force: neglected by Peel, 105–6, 231; need for, 233, 235, 238–9, 241; created, 241–2; strength, 242, 244; publicity, 243–4; personnel changes, 244; Dickens takes interest in, 244; and guided tours of London low life, 244; considered deficient, 244, 351, 353, 354; Secret Service Department created, 245, 352–3
Dewsbury: disturbances at (1838), 289
Dickens, Charles: visits Great Exhibition, 284; *Oliver Twist*, 88–9; interest in new detective police, 244
Dickson, Lieutenant-Colonel Lothian, 330, 334, 336–7, 340, 346
Director of Public Prosecutions: role created, 170
dismounted patrols, 159
dispersal powers, 189–90, 199–200, 211, 289, 312–13, 341–2
Disraeli, Benjamin: backs People's Charter, 218–19; Chancellor under Derby (1866), 330; urges dismissal of Mayne, 351
divisional superintendents, 233
divisional surgeons, 159
Divisions, 102, 106, 142, 319
Dixon, Superintendent James, 189, 193
Dochfour, Inverness, 267–8, 269
docks, 80–1
dockyard police, 318–19, 385
dog muzzling, 356
dog stealing, 228–30
Douro, Marchioness (*later* Duchess of Wellington), 269
Douro, Marquess *see* Wellesley, Arthur Richard
Dowling, Matthew Maurice: appointed chief clerk (Commissioners' Office), 103; resigns following breach of trust, 107–8; later police career, 108 & n460, 275, 384–5
Dowling, Vincent George, 107n458
drains and sewers, 80, 81
Dresden: Mayne visits, 370
Drummond, Colonel George, 39, 40
drunkenness: in British Army, 22; in early Victorian society, 89, 143; in Metropolitan police, 142, 143–4
Dublin, 10, 12, 78, 348
Dublin, HMS, 63

Dumfriesshire Police Force, 386
Duncannon, John Ponsonby, Viscount, 130–2, 141, 150, 177, 206
Duncombe, Thomas, 304
Dundas, General Sir David, 20
Dundas, Robert (*later* 2nd Viscount Melville), 101
Dundee Police, 386
dung, 83
Durkin, Superintendent, 344–5

East End of London, 81, 82; cholera outbreak, 180 & n733
Edinburgh City Police Force, 386
Edward, Prince of Wales (*later* King Edward VII), 116, 262
electoral reform, 218, 330, 342–3
electric lighting, 82
Electric Telegraph Company, 285–6
electric telegraphy, 82, 284, 285–6, 329
Ellenborough, Edward Law, 1st Earl of, 177
Ellis, Mr (barrister), 307
Ellis, James, 237
Emsley, Clive, 387
English, Chief Officer Stephen, 386–7
English, Nicholas, 350
Enright, Inspector John, 385
Episcopacy, 11
Erskine, Major-General Sir William, 39, 40, 41
Estremoz, Portugal, 27
Eugénie, Empress of the French: state visits to England, 294–5, 368
Euston railway station, 84
Evening Mail, 173
Everest, George, 355
executions: last in public, 350
Exeter Hall, Strand, 247

Farr, Dr William, 165
fast-day riots (March 1832), 114, 180–1
Feilding, Lieutenant-Colonel William, 352–3
Feltham, Inspector George, 232
Fenchurch Street railway station, 85
Fenian Brotherhood, 347
Fenians: formed, 347; arms smuggling, 350; raids (1866), 347; Manchester jail break and trial, 347–8; hangings at Salford Gaol, 348; arrest of Burke and Casey, 348; plot to storm Chester Castle, 350; Clerkenwell Prison

415

Index

bombing and trial (1867–8), 348–50; trial of Burke, Casey and Shaw, 350; execution of Michael Barrett, 350; terrorist threat, 185, 352; and Secret Service Department, 352–3
Ferguson, George, 268
Ferguson, Sir James, 355
Ferrol, Spain, 19
Fido, Martin, *The Official Encyclopedia of Scotland Yard* (with Keith Skinner), 358–9
Field, Detective Inspector Charles, 166–70, 234, 244
Fielden, John, 218
Fielding, Henry, 87
Fielding, John, 87
fines: for assaults on police officers, 163–4; for police misconduct, 144 & n600
Finsbury Square: fast-day riots (1832), 114, 180–1; Chartist meetings, 257; Reform Bill rally (1866), 333–4
fire brigades: development and operation, 206–7, 318
fires: Houses of Parliament (1834), 83, 205–6; Wells Street (1829), 162, 174; Tooley Street (1861), 318; Whitehall Palace (1698), 82
Fisher, John W., 159, 162, 315
fishing, 265
Fitzgerald, William, 75
Fitzroy, Henry, 291 & n1221, 292–3
Fitzroy, Lord *see* Somerset, Lord Fitzroy
flogging: in the military, 22; of juvenile offenders, 328–9
Floors Castle, Roxburghe, 268, 271, 276, 364
fog, 80
foot patrols, 87–8, 111
Ford, John, 87
Fordham, Edward, 182–3
foreign criminals, 283
forlorn hope: at Badajoz, 47; at Ciudad Rodrigo, 44; at Morne Fortuné, 14; at San Sebastian, 56
Fox, Lieutenant-Colonel Lane, 338
Francis, John, 240–1
Franco–Austrian War (1809), 34
Fraser, Colonel James (City Police Commissioner), 346
Fraser, Major-General Alexander, 28
Freame, Philadelphia Hannah (*later* Dawson), 9
Freame Mount (house), Cootehill, 9, 10

Frederick Street Murder case, Marylebone (1837), 231–2, 233–4
Frederick William, Crown Prince (*later* Frederick III, King of Prussia and German Emperor), 368
Freeman, Superintendent Samuel, 388
French Revolution, 247
Fuentes de Oñoro: battle of (1811), 41–2; British troops overwinter in (1812–13), 49
Fursey, George, 192–3, 194, 197–8, 197n802
Fussell, Joseph, 259 & n1055

Gabelee, Mr Justice, 197
Gaelic Ireland, 7
Gale, Sarah, 233
game bird shooting, 265
Gardner, Constable William, 238
Gardner's Lane station house, 182, 240, 243, 262
Garibaldi, Giuseppe: visits London, 325
Garibaldi riots (1862–4), 322–5; Primrose Hill meeting, 325–6
Garibaldi's Working Men's Committee, 325–6
garrotting panics (1856 and 1862), 320–1
Gawler, George, 266–7, 267n1098
Gay, William, 232
Gearing, Constable William, 312
General Game Certificate, 265
George III, King, 19, 83
George IV, King (*earlier* Prince Regent): Carlton House home, 91; reviews 1/52nd Regiment, 78; and crisis over Queen Caroline, 101; death, 176n719
Gernon, Superintendent Andrew, 348–9, 352
Gerrett, Sergeant William, 242
Gibbs (manservant), 370
Gibbs, Superintendent (of B Division), 298
Gibbs, Brevet Lieutenant-Colonel Edward, 48
Gibson, John B., 200
Gladstone, William Ewart: introduces Reform Bill (1866), 330
Glenmore Lodge, 270
Glover, Michael, *The Peninsular War 1807–1814: A Concise Military History*, 31, 46
Goff, Sergeant Charles, 235, 242
Gold Coast, 90

Index

Gold/Silver/Bronze hierarchy of command, 188
Golden, Thomas, 103
Goldsmid, Sir Francis, 266
Good, Daniel, 238-9
Goodman, Sergeant George, 224-5
Goodwood House, West Sussex, 264, 265, 274
Goodwood Races, 265-6, 281
Goodyer, Inspector Frederick, 182-3, 385
Gordon, Sir James Willoughby, 1st Baron, 25, 49, 209
Gordon Castle, 264, 269
Gothenburg, 26
Gould, Richard, 235-6
Graham, Sir James: character, 363-4; and Chartist agitation, 224, 226, 227; banning order, 224; and attempt on life of Queen Victoria, 240; and detective department, 241-2; reviews royal protection and security, 243; and police gratuities, 165
Graham, Lieutenant-General Sir Thomas (*later* Baron Lynedoch), 55, 56, 91
Granby Street (Lambeth): venue for prostitutes, 89
Grand Juries: support for New Police, 181-2
Grantham, Lord (*later* 2nd Earl de Grey), 91
Grantham, Constable Joseph, 161
gratuities for police officers, 144, 151, 163, 165, 179
Great Camp *see* Chobham Common Great Camp
Great Exhibition (1851), 282-5
Great Mews, 82
Green, Catherine, 152-3
Green Street, Mayfair, 361-2
Greenacre, James, 232-3
Greenwich: bread riots (1867), 344
Greenwich Police Court, 153-4
Gregory, William, 96
Gregson, William, 100 & n428
Greig, Major John, 347
Grenadier Guards, 205-6; and Garibaldi riots (1862), 322-3; and Hyde Park riots (1866), 335, 338, 340; on standby at Hyde Park, 346
Grey, Charles, 2nd Earl: advocates parliamentary reform, 175; forms government (1830), 177; introduces Reform Bill, 178
Grey, General Charles (Queen Victoria's private secretary), 373
Grey, Lady Elizabeth, 212
Grey, Sir George: petitioned over taxation, 248; introduces Bill for amalgamation of Metropolitan and City police, 120; stops Field's pension, 168-9; and Chartist unrest, 255, 259; presents Rowan to Queen Victoria, 262; interviews Robert Pate, 282; and Great Exhibition, 283-4; and state visit of Emperor Napoleon (1855), 295; and Hyde Park disturbances (1855), 297-8, 305, 310-12; and relations between Mayne and Hay, 305-6; criticises bail and custody arrangements, 312; and metropolitan fire service, 318; debates attack on Pilkington, 320; debates reception of Princess Alexandra, 119; and corporal punishment of child offenders, 328, 329; and Trafalgar Square demonstrations (1866), 331; clamour for his dismissal, 338-9
Grifs, Sergeant Henry, 150
Grimwood, Eliza, 234-5
Grimwood, Superintendent W., 162-3, 174n706
Grocott, Mrs (cook), 166-7
Grosvenor, Lord Robert (*later* 1st Baron Ebury): introduces Sunday Trading Bill (1855), 296; meeting with Mayne, 300; Park Street home safeguarded, 298, 303; withdraws Bill, 304; connection to Chester Square, 367
Guards Brigade: at Waterloo, 70, 71, 72, 73
Gummer, Sergeant Vincent, 312
Gurney, Mr. Baron, 153
Gurney, John, 190n772, 191, 193
Gurwood, Lieutenant John, 44, 45, 46
Gustavus IV, King of Sweden, 26

hackney carriages, 155
Haddingtonshire, 386
Hadow, Reverend William E., 368
Hall, Mr (magistrate), 183, 241
Hamilton, William, 262
Hampshire Constabulary, 287
Hannell, Mary, 237
Harcourt, Sir William, 376
Hardinge, Sir Henry (*later* 1st Viscount

Index

Hardinge), 274–5, 286
Hardy, Gathorne: succeeds Walpole as Home Secretary, 156; questioned in House on street outrages, 346; on police mishandling of Clerkenwell bombing, 351, 352; orders internal inquiry into Metropolitan police, 244–5, 354–5
Harris, Captain William: evidence to Select Committee on Police (1852–3), 287, 314n1307; appointed first assistant commissioner, 287, 314; and Garibaldi riots (1862), 323, 324; and Hyde Park riots (1866), 335, 336; connected to electric telegraph, 329; military powers, 353; takes over work responsibilities from Mayne, 358; and death of Mayne, 371, 372; at Mayne's funeral, 372
Hartley, Inspector, 142
Harvey, Daniel Whittle (City Police Commissioner): liaison with Rowan and Mayne (1848), 257–8, 260; rumoured successor to Rowan, 262; and Wellington's funeral, 286; and state visit of Emperor Napoleon (1855), 294–5; possible distrust of Mayne, 295; death, 116
Hay, Captain William: succeeds Rowan as commissioner, 262, 280; questions Robert Pate, 282; sidelined by Mayne, 284, 286, 290, 295; made Companion of the Order of the Bath, 285; proposes new policing system, 291–2, 293; betrays Mayne, 287; deteriorating relationship with Mayne, 290–3, 305–6; death, 280, 314
Hay, Lady Elizabeth *see* Douro, Marchioness
Hay, Lady Susan, 267, 269
Haye Sante, La (Waterloo), 69
Haynes, Inspector John, 242
healthcare and medical services, for police, 159
Hearn, Constable, 243
Hearts of Oak (protest movement) *see* Oakboy movement
Heesom, Hannah, 93
Hendaya, Spain, 57
Henderson, Sir Edmund, 374, 376
Henderson, Gilbert, 307
Henry, Mr. (magistrate), 152
Henry, Sir Edward, 377

Heron, Major Basil, 16
Heyer, Georgette, *The Spanish Bride*, 48n212
Heywood, John, 15
Hibbert, Charles (clothier to police), 109
Hill, George, 234
Hill, Sir Rowland: commands Light Division, 48; abandons Madrid and retreats across Spain, 49; at battle of Orthez, 60; at battle of Toulouse, 61; joins Wellington for 1815 campaign, 66; promotions list, 72–3; at scene of Parliament fire (1834), 206
Hillsden, Constable (of P Division), 343
Hinkman, Inspector, 243
History of the War of the Peninsula (Napier), 92–3
Hobler, Mr (solicitor), 236
Hodgkinson, Anne, 350
Hodgson, Captain Charles, 116
Hodgson, Kirkman, 121
holidays, 86–7
Holmes, Richard, *Wellington: The Iron Duke*, 41, 42, 53
Home Office: early relations with Metropolitan Police, 123, 125, 129–30; *see also* Phillipps, Samuel; Yardley, Charles
Hook, Captain William, 206
Hope, Lieutenant-General Sir John, 27, 28
Hornsby, Inspector, 146
horse patrol, 111, 138, 209
Hougoumont, Château d' (Waterloo), 69–70
housebreaking, 183
Household Words (magazine), 244
Houses of Parliament *see* Parliament
Howell, George, 330
Howick, Sir Henry Grey, Viscount (*later* 3rd Earl Grey), 145
Hubbard, William, 234
Huddersfield: disturbances at (1837), 289
Hue and Cry (magazine), 233 & n949
Hughes, Superintendent Samuel: early police career, 152; investigates Edward Oxford case (1840), 240; charged with improper conduct, 152; and Hyde Park disturbances (1855), 298, 299, 300, 301–2; conduct investigated, 307; evidence to Royal Commission into Hyde Park disturbances (1855), 307; censured, 309–11; Mayne reprimands,

418

Index

310, 311
Hume, Joseph, 176
Hunt, Brevet Lieutenant-Colonel John, 29, 56
Hunter, Chief Constable, 96
Hunter, Superintendent Thomas, 191–2
Hyde Park: Great Exhibition (1851), 282–5; Sunday trading riots (1855), 296–305, 306–13; Garibaldi riots (1862), 322–5; Reform Bill riots (1866), 332–8, 339–40; and public right of assembly, 333, 341–2, 345; peaceful rally by Reform League (6 May 1867), 344–6; memorial procession for executed Fenians (24 Nov 1867), 348
hygiene, public, 81–2, 86
Hythe barracks, Kent, 24, 25

Illustrated Times, 168, 341, 353–4
Imperial Guard (French): at Waterloo, 70–1
income tax: imposition during peacetime, 247 & n1010
India: First Anglo-Sikh War (1845–6), 272–3
indictments, preparing, 211
Inglis, Sir Robert, 221
Innes-Ker, Lord Charles, 279
inspecting superintendents, 355
insurance companies: and fire brigades, 207–8
intent, criminal, proof of, 211
Internal Departmental Committee on System of Policing in the Metropolis (1868), 244–5, 354–6
Ireland, 7, 8, 10, 11–12, 15; British Rule in, 347
Irish Catholics: uprising (1641), 8, 10
Irish Confederates, 258
Irish Rebellion (1641), 8, 10
Irish Rebellion (1798), 15
Irish Revolutionary Brotherhood (*later* Irish Republican Brotherhood), 347
Isabella II, Queen of Spain, 330
Isle of Man, 15
Islington Agriculture Hall: Reform Movement meeting, 340
Islington Green: Chartist meeting, 223–4

Jackson, Inspector Robert, 155–6, 157
Jacob's Island (Bermondsey slum), 88
James I of England and VI of Scotland,
King, 7
Johnson, Superintendent James, 189, 193, 235
Jones, George, 267 & n1102
Jones, Jane, 238
Jones, Superintendent John, 386
Jones, Thomas, 174
Jourdan, Marshal Jean-Baptiste, 52
Justice, Anne, 349–50
Justices of the Peace, Metropolis Act (1829), 95, 124–5
juvenile crime, 210–12

Keane, John, 388
Keating, Mr Justice, 156–7
Keller, Lisa, *Triumph of Order: Democracy and Public Space,* 86
Kelly, Captain Thomas, 347–8, 350
Kempt, Henry, 174
Kempt, Major-General James, 51, 52, 57
Kennedy, Colonel James Shaw: military career, 96–7; Craufurd's aide-de-camp, 44, 97; offered job as police commissioner, 97–9; later career in police, 98–9; *An Autobiographical Memoir and Notes of the Battle of Waterloo,* 73, 74
Kennington Common: Chartist meetings and demonstrations, 226, 252–5
Kensal Green Cemetery, 86, 228, 279, 315, 363, 372–3
Kensington: funeral procession of Duke of Sussex, 228
Kensington Palace, 227
Kerr, Lord Charles, 279
Key, John, 176
Kincaid, Lieutenant John: at Ciudad Rodrigo, 45; on Craufurd, 46; dines with old friends and colleagues, 273; government inspector of prisons, 273n1138
Kingston-upon-Hull Police Force, 385
Kinhan, Constable John, 141
knackers-yards, 81

La Bayonette redoubt, 57
Labalmondière, Captain Douglas: appointed Inspecting Superintendent, 281; and Great Exhibition, 284; and Wellington's lying-in-state ceremony, 286; royal security duties, 290, 295, 314; appointed second assistant commissioner,

Index

314; polices Royal illuminations (10 March 1863), 118; and Hyde Park demonstrations (1866), 335, 336; connected to electric telegraph, 329; and Clerkenwell bombing, 348–9; and military powers, 353; takes over work responsibilities from Mayne, 358; and death of Mayne, 372; acting chief commissioner, 372; at Mayne's funeral, 372
Labouchere, Henry (*later* 1st Baron Taunton), 122
Lamb, George, 128
Larceny Act (1827), 229–30
Larpent, Francis, 50
Last, Robert, 361–2
Lauderdale, James Maitland, 9th Earl of, 276
Law Enforcement Action Partnership, 380
Lawson, Elizabeth, 174
Lazenby, Superintendent (of D Division), 130–2, 150
Leach, Constable Charles, 312
Leach, Captain Jonathan, 34, 35
Lee, Captain W.L. Melville, 104n448, 383
Lee, Richard, 184, 190, 193
Leeke, Ensign William, 67
legal aid, for police officers, 170
Leicester City Police, 385
Lemeschal, Peter, 234–5
Lennox, Elizabeth (*later* Stuart), 276
Lennox, Lord *see* Richmond, Henry Gordon-Lennox, 6th Duke of
Lennox, Lord John George, 276–7
Lentz, Susan A., 381
Lesaca, Spain, 55
levee ceremonies, 262 & n1068, 364–5
Lever, John, 146–7
Leveson-Gower, Lord Francis, 96
Lewes: bonfire night riots, 289
Lewis, Sir George C., 122
Liberal party, and Gladstone's 1866 Reform Bill, 330; *see also* Whigs
Liddell, John, 367
Liddell, Sir Augustus, 352–3
Life Guards, 335, 338, 346
Light Brigade *see* Light Division
Light Division (*earlier* Light Brigade): formed, 31, 33; arrives in Lisbon, 34–5; Captain Leach on, 34, 35; reaches Talavera, 35; forced marching, 35; designated Light Division, 36; at battle of the river Coa, 36–8; at Bussaco, 38; winters in Torres Vedras (1810–11), 39; pursues French into Spain, 39–40; at Sabugal, 40; at battle of Fuentes de Oñoro, 41–2; inspected by Wellington, 42; at Ciudad Rodrigo, 43–5; assault on Badajoz, 47; casualties, 47–8; arrives at Salamanca (1812), 48; retreats across Spain, 49; overwinters at Fuentes de Oñoro (1812–13), 49; advances towards Salamanca, 51–2; at battle of Vitoria, 52–3; assault on San Sebastian, 56; campaign in Pyrenees, 56–8; at battle of Nivelle, 59; attacked at Arcangues, 59; at battle of Orthez, 60–1; at battle of Toulouse, 61–2; reputation and military achievements, 25, 64; at Chobham Common Great Camp, 290
Ligny, Belgium, 67; battle of (1815), 68
Lincoln's Inn Fields: Chartist meetings, 223, 224
Lindsay, Major-General James, 346, 353
Lisbon, 19, 27, 34–5
List, Inspector Alfred, 386
Liverpool: Fenian raids (1866), 347
Liverpool Dockyard Police, 385
Lloyd's Weekly Newspaper, 376
lodging houses, 155
Logan, Colonel, 271 & 1126
loitering, 211
London: cemeteries and burial grounds, 86; garrotting panics (1856 and 1862), 320; improvements and rebuilding, 82–3; as industrial and trading centre, 80–1; markets, 85–6; pollution, 81–2, 86; population, 82; rail network, 84–5; rich and poor districts, 81; slums and living conditions, 81–2, 86, 88–9 & n391; transport and traffic problems, 83–4; underground railway, 85
London Bridge, 84
London City Press, 356
London Daily News, 167–8, 340–1
London Evening News, 280
London Evening Standard: campaign against New Police, 171–2, 239; Field advertises in, 169; criticises Mayne, 356; on deteriorating police standards after Mayne's death, 376
London Fire Engine Establishment (LFEE), 207, 208, 318

Index

London Hackney Carriage Act (1853), 155
London Working Men's Association, 218, 334
Long, Constable John, 161, 163
Lords, House of: and police reform proposals, 94; defeats Reform Bill (1831), 178; and Sunday trading proposals, 317–18; police deployment at State Closing of Parliament, 225
Louis Napoleon (*later* Napoleon III, Emperor of the French) *see* Napoleon III, Emperor of the French
Louis Philippe, King of the French: deposed (1848), 247
Lovett, William, 218
Lowe, Sergeant, 254–5
Lowry, Superintendent Edward, 104
Loxton, Superintendent, 325–6
Luddites, 175
Ludolf, Count Guglielmo de, 143
Lugo, Spain, 29
Lulworth Castle: Peel rents, 101
Lund, Sergeant John, 224–5

macadam (road surface), 83–4
MacDonnell, Alexander, 3rd Earl of Antrim, 11
Maceroni lances, 188 & n761, 200
Mackay, Chief Officer Donald, 386
Mackenzie, Colonel Kenneth (*later* Sir Kenneth Douglas): commands 52nd Regiment, 21, 23; develops light infantry training methods, 23, 24; commended by Moore, 25
MacLeod, Major Charles, 37
MacMahon, Captain Charles, 388
MacPhedris, Eliza (*later* Rowan), 11
Madgett, Constable Charles, 312
Madrid, 48, 49
magistracy *see* Police Offices
Magistrates' Courts Act (1839), 235
Maguire, Connor, 8
Maiden Lane railway station, 85
Maidstone (warship), 90
Maisonette, Ingatestone (Mayne's summer residence), 220–1, 362
Maissey, Superintendent (of G Division), 225
Maitland, Major-General Sir Peregrine, 70, 264
Maitland, Brigadier General Thomas, 19
Malden, Charles Edward, 365

Mallalieu, Superintendent Francis: background, 288, 385, 387; Chartist demonstrations, 254; evidence to Select Committee on Police (1852–3), 287, 288; and Hay's proposed new policing system, 291, 293; receives death threat for Mayne, 153–4; appointed Inspecting Superintendent of Dockyard Police, 319
Malmesbury, Countess of, 366
Manby, Captain George, 206
Mancer, Sarah, 237
Manchester: Peterloo massacre (1819), 174n707, 181; Fenian attack on police van, 347–8; trial of Fenians, 348
Manchester Police, 99, 384
Mansion House (City), 117
March, Lord *see* Richmond, Charles Gordon-Lennox, 5th Duke of
Marine Police, 87, 217
markets, 85–6
Marlborough Street Police Office, 148
Marmont, Marshal Auguste, 48
marriage restrictions, in Metropolitan Police, 158
Marriott, Mr (magistrate), 183
Martin, Superintendent George: meritorious conduct, 150–1; charged with common assault, 151; and Chartist disturbances in Birmingham, 220; evidence to Select Committee on Police (1852–3), 250, 287, 288–9; and Hyde Park riots (1855), 298, 301; evidence to Royal Commission into Hyde Park disturbances (1855), 307
Marylebone Police Court, 125
Marylebone Police Office, 231–2, 233, 234
Marylebone Police Station House, 130
Masséna, Marshal André: advance on Lisbon, 36; winters in Santarém, 39; forced back into Spain, 39–40; defeat at Sabugal, 40; defeat at Fuentes de Oñoro, 41–2
Massey, William, 310 & n1292
Mather, E.C., *Public Order in the Age of the Chartists*, 216, 221–2, 250
Maule, Fox (*later* 11th Earl of Dalhousie), 115, 221 & n902
May, Edmund, 155
May, Superintendent John: appointed superintendent, 103–4; tours police stations, 108; and Cold Bath Fields

Index

riots, 188, 189, 190n772, 191, 192; and Chartist disturbances in Birmingham, 220; escorts Dassett to Cabinet Office, 243; Charing Cross affray, 251; illness, 281; and Hyde Park riots, 298, 299; evidence to Royal Commission into Hyde Park disturbances (1855), 299–300, 307; death, 307

Mayne, Anne (*née* Morton), 8

Mayne, Barbara (*née* Sedborough), 8

Mayne, Carvick Cox (RM's son), 362, 364; early death, 366

Mayne, Catherine (RM's sister), 15

Mayne, Catherine (*later* Heron; RM's sister), 15–16, 227; death, 371

Mayne, Charles (RM's brother), 15, 16

Mayne, Charles (RM's grandfather), 9, 10

Mayne, Charles Edward (RM's son), 316, 367–8

Mayne, Dawson (RM's brother), 16–17, 362, 372

Mayne, Dorothea (RM's grandmother), 9, 10

Mayne, Dorothea (RM's sister), 15

Mayne, Edward (RM's brother), 15, 372

Mayne, Edward (RM's father), 10, 15, 16

Mayne, Edward (RM's grandson), 372

Mayne, Edward (RM's great-uncle), 9–10

Mayne, Edward (RM's son), 364

Mayne, Frances Rebecca (RM's sister), 16, 17

Mayne, Georgina Marianne (*later* Broke; RM's daughter), 371; birth, 363; at Nuthurst Lodge, 364; with father in Hyde Park (24 June 1855), 297; presented to Queen Victoria, 367; accompanies father to Mansion House banquet, 369; introduced to Garibaldi, 325; marriage to Horace Broke, 363

Mayne, Georgina Marianne (*née* Carvick; RM's wife): family background, 360; courtship and marriage to Richard Mayne, 360, 361; presented to Queen Adelaide, 361; moves into Mayfair home, 361; birth of children, 362, 363, 364, 365, 367; summer breaks in Essex, 362; letters from husband, 220–1, 222, 224, 225–6, 226–7, 253–4, 261, 270, 272, 300, 304–6, 307–8, 362–4, 369, 370–1; with family at Nuthurst Lodge, 364; moves with family to New Street (St James's), 365; and early death of first son, 365–6; final move to Chester Square, 367; presents daughter Georgina to Queen Victoria, 367; accompanies husband on official engagements, 316–17, 319, 325, 368–9; holidays, 369–70; presents daughter Sarah to Queen Victoria, 371; executor of husband's will, 373; Civil List pension, 373, 374; death, 373

Mayne, John (1641–1710), 8

Mayne, John (d. 1641), 8

Mayne, John (RM's brother), 15

Mayne, Katherine Emily (RM's daughter): birth, 365; illness and death, 356–7, 369, 371, 372

Mayne, Margaret (RM's sister), 17

Mayne, Mary Elizabeth (Dawson's wife), 16–17

Mayne, Rebecca (*née* Pearce), 8, 9

MAYNE, RICHARD:

Personal life: ancestors in Ireland, 7, 8–9; family background, 10, 15–16, 16–17; birth, 16; schooling and university education, 16; career as barrister, 16, 89–90, 93; member of Athenaeum, 91–2 & n408; courtship and marriage to Georgina Carvick, 360, 361; legal action against father-in-law, 360–1; presented to Queen Adelaide and William IV, 361; moves into Mayfair home, 361; catches butler stealing, 361–2; birth of children, 362, 363, 364, 365, 367; letters to wife (*see* Mayne, Georgina Marianne: letters from husband); with family at Nuthurst Lodge, 364; at Queen Victoria's levees, 364–5; made Companion of the Order of Bath, 256; moves with family to New Street (St James's), 365; and early death of first son, 365–6; mingles with London's High Society, 366; final move to Chester Square, 367; at official and semi-official engagements, 368–9, 370; holidays, 356, 369–70; death of daughter Katherine, 356–7; failing health, 357–8; rumours of a baronetcy, 358; death, 371; Memorial Fund, 371–2; funeral procession and burial, 372; monument, 372–3; will and estate, 373; tribute, 374

Second joint commissioner (1829–49): sponsors for candidature, 100–1;

appointed commissioner, 100, 101–2, 377; sworn as Justice of the Peace, 102; relationship with Rowan, 102; drafts initial plan for New Police, 102–3; co-formulates 'Principles of Policing', 104, 378–9, 382–3, 384; personality clash with Phillipps, 129, 177; and Fordham fraud case, 182; and fast-day riots (March 1832), 180–1; mercy petition for James Sutton, 174; and Cold Bath Fields meeting (1833), 185–7, 195–7, 201; evidence to Select Committee on Petition of Frederick Young and Others (1833), 203; evidence to Select Committee on Police of the Metropolis (1834), 113, 114, 126, 133, 159–60, 163–4, 181, 198, 204; and Wovenden affair, 131–2; introduces 'route papers' communication system, 232; evidence to Select Committee on Metropolitan Police Offices (1837–8), 139, 214–17; and Lord Russell murder case (1840), 236–7; and Edward Oxford case, 240; develops detective department, 241–2; and Clerkenwell Green assault case (5 September 1842), 224–5; evidence to Select Committee on Dog Stealing (1844), 228–9; omnibus and coach regulations, 246–7; and Trafalgar Square riots (March 1848), 247–9, 250; meeting with Feargus O'Connor, 253–5; and Chartist unrest, 254–6, 259–60, 261; on Rowan's absences and failing health, 270, 271, 272, 277–8, 363; takes over work responsibilities from Rowan, 276, 281

First joint commissioner (1850–55): relations with Labalmondière, 281; charges Robert Pate, 282; and policing of Great Exhibition, 283–5; knighted, 285; and policing of Wellington's funeral, 286; thrown from horse, 286; at inquest into loss of life at Chelsea Hospital, 287; relations with Hay, 284, 286, 287, 290–3, 295, 305–6; and policing of state visit of Emperor Napoleon (1855), 294–5; opposes Sunday Trading Bill, 296, 306; and Hyde Park riots (1855), 297–8, 299–300, 301–2, 305, 313; appears before Committee of House of Commons, 306; evidence to Royal Commission into Hyde Park disturbances (1855), 307–8; reprimands Hughes, 310, 311; takes disciplinary action against accused officers, 311–12

Sole commissioner (1855–68): becomes sole commissioner, 314; and policing of Feargus O'Connor's funeral, 315; testifies at inquest on Elizabeth Saunders, 315; death threats against, 154, 321; in Paris, 368; attends police concert in Southwark (1860), 316–17; and garrotting outbreak (1862), 320–1; and Charles Field case, 166, 168–70; and Garibaldi riots (1862), 323–4; and policing of Royal procession and wedding (7–10 March 1863), 116, 118; evidence to Commission of Inquiry into Transportation and Penal Servitude (1863), 321; meets Garibaldi, 325; described by Cavanagh, 326; work ethic, 326, 360; relations with Yardley, 326–7; increasingly autocratic and inflexible, 314–15; criticised in press, 328; dismisses Inspector Jackson, 155–6; and Trafalgar Square demonstrations (1866), 331–2; issues ban on Hyde Park meeting (23 July 1866), 332–3, 340; and Hyde Park riots, 334–6, 338, 339, 340, 342; surrounded and injured by mob, 337, 339; criticised and disparaged in press, 340–1; offers resignation, 342; and Fenian raids in Liverpool, 347; and Hyde Park meeting (6 May 1867), 345–6; and street robbery, 346; and Clerkenwell Prison bombing, 349, 350–2; judged increasingly unfit for office, 352, 354; offers resignation for second time, 352; largely sidelined over Secret Service arrangements, 352; attacked by press, 353–4, 356, 357; before Internal Departmental Committee, 355; introduces petty and unpopular regulations, 356; writes to *The Times*, 357; libel action against, 154, 156–7; workload reduces, 358; assessment of last year in office, 358; deteriorating police standards after his death, 375–7; overshadowed by Peel, 377–8; achievements and legacy, 358–9, 373, 379, 389–90

Views on: centralized London police

force, 120–1, 122–3; commissioner uniforms, 209; corporal punishment of child offenders, 328–9; Culley murder, 198; electric telegraphy, 285–6, 329; fire brigade service, 318; indictment process, 211; juvenile crime, 210–11; marriage restrictions on the police, 158; plain clothes officers, 293–4; policing in the West Indies, 387; religion, 307–8, 363; riot and crowd control strategy, 313; salary increase, 210; Sunday trading, 296, 306, 317–18; surgeons' duties, 159–60; ticket-of-leave system, 320, 321

Mayne, Richard Charles (RM's son): birth, 362; Rowan made godfather, 362; at Nuthurst Lodge, 364; letter from father, 271; Royal Navy career, 362, 368, 369; formal dinners and banquets, 366, 369; in Rowan's will, 279; presents paper to Royal Geographical Society, 369; occupies Chester Square, 373

Mayne, Robert (RM's brother), 17
Mayne, Robert (1679–1753), 8–9
Mayne, Robert Dawson (RM's son), 316, 364, 370, 372
Mayne, Sarah (RM's sister), 15
Mayne, Sarah (née Fiddes; RM's mother), 10, 15; death, 365
Mayne, Sarah Fanny (later Malden; RM's daughter), 365, 373; presented to Queen Victoria, 371
Mayne, William (RM's brother), 16, 371, 372
Mayne, William (RM's nephew), 372
Mayne, William (RM's uncle), 10
Mayne, William John (RM's son), 364, 372
Mayo, Richard Bourke, 6th Earl of, 351
McDonald, Alexander, 9
McLean, Superintendent Andrew, 203, 226
McManus, Inspector Andrew, 385
McQueen, Steve, 367
Mee, James, 184, 190, 191, 192, 193
Meighan, Elizabeth, 263
Meighan, William, 263
Mein, Brevet Major William, 57–8
Melbourne, William Lamb, 2nd Viscount: seeks preferment for Kinhan, 141; Home Secretary, 177; antagonism towards police commissioners, 129–30, 177; receives complaints about police, 147; presents Mayne to Queen Adelaide and William IV, 361; gratuity payments, 162, 163, 179; and White Conduit House affair, 128–9; duplicitous character, 127, 198–9; bans fast-day processions, 180; and Cold Bath Fields protest, 185–7, 197, 198–9; Prime Minister (1834), 130; at scene of Parliament fire (1834), 206

Melville, Henry Dundas, 1st Viscount, 101
Metropolitan Board of Works, 318
Metropolitan Building Act (1855), 315
Metropolitan Fire Brigade: created, 318
Metropolitan Fire Brigade Act (1865), 318
Metropolitan Market (Islington), 85–6
Metropolitan Police: acceptance and active support for, 173, 181–2, 216, 217, 389; accommodation, 160 (see also station houses); advertising and publicity, 182; assaults on, 144, 162–3, 173–4, 176; auxiliary military support, 205–6, 338, 340, 353; batons and baton charges, 108, 181; beats, 106, 144; brass bands, 316–17, 319; brutality allegations against, 146, 194, 199–200, 224–5, 258, 303, 304, 308, 309–10, 312, 336, 337; City boundary and jurisdiction issues, 112–14, 177, 180, 181; clerical staff, 103; complaints against, 144–9; and corporal punishment of child offenders, 328–9; corruption, susceptibility to, 172; cricket teams, 315–16; crime prevention, early emphasis on, 105, 235; criticised in newspapers, 146, 147, 171–3, 238–9, 328, 340–1, 353–4, 356, 357; crowd and riot control, 113–14, 181, 199–200, 219, 221–2, 312–13 (see also riots and disturbances); death, injury and ill-health benefits, 160–2, 163–6; deployment outside Metropolitan District, 204, 216–17, 219–20, 347; detective branch, lack of before 1842, 233, 235, 238–9, 241; dismissals, 143–4, 149; divisions, 102, 106, 142, 319; dockyard divisions, 318–19; drill, 288; drunkenness and drinking

Index

on duty, 142, 143–4; effectiveness, 173; and electric telegraphy, 284, 285–6, 329; equipment, 108–09; and fire authorities, 206–8; gallantry and bravery, 162, 174; gratuities, 144, 151, 163, 165, 179; healthcare and medical services, 159; internal discipline, 142, 143–4, 146–7, 148–9, 311–12; jurisdiction area, 217; legal aid for officers, 170; liaison with City police, 113; major events policing, 116–17, 118, 225; marriage restrictions urged by Peel, 158; military nature/militarisation, 133–4, 144, 195; moral influence, 216, 217; murdered or fatally injured on duty, 161, 162; as national model, 383, 384, 387–9; nicknames for, 171; numbers and strength, 103, 217, 319, 354, 356; off-duty activities, 315–17; operation, 108; organisation and structure, 102–3, 106–7, 355–6; and parallel systems of policing in the Metropolis, 111, 124–5, 138, 139, 231; patronage, 141–2, 378; pay, 172, 210, 221, 281–2; pension scheme, 160–1, 163–6, 169, 281; plain clothes officers, deployment of, 183, 188, 204, 231, 233, 293–4, 315, 321; police/military cooperation, 205–6, 338, 340, 353; political surveillance, 203–4, 231; popular opposition to, 171; private inquiry work, 166–9; promotion, 104, 141, 142, 143, 378–9; prosecuted at police courts, 149–52, 224–5; public image, 146, 147, 389; rapid mobilisation of constables, 329; recruitment and selection, 103–4, 141–2, 171, 288, 378–9; resignations, 144, 149, 163; rewards, 236, 237, 238; riot control (*see* crowd and riot control); running costs, 120; Solicitors Department, 170; as spies, 203–4, 231; strike action (1872), 282; superannuation fund, 160–1, 163–6, 281–2; and ticket-of-leave men, 319–20, 321; training, 288; uniforms, 108, 109, 180n735, 209–10; visibility of, 172; working class and, 171

Metropolitan Police, history: policing before 1829, 87–8, 94; Marine Police established, 87; Peel introduces Metropolitan Police Act (1829), 94–5, 378; first two commissioners appointed, 95–100, 101–2, 377; receiver appointed, 102; development of Principles of Policing, 104–7, 378–84; Whitehall Place (headquarters), 109–10; and proposed amalgamation with City Police, 114–15, 119–23, 139; relations with London magistrates, 125–8, 129–32, 133–7, 138–9; early relations with Home Office, 123, 125, 129–30; increased authority and jurisdiction after 1839, 139–40; deteriorating standards after Mayne's death, 375–7

Metropolitan Police Act (1829), 94–5, 109, 160, 161, 164, 185, 378; City of London exempt, 112

Metropolitan Police Act (1838), 260

Metropolitan Police Act (1839), 115, 140, 217, 235

Metropolitan Police Act (1856), 314

Metropolitan Police Courts Act (1839), 139–40

Metropolitan Police Courts Act (1840), 139–40

Metropolitan Police Fund, 165

Metropolitan Streets Act (1867), 356

Meyer, Charles, 360

Meyer, Thomas, 360

Middlesex County Cricket Club, 317n1328

Middlesex Justices Act (1792), 87, 95, 124

Military and Country Club, St James's Street, 275 & n1149

Military General Service Medal, 73

Miller, Inspector James, 235

Miller, Wilbur, *Cops and Bobbies: Police Authority in New York and London, 1830–1870*, 379, 380–1, 389

Milton Street Committee, 194–5

Mitchel, John, 257

Mitchell, Mr (attorney), 307

Mitchell, Constable John, 234

mode of trial, 210

Moir, Peter, 379–80

Mondego Bay, Portugal, 26–7

Monro, James, 377

Mont St Jean, Belgium, 72

Montgomery-Moore, Lady Jane, 74

Moore, Edward, 109

Moore, Captain John, 369

Moore, Major-General John: commands

Index

52nd Regiment, 19; advances Rowan's career, 20–1; military training reforms, 22–4, 31; in charge of defence of Kent coast, 23; appoints Mackenzie commanding officer, 23; commends Mackenzie, 25; expedition to Sweden, 26; commands British troops in Peninsula, 27–8; retreat to Corunna, 28, 29–30, 93; mortally wounded, 30; training methods adapted for New Police, 22, 32, 106–7, 384, 391

Moorsom, W.S. (ed.), *Historical Record of the Fifty-Second Regiment (Oxfordshire Light Infantry)*, 31, 58

Morne Fortuné (fort), St Lucia, 14

Morning Advertiser, 180, 181, 182, 238, 239, 255, 304

Morning Herald, 172

Morning Post, 123, 172–3, 276, 347; criticises Mayne, 356, 357

Morris, Ruth, 130–1

Moscow, 50

Mount Moat, Highwood Hill, 361

Mount Sedborough, County Fermanagh, 8

Mullany, Patrick, 349–50

Mulvaney (detective), 347

murder: numbers, 241; public fascination, 231–2

Murdoch, John (alias Williams), 321n1355

Murray, Superintendent, 226

Murray, Charles Knight (magistrate), 139

Murray, Lieutenant-General Sir George, 95, 99

Murray, James, 263, 266

Murray, Maria, 263

Napier, Lieutenant-General George: background, 20; joins 52nd Regiment, 20; on Mackenzie, 23, 24; on moral training, 31–2; leads storming party at Ciudad Rodrigo, 44; wounded, 45; loses arm, 46; at battle of Orthez, 60–1; jaunt with Rowan, 62–3; returns to Chatham, 63–4; estimation of Colborne, 77–8; in Rowan's will, 279

Napier, Major Charles, 37; statue in Trafalgar Square, 83

Napier, Major-General Sir William, 64, 92–3

Napoleon I (Bonaparte), Emperor of the French: rise to power, 18; planned invasion of Britain, 19–20; leads army to Peninsula, 28; returns to France, 29; and Franco–Austrian War, 34; retreats from Moscow, 49–50; sends Soult to Spain, 55; abdicates, 61; surrenders, 62; escapes from Elba, 65; advances through France, 65, 66; crosses Belgian frontier, 67; conduct at battle of Waterloo, 69–72; casualties, 72

Napoleon III, Emperor of the French: state visits to England, 294–5, 368; receives Mayne in Paris, 368

National Charter Association (NCA), 223

National Gallery, 82, 87

National Mercantile Life Assurance Company: Mayne attends anniversary lunch (1846), 365

National Political Union (NPU), 127–8

National Union of the Working Classes (NUWC): formation, 175; organisation and membership, 184; revolutionary strategy, 188; and fast-day riots (March 1832), 114, 180–1; planned meeting at Cold Bath Fields, 184–5; legality of meeting, 185–6, 201; meeting banned, 187; procession and assembly of demonstrators, 190–1; arrest of Gurney, 191; advance of police, 191–2; fighting and dispersal of crowd, 192, 193; attack on C Division, 192–3; Constable Culley killed, 193; arrests, 193–4 & n791; petition on police spies, 203

Nelthorpe, Eliza Sarah, 364

Nelthorpe, James Tudor, 360–1, 364

Neuilly, 74

New Steyne Hotel, Brighton, 92

New Street (St James's): Mayne resides at, 365

New York: early policing, 388–9

Newgate Gaol, 130, 350

Newport Police, 386

newspapers: opposition to New Police, 171–3; criticisms of police, 146, 147, 171–3, 238–9; criticisms of Mayne, 328, 340–1, 353–4, 356, 357

Ney, Marshal Michel, 36, 37, 38, 39; at Waterloo, 70

Nicolay, Colonel William, 70

Nine Elms railway station, 85

Index

Nine Years War (1594–1603), 7
Nivelle, battle of (1813), 58–9
Norfolk Hotel, Brighton, 277
Norfolk Street, Park Lane, 278–9
Normanby, Constantine Phipps, 1st Marquess of, 214
North America: early policing, 388–9
Northumberland, Duchess of, 366, 367, 368, 369
Northumberland, Duke of, 366, 368
Nottingham: Reform Bill riots (1831), 178
Nuthurst Lodge, Sussex, 364

Oakboy movement, 9–10
O'Brien, Superintendent (of C Division), 298, 299, 303, 307
obstructing police in execution of duty, 327
obstruction of thoroughfares, police powers, 145, 217, 226, 246, 356
O'Connell, Daniel, 221
O'Connor, Feargus, 247, 253–5, 256, 315
O'Hara, Sergeant Edward, 385
O'Keefe, John, 350
Old Bailey trials: Catherine Green (1831), 153; James Sutton (1832), 174; George Fursey (1833), 197; Robert Last (1834), 362; Greenacre and Gale (1837), 233; Richard Gould (1840), 235–6; Edward Oxford (1840), 240; John Francis (1842), 241; John Bean (1842), 243; Joseph Fussell (1848), 259; William Hamilton (1849), 262; Robert Pate (1850), 282; garrotters (1862), 321; Fenians (1868), 350
O'Mahony, John, 347
omnibuses, 83, 246
Orange Tree conspiracy (1848), 260–1
Orthez, battle of (1814), 59–61
Osborne, HMS, 370
Osborne, Lord William G., 343
Otway, Sergeant, 236
Oxford, Edward, 239–40
oyster shops, regulation of, 205

Pack, Major-General Sir Denis, 76
Paddington: Chartist meeting, 226
Paddington railway station, 84
Paget, Lord Alfred, 118
Paget, Major-General Sir Edward, 28–9
Pall Mall Gazette: on Hyde Park riots, 341; on breaches of the peace, 347; on deteriorating police standards, 375, 377
Palmer, William, 168
Palmerston, Henry John Temple, 3rd Viscount, 291
Pamplona, 53
Papelotte (hamlet, Waterloo), 69
Paris, 74–5
parish constables, 88, 290
Park, Sir James Alan (Mr Justice), 101, 174
Park Street (Mayfair), 298, 303
Parker, Mr (equipment supplier to police), 109
Parliament: burnt down, 83, 205–6; policing of, 111, 145, 225; *see also* Commons, House of; Lords, House of
parliamentary reform, 175, 178, 218
Parliamentary Select Committee inquiries: Police of the Metropolis (1828), 94, 112; Petition of Frederick Young and Others (1833), 203–4; Cold Bath Fields Meeting (1833), 184, 191, 198–202; Police of the Metropolis (1834), 103, 104, 108, 112–13, 114–15, 126–7, 133–5, 159–60, 163–4, 181, 198, 204–5, 382; Metropolitan Police Offices (1837–8), 113, 115, 137–9, 214–17, 379; Metropolis Improvements (1840), 81; Dog Stealing (1844), 228–30; Sale of Beer Regulation (1848), 260; Police (1852–3), 250, 287–90; Transportation (1856), 320; System of Police (1868), 329
Partridge, Constable, 243
Paschal, Lieutenant-Colonel G.F., 154–5, 156, 384
Pate, Robert, 282
Patriot War (1837), 14
Patteson, Mr Justice, 122
Paulet, Major-General Lord Frederick, 335, 338, 339, 342
Pearce, Superintendent Nicholas: arrests Chartists, 222; and Birmingham Post Office robbery (1840), 237; and Courvoisier murder case, 236–7; joins Detective Force, 242; promoted superintendent, 244; charged with exceeding his duty, 152; and Trafalgar Square riots, 249; and Great Exhibition, 284; and Hay's policing proposals, 291, 293

427

Index

Peel, Julia, Lady, 90, 148, 161
Peel, Sir Robert: introduces police force to Ireland, 94; dines with Wellington after Waterloo, 75; relations with Viscount Melville, 101; Home Secretary (1822), 88; attempts to establish London day patrol, 88, 94; introduces Metropolitan Police Act, 94–5, 378; excludes City, 112; seeks candidates to head up New Police, 95–9; appoints Rowan and Mayne, 99–100, 101–2, 205, 377; view of Gregson, 100; sets out initial plan for New Police, 102–3; and Principles of Policing, 104–7, 245, 378–83; fails to address detective role, 105–6, 231; against cronyism and jobbery, 141, 142, 378–9; urges police marriage restrictions, 158; reprimands Dowling, 107–8; failures of management, 111, 124–5, 231; limited role in development of Metropolitan police, 379; and medical services for police, 159; receives death threat, 176; and fears of public unrest (9 November 1830), 176; continues to support Rowan and Mayne in opposition, 177; approves salary increase for commissioners, 221; questions witnesses in Francis case, 241; introduces Bill for Protection of her Majesty's Person, 243; Rowan seeks favour from, 266; as father of modern policing, 377–8
Pegler, Constable Samuel, 232, 233
Penal Servitude Act (1853), 319–20, 321
Pennethorne, James, 81
Penny, Constable (of A Division), 343
pension scheme, police, 160–1, 163–6, 169, 281
Peterloo Massacre (1819), 174n707, 181
Peters, Sergeant Thomas, 148–9
Phillipps, Samuel: Under-Secretary of State at Home Office, 125; correspondence with commissioners, 126–7, 128, 129–30, 135–6, 150–1, 163, 209–10; correspondence with Roe, 128–9; personality clash with Mayne, 129, 177; writes to Peel on Police Regulations leak, 382–3; and hospital provision for police, 159; and Cold Bath Fields protest (13 May 1833), 185, 187, 189–90, 197; evidence to Select Committee on Cold Bath Fields Meeting (1833), 199; evidence to Select Committee on Metropolitan Police Offices (1837–8), 137–8; and superannuation fund proposal, 164; retirement, 256
Picton, Lieutenant-General Thomas, 60, 61
Pike, Michael S., *The Principles of Policing*, 382
Pilkington, Hugh, 320
Pitfour estate, Buchan, 268
Place, Francis, 127, 181, 197n802, 218
plain clothes officers, 183, 188, 204, 231, 233, 293–4, 315, 321
Plantation of Ulster, 7, 10
Plume, Constable Henry, 162
Police Gazette, 233n949
Police Offices: created, 87, 111, 124; patrols established, 87–8; judicial and policing powers, 87, 94–5, 106, 111, 124–5; constables attached to, 111, 124, 125, 138, 171, 231; relations with New Police, 125–8, 129–32, 133–7, 138–9; prosecutions against police officers, 149–52, 224–5; detective role, 231, 235; Parliamentary inquiry into, 113, 115, 137–9, 214–17, 379; diminished authority and responsibility after 1839, 139–40, 235; renaming, 236n960; *see also names of specific offices*
Police Pension Act (1890), 166
Police Regulations Act (1853), 388
Pollock, Sir Frederick, 241
Ponsonby, John William, Viscount Duncannon *see* Duncannon, John Ponsonby, Viscount
Poor Law Commission, 212
poor laws and relief, 212, 344 & n1433
Poor Man's Guardian, 180
Poor Man's Guardian Society, 247
Popay, Sergeant William, 203–4, 231
Portsmouth Dockyard Police, 319
Portugal, 26–7, 34, 35–6, 60n257; light infantry battalions, 35; cacadores battalions, 37, 39, 40, 43, 62
Powder Magazine (gunpowder store), Hyde Park, 324 & n1362
pre-trial hearings, 124
Presbyterians in Ireland, 10
prevention of crime, emphasis on, 105, 235

Index

Price, Colonel C. (of Royal Horse Artillery), 117
Primrose Hill meeting (1864), 325–6
Prince Regent *see* George IV, King
Principles of Policing: development, 104–7, 378–84; Moore's influence on, 22, 32, 106–7, 384, 391; leaked to press, 107–8, 382–3; Reith's Nine Principles of Policing, 391–5
private inquiry work, 166–9
Prosecution of Offences Act (1879), 170
prostitution: venues and districts, 89, 205
protest and assemblies law, 185–6, 247–9, 333, 341–2, 345
Prussia: in 1815 campaign against Napoleon, 67, 68
Public Carriage Office, 154, 155, 358
public houses, supervision of, 205
public nuisance, 204–5
Pulteney, Lieutenant-General Sir James, 19, 20
Punch, 80
Putney Bridge, 84
Pyrenees: Wellington's campaign in, 55, 56–8

Quatre Bras, Belgium, battle of (1815), 68
Quiberon Bay, 18–19

railways: development, 84–5, 216
rattles, 108–9
Rawlinson, Miss (rescued from fire), 162, 174
Rawlinson, Mr (magistrate), 125, 233
Rebecca riots (1839–43), 288–9
Receiving House of the Royal Humane Society, 300 & n1250, 302
recruitment of police officers, 103–4, 171, 288, 378–9
Redwood, Constable Henry, 193, 197
Reform Act (1867), 342–3
Reform Bill (1831–2), 178
Reform Bill (1866), 330
Reform League: formation and aims, 330 & n1376; Trafalgar Square demonstrations, 330–2; Hyde Park protest and riots, 332–8, 339–40; deputation to Home Secretary, 342; peaceful rally (6th May 1867), 344–6
Reform Movement, 340
refugees, 283
Reiner, Robert, 381, 382

Reith, Charles, 105; develops Nine Principles of Policing, 381–2, 383, 384, 391–5; on Lord Melbourne, 198–9; on Charlotte Serocold, 278; on legacy of Rowan and Mayne, 390
religion in Ireland, 10–11
Representation of the People Act (1884), 343
Republican (newspaper), 174
rewards, 236, 237, 238
Reynolds's Weekly Newspaper: criticisms of Mayne, 328, 340
Rhynd, William, 234
Richards, Mr, 148
Richmond, Charles Gordon-Lennox, 5th Duke of: wounded at Orthez, 61; campaigns for institution of Military General Service Medal, 73; baptism party for son Alexander, 90; dukedom and political career, 264; estates, 264; recommends candidates for Metropolitan Police, 142; finds position for William Rowan, 264; friendship and correspondence with Rowan, 214, 263–6, 269, 270, 271–2, 273–4, 275, 277; and Gawler's book on Waterloo, 267; letters from Mayne, 277–8, 281; in Rowan's will, 279
Richmond, Charles Lennox, 4th Duke of: appointed Commander of British forces (Sussex district), 20; commands reserve force in Brussels, 67; with Wellington at Brussels ball, 68; meets Peel after Waterloo, 75
Richmond, Charlotte, Duchess of, 75; Brussels ball (1815), 67–8
Richmond, Henry Gordon-Lennox, 6th Duke of, 320
Riot Act, 189–90, 289
riot and crowd control, 113–14, 117–18, 119, 181, 199–200, 219, 221–2, 312–13; *see also* dispersal powers; protest and assemblies law
riots and disturbances: Birmingham (1839), 220–1, 313; Bishop Bonner's Fields (4 June 1848), 258; bread riots (1867), 344; Charing Cross (8 March 1848), 251; at City boundary, 112, 113–14, 162, 177, 180, 181; Clerkenwell Green (19 August 1842), 224–5; Clerkenwell Green (31 May 1848), 257; Cold Bath Fields (1833), 184–202; Dewsbury (1838),

289; fast-day (March 1832), 114, 180–1; Garibaldi riots (1862–4), 322–5; Huddersfield (1837), 289; Hyde Park (1866), 332–8, 339–40, 342; Lewes bonfire night riots, 289; Lord Mayor's Day disturbances (8–9 November 1830), 114, 162, 176–7; Peterloo Massacre (1819), 174n707, 181; Rebecca riots (1839–43), 288–9; Reform Bill (1830–1), 175–6, 178–9; Seven Dials (11 October 1829), 173; Sunday trading riots (1855), 296–305, 306–13; Swing (1830), 175 & n710; Trafalgar Square (6–8 March 1848), 247–52; West End riots (1886), 376
River Police, 111, 115, 138, 140; *see also* Marine Police
Roach, Lawrence, 377
roads, 83–4
Roe, Sir Frederick: appointed chief magistrate at Bow Street, 127; and White Conduit House affair, 128; conflict with New Police, 129; and Wovenden affair, 130–1; evidence to Select Committee on Police of the Metropolis (1834), 133–4; ennobled, 133; and Charles Taylor case, 233–4; and William IV's funeral, 135–7; and Inspector Martin case, 151; evidence to Select Committee on Metropolitan Police Offices (1837–8), 138–9; resigns, 140
rookeries, 88–9 & n391
Rose, William Anderson (Lord Mayor of London), 120
Rose Lane (Spitalfields), 81
Rosslyn, James St Clair, 2nd Earl of, 99–100
Rothes, Countess of, 368
Rotunda (Blackfriars), 174–5, 176, 184
'route papers' communication system, 232
Rowan, Reverend Andrew, 10, 11
ROWAN, CHARLES:
Personal life: ancestors in Ireland, 7, 10–11; family background, 11, 12, 13–15; birth, 12; schooling and upbringing, 12; whereabouts unknown (1822–5), 90; at baptism of Duke of Richmond's son, 90; member of United Service Club, 91–2; stays in Brighton, 92; and William Napier's *History of the War of the Peninsula*, 92–3; occupies rooms at Whitehall Place, 109, 263, 364; seeks position for brother William, 264; friendship and correspondence with Duke of Richmond, 264–6, 269, 270, 271–2, 273–4, 275, 277; summer holidays in Scotland, 265, 267–8, 269, 270, 271–2, 364; love of game shooting and fishing, 265, 270, 271; godfather to Richard Charles Mayne, 362; influenza attack (1837), 269; as disappointed suitor of Lady Elizabeth Hay, 269; relations with Dalhousie family, 269–70, 271; relations with Marquess of Tweeddale, 270, 274; seeks position for former servant (Murray), 265–6; assists sister-in-law Sally, 266; moves to Bolton Street, 263, 275; failing health, 270, 272, 273, 275–6; frequent visitor to Apsley House, 272; depicted in Salter's *Waterloo* painting, 272; dines with Harry Smith and colleagues, 273; visit to Goodwood House, 274; dinner parties in London, 274; further trips to Scotland, 275, 276; tumour diagnosed, 275; social life, 276–7; last visit to Scotland, 276; deteriorating condition, 277–8; death, 278; mystery of his relationship with Charlotte Serocold, 278–9; burial, 279; estate and bequests, 279
Military career: joins 52nd Regiment, 13, 18; made lieutenant, 18; at Quiberon, 18–19; first military action at Ferrol, 19; financial straits and career advancement, 20–1; promoted captain, 21; in Sicily, 26; Gothenburg expedition, 26; in Portugal, 26–7; advances into Spain, 27–8; retreats to Corunna, 28–30; at Corunna, 30; evacuated to England, 30; brigade major of Light Division, 33, 35, 40; promoted brevet major, 33; becomes Craufurd's chief-of-staff, 33–4; pay, 34; arrives in Lisbon, 34–5; reaches Talavera, 35; withdraws to Portugal, 35–6; at battle of the river Coa, 36–8; at Bussaco, 38; winters in Torres Vedras, 39; pursues French into Spain, 39–40; at Sabugal, 40; assistant adjutant-general role, 40–1, 51; in battle of Fuentes de Oñoro, 41–2; sells difficult horse to Harry

Index

Smith, 42; dines with Wellington, 43; at assault on Ciudad Rodrigo, 43–5; on Craufurd, 45; promoted brevet lieutenant-colonel, 48; in winter quarters (1812–13), 49; jaunt with George Napier, 62–3; returns to Chatham, 63–4, 65; with 1/52nd Regiment in Ireland, 65; joins allied army against Napoleon, 65–6; Clinton doubts, 66; at Duchess of Richmond's Brussels ball, 67–8; movements before Waterloo, 68–9; at Waterloo, 69–72; possible victim of friendly fire, 71; recommended for promotion, 73; awarded military honours, 73; movements after Waterloo, 74; enters Paris, 74–5; stationed in France, 75–6; regimental second-in-command, 75–6, 78; returns to England (1818), 76; policing and domestic peacekeeping in Midlands, 76; commanding officer in Dublin, 78; retires from army, 78; recommends Gawler's book on Waterloo, 266–7; military legacy, 74; visits slave forts in Africa, 90–1

Police commissioner: applies for post, 95–6; appointed, 99, 102, 377; sworn as Justice of the Peace, 102; relationship with Mayne, 102; drafts initial plan for New Police, 102–3; co-formulates Principles of Policing, 104–7, 378–9, 382–3, 384; recruits officers, 103–4; designs uniform, 108; proposes reforms to magistracy, 126–7, 133; and Reform Bill riots (1830–1), 176, 178–9; and White Conduit House affair (1831), 127–8; relations with Phillipps, 129; and Fordham fraud case, 182; and fast-day riots (March 1832), 180; mercy petition for James Sutton, 174; and Cold Bath Fields meeting (1833), 185–7, 188–90, 191, 192, 193, 195–7, 201; evidence to Select Committee on Cold Bath Fields Meeting (1833), 199; evidence to Select Committee on Petition of Frederick Young and Others (1833), 203; evidence to Select Committee on Police of the Metropolis (1834), 103, 104, 108, 112–13, 126–7, 160, 163, 204–5, 382; and Wovenden affair, 130, 131–2; at scene of Parliament fire (1834), 206; as defendant in court, 152–3; and James Greenacre case, 233; and William IV's funeral, 135–7; evidence to Select Committee on Metropolitan Police Offices (1837–8), 113, 139, 214–17; appointed to Royal Commission on County Constabularies, 212, 213–14; and attempts on life of Queen Victoria, 240–1, 243; develops detective department, 241–2; and policing of Duke of Sussex's funeral, 227–8; and Chartist unrest, 253, 257–8, 259–60, 260; evidence to Select Committee on Sale of Beer Regulation (1848), 260; knighted, 261–2; presented to Queen Victoria, 262; rumours of retirement, 262; hands over work responsibilities to Mayne, 276, 281; stands down as Commissioner, 276; succeeded by Hay, 280; overshadowed by Peel, 377–8; achievements and legacy, 379, 389–90

Rowan, Charles (CR's uncle): in 52nd Regiment, 13, 18, 21, 24n88
Rowan, Elinor (*later* Heywood; CR's sister), 15
Rowan, Eliza (*née* Wilson; CR's mother), 11, 12, 15
Rowan, Elizabeth (CR's sister), 15, 279
Rowan, Frederica Maclean (CR's niece), 14, 266
Rowan, Frederick (CR's brother), 14; death, 266
Rowan, Hill Wilson (CR's brother), 279
Rowan, James (CR's brother), 13, 14, 279
Rowan, John (CR's brother), 13, 279
Rowan, John (CR's grandfather), 11
Rowan, Reverend John, 11
Rowan, Robert (CR's brother), 13, 20, 21, 26, 279
Rowan, Robert (CR's father), 11, 12, 15
Rowan, Robert (CR's great-grandfather), 11
Rowan, Rose (*née* Stewart; CR's grandmother), 11
Rowan, Sarah (*née* Prom; 'Sally'; CR's sister-in-law), 14, 266, 279
Rowan, William (CR's brother): joins 52nd Regiment, 13–14, 24; promoted lieutenant, 25; promoted captain, 27; in Peninsular War, 28, 29, 51; at battle of Nivelle, 59; at Waterloo, 71, 72; later military career, 14, 78; Military

Index

Secretary to Sir John Colborne, 14, 264; in Charles's will, 279; death, 14
Rowe, Michael, *Introduction to Policing*, 387, 389
Rowley, Elizabeth (*later* Ferguson), 268
Roxburghe, James Innes-Ker, 6th Duke of, 268, 276, 279
Royal Commission for the Exhibition of 1851, 283, 284–5
Royal Commissions of Inquiry: Poor Laws (1832–4), 212; County Constabularies (1836–9), 212–14; City of London (1853–4), 115; Hyde Park disturbances (1855), 299–300, 306–10, 313
Royal Exchange: opening ceremony (1844), 246
Royal Geographical Society, 369
Royal Horse Artillery, 41, 117–18
Royal Horse Guards, 98, 339, 342
Royal Irish Constabulary, 94, 98, 158
royal parks, law on protest and assemblies, 333, 341–2, 345
royal protection and security work, 243
royal residences, policing, 111, 140
Royal Victoria Theatre, London, 247
Rush, James Blomfield, 321 & n1354
Russell, John, 185
Russell, Lord John (*later* 1st Earl), 150–1; proposes amalgamation of City and Metropolitan police, 115; and William IV's funeral, 135, 136; Count de Ludolf writes to, 143; and commissioner uniforms, 209–10; and Royal Commission on County Constabularies, 212, 213; introduces County Police Bill, 214; approves salary increase for commissioners, 221n903; uncle murdered, 236; preparations for Chartist demonstration (10 April 1848), 253; introduces Reform Bill (1866), 330; resigns, 330
Russell, Lord William, 236–7
Ryan, Superintendent Daniel, 348
Ryde, Isle of Wight: Mayne holidays at, 370

Sabugal, Portugal, battle of (1811), 40
Sadler's Wells Theatre, London, 247
Saffron Hill (Holborn slum), 88–9
Sahagún, Spain, 28–9
Saint-Jean-de-Luz, 58

Salamanca, 27, 52; battle of (1812), 48
Sale, Nigel, *The Lie at the Heart of Waterloo*, 71
Sale of Beer Act (1854), 296
Salford Gaol: execution of Fenians (1867), 348
Salter, William: *Sir Charles Rowan* (painting), 279; *The Waterloo Banquet 1836* (painting), 272
San Sebastian, 53, 55–6
Sandrock, Superintendent (of F Division), 233
Santarém, Portugal, 39
Saunders, Elizabeth: inquest on, 315
Savage, Constable, 183
Scotland: early policing, 386
Scotland Yard, 109, 187, 329, 348, 376
Scott, Sir Harold, 377
Secret Service Department, 245, 352–3
section houses, 160, 299
Sedborough, John (d. 1629), 8
Sedborough Mayne family, 8
Seditious Meetings Act (1817), 247–9
Select Committees *see* Parliamentary Select Committee inquiries
Selling and Hawking of Goods on Sunday Prevention Bill (1860), 317
Selway, Sergeant James, 150
Serocold, Charlotte Eleanor (*née* Vansittart), 278–9
Serocold, Reverend Edward Pearce, 278
Seven Dials (Holborn): street unrest (11 October 1829), 173
sewers and drains, 80, 81
Shackell, Inspector Joseph, 165, 244
Sharpe, Alexander, 259 & n1055
Shaw, Sergeant Frederick, 242
Shaw, Henry (alias Mullady), 350
Shaw, Colonel James *see* Kennedy, Colonel James Shaw
Shaw Levefre, Charles, 212, 213
Shepherd, Sergeant James, 234
Shoobart, Mr (complainant), 147–8
Shorncliffe Camp, 21, 23–5; Standing Orders papers, 271
Shropshire Constabulary, 16
Sibthorp, Colonel Charles, 221
Sicily, 26
Sidney, Alderman Thomas, 120
Sierra Leone, 90
Silver, Sergeant, 282
Sivier's Hotel, Ryde, 370
Skene, Superintendent Alexander, 104

Index

Skerrett, Brigadier-General John, 56, 57
Skinner, Keith, *The Official Encyclopedia of Scotland Yard* (with Martin Fido), 358–9
slaughterhouses, 81
slave trade, 90
slums, 81–2, 86, 88–9 & n391
Smith, Sir Harry: retreats to Corunna, 29–30; on Talavera battlefield, 35; anecdotes about Rowan, 42–3; at Badajoz, 47; marries Spanish girl in Badajoz, 48; in winter quarters (1812–13), 49; on Wellington's reaction to Vera engagement, 57; in First Anglo-Sikh War, 272–3; vote of thanks in House of Commons, 273
Smith, Juana, 48 & n212, 49, 273
Smith, W.F.N., 386
Smith, Constable William, 240
Smithfield Market, 85–6
Snow, Peter, *To War with Wellington: From the Peninsula to Waterloo*, 37, 41–2, 53
snowball throwing, 356
Sobraon, battle of (1846), 273 & n1132
social season, 366
Somerset, Edward Seymour, 12th Duke of, 368, 369
Somerset, Lord Fitzroy (*later* 1st Baron), 264n1083, 274 & n1144
Sorauren, Spain, battle of (1813), 55
Soult, Marshal Nicolas: commands French forces in Spain, 28, 29, 55; campaign in Pyrenees, 55, 56–7; defeated at Nivelle, 58–9; at battle of Orthez, 59–61; at Toulouse, 61–2
South Western Railway Company, 85, 89
Southampton City Police, 385
Southwark Bridge, 84
Southwark police brass band, 316–17
Southwark Police Court, 235
Spechnell, Joseph, 235
special constables, 289
Spitalfields Market, 86
spying and political surveillance, 203–4, 231
St Anne's Church, Soho, 195
St Boes, France, 60
St Clair, Lieutenant-Colonel James Alexander, 99
St Giles (Holborn slum), 88 & n391
St Pancras railway station, 85
station houses, 130, 160, 182, 240, 243, 262, 299
steam boats, 84
Stenning, Philip C., 381
Stephen, Sergeant Thornton, 242
Stephens, James, 347
Stepney Green: Chartist meeting, 223
Steward, Reverend J., 372
Stewart, Lieutenant-General Charles, 55
Stewart, Lieutenant-Colonel John, 161
Stewart, Letitia (*later* Rowan), 11
Stewart, Margaret (*later* Rowan), 11
Stirling, Thomas (coroner), 194
Stockdale, Superintendent Jeremiah Box, 386
Stockton, Samuel, 195
Stoddart, Mr., 152
Stokes, Constable (of A Division), 343
Stokes, Inspector, 326
Stokes, Mary, 237
stolen property, police powers, 215
Stone, Staffordshire: Chartist protest, 225
street games, 356
street lighting, 81, 82
street paving, 84
street robbery, 346–7
Stuart, Alexander, 276
Stuart, Inspector, 385
Summary Jurisdiction Act (1848), 328
Sunday trading, 215, 260, 296–7, 317–18
Sunday Trading Bill (1855), 296, 304
Sunday trading riots (1855): background, 296–7; planned meeting for 1 July, 297–8; banning order, 298; police deployment, 298–9; briefing and police operation, 299–300, 301–3, 313; assembly of demonstrators, 300–1; riot, 301–3; casualties, arrests and convictions, 303–4; aftermath, 304; calls for inquiry, 304–5; Royal Commission of inquiry into, 299–300, 306–10, 313; serious misconduct charges upheld, 310–11; disciplinary action against accused officers, 311–12; lessons learned, 312–13
superannuation fund, police, 160–1, 163–6, 281–2
superintendents: divisional, 233; general instructions for, 106–7; inspecting, 355; recruitment and selection of, 103–4
surgeons, superintending and divisional, 159–60
Sussex, Augustus Frederick, Duke of:

Index

lying-in-state and funeral, 227–8
Sutherland, Duke and Duchess of, 325
Sutton, James, 173–4
Sweden: seeks British aid, 26
Swing riots (1830), 175 & n710
swords, for police use, 108

Tagus River, 35
Talavera, Spain, battle of (1809), 34, 35
Tatham, Edward, 182
Tatham, Henry, 109, 182
Taylor, Charles, 233–4
Taylor, Frederick, 153
Taylor, William Cooke, 377
Teague, Inspector (of City Police), 235
Teasdale, Constable James, 312
Tedman, Inspector (of D Division), 237, 238
Temple Bar (City), 112, 114, 116, 162, 177, 180
Templeton, John, 235–6
Tenterden, Lord, 153
Terry, Constable John, 162–3, 174
Terry, Inspector John, 86
Thames, river: bridges, 84; excursions and day trips, 84; policing, 87, 111, 115, 138, 140, 217; sewage and waste disposal, 80
Thames Division, 140, 217
Thames Police Office, 126, 138, 234
Thames River Police *see* Marine Police; River Police
Thames Tunnel, 84
Thatcher, Margaret, 367
theatres: and coach traffic, 246–7; popularity, 87; as venue for prostitution, 89
Theatres Act (1843), 87
Thirlestane Castle, 276
Thomas, Superintendent Joseph: background, 181n738; appointed superintendent, 103; riot control, 173, 181; Deputy Chief Constable of Manchester, 384
Thompson, Sergeant Henry, 143
Thomson, Inspector James, 348
Thornton, Mr (church warden), 233
Thorpe, Constable George, 312
Thring, Henry, 355
Thurmond Smith, Phillip, *Policing Victorian London*, 333
ticket-of-leave system, 319–20, 321
Times, The: and criticism of New Police, 147, 173; on state visit of Emperor Napoleon (1855), 295; on Sunday trading, 296; on Hyde Park demonstrations (1855), 300 & n1249; on police brutality, 304; letter from Mayne, 357
Tompkins, Esther, 182
Tooley Street fire (1861), 318
Torrens, Major-General Sir Henry, 77
Torres Vedras, Lines of, 38–9
Toulouse, battle of (1814), 61–2
trade depression (1848), 247
Trafalgar Square: construction and development, 82–3, 87; Chartist demonstrations and riots (6–8 March 1848), 247–52; Reform Bill demonstrations (1866), 330–2; Reform Bill protest (1866), 336–7; West End riot (1886), 376
Traill, James (magistrate), 139, 226
transportation (penal), 319, 321
Treason Act (1848), 257n1040
Tremlett, John, 321
trespass, 342
Trinity College, Cambridge, 16
Trinity College, Dublin, 16
Tristan, Flora, 89
Triumphal Arch, 297n1234
Trounce, Constable William, 241
Turner, Mr and Mrs (of Cavendish Square), 237–8
Turvey, Constable, 150
Tweeddale, George Hay, 8th Marquess of, 265, 268, 269, 270, 274, 276, 364, 386; in Rowan's will, 279
typhus, 28, 82
Tyrell, Sergeant, 183

Ulster Plantation, 7, 10
underground railway, 85
Underhill, Superintendent Stephen, 386
Undertakers, 7, 10
uniforms, police, 108, 109, 180n735, 209–10
Union, Act of (1707), 7
Union Hall Police Office, 232
Union Tavern, Cold Bath Fields, 190
United Irishman, 257 & n1040
United Service Club, 91–2, 182, 269; attacked by mob, 178; Wellington dines at, 274
universal suffrage, 218, 330, 343
unsolved crime reporting, 232

Index

vagrancy, 204–5, 211, 215, 290
Valencia, 48
Vandeleur, Major-General Sir John, 51, 52, 53
Vera, Spain, 56–8
Victoria, Princess, the Princess Royal (*later* Crown Princess Frederick), 367
Victoria, Queen: assassination attempts on, 239–41, 242–3, 262, 282; leaves London during Chartist demonstrations, 253; State Closings of Parliament (1839 and 1842), 222, 225; ennobles Rowan, 261–2; levees and Drawing Room receptions, 256, 262 & n1068, 361, 364–5, 367, 371; travels from Maiden Lane station, 85; visits Great Exhibition, 284; reviews troops at Chobham Common Great Camp, 290; state visit to France (1855), 314; state visit of Napoleon III (1857), 368; banquet at Prussia House, 368; concerns over Fenian threat, 353; offers condolences on Mayne's death, 373
Victoria Park: demonstrations and meetings, 333–4
Victoria Police (Australia), 388
Vigo, Spain, 29
Vimeiro, Portugal, battle of (1808), 27
Vine Street Police Station, 300, 301, 302, 307, 312
Vitoria, battle of (1813), 52–3
Vyvyan, Sir Richard, 109

Waddington, Horatio, 291, 305 & n1272, 306, 307, 341–2
Wade, Constable Thomas, 312
Waldegrave, George, 368–9
Wales: early policing, 219–20, 288–9, 386
Walker, Chief Superintendent, 155, 156, 339
Walker, Mr (magistrate), 180
Walmer Castle, 286
Walpole, Spencer: and Jackson suspension incident, 156; bans Reform League demonstration, 332, 333; questioned in House, 340; criticised, 340, 342; deputation from Reform League, 342; bans Reform League meeting, 344–5; and Colonel Paschal affair, 156; resigns (1867), 156, 346

Walsh, John, 141
Walsworth, James: arson case (1828), 93
Walter, Henry, *Events of a Military Life*, 47
War of 1812, 65
War of the First Coalition (1792–97), 18
War of the Second Coalition (1798–1802), 19
warrants for arrest, 126, 236
watchmen, 88, 112
Waterloo, battle of (1815): battle site, 69; Wellington's forces deployed at, 69; conduct of, 69–72, 74; casualties, 72; promotions and military honours, 73
Waterloo Gold Medal, 73
Waterloo railway station, 85, 89
Watson, Sir Frederick, 135 & n560
Webb, Inspector, 303
Webb, Sergeant Arthur, 224–5
Webb, Constable Henry, 243
Webb, Thomas, 237
Wedderburn, Lieutenant-Colonel Alexander, 95–6
Wellesley, Arthur Richard, Marquess Douro (*later* 2nd Duke of Wellington), 269, 270
Wellington, Arthur Wellesley, Duke of: Irish ancestry, 7; victory at Vimeiro, 27; questioned over Convention of Cintra, 27; returns to Portugal (1809), 34; victory at Talavera, 34; supported by Light Brigade, 35; viscountcy, 35; assembles troops around Almeida, 36; on Craufurd at Coa, 38; at Bussaco, 38; withdraws south, 38–9; winters in Torres Vedras (1810–11), 39; pursues French into Spain, 39–40; victory at Sabugal, 40; victory at Fuentes de Oñoro, 41–2; inspects Light Division, 42; praises attack on redoubt at Ciudad Rodrigo, 43–4; on death of Craufurd, 45; at siege and taking of Badajoz, 46–7; advances on Salamanca (1812), 48; occupies Madrid, 48; besieges Burgos, 48–9; retreats from Burgos and Madrid, 49; in winter quarters (1812–13), 49; strategy in Spain (1813), 51–2; victory at Vitoria, 52–3; campaign in Pyrenees, 55, 56–8; and siege of San Sebastian, 55; advances into southern France, 58–61; battle at Orthez, 59–61; battle of Toulouse,

61–2; victory in Peninsula, 62; reviews Peninsular army, 62; takes command of allied army in Netherlands, 66; army dispersed along Belgian frontier, 67; in Brussels, 67–8; at Quatre Bras, 68; forces deployed at Waterloo, 69; member of United Service Club, 91; conduct of battle at Waterloo, 69–72, 74; casualties, 72; submits names for military honours, 73; writes Waterloo Despatch, 73; dines with Peel after Waterloo, 75; Waterloo Banquets, 272; presents Metropolitan Police Bill in House of Lords, 94; possibly recommends Rowan to Peel, 99; assassination threat (1830), 176; and fears of public unrest (9 November 1830), 176; Apsley House attacked, 179; resigns premiership (November 1830), 177, 377; caretaker prime minister (1834), 207; questions witnesses in Francis case, 241; dines at United Service Club, 274; preparations for Chartist demonstration (10 April 1848), 253; at soirées of Angela Burdett-Coutts, 276, 277; death, 286; lying-in-state, 286, 287; funeral procession, 287
Wells Street fire (1829), 162, 174
West African Squadron, 90
West Indies: early policing, 387
Westminster, Richard Grosvenor, 2nd Marquess of, 367
Westminster Bridge, 84
Westminster Hospital: facilities for police patients, 159
Whalley, Sir Samuel, 194–5
Whicher, Sergeant Jonathan, 242
Whigs, 115, 135, 175, 177, 377–8; general election victory (1831), 129
Whinyates, Lieutenant Edward, 38
White, James, 231–2, 233
White Conduit House, 127–9, 223
Whitechapel, 81
Whitehall Palace fire (1698), 82
Whitehall Place (No. 4): Police headquarters, 109, 240, 243, 246, 259; bachelor rooms for Rowan, 109–10, 263, 364; electric telegraph installed, 284, 285

Wiggins, Inspector William, 130
Wilhelmina, Queen of the Netherlands, 367
William, Colonel George, 145
William IV, King: accession, 176n719; Mayne presented to, 361; visit to City of London cancelled (9 November 1830), 176; death, 135
Williams, John, 152–3
Williamson (detective), 347
Willis's Rooms, St James, 247
Wilson, Eliza *see* Rowan, Eliza
Wilson, Hill, 11
Wilson, Constable Robert, 142
Wilson, Colonel Samuel, 346–7
Windmill, The (public house), Lambeth, 146–7
Windsor Castle, 118, 135
Wolverhampton Borough Police, 385
Wood, Sir Charles, 368
Wood, Colonel Sir David, 116, 118
Woodthorpe, Henry, 113
working class: recruited for police, 171
Wortley, James, 306–7
Wovenden, Inspector Squire, 130–2, 150
Wray, John, 102, 103, 163
Wyke Manor, Yorkshire (Carvick family home), 360
Wylde, Colonel William, 241
Wynne, Mr (solicitor), 236

Yardley, Charles: Chief Clerk to the Commissioners, 108; work ethic, 326; relations with Mayne, 326–7; correspondence duties, 113, 275; sits in on Courvoisier committal proceedings, 236; go-between for Mayne and Hay, 290–1; on Hay's proposed new policing system, 291, 293; retirement, 155 & n633, 327
Yardley, E. (magistrate), 327
Yester House, near Gifford, 268, 276
York, Prince Frederick, Duke of, 20, 25
York Police, 385

zoos, 87